D1496523

INTRODUCTION TO STELLAR ATMOSPHERES AND INTERIORS

INTRODUCTION TO STELLAR ATMOSPHERES AND INTERIORS

EVA NOVOTNY

National Aeronautics and Space Administration
Manned Spacecraft Center
and the University of Pennsylvania

New York   London   Toronto
OXFORD UNIVERSITY PRESS
1973

ACKNOWLEDGMENTS

Figure 1-2: Figure 6.5 p. 272, E. Pettit, *Astrophysics,* ed. J. A. Hynek. Copyright © 1951 by McGraw-Hill Book Company; reprinted by permission of McGraw-Hill Book Company.
Figure 1-4: Figure 23-3, p. 450, G. Abell, *Exploration of the Universe,* second ed. Copyright © 1964, 1969 by Holt, Rinehart and Winston, Inc; reprinted by permission of Holt, Rinehart and Winston, Inc.
Figures 1-6, 1-7: Figure 14, p. 213, P. van de Kamp, *Handbuch der Physik,* ed. S. Flügge, volume L (1958). Reprinted by permission of Springer-Verlag.

Table 4-2: Table of the solar atmosphere, O. Gingerich, R. W. Noyes, W. Kalkofen, and Y. Cuny, *Solar Physics,* **18,** 347 (1971). Reprinted by permission of D. Reidel Publishing Company.
Tables 4-3, 4-4: Tables 3, 2, J. R. Auman, Jr, *The Astrophysical Journal,* **157,** 799 (1969). Copyright © 1969 by the University of Chicago; all rights reserved; reprinted by permission of the University of Chicago Press.
Tables 4-6 to 4-12: Tables, pp. 407, 415, 425, 430, 436, 437, 438, in *Theory and Observation of Normal Stellar Atmospheres,* ed. O. Gingerich (1969). Copyright © 1969 by The Massachusetts Institute of Technology; reprinted by permission of The M.I.T. Press, Cambridge, Massachusetts.

Figures 5-2, 5-5, 5-8, 5-9: Figures 5, 4, 10a, 10b, pp. 256, 86, 289, L. H. Aller, *Astrophysics: The Atmospheres of the Sun and Stars,* first ed. (1953). Copyright © 1953 by The Ronald Press Company, New York; reprinted by permission of the publisher.
Figure 5-3: Figure 2, R. G. Athay and R. C. Canfield, *The Astrophysical Journal,* **156,** 695 (1969). Copyright © 1969 by The University of Chicago; all rights reserved; reprinted by permission of The University of Chicago Press.
Figure 5-4: Figure 7, R. Schild, D. M. Peterson, and J. B. Oke, *The Astrophysical Journal,* **166,** 95 (1971). Copyright © 1971 by The University of Chicago; all rights reserved; reprinted by permission of The University of Chicago Press.
Figure 5-6: Figure 1, C. H. Payne, *Harvard Circular, 256* (1924). Reprinted by permission of Harvard College Observatory.
Table 5-1: Table XX, p. 111, R. v. d. R. Woolley and D. W. N. Stibbs, *The Outer Layers of a Star.* Reprinted by permission of The Clarendon Press, Oxford.

Figure 6-6: Figure 11-10, p. 358, M. Russell Wehr and James A. Richards, Jr., *Physics of the Atom,* second ed. (1967). Reprinted by special permission of Addison-Wesley Publishing Company, Reading, Mass.

Figure 7-2: Figure 1, L. G. Henyey, R. LeLevier, and R. D. Levée, *Publications of the Astronomical Society of the Pacific,* **67,** 154 (1955). Reprinted by permission of the *Publications of the Astronomical Society of the Pacific.*
Figures 7-3 A, 7-5 A, 7-5 B, 7-5 C, 7-6, 7-8: Figures 17, 2, 3, 4, 16, 1, I. Iben, Jr., *The Astrophysical Journal,* **141,** 993 (1965). Copyright © 1965 by The University of Chicago; all rights reserved; reprinted by permission of The University of Chicago Press.
Figure 7-3 B: Figure 2b, A. S. Grossman and H. C. Graboske, Jr, *The Astrophysical Journal,* **164,** 475 (1971). Copyright © 1971 by The University of Chicago; all rights reserved; reprinted by permission of The University of Chicago Press.
Figure 7-4: Figure 1, p. 212, in *Stellar Evolution: Proceedings of a Symposium held November 1963,* eds. R. F. Stein and A. G. W. Cameron (1966). Reprinted by permission of Plenum Publishing Corporation.
Figure 7-7: Figure 1, I. Iben, Jr., and R. J. Talbot, *The Astrophysical Journal,* **144,** 968 (1966). Copyright © 1966 by The University of Chicago; all rights reserved; reprinted by permission of The University of Chicago Press.
Figures 7-9, 7-25: Figures 3, 4, I. Iben, Jr, *Annual Review of Astronomy and Astrophysics,* **5,** 571 (1967). Reprinted by permission of Annual Reviews, Inc.
Figures 10 A, 10 B, 7-26 A, 7-26 B: Figures 8, 9, 10, 11, I. Iben, Jr., *The Astrophysical Journal,* **147,** 624 (1967). Copyright © 1967 by The University of Chicago; all rights reserved; reprinted by permission of The University of Chicago Press.
Figures 7-11 A, 7-11 B: Figures 2, 1, S. Torres-Peimbert, E. Simpson, and R. K. Ulrich, *The Astrophysical Journal,* **155,** 957 (1969). Copyright © 1969 by The University of Chicago; all rights reserved; reprinted by permission of The University of Chicago Press.
Figures 7-12, 7-28 A, 7-28 B, 7-28 C, 7-28 D: Figures 4, 5, 8, 10, 12, I. Iben, Jr, *The Astrophysical Journal,* **143,** 483 (1966). Copyright © 1966 by The University of Chicago; all rights reserved; reprinted by permission of The University of Chicago Press.
Figures 7-13, 7-14: Figures 2, 3, R. Stothers, *The Astrophysical Journal,* **138,** 1074 (1963). Copyright © 1963 by The University of Chicago; all rights reserved; reprinted by permission of The University of Chicago Press.
Figure 7-15 A: Figure 1, P. Demarque, *The Astrophysical Journal,* **132,** 366 (1960). Copyright © 1960 by The University of Chicago; all rights reserved; reprinted by permission of The University of Chicago Press.

Table 7-4 A: Table 3, I. Iben, Jr, *The Astrophysical Journal,* **141,** 993 (1965). Copyright © 1965 by The University of Chicago; all rights reserved; reprinted by permission of The University of Chicago Press.

Table 7-5: Table 1, R. Stothers, *The Astrophysical Journal,* **138,** 1074 (1963). Copyright © 1963 by The University of Chicago; all rights reserved; reprinted by permission of The University of Chicago Press.

Table 7-6: Table 3, J. P. Cox and R. T. Giuli, *The Astrophysical Journal,* **133,** 755 (1961). Copyright © 1961 by The University of Chicago; all rights reserved; reprinted by permission of The University of Chicago Press.

Table 7-7: Tables III, IV, I. Iben, Jr, *Annual Review of Astronomy and Astrophysics,* **5,** 571 (1967). Reprinted by permission of Annual Reviews Inc.

Table 7-8: Table 1, M. Schwarzschild and H. Selberg, *The Astrophysical Journal,* **136,** 150 (1962). Tables 1 – 5, M. Schwarzschild and R. Härm, ibid., **136,** 158 (1962). Copyright © 1962 by The University of Chicago; all rights reserved; reprinted by permission of The University of Chicago Press.

Table 7-9: Tables 1, 3, R. Stothers, *The Astrophysical Journal,* **140,** 510 (1964); Tables 2, 3, 4, R. Stothers, ibid., **143,** 91 (1966). Copyright © 1964 and copyright © 1966 by the University of Chicago; all rights reserved; reprinted by permission of The University of Chicago Press.

Table 7-10: Table 27, p. 427, S. Chandrasekhar, *Introduction to the Study of Stellar Structure.* © 1939 by The University of Chicago; all rights reserved; reprinted by permission of the University of Chicago Press.

Table 7-11: Published by permission of S. C. Vila.

Tables 7-12 to 7-36: Published by permission of I. Iben, Jr.

Tables 7-37, 7-38: Published by permission of Z. Abraham.

Table 10-6: Table 28.2, p. 255, Martin Schwarzschild, *Structure and Evolution of the Stars.* Copyright © 1958 by Princeton University Press; reprinted by permission of Princeton University Press.

Tables 10-11, 10-12: "Tables of Emden Functions," The Royal Society, The British Association for the Advancement of Science, *Mathematical Tables,* **II** (1932). Reprinted by permission of The Royal Society.

Table 10-15: Table 3, P. M. Morse, *The Astrophysical Journal,* **92,** 27 (1940). Copyright © 1940 by The University of Chicago; all rights reserved; reprinted by permission of The University of Chicago Press.

Table 10-16: Table 4, A. N. Cox and J. N. Stewart, *The Astrophysical Journal, Suppl.* **19,** 243 (1970). Copyright © 1970 by The University of Chicago; all rights reserved; reprinted by permission of The University of Chicago Press.

PREFACE

This book is written at the intermediate level and is intended for those who wish to study the principal concepts and results of the theories of stellar atmospheres and interiors. The equations and methods have been restricted to simple forms, for example, Eddington's first approximation for the radiative transfer problem; however, references to more advanced treatments are cited.

The book has four major divisions. Part One considers the observational data pertinent to studies of the atmosphere or interior of a star. Parts Two and Three consider the atmosphere and interior of a star, respectively; these two parts have been written in such a way that they may also be read in reverse order or independently of one another. When overlapping of material in these two parts occurs, the reader is referred to specific sections in other places of the book. Part Four consists of detailed calculations of a model atmosphere and a number of model interiors.

The book may be used as a text for an undergraduate course and, in fact, has been expanded from lectures presented in a course in introductory astrophysics at the University of Pennsylvania. This has been taken by advanced undergraduates and occasionally by beginning graduate students. For a one-semester course, the instructor will find it necessary to be selective, as the material has grown rather extensive in the effort to include all important topics that are appropriate at this level.

The inclusion of a model calculation as a term project in a course on stellar atmospheres or interiors is well worth while, and a number of such problems are suggested at the end of Part Four. The model atmosphere for a star with $T_{eff} = 6000°$ K is the most easily calculated of the solutions requiring numerical integration. The model interior for the star having a radiative core and a convective envelope is the most difficult because four differential equations must be solved simultaneously in the core. Since the aim of these exercises is one of instruction in basic concepts, the equations have been kept at a minimum of complexity and the computations may be performed on a desk calculator. The integrations for the stellar interiors, however, may also be programmed for an automatic calculator. In addition to the term projects, short problems appropriate to the various chapters are also provided.

Numerous tables have been provided for instruction and reference, such as recent data on binary systems, model atmospheres (including several from the Harvard-Smithsonian grid), and model interiors (including detailed models from the evolutionary sequences calculated by I. Iben, Jr.).

The references quoted in this book by no means include all those that are important or relevant; the choices have been limited to material that seemed best suited to the immediate purpose. Additional references will be obtained by consulting the works cited.

It is a pleasure to thank all those who have contributed to the preparation of this book. Mrs. Z. Abraham, L. Binnendijk, J. Davis, B. H. Feierman, I. Iben, Jr., D. M. Popper, S. C. Vila, and the University of Michigan have generously provided data for tables or figures. A. B. Hull, G. C. Kilambi, G. E. McCluskey, and the staffs of the Manned Spacecraft Center and the Department of Astronomy of the University of Pennsylvania have kindly assisted in various ways. The proofs were checked while the author enjoyed the hospitality of the Department of Astronomy of the University of Manchester. Special thanks are extended to T. R. Carson, I. Iben, Jr., and D. W. N. Stibbs, who have read drafts of various chapters and made many valuable comments. Grateful acknowledgment is also made of the many publishers and authors whose work is reproduced in this book. Finally, it is a pleasure to express appreciation to those who have typed the manuscript, especially Mrs. P. C. Juday, who aided with the typing and also assisted with other tasks during the later stages of the work.

The University   E. N.
Manchester
February 1973

CONTENTS

PART ONE

OBSERVATIONAL DATA

1

OBSERVATIONAL DATA

Stars are believed to form from clouds of interstellar material. The chemical elements and their proportions that are initially present in the newly created star are therefore those inherited from the cloud. The total mass is similarly determined in the process of formation, although some adjustment of the mass may occur in the early stages before a bona fide star is produced. We may consider that the initial mass and initial chemical composition are fundamental quantities for any given star. If we neglect such possible complications as rotation and magnetic fields, then we ought to be able to predict all other properties of the star at any time during its evolution. For example, we should be able to calculate the radius and luminosity and to derive in detail all the features of the spectrum. The ultimate test of the theories of stellar atmospheres and interiors is the comparison of calculated results with the observational data.

Nearly all observational information about a star is obtained by measuring its radiant energy as received at the Earth: the amount of energy per second, its distribution with wavelength, and the direction in space along which it travels. In the case of the Sun, particles in the form of a *solar wind* consisting of ions and electrons are received, as well as neutrinos. These, however, have as yet made little contribution to our understanding of the atmosphere or interior of the Sun. In this chapter we shall discuss what can be discovered about the stars from a study of their emitted electromagnetic energy. Our concern will be with the principles involved, rather than with actual techniques of observation and analysis.

1 MAGNITUDES, SPECTRA, AND RELATED QUANTITIES

1-1 MAGNITUDE

The brightness of a star, as viewed from the Earth, is usually expressed as a *magnitude*. The faintest stars visible to the unaided eye are assigned magnitude $+6$, while a very bright star has magnitude about 0. Measurement of the energy received per second shows that a difference of 5 magnitudes corresponds to a ratio of 100 in the energy received per second.* A step of one magnitude then represents a ratio of

$$\sqrt[5]{100} = 2.512.$$

In general, the ratio of the energies l_1 and l_2 received per second from two sources of magnitude m_1 and m_2 is

$$\frac{l_1}{l_2} = (\sqrt[5]{100})^{-(m_1 - m_2)}$$

$$\frac{l_1}{l_2} = 10^{-0.4(m_1 - m_2)}. \tag{1-1}$$

The negative sign in the exponent expresses the convention that increasing magnitude corresponds to decreasing brightness.

Usually, magnitudes are measured in a restricted wavelength range. For example, the filters used to obtain the magnitudes m_U, m_B, m_V, or, as they are commonly designated, U, B, V, respectively, admit the following approximate ranges and peak transmissions:

Ultraviolet U	Blue B	Visual V
3000–4000 Å	3600–5500 Å	4800–6800 Å
3600 Å	4200 Å	5200 Å

The observing technique for obtaining these magnitudes depends on photoelectric measurement. Photographically determined magnitudes are commonly expressed as m_{pg} (*photographic*) and m_{pv} or m_v (*photovisual*). The plates used are sensitive in the blue, violet, and near ultraviolet for m_{pg} and in the yellow and green for m_{pv}. The term *visual magnitude* arises from the fact that the eye is most sensitive in this wavelength range.

The measured U, B, and V magnitudes of stars having a very low abundance of elements heavier than helium (so-called *metals*) should be adjusted before utilization in certain problems. These stars have a different spectral distribution from that of stars with approximately solar abundance because of the weakness of the absorption lines of the metals. These lines are especially prevalent in the ultraviolet and blue regions, and, as a consequence of the relative *lack* of absorption in these wavelengths by stars deficient in metals,

---

* Magnitudes were assigned in ancient times. For precise modern work, those values have been adjusted to a scale in which a difference of 5 magnitudes corresponds to a ratio of *exactly* 100 in the energies.

such stars produce an excess of short-wavelength radiation. Tables giving the required corrections are available.*

When the entire spectral range is included, a *bolometric magnitude* is measured. A bolometric magnitude can also be calculated from the visual magnitude by means of a *bolometric correction*, BC, usually defined as

$$m_{bol} = m_{pv} + BC. \qquad (1\text{-}2A)$$

This is necessarily the same as the corresponding equation for the absolute magnitude $\mathscr{M}$, to be defined in the following paragraph:

$$\mathscr{M}_{bol} = \mathscr{M}_{pv} + BC. \qquad (1\text{-}2B)$$

Since the V and the pv scales agree within a hundredth of a magnitude,† we may also write

$$\mathscr{M}_{bol} = \mathscr{M}_{V} + BC \qquad (1\text{-}2C)$$

and

$$m_{bol} = m_{V} + BC. \qquad (1\text{-}2D)$$

The determination of a bolometric correction requires a knowledge of the amount of energy produced by the star in the ultraviolet and infrared, as well as in the visible region of the spectrum. Absorption by interstellar matter and by the terrestrial atmosphere must be considered in the interpretation of observational data, and this introduces uncertainty into the values of the bolometric corrections.

The measured *apparent magnitudes* give no information about intrinsic brightness, since a star may appear very bright simply as a result of being relatively near the Earth. The *absolute magnitude* describes the rate at which a star emits radiation; it is the apparent magnitude that would be observed if the distance of the star were 10 parsecs. (A *parsec*, abbreviated *pc*, is about 3.26 light years.) The absolute magnitude of the Sun is about $+5$, and it would be one of the fainter stars in the sky if it were removed to the standard distance. The relation between the apparent magnitude m and the absolute magnitude $\mathscr{M}$ is obtained from eq. (1-1) together with the

---

* In practice, the stars of the Hyades cluster are adopted as standard. The corrections are given as functions of the observed value of $B - V$ (see Section 1-3) and the *ultraviolet excess*, $\delta(U - B)$, which is the difference $(U - B)_{star} - (U - B)_{Hyades}$ at the given value of $B - V$. In the Hyades stars, the numerous absorption lines cause blocking of the radiation (particularly in the short wavelengths) and consequent redistribution into other wavelengths. In stars deficient in metals, the relative absence of these effects results in a brighter V magnitude and fainter U and B magnitudes, with increases in both $B - V$ and $U - B$. For a detailed discussion and tables of the corrections, see R. L. Wildey, E. M. Burbidge, A. R. Sandage, and G. R. Burbidge, 1962 (140a).

† C. W. Allen, 1963 (10), p. 197.

inverse square law. Writing d for the distance (in parsecs), we have

$$\frac{l \text{ (at } d)}{l \text{ (at 10 pcs)}} = \frac{10^2}{d^2} = 10^{-0.4(m - \mathcal{M})}$$

or

$$\mathcal{M} = m + 5 - 5 \log d. \tag{1-3}$$

The quantity $m - \mathcal{M}$ is called the *distance modulus*. A correction must be made to the measured apparent magnitude for the dimming by interstellar dust, which is concentrated in the spiral arms of the Galaxy.

Distance is found most directly by measurement of the *trigonometric parallax* of a star. As the Earth revolves about the Sun, the star is viewed from differing vantage points and consequently appears displaced relative to more distant stars. Expressed in seconds of arc, the semi-major axis of the extremely small ellipse described by the star relative to (hypothetical) fixed stars is the *parallax*, defined as the angle subtended at the star by the radius of the orbit of the Earth.* The parallax varies inversely as the distance to the star and is less than $1''$ even for the nearest star, Proxima Centauri. The minuteness of stellar parallaxes restricts their measurement to those of stars that are within some dozens of parsecs or light years. For more distant objects, other methods of obtaining distance must be employed. Among these is the method of *spectroscopic parallaxes*, which is based on slight differences between the spectra of stars that have equal surface temperatures but different radii and hence different luminosities (see Sections 1-2 and 1-4). The luminosity, or absolute magnitude, is deduced by examination of the spectrum, and the distance is then calculated from eq. (1-3).

1-2 LUMINOSITY

Equation (1-1) permits the calculation of the comparative rates at which energy is emitted by two stars if they are equally distant from the Earth, or, in practical terms, if $m_1 - m_2$ is replaced by $\mathcal{M}_1 - \mathcal{M}_2$. In particular, the *luminosity* L, which is the amount of energy emitted per second in all wavelengths, can be found relative to that of the Sun, $L_\odot$, from the relation

$$\frac{L}{L_\odot} = 10^{-0.4(\mathcal{M}_{\text{bol}} - \mathcal{M}_{\text{bol} \odot})}. \tag{1-4}$$

The absolute bolometric magnitude of the Sun is†

$$\mathcal{M}_{\text{bol} \odot} = +4.76. \tag{1-5}$$

To determine $L_\odot$, the *solar constant* must be measured. This is the amount

---

* The *parsec* is then defined as the distance corresponding to a parallax of $1''$. The name *parsec* is, in fact, derived from the words "*parallax second.*"
† This value is based on an apparent visual magnitude -26.74 as given by H. L. Johnson, 1965 (101) and an adopted bolometric correction $BC_\odot = -0.07$.

of radiation falling normally on one square centimeter at the Earth per second, corrected for absorption by the terrestrial atmosphere and measured when the Earth is at its mean distance of 1.496×10^{13} cm from the Sun. We have*

$$\text{solar constant} = 1.948 \text{ cal cm}^{-2} \text{ min}^{-1}$$

$$= 1.359 \times 10^6 \text{ erg cm}^{-2} \text{ sec}^{-1}$$

and

$$L_\odot = \text{solar constant} \times 4\pi \text{ (mean distance)}^2$$

$$L_\odot = 3.82 \times 10^{33} \text{ erg sec}^{-1}. \tag{1-6}$$

1-3 COLOR INDEX

A significant quantity is obtained when two magnitudes measured at different wavelengths are subtracted. This is called the *color index* and is related to the surface temperature of a star (Tables 1-1A, 1-1B), providing a measure of this important characteristic with relative ease. A correction is necessary because interstellar dust removes shorter wavelengths more efficiently than longer ones, thus causing a *reddening* of the light.

If a star has a very low abundance of metals, a correction for the relative lack of line blanketing is necessary before a comparison is made with stars of a metal abundance approximating that of the Sun. Tables are available that give the corrections to $B - V$ and $U - V$ for this effect.†

1-4 TEMPERATURE

There is no unique definition of temperature; the numerical value depends on the process or phenomenon used in its determination. Several possible definitions compare the star with an ideal black body, and we first summarize the theoretical radiation laws.

Figure 1-1 shows several black body curves for various temperatures, calculated from the Planck function $B_\lambda(T)$, giving the energy radiated per cm² per second into unit solid angle and in unit wavelength interval:

$$B_\lambda(T) = \frac{2hc^2}{\lambda^5} \frac{1}{e^{hc/\lambda kT} - 1}, \tag{1-7A}$$

* The value given for the solar constant is the average of the determinations by (1) D. Labs and H. Neckel, 1968 (137), who find 1.958 cal cm^{-2} min^{-1}; (2) E. G. Laue and A. J. Drummond, 1968, (138), who find 1.952 cal cm^{-2} min^{-1}; and (3) the Goddard Space Flight Center, 1968 (139), with the result of 1.936 ± 0.041 cal cm^{-2} min^{-1}.
† R. L. Wildey, E. M. Burbidge, A. R. Sandage, and G. R. Burbidge, 1962 (140a). Also see Section 1-1.

Table 1-1A Relation between Spectral Type, Color Index, Effective Temperature, Bolometric Correction, Absolute Magnitude, and Luminosity.*

Main Sequence (Luminosity Class V)

Sp (V)	U − V	B − V	T_{eff}	$\log T_{eff}$	BC	$\mathcal{M}_v$†	$\mathcal{M}_{bol}$†	$\log L/L_\odot$†
O5	−1.47	−0.32	(54000)	(4.732)	(−4.76)	...	...	...
O6	−1.46	−0.32	(45000)	(4.653)	(−4.10)	−4.0	−8.1	+5.1
O7	−1.45	−0.32	(43300)	(4.636)	(−3.96)	−3.9	−7.9	+5.1
O8	−1.44	−0.31	(40600)	(4.608)	(−3.75)	−3.8	−7.5	+4.9
O9	−1.43	−0.31	(37800)	(4.577)	(−3.51)	−3.6	−7.1	+4.7
O9.5	−1.40	−0.30	(36200)	(4.559)	(−3.37)	−3.5	−6.9	+4.7
B0	−1.38	−0.30	29200	4.465	−2.85	−3.3	−6.2	+4.4
B0.5	−1.29	−0.28	25800	4.412	−2.56	−2.8	−5.4	+4.1
B1	−1.19	−0.26	23000	4.362	−2.30	−2.3	−4.6	+3.7
B2	−1.10	−0.24	21000	4.322	−2.09	−1.9	−4.0	+3.5
B3	−0.91	−0.20	17600	4.245	−1.68	−1.1	−2.8	+3.0
B5	−0.72	−0.16	15200	4.182	−1.33	−0.4	−1.7	+2.6
B6	−0.63	−0.14	14300	4.155	−1.18	0.0	−1.2	+2.4
B7	−0.54	−0.12	13500	4.130	−0.93	+0.3	−0.6	+2.1
B8	−0.39	−0.09	12300	4.090	−0.55	+0.7	+0.1	+1.9
B9	−0.25	−0.06	11400	4.057	−0.40	+1.1	+0.7	+1.6
B9.5	−0.13	−0.03	10600	4.025	−0.30	+1.3	+1.0	+1.5
A0	0.00	0.00	9600	3.982	−0.21	+1.5	+1.3	+1.4
A1	+0.06	+0.03	9330	3.970	−0.15	+1.7	+1.5	+1.3
A2	+0.12	+0.06	9040	3.956	−0.10	+1.8	+1.7	+1.2
A3	+0.17	+0.09	8750	3.942	−0.06	+2.0	+1.9	+1.1
A4	+0.21	+0.12	8480	3.928	−0.03	+2.1	+2.1	+1.1
A5	+0.25	+0.14	8310	3.920	−0.02	+2.2	+2.2	+1.0
A7	+0.30	+0.19	7920	3.899	+0.01	+2.4	+2.4	+0.9
F0	+0.37	+0.31	7350	3.866	−0.01	+3.0	+3.0	+0.7
F2	+0.39	+0.36	7050	3.848	−0.03	+3.3	+3.3	+0.6
F3	+0.41	+0.40	6850	3.836	−0.04	+3.5	+3.5	+0.5
F5	+0.43	+0.43	6700	3.826	−0.04	+3.7	+3.7	+0.4
F6	+0.48	+0.47	6550	3.816	−0.04	+4.0	+4.0	+0.3
F7	+0.54	+0.51	6400	3.806	−0.04	+4.3	+4.3	+0.2
F8	+0.60	+0.54	6300	3.799	−0.05	+4.4	+4.4	+0.1
G0	+0.70	+0.59	6050	3.782	−0.06	+4.7	+4.6	+0.1
G1	+0.75	+0.61	5930	3.773	−0.06	+4.9	+4.8	0.0
G2	+0.79	+0.63	5770	3.761	−0.07	+5.0	+4.9	−0.1
Sun (G2)	+0.70	+0.64	5770	3.761	−0.07	+4.83	+4.76	0.0
G5	+0.86	+0.66	5660	3.753	−0.09	+5.2	+5.1	−0.1
G8	+1.06	+0.74	5440	3.736	−0.13	+5.6	+5.5	−0.3
K0	+1.29	+0.82	5240	3.719	−0.19	+6.0	+5.8	−0.4
K1	+1.44	+0.86	5110	3.708	−0.24	+6.2	+6.0	−0.5
K2	+1.60	+0.92	4960	3.695	−0.30	+6.4	+6.1	−0.5
K3	+1.79	+0.99	4800	3.681	−0.40	+6.7	+6.3	−0.6
K4	+1.98	+1.07	4600	3.663	−0.50	+7.1	+6.6	−0.7
K5	+2.18	+1.15	4400	3.643	−0.62	+7.4	+6.8	−0.8
K7	+2.52	+1.30	4000	3.602	−0.89	+8.1	+7.2	−1.0

Table 1-1A (*continued*)

Sp (V)	U − V	B − V	T_{eff}	log T_{eff}	BC	$\mathcal{M}_v$†	$\mathcal{M}_{bol}$†	log $L/L_\odot$†
M0	+2.67	+1.41	3750	3.574	−1.17	+8.7	+7.5	−1.1
M1	+2.70	+1.48	3700	3.57	−1.45	+9.4	+7.9	−1.3
M2	+2.69	+1.52	3600	3.56	−1.71	+10.1	+8.4	−1.5
M3	+2.70	+1.55	3500	3.54	−2.0	+10.7	+8.7	−1.6
M4	+2.70	+1.56	3400	3.53	−2.3	+11.2	+8.9	−1.7
M5	+2.80	+1.61	3200	3.51	−2.6	+12.3	+9.7	−2.0
M6	+2.99	+1.72	3100	3.49	−2.9	+13.4	+10.5	−2.3
M7	+3.24	+1.84	2900	3.46	−3.4			
M8	(+3.50)	(+2.00)	2700	3.43	−4.0			
	(+3.2)	(+2.0)	(2500)	(3.40)	(−4.6)	+16.6	+12.0	−2.9
		(+2.3)	(2250)	(3.35)	(−5.8)	+18.9	+13.1	−3.3

* Parentheses indicate values that are less certain; with the exception of U − V and B − V for spectral type M8, they indicate values based on observations of a single star.
† The last three columns refer to an adopted zero-age main sequence in the range of spectral types O6 to K5.
This table is based on the following sources (listed in the Bibliography), with interpolations as necessary using the variable in parentheses. The omission of a reference implies that a quantity has been obtained by interpolation in the present table. U − V *and* B − V: (113). T_{eff}: O5 to O9.5 (199l); B0 to A7 (B − V) (199u); F0 to G1 (136); G2 to M0 (113); M3 to end (V − I)^a (199o). BC: O6 to B0.5 (T_{eff}) (199m); B1 to B6 (T_{eff}) (199n); B8 to F3 (B − V) (199k); G2 to M0 (113)^b; M3 to end (V − I)^a (199o). $\mathcal{M}_v$: O6 to K5 (199p) p. 407; K7 to M4 (199p) p. 401; M5 to M6 (199q). *Solar values:* U − V, B − V, and $\mathcal{M}_v$ from (101); T_{eff} from $R_\odot$ and $L_\odot$; BC$_\odot$ is an adopted value.
^{a} I = infrared magnitude
^{b} The zero point has been adjusted so that BC$_\odot$ = −0.07.

Table 1-1B   Relation between Spectral Type, Color Index, Effective Temperature, and Bolometric Correction. [From H. L. Johnson, 1966 (113), pp. 196 and 200.]*

Giants (Luminosity Class III)

Sp (III)	U − V	B − V	T_{eff}(°K)	log T_{eff}	BC
G5	+1.55	+0.92	5010	3.700	−0.27
G8	+1.64	+0.95	4870	3.688	−0.28
K0	+1.93	+1.04	4720	3.674	−0.37
K1	+2.13	+1.10	4580	3.661	−0.43
K2	+2.32	+1.16	4460	3.649	−0.49
K3	+2.74	+1.30	4210	3.624	−0.66
K4	+3.07	+1.41	4010	3.603	−0.86
K5	+3.34	+1.54	3780	3.578	−1.15
M0	+3.43	+1.55	3660	3.564	−1.24
M1	+3.48	+1.56	3600	3.56	−1.32
M2	+3.51	+1.59	3500	3.54	−1.48
M3	+3.51	+1.60	3300	3.52	−1.87
M4	+3.32	+1.59	3100	3.49	−2.51
M5	+3.00	+1.55	2950	3.47	−3.30
M6	+2.43	+1.54	2800	3.45	−4.22

Table 1-1B (*continued*)

Supergiants (Luminosity Class I)

Sp (I)	U − V Ia	Ib	B − V	T_{eff}(°K)	log T_{eff}	BC
O9	−1.46	−1.46	−0.31	—	—	—
O9.5	−1.44	−1.44	−0.30	—	—	—
B0	−1.38	−1.37	−0.27	21000	4.32	−2.36
B0.5	−1.32	−1.30	−0.25	18500	4.27	−2.06
B1	−1.26	−1.24	−0.22	16000	4.20	−1.89
B2	−1.15	−1.10	−0.18	14000	4.15	−1.60
B3	−1.03	−0.98	−0.14	12800	4.11	−1.34
B5	−0.86	−0.78	−0.10	11500	4.06	−0.98
B6	−0.80	−0.74	−0.08	11000	4.04	−0.92
B7	−0.73	−0.67	−0.06	10500	4.02	−0.82
B8	−0.64	−0.57	−0.03	10000	4.00	−0.71
B9	−0.58	−0.50	−0.01	9700	3.99	−0.59
A0	−0.47	−0.40	+0.01	9400	3.97	−0.45
A1	−0.35	−0.29	+0.03	9100	3.96	−0.37
A2	−0.22	—	+0.05	8900	3.95	−0.28
	I					
A5	+0.05	+0.11	8300	3.92	−0.06
F0	+0.45	+0.19	7500	3.88	+0.07
F2	+0.55	+0.25	7200	3.86	+0.06
F5	+0.66	+0.37	6800	3.83	+0.04
F8	+1.01	+0.55	6150	3.79	+0.01
G0	+1.24	+0.70	5800	3.76	−0.03
G2	+1.47	+0.85	5500	3.74	−0.11
G5	+1.83	+1.01	5100	3.71	−0.20
G8	+2.07	+1.03	5050	3.70	−0.22
K0	+2.38	+1.12	4900	3.69	−0.29
K1	+2.60	+1.18	4700	3.67	−0.35
K2	+2.83	+1.25	4500	3.65	−0.42
K3	+3.10	+1.38	4300	3.63	−0.57
K4	+3.35	+1.49	4100	3.61	−0.75
K5	+3.51	+1.62	3750	3.57	−1.17
M0	+3.57	+1.63	3660	3.56	−1.24
M1	+3.61	+1.63	3600	3.56	−1.33
M2	+3.62	+1.64	3500	3.54	−1.46
M3	+3.60	+1.64	3300	3.52	−1.87
M4	+3.36	+1.64	3100	3.49	−2.51
M5	(+3.00)	+1.62	2950	3.47	−3.30

* It should be noted that some entries in Tables 1-1A and 1-1B are inconsistent in that the more luminous stars of a given spectral class would be expected to have lower effective temperatures.

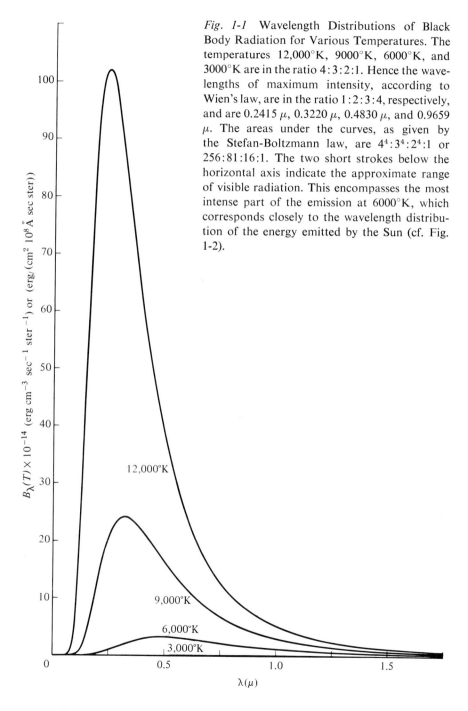

Fig. 1-1 Wavelength Distributions of Black Body Radiation for Various Temperatures. The temperatures 12,000°K, 9000°K, 6000°K, and 3000°K are in the ratio 4:3:2:1. Hence the wavelengths of maximum intensity, according to Wien's law, are in the ratio 1:2:3:4, respectively, and are 0.2415 μ, 0.3220 μ, 0.4830 μ, and 0.9659 μ. The areas under the curves, as given by the Stefan-Boltzmann law, are $4^4:3^4:2^4:1$ or 256:81:16:1. The two short strokes below the horizontal axis indicate the approximate range of visible radiation. This encompasses the most intense part of the emission at 6000°K, which corresponds closely to the wavelength distribution of the energy emitted by the Sun (cf. Fig. 1-2).

where

$$\lambda = \text{wavelength in centimeters,}$$
$$T = \text{absolute (Kelvin) temperature,}$$
$$h = \text{Planck's constant,}$$
$$c = \text{speed of light,}$$
$$k = \text{Boltzmann's constant.}$$

Written in terms of frequency rather than wavelength, this formula becomes

$$B_\nu(T)\, d\nu = B_\lambda(T)\, d\lambda$$

$$B_\nu(T) = \frac{2h\nu^3}{c^2} \frac{1}{e^{h\nu/kT} - 1}. \tag{1-7B}$$

As the temperature is increased, each point of the curve is raised, and the wavelength λ_m at which maximum emission occurs is shifted to shorter wavelengths. The latter relation is expressed by Wien's law, which is obtainable from Planck's law by differentiation*:

$$\lambda_m T = 0.2898. \tag{1-8}$$

Although stars are not true black bodies, their spectral distributions can often be approximated by black body curves, once the absorption lines have been smoothed out (Fig. 1-2). If a temperature is to be assigned by matching the stellar curve with one of the Planckian curves, some criterion of best fit must be chosen; for different criteria, different curves and hence different temperatures may result.

One possible criterion is that the two curves should have the same height at some definite wavelength, after multiplication of the Planckian curve by π to eliminate the dependence on unit solid angle and thus make possible a comparison of the fluxes [see Chapter 2: eq. (2-14) and example (h) of Section 5]. Note that this *brightness temperature* varies with the wavelength under consideration. It is necessary to know the ratio of the radius of the star to its distance, that is, its angular radius, since the energy per second detected by a receiver on the Earth depends upon the quantity (radius of star)^2/distance^2.

A *color temperature* can usually be assigned even if this ratio is unknown, since it is given by the *distribution* of energy in a given wavelength range; the absolute height of the stellar curve is not considered. For some stars, in some wavelength ranges, it may be impossible to fit the stellar and black body curves and, in that case, no color temperature can be defined.

The *effective temperature* (T_{eff}) is determined from the Planckian curve (multiplied by π) having the same total energy output as the star, regardless

* See F. K. Richtmyer and E. H. Kennard, 1947 (100), p. 182.

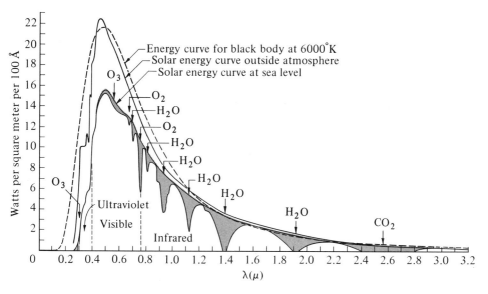

Fig. 1-2 Wavelength Distribution of the Solar Radiation. The lowest curve shows the flux received at the earth per 100 Å intervals as a function of wavelength. The molecules responsible for the heavy absorption regions are indicated. Radiation of wavelength less than 2900 Å is absorbed by the terrestrial atmosphere. The upper solid curve is an extrapolation to zero air mass, i.e., to outside the terrestrial atmosphere. This curve approximates the flux that would be received at the Earth from a black body at 6000°K at the distance of the Sun. [From *Astrophysics*, ed. J. A. Hynek, article by E. Pettit. Copyright 1951 by McGraw-Hill Book Company. Used with permission of McGraw-Hill Book Company.]

of how the energy may be distributed with wavelength. Integrating the Planck function over wavelengths or frequencies, we have*

$$B(T) = \int_0^\infty B_\lambda(T)\,d\lambda$$

$$= 2hc^2 \int_0^\infty \frac{1}{\lambda^5} \frac{1}{e^{(hc/\lambda kT)} - 1}\,d\lambda.$$

Let

$$x = \frac{hc}{kT}\frac{1}{\lambda}$$

or

$$\lambda = \frac{hc}{kT}\frac{1}{x}.$$

* *Ibid.*, p. 182.

Then

$$d\lambda = -\frac{hc}{kT}\frac{1}{x^2}\,dx$$

and

$$B(T) = 2hc^2\frac{k^4T^4}{h^4c^4}\int_0^\infty x^3\frac{1}{e^x-1}\,dx$$

$$= \frac{2k^4}{h^3c^2}T^4\frac{\pi^4}{15}$$

$$B(T) = \frac{\sigma}{\pi}T^4, \tag{1-9}$$

where σ is the Stefan–Boltzmann constant. If F is the total flux, that is, the total energy emitted per second per cm², then

$$F = \pi B(T) = \sigma T^4. \tag{1-10}$$

This is the Stefan-Boltzmann law. But, if R is the radius of the star,

$$L = F \times 4\pi R^2;$$

therefore

$$F = \sigma T_{\text{eff}}^4 = \frac{L}{4\pi R^2}, \tag{1-11}$$

from which the effective temperature may be found if the luminosity and radius are known or if the angular radius R/d is known:

$$\begin{array}{c}\text{energy received at Earth}\\\text{per cm}^2\text{ per sec}\end{array} = \frac{L}{4\pi d^2}$$

$$= \sigma T_{\text{eff}}^4\left(\frac{R}{d}\right)^2. \tag{1-12}$$

From the luminosity and radius of the Sun, we find

$$T_{\text{eff}} = 5770°\text{K}.$$

The disparity between the values from the various definitions of the temperature can be considerable. For example, a star with $T_{\text{eff}} = 10,800°$K has a color temperature of 15,300°K at 5000 Å; 16,700°K at 4250 Å; and 10,000°K at 3500 Å.*

Other definitions of temperature will be considered in Chapter 3.

---

* From D. L. Harris III (K. Aa. Strand, ed.), 1963 (1).

1-5 SURFACE GRAVITY

The acceleration due to gravity near the surface of a star is one of the factors determining the atmospheric structure. It also influences the finer details of the spectrum and, in fact, can be estimated from spectroscopic analysis.

If the mass M and radius R of a star are known, the surface gravity g is calculated from its definition,

$$g = \frac{GM}{R^2},$$
(1-13)

where G is the constant of gravitation. For most stars, however, M and R cannot be determined directly.

1-6 SPECTRAL TYPE

The spectra of stars are classified according to the identification and strengths of their spectral lines. Although the chemical compositions of most stars in the vicinity of the Sun are very similar, the spectra differ because of the range in surface temperatures and, to a lesser extent, because of differences in surface gravities. The latter effect is subtle, however, and the stars can be classified according to a continuous sequence of *spectral types*, or *spectral classes*, designated

O, B, A, F, G, K, M.

Additional spectral types that do not form part of this sequence because of significant differences in chemical composition are R, N, and S, paralleling the spectra of the K and M stars; and several other spectral classes also exist.

To allow further refinement of spectral type assignments, decimal subdivisions are used, for example, F0, F8. The spectral type of the Sun is G2.

For historical reasons, classes O, B, and A are sometimes referred to as *early type* and classes K and M as *late type*. The terms *early* and *late* may also be used to denote approximate subdivisions of a single spectral class; for example, G2 may be called *early G*, while G8 may be called *late G*.

Prefixes and suffixes are also employed. Those occurring in Tables 1-3 to 1-5 are *d* (indicating a dwarf, that is, a main-sequence star), *D* (a white dwarf, that is, a very underluminous star), *e* (emission lines apparent in the spectrum), *m* (abnormally strong metallic lines), and *p* (peculiar spectrum). Luminosity classes are designated by Roman numerals and are described in the next section.

Some of the characteristics of the various spectral classes are described in Table 1-2. Typical spectra are illustrated in Fig. 1-3. The corresponding effective temperatures are given in Tables 1-1A and 1-1B.

Table 1-2   Description of Principal Spectral Classes.

CLASS	COLOR OF STAR	SOME SPECTRAL CHARACTERISTICS *
O	Blue-white	H weak. He I, He II. C III, N III, O III. Si IV.
B	Blue-white	H stronger. He I (and He II in class B0). C II, N II, O II. Si II, Si III, Si IV. Mg II, Fe III. Also Ti II, Cr II, Fe II in later class B.
A	White	H very strong. (He I faint here and in classes below.) O I. Si II. Mg II, Ca II, Ti II, Mn I, Fe I, Fe II.
F	Yellow-white	H strong. Ca II, Cr I, Cr II, Fe I, Fe II, Sr II.
G	Yellow	H less strong. Ca II strong. Neutral and ionized metals.
K	Orange	H weak. Ca I, Ca II. Neutral metals, TiO bands.
M	Red	H very weak. Neutral metals. TiO very strong in later class M.

* The Roman numeral I signifies a neutral atom, II signifies the first ion, III the second ion, etc.

1-7 THE HERTZSPRUNG–RUSSELL DIAGRAM. LUMINOSITY CLASS

The *Hertzsprung–Russell diagram*, or H–R diagram, is a plot of luminosity or absolute magnitude against spectral type (Fig. 1-4). Most stars in the vicinity of the Sun lie on the *main sequence*, a continuous band that runs from the hot, luminous stars at the upper left to the cooler, fainter stars at the lower right. Main-sequence stars are also called *dwarfs* to distinguish them from the *subgiants*, *giants*, and *supergiants* occupying the area above the main sequence in the diagram. The *subdwarfs* and *white dwarfs* fall below the

Fig. 1-3 Representative Stellar Spectra. The name of the line, the wavelength in Ångstrom units, and the element responsible are given in some cases. (Department of Astronomy, The University of Michigan.)

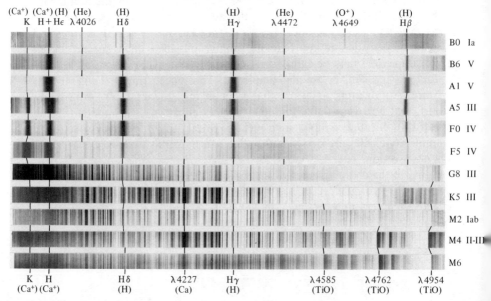

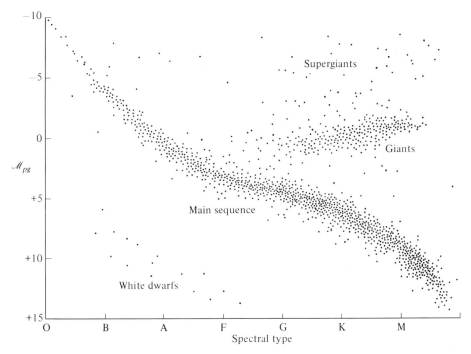

Fig. 1-4 The Hertzsprung–Russell Diagram. The distribution shown here for stars of known distance is characteristic of the stars in the general vicinity of the Sun. [After G. O. Abell, 1969 (7), p. 450.]

main sequence. It should be noted that not all white dwarfs are actually white in color.

The terms *dwarf* and *giant* represent the radii of the stars, as well as their luminosities. Equation (1-11) shows that, for a given effective temperature (or, approximately, spectral type), a large luminosity requires a large radius. Radii are largest at the upper right in the diagram, smallest at the lower left.

A Roman numeral may be affixed to the spectral type to indicate the position of a star in the Hertzsprung–Russell diagram. Main-sequence stars are denoted by the number V, subgiants by IV, giants by III, bright giants by II, and supergiants by Ib and Ia, the last being brightest of all. Stars below the main sequence are not usually assigned luminosity classes (see Fig. 1-5).

2 MASSES, RADII, AND LUMINOSITIES

The mass of a star can be measured only by its gravitational effects. One such effect is the red shift of radiation escaping from the surface of an extremely dense object, such as a white dwarf. For other stars, the presence of a nearby body is necessary. This restricts the masses that can

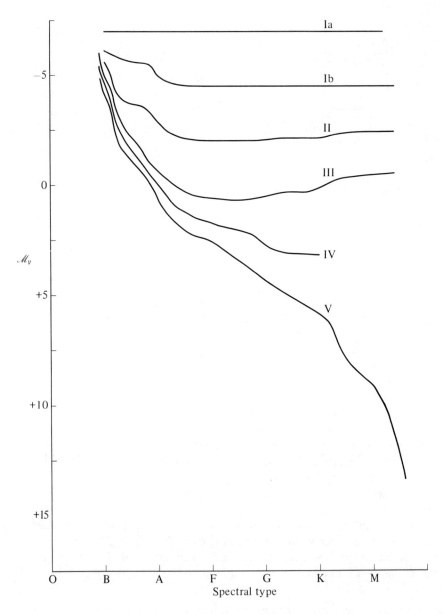

Fig. 1-5 Luminosity Classes. Absolute magnitude is plotted as a function of spectral type. Class I contains supergiants; class II, bright giants; class III, giants; class IV, subgiants; and class V, the main sequence. [From data given by P. C. Keenan (K. Aa. Strand, ed.), 1963 (1).]

be measured by the latter technique to that of the Sun and the binary stars.

The radii of a few dozen stars have been found from measurement of their angular radii by means of an interferometer. Radii can also be deduced for some binary stars. The radius of the Sun can be found from its observed angular radius.

2-1 THE SUN

The proximity of the Sun makes possible an accurate and direct determination of its properties. For a measurement of its mass, the gravitational acceleration experienced by the Earth can be used. The orbit of the Earth is nearly circular, and we may take the radial acceleration produced by the Sun to be

$$\text{acceleration} = \frac{GM_\odot}{d^2},$$

where

$$G = \text{constant of gravitation,}$$
$$M_\odot = \text{mass of the Sun,}$$
$$d = \text{mean distance of Earth from Sun}$$
$$= 1 \text{ astronomical unit (1 AU)}$$
$$= 1.496 \times 10^{13} \text{ cm.}$$

On the other hand, this acceleration can also be expressed purely kinematically:

$$\text{acceleration} = \frac{v^2}{d},$$

where

$$v = \text{orbital speed of the Earth about the Sun}$$
$$= \frac{2\pi d}{1 \text{ year}}$$
$$= 2.978 \times 10^6 \text{ cm sec}^{-1};$$

and therefore

$$M_\odot = \frac{v^2 d}{G}$$
$$= 1.990 \times 10^{33} \text{ gm.}$$

A more accurate value is

$$M_\odot = 1.991 \times 10^{33} \text{ gm.} \tag{1-14}$$

The radius $R_\odot$ of the Sun can be determined from a measurement of its angular radius $R_\odot''$,

$$R_\odot'' = 15' \, 59''.63.$$

Then

$$R_\odot = R_\odot"d/206265$$
$$= 6.960 \times 10^{10} \text{ cm,} \qquad (1\text{-}15)$$

where the factor 206265 is the number of seconds of arc in one radian.

2-2 BINARY STARS

A. VISUAL BINARY STARS

When both components of a mutually revolving pair of stars are visible (with telescopic aid), the system is a *visual binary*.

The masses must be determined in two steps, in which the ratio and the sum of the masses are found. We illustrate by reference to the system 99 Herculis. Figure 1-6 shows at left the relative orbit of star B about star A. (The relative orbit of A about B could just as well be considered.) The semi-major axis of this elliptical orbit, which is also the mean separation of the stars, subtends an angle

$$a" = 1."03$$

as viewed from the Earth. (We are speaking of the orbit as corrected for projection effects, so that, effectively, it is viewed face-on.) This corresponds to a linear dimension

$$a = 18.7 \text{ AU}$$

at the distance to the system of 3.8×10^6 AU.

Newton's modification of Kepler's harmonic law,

$$\mathscr{P}^2(M_A + M_B) = a^3, \qquad (1\text{-}16)$$

can now be used to calculate the sum of the masses $M_A + M_B$, expressed in units of the solar mass. The period $\mathscr{P}$ of revolution of the system, expressed in sidereal years,* has the value

$$\mathscr{P} = 56.0 \text{ years}$$

for 99 Herculis. Then

$$M_A + M_B = 2.1 \; M_\odot,$$

or, as given in the published solution,†

$$M_A + M_B = 2.0 \; M_\odot.$$

---

* The sidereal year is the time required for one revolution of the Earth about the Sun with respect to a fixed star.
† P. van de Kamp, 1958 (32), p. 213. More recent values for this system are given in Table 1-3.

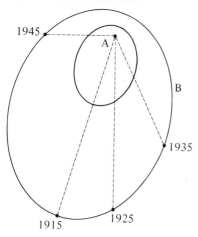
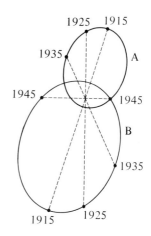

Fig. 1-6   The Orbits of the Components of the Visual Binary System 99 Herculis.
Left: Relative orbit of star B about star A (larger ellipse) and of the center of mass of the system about star A (smaller ellipse).
Right: Orbits of the two components about their center of mass, located at the intersection of the lines connecting the stars.
   The dots are much larger than the actual stars in relation to the size of the orbit. [Adapted from P. van de Kamp, 1958 (32), p. 213.]

   To find the ratio of the masses, we examine the motions of stars A and B with respect to more distant, and therefore relatively motionless, stars (Fig. 1-7). The center of mass of the system is identified as that point on the line joining the components that moves in a straight line, since other bodies are so distant that their gravitational forces on the system do not cause a measurable deviation from rectilinear motion. Measurement of the relative distances of the two components from this point yields the ratio of the masses:

$$\frac{M_B}{M_A} = \frac{\text{distance of A}}{\text{distance of B}} = 0.6.$$

Combining the information about the masses, we get finally

$$M_A = 1.3\ M_\odot$$
$$M_B = 0.7\ M_\odot.$$

   For comparison with the other motions, the orbits of the two stars about their center of mass are shown at the right in Fig. 1-6. These ellipses have the same eccentricity as the relative orbit.
   Visual binaries have no special properties amenable to determination of their radii, and these must be found from eq. (1-11) with temperatures determined from the spectra. Luminosities are measured as in Section 1-2.

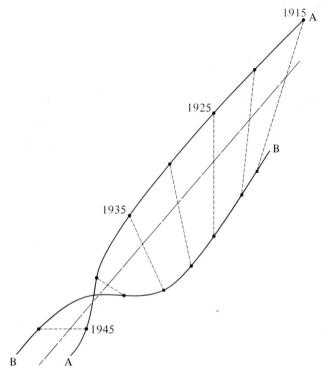

Fig. 1-7 Motions of the Components of the Visual Binary System 99 Herculis with Respect to Fixed Background Stars. The motion of the center of mass is indicated by the long dashed line. [Adapted from P. van de Kamp, 1958 (32), p. 213.]

B. ECLIPSING AND SPECTROSCOPIC BINARY STARS

Some double-star systems are so oriented in space as to produce periodic eclipses. The *light curve* of the system, which is a plot of the brightness against time (Fig. 1-8), yields much information. For example, the *inclination*, which is the angle between the plane of the orbit and the plane perpendicular to the line of sight to the system, can be deduced. If the inclination is about 90°, that is, if the orbital plane is viewed nearly edgewise, one eclipse is total and the light of the system remains constant as the hidden star passes from one edge to the other of the occulting star. This is the case in Fig. 1-8 for the primary eclipse.* The secondary eclipse is annular (i.e., with a ring of light surrounding the transiting star) and would also be constant at minimum

---

* Primary eclipse is defined as the deeper of the two eclipses in any system.

light if the larger star in back were uniformly bright over its disk. Because any star is brightest at the center of its disk, however, the profile of the minimum is rounded at the bottom. If partial eclipses occur, there is only one instant of maximum obscuration, hence one instant when the light of the system reaches a minimum. The contours of the minima are then similar to that of the annular eclipse in Fig. 1-8.

The radii of the stars can be found in units of the mean separation. Figure 1-9 illustrates the case of a circular orbit with an inclination of 90°, both of

Fig. 1-8 Light Curve of the Binary System AR Lacertae. The ordinate is the difference between the magnitude of a comparison star of constant light and the magnitude of the binary system. The abscissa is time expressed in days, measured from the middle of primary eclipse. The period of revolution is 1.983 days. [F. B. Wood, 1946 (102).]

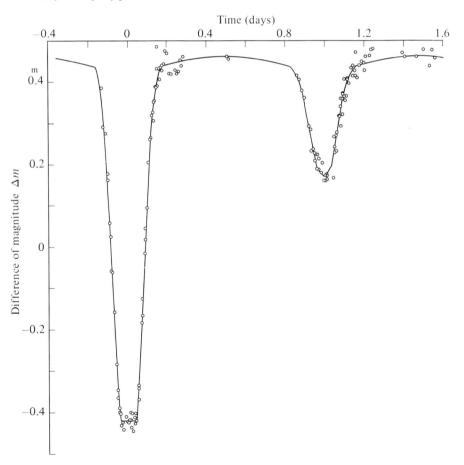

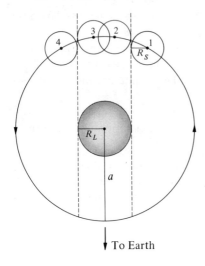

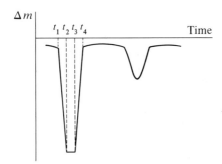

Fig. 1-9   The System AR Lacertae.
Upper: Scale drawing of the stars and orbit. Any possible tidal distortions of the components have been neglected.
Lower: Points of the light curve corresponding to the positions in the upper figure.

which conditions apply to the system AR Lacertae. From the diagram, we see that

$$\frac{t_4 - t_1}{\mathscr{P}} \approx \frac{2(R_{\mathrm{L}} + R_{\mathrm{S}})}{2\pi a} \tag{1-17}$$

$$\frac{t_3 - t_2}{\mathscr{P}} \approx \frac{2(R_{\mathrm{L}} - R_{\mathrm{S}})}{2\pi a}. \tag{1-18}$$

Measurement of the curve, Fig. 1-8, gives

$$t_4 - t_1 = 0.328 \text{ days}$$
$$t_3 - t_2 = 0.082 \text{ days};$$

and since
$$\mathscr{P} = 1.983 \text{ days},$$
we have

$$\frac{R_L}{a} = 0.325 \ (0.319)$$

(1-19)

$$\frac{R_S}{a} = 0.195 \ (0.194).$$

The numbers in parentheses are from the solution published by Wood.* Figure 1-9 represents the system to scale.

The relative luminosities are found by measuring the depth of the total eclipse,† which happens to be the primary eclipse in the case of AR Lacertae. The depth of the total eclipse (Fig. 1-8) is

$$\Delta m = 0\overset{m}{.}86,$$

which can be converted by means of formula (1-1) to the fraction of the total light remaining during totality. This is the luminosity of the occulting star divided by the sum for the two components. The occulting star is in this case the cooler star: the *area* that is obscured as the two disks are projected one upon the other must be the same regardless of which star is in front; hence the greater loss of light (primary eclipse) occurs when it is the hotter star that is obscured [cf. eq. (1-10)]. If C indicates the cooler and H the hotter star, then

$$\frac{L_C}{L_H + L_C} = 0.453 \ (0.457).$$

The hotter component must then provide the remainder of the light,

$$\frac{L_H}{L_H + L_C} = 0.547 \ (0.543).$$

The shading of the larger star in Fig. 1-9 indicates that its surface brightness is less. In this system, the smaller star is the hotter and also the more luminous component. The values of L_H and L_C individually can be obtained if the distance to the system is known and the apparent magnitude of the system is measured [see eqs. (1-3) and (1-4)].

Spectroscopic binaries reveal themselves by the periodic Doppler oscillations of their spectral lines about a mean position. Unless the ratio of the luminosities of the components is less than about two, only the brighter spectrum is visible. Complete information about the system can be obtained only if both spectra can be measured.

* F. B. Wood, 1946 (102).
† More precisely, we find not the relative luminosities but the relative amounts of energy radiated per second in the wavelength range in which the observations were made.

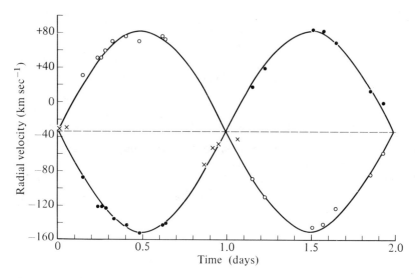

Fig. 1-10 The Radial Velocities of AR Lacertae. This is a spectroscopic (as well as an eclipsing) binary system, for which the spectra of both components are measurable. *Black dots* refer to the component designated *H* in the text, the *white dots* to component *C*. *Crosses* represent blended spectral lines of the two stars. The abscissa has the same zero point as in Fig. 1-8. [R. F. Sandford, 1951 (103).]

The Doppler displacements, translated into radial velocities* from the (non-relativistic) formula

$$\frac{\text{shift in wavelength}}{\text{unshifted wavelength}} = \frac{\text{radial velocity}}{\text{speed of light}}, \qquad (1\text{-}20)$$

are plotted against time in a *radial velocity curve*.

Figure 1-10 shows the radial velocity curves of both components of AR Lacertae. The center of mass of this system is approaching at a rate of 33.7 km sec^{-1}, which is the radial velocity at which the two curves coincide. This equality for the two components is possible only at the times when the stars are moving perpendicularly to the line to the observer and the radial velocities due to *orbital* motion are zero (Fig. 1-11). The amplitudes of the curves give the orbital speeds in the case of a circular orbit, except for a

---

* *Radial velocity* is the component of the relative velocity of the source and observer along the observer's line of sight to the source. Recession is measured as positive and approach as negative, corresponding to an increase or decrease in wavelength, respectively.

factor dependent on the inclination. For AR Lacertae, the inclination, as given by the light curve, is 90°; hence the measured amplitudes of 116 km sec⁻¹ give directly the speeds of revolution about the center of mass. From Fig. 1-10, we see that the two stars of AR Lacertae must have nearly equal masses. More careful measurement of the curves shows that

$$\frac{M_{\rm C}}{M_{\rm H}} = 0.995,$$

Fig. 1-11 Correspondence between Positions in the Orbit and Points on the Radial Velocity Curve. The cases of a mass ratio of 2:1 for stars A and B is illustrated.
Upper Left: Orbits of the two components about the center of mass, marked +.
Upper Right: Relative orbit of star B about star A.
Lower: The corresponding radial velocity curves. The amplitude of curve B is twice that of A.

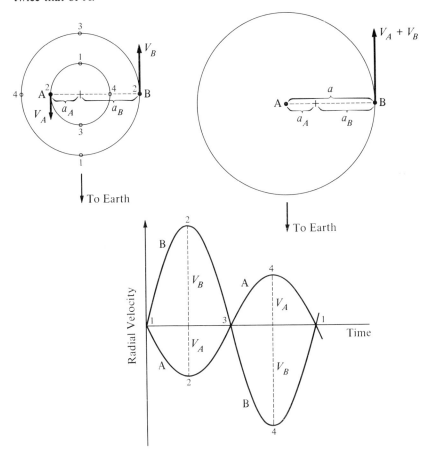

where the subscripts can again be taken to indicate the cooler and hotter stars, respectively, by correlating the information contained in Figs. 1-8 to 1-11.

The sum of the masses is obtained from the modified harmonic law, eq. (1-16); but we must first know the size of the relative orbit. The distance traveled by either star about the other, considered as fixed, can be found as

$$2\pi a = \mathscr{P} \times \text{speed in relative orbit.}$$

The latter factor is just the sum of the two speeds about the center of mass (see Fig. 1-11):

$$\text{speed in orbit} = v_\text{H} + v_\text{C} = 232 \text{ km sec}^{-1};$$

and with $\mathscr{P} = 1.983$ days,

$$a = 6.33 \times 10^6 \text{ km}$$
$$= 0.0423 \text{ AU.}$$

Then,

$$M_\text{H} + M_\text{C} = \frac{a^3}{\mathscr{P}^2} = 2.57 \ M_\odot$$

or, more accurately,

$$M_\text{H} + M_\text{C} = 2.59 \ M_\odot;$$

and finally*

$$M_\text{H} = 1.30 \ M_\odot$$
$$M_\text{C} = 1.29 \ M_\odot.$$

With the value just found for a, the actual dimensions of the stars can now be found from eqs. (1-19), giving

$$R_\text{L} = R_\text{C} = 2.02 \times 10^6 \text{ km} = 2.90 \ R_\odot$$
$$R_\text{S} = R_\text{H} = 1.23 \times 10^6 \text{ km} = 1.76 \ R_\odot.$$

Both stars in this system are larger than the Sun, even though their separation is only about one-tenth the distance of Mercury from the Sun! This situation is typical of spectroscopic and eclipsing systems. Indeed, if the stars were separated sufficiently to form a visual binary, their orbital motions would be so slow that no Doppler shift could be detected, and eclipses would occur so infrequently that they would probably not be noticed.

C. OBSERVATIONAL RESULTS

An accurate determination of the mass can be made for only a small number of stars. For a visual binary system, the observationally derived mass

---

* R. F. Sanford, 1951 (103). See Table 1-4 for more recent values for this system.

is sensitive to the parallax, which enters with the third power in the equation for the sum of the masses. Thus only the nearest visual binaries, having large parallaxes, yield good measurements of the mass. At the same time, proximity to the Earth is favorable for the observation of the separation of the stars. For the eclipsing and spectroscopic systems, on the other hand, parallax does not enter the derivation of the masses, and reliable values can be obtained even for more distant systems. Tables 1-3 to 1-5 list the observed properties, as well as some calculated ones, of a number of binary components. The W Ursae Majoris stars, in Table 1-5, are pairs so close as to be nearly in contact. The large tidal distortions of the components must be taken into account when a solution of the light curve is made, but the theory is difficult and further refinements are needed.

2-3 THE MASS-LUMINOSITY RELATION

Accurate and fundamentally determined luminosities can be found for the nearest stars, which have large trigonometric parallaxes. A few dozen visual binary systems are sufficiently close to the Earth to provide data for the *mass-luminosity relation*, but eclipsing and spectroscopic systems tend to be too distant for the trigonometric parallax to be reliable. Figure 1-12 shows the fundamentally derived mass-luminosity relation.

Once the mass-luminosity relation is established, it can be used for estimating the masses of other main-sequence stars for which luminosities are known. The relation does not apply to white dwarf stars, which have very low luminosities, nor does it necessarily apply to stars above the main sequence. Examples of such departures are apparent in Fig. 1-12. An estimated mean line through the points may be described by the following relations:

$$\log (L/L_\odot) > -1.2, \qquad \log (L/L_\odot) = 4.1 \log (M/M_\odot) - 0.1$$
or
$$\mathcal{M}_{bol} < 7.8, \qquad \mathcal{M}_{bol} = -10.1 \log (M/M_\odot) + 4.9;$$

for faint stars, the data are insufficient to obtain a reliable expression, but the two points of lowest luminosity in Fig. 1–12 (representing the components of L 726-8) conform to the same relation. Eggen [see ref. (140)] finds evidence for two separate mass-luminosity relations among observed binary systems.

2-4 THE MASS-RADIUS RELATION

Stellar radii can be determined fundamentally for eclipsing binaries that are also spectroscopic binaries having both spectra visible. The light curve gives the radii relative to the mean separation of the stars, while the radial-velocity curve (together with the inclination found from the light curve) yields the absolute value of the mean separation. It is then possible to determine absolute dimensions without a knowledge of the parallax.

Table 1-3   Visual Binary Systems (Including Systems Observed Interferometrically).*

SYSTEM	R.A. [a] Decl.	$M/M_\odot$	$\log \dfrac{M}{M_\odot}$	$\log \dfrac{L}{L_\odot}$	$\mathscr{M}_{bol}$ [b]	$\mathscr{M}_V$ [c]	m_V [c]
ADS 671[A]	00^{h}43^{m}0	0.86^F [146]	−0.07	+0.07	4.59	4.65	3.45 [142]
= η Cas	+57°17′	0.56	−0.25	−1.13	7.59	8.71	7.51
L 726–8[B]	01 34.0	0.17^F [151]	−0.76	−3.50	13.5	16.2	13.4 [140, 149]
	−18 28	0.13	−0.88	−3.70	14.0	16.7	13.9
BD + 68°278 B, C	03 38.2	0.45 [152]	−0.35	...	...	10.0	11.6 [152]
	+68 21	0.36	−0.44	...	...	10.0	11.6
ADS 3093 B, C[B]	04 10.7	0.44 [1]	−0.36	(−1.99)^L	(9.73)^L	11.07	9.52 [154]
= o² Eri B, C	−07 49	0.19	−0.72	−2.05	9.9	12.65	11.10
ADS 3841 A[B,C]	05 09.3	2.1^C [1]	+0.33	+1.94	−0.1	0.2	0.8 [140, 140]
= α Aur A	+45 54	2.4	+0.38	+1.90	0.0	0.2	0.8
Ross 614 A, B	06 24.3	0.15^F [157]	−0.82	−2.34	10.6	12.91	10.90 [140]
	−02 44	0.07	−1.15	...	...	16.41	14.10
ADS 5423[B,D]	06 40.8	2.21^F [1]	+0.344	+1.43	1.18	1.39	−1.47 [140]
= α CMa	−16 35	0.95	−0.02	−1.98	9.7^D	11.22	8.36 [140,159]
ADS 6251[B]	07 34.1	1.76^F [1]	+0.245	+0.87	2.61	2.65^{UV}	0.38 [140]
= α CMi	+05 29	0.65	−0.19	...	...	13.0:	10.7 [154]
ADS 6420	07 47.1	0.64 [162]	−0.19	+0.05	4.64	4.70^{UV}	5.72 [140]
= 9 Pup	−13 38	0.81	−0.09	−0.11	5.04	5.15^{UV}	6.17
ADS 6650 A, B	08 06.5	0.99 [1]	−0.00	+0.32	3.95	4.00	5.64 [140, 1]
= ζ¹ Cnc A, B	+17 57	0.85	−0.07	+0.19	4.29	4.35	5.99
BD + 77°361	09 06.3	0.75 [166]	−0.12	...	...	9.0	10.7 [1]
	+77 40	0.68	−0.17	...	...	9.3	11.0
ADS 7284	09 12.0	0.62 [1]	−0.21	...	...	6.8	8.0 [140, 140]
= Σ 3121	+29 00	0.64	−0.19	...	...	6.8	8.0
CD − 39°5580	09 26.8	1.30 [1]	+0.114	...	...	3.12	4.09 [140, 140]
= ψ Vel	−40 02	1.25	+0.097	...	...	3.65	4.62
ADS 8035 A[B,E]	10 57.6	1.53 [199t], [199f]	+0.185	+2.27	−0.91	−0.54	1.87 [199f, 199]
= α UMa A	+62 17	1.47	+0.167	+0.95	+2.39	+2.43	4.84
ADS 8630	12 36.6	1.18 [1]	+0.072	+0.58	3.31	3.33^{UV}	3.53 [140, 140]
= γ Vir	−00 54	1.13	+0.053	+0.58	3.31	3.33^{UV}	3.53
ADS 8804[B]	13 05.1	1.40 [1]	+0.146	+0.46	3.61	3.65^{UV}	5.02 [140, 141]
= α Com	+18 03	1.46	+0.164	+0.42	3.71	3.75^{UV}	5.12
BD − 10°3672[B,G]	13 19.9	10.9 [199e]	+1.037	+4.17 [199e]	−5.8	−3.5 [199e]	...
= α Vir	−10 38	6.8	+0.83	...	...	−1.5	...
ADS 9031	13 44.5	0.4 [173]	−0.4	−0.76	6.66	7.41	7.59 [140, 140]
= Σ 1785	+27 29	0.4	−0.4	−0.94	7.10	7.85	8.03

Sp [d]	B − V [d,e]	T_{eff}(°K) [f]	$\log T_{eff}$ [f]	$R/R_\odot$ [g]	$\log \dfrac{R}{R_\odot}$ [g]	$\bar{\rho}$ [h] (gm cm^{-3})	$g \times 10^{-4}$ [h] (cm sec^{-2})	P(yr) [a]	π [i]
[147] 0 V	[142] +0.57	6,050	3.782	[148] 1.08	+0.033	1.0	2.0	[146] 480	[146] 0″.174
[199zi] 10 V	+1.39	3,800	3.580	0.6	−0.20	3	4	11″.994	
[150] M5.5e	...	3,150	3.50	0.06	−1.22	1100	130	[151] 25	[1] 0.370
M5.5e	...	3,150	3.50	0.05	−1.32	1700	160	2″.13	
[152] [M0]	...	...	...	...	...	...	...	[153] 57.7	[152] (0.048)
...	...	...	...	...	...	...	...	0″.67	
[154] A	[154] +0.03	[199j] 15,000	4.185	[199j] 0.015	−1.82	1.8×10^5	5×10^3	[154a] 247.92	[1] 0.204
M4e	+1.68	3,100	3.49	0.3	−0.48	8	5	6″.894	
[193] 5 III	[140] [+0.80]	5,010	3.700	12	+1.09	0.0015	0.04	[156a] 0.2848^c	[1] 0.075
0 III	...	5,400	3.732	10	+1.01	0.003	0.06	0″.0536	
[140] M4e	...	3,400	3.53	0.19	−0.71	30	11	[157] 16.5	[1] 0.252
...	...	...	...	...	...	...	...	0″.98	
[145] 1 V	[140] +0.02	[199k] 9,910	3.996	[158] 1.75	+0.243	0.6	2.0	[160] 50.09	[1] 0.376
[154] A	...	[199zd] 32,000	4.51	[199zd] 0.0078	−2.11	2.8×10^6	4.3×10^4	7″.50	
[142a] 5 IV–V	[140] +0.40	[199k] 6,470	3.811	[158] 2.14	+0.330	0.25	1.1	[161] 40.65	[1] 0.287
[199i] F	...	...	...	...	...	...	...	4″.548	
[142a] 1 V]	[140] +0.57	5,930	3.773	1.0	0.00	0.9	1.8	[164] 23.18	[162] (0.063)
...	+0.65	5,580	3.747	0.9	−0.03	1.4	2.5	0″.58	
[144] 3 V	[140] [+0.54]	6,300	3.799	1.2	+0.09	0.8	1.8	[165] 59.7	[1] (0.047)
0	...	6,050	3.782	1.1	+0.05	0.8	1.8	0″.884	
[1] 5]	[166a] [+1.32]	...	...	...	...	...	...	[167] 16.6	[166] (0.045)
...	...	...	...	...	...	...	...	0″.33	
[140] K4]	[140] [+1.02]	...	...	...	...	...	...	[168] 34.2	[1] (0.058)
...	...	...	...	...	...	...	...	0″.66	
[142a] 2 IV]	[140] [+0.36]	...	...	...	...	...	...	[169] 34.11	[1] (0.064)
...	...	...	...	...	...	...	...	0″.920	
[142a] 0 III	[140] [+1.08]	[199f] 4,720	3.674	20	+0.31	2.6×10^{-4}	0.010	[199f] 44.2	[199f] (0.033)
[199z] ...	...	...	...	...	...	...	...	0″.595	
[147] V	[142] +0.35	6,950	3.842	[170] 1.67	+0.223	0.36	1.2	[171] 171.37	[1] (0.092)
V	+0.35	6,950	3.842	1.3	+0.13	0.7	1.7	3″.746	
[144] V	[140] [+0.45]	6,700	3.826	1.3	+0.10	1.0	2.4	[172] 25.83	[1] (0.054)
V	...	6,700	3.826	1.2	+0.08	1.2	2.8	0″.672	
[142a] V	[142a] [−0.23]	[199e] 22,400	4.350	[199e] 8.1	+0.91	0.029	0.46	[199e] 0.0109914	[199e] 0.0119
[199k] V?	...	...	...	...	...	...	...	0″.00154	
[173] 6	[140] [+1.12]	4,200	3.623	0.8	−0.10	1.2	1.8	[173] 155.71	[173] (0.092)
[174]	...	4,200	3.623	0.6	−0.19	2	3	2″.475	

Table 1-3 (*continued*)

SYSTEM	R.A. [a] Decl.	$M/M_\odot$	$\log \dfrac{M}{M_\odot}$	$\log \dfrac{L}{L_\odot}$	$\mathcal{M}_{bol}$ [b]	$\mathcal{M}_V$ [c]	m_V [c]
CPD − 60°5483 A, B	14h32m8	1.07F	+0.029	+0.18	4.30	4.37	[1] −0.04
= α Cen A, B	−60°25′	0.88	−0.06	−0.23	5.34	5.58	1.17
ADS 9413H	14 46.8	0.83F [1]	−0.08	−0.28	5.46	5.60UV	[140] 4.75
= ξ Boo	+19 31	0.73	−0.14	−1.05	7.38	7.78	6.91
ADS 9617	15 19.1	1.10 [176]	+0.041	+0.17	4.34	4.41UV	[140, 141] 5.59
= η CrB	+30 39	1.00	0.000	+0.04	4.65	4.72UV	5.90
ADS 10157I	16 37.5	1.22F [1]	+0.086	+0.73	2.94	3.00	[140, 140] 2.89
= ζ Her	+31 47	0.66	−0.18	−0.26	5.41	5.60	5.49
BD + 45°2505	17 10.6	0.31F [1]	−0.51	...	...	10.94	[179, 140] 9.96
= Fu 46	+45 47	0.24	−0.62	...	...	11.31	10.33
CD − 34°11626 A, BJ	17 12.1	0.77J [1]	−0.11	−0.74	6.61	7.01	[140] 6.30
= Melb 4 A, B	−34 53	0.54	−0.27	−1.01	7.29	7.91	7.20
ADS 10598	17 25.2	1.14 [199w]	+0.057	−0.02	4.82	4.95	[140, 199w] 6.02
= Σ 2173	−00 59	1.08	+0.033	−0.05	4.89	5.02	6.09
ADS 10660	17 34.0	1.34F [183]	+0.127	+0.16	4.36	4.42UV	[140] 5.33
= 26 Dra	+61 57	0.79	−0.10	−0.74	.6.62	7.16	8.06
ADS 11046K	18 00.4	0.90 [1]	−0.05	−0.30	5.50	5.69	[140] 4.20
= 70 Oph	+02 31	0.66	−0.18	−0.79	6.74 ·	7.49	6.00
ADS 11077M	18 03.2	1.21F [1]	+0.083	+0.34	3.91	3.97UV	[140, 141] 5.10
= 99 Her	+30 33	0.66	−0.18	−0.80	6.75	7.29	8.36
ADS 11871	18 53.3	2.19F [1]	+0.340	+0.36	3.87	3.94UV	[140, 141] 5.36
= β 648	+32 46	1.23	+0.090	−0.40	5.75	6.16	7.54
BD + 4°4510	20 34.6	0.69 [188]	−0.16	...	...	7.3	[143] 8.3
= Lal 39836	+04 37	0.65	−0.19	...	...	8.0	9.0
ADS 14773	21 09.6	1.26 [190a]	+0.100	+0.31	3.98	4.02UV	[140, 140] 5.26
= δ Equ	+09 36	1.20	+0.079	+0.31	3.98	4.02UV	5.26
ADS 14787	21 10.8	1.14F [191]	+0.057	+0.92	2.47	2.51UV	[140, 141] 3.86
= τ Cyg	+37 37	0.61	−0.21	−0.01	4.78	4.85UV	6.21
ADS 15972	22 24.4	0.26F [1]	−0.58	−2.03	9.8	11.84	[140, 140] 9.82
= Krü 60	+57 12	0.16	−0.80	−2.57	11.2	13.49	11.47
ADS 17175	23 56.9	0.87F [1]	−0.06	−0.20	5.27	5.34	[142, 1] 5.80
= 85 Peg	+26 33	0.69	−0.16	...	...	8.38	8.84

Sp [d]	B − V [d,e]	T_{eff}(°K) [f]	$\log T_{eff}$ [f]	$R/R_\odot$ [g]	$\log \dfrac{R}{R_\odot}$ [g]	$\bar{\rho}$ [h] (gm cm⁻³)	$g \times 10^{-4}$ [h] (cm sec⁻²)	P(yr) a	π [i]
[144] 52 V	...	5,770	3.761	1.2	+0.09	0.8	1.9	[144] 80.089	[1] 0″.761
K1	...	5,110	3.708	1.0	−0.01	1.3	2.5	17″.665	
[142a] 58 V	[140] +0.70	5,420	3.734	[148] 1.01	+0.004	1.1	2.2	[175] 149.95	[1] 0.149
[144] K4 V	+1.0	4,600	3.663	0.5	−0.33	10	9	4″.884	
[144] 52 V	[140] [+0.58]	5,770	3.761	1.2	+0.08	0.9	2.0	[177] 41.623	[176] (0.059)
52 V	...	5,770	3.761	1.1	+0.02	1.2	2.5	0″.907	
[142a] 50 IV	[140] [+0.64]	5,990	3.777	2.1	+0.33	0.17	0.7	[178] 34.38	[1] 0.105
[144] K0	...	5,240	3.719	0.9	−0.05	1.3	2.2	1″.369	
[140] dM4	[140] [+1.49]	...	...	...	...	...	...	[180] 12.98	[1] 0.157
...	...	...	...	...	...	...	...	0″.71	
[140] K3 V	[144] [+1.04]	4,800	3.681	0.6	−0.21	5	6	[180a] 42.06	[1] 0.139
K5 V	...	4,400	3.643	0.5	−0.27	5	5	1″.837	
[199w] 58 IV–V:	[140] [+0.72]	5,500	3.740	1.1	+0.03	1.3	2.7	[182] 46.08	[199w] 0.061
58 IV–V:	...	5,500	3.740	1.0	+0.02	1.4	2.8	1″.02	
[142] 50 V	[140] +0.56	6,100	3.785	1.1	+0.03	1.5	3	[184] 74.16	[183] (0.066)
...	+1.10	4,500	3.653	0.7	−0.16	3	4	1″.50	
[142] K0 V	[140] +0.78	5,240	3.719	[148] 1.17	+0.068	0.8	1.8	[185] 87.85	[1] 0.199
[148] K6 V	+1.15	4,200	3.623	0.8	−0.12	2	3	4″.56	
[144] '7 V	[140] +0.50	5,930	3.773	1.4	+0.15	0.6	1.7	[186] 53.7	[1] (0.061)
...	+1.10	4,500	3.653	0.7	−0.19	3	4	1″.07	
[144] 50 V	[140] +0.56	5,770	3.761	1.5	+0.18	0.9	2.6	[187] 61.2	[1] (0.053)
...	+1.00	4,800	3.681	0.9	−0.04	2	4	1″.24	
[143] K5 V]	...	...	...	...	...	...	...	[189] 37.0	[188] (0.062)
...	...	...	...	...	...	...	...	0″.76	
[142a, 190a] '7 V	[140] [+0.49]	6,400	3.806	1.2	+0.07	1.1	2.5	[190a] 5.708	[190a] 0.057
'7 V	...	6,400	3.806	1.2	+0.07	1.1	2.4	[141a] 0″.245	
[142a] '0 IV	[140] +0.38	6,900	3.84	2.0	+0.30	0.2	0.8	[191] 49.9	[191] (0.054)
...	+0.60	5,770	3.761	1.0	0.00	0.9	1.7	0″.88	
[1] M3	[140] [+1.65]	3,500	3.54	0.26	−0.58	20	11	[192] 44.46	[1] 0.254
M4e	...	3,400	3.53	0.15	−0.82	60	19	2″.386	
[144] 52 V	[142] [+0.68]	5,770	3.761	0.8	−0.10	2	4	[192a] 26.27	[1] (0.081)
...	...	...	...	...	...	...	...	0″.83	

Table 1-3 (*continued*)

* For each system, unless otherwise noted, the upper row of entries refers to component A and the lower row refers to component B.

Solar values are $M_\odot = 1.991 \times 10^{33}$ gm, $L_\odot = 3.82 \times 10^{33}$ erg sec^{-1}, $\mathcal{M}_{bol\odot} = +4.76$, $\mathcal{M}_{V\odot} = +4.83$, Sp = G2 V, $T_{eff} = 5770°$K, $R_\odot = 6.960 \times 10^{10}$ cm, $\bar{\rho} = 1.41$ gm cm^{-3}, $g_\odot = 2.74 \times 10^4$ cm sec^{-2}.

The reliability of the determinations varies widely. For example, the masses for η Cas may be considered known within approximately 7 per cent, but the masses for BD $+77°361$ are determined within about 30 per cent. Systems for which the value of the parallax is enclosed in parentheses are less reliable. A colon indicates uncertainty.

References, given in parentheses, are listed in the Bibliography. Except in the columns for $R/R_\odot$ or T_{eff}, or unless otherwise noted, the reference applies to both components. Reference (1) here implies the article by D. L. Harris, III, K. Aa. Strand, and C. E. Worley (K. Aa. Strand, ed.), 1963 (1).

[a] The right ascension and declination are given for the year 1900.

[b] $\mathcal{M}_{bol}$ is found with a bolometric correction corresponding to B − V or the spectral type, as given by Table 1-1A or Table 1-1B. See note UV.

[c] Observed photoelectric V magnitudes are given where available. Where two references are enclosed in one pair of parentheses, the first refers to the combined V magnitude and the second to Δm.

[d] Brackets indicate that the quantity refers to the combined light of the system. (Brackets have been judged to be appropriate in certain cases not made clear in the references quoted.)

[e] B − V is the observed color index, i.e., it is not corrected for line blanketing effects. See note UV.

[f] T_{eff} is found from B − V or the spectral type, as given by Table 1-1A or 1-1B, unless a reference is quoted. See note UV.

[g] $R/R_\odot$ is calculated from $L/L_\odot$ and T_{eff} unless a reference is quoted; hence $R/R_\odot$ is generally not a direct observational value. The radii of α CMa A, α CMi A, and α Vir A may be regarded as direct observational values, being based on interferometric measurements. The published radii for some stars are not consistent with $L/L_\odot$ and T_{eff} as adopted in this table. The published values have been adjusted to the parallaxes adopted here. In this column, a reference applies to only one component, not to both.

[h] The values of $\bar{\rho}$ and g are calculated with the use of $R/R_\odot$, hence they are not direct observational values except for α CMa A, α CMi A, and α Vir A. Revisions by factors of 2 or 3 may prove necessary for some values.

[i] Absolute trigonometric parallax, except for α Vir, Σ 2173, and δ Equ. Parentheses indicate that among the published measured values, the maximum exceeds the minimum value by a factor of about 1.5 or greater, or, for ψ Vel and β 648, that only two or three measurements have been published. The parallax of α Vir is obtained from a combination of interferometric and spectroscopic data, while those of Σ 2173 and δ Equ are derived from a combination of visual and spectroscopic data.

[A] No evidence has been found for a previously suggested companion. Ref. (146).

[B] Additional designations: L 726-8 B = UV Ceti, α Aur = Capella, α CMa = Sirius, α CMi = Procyon, o^2 Eri = 40 Eri, α Com = 42 Com, α UMa = Dubhe, α Vir = Spica, Melb 4 = HD 156384.

[C] Observed interferometrically. Although the orbit and mass ratio are not well determined, this system has been included because it has giant components.

[D] Each component is possibly binary. Refs. (143), (154), and (160a). For α CMa B, the bolometric correction −1.5 used in ref. (158a) is adopted.

[E] The components of α UMa A are not well resolved except near maximum separation, and the orbit has been determined by treating the system as an unresolved astrometric binary with the use of parallax plates and visual observations of position angle.

[F] The mass ratio is that determined by B. H. Feierman [1970, private communication, or 1971 (199t)].

[G] Observed interferometrically. The primary component is intrinsically variable. Ref. (199zj).

[H] One component is possibly binary. Ref. (175a).

[I] Component A is possibly binary. Ref. (193).

[J] The mass ratio is not well determined.

[K] Component A has been reported as a spectroscopic binary, but this is not supported. Refs. (143) and (193).

[L] $L/L_\odot$ and $\mathcal{M}_{bol}$ are calculated from $R/R_\odot$ and T_{eff}.

[M] Note added in proof. A new study (199zl) yields $M_A = 0.90\ M_\odot$ and $M_B = 0.59\ M_\odot$.

[UV] Ultraviolet excess is observed and a correction (−0.01 to −0.06 mag) is included in $\mathcal{M}_V$ (although the *observed* value is given for m_V). When the ultraviolet excess is known only for the combined light of the system, but the spectral types are the same, the correction is applied to each component.

In cases where B − V has been used to determine the bolometric correction or T_{eff}, a correction ($\leqslant 0.11$) has also been applied to B − V (although the *observed* value is given here.) See refs. (140) and (140a).

An ultraviolet excess is also observed for 85 Peg [ref. (141a)].

Fig. 1-12 The Mass-Luminosity Relation for Visual Binary Stars. The data from Table 3 are plotted. *Large dots* indicate higher reliability than *small dots*, but possible duplicity of some components is not considered; consult Table 1-3. The *circle* represents the Sun. The *horizontal segments* show the displacements in log $(M/M_\odot)$ produced by errors of 10 and 25 per cent in the mass. The *vertical segment* shows the displacement in log $(L/L_\odot)$ produced either by an error of 10 per cent in the parallax or by an error of 0.2 mag in $\mathcal{M}_{bol}$.

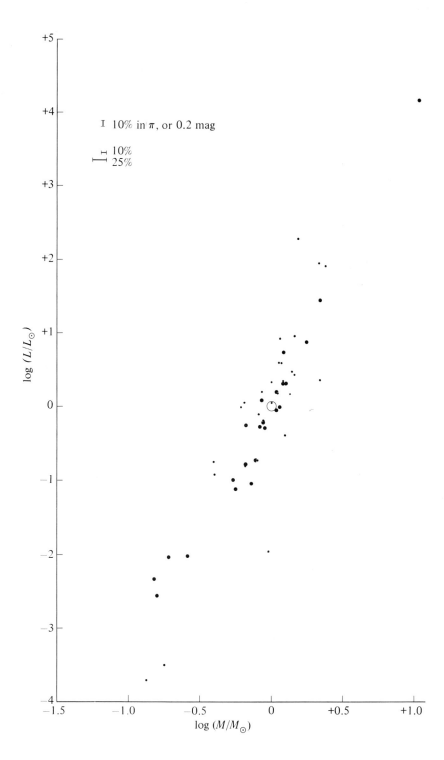

Table 1-4   Eclipsing and Spectroscopic Binary Systems (Exclusive of W Ursae M. Systems).*

SYSTEM	R.A.[a] Decl.	$M/M_\odot$	$\log \dfrac{M}{M_\odot}$	$R/R_\odot$	$\log \dfrac{}{R}$
XY Cet	02ʰ54ᵐ3	1.75 (199za)	+0.243	1.95 (199za)	+0.2
= HD 18597	+3°07′	1.63	+0.212	1.89	+0.2
ζ Aur[A]	04 55.5	5.6 (197)	+0.75	...	...
= HD 32068/9	+40 56	8.3	+0.92	160: (197)	+2.2
AR Aur	05 11.8	2.55[P]	+0.406	1.9[P]	+0.2
= HD 34364	+33 39	2.30	+0.362	1.7	+0.2
β Aur	05 52.2	2.35 (199zb, 199zc)	+0.371	2.5 (199zc)	+0.4
= HD 40183	+44 56	2.27	+0.356	2.5	+0.4
RR Lyn	06 18.0	2.09 (199za)	+0.320	2.52 (199za)	+0.4
= HD 44691	+56 20	1.58	+0.199	1.95	+0.2
WW Aur	06 26.0	1.81[P]	+0.258	1.95[P]	+0.2
= HD 46052	+32 31	1.75	+0.243	1.90	+0.2
YY Gem =	07 28.2	0.58 (197)	−0.24	0.60 (197)	−0.2
BD +32°1582	+32 06	0.58	−0.24	0.60	−0.2
VZ Hya	08 26.7	1.23[P]	+0.090	1.34[P]	+0.1
= HD 72257	−05 59	1.12	+0.049	1.10	+0.0
RZ Cnc	08 32.9	3.1 (197)	+0.49	11: (197)	+1.0
= HD 73343	+32 08	0.55	−0.26	13:	+1.1
UV Leo	10 33.0	[0.98][P]	[−0.01]	[1.07][P]	[+0.0
= HD 92109	+14 47				
RS CVn[A]	13 06.0	1.35 (197)	+0.130	1.7: (197)	+0.2
= HD 114519	+36 28	1.40	+0.146	4:	+0.6
ZZ Boo	13 51.6	1.76 (199x)	+0.245	2.26 (199x)	+0.3
= HD 121648	+26 25	1.68	+0.225	2.17	+0.3
BH Vir[B]	13 53.3	0.87 (199)	−0.06	1.05 (199)	+0.0
= HD 121909	−01 11	0.90	−0.05	1.15	+0.0
WZ Oph	17 01.8	[1.12][P]	[+0.049]	[1.34][P]	[+0.
= HD 154676	+07 55				
U Oph	17 11.4	5.30 (197)	+0.724	3.4 (197)	+0.5
= HD 156247	+01 19	4.65	+0.667	3.1	+0.4
TX Her[A]	17 15.4	1.60[P]	+0.204	1.53[P]	+0.
= HD 156965	+42 00	1.42	+0.152	1.38	+0.
Z Her[B]	17 53.6	1.22 (197)	+0.086	1.6	+0.
= HD 163930	+15 09	1.10	+0.041	2.6	+0.

$\dfrac{L}{L_\odot}$ [b]	$\mathcal{M}_{bol}$	Sp	$T_{eff}(°K)$ [c]	$\log T_{eff}$ [c]	$\bar{\rho}$ (gm cm^{-3})	$g \times 10^{-4}$ (cm sec^{-2})
.25 [199za]	+1.63	A^E	8,500	3.93	0.3	1.3
.13	+1.93	A^E	8,000	3.91	0.3	1.3
..	...	B6.5 V [194]	13,900	4.143	...	...
▪.8:	−4.7:	K4 Ib	4,100	3.618	3×10^{-6}:	9×10^{-4}:
.73^P	+0.43	B9 [194]	11,400	4.057	0.5	1.9
.56	+0.86	B9	10,900	4.037	0.7	2.2
.70	+0.51	[A2 V] [144]	9,700 [199zc]	3.99	0.2	1.0
.70	+0.51				0.4	1.0
.42 [199za]	+1.21	A^E	8,200	3.92	0.2	0.9
.06	+2.11	...	7,600	3.88	0.3	1.1
.29^P	+1.53	A3$^{(m)}$ [145]	8,700	3.940	0.34	1.31
.18	+1.81	A3$^{(m)}$?	8,270	3.918	0.36	1.33
.21	+7.78	dM1e [194]	3,700	3.568	3.8	4.4
.21	+7.78	dM1e	3,700	3.568	3.8	4.4
.47^P	+3.58	F5 [194]	6,540	3.816	0.72	1.88
.24	+4.16	F5	6,330	3.801	1.19	2.54
.7:	+0.5:	K1 III [197]	4,580	3.661	3×10^{-3}:	7×10^{-2}:
.6:	+0.8:	K4 III	4,010	3.603	4×10^{-3}:	9×10^{-3}:
.02]^P	[+4.71]	G0 V [194]	[5,660]	[3.753]	[1.13]	[2.35]
		G1 V				
7:	+2.9:	F4 IV–V [194]	6,700	3.826	0.4:	1.3:
0:	+2.4:	K0 IV	5,000	3.699	0.03:	0.24:
02	+2.22	F2 IV–V [199x]	6,900	3.839	0.21	0.95
98	+2.31	F2 IV–V	6,900	3.839	0.23	0.98
16	+4.35	F8 IV–V [194]	6,200	3.792	1.06	2.16
12	+4.46	G2 V	5,770	3.761	0.83	1.87
35]^P	[+3.88]	F8 V [194]	[6,110]	[3.786]	[0.66]	[1.71]
		F8 V				
75	−2.10	B5 [194]	15,200	4.182	0.19	1.3
56	−1.64	B6	14,300	4.155	0.22	1.3
93^P	+2.43	A5 [194]	8,000	3.903	0.63	1.87
64	+3.16	F0	7,100	3.851	0.76	2.05
51	+3.23	F5 IV [194]	6,500	3.813	0.4	1.3
58	+3.31	K0 IV	5,000	3.699	0.09	0.4

Table 1-4 (*continued*)

SYSTEM	R.A. [a] Decl.	$M/M_\odot$	$\log \dfrac{M}{M_\odot}$	$R/R_\odot$	$\log \dfrac{R}{R}$
MM Her =	$17^h54^m.5$	1.22 [(199y)]	+0.086	2.8 [(199y)]	+0.4:
BD +22°3245	+22°09′	1.19	+0.075	1.5	+0.18
V451 Oph	18 24.5	2.78 [(199v)]	+0.444	2.6 [(199v)]	+0.4
= HD 170470	+10 49	2.36	+0.373	2.1	+0.3
RX Her	18 26.0	2.75P	+0.439	2.45P	+0.3
= HD 170757	+12 33	2.33	+0.367	1.95	+0.2
Z Vul[B]	19 17.5	5.4 [(197)]	+0.73	4.7 [(197)]	+0.6
= HD 181987	+25 23	2.3	+0.36	4.7	+0.6
V1143 Cyg[D]	19 36.4	1.34P [(195)]	+0.127	1.40P [(195)]	+0.1
= HD 185912	+54 44	1.30	+0.114	1.22	+0.0
V477 Cyg	20 01.6	1.78P	+0.250	1.52P	+0.1
= HD 190786	+31 42	1.34	+0.127	1.20	+0.0
31 Cyg[D] =	20 10.5	6.21 [(198)]	+0.793	6: [(198a)]	+0.8
HD 192577/8	+46 26	9.31	+0.969	200:	+2.3
Y Cyg	20 48.1	17.4 [(197)]	+1.240	5.9 [(197)]	+0.7
= HD 198846	+34 17	17.2	+1.235	5.9	+0.7
EI Cep[A]	21 28.9	1.68 [(199v)]	+0.225	2.3 [(199v)]	+0.3
= HD 205234	+75 58	1.78	+0.250	3.0	+0.4
CM Lac	21 56.1	1.88P	+0.274	1.59P	+0.2
= HD 209147	+44 04	1.47	+0.167	1.47	+0.1
AR Lac[A]	22 04.6	1.32 [(197)]	+0.121	1.8: [(197)]	+0.2
= HD 210334	+45 15	1.31	+0.117	3.0:	+0.4
CO Lac	22 42.5	4.5 [(199s)]	+0.65	2.9 [(199s)]	+0.4
	+56 19	3.7	+0.57	2.4	+0.3

* Except as otherwise noted, the two rows of entries for each system refer to the two compo
Brackets indicate the average for similar components.

A colon indicates uncertainty.

Solar values are $M_\odot = 1.991 \times 10^{33}$ gm, $R_\odot = 6.960 \times 10^{10}$ cm, Sp = G2 V, T_e
$5780°K$ (this table), $\mathscr{M}_{bol\odot} = 4.76$, $\bar{\rho}_\odot = 1.41$ gm cm^{-3}, $g_\odot = 2.74 \times 10^4$ cm sec^{-2}.

Most of the masses are known to a precision of roughly 5 per cent. However, the unce
for the K-type component of 31 Cyg is about 20 per cent.

References, given in parentheses, are listed in the Bibliography. A reference applies t
components, unless otherwise noted.

[a] The right ascension and declination are given for the year 1900.

[b] Log $(L/L_\odot)$ is calculated from the radius and temperature and therefore should not be re
as a direct observational value.

$\dfrac{L}{L_\odot}$ [b]	$\mathscr{M}_{bol}$	Sp	$T_{eff}(°K)$ [c]	$\log T_{eff}$ [c]	$\bar{\rho}$ (gm cm^{-3})	$g \times 10^{-4}$ (cm sec^{-2})
).69	+3.02	G8 IV [(199y)]	5,150	3.712	0.08	0.4
).09^c	+4.52^c	...	5,000^c	3.70	0.5	1.5
▪.95 [(199v)]	−0.12	A0 [(194)]	11,000	4.041	0.22	1.1
▪.55	+0.89	(A2)	9,700	3.987	0.35	1.4
▪.78^p	+0.31	B9.5 [(194)]	10,300	4.013	0.26	1.26
▪.46	+1.11	A1	9,600	3.982	0.44	1.68
▪.22	−3.29	B3–4 [(194)]	17,000	4.230	0.073	0.67
2.10	−0.48	A2–3	8,900	3.949	0.031	0.29
▪.49^p	+3.53	F5 V [(194)]	6,500	3.813	0.69	1.88
).41	+3.73	F5 V	6,600	3.820	1.01	2.40
.22^p	+1.71	A3 [(194)]	9,450	3.975	0.71	2.11
▪.45	+3.63	F5	6,850	3.836	1.09	2.55
▪.4:	−3.7:	B4 V [(194)]	16,400	4.215	0.04:	0.5:
▪.0:	−5.2:	K3.5 Ib	4,200	3.62	2×10^{-6}:	6×10^{-4}:
▪.56	−6.65	O9.8 V [(199b)]	32,700	4.514	0.12	1.4
▪.56	−6.65	O9.8 V	32,700	4.514	0.12	1.4
.1 [(199v)]	+2.0	F2 [(194)]	7,200	3.857	0.19	0.9
.25	+1.63	F2	6,900	3.839	0.09	0.5
.24^p	+1.66	A2 V [(194)]	9,350	3.861	0.66	2.04
.78	+2.81	A8 V	7,450	3.872	0.65	1.87
▪5:	+3.5:	G2 [(194)]	5,770	3.761	0.32:	1.1:
▪8:	+2.8:	K0	5,240	3.719	0.07:	0.4:
▪0:	−0.19:	B8.5 IV: [(199s)]	10,600:	4.025	0.26:	1.5:
▪8:	−0.22:	B9.5 V:	10,600:	4.025	0.38:	1.8:

s found from the spectral type as given by Table 1-1A or 1-1B except for β Aur, the second-
mponent of MM Her, or in cases where a reference is quoted for $\log (L/L_\odot)$. In the last
$_{\text{eff}}$ as given here corresponds to the published values of $L/L_\odot$ and $R/R_\odot$.
dly metallic-line star.
nsic variability may be present. Ref. (194).
nsic variability is present. Ref. (194).
$L/L_\odot$) is based on the value for the primary components and the observational result that
ary)/L(secondary) = 0.88/0.12. Then T_{eff} is derived from $L/L_\odot$ and $R/R_\odot$.
tional designations: V1143 Cyg = HR 7484; 31 Cyg = o^1 Cyg = ADS 13554 A.
rent criteria indicate a spectral type of early A or F0. See ref. (199za).
lata are from a list supplied by D. M. Popper (1970, private communication). See also
36) and (197).

Table 1-5   W Ursae Majoris Systems.* [Adapted from L. Binnendijk, 1970 (199a

SYSTEM	R.A. [a] Decl.	$M/M_\odot$	$\log \dfrac{M}{M_\odot}$	$R_a/R_\odot$ [b]	R_b/R
YY Eri	04^h07^m4	0.95	−0.02	1.07	0.9
= HD 26609	−10°44′	0.56	−0.25	0.64	0.5
RZ Tau	04 30.8	1.65	+0.217	1.47	1.2
= HD 285892	+18 33	0.89	−0.05	0.73	0.6
W UMa	09 36.7	1.08	+0.033	1.17	1.0
= HD 83950	+56 25	0.65	−0.19	0.67	0.5
AH Vir	12 09.3	1.38	+0.140	1.47	1.3
= HD 106400	+12 23	0.58	−0.24	0.73	0.6
RZ Com =	12 30.1	1.59	+0.201	1.31	1.1
BD +24°2475	+23 53	0.77	−0.11	0.70	0.6
44 Boo B[A]	15 00.5	0.87	−0.06	0.89	0.7
= HD 133640 ftr	+48 03	0.48	−0.32	0.62	0.5
V566 Oph	17 51.9	1.27	+0.104	1.49	1.3
= HD 163611	+5 00	0.43	−0.37	0.61	0.5
V1073 Cyg[A]	21 20.8	1.40	+0.146	2.26	2.0
= HD 204038	+33 16	0.48	−0.32	1.37	1.2
GK Cep[A]	21 29.7	2.72	+0.435	2.60	2.4
= HD 205372	+70 23	2.50	+0.398	2.47	2.2
SW Lac	22 49.1	1.22	+0.086	1.06	0.9
= HD 216598	+37 23	1.07	+0.029	0.85	0.7

* Except as otherwise noted, the two rows of entries for each system refer to the two comp
[a] The right ascension and declination are given for the year 1900.
[b] The radii of the prolate spheroid assumed for each star are R_a along the line of centers
components and R_b perpendicular to this direction.

Interferometric measurements are becoming increasingly important as a fundamental means of obtaining stellar radii. This method is applicable to single stars, as well as to binary components.

Figure 1-13 presents the empirical mass-radius relation as determined from those stars in Tables 1-3 to 1-5 that have fundamentally determined radii.

2-5 THE RELATION BETWEEN LUMINOSITY AND EFFECTIVE TEMPERATURE

We have shown a Hertzsprung–Russell diagram in Fig. 1-4. While the relation between luminosity and effective temperature, often called by the same name, is in some ways equivalent to that between the absolute magnitude at some wavelength and the spectral type, different observational data are needed in the two cases. The luminosity, or absolute bolometric magnitude, requires a knowledge not only of the magnitude at a specific wavelength but at *all* wavelengths. A spectral type is derived from the

$\log \dfrac{R_a}{R_\odot}$ [b]	$\log \dfrac{R_b}{R_\odot}$ [b]	$\log \dfrac{L}{L_\odot}$ [c]	$\mathscr{M}_{bol}$ [c]	Sp[d]	$\bar{\rho}\left(\dfrac{gm}{cm^3}\right)$
−0.029	−0.03	−0.04	4.9	G5	1.42
−0.19	−0.24	−0.44	5.9	G4	3.8
+0.167	+0.107	+0.76	2.9	F0	0.97
−0.14	−0.19	+0.04	4.7	F3	4.2
+0.068	+0.017	+0.16	4.4	F8	1.20
−0.17	−0.23	−0.24	5.4	F6	3.9
−0.167	+0.127	0.00	4.8	K0	0.74
−0.14	−0.18	−0.56	6.2	G9	2.6
−0.117	+0.045	−0.08	5.0	K0	1.39
−0.15	−0.22	−0.56	6.2	G9	4.3
−0.05	−0.10	−0.20	5.3	G2	2.21
−0.21	−0.27	−0.40	5.8	G0	3.7
−0.173	+0.124	+0.52	3.5	F4	0.68
−0.21	−0.26	−0.36	5.7	F8	3.3
−0.354	+0.301	+1.4	1.2	A3m	0.218
−0.137	+0.093	+0.72	3.0	A8	0.321
0.415	+0.384	+1.6	0.7	A2	0.252
0.393	+0.360	+1.6	0.9	A2	0.272
0.025	−0.05	+0.04	4.7	G3	2.00
0.07	−0.14	−0.08	5.0	G1	3.42

on trigonometric parallax for W UMa and 44 Boo; otherwise not a direct observational

pectral type of the fainter component is inferred, rather than observed, for some systems.
tional designations: 44 Boo = i Boo = 44 i Boo; V1073 Cyg = BV 342; GK Cep =

characteristic absorption lines in the spectrum, while an effective temperature must be derived from the luminosity and radius. Although the properties of the spectrum are indeed largely determined by the luminosity and radius of the star, it is clear that the two abscissae are not entirely equivalent. Similarly, the use of a color index as the abscissa has a somewhat different significance.

The effective temperature may be determined fundamentally for an eclipsing and spectroscopic system of known parallax for which the absolute radii and luminosities can be found. A fundamentally derived value of T_{eff} can also be obtained from interferometric measurements of the angular radius, together with the measured flux at some wavelength and the distribution of the flux with wavelength [see eq. (1-12)].

Figure 1-14 illustrates the relation between luminosity and effective temperature for stars for which luminosities are known from the apparent magnitudes and trigonometric parallaxes. For lack of stars with fundamentally derived effective temperatures, however, we have plotted visual binary systems, obtaining T_{eff} from the color index or spectral type through the use of Table 1-1.

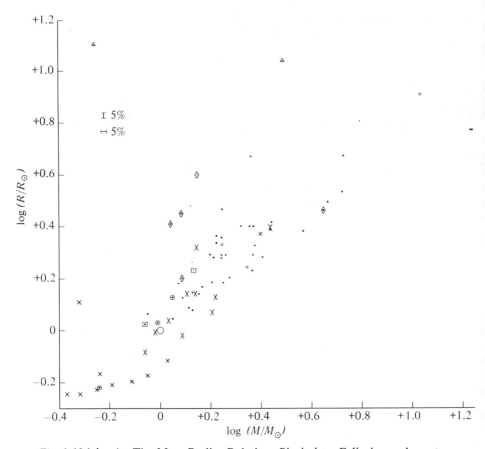

Fig. 1-13 (above)   The Mass-Radius Relation. *Black dots:* Eclipsing and spectro-scopic binary stars from Table 1-4. *Encircled black dots:* superposition of two points. *White dots:* α CMa A, α CMi A, and α Vir A (Table 1-3). *Large dots* (both black and white) indicate higher reliability than *small dots*, but intrinsic variability or possible duplicity of some components is not considered; consult Tables 1-3 and 1-4. *Circle:* the Sun. *Squares:* luminosity class IV–V. *Diamonds:* luminosity class IV. *Triangles:* luminosity class III. *Dash:* uncertain spectral classification. *Large crosses:* primary components of W Ursae Majoris systems. *Small crosses:* secondary components of W Ursae Majoris systems. [Reliability for these systems is not indicated. The ordinate for these tidally distorted stars is $\log (\sqrt[3]{R_a R_b^2}/R_\odot)$.] The horizontal and vertical segments show the displacements produced by an error of 5 per cent in $M/M_\odot$ or $R/R_\odot$, respectively.

Fig. 1-14 (on facing page)   The Hertzsprung–Russell Diagram for Visual Binary Stars. The data of Table 1-3 are plotted. Different masses are represented by the various symbols, according to the key in the figure. Possible duplicity of some stars is not considered; consult Table 1-3. The *vertical segment* at the upper right shows the displacement in $\log (L/L_\odot)$ produced either by an error of 10 per cent in the parallax or an error of 0.2 mag in $\mathcal{M}_{\text{bol}}$. The *horizontal segment* shows the maxi-mum displacement in $\log T_{\text{eff}}$ produced by an error of one subclass in spectral type.

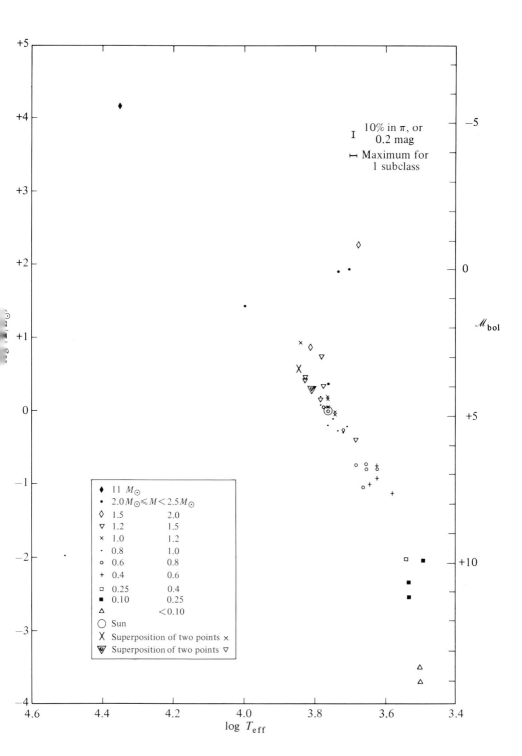

3 CHEMICAL COMPOSITION, AGE, AND POPULATION TYPE

3-1 RELATIVE ABUNDANCES OF THE ELEMENTS

Hydrogen is the most abundant element in the interstellar medium and also in stars that are not highly evolved. Helium is next in abundance, while all other elements comprise only a few per cent or less of the mass. Table 1-6A lists observed abundances of the elements, giving values for the solar photosphere when available. Table 1-6B summarizes the observational and theoretical values of the solar abundance of helium. (The quantity Y is defined below.) These tables indicate a general trend of decreasing abundance with increasing atomic number, with the conspicuous exceptions of the very low values for Li, Be, and B.

The amount of elements heavier than helium, relative to the hydrogen abundance, varies widely in different types of stars, being less than a hundredth of the solar value in very old stars. Whether helium in these cases is also underabundant with respect to hydrogen is not yet known, although there is now evidence that the fraction (by mass) of helium lies approximately in the range 0.2 to 0.4.* This abundance is similar to that in the Sun and other stars having approximately the solar abundance of heavier elements. A spectroscopic determination of the helium content is difficult for most stars, including the Sun, because the helium lines are weak except at very high temperatures (cf. Fig. 1-3).

If chemical composition is described by the parameters

X = fraction of hydrogen (by mass)
Y = fraction of helium (by mass)
Z = fraction of all other elements collectively (by mass),

Tables 1-6A and 1-6B yield the following range of values for the Sun. If

$$N_{He}/N_H = 0.037, \quad X = 0.86, \quad Y = 0.13, \quad Z = 0.018.$$

If

$$N_{He}/N_H = 0.14, \quad X = 0.63, \quad Y = 0.35, \quad Z = 0.013.$$

3-2 POPULATION TYPE

The stars may be broadly classified into two *population types*, although it is recognized that a strict dichotomy is an oversimplification. There is, in fact, a gradation from extreme Population I to extreme Population II. Population I stars, which include the Sun, are found in the spiral arms of the Galaxy and revolve about the galactic center with velocities similar to that of

---

* See P. Demarque, J. G. Mengel, and M. L. Aizenman, 1971 (403) and the references quoted therein; also see M. Schwarzschild, 1970 (399).

Table 1-6A   Relative Abundances of the Elements. Except for the elements specially marked, the values are for the solar photosphere or sunspots. The abundances are given both by numbers of atoms, N, and by mass, AN. The scales are normalized to the value $N(H) = 10^{12}$.*

AT. NO.	AT. WT.	ELEMENT	log N	N	AN	REF.
1	1.008	H	12.00	1.0 (12)	1.0 (12)	—
2	4.003	He		See Table 1-6B		
3	6.939	Li	0.80§	6.3 (0)§	4.4 (1)§	(118a)
4	9.012	Be	1.17	1.5 (1)	1.3 (2)	(119)
5	10.811	B	< 2.5	< 3 (2)	< 3 (3)	(120)
6	12.011	C	8.55	3.5 (8)	4.3 (9)	(121)
7	14.007	N	7.93	8.5 (7)	1.2 (9)	(121)
8	15.999	O	8.77	5.9 (8)	9.4 (9)	(121)
9	18.998	F†	6.01	1.0 (6)	1.9 (7)	(25)
10	20.183	Ne‡	7.88	7.6 (7)	1.5 (9)	(122)
11	22.990	Na	6.30	2.0 (6)	4.6 (7)	(135a)
12	24.312	Mg	7.48	3.0 (7)	7.3 (8)	(124)
13	26.981	Al	6.40	2.5 (6)	6.8 (7)	(123)
14	28.086	Si	7.55	3.5 (7)	1.0 (9)	(125)
15	30.974	P	5.43	2.7 (5)	8.3 (6)	(123)
16	32.064	S	7.21	1.6 (7)	5.2 (8)	(123)
17	35.453	Cl	⩽5.5	⩽3 (5)	⩽1.1 (7)	(126)
18	39.948	A†	6.88	7.6 (6)	3.0 (8)	(25)
19	39.102	K	5.05	1.1 (5)	4.4 (6)	(123)
20	40.08	Ca	6.33	2.1 (6)	8.6 (7)	(124)
21	44.956	Sc	3.04	1.1 (3)	4.9 (4)	(127)
22	47.90	Ti	4.50	3.2 (4)	1.5 (6)	(127)
23	50.942	V	3.92	8.3 (3)	4.2 (5)	(127)
24	51.996	Cr	5.65	4.5 (5)	2.3 (7)	(128)
25	54.938	Mn	4.88§	7.6 (4)§	4.2 (6)§	(127)
26	55.847	Fe	7.5§	3.2 (7)§	1.8 (9)§	(129)
27	58.933	Co	4.5§	3 (4)§	2 (6)§	(129a)
28	58.71	Ni	6.30§	2.0 (6)§	1.2 (8)§	(139a)
29	63.546	Cu	4.16	1.4 (4)	9.1 (5)	(130)
30	65.37	Zn	4.42	2.6 (4)	1.7 (6)	(131)
31	69.72	Ga	2.84§	6.9 (2)§	4.8 (4)§	(131)
32	72.59	Ge	3.32	2.1 (3)	1.5 (5)	(131)
33	74.922	As†	2.10	1.3 (2)	9.4 (3)	(25)
34	78.96	Se†	3.33	2.1 (3)	1.7 (5)	(25)
35	79.904	Br†	2.64	4.4 (2)	3.5 (4)	(25)
36	83.80	Kr†	3.20	1.6 (3)	1.3 (5)	(25)
37	85.47	Rb	2.63	4.3 (2)	3.6 (4)	(132)
38	87.62	Sr	2.82	6.6 (2)	5.8 (4)	(124)
39	88.905	Y	1.43§	2.7 (1)§	2.4 (3)§	(133)
40	91.22	Zr†	2.80	6.3 (2)	5.8 (4)	(25)
41	92.906	Nb†	1.50	3.2 (1)	2.9 (3)	(25)
42	95.94	Mo†	1.88	7.6 (1)	7.3 (3)	(25)
43	—	Tc	—	—	—	
44	101.07	Ru†	1.44	2.8 (1)	2.8 (3)	(25)
45	102.905	Rh†	0.80	6.3 (0)	6.5 (2)	(25)
46	106.4	Pd†	1.26	1.8 (1)	1.9 (3)	(25)
47	107.868	Ag	0.75	5.6 (0)	6.1 (2)	(134)

Table 1-6A (*continued*)

AT. NO.	AT. WT.	ELEMENT	log N	N	AN	REF.
48	112.40	Cd	1.86	7.2 (1)	8.1 (3)	(134a)
49	114.82	In	1.71	5.1 (1)	5.9 (3)	(131)
50	118.69	Sn	1.71§	5.1 (1)§	6.1 (3)§	(131)
51	121.75	Sb†	0.95	8.9 (0)	1.1 (3)	(25)
52	127.60	Te†	2.04	1.1 (2)	1.4 (4)	(25)
53	126.904	I†	1.35	2.2 (1)	2.8 (3)	(25)
54	131.30	Xe†	2.06	1.1 (2)	1.5 (4)	(25)
55	132.905	Cs†	1.15	1.4 (1)	1.9 (3)	(25)
56	137.34	Ba	1.90	7.9 (1)	1.1 (4)	(124)
57	138.91	La	1.81	6.5 (1)	9.0 (3)	(135)
58	140.12	Ce	1.88	7.6 (1)	1.1 (4)	(135)
59	140.907	Pr	1.63	4.3 (1)	6.0 (3)	(135)
60	144.24	Nd	1.82	6.6 (1)	9.5 (3)	(135)
61	—	Pm	—	—	—	—
62	150.35	Sm	1.66	4.6 (1)	6.9 (3)	(135)
63	151.96	Eu	1.0	1.0 (1)	1.5 (3)	(133a)
64	157.25	Gd	1.12	1.3 (1)	2.1 (3)	(135)
65	158.924	Tb†	0.24	1.7 (0)	2.8 (2)	(25)
66	162.50	Dy	1.11	1.3 (1)	2.1 (3)	(135)
67	164.930	Ho†	0.38	2.4 (0)	4.0 (2)	(25)
68	167.26	Er	0.76§	5.8 (0)§	9.6 (2)§	(135)
69	168.934	Tm	0.43	2.7 (0)	4.5 (2)	(135)
70	173.04	Yb	0.81§	6.5 (0)§	1.1 (3)§	(135)
71	174.97	Lu	0.84§	6.9 (0)§	1.2 (3)§	(135)
72	178.49	Hf†	0.40	2.5 (0)	4.5 (2)	(25)
73	180.948	Ta†	0.75	5.6 (0)	1.0 (3)	(25)
74	183.85	W†	0.60	4.0 (0)	7.3 (2)	(25)
75	186.2	Re†	0.90	7.9 (0)	1.5 (3)	(25)
76	190.2	Os†	1.40	2.5 (1)	4.8 (3)	(25)
77	192.2	Ir†	1.20	1.6 (1)	3.0 (3)	(25)
78	195.09	Pt†	0.70	5.0 (0)	1.0 (3)	(25)
79	196.967	Au†	0.65	4.5 (0)	8.8 (2)	(25)
80	200.59	Hg	<3.0	<1 (3)	<2 (5)	(131)
81	204.37	Tl	≳0.2§	≳1.6 (0)§	≳3 (2)§	(131)
82	207.19	Pb	1.90	7.9 (1)	1.6 (4)	(131)
83	208.980	Bi†	0.40	2.5 (0)	5.2 (2)	(25)
...	...	...	...	...	...	...
90	232.038	Th†	−0.02	9.5 (−1)	2.2 (2)	(25)
92	238.03	U†	−0.30	5.0 (−1)	1.2 (2)	(25)

Excluding H and He, $\sum N = 0.00124 \times 10^{12}$, $\sum AN = 0.0212 \times 10^{12}$.

* In the columns for N and AN, the number in parentheses is the power of 10 by which the entry is to be multiplied. The atomic weights are based on the isotope C^{12}; values are from ref. (199r).
  References are listed in the Bibliography. Ref. (25) here implies p. 417 of the 2nd edition of the book.
  Note added in proof. R. Foy (1972, *Astron. Ap.* **18**, 26) finds log N(Fe)7.28 and H. Molnar (1972, *Astron. Ap.* **20**, 69) derives log N(Eu) = 0.70, log N(La) = 2.14, and log N(Sm) = 2.30.
† Data from early-type stars and chondritic meteorites is included in the listing from which the value is taken.
‡ Data from solar cosmic rays is used.
§ The value of N is not highly reliable. The uncertainty for some elements not explicitly marked may also be considerable.

Table 1-6B   The Solar Helium Abundance.

METHOD	N_{He}/N_H	Y	REF.[*]
Mean solar wind: ratio of numbers of α-particles to protons	0.037 (range 0.01 to 0.15[+])	0.13	(199ze) (115)
Model solar interior: requirements of age ($\geq 4\frac{1}{2} \times 10^9$ years) and observed neutrino flux	0.05 (upper limit 0.086)	0.16 ± 0.01[+] (upper limit ~ 0.25)	(117)
Solar cosmic rays: cosmic-ray ratio of He to medium nuclei, together with spectroscopic data for C, N, O relative to H	0.063 (range 0.055 to 0.071)	0.20	(116) (cf. 122)
Solar chromosphere and prominences: spectroscopic determination from eclipse data	0.065	0.20	(199zf)
Model solar atmosphere: prediction of intensities in wings of two calcium lines and at two points of continuum	0.14[-]	0.35	(118)

[*] The references are given in the Bibliography.

the Sun. They are believed to have formed comparatively recently. The Sun appears to be about 4.5 billion years old, but hot main-sequence stars have ages of only some millions of years. These stars have chemical compositions similar to that of the Sun.

Population II stars have orbits that may be highly inclined to the plane defined by the spiral arms. The orbits have higher eccentricities than those of the Population I stars, and, consequently, their orbital velocity vectors are not parallel to that of the Sun when they are in the vicinity of the Sun. Their velocities relative to the Sun are therefore large, and they are called *high-velocity stars*. They were apparently formed some 10 billion years ago[*] from clouds composed predominantly of hydrogen and perhaps helium, and they contain very little of the heavier elements. Transmutation of hydrogen and helium into heavier elements in these stars, together with subsequent release (by one means or another) into the interstellar medium, has caused an enrichment of that medium in these heavier elements. The Population I stars, formed subsequently from the interstellar matter, therefore contain 10 or 100 times as much of these elements.[†]

[*] A. Sandage, 1970 (199zg) has found that globular clusters, which are composed of Population II stars, have ages of about 10 billion years.
[†] The relation between age and composition is not a simple one, however. See the review article by I. R. King, 1971 (199zh).

3-3 STAR CLUSTERS

Clusters are basically of two types: *galactic* or *open clusters* containing Population I stars and *globular clusters* containing Population II stars. The former are amorphous aggregates found in the spiral arms; the latter are globular in form and are located in and around the Galaxy. Clusters belonging to galaxies other than our own are also observed.

Important observational evidence is provided by clusters, against which theories of stellar evolution may be tested. Presumably, the stars in any given cluster were formed at comparable times from the same large cloud of material and had about the same initial chemical composition. They therefore have similar ages, and the differences in their properties are due mainly to differences in their masses. The larger the mass, the more rapid is the evolution; and the cluster therefore displays various stages in the development of a star.

The fact that all the members of a cluster are at approximately the same distance from the Earth makes possible a comparison of their relative

Fig. 1-15   The Color-Magnitude Diagram of NGC 2264. This is a young galactic cluster. *Black dots* represent photoelectric, and *white dots* photographic, observations. *Vertical lines* indicate known light-variables; *horizontal lines* indicate stars having spectra showing the line *H*α in emission. The reddening is small, and the observed values of the magnitudes and colors have been plotted. *Lines* represent the standard main sequence and giant branch of Johnson and Morgan, corrected for the uniform reddening of the cluster. [After M. F. Walker, 1956 (105).]

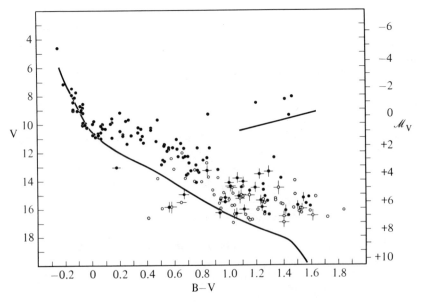

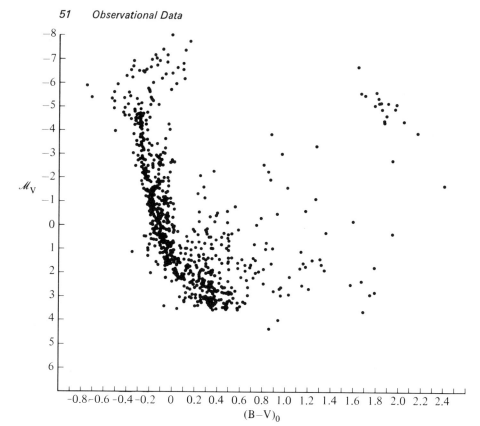

Fig. 1-16   The Color-Magnitude Diagram of the Galactic Clusters *h* and χ Persei. The color index has been corrected for interstellar reddening. [R. L. Wildey, 1964 (106).]

luminosities. For any two stars, the difference of absolute magnitudes must be the same as the difference of apparent magnitudes,

$$\mathcal{M}_1 - \mathcal{M}_2 = m_1 - m_2$$

by eq. (1-3). Therefore, if these are bolometric magnitudes,

$$\frac{L_1}{L_2} = 10^{-0.4(m_1 - m_2)}$$

by eq. (1-1). A plot of apparent magnitude against color index (say V versus B − V) is then essentially equivalent to a Hertzsprung–Russell diagram. Several such *color-magnitude diagrams* are shown in Figs. 1-15 to 1-19.* The

---

* The term *color* may be confusing in this context, inasmuch as each magnitude is measured in some particular range of wavelengths, i.e., in some particular color. However, the color index is actually a measure of the color of the star as it appears to the eye, as can be seen by comparing Tables 1-1 and 1-2.

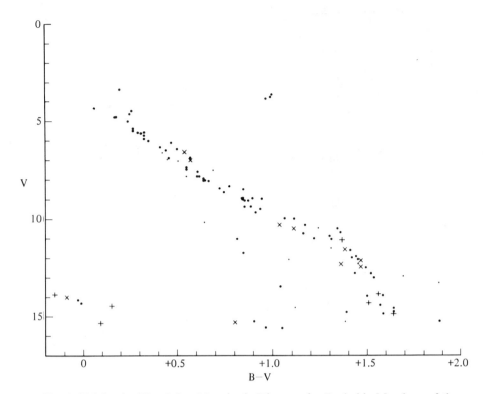

Fig. 1-17 (above)   The Color-Magnitude Diagram for Probable Members of the Hyades, a Galactic Cluster. *Large dots* indicate a probability of membership of 90 per cent or greater, *small dots* 80 to 89 per cent, and *crosses* 50 to 79 per cent in Table I of W. F. van Altena, 1969 (107). *Plus symbols* represent additional probable members from his Tables IIIA and IIIC. A number of the points plotted represent binary systems. White dwarfs and other subluminous stars are apparent in this diagram. The cluster is unreddened. [Data from W. F. van Altena, 1969 (107).]

Fig. 1-18 (on facing page, above)   The Color-Magnitude Diagram of M67. This is an old galactic cluster. No correction has been made to reddening in this figure. The scale of $\mathscr{M}_V$ is based on the distance modulus determined by O. J. Eggen and A. R. Sandage, 1964 (109). [After H. L. Johnson and A. R. Sandage, 1955 (108).]

Fig. 1-19 (on facing page, below)   The Color-Magnitude Diagram of M5. This is a typical globular-cluster diagram. No correction for reddening was necessary because the cluster lies well removed from the dust of the spiral arms. [After H. Arp, 1962 (110).]

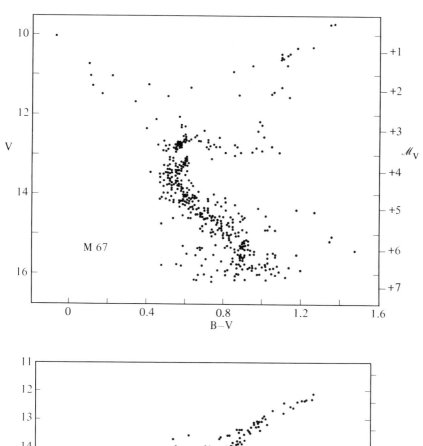

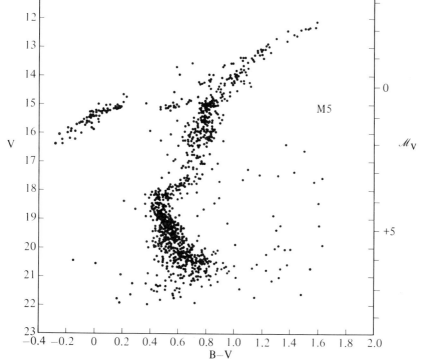

last of these is for a globular cluster, while the others are for galactic clusters. In Fig. 1-15, the less massive stars have not yet had time to attain the characteristics of the main sequence but are approaching that band from above. Figures 1-16 to 1-19 are for progressively older clusters, in which the massive stars that had been at the upper end of the main sequence have already evolved into giants. The age of a cluster can, in fact, be inferred from the absolute magnitude of the brightest main-sequence stars: the older the cluster, the fainter the stars at the upper end of the main sequence. Note also the resemblance between the old galactic cluster M67 and the globular cluster; the occupied portions of the diagram are qualitatively similar, although the giant region is less populous in M67.

The absolute magnitudes of the stars in a cluster can be derived by superposing the unevolved main sequence, plotted in terms of apparent magnitude, upon that of a cluster of known distance, plotted in terms of absolute magnitude. The difference $m - \mathcal{M}$ is called the *distance modulus* [cf. eq. (1-3)]. For accuracy, the effect of changes in chemical composition from one cluster to another must be taken into account, and a small vertical separation between the main sequences in the superposed diagrams must be allowed.

It should be realized that the lower end of the main sequence in an observed color-magnitude diagram does not necessarily mark the end of the main sequence in the actual cluster, as there may be other stars that are too faint to measure.

PROBLEMS

1. If a star with the same intrinsic properties as the Sun existed in the Hyades cluster (at a distance of 44 pcs), what would be its position in Fig. 1-17?

2. Choose a star in Fig. 1-17 for the Hyades cluster and adopt the value 44 pcs for its distance. Assume that the statistical relations discussed in this chapter may be applied.
   (a) Find the absolute visual magnitude $\mathcal{M}_V$, absolute bolometric magnitude, mass, radius, luminosity, effective temperature, spectral type, surface gravity, and mean density.
   (b) If the star is actually 30 per cent more massive than the value determined in part (a), how will its other properties be affected?
   (c) If the star is actually a field star at a distance 30 per cent greater than assumed, how will its properties be affected?

3. Two stars, at a distance of 50 parsecs from the Earth, form a binary system with a mean separation equal to that of Jupiter from the Sun (5 AU). Each of the stars is comparable to the Sun.

(a) Assuming that the orientation of the orbit is favorable for the occurrence of eclipses, how often do eclipses take place?

(b) If eclipses are to occur, how much may the orbital plane depart from the position in which it would be viewed edge-on? (Note that 1 parsec = 206,265 AU and that 1 radian = 206,265 seconds of arc.)

(c) Can this system be detected as a spectroscopic binary with an instrument capable of measuring a shift of 0.1 Å in a spectral line at 4000 Å?

(d) The theoretical resolving power of a telescope, expressed in radians, is 1.2 λ/D, where λ is the wavelength of the light and D (expressed in the same units as λ) is the diameter of the objective lens or mirror. What is the minimum diameter for the objective of a telescope that can reveal the system as a visual binary?

4. A *dynamical parallax* can be determined for a visual binary system having known apparent magnitude for each component and known period and mean separation (in seconds of arc) in the orbit corrected for projection effects. An initial trial value for the sum of the masses yields the parallax, which is used to derive the absolute magnitudes. New values are then obtained for the masses by use of the mass-luminosity relation, and the process is repeated until self-consistency is attained. Choose a main-sequence system in Table 1-3 and derive its dynamical parallax. Compare the results for the parallax and the masses with the values given in the table.

5. For the solar composition, calculate the value of X corresponding to $Z = 0.015$.

6. Make a rough verification of the right-hand scale of Fig. 1-18 for M67 by assuming that

(a) the Sun at the distance of this cluster would lie on (or near) the main sequence of the cluster;

(b) the main sequence of this cluster contains stars similar to stars on the main sequence of the Hyades cluster. Use the value +3 for the distance modulus of the Hyades.

PART TWO

STELLAR ATMOSPHERES

2

THE TRANSFER OF RADIATION

It is the astronomer, not the star, that draws a boundary between a stellar atmosphere and interior. The outer layers merge smoothly with the interior regions, and the same physical principles must operate in both. Nevertheless, it is convenient to discuss the atmosphere and interior separately, since only the atmosphere is susceptible to direct observation and, furthermore, since approximations that are valid in one part of the star may not be so in the other. We begin by studying the atmosphere, which consists of those layers from which a significant amount of radiation reaches the surface without absorption by the overlying strata. Our discussion will be limited to the photospheric layers, which are the brilliant layers at the surface.* Chromospheres and coronae will not be considered.

This chapter is concerned with the passage of radiation through matter. We shall study the absorption and emission of radiant energy, the angular dependence of the intensity, the theoretical and observed intensities for the solar surface, and the temperature distribution as deduced from the radiation field.

1 DEFINITIONS

1-1 SPECIFIC INTENSITY I_ν

Intuitively, we think of *intensity* as being a measure of brightness. For example, we say that the light from a 100-watt bulb is more intense than that from a 25-watt bulb, or that the surface of the 100-watt bulb looks brighter. (We are assuming that the surfaces of the bulbs are frosted.) What is perceived is the amount of energy passing per second along a bundle of rays coming from any small area of the bulb. More generally, we can define the intensity not only at any point of a radiating surface, but also at any point in space. We must specify also the direction of the rays under consideration, because the radiation need not be isotropic. In the application to spherically symmetrical atmospheres, the position of a point can be specified by a single co-ordinate, namely, the distance x from the stellar surface; and the direction

---

* The *photosphere* is sometimes considered a single, idealized layer at a specific optical depth, such as $\tau = \frac{2}{3}$ or 1. See Section 2-1 for the definition of τ.

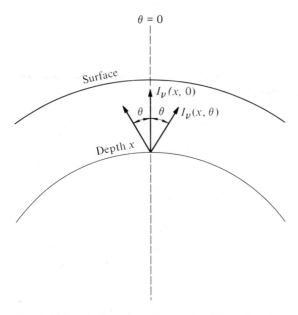

Fig. 2-1   Intensity at Depth *x* and in Direction θ.

can be specified by the angle θ between the ray and the normal to the layer (Fig. 2-1).*

Let us now define the intensity more precisely. Suppose that it is desired to find the intensity at point *P* and in the direction *PP'* in Fig. 2-2A. We find the intensity by considering the amount of energy passing in a given time through a small area $\Delta\sigma$ about *P* and into directions nearly parallel to *PP'*. Then we allow the time interval and the area to approach zero, while the permissible rays are required to approach the direction *PP'* more and more closely. Furthermore, only the range of frequencies between ν and $\nu + \Delta\nu$ will be considered, so that we obtain the intensity at frequency ν if the range $\Delta\nu$ is made to decrease toward zero.

* The reader who wishes to omit the mathematical description of the intensity may proceed directly to the verbal definition following eq. (2-2). In the subsequent equations, $d\omega$ is an element of solid angle.

Fig. 2-2A   Radiation passing through a small area $\Delta\sigma$ about point *P* and into directions nearly parallel to *PP'*.

Fig. 2-2B   Radiation from each point of $\Delta\sigma$ flowing into solid angle $\Delta\omega$ about an axis parallel to *PP'*.

Fig. 2-2C   The Envelope of the Cones in Fig. 2-2B. The elemental area $\Delta\sigma$ is assumed to be circular.

Fig. 2-2D   Bundles of parallel rays passing through a circular element $\Delta\sigma$ into a solid angle $\Delta\omega$ about *PP'*.

A

B

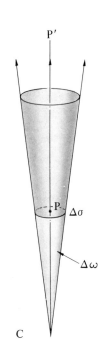

C

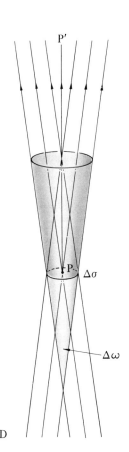

D

For the moment, let us suppose that P is a point of a radiating surface and that PP' is normal to the surface. Let $\Delta\sigma$ be the small area about P, and let $\Delta\omega$ be the solid angle of a cone with vertex at P that contains rays nearly parallel to PP'.* Draw similar cones for each point of $\Delta\sigma$ (Fig. 2-2B). The enveloping surface is a truncated cone with base $\Delta\sigma$ and solid angle $\Delta\omega$ (Fig. 2-2C).

If P is instead a point in space, we consider all the bundles of parallel rays that pass through $\Delta\sigma$ but remain within the enveloping truncated cone of solid angle $\Delta\omega$ (Fig. 2-2D). The result is identical with that of Fig. 2-2C. Then, if ΔE_ν is the amount of energy at frequencies between ν and $\nu + \Delta\nu$ passing in time Δt through (or from) the area $\Delta\sigma$ into the truncated cone of solid angle $\Delta\omega$, it is found experimentally that the ratio of ΔE_ν to the product $\Delta\nu \, \Delta t \, \Delta\sigma \, \Delta\omega$ has a definite limit as the quantities $\Delta\nu$, Δt, $\Delta\sigma$, $\Delta\omega$ approach zero in any manner. This limit is the *specific intensity* I_ν of radiation of frequency ν at point P in the direction of the normal to $\Delta\sigma$:

$$I_\nu = \lim_{\substack{\Delta\nu \to 0 \\ \Delta t \to 0 \\ \Delta\sigma \to 0 \\ \Delta\omega \to 0}} \frac{\Delta E_\nu}{\Delta\nu \, \Delta t \, \Delta\sigma \, \Delta\omega}. \tag{2-1}$$

This is usually called simply the *intensity*.

If PP' is oriented at some angle θ with the normal to $\Delta\sigma$, as in Fig. 2-3, we again draw a cone of solid angle $\Delta\omega$ about PP' with vertex at P. Similar cones of solid angle $\Delta\omega$ and axes parallel to PP' are then drawn through every other point of $\Delta\sigma$, producing an enveloping surface as before.† The energy ΔE_ν in frequencies between ν and $\nu + \Delta\nu$ that streams in time Δt from every point of $\Delta\sigma$ into a solid angle $\Delta\omega$ about the direction defined by θ has an intensity

$$I_\nu(\theta) = \lim_{\substack{\Delta\nu \to 0 \\ \Delta t \to 0 \\ \Delta\sigma \to 0 \\ \Delta\omega \to 0}} \frac{\Delta E_\nu}{\Delta\nu \, \Delta t \, \Delta\sigma \cos\theta \, \Delta\omega}, \tag{2-2}$$

where the factor $\cos\theta$ expresses the fact that the rays are now confined by the projected area $\Delta\sigma \cos\theta$, rather than by $\Delta\sigma$ itself.

The *specific intensity* I_ν of radiation of frequency ν at a point P and in a given direction is thus the amount of energy per unit frequency interval at ν per unit time interval per unit area per unit solid angle passing into the

* In general, the shape of $\Delta\sigma$ is arbitrary; but since the geometry involving a circular area is most readily visualized, we assume this shape in the following text and illustrations.
† In this case, the enveloping surface is no longer a cone, since the rays defining it do not, in general, have a common apex.

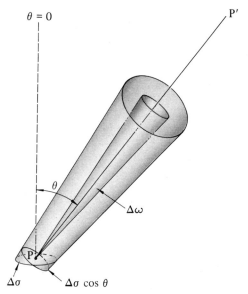

$\theta = 0$

P'

θ

$\Delta\omega$

P

$\Delta\sigma$ $\Delta\sigma \cos\theta$

Fig. 2-3   Radiation passing into a solid angle $\Delta\omega$ about *PP'*, which is inclined at an angle θ to the normal to the circular element $\Delta\sigma$.

specified direction at *P*. In the cgs system, the units of I_v are erg $(\text{cycle/sec})^{-1}$ $\text{sec}^{-1} \text{cm}^{-2} \text{sterad}^{-1}$.

Once the passage to the limit $\Delta\omega \to 0$ has been made, the beam is no longer divergent. Therefore, there is no dilution of energy as the beam travels through space, and *the intensity is independent of the distance from the source.* The solar disk would appear just as bright from Saturn as it does from the Earth.

No optical instrument can make a radiating surface appear more intense, since it cannot increase the amount of energy passing along a ray. A telescope gathers more light than the eye, but spreads it over an enlarged image. Hence, the unresolved continuum of stars in the Andromeda Galaxy appears just as disappointingly faint when viewed through a telescope as it does to the naked eye. See Section 5, example (i).

The intensity can be measured only for sources that present a finite angular size to the observer, such as the Sun or a planet. See Section 5, example (j). The relative intensities of various portions of the disk of an eclipsing binary component can be derived from the light curve, but the values are not precise.*

* The limb-darkening coefficient x is the quantity derived, where $I(\theta) = I_{\theta=0}(1 - x + x \cos\theta)$. The values of x obtained from observations in the visible wavelength range are usually between 0.4 and 0.8. Compare Section 4-2B, eq. (2-45).

1-2 MEAN INTENSITY J_ν

We shall often consider the mean value J_ν of the intensities at a point. The contributions $I_\nu(x, \theta)\, d\omega$ from all directions are summed and then divided by the solid angle contained in a sphere:

$$J_\nu(x) = \frac{\displaystyle\int_{\text{sphere}} I_\nu(x, \theta)\, d\omega}{\displaystyle\int_{\text{sphere}} d\omega}$$

or

$$J_\nu(x) = \frac{1}{4\pi} \int_{\text{sphere}} I_\nu(x, \theta)\, d\omega. \tag{2-3}$$

We postpone for the moment the technique of performing the integration (see Section 1-5).

1-3 FLUX F_ν AND THE QUANTITY H_ν

The *flux* F_ν is the rate at which energy at frequency ν flows through (or from) a unit surface either into a given hemisphere or in all directions,

Fig. 2-4A   The Outward Flux. Radiation from all directions for which $\theta \leqslant \pi/2$ is included.

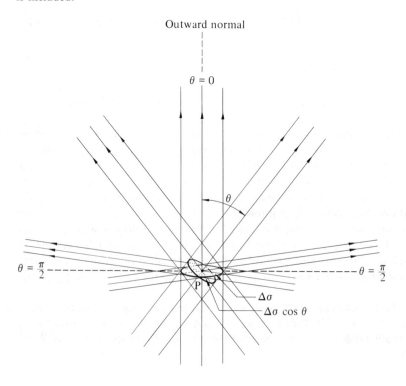

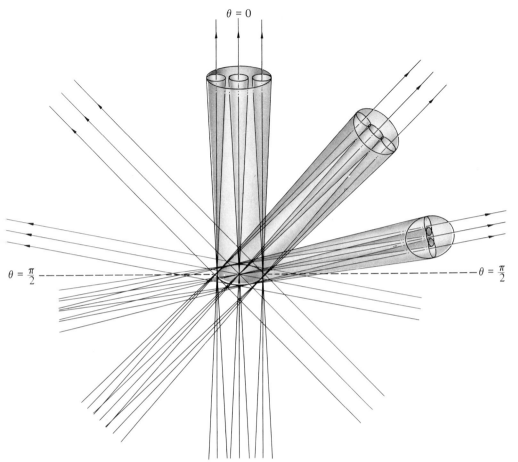

$\theta = 0$

$\theta = \dfrac{\pi}{2}$ — $\theta = \dfrac{\pi}{2}$

Fig. 2-4B   The Outward Flux. This diagram should be compared with Figs. 2-3 and 2-4A.

depending on which is specified. For example, the *outward flux*, directed away from the center of the star, includes all the radiation going in directions between $\theta = 0$ and $\theta = \pi/2$.* This is illustrated in Fig. 2-4A, which shows how Fig. 2-2D would appear if radiation were passing in all outward directions. Figure 2-4B includes cones such as those in Fig. 2-3.

---

* The reader who has omitted the detailed discussion in Section 1-1 should proceed directly to eq. (2-5), which expresses the outward flux $F_\nu{}^+$ as the integral (over all outward directions) of the intensity multiplied by the elemental solid angle and the projection factor $\cos \theta$, which restricts the cross-sectional area of a beam traveling in the direction θ.

To find the flux at point P, we must sum the contributions of all beams traveling in the specified range of directions. Any one beam, oriented at an angle θ with the normal to the surface $\Delta\sigma$ at P, makes a contribution ΔF_ν, which is the energy ΔE_ν per frequency interval $\Delta\nu$ at ν per time Δt per area $\Delta\sigma$ of the surface through which the flux is being measured:

$$\Delta F_\nu = \frac{\Delta E_\nu}{\Delta\nu \, \Delta t \, \Delta\sigma},$$

which we may write as

$$\Delta F_\nu = \frac{\Delta E_\nu}{\Delta\nu \, \Delta t \, \Delta\sigma \cos\theta \, \Delta\omega} \cos\theta \, \Delta\omega.$$

As the quantities $\Delta\nu$, Δt, $\Delta\sigma$, and $\Delta\omega$ become very small, the quotient on the right-hand side of the equation approaches the specific intensity I_ν. Thus we have

$$\Delta F_\nu = I_\nu \cos\theta \, \Delta\omega. \tag{2-4}$$

The physical meaning of the factor $\cos\theta$ is that the cross section of the beam passing through $\Delta\sigma$ in the direction θ is restricted to $\cos\theta \, \Delta\sigma$. Integration over the outward hemisphere now yields the *outward flux* $F_\nu^+(x)$:*

$$F_\nu^+(x) = \int_{\substack{\text{outward} \\ \text{hemisphere}}} I_\nu(x, \theta) \cos\theta \, d\omega. \tag{2-5}$$

Similarly, the *inward flux*, for directions with $\theta = \pi/2$ to π, is given by

$$F_\nu^-(x) = \int_{\substack{\text{inward} \\ \text{hemisphere}}} I_\nu(x, \theta) \cos\theta \, d\omega. \tag{2-6}$$

The *net flux* is simply the difference of the outward and inward fluxes,

$$F_\nu(x) = F_\nu^+(x) - F_\nu^-(x).$$

We may also write

$$F_\nu(x) = \int_{\text{sphere}} I_\nu(x, \theta) \cos\theta \, d\omega. \tag{2-7}$$

For an isotropic radiation field (for example, at the center of a star), the net flux is zero.

Unlike intensity, outward flux diminishes with increasing distance from the source, because the maximum angle between the rays and the normal to the surface decreases (Fig. 2-5A); as the area at which the flux is measured is moved farther from the source, the range of angles from which rays are incident becomes smaller. For a point source, the flux diminishes as the inverse square of the distance (Fig. 2-5B).

The flux received by an observer, unlike the intensity, can be measured for

* Some authors include a factor π in the definition, letting πF equal flux.

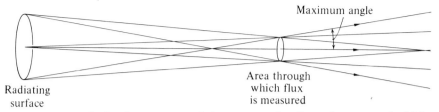

Fig. 2-5A   Radiation from an extended source passing through an area at which it is measured.

any source, regardless of whether the source appears as a point or has finite extent. See Section 5, example (f).

We also introduce the quantity

$$H_\nu(x) = \frac{\displaystyle\int_{\text{sphere}} I_\nu(x,\,\theta)\cos\theta\;d\omega}{\displaystyle\int_{\text{sphere}} d\omega}$$

$$= \frac{1}{4\pi}\int_{\text{sphere}} I_\nu(x,\,\theta)\cos\theta\;d\omega \tag{2-8}$$

$$= \frac{1}{4\pi}F_\nu(x). \tag{2-9}$$

This is useful in eliminating the factor 4π in certain equations.

1-4 THE QUANTITY K_ν

We next define

$$K_\nu(x) = \frac{\displaystyle\int_{\text{sphere}} I_\nu(x,\,\theta)\cos^2\theta\;d\omega}{\displaystyle\int_{\text{sphere}} d\omega}$$

$$= \frac{1}{4\pi}\int_{\text{sphere}} I_\nu(x,\,\theta)\cos^2\theta\;d\omega \tag{2-10}$$

Fig. 2-5B   Radiation from a point source passing through an area at which it is measured. The amount of radiation falling upon the area decreases as the inverse square of the distance from the source.

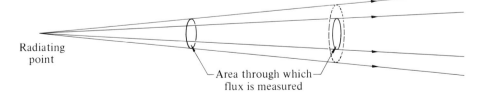

and show that it is related to the pressure of the radiation of frequency ν, $P_{\text{rad }\nu}(x)$.

Pressure is given numerically as the force per unit area acting normally on a surface. If the subscript n denotes a normal component, we may write

$$\text{pressure} = \text{force}_n/\text{area}$$

$$= \text{mass} \times \text{acceleration}_n/\text{area}$$

$$= \left[\frac{d}{dt} (\text{mass} \times \text{velocity})_n \right] \Big/ \text{area}$$

$$= \left[\frac{d}{dt} (\text{momentum})_n \right] \Big/ \text{area}.$$

Hence, the pressure can be expressed as the rate of transfer of the component of momentum that is normal to a unit surface. For radiation, the momentum is the energy divided by the speed of light.* From eq. (2-4), we find that the total amount of momentum transferred in time Δt by a beam of solid angle $\Delta\omega$ across a surface of area $\Delta\sigma$ for which the normal makes an angle θ with the direction of the beam is

$$\frac{1}{c} I_\nu \cos\theta \, \Delta\omega,$$

the factor $\cos\theta$ resulting from the limited size of the beam due to the projection of the area $\Delta\sigma$. To obtain the component of this momentum transferred normally to the surface, we must multiply by an additional factor $\cos\theta$. Finally, we sum over all directions†:

$$P_{\text{rad }\nu}(x) = \frac{1}{c} \int_{\text{sphere}} I_\nu(x, \theta) \cos^2\theta \, d\omega. \qquad (2\text{-}11)$$

Therefore

$$K_\nu(x) = \frac{c}{4\pi} P_{\text{rad }\nu}(x). \qquad (2\text{-}12)$$

* Compare
$$\text{momentum} = \text{mass} \times \text{velocity} = \text{mass} \times c.$$
But
$$\text{energy} = \text{mass} \times c^2.$$
Therefore
$$\text{momentum} = \text{energy}/c.$$

† We sum indifferently over all directions. Considering energy to be carried by discrete photons of momentum p ($=$ energy/c) traveling normally to a unit cross section, we find the amount of momentum carried per second to be (momentum/photon) $\times$ number of photons passing per second, which is proportional to $p \times c$. Radiation flowing in the opposite direction carries momentum proportional to $(-p) \times (-c) = p \times c$ as before, so that the contributions to the radiation pressure are to be added numerically.

This quantity, like H_ν, is merely a multiple of a physical quantity and is introduced to avoid the need of writing constants in certain equations.

1-5 THE INTEGRATION OVER SOLID ANGLE

For the sphere in Fig. 2-6, the solid angle $d\omega$ is related to the shaded area dA by

$$\frac{d\omega}{4\pi} = \frac{dA}{4\pi r^2}$$

or

$$d\omega = \frac{dA}{r^2}.$$

But dA may be approximated as the area of a rectangle,

$$dA = (r\,d\theta)(r\sin\theta\,d\varphi).$$

Therefore

$$d\omega = \sin\theta\,d\theta\,d\varphi. \qquad (2\text{-}13)$$

An integral over a sphere may be written as

$$\int_{\varphi=0}^{2\pi} \int_{\theta=0}^{\pi} \cdots d\theta\,d\varphi,$$

Fig. 2-6 The solid angle $d\omega$ in polar coordinates equals $\sin\theta\,d\theta\,d\varphi$.

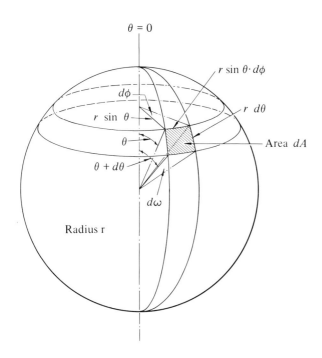

while integrals over the outward and inward hemispheres may be written as

$$\int_{\varphi=0}^{2\pi} \int_{\theta=0}^{\pi/2} \cdots d\theta \, d\varphi \quad \text{(outward)}$$

$$\int_{\varphi=0}^{2\pi} \int_{\theta=\pi/2}^{\pi} \cdots d\theta \, d\varphi \quad \text{(inward)}.$$

As an example, we find the solid angle contained in a sphere:

$$\int_{\text{sphere}} d\omega = \int_{\varphi=0}^{2\pi} \int_{\theta=0}^{\pi} \sin\theta \, d\theta \, d\varphi$$

$$= 2\pi[-\cos\theta]_0^\pi$$

$$= 4\pi.$$

As another example, we find the relation between outward flux and intensity when I_ν is independent of θ. We have

$$F_\nu^+ = \int_{\substack{\text{outward} \\ \text{hemisphere}}} I_\nu \cos\theta \, d\omega$$

$$= I_\nu \int_{\varphi=0}^{2\pi} \int_{\theta=0}^{\pi/2} \cos\theta \cdot \sin\theta \, d\theta \, d\varphi$$

$$= 2\pi I_\nu [\tfrac{1}{2} \sin^2\theta]_0^{\pi/2}$$

$$= \pi I_\nu, \tag{2-14}$$

and the outward flux is equal to the intensity multiplied by π.

2 ABSORPTION AND EMISSION OF RADIATION

2-1 ABSORPTION

Consider radiation passing through a slab of thickness dz (Fig. 2-7). The absorbed intensity is proportional both to the initial intensity I_ν and to the path length dz. Denoting the proportionality constant by κ_ν', we have

$$dI_\nu = -\kappa_\nu' I_\nu \, dz.$$

The constant κ_ν' is the *absorption coefficient*, expressed in this equation in cm^{-1}. Frequently the proportionality constant is set equal to $\kappa_\nu \rho$, where ρ is the density of the material:

$$dI_\nu = -\kappa_\nu \rho I_\nu \, dz. \tag{2-15}$$

The product $\kappa_\nu \rho$ has dimensions of cm^{-1}, while κ_ν has dimensions of $\text{cm}^2 \, \text{gm}^{-1}$. For this reason, κ_ν is called the *mass absorption coefficient*. It is this coefficient that we shall use henceforth.

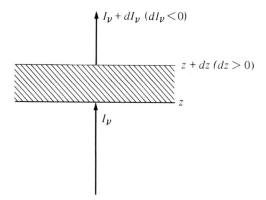

Fig. 2-7 The intensity I_ν changes by an amount $-dI_\nu$ upon passage through a slab of thickness dz.

Integrating eq. (2-15) between some definite limits designated by subscripts 1 and 2, we now have

$$\log_e I_\nu|_{I_{\nu 1}}^{I_{\nu 2}} = \log_e \frac{I_{\nu 2}}{I_{\nu 1}} = -\int_{z_1}^{z_2} \kappa_\nu \rho \, dz$$

$$I_{\nu 2} = I_{\nu 1} \exp \left(-\int_{z_1}^{z_2} \kappa_\nu \rho \, dz \right). \tag{2-16}$$

Let us apply this to find the intensity reaching the surface after attenuation of the radiation coming from depth x in the star. By convention, $x = 0$ at the stellar surface and decreases algebraically with increasing depth (Fig. 2-8). Since $I_{\nu 1}$ is the initial intensity [in this case to be called $I_\nu(x)$] and z_1 is the level of origin (in this case x), we find that, at the surface (corresponding to $z_2 = 0$),

$$I_\nu(0) = I_\nu(x) \exp \left(-\int_{x}^{0} \kappa_\nu \rho \, dx \right). \tag{2-17}$$

Fig. 2-8 The Relation between τ and x.

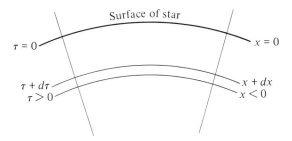

We now introduce the *optical depth* τ_ν, which is a dimensionless quantity:

$$d\tau_\nu = -\kappa_\nu \rho \, dx$$

$$\tau_{\nu 2} - \tau_{\nu 1} = -\int_{x_1}^{x_2} \kappa_\nu \rho \, dx. \tag{2-18}$$

Note that τ_ν and x increase in opposite directions. If we fix $\tau_{\nu 1} = 0$ and $x_1 = 0$ at the surface of the star (Fig. 2-8), then

$$\tau_{\nu 2} = -\int_0^{x_2} \kappa_\nu \rho \, dx$$

$$-\tau_{\nu 2} = -\int_{x_2}^0 \kappa_\nu \rho \, dx. \tag{2-19}$$

The subscript 2 is no longer needed and will henceforth be omitted. Then

$$I_\nu(0) = I_\nu(x) \, e^{-\tau_\nu}$$

or

$$I_\nu(0) = I_\nu(\tau_\nu) \, e^{-\tau_\nu}. \tag{2-20}$$

The optical depth of a layer determines the fraction of the intensity from that layer that reaches the surface without absorption. For example, from a layer at optical depth $\tau_\nu = 2$, the fraction $e^{-2} \approx 0.14$ of the original intensity survives to reach the surface.

As another illustration of the meaning of optical depth, consider a star for which the apparent magnitude would be $+2$ if measured above the atmosphere of the Earth. If its magnitude is $+3$ as measured at the surface of the Earth, then the star has been dimmed by a factor 2.512. Then

$$\frac{1}{2.512} = e^{-\tau},$$

and

$$\tau = 0.92$$

is the optical depth of the terrestrial atmosphere along the line between the star and the observer and in the spectral region in which the magnitude is measured.

2-2 EMISSION

We consider isotropic emission from an element of matter having mass dm. The amount of energy radiated per gram at frequencies between ν and $\nu + d\nu$ is proportional to $d\nu$ and to the time interval dt. Letting the proportionality constant be $4\pi j_\nu$, where j_ν is the *emission coefficient*, we have

$$\left. \begin{array}{l} \text{amount of energy emitted per gram} \\ \text{at frequencies between } \nu \text{ and} \\ \nu + d\nu \text{ in time } dt \end{array} \right\} = 4\pi j_\nu \, d\nu \, dt. \tag{2-21}$$

The amount of this energy that is radiated into the solid angle $d\omega$ is

$$4\pi j_\nu \, d\nu \, dt \, \frac{d\omega}{4\pi} = j_\nu \, d\nu \, dt \, d\omega. \qquad (2\text{-}22)$$

We shall use this expression in the next section.

3 THE EQUATION OF TRANSFER

3-1 DERIVATION

Consider energy passing through a frustum of a cone of solid angle $d\omega$ and height ds (Fig. 2-9). We shall find the change in the intensity due to absorption and emission within the frustum.

$$dI_\nu = \text{intensity emitted} - |\text{intensity absorbed}|.$$

We first find the intensity emitted. The coefficient j_ν is measured per gram, and we therefore must compute the mass of the frustum from its density ρ and volume dV. We see from the following considerations that the volume can be approximated by that of a cylinder. The solid angle $d\omega$ can be drawn

Fig. 2-9   Radiation is absorbed in the truncated cone of solid angle $d\omega$ and is emitted into the solid angle $d\omega$ by each particle of matter within the truncated cone.

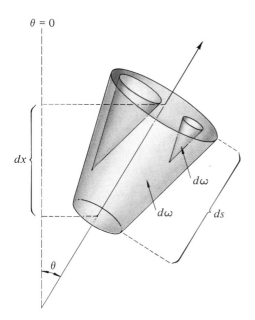

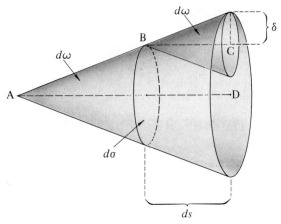

Fig. 2-10   The radius δ is much less than ds because $d\omega$ is a very small angle.

as in Fig. 2-10 with its vertex at point B, where the axis BC is parallel to the axis AD. Then

$$d\omega \approx \frac{\pi\delta^2}{(ds)^2}.$$

But $d\omega$ is a very small angle; hence

$$\delta \ll ds,$$

and if the diameter of the base of the frustum is comparable with the height, the figure must be very nearly a cylinder.* Therefore, by eq. (2-22),

$$\text{energy emitted} = (j_\nu \, d\nu \, dt \, d\omega)(\rho \, d\sigma \, ds).$$

By the definition of intensity, eq. (2-1) or eq. (2-2) with $\cos \theta = 1$,

$$\text{intensity emitted} = \frac{\text{energy emitted}}{d\nu \, dt \, d\sigma \, d\omega},$$

and thus

$$\text{intensity emitted} = j_\nu\rho \, ds. \tag{2-23}$$

On the other hand, by eq. (2-15),

$$-|\text{intensity absorbed}| = -\kappa_\nu\rho I_\nu \, ds.$$

Therefore,

$$dI_\nu = j_\nu\rho \, ds - \kappa_\nu\rho I_\nu \, ds.$$

* The reader can satisfy himself that the volume of the frustum $(\frac{1}{3})(A_1 + A_2 + \sqrt{A_1 A_2}) \times$ height (where A_1, A_2 are the areas of the bases) equals that of a cylinder if higher-order terms are neglected.

Since, from Fig. 2-9,

$$ds = dx \sec \theta,$$

it follows that

$$dI_\nu = j_\nu \rho \, dx \sec \theta - \kappa_\nu \rho I_\nu \, dx \sec \theta \qquad (2\text{-}24)$$

or

$$\cos \theta \, \frac{dI_\nu}{\kappa_\nu \rho \, dx} = -I_\nu + \frac{j_\nu}{\kappa_\nu}. \qquad (2\text{-}25)$$

In terms of optical depth, we have

$$\cos \theta \, \frac{dI_\nu}{d\tau_\nu} = I_\nu - \frac{j_\nu}{\kappa_\nu}. \qquad (2\text{-}26)$$

Either eq. (2-25) or eq. (2-26) is called the *equation of transfer*.

To avoid the problems of dealing with individual frequencies, we integrate eq. (2-24) over the spectrum:

$$d \int_0^\infty I_\nu \, d\nu = \rho \, dx \sec \theta \int_0^\infty j_\nu \, d\nu - \rho \, dx \sec \theta \int_0^\infty \kappa_\nu I_\nu \, d\nu.$$

Let

$$I = \int_0^\infty I_\nu \, d\nu$$

and

$$j = \int_0^\infty j_\nu \, d\nu.$$

For simplicity, we take κ_ν to be independent of ν, calling it κ; whether or not this is a justifiable assumption we shall see in the following chapter. Then

$$\int_0^\infty \kappa_\nu I_\nu \, d\nu = \kappa \int_0^\infty I_\nu \, d\nu = \kappa I,$$

and the equation of transfer becomes

$$\cos \theta \, \frac{dI}{\kappa \rho \, dx} = \frac{j}{\kappa} - I \qquad (2\text{-}27)$$

or

$$\cos \theta \, \frac{dI}{d\tau} = I - \frac{j}{\kappa}, \qquad (2\text{-}28)$$

where

$$d\tau = -\kappa \rho \, dx. \qquad (2\text{-}29)$$

An atmosphere having κ_ν independent of ν is called a *gray atmosphere*. This does not imply that the emergent radiation has no dependence on frequency.

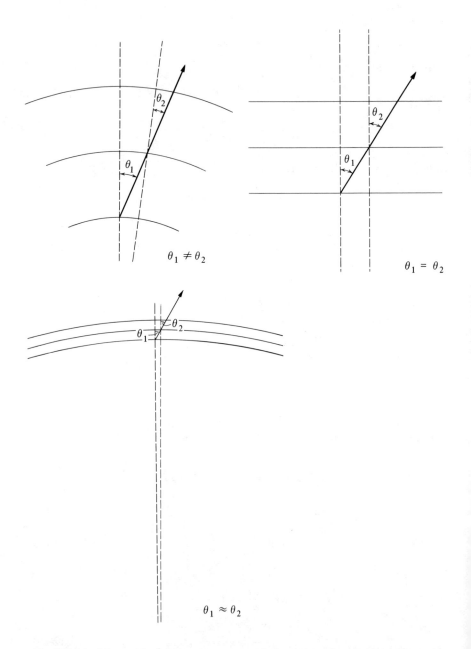

$\theta_1 \neq \theta_2$

$\theta_1 = \theta_2$

$\theta_1 \approx \theta_2$

Fig. 2-11A The angle θ between a ray and the outward normal to successive atmospheric layers is not constant in a deep atmosphere.
Fig. 2-11B The angle θ is constant in a plane-parallel atmosphere.
Fig. 2-11C The angle θ is nearly constant if the atmosphere is shallow.

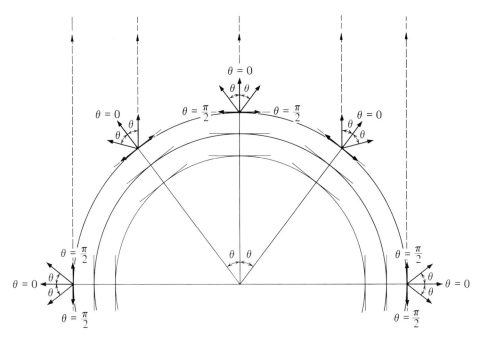

Fig. 2-12 Radiation traveling into a given direction in space (say, toward the top of the diagram) leaves the atmosphere at various points of the observed disk at different angles θ.

3-2 PLANE-PARALLEL ATMOSPHERES

The equation of transfer as written above refers to a plane-parallel atmosphere, as will now be explained.*

A ray traveling through various atmospheric layers as in Fig. 2-11A does not maintain a constant angle with the outward normals to the successive layers. However, in our derivation of the equation of transfer, we assumed that θ is the same at the bottom and at the top of the truncated cone. This condition can be strictly met only in an atmosphere that is stratified in parallel planes, as in Fig. 2-11B. It can be approximately met in a real atmosphere whose thickness is only a small fraction of the total radius (Fig. 2-11C). This is true for most stars. In the Sun, for example, the atmosphere is several hundred kilometers deep, while the solar radius is 7×10^5 km. The atmosphere thus occupies only about 0.1 per cent of the total radius, and the change in the angle θ from the bottom to the top of the atmosphere is correspondingly small.

The plane-parallel approximation does not require the atmosphere to be

* For an outline of the derivation of the equation of transfer in the general case, consult M. Schwarzschild, 1958 (50), p. 38 et seq.

flat; the parallel planes are to be drawn normal to the individual radii, as in Fig. 2-12. Note that radiation traveling in a given direction from the star (toward the Earth, say) leaves the star at angle $\theta = 0$ at the center of the observed disk and at increasingly larger angle θ toward the limb,* where $\theta = \pi/2$. To predict the change in the intensity of the disk from center to limb, it is sufficient to study the angular distribution of the intensity emerging at any point of the stellar surface. We shall use this fact in Section 4-2B.

4 SOLUTION OF THE EQUATION OF TRANSFER

4-1 TWO THEOREMS

We first derive two results that will be useful in the following sections.

A. Multiply the equation of transfer (2-28) by $d\omega$ and integrate over a sphere:

$$\int_{\text{sphere}} \cos \theta \, \frac{dI}{d\tau} \, d\omega = \int_{\text{sphere}} I \, d\omega - \int_{\text{sphere}} \frac{j}{\kappa} \, d\omega.$$

The differentiation with respect to τ is independent of the integration over angle, and we may write

$$\frac{d}{d\tau} \int_{\text{sphere}} I \cos \theta \, d\omega = \int_{\text{sphere}} I \, d\omega - \int_{\text{sphere}} \frac{j}{\kappa} \, d\omega.$$

The integral on the left is the flux F, by eq. (2-7). The first integral on the right is $4\pi J$, where J is the mean intensity [eq. (2-3)]. Neither j nor κ has angular dependence, and so

$$\frac{d}{d\tau} F = 4\pi J - 4\pi \frac{j}{\kappa}.$$

Since the atmospheres we are considering do not contain energy sources (e.g., nuclear sources) or sinks, the condition of *radiative equilibrium* is that the energy absorbed by any element of matter must equal that emitted, and hence the amount of energy entering any shell at given stellar radius must equal that leaving it each second. The flux is therefore constant with optical depth, and

$$\frac{d}{d\tau} F = 0. \tag{2-30}$$

(The area of each layer is about the same, namely $4\pi R^2$, since we are dealing with shallow atmospheres.) Thus

$$0 = 4\pi J - 4\pi \frac{j}{\kappa}$$

or

$$J = \frac{j}{\kappa}. \tag{2-31}$$

---

* The perimeter of the observed disk is called the *limb*.

This result may be compared with the Kirchhoff–Planck law,

$$B_\nu(T) = \frac{j_\nu}{\kappa_\nu}, \tag{2-32}$$

where $B_\nu(T)$ is the Planck function.

B. Next we multiply the equation of transfer by $\cos\theta\, d\omega$ and then integrate:

$$\frac{d}{d\tau}\int_{\text{sphere}} I\cos^2\theta\, d\omega = \int_{\text{sphere}} I\cos\theta\, d\omega - \frac{j}{\kappa}\int_{\text{sphere}}\cos\theta\, d\omega.$$

Since

$$\int_{\text{sphere}}\cos\theta\, d\omega = 0,$$

we have

$$\frac{d}{d\tau}(4\pi K) = 4\pi H.$$

Therefore,

$$\frac{dK}{d\tau} = H \tag{2-33}$$

$$K = H\tau + \text{const.} \tag{2-34}$$

4-2 EDDINGTON'S FIRST APPROXIMATION*

A. SOLUTION FOR THE INTENSITIES

In a first approximation, which is the only one that we shall discuss, Eddington represented the radiation field at any point by a constant intensity $I_1(\tau)$ over the outward hemisphere and a constant intensity $I_2(\tau)$ over the inward hemisphere (Fig. 2-13):

$$I(\tau, \theta) = \begin{cases} I_1(\tau) & 0 \leqslant \theta < \pi/2 \\ I_2(\tau) & \pi/2 < \theta \leqslant \pi, \end{cases} \tag{2-35}$$

where I_1 and I_2 must be found as functions of τ.

Let us first find expressions for J, H, and K as functions of I_1 and I_2. We have

$$\begin{aligned}
J &= \frac{1}{4\pi}\int_{\text{sphere}} I\, d\omega \\
&= \frac{1}{4\pi}\cdot 2\pi\left[\int_0^{\pi/2} I_1\sin\theta\, d\theta + \int_{\pi/2}^{\pi} I_2\sin\theta\, d\theta\right] \\
&= \tfrac{1}{2}I_1[-\cos\theta]_0^{\pi/2} + \tfrac{1}{2}I_2[-\cos\theta]_{\pi/2}^{\pi} \\
&= \tfrac{1}{2}(I_1 + I_2).
\end{aligned} \tag{2-36}$$

* Eddington's second and his amended second approximations, as well as other solutions of the equation of transfer, are discussed by R. v. d. R. Woolley and D. W. N. Stibbs, 1953 (26).

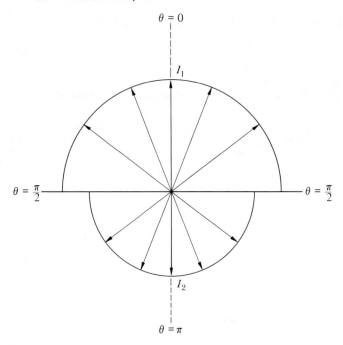

Fig. 2-13 In Eddington's first approximation, all outward radiation has intensity I_1 and all inward radiation has intensity I_2.

This result could have been obtained intuitively, since J, the mean intensity, is a simple average of the intensities I_1 and I_2, or $\frac{1}{2}(I_1 + I_2)$.

Next we have

$$H = \frac{1}{4\pi} \int_{\text{sphere}} I \cos \theta \, d\omega$$

$$= \frac{1}{4\pi} \cdot 2\pi \left[\int_0^{\pi/2} I_1 \cos \theta \sin \theta \, d\theta + \int_{\pi/2}^{\pi} I_2 \cos \theta \sin \theta \, d\theta \right]$$

$$= \tfrac{1}{2}I_1 \cdot \tfrac{1}{2} \sin^2 \theta |_0^{\pi/2} + \tfrac{1}{2}I_2 \cdot \tfrac{1}{2} \sin^2 \theta |_{\pi/2}^{\pi}$$

$$= \tfrac{1}{4}(I_1 - I_2). \tag{2-37}$$

Again the result can be understood from another point of view. By definition, H is $(4\pi)^{-1}$ times the net flux. In the present case, we can compute the net flux by subtracting the inward intensity from the outward intensity, giving a net value $I_1 - I_2$ in any outward direction. The energy passing per second into a solid angle $d\omega$ through a projected area of 1 cm² is then $(I_1 - I_2) \cos \theta \, d\omega$, and the sum of such contributions over the outward hemisphere yields

$$F = (I_1 - I_2) \int_{\text{hemisphere}} \cos\theta \, d\omega$$

$$= \pi(I_1 - I_2)$$

and

$$H = \tfrac{1}{4}(I_1 - I_2).$$

Next,

$$K = \frac{1}{4\pi} \int_{\text{sphere}} I \cos^2\theta \, d\omega$$

$$= \frac{1}{4\pi} \cdot 2\pi \left[\int_0^{\pi/2} I_1 \cos^2\theta \sin\theta \, d\theta + \int_{\pi/2}^{\pi} I_2 \cos^2\theta \sin\theta \, d\theta \right]$$

$$= \tfrac{1}{2}(I_1[-\tfrac{1}{3}\cos^3\theta]_0^{\pi/2} + I_2[-\tfrac{1}{3}\cos^3\theta]_{\pi/2}^{\pi})$$

$$= \tfrac{1}{6}(I_1 + I_2)$$

$$K = \tfrac{1}{3}J. \tag{2-38}$$

This is the average intensity J, multiplied by the average value of $\cos^2\theta$ over a sphere.

Now we find $J(\tau)$, from which $I_1(\tau)$ and $I_2(\tau)$ will be derived. From eqs. (2-34) and (2-38), we have

$$\tfrac{1}{3}J(\tau) = H\tau + \text{const.} \tag{2-39}$$

To evaluate the constant, we first write

$$\tfrac{1}{3}J(0) = \text{const} \tag{2-40}$$

and use the boundary condition that there is no radiation incident from outside the star, namely,

$$I_2(0) = 0.$$

From eqs. (2-36) and (2-37), we find

$$J(0) = 2H.$$

Then

$$\text{const} = \tfrac{2}{3}H,$$

and

$$J(\tau) = H(2 + 3\tau). \tag{2-41}$$

This relation is useful because it expresses J in terms of the optical depth τ and one of the fundamental properties of a star, H, which is $(4\pi)^{-1}$ times the net flux:

$$H = \frac{1}{4\pi} \frac{L}{4\pi R^2}.$$

We are now ready to find $I_1(\tau)$ and $I_2(\tau)$. From eqs. (2-36) and (2-37), we have

$$J + 2H = I_1.$$

Using eq. (2-41), we find

$$I_1(\tau) = H(4 + 3\tau). \tag{2-42}$$

Again from eqs. (2-36) and (2-37), we obtain

$$J - 2H = I_2$$

and

$$I_2(\tau) = 3H\tau. \tag{2-43}$$

The intensities $I_1(\tau)$ and $I_2(\tau)$ differ by 4π for all values of τ. Figure 2-14 illustrates the intensities at various depths. As τ increases, the radiation field becomes more nearly isotropic, although the difference $I_1 - I_2$, which determines the net flux, remains constant.

B. LIMB-DARKENING*

The solar disk is darker at the edge, or limb, than at the center. This is true also of other stars, as the light curves of eclipsing binaries reveal. The variation in the intensity with position on the disk must be due to a dependence of the intensity on the angle θ that a ray makes with the outward normal (see Section 3-2). It is therefore necessary to find I as a function of θ, in a somewhat better approximation than that of eq. (2-42).

We proceed by calculating the intensity emitted by an element of matter at an arbitrary level within the atmosphere and the amount by which this intensity is attenuated as the radiation traverses the overlying layers. We shall then add the contributions from all levels.

Again we consider a truncated cone that emits an intensity equal to

$$j\rho \, ds = j\rho \, dx \sec \theta,$$

according to eq. (2-23) and Fig. 2-9. When this radiation reaches the surface, it will have been diminished by an exponential factor involving the optical thickness of the path [cf. eq. (2-20)]. Here, the ray may be inclined at angle θ with the normal, and the optical thickness becomes $\tau \sec \theta$. The contribution of the layer to the emergent intensity is then

$$dI = j\rho \, dx \sec \theta \, e^{-\tau \sec \theta}.$$

But

$$d\tau = -\kappa\rho \, dx,$$

and therefore

$$dI = -\frac{j}{\kappa} \, d\tau \sec \theta \, e^{-\tau \sec \theta}.$$

---

* We consider only the gray case in this section. A brief discussion of the solar limb-darkening in monochromatic light is given in Chapter 4, Section 3-3.

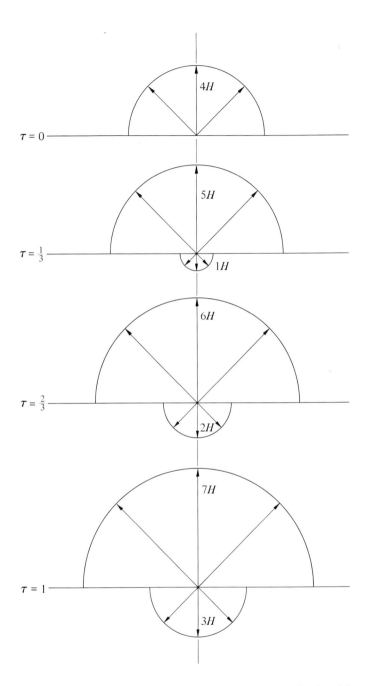

$\tau = 0$

$4H$

$\tau = \frac{1}{3}$

$5H$

$1H$

$\tau = \frac{2}{3}$

$6H$

$2H$

$\tau = 1$

$7H$

$3H$

Fig. 2-14 The intensities I_1 and I_2 increase with depth while maintaining a constant difference $4H$.

83

Table 2-1 Limb-Darkening for the Sun, $I(0, \theta)/I(0, 0)$. [After L. H. Aller, 1963 (25).]

Cos θ	EDDINGTON APPROXIMATION	OBSERVED INTENSITY
1.00	1.000	1.000
0.90	0.940	.0.944
0.80	0.880	0.898
0.70	0.820	0.842
0.60	0.760	0.788
0.50	0.700	0.730
0.40	0.640	0.670
0.30	0.580	0.602
0.20	0.520	0.552
0.10	0.460	0.450
0.00	0.400	

By eq. (2-31), this becomes

$$dI = -J(\tau)\, d\tau \, \sec \theta \, e^{-\tau \sec \theta}.$$

Summing the contributions from all layers of the atmosphere, we find that $I(\tau, \theta)$ at the surface becomes

$$I(0, \theta) = -\int_{\infty}^{0} J(\tau)\, e^{-\tau \sec \theta}\, d\tau \, \sec \theta. \qquad (2\text{-}44)$$

The quantity multiplying $e^{-\tau \sec \theta}\, d\tau \, \sec \theta$ is called the *source function*, since it gives essentially the amount of energy originating at any layer. In this case, the source function is identical with the mean intensity J.

Having found an expression for J from Eddington's first approximation [eq. (2-41)], we may use it to evaluate the integral:

$$I(0, \theta) = \int_{0}^{\infty} H(2 + 3\tau)\, e^{-\tau \sec \theta}\, d\tau \, \sec \theta$$

$$= 2H \int_{0}^{\infty} e^{-\tau \sec \theta}\, d\tau \, \sec \theta + 3H \int_{0}^{\infty} \tau\, e^{-\tau \sec \theta}\, d\tau \, \sec \theta.$$

The first integral is of the form

$$\int_{0}^{\infty} e^{-y}\, dy = -e^{-y}\big|_{0}^{\infty},$$

with $y = \tau \sec \theta$. The value of the integral is unity. Hence the first term contributes $2H$. If we write the second term on the right as

$$3H \frac{1}{\sec \theta} \int_{0}^{\infty} \tau \sec \theta \, e^{-\tau \sec \theta}\, d\tau \, \sec \theta,$$

the integral takes the form

$$\int_0^\infty ye^{-y}\,dy.$$

Integrating by parts, with $e^{-y}\,dy$ as the differential of the function $-e^{-y}$, we have

$$\int_0^\infty ye^{-y}\,dy = -ye^{-y}\Big|_0^\infty - \int_0^\infty -e^{-y}\,dy$$

$$= -ye^{-y}\Big|_0^\infty - e^{-y}\Big|_0^\infty$$

$$= 1,*$$

so that the second term is $3H\cos\theta$. Therefore,

$$I(0,\theta) = H(2 + 3\cos\theta). \tag{2-45}$$

The values $I(0,0) = 5H$ and $I(0,\pi/2) = 2H$ from this expression may be compared with $I_1(0) = 4H$ given by eq. (2-42). Eddington's first approximation evidently gives the same result as eq. (2-45) if $\cos\theta = \tfrac{2}{3}$.

The intensity decreases with increasing θ, as might be expected; the larger the angle θ, the greater is the distance that the ray must travel through the atmosphere and hence the greater the absorption.

Table 2-1 compares values calculated from this equation with the observed values for the Sun. The tabulated quantities are actually $I(0,\theta)/I(0,0)$, that is, the intensity at θ divided by the intensity at the center of the disk. The agreement between the observations and the simple theory is good.

C. TEMPERATURE DISTRIBUTION

Before a definite temperature can be ascribed to a sample of matter, it must be stated what phenomenon is being characterized by this value. Just as we have seen, in Section 1-4 of Chapter 1, that various possibilities exist for defining the temperature of a radiation field, so we may consider several different ways to assign a temperature to the gaseous particles. The three defining phenomena that will be of interest here are the velocity distribution, the degree to which bound electrons are excited to levels above the ground level, and the degree of ionization that has taken place.

The *kinetic temperature* is given by the Maxwell–Boltzmann law for the velocity distribution of the particles. If $N(v_z)$ is the number of particles having

* The reader who is not convinced that

$$ye^{-y} = \frac{y}{e^y} \to 0 \quad \text{as} \quad y \to \infty$$

can apply l'Hôpital's rule,

$$\lim_{y\to\infty} \frac{f(y)}{g(y)} = \lim_{y\to\infty} \frac{f'(y)}{g'(y)}.$$

a velocity component between v_z and $v_z + dv_z$ in rectangular co-ordinates along a direction z, then

$$N(v_z)\,dv_z \propto \exp\left(-\text{const}\,v_z{}^2/T\right),$$

where T is the kinetic temperature. This velocity-distribution law is further discussed in Section 4 of Chapter 3.

The *excitation temperature* occurs in the Boltzmann law, describing the relative numbers of atoms or ions of a given element, in a definite stage of ionization, that have been raised to some level A above the ground level:

$$\frac{N\text{ (level }A)}{N\text{ (ground level)}} \propto \exp\left(-\frac{\text{const}}{T}\right).$$

This relation is described in Chapter 3, Section 2.

The *ionization temperature* is determined by the relative numbers of ions of a given element that are in the various possible stages of ionization. If some atoms have lost r electrons and other atoms have lost $r + 1$ electrons, then

$$\frac{N(r + 1)}{N(r)} \propto T^{3/2} \exp\left(-\frac{\text{const}}{T}\right) \times f(T),$$

where $f(T)$ is a function having little dependence on T. This is the Saha equation, considered in Chapter 3, Section 3.

The constants in these three relations depend upon the element in question and also upon the degree of ionization or excitation in the case of the Boltzmann and Saha equations.

The important point is that all of these values of T may be different the one from the other and also from the one or more temperatures applicable to the co-existing radiation.

However, inside a closed container in which the walls are maintained at constant temperature (as measured by a thermometer), conditions become less complicated. There are interactions among the gas particles, the photons, and the walls of the container. Collisions produce exchanges of energy among the various particles. The absorption of photons by atoms and ions and the subsequent re-emission of photons result in interchanges of energy between the particles and the radiation field. Furthermore, each process must proceed at the same rate as its inverse, that is, at an equilibrium rate. These interactions ensure that all the definitions of temperature, given above, yield the same value of T. The matter is said to be in *thermodynamic equilibrium*. One particularly important relation that is valid under these conditions is Kirchhoff's law (or the Kirchhoff–Planck law),

$$j_\nu = \kappa_\nu B_\nu(T), \tag{2-46}$$

which will be useful later.*

* For a more detailed discussion of thermodynamic equilibrium, see E. R. Mustel (V. A. Ambartsumyan, ed.), 1958 (30).

In view of the simplification afforded by thermodynamic equilibrium, we ask whether it might be applicable to a stellar atmosphere. We must ask whether the matter and radiation in a sample volume behave approximately as if they were enclosed in a box maintained at constant temperature. Specifically, we must investigate the mean free paths of the particles and photons and the magnitude of the temperature gradient.

From the results for the Sun in Table 4-2, we see that the temperature varies by roughly 10 degrees/km, or 0.1 per cent/km. We are thus justified in considering the temperature to be constant over small distances.

A simple argument will suffice to give the order of magnitude of the mean free path of the particles. We find the total target area within a 1-cm cube:

$$\text{total target area in 1 cm}^3 = \text{cross section/particle}$$

$$\times \text{ number of particles in 1 cm}^3$$

$$= \pi \, (\text{radius of particle})^2$$

$$\times \frac{\text{number of grams/cm}^3}{\text{number of grams/particle}}.$$

The chief constituent of an atmosphere is usually neutral hydrogen in the ground state, and so we may take the radius of a typical particle to be 0.5 Å, corresponding to the radius of the first Bohr orbit of hydrogen. The number of grams per cm^3, ρ, is of the order of 10^{-7} (see Table 4-2), and the mass of a hydrogen atom is 1.7×10^{-24} gm. Thus

$$\frac{\text{total target area}}{\text{in 1 cm}^3} = \pi \times (0.5 \times 10^{-8} \text{ cm})^2 \times \frac{10^{-7} \text{ gm cm}^{-3}}{1.7 \times 10^{-24} \text{ gm}}$$

$$\approx 5 \text{ cm}^2 \text{ in 1 cm}^3.$$

Since this is larger than the 1 cm^2 face of the cube, it is unlikely that an incident particle will traverse the cube without collision; the mean free path is less than 1 cm. Therefore the particles are, more or less, confined to a small volume and behave approximately as if they were in an enclosure at constant temperature.

The photons, however, travel over great distances before being absorbed. An optical depth of unity is reached at a geometrical depth of about 170 km (see Table 4-2), which means that e^{-1} or 0.4 of the original energy of the photons, and a similar fraction of the number of photons originating at this depth, reach the surface without being obstructed. Their mean free path is therefore large, and the walls of the hypothetical enclosing box are consequently not at the same temperature. Moreover, the radiation field is not isotropic; the intensity is greatest in the outward direction and least in the inward direction.

Nevertheless, it is a fairly good approximation to assume *local thermo-dynamic equilibrium* (LTE)*; it is acknowledged that there exists a gradual change in temperature from one atmospheric level to another, but this is small for moderate changes in height. Hence the laws of Maxwell, Boltzmann, Saha, and Kirchhoff may be applied in considerations pertaining to the continuum. To determine the temperature, then, we may use the law

$$\frac{j_\nu}{\kappa_\nu} = B_\nu(T),$$

or, for a gray atmosphere,

$$\frac{j}{\kappa} = \int_0^\infty B_\nu(T)\, d\nu = B(T)$$

$$= \frac{\sigma}{\pi} T^4$$

by eq. (1-9). Then, with the aid of eq. (2-31), we get

$$J(\tau) = B(T); \tag{2-47}$$

and using eq. (2-41), we find

$$\frac{\sigma}{\pi} T^4 = H(2 + 3\tau).$$

This can be expressed in terms of the surface temperature T_0. At $\tau = 0$,

$$\frac{\sigma}{\pi} T_0{}^4 = 2H, \tag{2-48}$$

and consequently

$$T^4 = T_0{}^4(1 + \tfrac{3}{2}\tau). \tag{2-49}$$

To introduce the effective temperature T_{eff}, we recall eq. (1-10):

$$F = \sigma T_{\text{eff}}{}^4.$$

The definition of H then yields

$$2H = \frac{\sigma}{2\pi} T_{\text{eff}}{}^4.$$

This can be compared with eq. (2-48), giving

$$T_{\text{eff}} = \sqrt[4]{2}\, T_0 = 1.189\, T_0. \tag{2-50}$$

Finally, we may write

$$T^4 = \tfrac{1}{2} T_{\text{eff}}{}^4(1 + \tfrac{3}{2}\tau). \tag{2-51}$$

* Caution must be exercised in some cases in which local thermodynamic equilibrium is assumed. For a discussion of departures from LTE in the formation of spectral lines in early-type stars, see O. Gingerich, ed., 1969 (35), several papers and discussions in Part II; also D. Mihalas, 1970 (41).

From this equation, we see that the temperature reaches T_{eff} at the level

$$\tau = \tfrac{2}{3}. \tag{2-52}$$

For the Sun,

$$T_{\text{eff}} = 5770°\text{K} \quad \text{and} \quad T_0 = 4850°\text{K}. \tag{2-53}$$

The model for the solar atmosphere calculated in Part Four uses eq. (2-51), and hence condition (2-52) is fulfilled. (Note, however, that the model adopts an older value of the luminosity, and T_{eff} and T_0 are therefore different from the values given here.)

5 EXAMPLES FOR THE SOLAR RADIATION

We shall now illustrate some of the concepts presented in this chapter by finding the intensity and flux of the solar radiation, both at the surface of the Sun and at the position of the Earth. We shall consider some of the relationships between these quantities and also some schematic methods for measuring them.

(a) The bolometric flux emitted at the solar surface is the total amount of energy radiated per second per cm². According to eq. (1-11), this can be expressed as the luminosity L divided by the total surface area:

$$F_{\odot} = \frac{L}{4\pi R^2}$$

$$= \frac{3.91 \times 10^{33}}{4\pi (6.960 \times 10^{10})^2}$$

$$= 6.42 \times 10^{10} \frac{\text{erg}}{\text{sec cm}^2}.$$

(b) The bolometric intensity, which is the same at the solar surface and at the Earth, can be computed from example (a) if we suppose, for the moment, that the radiation is isotropic over the outward hemisphere [cf. example (h)]. Using eq. (2-14), we have

$$I = \frac{F_{\odot}}{\pi}$$

$$= 2.04 \times 10^{10} \frac{\text{erg}}{\text{sec cm}^2 \text{ sterad}}.$$

(c) The mean bolometric intensity at the Sun is simply one-half this value, since there is no inward radiation at the surface:

$$J_{\odot} = 1.02 \times 10^{10} \frac{\text{erg}}{\text{sec cm}^2 \text{ sterad}}.$$

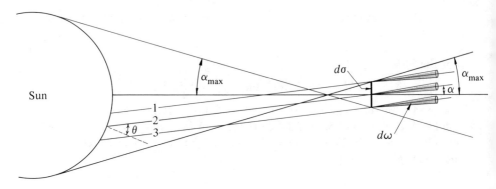

Fig. 2-15A   Radiation from the Sun passing through an area $d\sigma$ with the normal passing through the center of the Sun. The rays 1, 2, and 3 come from a portion of the solar surface that is comparable in size with $d\sigma$.

(d) The bolometric flux received from the Sun at the Earth can be expressed in terms of the luminosity L and distance d to the Sun, considering the Sun to be a point source:

$$F_{\oplus} = \frac{L}{4\pi d^2}$$

$$= \frac{3.91 \times 10^{33}}{4\pi(1.496 \times 10^{13})^2}$$

$$= 1.39 \times 10^6 \frac{\text{erg}}{\text{sec cm}^2}.$$

Note that this is the solar constant if the Earth is at its mean distance from the Sun (see Chapter 1, Section 1-2).

Fig. 2-15B   The Relation between the Angles α and θ. Portions of Fig. 2-15A are shown. The line PQ is perpendicular to the line from $d\sigma$ to the center of the Sun. The distance d is measured between $d\sigma$ and Q and is approximately equal to the distance between $d\sigma$ and the center of the Sun.

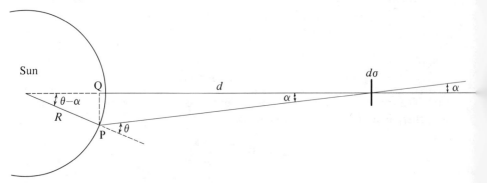

(e) The flux can also be calculated from its definition, if the intensity distribution $I(\theta)$ is known. In Fig. 2-15A, a ray from the Sun falling on the small circular area $d\sigma$, which is placed normally to the central ray from the Sun, is inclined to the normal to $d\sigma$ by an angle α. The maximum value of α is α_{max}, which is the angular radius of the Sun. Although α plays the same role as θ did before, we have introduced a different symbol to avoid confusion with the angular distance of any point on the Sun from the center of the disk (as in Fig. 2-12 or Fig. 2-16). (We note parenthetically, from Fig. 2-15B, that θ defined in this way is not strictly the same as the angle measured at the center of the Sun between the normal to $d\sigma$ and the radius vector to the point at which the ray emerges from the solar surface.) If d is the distance from the element $d\sigma$ to the nearest point of the solar surface, or approximately the distance between the centers of the Earth and the Sun, the relation between α and θ is

$$\tan \alpha = \frac{R \sin (\theta - \alpha)}{d}$$

$$\approx \frac{R \sin \theta}{d}.$$

The intensity in any direction α is determined by the rate at which energy flows into cones of solid angle $d\omega$ about all the parallel rays inclined at angle α with the normal to the surface. The flux is then given by

$$F_\oplus = \int_0^{\alpha_{max}} I(\alpha) \cos \alpha \, d\omega$$

$$= 2\pi \int_0^{\alpha_{max}} I(\alpha) \cos \alpha \sin \alpha \, d\alpha.$$

To complete the example in an approximate manner, we again take I to be isotropic for all outward directions at the surface of the Sun. Then

$$F_\oplus = 2\pi I \cdot \tfrac{1}{2} \sin^2 \alpha |_0^{\alpha_{max}};$$

and if we set

$$\alpha_{max} \approx \frac{R}{d}$$

$$= 5 \times 10^{-3} \text{ radian}$$

and

$$\sin \alpha \approx \alpha,$$

we find that

$$F_\oplus \approx \pi I \left(\frac{R}{d}\right)^2.$$

To compare this with example (d), we replace πI by $F_\odot$, which yields

$$F_\oplus \approx \frac{L}{4\pi R^2}\left(\frac{R}{d}\right)^2 = \frac{L}{4\pi d^2},$$

as before.

(f) To *measure* the flux $F_\oplus$ received at the Earth, we must use a device that will register the amount of energy flowing per second through a given area placed normally to a ray from the center of the solar disk and allowing all incident rays to be measured. In Fig. 2-15A, $d\sigma$ could represent the area of such a detector.

(g) The mean intensity $J_\oplus$ can be readily found by retaining the assumption of isotropy of $I(\theta)$ at the Sun. We have

$$J_\oplus = \frac{1}{4\pi}\int_0^{\omega\,\text{max}} I\,d\omega$$

$$= \tfrac{1}{2}I\int_0^{\alpha\,\text{max}} \sin\alpha\,d\alpha$$

$$= \tfrac{1}{2}I[-\cos\alpha]_0^{R/d}.$$

Fig. 2-16   The Solar Disk. The area of the annulus is

$$da = 2\pi R\sin\theta\cdot R\,d\theta\cos\theta.$$

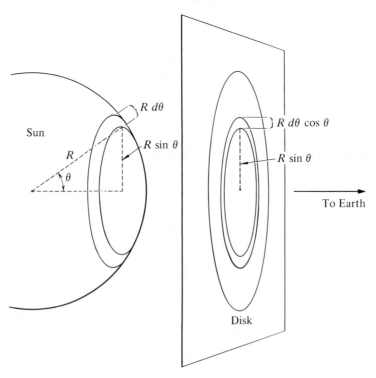

A Taylor expansion of cos α,

$$\cos \alpha = 1 - \frac{\alpha^2}{2} + \cdots,$$

yields

$$J_{\oplus} \approx \tfrac{1}{2}I\left[\frac{\alpha^2}{2}\right]_0^{R/d}$$

$$= \tfrac{1}{4}I\left(\frac{R}{d}\right)^2$$

$$= \frac{1}{4\pi}F_{\oplus}.$$

We note that J, unlike I, varies with distance.

(h) We now show that the value of I in example (b) is appropriate to the mean value of $I(\theta)$ averaged over the solar disk. Imagine the visible surface of the Sun to be projected orthogonally on a plane perpendicular to the line between the center of the solar disk and the observer, as in Fig. 2-16. Then the mean intensity I_{mean} is given by

$$I_{\text{mean}} = \frac{\displaystyle\int_{\text{annulus}} I(\theta)\, da}{\displaystyle\int_{\text{annulus}} da}$$

$$= \frac{\displaystyle\int_0^{\pi/2} I(\theta) \cdot 2\pi R \sin\theta \cdot R\, d\theta \cos\theta}{\displaystyle\int_0^{\pi/2} 2\pi R \sin\theta \cdot R\, d\theta \cos\theta}$$

$$= \frac{\displaystyle\int_{\text{hemisphere}} I(\theta) \cos\theta\, d\omega}{2\pi[\tfrac{1}{2}\sin^2\theta]_0^{\pi/2}}$$

$$= \frac{F_{\odot}^{+}}{\pi}.$$

Thus the mean intensity averaged over the disk is the same as the isotropic intensity that would yield the same flux.

(i) To demonstrate that intensity remains unchanged in the passage of radiation through a lens, we consider Fig. 2-17A. The object from which the light originates is at the left, and a small circular section of area $d\sigma$ and height dh is shown. The rays from the point on the optic axis that spread into a solid angle $d\omega$ intercept an area $d\Sigma$ at the lens. By the usual ray-tracing technique, we can locate the position and size of the image, for which area and height are, respectively, $d\sigma'$ and dh'. After refraction by the lens, the rays are bounded by a cone of solid angle $d\omega'$.

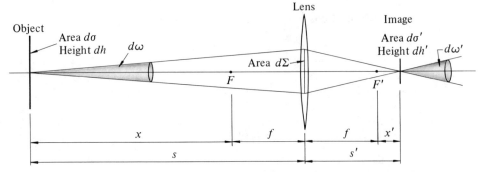

Fig. 2-17A Radiation Passing through a Thin Lens. A small area $d\sigma$ of an object, and the image of that small area, are shown. The focal points of the lens are F and F', and the focal length is f.

The intensity of the object is determined by the energy per unit time leaving $d\sigma$ to flow into the solid angle $d\omega$ (from each point of $d\sigma$). At the image, the same amount of energy flows per unit time through $d\sigma'$ into solid angle $d\omega'$. Hence the relative intensities depend on the relative values of the products $d\sigma\, d\omega$ and $d\sigma'\, d\omega'$. To evaluate these, we use the following thin-lens relations, with the notation of Fig. 2-17A:

$$\frac{s'}{s} = \frac{f}{x}$$

and

$$\frac{dh}{dh'} = \frac{x}{f}.$$

But

$$d\omega = \frac{d\Sigma}{s^2},$$

$$d\omega' = \frac{d\Sigma}{s'^2},$$

Fig. 2-17B Radiation Passing through a Thin Lens. The rays in Fig. 2-17A are again shown, together with three additional rays from the bottom point of $d\sigma$.

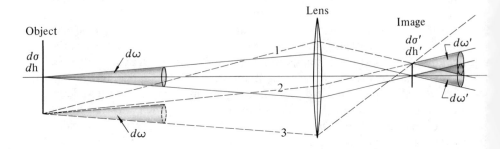

and

$$\frac{d\sigma}{d\sigma'} = \left(\frac{dh}{dh'}\right)^2 = \left(\frac{x}{f}\right)^2.$$

Therefore,

$$\frac{d\omega}{d\omega'} \cdot \frac{d\sigma}{d\sigma'} = 1,$$

and the intensities of the object and image are the same. Depending on the location of the surface $d\sigma$ with respect to F, $d\sigma'$ may be either smaller or larger than $d\sigma$; but the change will be compensated by the opposite change in $d\omega'$ with respect to $d\omega$. If the image were viewed by eye from a position to the right of the figure, the intensity of the image could be less than that of the object, if the pupil of the eye were not large enough to admit all the rays passing through $d\sigma'$; but the intensity cannot be made greater than it was originally. Note, however, that the *flux* at $d\sigma'$ is greater than that at $d\sigma$ for the case illustrated in Fig. 2-17A, since the same amount of energy passes per second through a smaller area.

If rays from some other point of $d\sigma$ are included, as in Fig. 2-17B, the situation is not so straightforward. In this figure, we have again shown the constructions in Fig. 2-17A, but have traced three additional rays through the lens. Two rays, labeled 1 and 2, from the bottom point of $d\sigma$ define a second cone of rays of solid angle $d\omega'$ at the image, with axis parallel to that of the first cone. These rays, however, leave the object at such an angle that they are not contained within the solid angle $d\omega$. The third ray is just on the boundary of the cone of solid angle $d\omega$ as it leaves the object, but lies outside $d\omega'$ at the image. These difficulties disappear, however, as $dh \rightarrow 0$, for then the diagram approaches the case of Fig. 2-17A.

The area $d\sigma$ described here is centered on the optic axis of the lens. A similar argument, however, can be presented for other points of the object.

(j) To *measure* $I(\theta)$, let us use the apparatus depicted in Fig. 2-18, where A′B′ represents the image of the solar disk formed by a telescope upon an opaque screen. A small opening of area $d\sigma$ in the screen allows radiation from a limited portion of the solar disk to pass through. Rays 1, 1′, and 1″ are virtually parallel and come from some point b on the solar disk, for which the image point is b′. Similarly, rays 2, 2′, and 2″ come from a single point a that is imaged at a′. From the figure, we see that a cone of rays arises from each point of the opening in the screen, the solid angle of the cones being determined by the size of the objective and its focal length. (We assume that $d\sigma$ is large enough so that diffraction effects may be neglected.) Let us call the solid angle $d\omega$. The detector measures the amount of radiation falling upon it per second, and this quantity divided by $d\sigma\, d\omega$ (also $d\nu$ if monochromatic

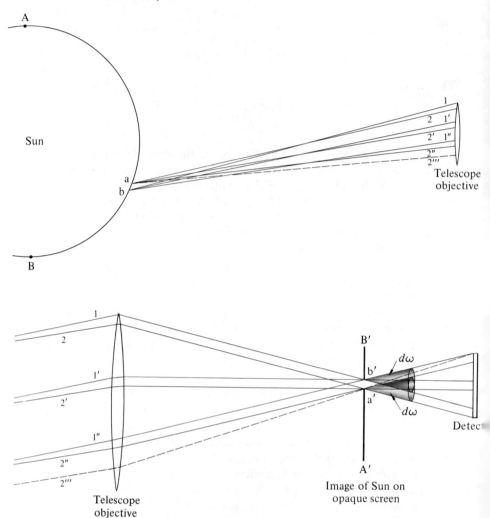

Fig. 2-18 Solar Intensity Measurement. In the upper diagram, rays from the Sun are shown arriving at the telescope objective, which is also shown (enlarged) in the lower diagram. The points A′ and B′ are the image points of A and B at the edge of the visible disk, and a′ and b′ are the image points of a and b. The solar image is formed upon an opaque screen that has an opening of area $d\sigma$ and height a′b′, allowing radiation to pass through to the detector.

radiation is observed) is approximately the intensity $I(\theta)$. We note that some rays, such as the one labeled 2‴, not falling within the cone of solid angle $d\omega$ are also measured, but their contribution vanishes as $d\sigma$ and $d\omega$ are made to approach zero.

PROBLEMS

1. Is it possible to define the intensity of radiation emitted by a point source?

2. The radius of the diffraction disk formed after passage of radiation from a point source through a circular aperture of diameter D is 1.2 λ/D radians, where λ and D are expressed in the same units. Compare the size of this disk with that of the geometrical image of a star, choosing definite numerical values for the quantities involved. This calculation demonstrates the essential reason that stellar intensities cannot, in general, be measured.

3. A lens forms an image of the Sun. Find an expression for the flux passing through this image in terms of known properties of the Sun and of the lens.

4. An enclosure is maintained at a temperature of 6000° K. Find the values of the intensity, mean intensity, net flux, and flux flowing into a hemisphere for the wavelength at which the intensity has the maximum value.

5. As radiation traverses a stellar atmosphere and reaches layers that are progressively higher and cooler, absorption results in a continual diminution of the intensity at any wavelength. How, then, can energy be conserved?

6. Repeat the demonstration of example (i) in Section 5 for an object point that is not on the optic axis of the lens.

3

PHYSICAL PROPERTIES OF GASES
ABSORPTION COEFFICIENTS

In Chapter 2, we introduced the absorption coefficient κ. On the assumption (whether or not it is well founded) that κ is independent of frequency, we were able to gain some insight into the character of the radiation field inside a stellar atmosphere. Nevertheless, if we are to make much further progress, we must have a better understanding of the dependence of the absorption upon frequency and of the properties of the absorbing matter itself. Even if we restrict our interest to a gray atmosphere, with κ independent of frequency, we must know how to evaluate a mean absorption coefficient. In our later study of the stellar interior, we shall also require a knowledge of this quantity. In this chapter, we therefore consider the physical mechanisms that contribute to absorption and then give formulae from which the appropriate coefficients may be calculated.

The numerical value of an absorption coefficient depends upon the number of atoms that are producing the absorption. It is not enough, however, to know merely how many particles of a given element are contained in a sample of the material. If we are concerned with a particular frequency ν for which we desire to know κ_ν, we must calculate the fraction of these particles that are capable of contributing to the absorption at that frequency. For example, to calculate κ_ν for hydrogen at a frequency corresponding to the line $H\alpha$ at $\lambda = 6563$ Å, we must know the fraction of the hydrogen atoms that have been excited to the second level and also the proportion of the hydrogen that is in the neutral state. An absorption coefficient may also depend upon the speed of an absorbing free electron, and the distribution of the free-electron speeds must therefore be known.

We thus must consider excitation, ionization, and the distribution of velocities and speeds. The averaging process for obtaining a mean coefficient will also be discussed, as will the opacity of the solar atmosphere.

1 THE BOHR THEORY FOR HYDROGEN-LIKE IONS

Absorption processes can be readily visualized in terms of the Bohr model of an atom, which we shall now briefly review. To avoid the complications that arise when the electrons interact among themselves as well as with the nucleus, we shall restrict the discussion to the case of hydrogen and hydrogen-like ions, that is, to ions that have lost all but one electron. Furthermore, since only the total energy of the electron in an orbit is needed to calculate the frequency of an absorption edge or spectral line, it will be sufficient to consider the orbits as circular; the total energy is independent of the orbital eccentricity when only one electron is present.

Fig. 3-1 The Bohr Atom. The first five electronic orbits are drawn to relative scale. The orbit for $n = \infty$ has infinite radius and is therefore indicated by a dashed line. Fragments of two hyperbolic orbits about the nucleus are similarly indicated. Examples of bound-bound, bound-free, and free-free transitions are designated by the symbols *b-b*, *b-f*, and *f-f*, respectively. Transitions from lower to higher n represent absorption and those in the reverse direction represent emission.

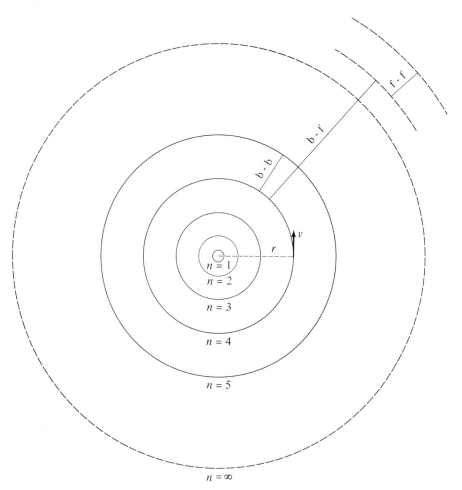

Let us refer to Fig. 3-1 and define the following quantities:

e = electronic charge (absolute value),

z = atomic number of the nucleus,

m' = reduced mass of the system

$$= \frac{\text{mass}_{\text{nucleus}} \times \text{mass}_{\text{electron}}}{\text{mass}_{\text{nucleus}} + \text{mass}_{\text{electron}}}$$

$\approx$ mass of electron,

n = principal quantum number of the nth orbit,

r_n = radius of the nth orbit,

v_n = speed of the electron in the nth orbit.

The total energy of the electron $\mathscr{E}_{i,n}$ is the sum of its kinetic and potential energies. Although not needed here, a subscript i has been introduced in anticipation of the following sections. This symbol designates the degree of ionization, with I representing the neutral atom, II the singly ionized particle, and so on. We have

$$\mathscr{E}_{i,n} = \tfrac{1}{2}m'v_n{}^2 - \frac{(ze)e}{r_n}. \tag{3-1}$$

The radial force F_n experienced by the electron is

$$F_n = -m'\frac{v_n{}^2}{r_n} = -\frac{(ze)e}{r_n{}^2}, \tag{3-2}$$

and therefore

$$\mathscr{E}_{i,n} = -\frac{ze^2}{2r_n}. \tag{3-3}$$

We can evaluate r_n by utilizing the postulate of the quantization of angular momentum,

$$m'v_n r_n = n\frac{h}{2\pi}, \tag{3-4}$$

where h is Planck's constant. Eliminating v_n between eqs. (3-2) and (3-4), we find

$$r_n = \frac{n^2}{z}\frac{h^2}{4\pi^2 m'e^2}, \tag{3-5}$$

and

$$\mathscr{E}_{i,n} = -\frac{2\pi^2 m'e^4}{h^2}\frac{z^2}{n^2}. \tag{3-6}$$

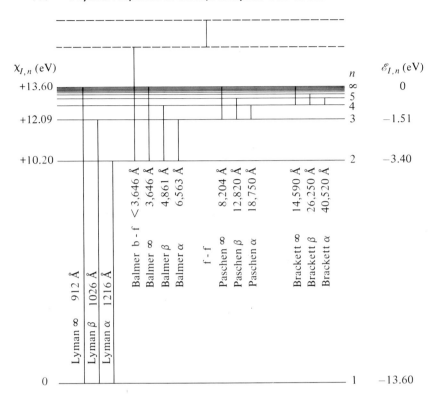

Fig. 3-2 Energy Levels in Hydrogen. For the first four series of hydrogen, the first and second spectral lines and that at the series limit are shown. The dashed horizontal lines represent two free energy states. A free-free transition (f-f) and a Balmer bound-free transition (b-f) are also shown.

As could have been anticipated, the magnitude of $\mathscr{E}_{i,n}$ increases with the atomic number of the nucleus, since the attraction is stronger with larger z; and it decreases with increasing n, since the attraction is less at greater separation between nucleus and electron. The energy $\mathscr{E}_{i,n}$ must be negative for a bound electron, because if the positive kinetic energy exceeded the negative potential energy, the electron would escape from the nucleus without returning.

Figure 3-2 shows the energy of the electron in various levels of the hydrogen atom. The same diagram could be used for hydrogen-like ions by multiplying all the energies by z^2 for the ion*; for example, for He^+, $\mathscr{E}_{II,1} = -13.60 \times 4 = -54.40$ eV. Note that the nth level lies at a fractional distance $1/n^2$

---

* The appropriate value of the reduced mass for the ion should be used for greater accuracy.

below the level $n = \infty$, since

$$\frac{\mathscr{E}_{i,\infty} - \mathscr{E}_{i,n}}{\mathscr{E}_{i,\infty} - \mathscr{E}_{i,1}} = \frac{\mathscr{E}_{i,n}}{\mathscr{E}_{i,1}} = \frac{1}{n^2}. \tag{3-7}$$

Also given in the figure is the energy with respect to the first orbit,

$$\chi_{i,n} = \mathscr{E}_{i,n} - \mathscr{E}_{i,1}. \tag{3-8}$$

Since $\mathscr{E}_{i,1}$ is the most negative of the energies, $\chi_{i,n}$ is always positive. It is called the *excitation potential* of level n, and $\chi_{i,\infty}$ is the *ionization potential* of the atom or ion.

An electron having an energy corresponding to a level that lies higher than $\mathscr{E}_{i,\infty}$ in this diagram, that is, one that has positive energy, must be a free electron. Since it is no longer bound to the atom, its energy is not quantized but may have any positive value. If the electron came from the level n by absorbing a photon of energy $h\nu$, then the kinetic energy of the electron (which in this case is also its total energy) is the difference between the absorbed energy, $h\nu$, and that expended in removing the electron from the field of the nucleus, $|\mathscr{E}_{i,n}|$:

$$\text{energy of electron} = h\nu - |\mathscr{E}_{i,n}|$$
$$= h\nu + \mathscr{E}_{i,n}.$$

We may retain eq. (3-6) for expressing this result if we adjust the quantum number n in such a way as to make the energy positive, that is, if we take $n = \sqrt{-1}\, n'$. The new quantum number n' is not restricted to integral quantities but may have any positive value, to be determined by the condition

$$\mathscr{E}_{i,n'} = h\nu + \mathscr{E}_{i,n}$$

$$+ \frac{2\pi^2 m' e^4}{h^2} \frac{z^2}{n'^2} = h\nu - \frac{2\pi^2 m' e^4}{h^2} \frac{z^2}{n^2}.$$

The orbit in this case is hyperbolic rather than elliptical, corresponding to the positive value of the total energy.

The energy $h\nu$ of a photon absorbed by a hydrogen-like ion must always equal the difference between the energies of the excited, or possibly free, electron in its initial and final states, n_a and n_b, respectively:

$$h\nu = \mathscr{E}_{i,n_b} - \mathscr{E}_{i,n_a} \tag{3-9}$$

$$= -\frac{2\pi^2 m' e^4}{h^2} z^2 \left(\frac{1}{n_b^2} - \frac{1}{n_a^2} \right). \tag{3-10}$$

For example, the red line of hydrogen, $H\alpha$ or Balmer α in Fig. 3-2 or Fig. 3-3, has a frequency

$$\nu = \frac{\mathscr{E}_{I,3} - \mathscr{E}_{I,2}}{h}$$

$$= -\frac{2\pi^2(9.1034 \times 10^{-28})(4.803 \times 10^{-10})^4}{(6.6256 \times 10^{-27})^3}\left(\frac{1}{3^2} - \frac{1}{2^2}\right)$$

$$= 45.68 \times 10^{13} \frac{\text{cycles}}{\text{sec}}$$

or, in terms of wavelength,

$$\lambda = \frac{c}{\nu}$$

$$= \frac{ch^3}{2\pi^2 m'e^4}\frac{1}{z^2}\left(\frac{1}{n_a^2} - \frac{1}{n_b^2}\right)^{-1} \tag{3-11a}$$

$$= 911.6 \frac{1}{z^2}\left(\frac{1}{n_a^2} - \frac{1}{n_b^2}\right)^{-1} \text{(Å)} \tag{3-11b}$$

$$= 6563 \text{ Å}.$$

The frequencies and wavelengths of the *series limits*, corresponding to $\mathscr{E}_{i,\infty} - \mathscr{E}_{i,n} = -\mathscr{E}_{i,n}$, may be similarly computed. A photon with a wavelength equal to that of the series limit will just be able to ionize an atom that has an electron in the nth orbit. All the energy of the photon in this case will be used to raise the electron out of the potential field of the nucleus, and there will be none left to supply the electron with kinetic energy. We have, from eq. (3-10),

$$\nu_n = \frac{2\pi^2 m'e^4}{h^3}z^2\frac{1}{n^2} \tag{3-12}$$

and

$$\lambda_n = \frac{ch^3}{2\pi^2 m'e^4}\frac{1}{z^2}n^2 = 911.6\frac{n^2}{z^2} \text{ (Å)}. \tag{3-13}$$

The wavelengths of the first five series limits of hydrogen are given in Table 3-1.

Table 3-1   Series Limits for Hydrogen.

SERIES	n	λ_n (Å)
Lyman	1	912
Balmer	2	3,646
Paschen	3	8,204
Brackett	4	14,590
Pfund	5	22,790

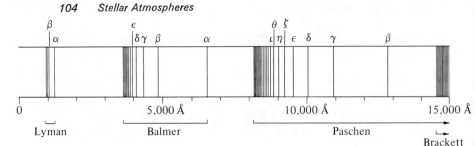

Fig. 3-3

Fig. 3-3   Spectral Series in Hydrogen between 0 and 15,000 Å. The Lyman and Balmer series are complete in this figure, but Paschen α (18,750 Å) lies to the right of the diagram. For the Brackett series, only the lines near the limit have wavelengths within the range of the figure.

A calculation of the wavelength of Lyman α gives 1216 Å. Since all other Lyman lines involve greater energy differences between the initial and final orbits, we see that the entire Lyman series lies in the ultraviolet (Figs. 3-2 and 3-3). The Balmer series lies in the visible and near ultraviolet, while all other series (except the Lyman) lie in the infrared. The *continuous* absorption in the visible, however, is due mainly to the Paschen continuum, with small contributions by the higher continua; the Balmer continuum falls in the ultraviolet, below 3646 Å.

2 EXCITATION

2-1 DEFINITIONS

The fraction of atoms (ions) of a given element that has an electron excited to a given level is given by the Boltzmann equation. Before stating this relation, we discuss the quantities involved.

It is assumed that all the particles being compared have been ionized to the same extent; that is, they are all neutral, or they all have lost the same number of electrons. We define $N_{i,x}$ as the number of atoms (ions)* that have been ionized to the degree i and excited to the level x.† We shall let $i = I$ represent the neutral stage, II represent the once-ionized stage, and so forth. For excitation, unless n is explicitly given, we shall use 0 for the ground state (which, of course, need not correspond to $n = 1$), 1 for the first excited state, 2 for the second excited state, and so on.

The number of atoms having an electron excited to a level x depends also upon the number of ways in which the electron can enter that level. If

---

* Throughout the remainder of this chapter, we generally use the term *atoms* as an abbreviation for *atoms or ions*, although the latter will occasionally be written to emphasize the applicability to ions.

† Since we shall be dealing with ratios only, it is immaterial here whether $N_{i,x}$ is the total number of particles or the number per cm³.

level x contains g_x sublevels (Zeeman states),* then the electron has not one but g_x possible ways to be raised to level x. Accordingly, g_x is called the *statistical weight* of level x. Each of the g_x sublevels corresponds to one complete set of quantum numbers, which, by the Pauli exclusion principle, must differ from one another in the value of at least one quantum number. The statistical weights for the ground states of various atoms and ions are given in Table 3-2A.†

* The designation *level* is here being used in a broad sense to include not only levels of quantum number $J = L + S$ but also, for example, an orbit of quantum number n. Then g_x represents, respectively, g_J or g_n.

† The horizontal and vertical progressions in this table may be compared with the electronic structures of the ions.

Table 3-2A   Statistical Weights.* [After A. Unsöld, 1968 (27).]

AT. NO.	ELEMENT	I	II	III	IV	V	VI	VII	VIII	IX	X	XI	XII	XIII	XIV	XV
1	H	2														
2	He	1	2													
3	Li	2*	1	2												
4	Be	1	2	1	2											
5	B	6	1	2	1	2										
6	C	9*	6	1	2	1	2									
7	N	4	9*	6	1	2	1	2								
8	O	9*	4	9	6	1	2	1	2							
9	F	6	9	4	9	6	1	2	1	2						
10	Ne	1	6	9	4	9	6	1	2	1	2					
11	Na	2	1	6	9	4	9	6	1	2	1	2				
12	Mg	1	2	1	6	9	4	9	6	1	2	1	2			
13	Al	6	1	2	1	6	9	4	9	6	1	2	1	2		
14	Si	9**	6	1	2	1	6	9	4	9	6	1	2	1	2	
15	P	4	9*	6	1	2	1	6	9	4	9	6	1	2	1	2
16	S	9*	4*	9*	6	1	2	1	6	9	4	9	6	1	2	1
17	Cl	6	9*	4	9*	6	1	2	1	6	9	4	9	6	1	2
18	Ar	1	6	9*	4	9	6	1	2	1	6	9	4	9	6	1
19	K	2*	1	6	9	4	9	6	1	2	1	6	9	4	9	6
20	Ca	1*	2*	1	6	9	4	9	6	1	2	1	6	9	4	9
21	Sc	10*	15**	10	1	6	9	4	9	6	1	2	1	6	9	4
22	Ti	21**	28**	21*	10	1	6	9	4	9	6	1	2	1	6	9
23	V	28**	25**	28*	21*	10	1	6	9	4	9	6	1	2	1	6
24	Cr	7**	6*	25	28*	21*	10	1	6	9	4			1	2	1
25	Mn	6	7*	6	25	28	21*	10	1	6	9				1	2
26	Fe	25**	30**	25	6	25	28	21	10	1	6	9		9	6	1
27	Co	28**	21**	28*	25	6	25	28	21	10	1	6				
28	Ni	21**	10*	21		25	6	25	28	21	10		6			9
29	Cu	2*	1	10												
30	Zn	1	2	1												

Table 3–2A (*continued*)

AT. NO.	ELEMENT	*I*	*II*	*III*		AT. NO.	ELEMENT	*I*	*II*
31	Ga	6	1	2		61	Pm		
32	Ge	9**	6	1		62	Sm	49	
33	As	4*	9*	6		63	Eu	8	
34	Se	9*	4*	9*		64	Gd	45	
35	Br	6	9*	4*		65	Tb	(66)	
36	Kr	1	6	9*		66	Dy		
37	Rb	2*	1	6		67	Ho		
38	Sr	1*	2*	1		68	Er		
39	Y	10*	1**	10**		69	Tm		
40	Zr	21**	28**	21**		70	Yb	1	
41	Nb	30**	25**	28		71	Lu	10	
42	Mo	7				72	Hf	21	
43	Tc					73	Ta	28	
44	Ru	35**				74	W	25	
45	Rh	28**				75	Re	6	
46	Pd	1**	10			76	Os	25	
47	Ag	2	1			77	Ir	28	
48	Cd	1	2			78	Pt	15	
49	In	6	1			79	Au	2	
50	Sn	9*	6			80	Hg	1	2
51	Sb	4*				81	Tl	6	1
52	Te	9*				82	Pb	9	6
53	I	6				83	Bi	4	
54	Xe	1				90	Th	21	
55	Cs	2*	1			92	U	85	
56	Ba	1*	2**						
57	La	10**	21**						
58	Ce	33							
59	Pr								
60	Nd	65							

* The Roman numeral *I* designates the statistical weight $g_{I,0}$ (i.e., for the ground term of the neutral atom), *II* designates $g_{II,0}$ (i.e., for the ground term of the first ion), etc. A single asterisk following the value of a statistical weight signifies the presence of another term within 2 eV of the ground term; a double asterisk, within 1 eV. In these cases, it may be necessary to calculate the partition function u_i as a sum, rather than to assume it to equal $g_{I,0}$ alone.

2-2 THE STATISTICAL WEIGHT FOR HYDROGEN*

We illustrate the calculation of g_n for the case of hydrogen or hydrogen-like ions. The set of quantum numbers may be taken alternatively as (n, l, m_l, m_s) or as (n, l, j, m_j). Since we are dealing with a single electron, we have $j = J$. Thus we have, recalling that $0 \leqslant l < n$, $-l \leqslant m_l \leqslant +l$, $m_s = \pm\frac{1}{2}$

* This section is not essential to the succeeding material.

and $j = l \pm s$, $s = \frac{1}{2}$, $-j \leqslant m_j \leqslant +j$:

$$\text{for } n = 1: (n = 1, l = 0, m_l = 0, \quad m_s = \pm\tfrac{1}{2})$$
$$\text{for } n = 2: (n = 2, l = 0, m_l = 0, \quad m_s = \pm\tfrac{1}{2})$$
$$(n = 2, l = 1, m_l = -1, m_s = \pm\tfrac{1}{2})$$
$$(n = 2, l = 1, m_l = 0, \quad m_s = \pm\tfrac{1}{2})$$
$$(n = 2, l = 1, m_l = +1, m_s = \pm\tfrac{1}{2}).$$

Alternatively,

$$\text{for } n = 1: (n = 1, l = 0, j = \tfrac{1}{2}, m_j = \pm\tfrac{1}{2})$$
$$\text{for } n = 2: (n = 2, l = 0, j = \tfrac{1}{2}, m_j = \pm\tfrac{1}{2})$$
$$(n = 2, l = 1, j = \tfrac{3}{2}, m_j = \pm\tfrac{3}{2})$$
$$(n = 2, l = 1, j = \tfrac{3}{2}, m_j = \pm\tfrac{1}{2})$$
$$(n = 2, l = 1, j = \tfrac{1}{2}, m_j = \pm\tfrac{1}{2}).$$

With either set of quantum numbers, we find $g_{n=1} = 2$ and $g_{n=2} = 8$. To find g_n for any n, we need only find the number of different possible sets of quantum numbers for that n, that is, the number of different sets of (n, l, m_l, m_s) or (n, l, j, m_j). Let us consider the representation using m_l, m_s. For a given n, we have the values as given in the following table.

l	m_l	m_s
0	0	$\pm\frac{1}{2}$
1	$0, \pm 1$	$\pm\frac{1}{2}$
2	$0, \pm 1, \pm 2$	$\pm\frac{1}{2}$
$\vdots$		
$n - 2$	$0, \pm 1, \pm 2, \cdots, \pm(n - 2)$	$\pm\frac{1}{2}$
$n - 1$	$0, \pm 1, \pm 2, \cdots, \pm(n - 2), \pm(n - 1)$	$\pm\frac{1}{2}$

The statistical weight is the number of entries under m_l (counting positive and negative values separately) multiplied by 2, since each is associated with the two values $m_s = \pm\frac{1}{2}$. See the table below.

m_l	Number with value m_l
0	n
$+1$	$n - 1$
-1	$n - 1$
$+2$	$n - 2$
-2	$n - 2$
$\vdots$	$\vdots$
$+(n - 2)$	2
$-(n - 2)$	2
$+(n - 1)$	1
$-(n - 1)$	1

Summing these, we have

$$\text{number of entries} = n + [2(n-1) + 2(n-2) + \cdots + 2(2) + 2(1)]$$

$$= n + 2[(n-1) + (n-2) + \cdots + 2 + 1].$$

We now apply the formula for the sum of an arithmetical series to the part in brackets:

$$\text{sum} = \frac{\text{number of terms}}{2} (\text{first term} + \text{last term})$$

$$= \frac{n-1}{2} [(n-1) + 1]$$

$$= \frac{n(n-1)}{2}.$$

Thus,

$$\text{number of entries} = n + 2 \cdot \frac{n(n-1)}{2}$$

$$= n^2.$$

This must be multiplied by 2 so as to account for the two values of m_s for each entry, giving finally

$$g_n = 2n^2. \tag{3-14}$$

For any atom, for a level J having sublevels $-J, \cdots, -1, 0, +1, \cdots, +J$, the statistical weight g_J is

$$g_J = 2J + 1. \tag{3-15}$$

2-3 THE BOLTZMANN EQUATION

We are now ready to write down the Boltzmann equation:

$$\frac{N_{i,x}}{N_{i,x'}} = \frac{g_{i,x} \exp(-\mathscr{E}_{i,x}/kT)}{g_{i,x'} \exp(-\mathscr{E}_{i,x'}/kT)}$$

$$= \frac{g_{i,x}}{g_{i,x'}} \exp[-(\mathscr{E}_{i,x} - \mathscr{E}_{i,x'})/kT]. \tag{3-16}$$

If x' is the ground level, then

$$\frac{N_{i,x}}{N_{i,0}} = \frac{g_{i,x}}{g_{i,0}} \exp[-(\mathscr{E}_{i,x} - \mathscr{E}_{i,0})/kT]$$

$$= \frac{g_{i,x}}{g_{i,0}} \exp(-\chi_{i,x}/kT). \tag{3-17}$$

It is often convenient to express $N_{i,x}$ in terms of the total number N_i of atoms of that species in that stage of ionization. If we sum eq. (3-17) over all states x, we have

$$N_i = \sum_x N_{i,x} = \frac{N_{i,0}}{g_{i,0}} \sum_x g_{i,x} \exp\left(-\chi_{i,x}/kT\right). \tag{3-18}$$

The sum

$$u_i = \sum_x g_{i,x} \exp\left(-\chi_{i,x}/kT\right) \tag{3-19}$$

is called the *partition function**; each of the additive terms gives the relative population for the corresponding x. It is a function of temperature and, of course, the identity of the atom or ion. It is also a function of pressure, which governs the number of unperturbed levels in the summation at a given temperature. Table 3-2B lists the partition functions for various ions. We now have

$$N_i = \frac{N_{i,0}}{g_{i,0}} u_i$$

and

$$\frac{N_{i,x}}{N_i} = \frac{g_{i,x}}{u_i} \exp\left(-\chi_{i,x}/kT\right). \tag{3-20}$$

In numerical work, it is convenient to replace the base e of the exponential term by the base 10 and to write $\chi_{i,x}$ in electron volts rather than in ergs. We have

$$e^{-\chi_{i,x}(\text{erg})/kT} = 10^{-\chi_{i,x}(\text{eV}) \times 1.6021 \times 10^{-12}(\text{erg/eV}) \cdot 1/kT \cdot \log_{10} e}$$

$$= 10^{-(5040.2/T)\chi_{i,x}(\text{eV})}$$

$$= 10^{-\theta\chi_{i,x}(\text{eV})},$$

where we have introduced the symbol

$$\theta = 1.6021 \times 10^{-12}\left(\frac{\text{erg}}{\text{eV}}\right) \frac{\log_{10} e}{k} \bigg/ T.$$

This is usually taken as

$$\theta = \frac{5040}{T}. \tag{3-21}$$

---

* Strictly, each term in the summation should be multiplied by a factor expressing the probability that the level has not been perturbed out of existence by neighboring particles. The highest terms are the first to be truncated.

Table 3-2B   Logarithms of Partition Functions.* [From T. L. Swihart, 1968 (6), pp. 274–275, based on unpublished calculations of A. N. Cox.]

The following ions have partition functions which are nearly independent of temperature and electron pressure as long as the abundance of the ion is not negligibly small:

ION	$\log u_i$	ION	$\log u_i$	ION	$\log u_i$
H I	0.30	O II	0.60	Mg III	0.00
He I	0.00	O III	0.95	Al II	0.00
He II	0.30	Ne I	0.00	Al III	0.30
Li II	0.00	Ne II	0.78	Si II	0.78
Li III	0.30	Ne III	0.95	Si III	0.00
C II	0.78	Na II	0.00	K II	0.00
C III	0.00	Na III	0.78	K III	0.78
N II	0.96	Mg II	0.30	Ca III	0.00
N III	0.78				

The following table gives $\log u_i$ for other ions as a function of temperature and electron pressure:

ION	$\log P_e$	TEMPERATURE (°K)			ION	$\log P_e$	TEMPERATURE (°K)		
		5,040	7,200	10,080			5,040	7,200	10,080
Li I	0	0.33	0.75	1.68	Si I	0	0.97	1.00	1.21
	2	0.32	0.44	0.91		2	0.96	0.99	1.06
	4	0.32	0.37	0.51		4	0.96	0.98	1.04
C I	0	0.96	0.98	1.01	K I	0	0.43	1.16	2.02
	2	0.95	0.98	1.01		2	0.35	0.62	1.19
	4	0.95	0.98	0.99		4	0.33	0.45	0.69
N I	0	0.60	0.62	0.66	Ca I	0	0.08	0.46	1.36
	2	0.60	0.62	0.66		2	0.07	0.30	0.79
	4	0.60	0.62	0.66		4	0.04	0.27	0.62
O I	0	0.95	0.95	0.97	Ca II	0	0.34	0.43	0.57
	2	0.95	0.96	0.97		2	0.33	0.42	0.56
	4	0.95	0.96	0.97		4	0.31	0.38	0.52
Na I	0	0.32	0.68	1.53	Fe I	0	1.47	1.85	2.83
	2	0.31	0.41	0.81		2	1.47	1.78	2.36
	4	0.30	0.36	0.51		4	1.47	1.74	2.26
Mg I	0	0.00	0.02	0.30	Fe II	0	1.38	1.55	1.79
	2	0.00	0.00	0.09		2	1.38	1.54	1.79
	4	0.00	0.00	0.06		4	1.38	1.52	1.75
Al I	0	0.78	0.84	1.33	Fe III	0	1.40	1.42	1.49
	2	0.78	0.79	0.91		2	1.40	1.42	1.49
	4	0.78	0.73	0.82		4	1.40	1.42	1.49

* The electron pressure is expressed in dyne cm^{-2}.

   Note in proof. A. N. Cox (1972) finds additive corrections as large as 2.3 for some entries.

Table 3-3 gives the number of hydrogen atoms having the electron in the 2nd or 3rd orbit, respectively, compared with the number in the ground level ($n = 1$), at various temperatures. As an example of the calculation of these

Table 3-3   Relative Populations of Levels in Hydrogen
($P_e = 10$ dyne cm^{-2}).

T	$\dfrac{N_{I,2}}{N_{I,1}}$	$\dfrac{N_{I,3}}{N_{I,1}}$
4,000°K	5.62×10^{-13}	5.25×10^{-15}
6,000	1.08×10^{-8}	6.28×10^{-10}
8,000	1.50×10^{-6}	2.17×10^{-7}
10,000	2.89×10^{-5}	7.25×10^{-6}
12,000	2.08×10^{-4}	7.52×10^{-5}
14,000	8.51×10^{-4}	4.00×10^{-4}
16,000	2.45×10^{-3}	1.40×10^{-3}
18,000	5.57×10^{-3}	3.71×10^{-3}
20,000	1.08×10^{-2}	8.08×10^{-3}

tabular entries, let us compute $N_{I,n=2}/N_{I,n=1} = N_{I,2}/N_{I,1}$ at 10,000°K.* We have

$$\frac{N_{I,2}}{N_{I,1}} = \frac{g_{I,2}}{g_{I,1}} 10^{-\theta \chi_{I,2}}$$

with $\chi_{I,2} = 10.20$ eV (see Fig. 3-2). Then

$$\frac{N_{I,2}}{N_{I,1}} = \frac{8}{2} 10^{-(5040.2/10,000) \times 10.20}$$

$$= 2.89 \times 10^{-5}.$$

To find $N_{I,2}/N_I$, we need the partition function u_I:

$$u_I = g_{I,1} + g_{I,2} \exp\left(-\chi_{I,2}/kT\right) + g_{I,3} \exp\left(-\chi_{I,3}/kT\right) + \cdots$$

$$= 2 + 8 \times 10^{-(5040.2/10,000) \times 10.20} + 18 \times 10^{-(5040.2/10,000) \times 12.09} + \cdots$$

$$= 2 + 5.78 \times 10^{-5} + 1.45 \times 10^{-5} + \cdots$$

$$\approx g_{I,1}.$$

Thus $N_{I,2}/N_I$ is very nearly equal to $N_{I,2}/N_{I,1}$, even for a temperature as high as 10,000°K.

It is often true, as in this example, that the partition function can be replaced by the statistical weight of the ground state. However, for the cases in Table 3-2 that are marked with one or two asterisks, it may be necessary to calculate u_i as a sum of terms rather than approximating it as $g_{i,0}$ alone.

* We could also write $N_{I,n=1}$ as $N_{I,0}$, since $n = 1$ is the ground level, represented by 0.

3 IONIZATION

The fraction of atoms that have been ionized to a given degree can be found from the Saha equation.* If N_e is the number of free electrons per cm³, then

$$\frac{N_{i+1,0}}{N_{i,0}} N_e = \frac{2(2\pi m k T)^{3/2}}{h^3} \frac{g_{i+1,0}}{g_{i,0}} \exp\left(-\chi_{i,\infty}/kT\right). \qquad (3\text{-}22)$$

We recall that $\chi_{i,\infty}$ represents the ionization potential, which is listed in Table 3-4.† This equation can be rewritten in terms of the total number of atoms in a given stage of ionization, rather than the number in the ground state. From eq. (3-20), we have

$$\frac{N_{i+1,0}}{N_{i+1}} = \frac{g_{i+1,0}}{u_{i+1}} \exp\left(-\chi_{i+1,0}/kT\right). \qquad (3\text{-}23)$$

But $\chi_{i+1,0}$ is the excitation potential of the ground state, which is zero. Therefore

$$N_{i+1,0} = N_{i+1} \frac{g_{i+1,0}}{u_{i+1}}.$$

Similarly,

$$N_{i,0} = N_i \frac{g_{i,0}}{u_i}, \qquad (3\text{-}24)$$

and thus

$$\frac{N_{i+1}}{N_i} N_e = \frac{2(2\pi m k T)^{3/2}}{h^3} \frac{u_{i+1}}{u_i} \exp\left(-\chi_{i,\infty}/kT\right). \qquad (3\text{-}25)$$

Another convenient form of the Saha equation uses the electron pressure, P_e, rather than N_e. This partial pressure due to the electrons can be evaluated in terms of the number of electrons per cm³ by rewriting the perfect gas law. If V is the volume of a sample of gas containing $\mathcal{N}$ moles of particles of a given species at partial pressure P and temperature T, then

$$PV = \mathcal{N}\mathcal{R}T, \qquad (3\text{-}26)$$

where $\mathcal{R}$ is the gas constant. Then, since

$$\mathcal{R} = N_0 k,$$

where $N_0 = $ Avogadro's number, we have

$$P = \frac{\mathcal{N} N_0}{V} kT.$$

---

* The derivation of this equation is given by L. H. Aller (25), p. 77 et seq. in the 1953 edition, or in more detail on p. 99 et seq. in the 1963 edition.
† It is worthwhile to examine the progression of the ionization potentials in Table 3-4, both vertically and horizontally, and to make a qualitative comparison with the electronic structure and the nuclear charge.

But $\mathscr{N}N_0$ is the total number of particles of the species in the volume V, hence*

$$P = NkT, \tag{3-27}$$

where N = number of particles per cm³. If these are electrons, then

$$P_e = N_e kT. \tag{3-28}$$

Thus the Saha equation can be written as

$$\frac{N_{i+1}}{N_i} P_e = \frac{2(2\pi m)^{3/2}}{h^3} (kT)^{5/2} \frac{u_{i+1}}{u_i} \exp(-\chi_{i,\infty}/kT). \tag{3-29}$$

For computational purposes, we can write

$$\log \frac{N_{i+1}}{N_i} = -\log P_e + \log \frac{2(2\pi m)^{3/2} k^{5/2}}{h^3} + \log \frac{u_{i+1}}{u_i} +$$

$$+ 2.5 \log T - \frac{5040}{T} \chi_{i,\infty} \ (\text{eV})$$

$$= -0.1761 - \log P_e + \log \frac{u_{i+1}}{u_i} +$$

$$+ 2.5 \log T - \frac{5040}{T} \chi_{i,\infty} \ (\text{eV}). \tag{3-30}$$

The transformation from base e to base 10 has again been made, for the last term, as in the preceding section. All logarithms in eq. (3-30) are to the base 10, and the pressure is in dyne cm⁻².

It should be noted that this formula compares one stage of ionization with the next. To compare the number of ions in a given stage with the total number in all stages, it may be necessary to apply the formula successively to several ionization stages. Usually, no more than two stages occur simultaneously to a significant degree at a given temperature.

By way of illustration, the Saha equation is applied to hydrogen and helium at an electron pressure $P_e = 10$ dyne cm⁻² and for various temperatures. This is approximately the electron pressure in the Sun at the level for which $T = T_{\text{eff}}$, and, although P_e increases inwardly in the Sun, the results of our calculation will serve to demonstrate roughly how the ionization of hydrogen and helium proceeds with depth in the solar atmosphere.

The absence of asterisks following the statistical weights for these elements in Table 3-2 implies that u_{i+1} may be taken as $g_{i+1,0}$ and u_i as $g_{i,0}$. For the helium ion, $g_{II,0} = 2$, corresponding to the two ways that the single electron can be placed in the ground state, that is, the first orbit. For the neutral atom, the second electron can be put into the ground state in only one way, with

---

* Equation (3-27) is derived from the Maxwell–Boltzmann distribution in Section 4-3.

Table 3–4   Ionization Potentials.* [C. E. Moore, 1970 (234).]

AT. NO.	ELEMENT	IONIZATION POTENTIAL (ELECTRON VOLTS)								
		I	II	III	IV	V	VI	VII	VIII	IX
1	H	13.598								
2	He	24.587	54.416							
3	Li	5.392	75.638	122.451						
4	Be	9.322	18.211	153.893	217.713					
5	B	8.298	25.154	37.930	259.368	340.217				
6	C	11.260	24.383	47.887	64.492	392.077	489.981			
7	N	14.534	29.601	47.448	77.472	97.888	552.057	667.029		
8	O	13.618	35.116	54.934	77.412	113.896	138.116	739.315	871.387	
9	F	17.422	34.970	62.707	87.138	114.240	157.161	185.182	953.886	1,103.089
10	Ne	21.564	40.962	63.45	97.11	126.21	157.93	207.27	239.09	1,195.797 1
11	Na	5.139	47.286	71.64	98.91	138.39	172.15	208.47	264.18	299.87 1
12	Mg	7.646	15.035	80.143	109.24	141.26	186.50	224.94	265.90	327.95
13	Al	5.986	18.828	28.447	119.99	153.71	190.47	241.43	284.59	330.21
14	Si	8.151	16.345	33.492	45.141	166.77	205.05	246.52	303.17	351.10
15	P	10.486	19.725	30.18	51.37	65.023	220.43	263.22	309.41	371.73
16	S	10.360	23.33	34.83	47.30	*72.68*	88.049	280.93	328.23	379.10
17	Cl	12.967	23.81	39.61	53.46	67.8	*97.03*	114.193	348.28	400.05
18	Ar	15.759	27.629	40.74	59.81	75.02	91.007	124.319	143.456	422.44
19	K	4.341	31.625	45.72	60.91	*82.66*	*100.0*	117.56	154.86	175.814
20	Ca	6.113	11.871	50.908	67.10	84.41	*108.78*	127.7	147.24	188.54
21	Sc	6.54	12.80	24.76	73.47	91.66	111.1	*138.0*	158.7	180.02
22	Ti	6.82	13.58	27.491	43.266	99.22	119.36	140.8	168.5	*193.2*
23	V	6.74	14.65	29.310	46.707	*65.23*	128.12	150.17	173.7	*205.8*
24	Cr	6.766	16.50	30.96	*49.1*	*69.3*	90.56	161.1	*184.7*	*209.3*
25	Mn	7.435	15.640	33.667	*51.2*	*72.4*	95	119.27	*196.46*	*221.8*
26	Fe	7.870	16.18	30.651	*54.8*	*75.0*	99	125	151.06	235.04
27	Co	7.86	17.06	33.50	*51.3*	*79.5*	*102*	*129*	*157*	186.13
28	Ni	7.635	18.168	35.17	*54.9*	*75.5*	*108*	*133*	*162*	*193*
29	Cu	7.726	20.292	36.83	*55.2*	*79.9*	*103*	*139*	*166*	*199*
30	Zn	9.394	17.964	39.722	*59.4*	*82.6*	*108*	*134*	*174*	*203*
31	Ga	5.999	20.51	30.71	64					
32	Ge	7.899	15.934	34.22	45.71	93.5				
33	As	9.81	18.633	28.351	50.13	62.63	127.6			
34	Se	9.752	21.19	30.820	42.944	*68.3*	81.70	155.4		
35	Br	11.814	21.8	36	*47.3*	*59.7*	*88.6*	*103.0*	192.8	
36	Kr	13.999	24.359	36.95	*52.5*	*64.7*	*78.5*	*111.0*	*126*	230.9
37	Rb	4.177	27.28	40	*52.6*	*71.0*	*84.4*	*99.2*	*136*	*150*
38	Sr	5.695	11.030	*43.6*	57	*71.6*	*90.8*	*106*	*122.3*	*162*
39	Y	6.38	12.24	20.52	*61.8*	*77.0*	*93.0*	*116*	*129*	*146.2*
40	Zr	6.84	13.13	22.99	34.34	81.5				
41	Nb	6.88	14.32	25.04	38.3	50.55	102.6	125		
42	Mo	7.099	16.15	27.16	46.4	61.2	68	126.8	153	
43	Tc	7.28	15.26	29.54						
44	Ru	7.37	16.76	28.47						
45	Rh	7.46	18.08	31.06						
46	Pd	8.34	19.43	32.93						
47	Ag	7.576	21.49	34.83						
48	Cd	8.993	16.908	37.48						
49	In	5.786	18.869	28.03	54					
50	Sn	7.344	14.632	30.502	40.734	72.28				
51	Sb	8.641	16.53	25.3	44.2	56	108			
52	Te	9.009	18.6	27.96	37.41	58.75	70.7	137		
53	I	10.451	19.131	*33*						
54	Xe	12.130	21.21	32.1						
55	Cs	3.894	23.1†							
56	Ba	5.212	10.004							
57	La	5.577	11.06	19.175						

* The Roman numeral *I* designates the first ionization potential $\chi_{I,0}$ (i.e., for the ground state of the neutral atom), *II* des[...] second ionization potential $\chi_{II,0}$ (i.e., for the ground state of the first ion), etc. Values in italics were interpolated or e[...] after all available data had been entered into the table. The conversion factor $1 \text{ cm}^{-1} = 0.000123981$ eV has been us[...]
† The value differs from that published in ref. (234). The change has been supplied by the author of the table, C. E. N[...] private communication (1972).

	IONIZATION POTENTIAL (ELECTRON VOLTS)										AT.
	XII	*XIII*	*XIV*	*XV*	*XVI*	*XVII*	*XVIII*	*XIX*	*XX*	*XXI*	NO.
											1
											2
											3
											4
											5
											6
											7
											8
											9
											10
9											11
2	1,962.613										12
	2,085.983	2,304.080									13
	523.50	2,437.676	2,673.108								14
	560.41	611.85	2,816.943	3,069.762							15
	564.65	651.63	707.14	3,223.836	3,494.099						16
	591.97	656.69	749.74	809.39	3,658.425	3,946.193					17
	618.24	686.09	755.73	854.75	*918*	4,120.778	4,426.114				18
	629.09	714.02	787.13	861.77	*968*	*1,034*	4,610.955	4,933.931			19
	656.39	726.03	816.61	895.12	*974*	*1,087*	*1,157*	5,129.045	5,469.738		20
2	685.89	755.47	829.79	926.00							21
	291.497	787.33	861.33	940.36							22
	308.25	336.267	895.58	974.02							23
	298.0	355	384.30	1,010.64							24
	314.4	*343.6*	404	435.3	1,133.2†						25
	330.8	*361.0*	*392.2*	457	489.5	1,266.1					26
	336	*379*	*411*	*444*	512	546.8	1,403.0				27
	352	*384*	*430*	*464*	*499*	*571*	607.2	1,547			28
	368.8	*401*	*435*	*484*	*520*	*557*	*633*	671	1,698		29
	310.8	*419.7*	*454*	*490*	*542*	*579*	*619*	*698*	738	1,856	30
											31
											32
											33
											34
											35
											36
											37
											38
	374.0										39
											40
											41
											42
											43
											44
											45
											46
											47
											48
											49
											50
											51
											52
											53
											54
											55
											56
											57

Table 3-4 (*continued*)

AT. NO.	ELEMENT	I	II	III	IV	V	VI	VII	VIII	IX	X
					IONIZATION POTENTIAL (ELECTRON VOLTS)						
58	Ce	5.47	10.85	20.20	36.72						
59	Pr	5.42	10.55	21.62	38.95	57.45					
60	Nd	5.49	10.72								
61	Pm	5.55	10.90								
62	Sm	5.63	11.07								
63	Eu	5.67	11.25								
64	Gd	6.14	12.1								
65	Tb	5.85	11.52								
66	Dy	5.93	11.67								
67	Ho	6.02	11.80								
68	Er	6.10	11.93								
69	Tm	6.18	12.05	23.71							
70	Yb	6.254	12.17	25.2							
71	Lu	5.426	13.9								
72	Hf	7.0	14.9	23.3	33.3						
73	Ta	7.89									
74	W	7.98									
75	Re	7.88									
76	Os	8.7									
77	Ir	9.1									
78	Pt	9.0	18.563								
79	Au	9.225	20.5								
80	Hg	10.437	18.756	34.2							
81	Tl	6.108	20.428	29.83							
82	Pb	7.416	15.032	31.937	42.32	68.8					
83	Bi	7.289	16.69	25.56	45.3	56.0	88.3				
84	Po	8.42									
85	At										
86	Rn	10.748									
87	Fr										
88	Ra	5.279	10.147								
89	Ac	6.9	12.1								
90	Th		11.5	20.0	28.8						
91	Pa										
92	U										
93	Np										
94	Pu	5.8									
95	Am	6.0									

Table 3-5 Ionization of Hydrogen ($P_e = 10$ dyne cm^{-2}).

T	$\dfrac{N_{II}}{N_I}$	$\dfrac{N_I}{N_I + N_{II}}$	$\dfrac{N_{II}}{N_I + N_{II}}$
4,000°K	2.46×10^{-10}	1.000	0.246×10^{-9}
6,000	3.50×10^{-4}	1.000	0.350×10^{-3}
8,000	5.15×10^{-1}	0.660	0.340
10,000	$4.66 \times 10^{+1}$	0.0210	0.979
12,000	$1.02 \times 10^{+3}$	0.000978	0.999
14,000	$9.82 \times 10^{+3}$	0.000102	1.000
16,000	$5.61 \times 10^{+4}$	0.178×10^{-4}	1.000
18,000	$2.25 \times 10^{+5}$	0.444×10^{-5}	1.000
20,000	$7.05 \times 10^{+5}$	0.142×10^{-5}	1.000

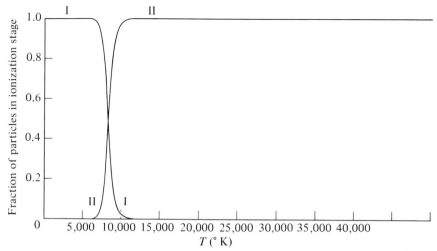

Fig. 3-4 Ionization of Hydrogen. An electron pressure $P_e = 10$ dynes cm^{-2} is assumed. For this electron pressure, hydrogen is almost completely neutral at temperatures below 6,000°K and almost completely ionized above 11,000°K.

Fig. 3-5 Ionization of Helium. An electron pressure $P_e = 10$ dynes cm^{-2} is assumed. For this electron pressure, helium is almost completely neutral at temperatures below 10,000°K, once ionized in the neighborhood of 20,000°K, and almost entirely twice ionized above 37,000°K.

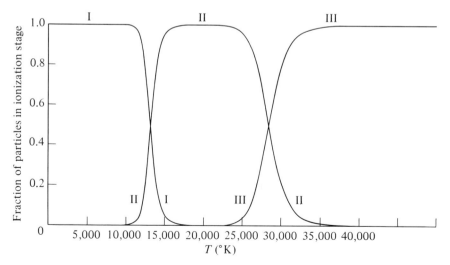

Table 3-6   Ionization of Helium ($P_e = 10$ dyne cm^{-2}).

T	$\dfrac{N_{II}}{N_I}$	$\dfrac{N_{III}}{N_{II}}$
4,000°K	1.44×10^{-23}	9.58×10^{-62}
6,000	7.70×10^{-13}	1.86×10^{-38}
8,000	2.49×10^{-7}	1.02×10^{-26}
10,000	5.45×10^{-4}	1.27×10^{-19}
12,000	9.97×10^{-2}	7.45×10^{-15}
14,000	4.37	2.01×10^{-11}
16,000	7.80×10^1	7.88×10^{-9}
18,000	7.59×10^2	8.48×10^{-7}
20,000	4.82×10^3	3.68×10^{-5}
22,000	2.24×10^4	8.24×10^{-4}
24,000	8.19×10^4	1.12×10^{-2}
26,000	2.50×10^5	1.03×10^{-1}
28,000	6.58×10^5	7.05×10^{-1}
30,000	1.54×10^6	3.77
32,000	3.28×10^6	1.65×10^1
34,000	6.45×10^6	6.13×10^1
36,000	1.19×10^7	1.98×10^2
38,000	2.06×10^7	5.71×10^2
40,000	3.41×10^7	1.49×10^3

T	$\dfrac{N_I}{N_I + N_{II} + N_{III}}$	$\dfrac{N_{II}}{N_I + N_{II} + N_{III}}$	$\dfrac{N_{III}}{N_I + N_{II} + N_{III}}$
4,000°K	1.000	0.144×10^{-22}	0.138×10^{-83}
6,000	1.000	0.770×10^{-12}	0.144×10^{-49}
8,000	1.000	0.249×10^{-6}	0.253×10^{-32}
10,000	0.999	0.544×10^{-3}	0.692×10^{-22}
12,000	0.909	0.0907	0.735×10^{-16}
14,000	0.186	0.814	0.164×10^{-10}
16,000	0.127×10^{-1}	0.987	0.777×10^{-8}
18,000	0.132×10^{-2}	0.999	0.847×10^{-6}
20,000	0.207×10^{-3}	1.000	0.368×10^{-4}
22,000	0.447×10^{-4}	0.999	0.823×10^{-3}
24,000	0.121×10^{-4}	0.989	0.0111
26,000	0.363×10^{-5}	0.906	0.0937
28,000	0.891×10^{-6}	0.586	0.414
30,000	0.136×10^{-6}	0.210	0.790
32,000	0.174×10^{-7}	0.0571	0.943
34,000	0.249×10^{-8}	0.0161	0.984
36,000	0.423×10^{-9}	0.502×10^{-2}	0.995
38,000	0.847×10^{-10}	0.175×10^{-2}	0.998
40,000	0.197×10^{-10}	0.671×10^{-3}	0.999

spin opposite to that of the electron already present. Hence, $g_{I,0} = 1$. Then, for helium,

$$\log \frac{N_{II}}{N_I} = -0.1761 - 1 + \log \tfrac{2}{1} + 2.5 \log 10,000 - \frac{5,040}{10,000} \times 24.58.$$

For the next (completely ionized) stage, $g_{III,0} = 1$, since the lone nucleus can exist in only one state. Thus

$$\log \frac{N_{III}}{N_{II}} = -0.1761 - 1 + \log \tfrac{1}{2} + 2.5 \log 10,000 - \frac{5,040}{10,000} \times 54.40.$$

Table 3-5 and Fig. 3-4 present the results for hydrogen, and Table 3-6 and Fig. 3-5 present those for helium.

4 VELOCITIES AND SPEEDS OF GAS PARTICLES*

4-1 THE MAXWELLIAN VELOCITY DISTRIBUTION

Under the conditions of thermodynamic equilibrium, and often when these conditions are not met, the velocities of the particles in a gas obey the Maxwellian distribution law, also known as the Maxwell–Boltzmann distribution law. Letting x, y, and z be orthogonal axes, we have

$N(v_x)\, dv_x =$ the number of particles having a velocity component along the x-axis between v_x and $v_x + dv_x$,

$N =$ total number of particles,

$m =$ mass of a particle.

Then

$$\frac{N(v_x)\, dv_x}{N} = \sqrt{\frac{m}{\pi \cdot 2kT}}\, \exp\left(-\tfrac{1}{2}mv_x{}^2/kT\right) dv_x \qquad (3\text{-}31)$$

or, letting

$$\alpha = \sqrt{\frac{2kT}{m}}, \qquad (3\text{-}32)$$

we have

$$\frac{N(v_x)\, dv_x}{N} = \frac{1}{\sqrt{\pi}}\, \exp\left[-(v_x{}^2/\alpha^2)\right] \frac{dv_x}{\alpha}. \qquad (3\text{-}33)$$

This function, which will be recognized as a Gaussian function, is plotted in Fig. 3-6. Similarly, the fraction of particles with velocity component

---

* British readers may prefer to substitute the term *space velocity* for *speed*. *Space velocity* in this sense, however, must not be confused with the American usage, which implies a vector quantity.

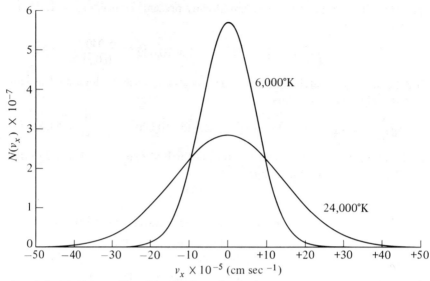

Fig. 3-6   The Maxwellian Distribution of Velocity Components. The distributions of velocity components for hydrogen at different temperatures are compared.

between v_y and $v_y + dv_y$ along the y-axis is

$$\frac{N(v_y)\,dv_y}{N} = \frac{1}{\sqrt{\pi}} \exp\left[-(v_y^2/\alpha^2)\right] \frac{dv_y}{\alpha},$$

and the fraction having velocity component between v_z and $v_z + dv_z$ along the z-axis is

$$\frac{N(v_z)\,dv_z}{N} = \frac{1}{\sqrt{\pi}} \exp\left[-(v_z^2/\alpha^2)\right] \frac{dv_z}{\alpha}.$$

The fraction of particles with velocity components between v_x and $v_x + dv_x$, v_y and $v_y + dv_y$, v_z and $v_z + dv_z$ along the x-, y-, and z-axis, respectively, is

$$\frac{N(v_x)\,dv_x}{N} \frac{N(v_y)\,dv_y}{N} \frac{N(v_z)\,dv_z}{N}$$

$$= \frac{1}{\pi^{3/2}} \exp\left[-(v_x^2/\alpha) - (v_y^2/\alpha) - (v_z^2/\alpha)\right] \frac{dv_x\,dv_y\,dv_z}{\alpha^3}. \quad (3\text{-}34)$$

It should be realized that the coefficient α produces the normalization

$$\int_{-\infty}^{+\infty} N(v_i)\,dv_i = N_i \quad (i = x, y, z); \quad (3\text{-}35)$$

hence,

$$\int_{-\infty}^{+\infty} \int_{-\infty}^{+\infty} \int_{-\infty}^{+\infty} \frac{N(v_x)\,dv_x}{N} \frac{N(v_y)\,dv_y}{N} \frac{N(v_z)\,dv_z}{N} = 1.$$

To make eq. (3-34) more meaningful intuitively, we can introduce a function of all three velocity components, $N(v_x, v_y, v_z)$, which is the number of particles with components between v_x and $v_x + dv_x$, v_y and $v_y + dv_y$, and v_z and $v_z + dv_z$. Then we can write

$$\frac{N(v_x, v_y, v_z)\,dv_x\,dv_y\,dv_z}{N} = \frac{1}{\pi^{3/2}} \exp\left[-(v_x{}^2 + v_y{}^2 + v_z{}^2)/\alpha^2\right] \frac{dv_x\,dv_y\,dv_z}{\alpha^3}.$$

$$(3\text{-}36)$$

4-2 THE MAXWELLIAN DISTRIBUTION OF SPEEDS

Frequently, one may wish to deal with the speeds of the particles rather than with the velocity components. In this case, we are not concerned with the direction in which a particle is moving. In Fig. 3-7, all particles with velocity vectors terminating on the indicated sphere have the same speed v, where

$$v^2 = v_x{}^2 + v_y{}^2 + v_z{}^2. \qquad (3\text{-}37)$$

Fig. 3-7   Velocity Vector Corresponding to Speed v. The radius of the sphere is the speed v. The velocity vector has components v_x, v_y, v_z, where $v^2 = v_x{}^2 + v_y{}^2 + v_z{}^2$.

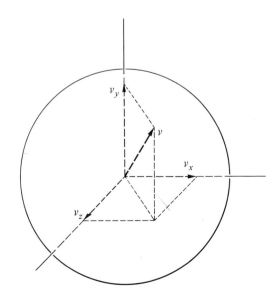

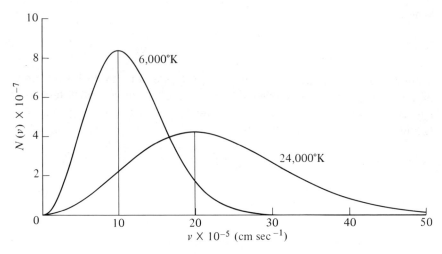

Fig. 3-8 The Maxwellian Distribution of Speeds. The distributions of speed for hydrogen at different temperatures are compared. The most probable speed at a given temperature is α, indicated by the vertical line in either case.

In place of the rectangular element of volume $dv_x\,dv_y\,dv_z$ in eq. (3-36), we now take an element of volume $4\pi v^2\,dv$ between the spherical shells of radius v and $v + dv$. Then the number of particles with speeds between v and $v + dv$ is, from eq. (3-36),

$$\frac{N(v)\,dv}{N} = \frac{1}{\pi^{3/2}} \exp\left[-(v^2/\alpha^2)\right] \frac{4\pi v^2\,dv}{\alpha^3} \tag{3-38A}$$

$$= \left(\frac{m}{2\pi kT}\right)^{3/2} \exp\left[-(mv^2/2kT)\right] 4\pi v^2\,dv. \tag{3-38B}$$

This distribution law is shown in Fig. 3-8.

Let us investigate the significance of the constant α. Differentiation of eq. (3-38A) gives

$$\frac{d}{dv}\left(\frac{N(v)}{N}\right) = \frac{4\pi}{\alpha^3 \pi^{3/2}} \exp\left[-(v^2/\alpha^2)\right]\left(2v - 2\frac{v^3}{\alpha^2}\right).$$

Setting this expression equal to zero, for the maximum of the function $N(v)$, we have

$$1 - \frac{v^2}{\alpha^2} = 0,$$

$$\therefore v = \alpha;$$

α is thus the most probable speed (see Fig. 3-8).

4-3 GAS PRESSURE

The pressure P exerted by a gas is the rate at which the particles transfer momentum normally across a unit area. We can ensure that we are dealing with the normal components by considering the particles to be traveling only along the directions of a set of orthogonal axes, so that one-sixth of all particles are moving in the positive x-direction, one-sixth in the negative x-direction, and so on.

Let us assume for the moment that all particles have the same speed v. Then, if a unit area is placed normally to one of the axes, the number of particles crossing it each second in one direction can be found as one-sixth of the number of particles in a cylinder of unit cross section and length v, as in Fig. 3-9:

Number crossing unit area per second from one direction

$$= \tfrac{1}{6} \times \text{ number per unit volume} \times \text{ volume of cylinder}$$

$$= \tfrac{1}{6}Nv.$$

The number of particles crossing the unit area per second in *both* directions is $\tfrac{1}{3}Nv$. To find the pressure, we must multiply by the momentum mv carried per particle, obtaining

$$P = \tfrac{1}{3}mNv^2.$$

If the particles have a Maxwellian distribution of speeds, then the number of particles having speed in the range v to $v + dv$ is $N(v)\, dv$ rather than N. Hence

$$P = \tfrac{1}{3}m \int_0^\infty N(v)v^2 \, dv. \qquad (3\text{-}39)$$

From eq. (3-38A), we have

$$\int_0^\infty N(v)v^2 \, dv = \frac{4}{\sqrt{\pi}\, \alpha^3} N \int_0^\infty \exp\left[-(v^2/\alpha^2)\right] v^4 \, dv,$$

Fig. 3-9 Transfer of Momentum in a Gas. In one second, one-sixth of the particles to the left of the central cross section pass through it to the right, and one-sixth of the particles on the right pass through to the left.

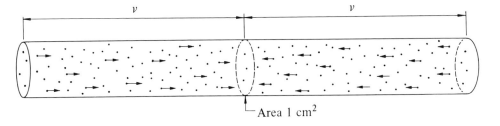

Area 1 cm^2

and it may be shown that

$$\int_0^\infty \exp\left[-(v^2/\alpha^2)\right] v^4 \, dv = \tfrac{3}{8}\sqrt{\pi}\,\alpha^5.$$

Therefore,

$$\int_0^\infty N(v)v^2 \, dv = \tfrac{3}{2}\alpha^2 N$$

and

$$P = \tfrac{1}{2}m\alpha^2 N$$

$$= NkT.$$

This is the perfect gas law, expressed in the form of eq. (3-27).

4-4 THE MEAN KINETIC ENERGY OF A PARTICLE

For an individual particle having speed v, the kinetic energy is $\tfrac{1}{2}mv^2$. The mean kinetic energy of particles whose speeds are distributed according to Maxwell's law is $\tfrac{1}{2}m\langle v^2 \rangle$, where $\langle v^2 \rangle$ is to be evaluated as

$$\langle v^2 \rangle = \frac{\displaystyle\int_0^\infty v^2 N(v) \, dv}{\displaystyle\int_0^\infty N(v) \, dv}.$$

The value of the numerator was given in the preceding section, while the denominator is simply N. Thus

$$\tfrac{1}{2}m\langle v^2 \rangle = \tfrac{3}{2}kT. \qquad (3\text{-}40)$$

We may also obtain this relation less rigorously from another point of view, using the results of the preceding section. For the case in which all particles have the same speed v, we have

$$P = \tfrac{1}{3}mNv^2 = NkT,$$

and therefore

$$\tfrac{1}{2}mv^2 = \tfrac{3}{2}kT.$$

For a distribution of speeds, v^2 may be replaced by $\langle v^2 \rangle$, yielding eq. (3-40).

5 ABSORPTION PROCESSES

5-1 ABSORPTION AND SCATTERING

When a photon encounters a particle and interacts with it, the photon may or may not survive. *Scattering* is a process that effectively deflects a photon from its course but does not alter the wavelength. *Absorption* is a process that converts a photon either into other photons of different wavelength or into other forms of energy. Thus, if a photon encounters an atom and raises a bound electron to a higher level, *scattering* occurs if the electron returns directly to the initial state, for then a photon of the original wavelength must be emitted (though not necessarily in the same direction); *absorption* occurs if the electron cascades downwards, emitting two or more photons of wavelength different from the original, or if the electron is then raised to a still higher level by another event. Absorption also takes place if the original photon raises the energy of an initially bound electron beyond the level of ionization and provides the freed electron with kinetic energy. The distinction between scattering and absorption is not always important, however, as the effect in both cases is to remove a photon from an incident beam. Thus one frequently includes both phenomena in the term *absorption*.

5-2 DESCRIPTION OF PHYSICAL PROCESSES

Bound-bound transitions involve the absorption of a photon and the excitation of an electron from one bound (elliptical, possibly circular) orbit to another of higher energy, or the emission of a photon by de-excitation of an electron to an orbit of lower energy. The difference between the energies of the initial and final orbits determines the energy, and hence the wavelength, of the absorbed or emitted photon. The transition produces a discrete line in the spectrum.

Bound-free transitions occur if the orbit of higher energy lies in the continuum. This orbit is hyperbolic rather than elliptical, or it is parabolic in the event that an electron in the nth orbit absorbs a photon of the minimum energy to produce ionization, $|\mathscr{E}_{i,n}|$.

Free-free transitions involve a change in the motion of the electron from one hyperbolic orbit to another, that is, from one free state to another. In this sense, the electron is still associated with a nucleus, even though it is not bound to it.

Bound-bound, bound-free, and free-free transitions are illustrated in Figs. 3-1 and 3-2.

Scattering is a deflection of a photon from its original path upon encounter with a particle. The scattering particle may be either charged or uncharged; it may be an electron, atom, ion, or a molecule. The effects that may produce a change in wavelength (such as the Compton effect producing a shift of 0.02 Å) may often be neglected, and we shall take the wavelengths of the incident and scattered photons to be the same. If the wavelength of the incident photon is much greater than that of a resonant wavelength of the particle, then *Rayleigh scattering* occurs. If the wavelength of the incident photon is much less, then *Thomson scattering* occurs. The latter case applies to free electrons, which have no resonant wavelength or, formally, a resonant wavelength of infinity (or a resonant frequency of zero). The term *electron scattering* customarily refers to this process. As will be seen from the formulae of Section 6, the efficiency of Thomson scattering is independent of wavelength, while that of Rayleigh scattering varies as λ^{-4}. The greatest efficiency occurs, of course, at the resonant wavelength; this corresponds to scattering in a spectral line.

Photodissociation may occur for molecules. If sufficient energy is supplied by an absorbed photon, the component atoms separate to become independent atoms.

5-3 THE DISTINCTION BETWEEN ELECTRON SCATTERING AND FREE-FREE ABSORPTION*

When electron scattering occurs, the path of a photon is altered, but the frequency remains essentially unchanged. When a free-free transition occurs, a photon is either emitted or absorbed. In the latter case, the electron has gained the energy of the photon to increase its own kinetic energy. This is possible only because of the presence of the associated nucleus; an electron in free space is unable to gain the energy of a photon, as we now demonstrate.

Let us compute the speed that an electron *would* have if it *were* to absorb a photon of frequency v, assuming the electron to be initially at rest with respect to the observer. The direction of its motion after the absorption must be the same as that of the incident photon if momentum is to be conserved.

The momentum of the system initially is that of the photon, hv/c (see the first footnote, p. 68). The momentum of the electron after the encounter is mv, where m is its relativistic mass and v is its speed relative to the observer. Since momentum must be conserved, we have

$$\frac{hv}{c} = mv$$

$$= \frac{m_0}{\sqrt{1 - (v^2/c^2)}} v,$$

where m_0 is the rest mass of the electron. Setting

$$\beta = \frac{v}{c},$$

we have

$$\frac{hv}{c} = \frac{m_0}{\sqrt{1 - \beta^2}} \beta c. \tag{3-41}$$

Next we apply the principle of conservation of mass and energy. We recall that the total energy of the electron may be written as mc^2, which consists

---

* This section is not essential to the succeeding material.

of kinetic energy $(m - m_0)c^2$ and rest energy m_0c^2:

$$h\nu + m_0c^2 = (m - m_0)c^2 + m_0c^2$$

or

$$h\nu = \frac{m_0}{\sqrt{1 - \beta^2}} c^2 - m_0c^2. \tag{3-42}$$

We now have *two* equations from which to find β (or v) for a given photon frequency, and the problem is therefore overdetermined. However, if we proceed by comparing eqs. (3-41) and (3-42), we obtain

$$\frac{1}{\sqrt{1 - \beta^2}} - 1 = \frac{\beta}{\sqrt{1 - \beta^2}}$$

or

$$1 - \beta^2 = (1 - \beta)^2.$$

The roots of this quadratic equation are β equals zero or unity, giving

$$v = 0 \quad \text{or} \quad c.$$

Hence, the electron either acquires no kinetic energy from the photon, and the electron is not scattered at all, or it acquires the relativistically inadmissible speed of light. Moreover, the solution $\beta = 0$ requires the photon to have zero frequency, while $\beta = 1$ requires infinite frequency. The equations of conservation of momentum and energy evidently cannot be satisfied simultaneously for a finite frequency, and a free electron therefore cannot absorb a photon.

5-4 ABSORPTION AND SCATTERING BY VARIOUS PARTICLES

We now reverse our point of view to consider which processes may take place for a given particle.

Free electrons produce Thomson scattering.* One may also list free-free absorptions here; however, because a nucleus must be present, we include this rather under the heading of *atoms and ions.*

Atoms and ions are capable of absorption by means of bound-bound, bound-free, and free-free transitions. In addition, Rayleigh scattering can occur.

Molecules produce absorption and scattering by all the processes stated for atoms and ions and also by photodissociation.

---

* We continue to disregard any change in the frequency of the photon (Compton effect). This approximation is valid for $h\nu \ll mc^2$, where ν is the frequency of the photon and m is the mass of the electron.

6 ABSORPTION COEFFICIENTS

6-1 MONOCHROMATIC ABSORPTION COEFFICIENTS

A. FORMULAE

To calculate the mass absorption coefficient κ_λ or κ_ν,* it is first necessary to know the *atomic absorption coefficient* $a(\lambda)$ or $a(\nu)$, which is calculated per absorbing atom or ion. This coefficient must then be multiplied by the number of absorbing atoms or ions per gram of stellar matter.

We now consider each of the absorption and scattering processes in turn.

a. *Bound-bound transitions.* These produce spectral lines and may often be neglected at high temperatures such as those in a stellar interior. In cooler regions, however, they may make an important contribution. Even at a temperature of a million degrees, where ionization is high and relatively few discrete transitions can be expected, the line coefficient exceeds the continuous coefficient (i.e., the coefficient for the background continuum) at some densities. Because of the difficulty of calculating the contribution of lines, however, absorption coefficients including line effects have been computed extensively only during the past ten years or so. The absorption coefficient within a spectral line is discussed in Chapter 5.

b. *Bound-free transitions.* We shall first discuss a formula that is applicable to neutral hydrogen and to ions in which only one electron is retained. The formula has often been applied to other systems because of the complexity of the multi-electron case, and it is therefore written with an effective nuclear charge z' to compensate, at least in part, for the electrostatic screening by the other bound electrons. Comparison with observations shows, however, that the calculated values for complex systems may be extremely inaccurate.

An expression for the bound-free coefficient was derived in 1923 by H. A. Kramers, using classical physics.† A quantum-mechanical correction g_{bf}, called a *Gaunt factor* (and not to be confused with a statistical weight g_x), was later introduced by J. A. Gaunt.‡ The quantity g_{bf} depends on the element, the bound level n, and the wavelength of the photon. Its value is usually close to unity in the region of interest. Kramers' expression, including the Gaunt factor, is

$$a_{bf}(\lambda, z', n) = \frac{64\pi^4}{3\sqrt{3}} \frac{me^{10}}{c^4 h^6} z'^4 \frac{g_{bf}}{n^5} \lambda^3 \qquad (\lambda < \lambda_n). \qquad (3\text{-}43)$$

The wavelength λ_n is that of the photon having the minimum energy to produce ionization from level n, that is, to raise the electron from n to ∞. By

---

* We shall use both κ_ν and κ_λ. These are numerically equal.
† H. A. Kramers, 1923 (200).
‡ J. A. Gaunt, 1930 (201).

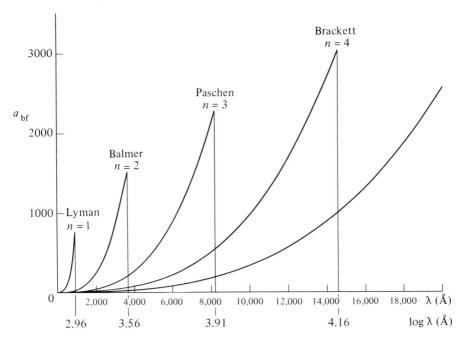

Fig. 3-10 The Bound-Free Absorption Coefficient of a Hydrogen-Like Atom. The coefficients of absorption from the first four levels, and part of the coefficient from the fifth level, are illustrated. The units are chosen such that $a_{bf} = 1$ at $\lambda = 100$ Å, $n = 1$; thus the ordinate is actually eq. (3-13),

$$a_{bf}(\lambda, z', n)/a_{bf}(\lambda = 100 \text{ Å}, z', n = 1).$$

$$\lambda_n = \frac{ch^3}{2\pi^2 me^4} \frac{n^2}{z'^2}. \tag{3-44}$$

We note from the expression for a_{bf} that an electron near a strongly attracting nucleus (small n and large z') is favorably situated for efficient absorption.

Figure 3-10 is a graph of the atomic coefficient for given n in units of the coefficient a_{bf} (100 Å, z', 1). The characteristic λ^3 dependence between absorption edges should be noted. The wavelengths λ_n are proportional to n^2, according to eq. (3-44). The corresponding ordinates are

$$\frac{a_{bf}(\lambda_n, z', n)}{a_{bi}(100 \text{ Å}, z', 1)} = \frac{\lambda_n^3/n^5}{\lambda_1^3/1}$$

$$= n.$$

The influence of the Gaunt factors has not been considered here.

To convert to the mass absorption coefficient $\kappa_{bf}(\lambda, z', n)$,* we multiply $a_{bf}(\lambda, z', n)$ by the number of atoms (ions) in state n and in the pertinent ionization stage i per gram of stellar material. The conversion consists of the factors

$$\left(\frac{N_{i,n}}{N_i}\right)_{z'} \cdot \left(\frac{N_i}{\sum N_i}\right)_{z'} \cdot \frac{1}{A_{z'}m_H} \cdot X_{z'}, \qquad (3\text{-}45)$$

which are:

$$\left(\frac{N_{i,n}}{N_i}\right)_{z'} = \left(\frac{\text{number of atoms in ionization stage } i \text{ and excitation state } n}{\text{number of atoms in ionization stage } i \text{ (and summed}}\atop{\text{over all states } n)}\right)_{z'};$$

$$\left(\frac{N_i}{\sum N_i}\right)_{z'} = \left(\frac{\text{number of atoms in ionization stage } i}{\text{number of atoms (summed over all ionization stages } i)}\right)_{z'};$$

$$\frac{1}{A_{z'}m_H} = \frac{1}{\text{atomic mass of atoms } z' \times \text{mass of H atom}}$$

$$= \frac{1}{(\text{mass/atom})_{z'}}$$

$$= \frac{\text{number of atoms } z'}{\text{gram of element } z'};$$

$$X_{z'} = \frac{\text{number of grams of element } z'}{\text{gram of stellar material}}.$$

The product of these four factors then gives

$$\frac{(\text{number of atoms in ionization stage } i \text{ and excitation state } n)_{z'}}{\text{gram of stellar material}},$$

as required. The first factor is found by application of the Boltzmann equation [eq. (3-20)], the second by repetitive use of the Saha equation [eq. (3-25)] for the various stages of ionization. The last factor refers to the known (or assumed) composition of the stellar material.

To find $\kappa_{bf}(\lambda)$, one must sum over all states n and all elements z', obtaining

$$\kappa_{bf}(\lambda) = \sum_{z'}\sum_{n} a_{bf}(\lambda, z', n)\left(\frac{N_{i,n}}{N_i}\right)_{z'}\left(\frac{N_i}{\sum N_i}\right)_{z'}\frac{1}{A_{z'}m_H} X_{z'}. \qquad (3\text{-}46)$$

Another important source of absorption in some stellar atmospheres is the negative ion of hydrogen, denoted by H^-. This has only one known bound state, from which bound-free absorption can take place. The extra electron is bound to the H atom with an energy of 0.754 eV, and the ionizing photon

---

* We have previously used the notation κ_λ (or κ_ν). It is now necessary to be explicit as to the absorption mechanism and its dependence on atomic properties.

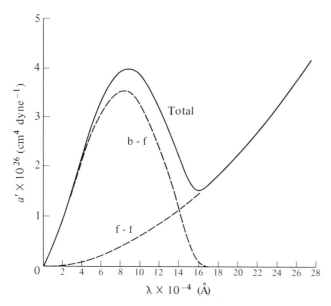

Fig. 3-11 The Absorption Coefficient of the Negative Hydrogen Ion at a Temperature of 6300°K ($\theta = 0.8$) due to Bound-Free and Free-Free Transitions. The quantity plotted is 10^{26} times the absorption coefficient per unit electron pressure and per neutral hydrogen atom in one cm^3. Thus the coefficient has the dimensions cm^{-1} and is not a mass absorption coefficient. [Adapted from N. A. Doughty and P. A. Fraser, 1966 (211).]

must have an energy at least as great as this. Its wavelength must therefore be less than

$$\lambda = \frac{hc}{h\nu} = \frac{hc}{0.754 \text{ eV}}$$
$$= 16,500 \text{ Å.}$$

The absorption coefficient as a function of wavelength is shown in Fig. 3-11 for a temperature of 6300°K. For wavelengths shorter than 14,000 Å, the principal contribution is from the bound-free process, while for wavelengths longer than 16,500 Å, free-free transitions are solely responsible for the absorption.

c. *Free-free transitions.* The atomic coefficient depends on the charge of the associated nucleus and also on the speed of the absorbing electron. For one electron and one nucleus of effective charge z' per cm^3, when the speed of the electron relative to the nucleus is in the range v to $v + dv$,

$$a_{\text{ff}}(\lambda, z', v) = \frac{4\pi}{3\sqrt{3}} \frac{e^6}{c^4 hm^2} z'^2 \frac{g_{\text{ff}}}{v} \lambda^3. \tag{3-47}$$

Here again there is a Gaunt factor, g_{ff}, usually close to unity.

The mass absorption coefficient is found from the integral

$$\kappa_{ff}(\lambda, z') = \int_0^\infty a_{ff}(\lambda, z', v) \frac{X_{z'}}{A_{z'}m_H} N_e(v) \, dv, \qquad (3\text{-}48)$$

where $N_e(v) \, dv$ is the number of electrons per cm^3 having speeds in the range v to $v + dv$, as given by eq. (3-38B). The factor $X_{z'}/A_{z'}m_H$ again gives the number of nuclei of element z' per gram of stellar material.

In particular, the imperfectly shielded nucleus of the H atom enables free-free transitions to take place. Since a hydrogen atom and an additional electron are involved, the interactions are considered as free-free transitions of the H$^-$ ion.*

d. *Electron scattering.* The electron-scattering coefficient per electron is

$$a_e = \tfrac{8}{3}\pi \left(\frac{e^2}{mc^2} \right)^2 \qquad (3\text{-}49A)$$

$$= 6.654 \times 10^{-25} \text{ cm}^2. \qquad (3\text{-}49B)$$

This is $\tfrac{8}{3}$ times the geometrical cross section calculated from the classical electron radius, e^2/mc^2. Note that it is independent of wavelength.

The mass coefficient is found by multiplying a_e by the number of electrons per gram of stellar matter, which is the ratio of the number of electrons per cm^3 and the number of grams of stellar matter per cm^3, ρ:

$$\sigma_e = a_e \frac{N_e}{\rho}$$

$$= 6.654 \times 10^{-25} \frac{N_e}{\rho}. \qquad (3\text{-}50)$$

In this equation, we have written σ rather than κ to emphasize that electron scattering is not a true absorption process.

Scattering by nuclei also exists, but it is negligible because the factor $1/m^2$ is small.

The formula given is for Thomson scattering, in which no change of wavelength occurs.

e. *Rayleigh scattering.* This type of scattering is produced by forced oscillation of orbital electrons by an electromagnetic wave for which the wavelength is much greater than that corresponding to a spectral line. The formula for Rayleigh scattering by a hydrogen atom is

$$\sigma_R = \sigma_e \left(\frac{\lambda_L}{\lambda} \right)^4, \qquad (3\text{-}51)$$

* Values of the free-free absorption coefficient of H$^-$ are tabulated by J. L. Stilley and J. Calloway, 1970 (202).

where $\lambda_L = 1026$ Å is a weighted average of the wavelengths of the Lyman lines. The wavelength of the incident radiation is compared with this value because nearly all the hydrogen atoms are in the ground state, from which Lyman absorption arises.

Rayleigh scattering by other elements can generally be neglected, although H_2 becomes an important scattering agent when its abundance is high.

B. GRAPHS OF MONOCHROMATIC COEFFICIENTS FOR STELLAR ATMOSPHERES

In a stellar interior, there is no need even to attempt to treat the monochromatic case. It suffices for the solution of the equations of stellar structure to consider a coefficient that has been averaged over frequency, as in Section 6-2; and the frequency dependence of the radiation is in any case unobservable. In a stellar atmosphere, on the other hand, both the monochromatic and the mean coefficients are of interest, and we shall now describe the results obtained by E. Vitense, which are presented in Figs. 3-12A to 3-12O.* The absorptions due to the H atom, the H^- ion, the H_2 molecule, the He atom, the He^+ ion, and several heavier elements are considered, as are Thomson scattering by electrons and Rayleigh scattering by H atoms.

Each curve must be computed for a particular electron pressure, and the value appears beside the curve as log P_e. The electron pressure enters the problem, for example, through the Saha equation, which must be applied to determine the degree of ionization of any element and hence the fraction of particles of that element capable of absorbing at a particular frequency according to any given mechanism. A method for calculating P_e is given in Section 7. Since the electron pressure depends upon the number of electrons that each atom can release, the curves must be calculated for a specific mixture of elements in definite proportions. Table 3-7 gives the composition assumed. The fraction of the total mass of this mixture that is due to hydrogen, namely 0.56, is lower than the approximate value believed to be present in the Sun.

The temperature is given in terms of the parameter $\theta = 5040/T$ [see eq. (3-21)]. The spectral type of a star with an effective temperature corresponding to θ is given in Table 3-8. Further information pertinent to the figures is given in Table 3-9.

The total coefficient, which is the sum for all absorption and scattering processes, is represented by the solid lines in the figures. (There is an additional solid-line curve, labeled G, in each figure, and this will be discussed later.) The contributions of the H atom by bound-free and free-free transitions are combined in the dotted curves, and the Rayleigh scattering is shown in the dashed curves. Electron scattering is independent of frequency, and the value

* E. Vitense, 1951 (203). Additional references for monochromatic absorption coefficients are given by G. Elste, 1968 (235) and various papers in O. Gingerich, ed., 1969 (35), including pp. 375 and 382.

Table 3-7 Abundances of Elements Assumed for the Absorption Coefficients in Figs. 3-12A to 3-12O and Fig. 3-13. For this composition, $X = 0.56$, $Y = 0.41$, and $Z = 0.03$. [After A. Rosa, 1948 (210).]

ATOMIC NUMBER z	ELEMENT	ABUNDANCE BY NUMBER (FOR $H = 25,100$)	ABUNDANCE BY MASS (FOR $H = 25,100$)	FRACTION BY MASS
1	H	25,100	25,100	0.5608
2	He	4,570	18,200	0.4066
6	C	6.31	75.9	0.0017
7	N	13.5	190	0.0042
8	O	24.5	389	0.0087
10	Ne	28.8	575	0.0128
11	Na	0.0575	1.32	0.0000
12	Mg	1.55	38.0	0.0008
13	Al	0.0955	2.57	0.0001
14	Si	1.41	39.8	0.0009
16	S	0.371	12.0	0.0003
19	K	0.00794	0.31	0.0000
20	Ca	0.0759	3.02	0.0001
26	Fe	2.34	132.0	0.0029
		$\Sigma = 29,750$	$\Sigma = 44,760$	$\Sigma = 1.0000$

Table 3-8 The Relation between $\theta = 5040/T$ and Temperature, with Corresponding Spectral Types if T Equals T_{eff}.*

θ	$T(°K)$	SPECTRAL TYPE
1.3	3,880	K8
1.2	4,200	K6
1.1	4,580	K4
1.0	5,040	K1
0.9	5,600	G5
0.8	6,300	F8
0.7	7,200	F1
0.6	8,400	A6
0.5	10,080	B9.5
0.4	12,600	B8
0.3	16,800	B4
0.2	25,200	B0.5
0.1	50,400	O5
0.07	72,000	O
0.05	100,800	O

* The relation between temperature and spectral type is that given by Table 1-1A.

Table 3-9   The Absorption Coefficients of Figs. 3-12 A to 3-12 O. [After E. Vitense, 1951 (203).]

$\dfrac{G}{\rule{3cm}{0.4pt}}$ Weighting factor for Rosseland mean absorption coefficient $\bar{\kappa}$.

$\rule{3cm}{0.4pt}$ Total coefficient $= [\kappa_\lambda(H) + \kappa_\lambda(H^-) + \kappa_\lambda(H_2) + \kappa_\lambda(He) + \kappa_\lambda(He^+) + \kappa_\lambda \text{ (metals)}](1 - e^{-h\nu/kT}) + \sigma_e + \sigma_R$.

$\cdots\cdots$ $\kappa_\lambda(H)$ (requires correction factor F given below).

$------$ σ_R

All coefficients are calculated per gram of stellar matter; the units are $cm^2\ gm^{-1}$.

Scale A   gives log [(any coefficient except $\kappa_\lambda(H))/P_e$]; for H, the scale gives $\log[\kappa_\lambda(H)/P_e] - \log F$.

Scale B   is used to find log $(\bar{\kappa}/P_e)$. The value of log $\bar{\kappa}/P_e$ is read on scale A at the height of the value of log P_e given by scale B.

Scale C   is used to find log σ_e/P_e. The value of log σ_e/P_e is read on scale A at the height of the value of log P_e given by scale B.

Table of log F

θ						$\log P_e =$					
	-1	0	0.5	1	1.5	2	3	4	5	6	7
1.3	-3.47	-4.47	-4.97	-5.47							
1.2	-2.27	-3.27	-3.77	-4.27							
1.1	-1.07	-2.07	-2.57	-3.07	-3.57	-4.07					
1.0	$+0.33$	-0.67		-1.67		-2.67	-3.67				
0.9	$+1.33$	$+0.33$	-0.17	-0.67		-1.67	-2.67				
0.8			$+1.07$	$+0.53$		-0.47	-1.47				
0.7			$+2.17$	$+1.71$		$+0.73$	-0.27	-1.27			
0.6			$+2.64$	$+2.51$		$+1.86$	$+0.92$	-0.07			
0.5			$+2.16$	$+2.16$		$+2.10$	$+1.73$	$+0.90$			
0.4			$+2.57$	$+2.57$		$+2.57$	$+2.55$	$+2.41$	$+1.84$		
0.3			$+1.90$	$+1.90$		$+1.90$	$+1.90$	$+1.90$	$+1.87$		
0.2				$+2.11$		$+2.11$	$+2.11$	$+2.11$	$+2.11$	$+2.11$	
0.1				$+2.01$		$+2.01$	$+2.01$	$+2.01$	$+2.01$	$+2.01$	
0.07				$+1.21$		$+1.21$	$+1.21$	$+1.21$	$+1.21$	$+1.21$	$+1.21$
0.05				$+1.58$		$+1.58$	$+1.58$	$+1.58$	$+1.58$	$+1.58$	$+1.58$

is indicated on scale C, as will be explained below. Discontinuities in the total-coefficient curves, caused by absorption edges, are labeled with the element responsible.

The ordinate scales require some explanation:

Scale A gives the logarithm of the mass absorption (or scattering) coefficient per unit electron pressure, that is, $\log(\kappa_\lambda/P_e)$ or $\log(\sigma/P_e)$. For example, for $\theta = 1.3$, $\log \lambda = 3.5$, and $\log P_e = 1$, the value of $\log \kappa_\lambda$ (the total coefficient) is $(-1.3 + 1) = -0.3$; and $\log \sigma_R$, due to Rayleigh scattering, is $(-3.6 + 1) = -2.6$. To obtain $\log \kappa_\lambda(H)$ for H alone, an additional scale correction is needed; the quantity $\log F$ (given in Table 3-9) for the appropriate θ and $\log P_e$ must be added to $\log \kappa_\lambda(H)$. This gives $\log \kappa_\lambda(H) = -1.6 - 5.47 + 1 = -6.1$.

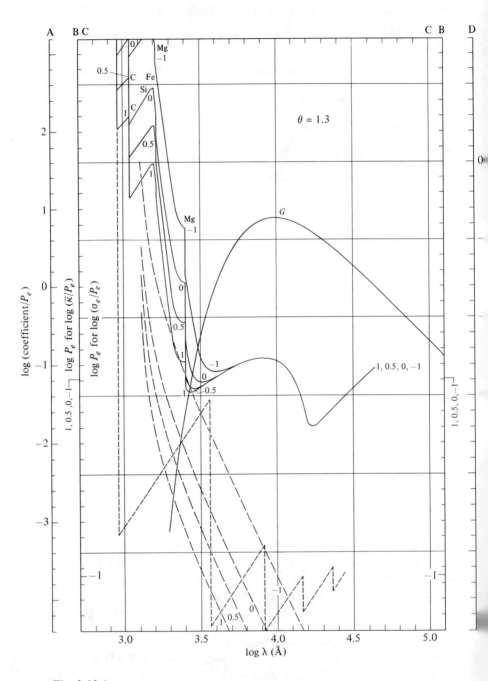

Fig. 3-12A

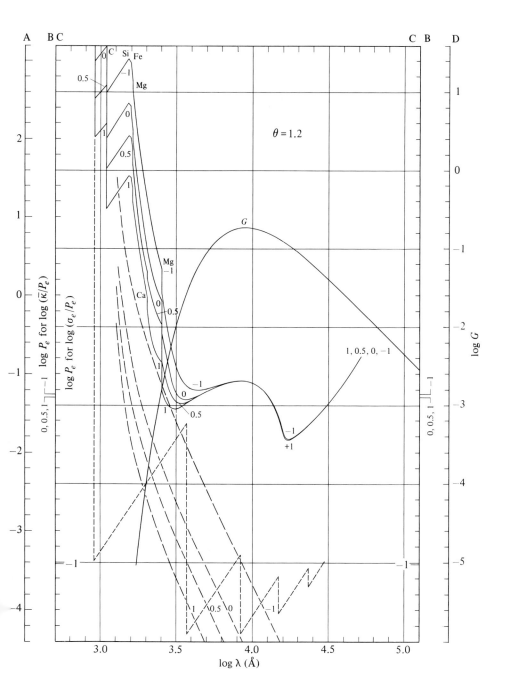

Fig. 3-12B

137

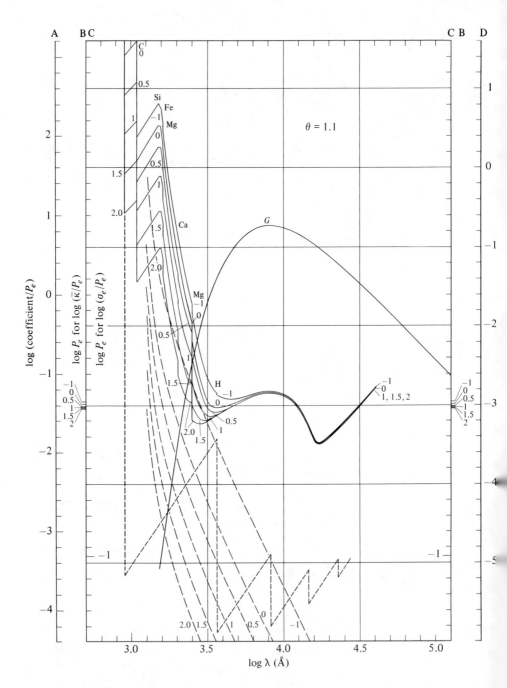

Fig. 3-12C

138

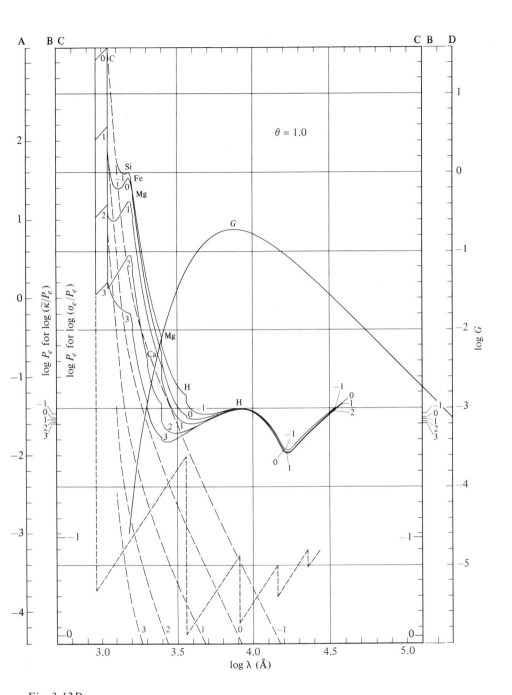

Fig. 3-12D

139

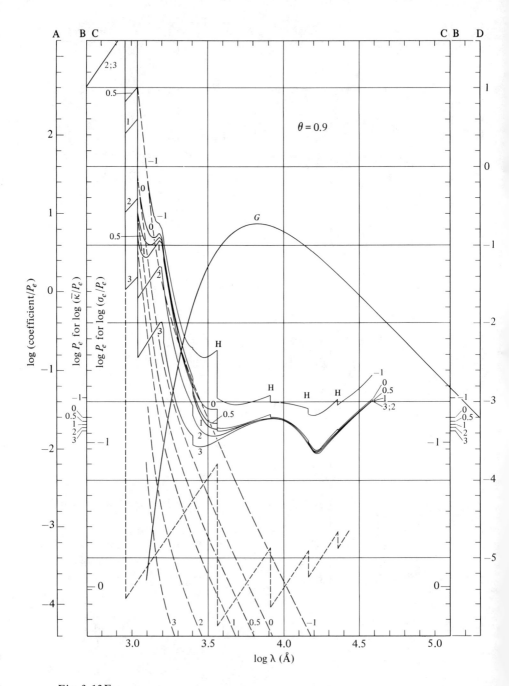

Fig. 3-12E

140

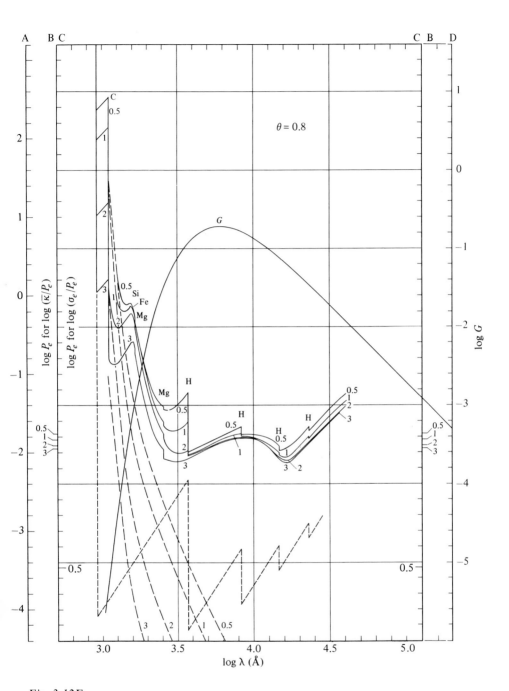

Fig. 3-12F

141

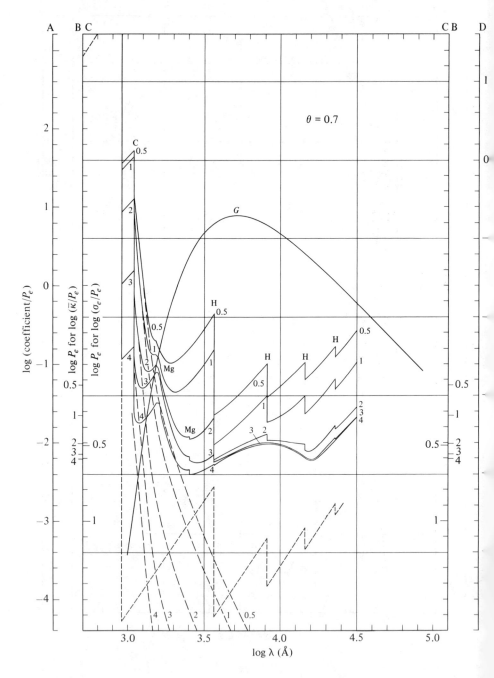

Fig. 3-12G

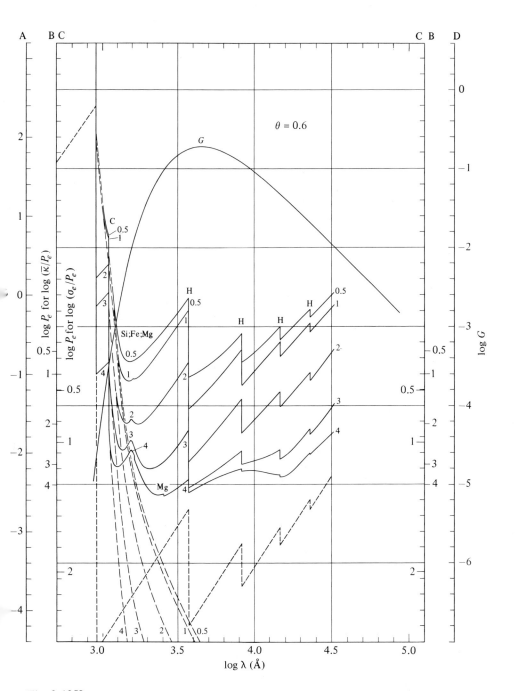

Fig. 3-12H

143

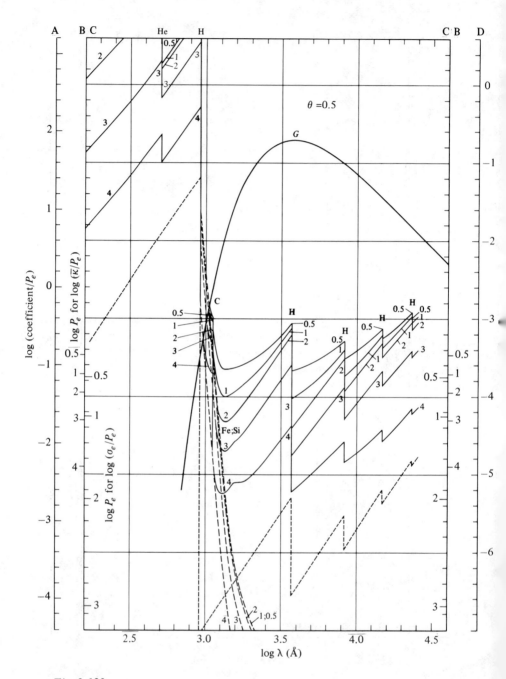

Fig. 3-12I

144

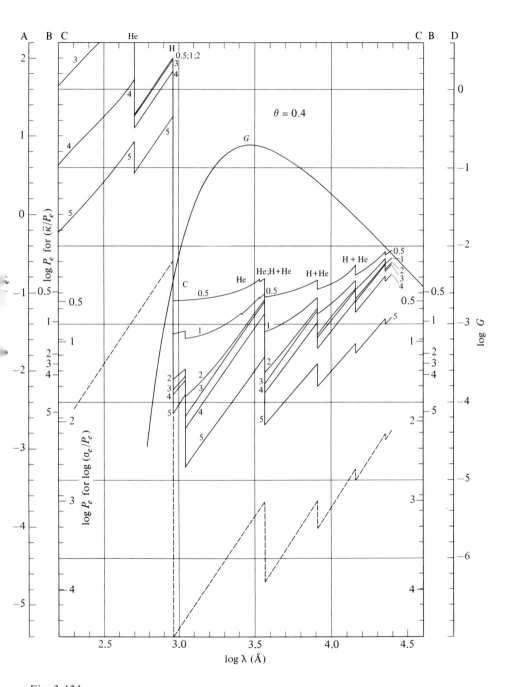

Fig. 3-12J

145

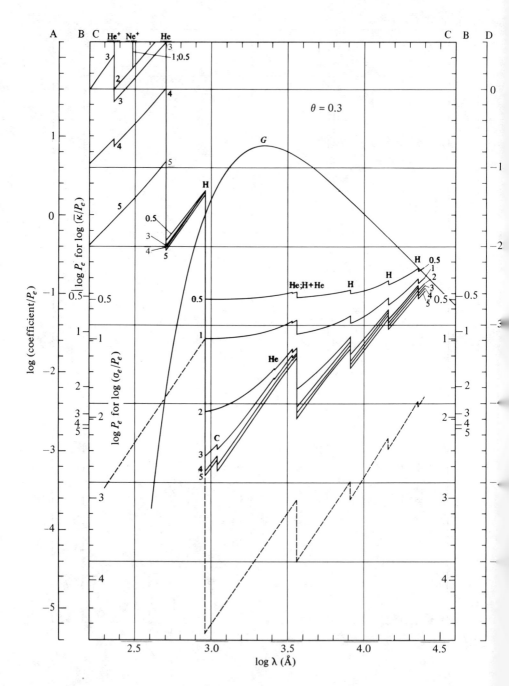

Fig. 3-12K

146

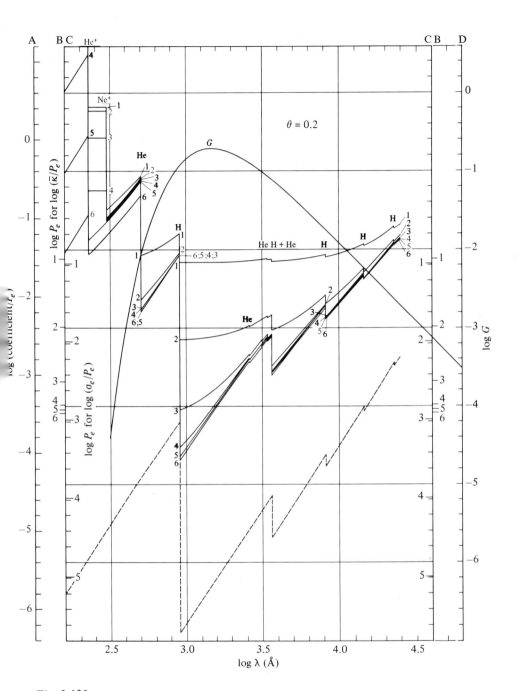

Fig. 3-12L

147

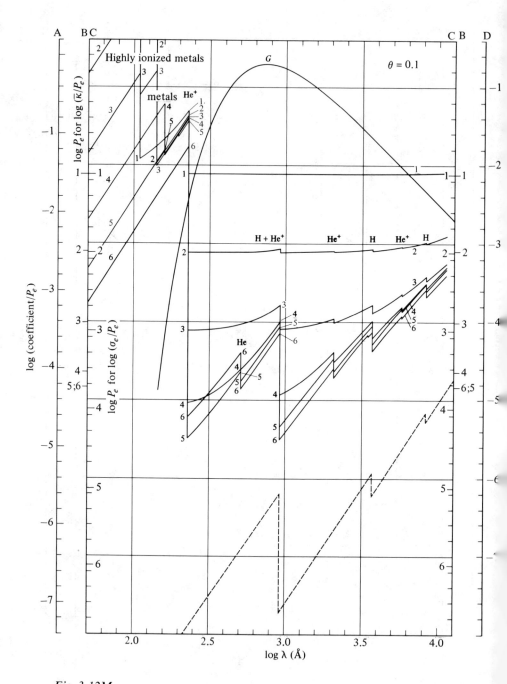

Fig. 3-12M

148

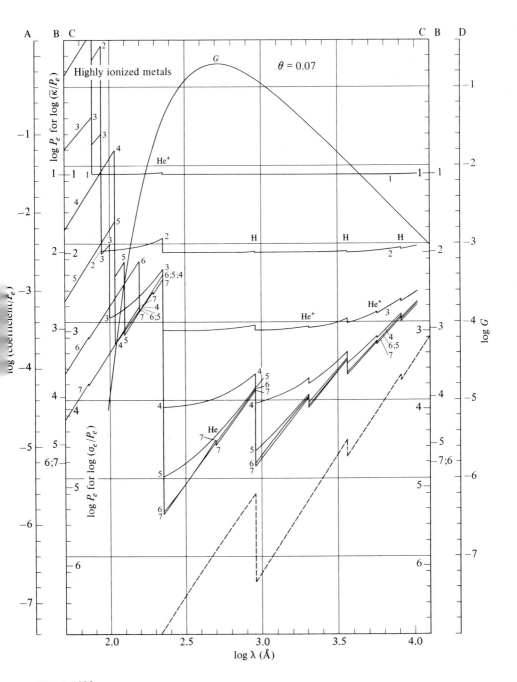

Fig. 3-12N

149

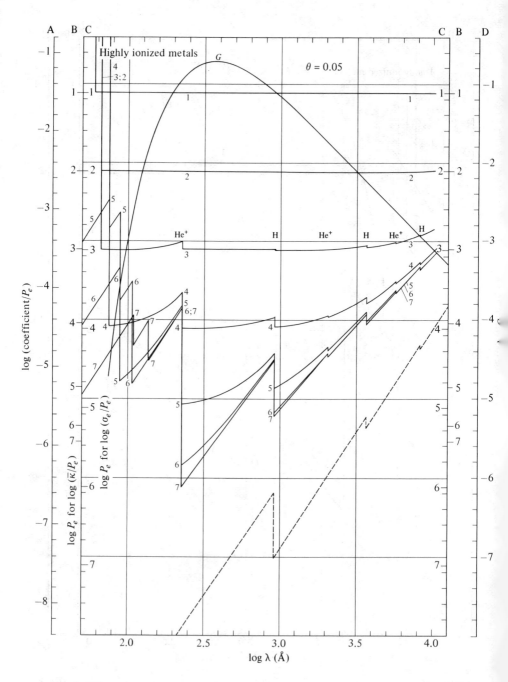

Fig. 3-12O

Scale B gives the log P_e for which log $(\bar{\kappa}/P_e)$ is computed, $\bar{\kappa}$ being the total coefficient averaged over wavelength. The value of log $(\bar{\kappa}/P_e)$ is read from scale A at the height of the log P_e value in question. For example, at $\theta = 1.3$, log $(\bar{\kappa}/P_e)$ has the same value -1.2 for log $P_e = 1, 0.5, 0, -1$. Hence, for log $P_e = 1$, we have log $\bar{\kappa} = -0.2$; for log $P_e = 0.5$, we have log $\bar{\kappa} = -0.7$, etc.

Scale C gives the log P_e for which log (σ_e/P_e) is computed. The value of log (σ_e/P_e) is read from scale A at the height of the log P_e value. Thus, at $\theta = 1.3$ and log $P_e = -1$, we find log $\sigma_e = (-3.7 - 1) = -4.7$.

Scale D gives log G, where G is the weighting function to obtain the Rosseland mean absorption coefficient $\bar{\kappa}$, discussed in Section 6-2.

We now turn to an examination of the curves themselves. The dotted, saw-toothed curves represent the contribution of neutral hydrogen, by bound-free plus free-free transitions. The absorption edges are clearly evident. This graph may be compared with Fig. 3-10. At low temperatures (large θ), there is no evidence of the absorption edges in the solid-line curves representing the total coefficient, indicating that the contribution of neutral hydrogen is negligible. This may be verified numerically; at $\theta = 1.3$, log $P_e = 1$, and log $\lambda = 3.56$ (Balmer limit), the difference in heights of the total-coefficient curve and the peak of the H curve is about 0.3; but from this must be subtracted the log F correction for the scale of the H curve, making the true difference in heights equal to $(+0.3 + 5.47) \approx 5.8$. Thus, the total-absorption coefficient is 6×10^5 times greater than the coefficient due to neutral hydrogen at this wavelength. With increasing temperature, the relative importance of H becomes greater, until at $\theta = 0.7$ it dominates the total-coefficient curves for the lower electron pressures. At $\theta = 0.7$, log $\lambda = 3.5$, and log $P_e = 0.5$, the difference in heights of the total-coefficient and the H curves is about 2.2, which is balanced by the scale correction log $F = 2.17$. Thus the curves are very nearly coincident at this wavelength, and neutral hydrogen is by far the most important source of continuous absorption.

This behavior can be readily understood. At low temperatures, almost all the hydrogen atoms are in the ground state, and only Lyman transitions, with wavelengths below 912 Å, are effective in absorbing. As the temperature increases, greater numbers of H atoms are excited to the second (Balmer) and higher levels (Table 3-3), making absorption in the far ultraviolet, visible, and infrared ranges more effective. At very high temperatures, however, hydrogen becomes ionized (Table 3-5), and its influence is thereby diminished, as seen from Figs. 3-12 I to 3-12 O.

Rayleigh scattering by neutral hydrogen atoms (dashed curves) similarly becomes ineffective at higher temperatures, when the single electron of the atom is lost.

At the higher temperatures, He and finally He$^+$ are excited. The positions of the absorption peaks of He$^+$ are closely correlated with those of H. Equation (3-13) gives

$$\lambda_n \propto \frac{n^2}{z^2},$$

and thus

$$\text{for H:} \begin{cases} n = & 1, \quad 2, \quad 3, \quad 4, \cdots \\ \dfrac{n^2}{z^2} = & 1, \quad 4, \quad 9, \quad 16, \cdots \end{cases}$$

$$\text{for He}^+: \begin{cases} n = 1, 2, 3, 4, 5, \quad 6, 7, \quad 8, \cdots \\ \dfrac{n^2}{z^2} = \tfrac{1}{4}, 1, \tfrac{9}{4}, 4, \tfrac{25}{4}, 9, \tfrac{49}{4}, 16, \cdots \end{cases}$$

We see that alternate entries for λ_n (or n^2/z^2) have the same values for H and He$^+$ (if we neglect the difference in the reduced masses). Therefore, there is a peak of He$^+$ not only at each H peak but also between any two successive H peaks.* Most of the coincident positions are labeled only as *H* in the graphs.

Electron scattering makes a negligible contribution at lower temperatures but becomes the principal mechanism at high temperatures and low electron pressures. At $T = 50{,}400°\text{K}$ ($\theta = 0.1$), absorption due to H and He$^+$ is more important than electron scattering at $\log P_e = 5$ or 6. However, at $\log P_e = 2$, the total-coefficient curve is already flattening into a straight line; and for $\log P_e = 1$, the curve is nearly a horizontal line at the same ordinate as $\log (\sigma_e/P_e)$: electron scattering dominates over all other processes. At the low electron pressures, H and He are so highly ionized as to be ineffective.

We can verify the numerical value of $\log \sigma_e$ in the case of complete ionization. In eq. (3-50), N_e/ρ is the number of electrons per gram of stellar matter and can be found as the number of electrons released by any atom (which is the atomic number) multiplied by the number of atoms of the element in 1 gm of stellar matter:

$$\frac{N_e}{\rho} = \sum_z z \frac{X_z}{A_z m_{\text{H}}} \tag{3-52}$$

(cf. Section A, b). Since 1 gm of the present mixture contains 0.56 gm of hydrogen, 0.41 gm of helium, and 0.03 gm of heavier elements, we have

$$\frac{N_e}{\rho} \approx \frac{0.56}{m_{\text{H}}} + \frac{2}{4}\frac{0.41}{m_{\text{H}}} + \frac{1}{2}\frac{0.03}{m_{\text{H}}},$$

---

* The *Pickering series* of He$^+$ is the corresponding phenomenon for bound-bound transitions; alternate lines of this series coincide with the Balmer lines of H.

where we have used the approximate value $\frac{1}{2}$ for the ratio z/A_z for all heavier elements. Then

$$\frac{N_e}{\rho} = 4.66 \times 10^{23}$$

$$\sigma_e = 0.310$$

$$\log \sigma_e = -0.508,$$

in agreement with the value read from the graphs.

We can now examine the curves to determine which absorption mechanisms prevail for various spectral types. The H^- ion is the major source of opacity for late F stars and for G and K stars. Neutral hydrogen is important for late A and early F types, although the H^- ion dominates at high electron pressure, and electron scattering contributes at low electron pressure. In early A and also in O and B stars, neutral hydrogen is again important, with the H^- ion contributing at high electron pressure for early A stars and electron scattering predominating at low electron pressure for O and B stars. Neutral helium plays a role in type B, and singly ionized helium must be considered for type O. The coolest stars, of type M, are not represented by any of the curves. For these stars, molecular absorption would have to be included.

6-2 MEAN ABSORPTION COEFFICIENTS
A. SOME ALTERNATIVE DEFINITIONS*

To avoid dealing with individual frequencies, it is often desirable to use an absorption coefficient that has been averaged over all frequencies (or wavelengths). This averaging may be performed in various ways, and we shall consider some examples.

From the equation of transfer (2-25), we have

$$\cos \theta \frac{dI_\nu}{\kappa_\nu \rho \, dx} = -I_\nu + \frac{j_\nu}{\kappa_\nu}.$$

Multiplication by $\cos \theta$ and subsequent integration over solid angle gives

$$\int_{\text{sphere}} \cos^2 \theta \frac{dI_\nu}{\kappa_\nu \rho \, dx} \, d\omega = -\int_{\text{sphere}} \cos \theta \, I_\nu \, d\omega + \int_{\text{sphere}} \cos \theta \frac{j_\nu}{\kappa_\nu} \, d\omega.$$

Since j_ν and κ_ν are independent of ω, and since

$$\int_{\text{sphere}} \cos \theta \, d\omega = 0,$$

---

* This section is not essential to the succeeding material.

we have

$$4\pi \frac{1}{\kappa_\nu} \frac{dK_\nu}{\rho\, dx} = -F_\nu,$$

or

$$4\pi \frac{dK_\nu}{\rho\, dx} = -\kappa_\nu F_\nu. \tag{3-53}$$

Integration over ν gives

$$\frac{4\pi}{\rho} \frac{d}{dx} \int_0^\infty K_\nu\, d\nu = -\int_0^\infty \kappa_\nu F_\nu\, d\nu.$$

We now define $\bar{\kappa}$ from the condition

$$\bar{\kappa} \int_0^\infty F_\nu\, d\nu = \int_0^\infty \kappa_\nu F_\nu\, d\nu,$$

that is,

$$\bar{\kappa} = \frac{\displaystyle\int_0^\infty \kappa_\nu F_\nu\, d\nu}{F}. \tag{3-54}$$

Let us also define a mean optical depth $\bar{\tau}$ from the relation

$$d\bar{\tau} = -\bar{\kappa}\rho\, dx. \tag{3-55}$$

Then we have

$$\frac{4\pi}{\rho} \frac{dK}{dx} = -\bar{\kappa}F$$

and

$$\frac{dK}{d\bar{\tau}} = H,$$

as we had for the gray atmosphere. This ensures that the total flux is the same for the gray and non-gray cases. In general, the unknown fluxes F_ν prevailing at each level of the atmosphere are required. If they are approximated by those computed in the gray case, then the temperature distribution $T(\bar{\tau})$ is, under certain conditions, exactly the same as for a gray atmosphere. This coefficient $\bar{\kappa}$, using gray-atmosphere fluxes, is called a *Chandrasekhar mean absorption coefficient*.

The coefficient defined by eq. (3-54) can be expressed in an alternative form. From eq. (3-53) we have

$$\frac{1}{\kappa_\nu} \frac{dK_\nu}{\rho\, dx} = -H_\nu.$$

Integration over v then gives

$$\frac{1}{\rho}\int_0^\infty \frac{1}{\kappa_v}\frac{dK_v}{dx}\,dv = -H,$$

and this suggests that we write

$$\frac{1}{\bar{\kappa}}\int_0^\infty \frac{dK_v}{dx}\,dv = \int_0^\infty \frac{1}{\kappa_v}\frac{dK_v}{dx}\,dv. \tag{3-56}$$

This mean coefficient $\bar{\kappa}$ is identical with that of eq. (3-54), as may be seen by the use of eq. (3-53), from which both expressions originate.

The form just introduced may be modified by replacement of K_v by $\frac{1}{3}J_v$, according to eq. (2-38):

$$\frac{1}{\bar{\kappa}}\int_0^\infty \frac{dJ_v}{dx}\,dv = \int_0^\infty \frac{1}{\kappa_v}\frac{dJ_v}{dx}\,dv$$

or

$$\frac{1}{\bar{\kappa}}\int_0^\infty \frac{dJ_v}{dT}\frac{dT}{dx}\,dv = \int_0^\infty \frac{1}{\kappa_v}\frac{dJ_v}{dT}\frac{dT}{dx}\,dv.$$

Since dT/dx is independent of v,

$$\frac{1}{\bar{\kappa}}\int_0^\infty \frac{dJ_v}{dT}\,dv = \int_0^\infty \frac{1}{\kappa_v}\frac{dJ_v}{dT}\,dv.$$

Neither J_v nor K_v is immediately known, and it is therefore convenient to replace J_v by $B_v(T)$, the Planck function. This permits calculation of $\bar{\kappa}$ without reference to any particular atmosphere, although some accuracy must be lost when this is applied to a given atmosphere since J_v is not actually equal to B_v. With increasing depth in the atmosphere, however, conditions approach those in local thermodynamic equilibrium more and more closely, and the approximation becomes an excellent one, particularly in the stellar interior. We thus have

$$\frac{1}{\bar{\kappa}} = \frac{\displaystyle\int_0^\infty \frac{1}{\kappa_v}\frac{\partial B_v(T)}{\partial T}\,dv}{\displaystyle\int_0^\infty \frac{\partial B_v(T)}{\partial T}\,dv}, \tag{3-57}$$

which is the *Rosseland mean absorption coefficient.** It should be borne in

---

* Strictly, the monochromatic absorption coefficient here should be multiplied by the *stimulated emission factor* $(1 - e^{-hv/kT})$, although this factor is not to be applied to a scattering coefficient. *Stimulated emission* is a process in which an atom emits a photon under the influence of an incident photon of the same wavelength. Since the induced photon travels in the same direction as the incident one, compensation should be made for this negative absorption.

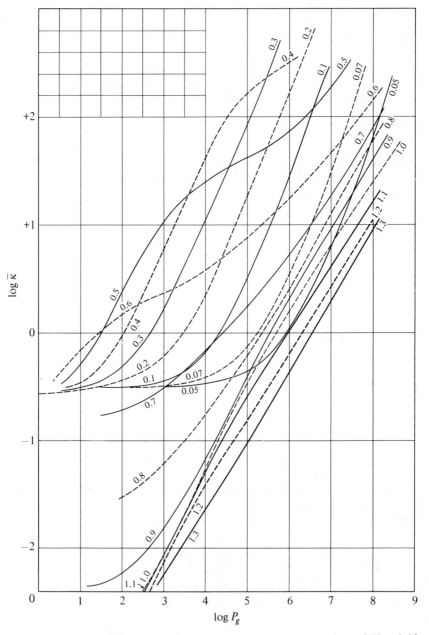

Fig. 3-13 The Rosseland mean absorption coefficient from the data of Figs. 3-12. [E. Vitense, 1951 (203).]

mind that κ_v is a sum for all contributing processes. The expression can be rewritten as

$$\frac{1}{\bar{\kappa}} = \int_0^\infty \frac{1}{\kappa_v} G \, d\left(\frac{h\nu}{kT}\right),$$

with

$$G = \frac{\partial B_v(T)/\partial T}{\displaystyle\int_0^\infty [\partial B_v(T)/\partial T] \, d\left(\frac{h\nu}{kT}\right)}.$$

The weighting function G is plotted in Fig. 3-12. The largest contributions to $1/\bar{\kappa}$ occur where G is largest and κ_v is smallest.

We shall henceforth use the Rosseland mean exclusively, although in certain situations a different choice of mean absorption coefficient may be more suitable.*

B. THE ROSSELAND MEAN ABSORPTION COEFFICIENT

The Rosseland mean based on the monochromatic coefficients in Fig. 3-12 has been evaluated and plotted by E. Vitense in Fig. 3-13. Note that the total gas pressure has been used in the latter figure, rather than electron pressure as was used in plotting the monochromatic coefficients. The conversion requires the use of the ionization equation. Curves showing the relation between gas pressure, electron pressure, and temperature are presented in Fig. 3-14 for the assumed chemical composition.† A portion of Fig. 3-12 appears on an enlarged scale in Figs. 9-2A to 9-2G.

Although various definitions of the mean coefficient are useful for the atmospheric layers, the Rosseland mean is universally used for the interior. Extensive tables of the numerical values of this mean for given chemical composition, temperature, and density have been published,‡ and these include the combined effects of the various absorption and scattering processes. (See Table 10-16, for example.) In practice, these tables may be stored in a large computer along with a program for the investigation at hand, and interpolation can be used between adjacent values to obtain the coefficient for the temperature, density, and composition in question; or one may, by trial and error, devise a formula that fits the tabulated values to the required accuracy. Particularly before such tables became available (and also before large computers were used), it was customary to use rather simple formulae

---

* See D. Mihalas, 1970 (41), pp. 37–41.

† A method for calculating electron pressure is given in Section 7.

‡ See the tables of A. N. Cox, J. N. Stewart, and D. D. Eilers, 1965 (371a); A. N. Cox and J. N. Stewart, 1965 (371b), 1970 (205) and 1970 (206); and W. D. Watson, 1970 (207). Atmospheric opacities are included in all of these except the last reference; also see the tables of M. S. Vardya, 1964 (204).

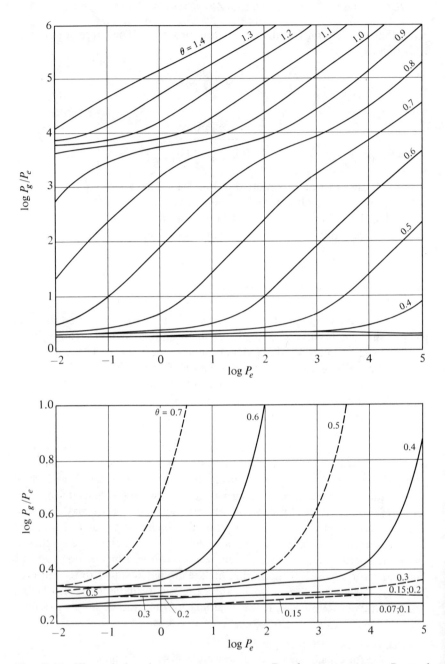

Fig. 3-14 The relation between gas pressure P_g, electron pressure P_e, and $\theta = 5040/T$ for the chemical composition of Table 3-7. [Adapted from A. Rosa, 1948 (210).]

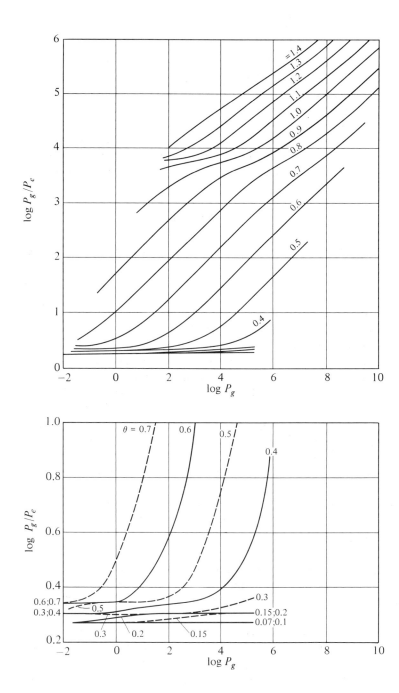

Fig. 3-14 continued

for $\bar{\kappa}_{bf}$ and $\bar{\kappa}_{ff}$ in the interior regions, where hydrogen and helium can be assumed to be completely ionized. The total coefficient may be expressed as a linear function of these two coefficients plus that for electron scattering when more than one process is operative simultaneously, although the correct procedure for obtaining a Rosseland mean is to average the reciprocal of the sum of the monochromatic coefficients. The formulae for $\bar{\kappa}_{bf}$, $\bar{\kappa}_{ff}$, and σ_e (which is already independent of frequency and needs no averaging) under conditions of complete ionization of hydrogen and helium are given below. The hydrogenic approximation is assumed for $\bar{\kappa}_{bf}$. No simple formula can be given for the contribution of absorption lines.

$$\bar{\kappa}_{bf} = 4.34 \times 10^{25} \frac{\bar{g}_{bf}}{t} Z(1 + X) \frac{\rho}{T^{3.5}} \tag{3-58}$$

$$\bar{\kappa}_{ff} = 3.68 \times 10^{22} \bar{g}_{ff}(1 - Z)(1 + X) \frac{\rho}{T^{3.5}} \tag{3-59}$$

$$\sigma_e = 0.20(1 + X). \tag{3-60}$$

Again, X is the fraction (by mass) of hydrogen in the stellar matter and Z is the fraction (by mass) of elements other than hydrogen and helium. The Gaunt factors averaged over frequency are denoted by $\bar{g}_{bf}$ and $\bar{g}_{ff}$. Another correction factor is t, the *guillotine factor*, for which the value is typically between 1 and 100. (See Table 10-15.) This name was introduced by Eddington with reference to the fact that when all electrons in an orbit have been lost by ionization, the "guillotine has fallen" on that element and it can no longer contribute to absorption from that orbit. The bound-free coefficient depends on the abundance Z of the heavier elements, since it is only these that have orbital electrons remaining to produce bound-free transitions. On the other hand, the free-free coefficient is proportional to the abundance of hydrogen plus helium, which is $(1 - Z)$. This proportionality arises from omission of the contribution of the heavier elements for the sake of obtaining a simpler formula. This is justifiable because $\bar{\kappa}_{ff}$ is important only when the abundance of heavier elements is low, and because the bound-free process is more efficient than the free-free process for the heavier elements. Electron scattering becomes the most important source of opacity when the density is low or the temperature is high, because the bound-free and free-free coefficients diminish, while the electron-scattering coefficient remains constant with respect to these variables.

We now show that the factor $(1 + X)$ arises from the dependence of these three coefficients on N_e. In the expression for $\bar{\kappa}_{bf}$, it is through $N_i/\sum N_i$ that N_e is introduced. Since hydrogen and helium are assumed to be completely ionized and the heavier elements nearly so, we may use eq. (3-52):

$$N_e = \rho \sum_z z \cdot \frac{X_z}{A_z m_H}.$$

If we now let

Y = fraction of helium in the stellar matter (by mass),

we get

$$N_e = \frac{\rho}{m_{\mathrm{H}}} (X + \tfrac{1}{2} Y + \tfrac{1}{2} Z),$$

where we have again made the approximation that $z/A_z \approx \tfrac{1}{2}$ for all heavier elements. Since

$$Y + Z = 1 - X,$$

we find

$$N_e = \frac{\rho}{2m_{\mathrm{H}}} (1 + X), \tag{3-61}$$

which shows the dependence we wished to demonstrate.

A process that we have not considered is conduction by electrons when the density is high. This can become more effective than radiation in transporting energy outwards through a star and can be accounted for by a suitable modification of the radiative opacity.*

6-3 THE CONTINUOUS ABSORPTION COEFFICIENT OF THE SOLAR ATMOSPHERE

The opacity of a stellar atmosphere at any wavelength is correlated with the intensity (or flux) that is able to escape at that wavelength; the greater the opacity, the less the amount of radiation that can penetrate the outer layers. This relationship makes it possible to determine $\kappa_\nu/\bar\kappa$ from observations of the surface intensity or flux.

If we repeat the derivation of Section 4-2B of Chapter 2 but include the frequency dependence, we find

$$I_\nu(\tau_\nu = 0, \theta) = \int_0^\infty B_\nu(T) e^{-\tau_\nu \sec \theta} \, d\tau_\nu \sec \theta, \tag{3-62}$$

where the Kirchhoff–Planck relation

$$\frac{j_\nu}{\kappa_\nu} = B_\nu(T)$$

has been used. Since we are interested in κ_ν, let us write

$$d\tau_\nu = -\kappa_\nu \rho \, dx$$

$$d\bar\tau = -\bar\kappa \rho \, dx,$$

* See A. N. Cox (L. H. Aller and D. B. McLaughlin, eds.), 1965 (58), pp. 223, 224.

giving

$$dr_v = \frac{\kappa_v}{\bar{\kappa}} d\bar{\tau}.$$

If we now make the simplifying assumption that $\kappa_v/\bar{\kappa}$ is independent of depth, we have

$$\tau_v = \frac{\kappa_v}{\bar{\kappa}} \bar{\tau},$$

and eq. (3-62) can be written in the form

$$I_v(0, \theta) = \int_0^\infty B_v(T) e^{-(\kappa_v/\bar{\kappa})\bar{\tau}\sec\theta} \frac{\kappa_v}{\bar{\kappa}} d\bar{\tau} \sec \theta. \qquad (3\text{-}63)$$

To a first approximation, $T(\bar{\tau})$ may be taken as the gray-atmosphere distribution given by eq. (2-51). Numerical values of the integral can then be calculated for given values of v, $\kappa_v/\bar{\kappa}$, $\sec \theta$, and T_{eff}. Conversely, one can extract the value of $\kappa_v/\bar{\kappa}$ corresponding to the observed value of $I_v(0, \theta)$ at given v, $\sec \theta$, and T_{eff}. A similar analysis can be made from the observed flux $F_v(0)$.*

The mechanism producing the observed variation of the absorption coefficient with wavelength in the solar atmosphere was not understood until 1939. It had been thought that continuous absorption of hydrogen and the metals might be responsible, but it was not clear why the absorption edges due to the metals were not evident. The problem was solved when R. Wildt demonstrated the high relative abundance of the negative hydrogen ion and proposed that it might be the main source of absorption in atmospheres like that of the Sun.† The theoretical ratio $\kappa_v/\bar{\kappa}$ due to H⁻ at various wavelengths is in fair agreement with the observed values. The H⁻ ion dominates the total-coefficient curves at the lower temperatures (higher θ) in Figs. 3-12.

Although the number of H⁻ ions in the solar atmosphere is very small, it is larger than the number of H atoms capable of absorbing in the same wavelength range. It is the Paschen and higher series that are operative here, and we have already seen in Table 3-3 that only one atom in 0.16×10^{10} can absorb in the Paschen continuum at the 6000°K temperature typical of the solar atmosphere. For the higher series, the population of the appropriate levels is even smaller. To find the number of H⁻ ions relative to the number of H atoms for a representative point in the solar atmosphere, we may use the Saha equation [eq. (3-30)] with $\log P_e = 1.3$ (see Table 4-2) and $T = 6000°K$. The parts played by the atom and ion are here reversed, as it is the

---

* Tables that facilitate the calculation of $\kappa_v/\bar{\kappa}$ from the observed intensities or fluxes are given by S. Chandrasekhar, 1950 (28), pp. 306, 307.
† R. Wildt, 1939 (208) and 1939 (209).

ion that loses an electron to become an atom. The statistical weight of the H^- ion, which is formed in the ground state, is unity. The partition functions may be replaced by statistical weights. Thus

$$\log \frac{N(H)}{N(H^-)} = -0.1761 - \log P_e + \log \frac{u(H)}{u(H^-)} + 2.5 \log T - \frac{5040}{T} \chi \text{ (eV)}$$

$$= -0.1761 - 1.3 + \log \tfrac{2}{1} + 2.5 \log 6000 - \frac{5040}{6000} \times 0.754$$

$$= 7.6;$$

$$\frac{N(H)}{N(H^-)} = 4 \times 10^7,$$

and the number of H^- ions is about 40 times larger than the number of sufficiently excited H atoms. This allows H^- to be the main source of opacity in the solar atmosphere.

7 ELECTRON PRESSURE

If the opacity coefficient $\bar{\kappa}$ is expressed in terms of the electron pressure P_e, it is necessary to find the relation between P_e and the gas pressure P_g and temperature T. This may be accomplished for a given chemical composition by the following method.

For a specified value of T and an estimated value of P_e, we calculate for each element the fraction of atoms that are once ionized and twice ionized. Higher stages may be neglected since they are applicable only to the heavier elements, which have low abundances and which contribute only after hydrogen and helium have already released large numbers of electrons. From the Saha equation, we find the ratios $(N_{II}/N_I)_z$ and $(N_{III}/N_{II})_z$ for each element z. We then calculate the fractions x_{IIz} and x_{IIIz} of atoms that are once and twice ionized from the following quantities, where

$$N_z = (N_I + N_{II} + N_{III})$$

if no ionization beyond stage III occurs:

$$\frac{1}{x_{IIz}} = \left(\frac{N}{N_{II}}\right)_z = \left(\frac{N_I}{N_{II}} + \frac{N_{II}}{N_{II}} + \frac{N_{III}}{N_{II}}\right)_z,$$

$$\frac{1}{x_{IIIz}} = \left(\frac{N}{N_{III}}\right)_z = \left(\frac{N_I}{N_{II}} \cdot \frac{N_{II}}{N_{III}} + \frac{N_{II}}{N_{III}} + \frac{N_{III}}{N_{III}}\right)_z.$$

The average number E of electrons per nucleus is next determined from the expression

$$E = \frac{\sum\limits_z N_z x_{IIz} + 2 \sum\limits_z N_z x_{IIIz}}{\sum\limits_z N_z}, \cdot$$

and the ratio P_g/P_e is given as

$$\frac{P_g}{P_e} = \frac{(N_{\text{ions}} + N_{\text{atoms}} + N_{\text{electrons}})kT}{N_{\text{electrons}}kT}$$

$$= \frac{N_{\text{nuclei}} + N_{\text{electrons}}}{N_{\text{electrons}}}$$

$$= \frac{E + 1}{E}.$$

Thus

$$P_e = P_g \frac{E}{E + 1}.$$

If this value of P_e disagrees with that initially assumed, a new estimate is made and the calculation is repeated with as many iterations as necessary to obtain consistency.

The relation for P_g/P_e, expressed conveniently as a function of P_g and T, is shown in Fig. 3-14 for the composition of Table 3-7.

PROBLEMS

1. Calculate the relative populations of the five lowest levels in a hydrogen atom at $T = 50,000°K$.

2. Using the data of Tables 4-2 and 7-38, calculate the mean thermal energy of an electron under the conditions at the center of the Sun and at the atmospheric level for which $T = T_{\text{eff}}$. Can the electron in either case ionize a hydrogen atom?

3. Consider a mixture of 2×10^{23} hydrogen atoms and 4×10^{23} nitrogen atoms per cm³. For a temperature of $5000°K$, find the mean kinetic energies and the most probable speeds of the atoms. Also find the partial pressures of the hydrogen and nitrogen atoms.

4. For pure hydrogen at $T = 10^4 °K$ and $\rho = 10^{-7}$ gm cm⁻³, determine the partial pressures of the atoms, ions, and electrons.

5. Refer to the monochromatic absorption coefficients of Fig. 3-12 H. (a) For $\log P_e = 0.5$ and 4, at the wavelength for which the contribution to the Rosseland mean reaches its maximum, find the values of the absorption coefficient due to hydrogen bound-free and free-free transitions and (by extrapolation, if necessary) the Rayleigh scattering coefficient and the electron-scattering coefficient. Compare these values with the total

coefficient and identify the major sources of opacity at the two values of the electron pressure.

(b) From the values of σ_e obtained in part (a), what qualitative conclusion can be drawn about the degree of ionization?

(c) Verify the answer to part (b) by calculating the relative numbers of hydrogen atoms and ions for the two values of the electron pressure.

4

MODEL ATMOSPHERES

A model atmosphere is a schematic representation of an actual atmosphere, expressible in the form of a tabulation of various quantities such as pressure and temperature as functions of depth in the atmosphere. In addition to being of interest in itself, a description of the physical structure of an atmosphere is a prerequisite for calculating the details of the flux emerging at the surface, which can then be compared with observations of the spectral distributions of actual stars both in the continuum and in the absorption lines.

We have seen in Chapter 2 how temperature may be related to optical depth for an atmosphere in radiative equilibrium, but the question of converting optical depth into geometrical depth was not considered. We shall first obtain the pressure as a function of optical depth by integrating the differential equation expressing the condition of *hydrostatic equilibrium*, namely, that the upward force on matter at any depth must be compensated by the downward force to maintain mechanical balance. An auxiliary integration will then give the optical depth as a function of geometrical depth.

The model depends on the mode by which energy is carried toward the stellar surface. Only radiation and convection need be considered for an atmosphere, because the low density of the gases makes conduction inefficient. Our primary concern will be with atmospheres in which radiation alone is responsible for the energy transfer, and we shall mention the more complicated case of convective transfer only briefly.

Tables and discussions of several model atmospheres and figures illustrating their monochromatic flux distributions will conclude the chapter.

1 THE EQUATIONS FOR MODEL ATMOSPHERES

The outermost layers of the stars are so rarefied that radiation passes easily through them. Since the total amount of radiant energy received by a small sample of matter in each second is the same as that radiated (even though the frequency distribution may be changed), these layers are in radiative equilibrium. In some stars, convection occurs beneath the radiative region, and the situation in which both radiation and convection transfer energy poses a difficult problem that we shall not treat quantitatively. The equations to be derived in Sections 1-1 and 1-2 are applicable regardless of the mode of transfer; but in Section 1-3, we shall be concerned specifically with radiative equilibrium.

We now collect the equations needed, within our limitations, for the determination of a plane-parallel atmosphere in which the acceleration due to gravity may be considered constant. The method of numerical solution of these equations will be deferred until Part Four.

1-1 THE EQUATION OF HYDROSTATIC EQUILIBRIUM

As in Fig. 2-8, the radial distance of a layer below the stellar surface is denoted by the variable x, which is zero at the surface and decreases algebraically in the inward direction. This corresponds to the optical depth τ, which is likewise zero at the surface but *increases* inwards.

Consider now an element of matter having mass dm, height dx, and cross-sectional area $d\sigma$ (see Fig. 4-1): if g is the acceleration due to gravity and P is the pressure at the depth x, then the requirement that the upward and downward forces on the element must be in balance gives the relation

$$(P + dP)\, d\sigma + g\, dm - P\, d\sigma = 0.$$

But, if ρ is the density of the matter at x, we have

$$dm = \rho\, dx\, d\sigma,$$

and therefore

$$\frac{dP}{dx} = -g\rho. \tag{4-1}$$

Fig. 4-1 The Forces on an Element of Matter. The mass of the element is dm and the cross-sectional area (perpendicular to the plane of the paper) is $d\sigma$. The acceleration due to gravity is g. For equilibrium, the sum of the forces must be zero.

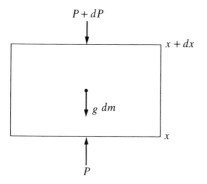

This is the equation of hydrostatic equilibrium. The acceleration due to gravity may usually be considered constant, since the atmospheres of most stars are shallow. We therefore take

$$g = \frac{GM}{R^2},$$

where

$$M = \text{mass of the star,}$$

$$R = \text{radius of the star.}$$

The numerical integration to be presented in Part Four requires that the value of the derivative of P at any level be expressed in terms of the values of the dependent and independent variables at that level, in this case, P and x. As a first step, then, let us transform from ρ to the gas pressure P_g by means of the perfect gas law.

1-2 THE PERFECT GAS LAW. RADIATION PRESSURE

For a mixture of gases, if

$$V = \text{volume of a sample of the mixture,}$$

$$\mathcal{N}_i = \text{number of moles of constituent } i \text{ in the sample,}$$

$$P_i = \text{partial pressure of constituent } i,$$

$$T = \text{absolute temperature,}$$

$$\mathcal{R} = \text{gas constant,}$$

then

$$\left(\sum_i P_i \right) V = \left(\sum \mathcal{N}_i \right) \mathcal{R} T$$

$$P_g V = \mathcal{N} \mathcal{R} T, \tag{4-2}$$

where

$$P_g = \text{total gas pressure,}$$

$$\mathcal{N} = \text{total number of moles in the sample.}$$

Since

$$\mathcal{R} = N_0 k,$$

which is the product of Avogadro's number and Boltzmann's constant, we can write

$$P_g = \frac{\mathcal{N} N_0}{V} kT.$$

But $\mathcal{N}N_0$ is the total number of particles in the sample, with each atom, ion, and free electron considered as one particle. Therefore, if we multiply both numerator and denominator of $\mathcal{N}N_0/V$ by the average mass per particle, we get

$$\frac{\mathcal{N}N_0}{V} = \frac{\text{mass of sample}}{\text{volume}} \cdot \frac{1}{\text{average mass per particle}}$$

$$= \frac{\rho}{\text{average mass per particle}}.$$

The average mass per particle is conveniently expressed as the product μH, where μ, called the *mean molecular weight*, is the average atomic mass per free particle and H is the mass of one atomic mass unit (but see below). The perfect gas law then becomes

$$P_g = \frac{k}{\mu H}\,\rho T. \tag{4-3}$$

The value of μ depends on the chemical composition of the material and also on the degree of ionization. Simple expressions can be obtained in the limiting cases of complete ionization and of complete neutrality of the constituents. Complete ionization may be assumed for the material in the stellar interior, and the formula for μ in this case is given by eq. (6-3) or eq. (6-4). We now consider the expression applicable in the case of complete neutrality. This is a good approximation in atmospheres similar to that of the Sun. If

$$z = \text{atomic number of an element,}$$

$$N_z = \text{number of atoms of the element per cm}^3,$$

$$m_z = \text{mass of an atom of the element,}$$

then

$$\mu H = \frac{\sum_z N_z m_z}{\sum_z N_z}.$$

If we now set

$$H = \text{mass in grams of 1 Atomic Mass Unit,*}$$

$$A_z = \text{atomic weight of the element,}$$

---

* In practice, H may be taken as the mass of the hydrogen atom. The substitution of $\text{mass}_H = 1.673 \times 10^{-24}$ gm for $\text{mass}_{1\text{AMU}} = 1.660 \times 10^{-24}$ gm is preferable if hydrogen is the main constituent of the gas and the atomic mass of hydrogen is taken simply as 1 rather than as 1.008.

then

$$\mu = \frac{\sum\limits_{z} N_z A_z}{\sum\limits_{z} N_z} \quad \text{(neutral gas)}. \tag{4-4}$$

For the mixture of gases listed in Table 3-7, we find

$$\mu = \frac{44,760}{29,750} = 1.505.$$

The pressure due to radiation can be determined from eq. (2-11). After integration over all frequencies, we obtain

$$P_{\text{rad}}(r) = \frac{1}{c} \int_{\text{sphere}} I(r, \theta) \cos^2 \theta \, d\omega.$$

If the intensity $I(r, \theta)$ may be adequately approximated by the Planck function $B(T)$, we find

$$\begin{aligned}
P_{\text{rad}} &= \frac{1}{c} B(T) \int_{\varphi=0}^{2\pi} \int_{\theta=0}^{\pi} \cos^2 \theta \sin \theta \, d\theta d\varphi \\
&= \frac{1}{c} B(T) \frac{4\pi}{3} \\
&= \frac{4}{3c} \sigma T^4
\end{aligned}$$

by eq. (1-9). Introducing the constant $a = 4\sigma/c$, we have

$$P_{\text{rad}} = \frac{1}{3} aT^4.$$

When both radiation and a perfect gas are present, the total pressure P is given as the sum of P_{rad} and P_g,

$$P = P_g + P_{\text{rad}}.$$

1-3 AN ALTERNATIVE FORM OF THE EQUATION OF HYDROSTATIC EQUILIBRIUM

If the equation of state contained only P and ρ, we could eliminate ρ from the differential equation (4-1) and solve it numerically to find $P(x)$. The fact that the temperature, as well, enters the equation creates a problem, as we do not have a $T(x)$ relation. At best, we have a $T(\tau)$ relation from radiative transfer theory, and we are thus obliged to replace x in the differential equation by τ.* The temperature distribution given by the theory is actually

---

* It is, in fact, possible in a simple case to avoid the replacement of τ by x. See problem 1 at the end of this chapter. Although the required condition is met in the present discussion, we shall proceed with the use of τ to illustrate the more general case.

expressed in terms of the *mean* optical depth, $\bar{\tau}$, which can then be used as the independent variable for the construction of a gray model atmosphere. This case will be discussed in detail. A gray model, however, may not be altogether satisfactory if accuracy is required, since it is not possible to define the mean absorption coefficient $\bar{\kappa}$ in a manner simultaneously consistent with all the equations of radiative transfer. The construction of a non-gray atmosphere is therefore necessary for a more realistic representation of the actual conditions in a star. The temperature distribution for the gray case can serve as a first approximation to that in the non-gray case; but, in general, this first non-gray model will suffer from variability of the total flux with depth. A series of models will generally have to be calculated, with successive trial corrections to the temperatures at various depths, until constancy of the flux is maintained.

   We now describe the calculation of *gray* atmospheres in radiative equilibrium. Recalling the definition of $\bar{\tau}$ [eq. (3-55)],

$$d\bar{\tau} = -\bar{\kappa}\rho \, dx,$$

we obtain

$$\frac{dP}{d\bar{\tau}} = \frac{g}{\bar{\kappa}}. \tag{4-5}$$

At first sight, this might appear even more intractable than the original equation, since we now require $\bar{\kappa}(\bar{\tau})$. Nevertheless, the problem is now expressed in a soluble form. Only the numerical value of $\bar{\kappa}$ is required, and this can be evaluated for given gas pressure P_g and temperature T. Figure 3-13 gives $\bar{\kappa}$ as a function of P_g and $\theta = 5040/T$. We shall make the simplifying assumption that radiation pressure is negligible, allowing us to set P_g equal to P. The temperature will be obtained from eq. (2-51), which is based on Eddington's first approximation for the case of radiative equilibrium:

$$T^4 = \tfrac{1}{2}T_{\text{eff}}^4(1 + \tfrac{3}{2}\bar{\tau}). \tag{4-6}$$

We therefore have $\bar{\kappa}$ for any given values of the dependent and independent variables in the differential equation (P and $\bar{\tau}$, respectively) and can proceed inwards, layer by layer, with the numerical solution. This provides a table of $P(\bar{\tau})$. The details of this calculation will be presented in Part Four.

   The correspondence between x and $\bar{\tau}$ can now be derived by reconsidering eq. (4-1) in the form

$$\frac{dP}{dx} = -g\left(\frac{\mu H}{k}\frac{P}{T}\right)$$

or

$$\frac{d\log_e P}{dx} = -\frac{\mu H}{k}g\frac{1}{T}.$$

Since the values of P and T for given $\bar{\tau}$ are already known, while x has not yet been related to these quantities, we use these equations in the form

$$\frac{dx}{d\log_{10} P} = -\log_e 10 \, \frac{k}{\mu H} \frac{1}{g} T, \tag{4-7}$$

with x as the dependent variable and $d \log_{10} P$ as the independent variable. A procedure for solving the equation is explained in Part Four.

It is also possible to integrate eq. (3-55), giving x directly as a function of $\bar{\tau}$:

$$\frac{dx}{d\bar{\tau}} = -\frac{1}{\bar{\kappa}\rho}.$$

This differential equation is unsatisfactory for use at small optical depths, however, as both $\bar{\kappa}$ and ρ increase rapidly in this region. The behavior of $dx/d\bar{\tau}$ is illustrated in Table 9-5B, which may be compared with the integration of $dx/d \log P$ in Table 9-5A.

2 CONVECTION IN STELLAR ATMOSPHERES

As the numerical integration proceeds, it is possible that convection may be encountered below some layer. This will occur if the magnitude of the temperature gradient in *radiative equilibrium* exceeds that for *convective equilibrium*, as will be discussed in Chapter 6, Section 4. In the upper regions, where convection is inefficient, radiation still transfers the greater part of the energy flux, and convection may be of little consequence. In the deeper layers, on the other hand, the radiative temperature distribution expressed by eq. (4-6) may no longer be applicable. In Chapter 6, we shall derive an expression for the temperature distribution in the fully convective case, but we shall not give the equations necessary when both convection and radiation are responsible for energy transfer.*

If the opacity in some layers is high, or if an abundant constituent of the atmosphere (usually hydrogen or helium) is in such a condition that two stages of ionization are present in comparable amounts, conditions are favorable for the maintenance of convection currents. These carry hot gases toward the cooler, upper regions and, conversely, carry cool gases downward. Both the ascending and descending currents contribute to a net transfer of energy outwards, the energy being in the form of the kinetic energy of the gas particles. Convection can thus supplement radiation in the transfer of energy. Although the outermost layers of all stars have radiation as the transfer mechanism, permitting the equations of radiative equilibrium to be

---

* See, for example, E. Vitense, 1953 (212); E. Böhm-Vitense, 1958 (213); J. P. Cox and R. T. Giuli, 1968 (52), Chapter 14, for descriptions of the mixing-length theory.

applied there, the convection in the lower layers of some atmospheres is so efficient that convective equilibrium must be considered.

In the Sun, convection is in evidence in the form of *granulation* seen on photographs. With high resolution, the granulation looks like cells in an irregular honeycomb pattern, similar to the Bénard cells in a convective fluid in laboratory experiments. Each granule is the top of a column of ascending material, while the narrow, darker spaces separating the granules are regions where the cooler gases sink back into the Sun. Even though convection takes place at such small optical depths that its pattern is easily visible [$\tau(5000 \text{ Å}) \gtrsim 1$], it remains inefficient as a means of carrying energy until an optical depth $\tau(5000 \text{ Å}) \sim 2$ is reached. For smaller optical depths,

Table 4-1   Adopted Model Atmosphere for the White Dwarf 40 Eridani B (o^2 Eri B).*

$$\theta_{\text{eff}} = 0.329, \quad T_{\text{eff}} = 15,300°\text{K}, \quad \log g = 7.720.$$

$$\text{H:He (by number)} = 0.900:0.100.$$

[After S. Matsushima and Y. Terashita, 1969 (199j).]

$\log \tau_{5000}$	T	$\log P_g$	$\log P_e$	$\log \rho$	$H^+/\Sigma H$	$x(m)$
-4.0	11,287	2.943	2.596	-9.173	0.906	1,221
-3.6	11,364	3.155	2.798	-8.958	0.872	1,101
-3.2	11,404	3.373	3.001	-8.729	0.819	980
-2.8	11,453	3.598	3.204	-8.490	0.752	858
-2.4	11,473	3.832	3.404	-8.235	0.664	736
-2.0	11,548	4.077	3.610	-7.972	0.577	615
-1.8	11,615	4.202	3.716	-7.840	0.540	554
-1.6	11,722	4.327	3.826	-7.712	0.514	494
-1.4	11,875	4.451	3.942	-7.589	0.498	435
-1.2	12,096	4.572	4.064	-7.477	0.500	377
-1.0	12,408	4.688	4.192	-7.379	0.524	320
-0.8	12,825	4.796	4.326	-7.297	0.571	263
-0.6	13,369	4.899	4.462	-7.230	0.641	205
-0.4	14,047	4.998	4.594	-7.173	0.724	144
-0.2	14,771	5.097	4.718	-7.112	0.795	76
0	15,605	5.201	4.840	-7.046	0.856	0
0.2	16,522	5.311	4.962	-6.971	0.901	-88
0.4	17,519	5.427	5.087	-6.887	0.931	-188
0.6	18,611	5.549	5.216	-6.796	0.952	-302
0.8	19,813	5.676	5.348	-6.702	0.966	-429
1.0	21,194	5.806	5.484	-6.606	0.977	-569
1.2	22,774	5.939	5.623	-6.509	0.984	-725
1.4	24,612	6.075	5.764	-6.413	0.989	-898
1.6	26,766	6.214	5.908	-6.314	0.993	$-1,092$
1.8	29,296	6.358	6.054	-6.212	0.995	$-1,313$
2.0	32,289	6.506	6.204	-6.107	0.997	$-1,564$

* The symbols and units are explained in the footnote to Table 4-2.

Table 4-2   Model Solar Atmosphere (Main Sequence G2).* This is a p
of the Harvard-Smithsonian Reference Atmosphere. [O. Gingerich,]
Noyes, W. Kalkofen, and Y. Cuny, 1971 (238).]

$$\theta_{\text{eff}} = 0.8720, \quad T_{\text{eff}} = 5,780°\text{K}, \quad \log g = 4.440.$$

H:He:Other elements (by number) = 941:94.1:1.

τ_{5000}	T (°K)	$\log P_g$	$\log P_e$	P_g	P_e
10^{-8}	8,930	−0.8187	−1.3168	1.518 (−1)	4.822 (
10^{-7}	8,320	−0.7724	−1.2721	1.689 (−1)	5.345 (
10^{-6}	7,360	−0.4245	−1.1054	3.763 (−1)	7.846 (
10^{-5}	5,300	+1.8319	−1.1695	6.790 (+1)	6.769 (
10^{-4}	4,170	+2.9386	−1.2133	8.682 (+2)	6.119 (
10^{-3}	4,380	+3.5387	−0.6260	3.457 (+3)	2.366 (
10^{-2}	4,660	+4.1035	−0.0480	1.269 (+4)	8.953 (
0.05012	4,950	+4.4936	+0.3817	3.116 (+4)	2.408 (
0.10000	5,160	4.6592	0.5966	4.562 (+4)	3.950 (
0.15849	5,330	4.7675	0.7569	5.854 (+4)	5.713 (
0.19953	5,430	4.8201	0.8476	6.608 (+4)	7.041 (
0.25119	5,540	4.8710	0.9478	7.430 (+4)	8.868
0.31623	5,650	4.9197	1.0523	8.311 (+4)	1.128
0.39811	5,765	4.9659	1.1635	9.244 (+4)	1.457
0.50119	5,890	5.0090	1.2847	1.021 (+5)	1.926
0.63096	6,035	5.0492	1.4232	1.120 (+5)	2.650
0.79433	6,200	5.0853	1.5782	1.217 (+5)	3.786
1.00000	6,390	5.1173	1.7516	1.310 (+5)	5.644
1.25892	6,610	5.1446	1.9443	1.395 (+5)	8.796
1.58489	6,860	5.1679	2.1520	1.472 (+5)	1.419
1.99526	7,140	5.1875	2.3701	1.540 (+5)	2.345
2.51189	7,440	5.2036	2.5879	1.598 (+5)	3.872
3.16228	7,750	5.2170	2.7968	1.648 (+5)	6.263
3.98107	8,030	5.2289	2.9731	1.694 (+5)	9.400
5.01187	8,290	5.2395	3.1271	1.736 (+5)	1.340
6.30957	8,520	5.2494	3.2565	1.776 (+5)	1.805
7.94328	8,710	5.2594	3.3595	1.817 (+5)	2.288
10.00000	8,880	5.2693	3.4487	1.859 (+5)	2.810
12.58925	9,050	5.2797	3.5349	1.904 (+5)	3.427
15.84893	9,220	5.2903	3.6183	1.951 (+5)	4.152
19.95262	9,390	5.3012	3.6989	2.001 (+5)	4.999
25.11886	9,560	5.3124	3.7769	2.053 (+5)	5.983

* The chromosphere lies above $\tau_{5000} \sim 10^{-4}$, the transition region is betwee
10^{-4} and 10^{-2}, and the photosphere lies below $\tau_{5000} \sim 10^{-1}$. The mode
vectively unstable for $\tau_{5000} \gtrsim 1$, but convection is efficient only below τ_{5000}
    In Tables 4-1 to 4-4, the optical depth τ_λ is evaluated either at 5000 Å or at 1.
temperature T is expressed in °K; the total pressure P, the gas pressure P_g
electron pressure P_e in dyne cm^{-2}; the density ρ in gm cm^{-3}; and the a
coefficient κ_λ in cm^2 gm^{-1}. The ratio H$^+$/ΣH is the fraction (by number) of a
gen that is ionized, $\epsilon_{\text{metals}}/\Sigma\epsilon$ is the fraction of all electrons contributed b
and F_C/F is the fraction of the total flux that is transferred by convection.
point of the geometrical depth (or height) x is arbitrary.

174

ρ	κ_{5000}	$H^+/\Sigma H$	$\epsilon_{metals}/\Sigma\epsilon$ (per cent)	x (km)
(-13)	0.146	5.11 (-1)	0.2	1,850
(-13)	0.146	5.09 (-1)	0.2	1,820
(-13)	0.0863	2.89 (-1)	0.3	1,620
(-10)	0.00258	9.13 (-4)	16.9	840
(-9)	0.00487	2.26 (-7)	99.7	557
(-8)	0.0139	4.06 (-7)	99.5	420
(-8)	0.0388	1.09 (-6)	98.6	283
(-8)	0.0799	3.43 (-6)	96.0	183
(-7)	0.110	8.49 (-6)	91.1	138
(-7)	0.140	1.69 (-5)	84.3	108
(-7)	0.160	2.47 (-5)	78.9	92.6
(-7)	0.187	3.68 (-5)	72.0	77.7
(-7)	0.221	5.29 (-5)	64.6	63.1
(-7)	0.264	7.51 (-5)	56.7	48.9
(-7)	0.323	1.07 (-4)	48.4	35.4
(-7)	0.407	1.58 (-4)	39.6	22.6
(-7)	0.527	2.37 (-4)	31.0	10.8
(-7)	0.706	3.65 (-4)	23.2	0.0
(-7)	0.978	5.79 (-4)	16.6	-9.6
(-7)	1.39	9.40 (-4)	11.6	-18.0
(-7)	2.02	1.55 (-3)	7.9	-25.3
(-7)	2.94	2.53 (-3)	5.4	-31.6
(-7)	4.24	4.04 (-3)	3.8	-37.1
(-7)	5.83	5.97 (-3)	2.9	-42.1
(-7)	7.76	8.38 (-3)	2.2	-46.8
(-7)	9.94	1.11 (-2)	1.8	-51.4
(-7)	12.2	1.38 (-2)	1.6	-56.0
(-7)	14.6	1.67 (-2)	1.4	-60.8
(-7)	17.4	1.99 (-2)	1.2	-65.8
(-7)	20.8	2.37 (-2)	1.1	-71.1
(-7)	24.7	2.79 (-2)	1.0	-76.7
(-7)	29.4	3.28 (-2)	0.9	-82.6

we may still use the equations of radiative equilibrium (specifically, the radiative temperature distribution) to construct a model solar atmosphere.

In the atmospheric models of Tables 4-6 to 4-12 at the end of this chapter, convection is not present for $T_{eff} \geqslant 9000°$K. Near 8000°K (spectral type A), there is a convective layer about 100 to 200 km in thickness for stars near the main sequence, but the fraction of the total flux transferred by convection decreases as the surface gravity decreases, that is, with increasing departure from the main sequence. In the giant stars, the rarefied gases have little capacity to transfer energy. At $\log g = 2$, convection is absent. The efficiency is still low in giant stars with $T_{eff} \sim 7000°$K; but at lower effective temperatures, convection is efficient and extensive for both main-sequence and giant stars, unless $\log g$ is very small (cf. Table 4-4). In fact, as will be seen in Part Three, the convective zones in later-type stars extend to large fractions of the total radius. In all the models described above, convection (if present) becomes significant when the optical depth reaches a value in the approximate range 2 to 6, which is just below the visible layers.

Table 4-3   Model for a Main-Sequence M6 Star.*

$\theta_{eff} = 1.680$, $T_{eff} = 3,000°$K, $\log g = 5.0$.

H:He: Other elements (by number) = 470:56:1.

[After J. R. Auman, Jr., 1969 (217).]

$\tau_{1.17\mu}$	T	$\log P_g$	$\log P_e$	F_C/F
0.04	2,596	5.732	−0.803	0.0276
0.06	2,678	5.826	−0.601	0.0479
0.10	2,775	5.940	−0.372	0.084
0.15	2,849	6.026	−0.204	0.123
0.20	2,899	6.085	−0.096	0.158
0.25	2,938	6.130	−0.013	0.189
0.30	2,969	6.167	+0.054	0.220
0.40	3,019	6.224	+0.155	0.274
0.60	3,088	6.303	+0.291	0.368
0.80	3,137	6.358	+0.386	0.446
1.00	3,175	6.401	+0.458	0.512
1.20	3,207	6.436	+0.515	0.564
1.40	3,233	6.465	+0.561	0.614
1.60	3,256	6.491	+0.602	0.649
2.00	3,295	6.533	+0.670	0.718
2.50	3,334	6.575	+0.738	0.759
3.00	3,366	6.610	+0.792	0.807
4.00	3,417	6.665	+0.876	0.855
6.00	3,490	6.742	+0.992	0.903
10.00	3,584	6.840	+1.138	0.937

* The symbols and units are explained in the footnote to Table 4-2.

Table 4-4   Model for a Giant M5 Star.*

$$\theta_{eff} = 1.680, \quad T_{eff} = 3,000°K, \quad \log g = 1.0.$$

H:He:Other elements (by number) = 470:56:1.

[After J. R. Auman, Jr., 1969 (217).].

$\tau_{1.17\mu}$	T	$\log P_g$	$\log P_e$	$\rho \times 10^8$	$\kappa_{1.17\mu}$	F_C/F*	$-x \times 10^{-5}$ (km)
0.04	2,295	2.060	−3.687	0.110	0.00367	0.00019	0
0.06	2,398	2.239	−3.436	0.148	0.00312	0.00022	0.46
0.10	2,553	2.513	−3.087	0.242	0.00226	0.00007	1.26
0.15	2,682	2.756	−2.786	0.388	0.00193	0	2.04
0.20	2,743	2.914	−2.607	0.542	0.00213	0	2.58
0.30	2,840	3.103	−2.381	0.794	0.00234	0	3.26
0.40	2,907	3.223	−2.232	1.01	0.00259	0	3.71
0.50	2,961	3.310	−2.123	1.20	0.00286	0.0000001	4.04
0.60	3,011	3.376	−2.032	1.37	0.00310	0.0000002	4.30
0.80	3,096	3.474	−1.890	1.65	0.00356	0.0000004	4.71
1.00	3,172	3.545	−1.775	1.88	0.00403	0.0000007	5.01
1.20	3,241	3.599	−1.672	2.06	0.00460	0.0000009	5.24
1.40	3,304	3.642	−1.583	2.22	0.00512	0.0000008	5.44
1.60	3,362	3.677	−1.499	2.36	0.00570	0.0000007	5.6
2.00	3,469	3.732	−1.348	2.58	0.00694	0.0000009	5.9
2.50	3,586	3.781	−1.191	2.77	0.00856	0.0000015	6.1
3.00	3,694	3.818	−1.057	2.92	0.0102	0.0000023	6.3
4.00	3,883	3.871	−0.838	3.14	0.0133	0.0000068	6.6
6.00	4,204	3.940	−0.555	3.39	0.0179	0.0000333	7.0
8.00	4,482	3.988	−0.373	3.54	0.0207	0.0000759	7.3
10.00	4,731	4.028	−0.236	3.68	0.0227	0.0000807	7.5

* Convection carries more than 0.1 of the total flux below $\tau_{1.17\mu} = 20$. The symbols and units are explained in the footnote to Table 4-2.

3 COMPARISONS OF MODEL ATMOSPHERES

3-1 MODELS OF DIFFERENT EFFECTIVE TEMPERATURES AND SURFACE GRAVITIES

A. THE ATMOSPHERIC STRUCTURE

The effective temperature and surface gravity are of primary importance in determining the structure of a stellar atmosphere. Tables 4-1 to 4-4 present some of the properties of the atmospheres of white dwarf, main-sequence, and giant stars and these, together with Table 4-6, will be discussed below. Tables 4-6 to 4-12 present a homogeneous set of additional models for various values of T_{eff} and g, corresponding to main-sequence stars of spectral types B, A, F, G, and K, as well as a giant star of spectral type G.

We have already noted that the temperature distribution and absorption coefficient for a gray atmosphere are but first approximations for model computation, but with modern computers one may evaluate the necessary quantities at many frequencies throughout the spectrum. Hence the independent variable in these tables is not $\bar{\tau}$ but τ_λ at some specific wavelength at which, in most cases, τ_λ approximates $\bar{\tau}$ for the Rosseland mean absorption coefficient. With the refined temperature distribution, we may no longer expect that T will equal T_{eff} at $\tau_\lambda = \frac{2}{3}$ and, indeed, departures are evident in these tables.

The surface gravities increase in these models by only a factor of 10 along the main sequence between the spectral types B0.5 and M6, but the white dwarf has a very much higher gravity. The greater compression of the gases induced by the stronger gravitational fields produces larger pressures in the atmospheres of the white dwarf and the late main-sequence stars. Even in these cases, however, the pressure is only of the order of 1 atm at sea level on Earth at $\tau_{5000} \sim 10$ (but note that the geometrical depth in the white dwarf

Fig. 4-2   The Flux Distributions for Early-Type, Main-Sequence Model Atmospheres. The effective temperatures in degrees Kelvin are indicated in the figure. For $T_{\text{eff}} = 50,000°$K and $40,000°$K, $\log g = 5$; for $T_{\text{eff}} = 30,000°$K, $\log g = 4$. The flux F_ν is expressed in erg cm^{-2} sec^{-1} (cycle/sec)$^{-1}$. The absorption edges are due to the atoms and ions indicated. These models are part of the same grid from which Tables 4-6 to 4-12 are selected. [After O. Gingerich, ed., 1969 (35), p. 403.]

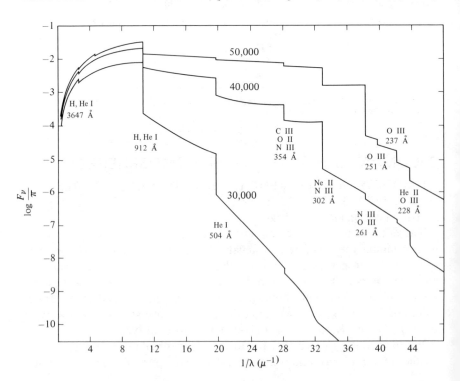

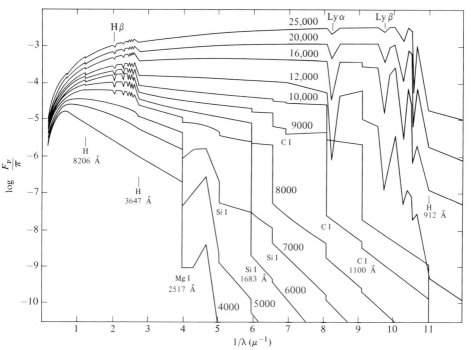

Fig. 4-3 The Flux Distributions for Main-Sequence Model Atmospheres. The effective temperatures in degrees Kelvin are indicated in the figure. In all cases, $\log g = 4$. The flux F_ν is expressed in erg cm^{-2} sec^{-1} (cycle/sec)$^{-1}$. The absorption edges are due to the atoms indicated. The Lyman and Balmer absorption edges and lines are shown, except for Hα. The Paschen edge is visible at 8206 Å. The true line profiles have been simplified. These models are part of the same grid from which Tables 4-6 to 4-12 are selected. [After O. Gingerich, ed., 1969 (35), p. 403.]

is measured in *meters*, not kilometers!). The surface gravity of the giant M star is so low that its pressure distribution is comparable to that of the early-type star. The pressure due to radiation is almost negligible in the models discussed here, although it makes a small contribution to the total pressure in the hot stars.

The electron pressure is lower in the cooler stars than in the hotter ones, since ionization is so retarded at the lower temperatures that few free electrons exist. With increasing depth in any given atmosphere, both the temperature and the electron pressure increase, and electrons make a greater contribution to the total pressure. For the solar atmosphere, Table 4-2 includes the degree of ionization of hydrogen and the percentage of all electrons that come from the so-called *metals* (actually all elements heavier than helium). The metals, in spite of their small abundance, supply a large fraction of all the electrons in the upper photosphere.

The densities may be compared with the density of air at sea level on Earth. In both the Sun and the white dwarf at $\tau_{5000} = 10$, the density is 0.0003 that of air. In the M dwarf and the M giant at this optical depth, the density is 100 times and $\frac{1}{10}$ this amount, respectively. Stellar atmospheres are therefore very rarefied.

B. MONOCHROMATIC FLUXES

Figures 4-2 and 4-3 show the flux of emitted radiation divided by π as a function of reciprocal wavelength, for main-sequence stars with effective temperatures between 50,000°K and 4000°K. Absorption edges are prominent in both Figs. 4-2 and 4-3. In the hot stars, multiple ionization occurs, and two or more elements may contribute to the production of an absorption edge at a specific wavelength: as eq. (3-13) shows, a change in the atomic number z can be compensated by a change in the quantum number n. In Fig. 4-3, hydrogen line absorption is prominent, especially in the Lyman series. The profiles of the hydrogen lines have been modified to facilitate the calculations.

Fig. 4-4   The Flux Distributions for Model Atmospheres with $T_{\text{eff}} = 3000°$K and log $g = 5, 1,$ or 0. F_ν is in arbitrary units. The high surface gravity corresponds to a main-sequence star and the low values to giant stars of spectral type M. The principal source of opacity is water vapor, H_2O. Solar metal abundances are assumed. [After J. R. Auman, Jr., 1969 (217).]

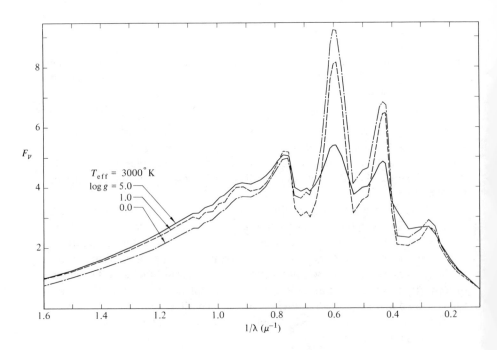

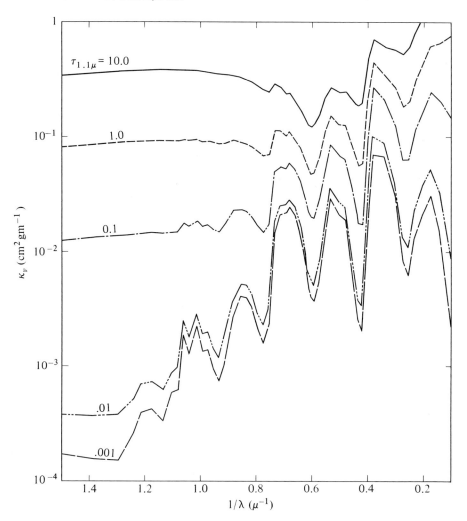

Fig. 4-5 The Monochromatic Absorption Coefficient for a Model with T_{eff} = 3000°K and log g = 5 (Main-Sequence M6 Star). The coefficient at various optical depths is shown. The distribution at small τ should be compared with that of Fig. 4-4. [After J. R. Auman, Jr., 1969 (217).]

The Lyman lines may be omitted for stars with effective temperatures of 10,000°K or less, because only a small fraction of the total flux is emitted at these wavelengths and the absorption by the Lyman lines is therefore negligible.

The flux distribution in Fig. 4-4, for a model with T_{eff} = 3000°K, is governed by water vapor absorption. The peaks and valleys should be compared with those in Fig. 4-5, which shows the absorption coefficient as a function of reciprocal wavelength; at small optical depths, that is, near the surface, large values of κ_ν correspond to small values of F_ν, showing that a large absorption coefficient at a given wavelength hinders the flow of radiation at that wavelength.

In Fig. 4-6, the flux distribution from one of the model atmospheres is compared with a black body curve, to emphasize that an effective temperature is a measure only of the *total* energy radiated in all wavelengths per second per cm², while the *distribution* with wavelength may be very different from that of a black body if the absorption coefficient depends strongly on wavelength.

The success of theoretical models in predicting observed fluxes over a

Fig. 4-6 Comparison of the Flux Distributions Emitted by a Model Atmosphere at $T_{\text{eff}} = 30,000°$K and a Black Body at $T = 30,000°$K. The model atmosphere is also represented in Fig. 4-2. Since F_ν has been divided by π, it is dimensionally equivalent to an intensity and is therefore compared directly with the Planck function $B_\nu(T)$.

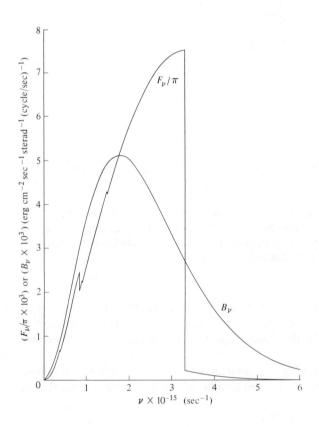

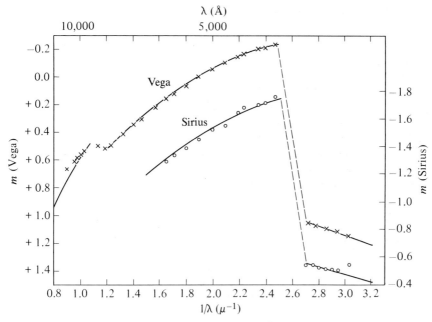

Fig. 4-7   Comparison of the Observed Spectral Distributions of Vega (α Lyrae) and Sirius (α Canis Majoris) with Those of Theoretical Models. The ordinate is apparent magnitude. *Crosses* represent the observations of Vega and *dots* the observations of Sirius. *Solid lines* show the distributions for the corresponding model atmospheres. The details of the theoretical distributions in the region of the closely spaced lines near the Balmer limit (3646 Å or 2.74 μ^{-1}) are not shown, and *dashed lines* simply connect the curves on either side of the discontinuity. [Adapted from R. Schild, D. M. Peterson, and J. B. Oke, 1971 (199u).]

wide range of wavelengths is illustrated in Fig. 4-7. Here the observed magnitudes of Vega and Sirius are compared with those derived from model atmospheres having $T_{eff} = 9650°$K and log $g = 4.05$ for Vega and $T_{eff} = 10,200°$K and log $g = 4.35$ for Sirius. The agreement in both cases is good.

A difficulty arises in portions of the violet and ultraviolet regions of many stars, including the Sun. More energy is emitted by main-sequence stars of spectral type A and later than can be accounted for theoretically. There is apparently a source of opacity that is not yet known and that has not been included in the models.*

---

* The problem for the main-sequence stars is discussed by J. Davis and R. J. Webb, 1970 (199k). The solar problem is considered by J. L. Linsky, 1970 (214) and S. Matsushima, 1968 (236). Also see O. Gingerich, ed., 1969 (35) for various pertinent papers and discussions and the footnote on p. 188.

3-2 SENSITIVITY TO ASSUMPTIONS

A model necessarily depends upon the theory adopted and the numerical values employed in its construction. In this section, we shall illustrate the sensitivity of atmospheric models to certain parameters.

Figure 4-8 shows the effect of the opacity on the relation between temperature and pressure. When additional opacity sources are included, the temperature at a given pressure is increased. The influence of opacity on emergent intensity is shown in Fig. 4-9. When the opacity in the ultraviolet region is increased, the amount of radiation emerging in that region is decreased. The significance of this figure lies in its pertinence to the problem of the ultraviolet flux mentioned above, which will be referred to again in the next section.

The convective parameter l/H, which describes the distance traveled by a

Fig. 4-8 The Effect of Opacity on the Relation between Temperature and Pressure. In the *lowest curve*, only H and H⁻ opacity are considered; in the *middle curve*, metal absorption is added; in the *upper curve*, an additional, hypothetical source has been included. The optical depths refer to a wavelength of 5000 Å. [S. Matsushima, 1968 (236).]

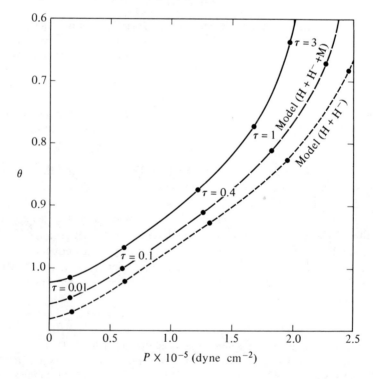

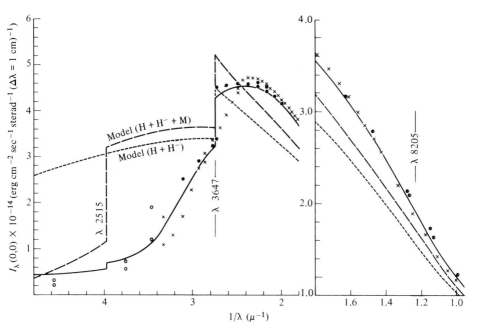

Fig. 4-9 The Variation of Intensity with Wavelength at the Center of the Solar Disk. The three curves correspond to those in Fig. 4-8. The hypothetical source of opacity for the solid-line curve in that figure was chosen to produce good agreement between the observations and the theoretical intensity distribution represented here by the solid line. The observations are those of J.-E. Blamont and R.-M. Bonnet, 1966 (218) (*circles*); R. Canavaggia, D. Chalonge, M. Egger-Moreau, and H. Oziol-Peltey, 1950 (219), and D. Labs and H. Neckel, 1962 (220) (both represented by *dots*); G. F. W. Mulders, 1939 (221) and 1935 (222) in the left-hand portion of the figure and 1935 (222) in the right-hand portion (*crosses*); and R. Peytureaux, 1955 (223) (*encircled points*). [S. Matsushima, 1968 (236).]

convective cell,* is important in determining the temperature distribution below the photosphere. In Fig. 4-10 are shown the results of assuming three alternative values, including the case $l/H = 0$ corresponding to the absence of convection. The stronger the convection, the more gradual is the change of T with τ.

* Specifically, l is the distance traveled by a convective cell before dissolving into the surrounding medium, and H is the distance over which pressure (or density, whichever is assumed) changes by a factor e. The quantity H is called the *scale height*.

3-3 THE SOLAR ATMOSPHERE

The solar temperature distribution can be determined empirically, as well as theoretically. One method makes use of eq. (3-62), which gives the emergent intensity at angle θ on the solar disk as

$$I_\nu(0,\, \theta) = \int_0^\infty B_\nu(T)\, e^{-\tau_\nu \sec \theta}\, d\tau_\nu \sec \theta. \tag{4-8}$$

Fig. 4-10 Comparison of Convective and Non-Convective (Radiative) Temperature Distributions. For all curves, $\log g = 4$. [O. Gingerich, ed., 1969 (35), p. 401.]

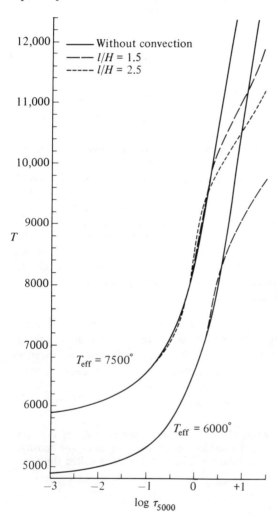

Table 4-5   The Model Atmospheres of Tables 4-6 to 4-12. These model atmospheres are selected from the grid of 68 models published by O. Gingerich, ed., 1969 (35). The characteristics of these selected models are described below.*

	$50,000°K \geq T_{eff} \geq 11,000°K$	$10,000°K \geq T_{eff} \geq 4000°K$
Relative abundances of elements by number (approximate)	H 1.00 He 0.10 C 3.55 (−4) N 8.54 (−5) O 5.91 (−4) Ne (= C) Mg 3.02 (−5) Al 2.51 (−6) Si 3.55 (−5)	H 1.00 He 0.10 C 3.55 (−4) Na 1.51 (−6) Mg 3.02 (−5) Al 2.51 (−6) Si 3.55 (−5) Fe 3.24 (−6)
Sources of opacity Parentheses indicate that the source is negligible	H I, He I, He II, H⁻, (He⁻), (H₂⁺), (Si I), (Mg I), (Al I), C I–V, N II–V, O II–V, Ne II–V, Rayleigh scattering from H and He, electron scattering, H lines	H, H⁻, H₂⁺, H lines, C, Mg, Si, electron scattering, Rayleigh scattering from H and H₂.
Radiation pressure	Included by setting $$g_{eff} = g - \frac{\sigma}{c}\bar{\kappa}T_{eff}{}^4,$$ where $\bar{\kappa}$ is the mean with respect to flux	Included but not important for $\log g = 4$
Convection	Negligible	Included for $T_{eff} \leq 8500°K$, with $\log l/H_p = 1.5$
Line blanketing by metals	Negligible	Included for $T_{eff} \leq 8500°K$

* In Tables 4-6 to 4-12, the optical depth τ_{5000} refers to a wavelength of 5000 Å. The temperature T is expressed in °K, the gas pressure P_g in dyne cm⁻², the electron density N_e in number of electrons per cm⁻³, the absorption coefficient κ_{5000} at 5000 Å in cm² gm⁻¹, the density ρ in gm cm⁻³, the effective gravity g_{eff} in cm sec⁻², and the height x in km. The ratio H⁺/ΣH is the fraction (by number) of hydrogen that is ionized, and F_C/F is the fraction of the total flux that is carried by convection. The zero point of x is arbitrary. In Tables 4-5 to 4-12, a number in parentheses is the power of 10 by which an entry is to be multiplied.

The intensity $I_\nu(0, \theta)$ is obtained from observations, making it possible to derive the relation between T and τ_ν.* If the absorption coefficient κ_ν varies considerably with ν, then τ_ν will vary appreciably, as well. The different layers of the atmosphere can thus be probed, and the empirical temperature distribution can be determined.

* Methods for deducing the correspondence between T and τ_ν are discussed by L. H. Aller, 1963 (25), p. 205 et seq.; by R. v. d. R. Woolley and D. W. N. Stibbs, 1953 (26), pp. 77 and 85–90; and by D. Mihalas, 1970 (41), pp. 208–211.

The Harvard-Smithsonian Reference Atmosphere, presented in Table 4-2, is an empirically based model. The highest layers considered here, extending inwards to $\tau_{5000} \sim 10^{-4}$, belong to the chromosphere. The temperature *decreases* inwards to a minimum value and thereafter increases both in the transition region ($10^{-4} \gtrsim \tau_{5000} \gtrsim 10^{-2}$) and in the photosphere ($\tau_{5000} \gtrsim 10^{-2}$). In the *photosphere*, the density and the opacity become much larger than in the higher layers, and the optical depth increases rapidly with geometrical depth. This fact causes the Sun to present a sharply defined disk. For example, from the layer at $\tau = 2$, we receive only e^{-2} or 0.135 of the radiation originating there. This layer, however, lies only a few hundred kilometers below the level at which $\tau = 0.05$ (say), from which 95 per cent of the radiation escapes directly.

The emergent intensities predicted by this model for the solar atmosphere are in good agreement with the observed values, both in comparisons of absolute intensities at the center of the disk, $I_\lambda(0, 0)$, and limb-darkening ratios, $I_\lambda(0, \theta)/I_\lambda(0, 0)$, over a broad range of wavelengths. There remains, however, a discrepancy in the ultraviolet (about 1700 Å to 3600 Å), where considerably less radiation is emitted than is expected from the model.* This indicates that there exists an unknown source of opacity in the ultraviolet The effect may possibly be explained as a veiling by numerous faint lines together with absorption far from the line center (that is, in the *wings*) of stronger lines. We have already noted in Fig. 4-9 how the ultraviolet continuum can be depressed by the inclusion of an additional (hypothetical) source of absorption in that wavelength region.

---

* Note added in proof. The situation is now improved. See S. P. Tarafdar and M. S. Vardya, 1972, *Ap. J.* **171**, 185.

Table 4-6 Model Atmosphere. Main sequence, spectral class B0.5. (See Table 4-5.)

$$T_{eff} = 25{,}000°K, \quad \log g = 4.$$

τ_{5000}	T	P_g	N_e	κ_{5000}	ρ	$\log g_{eff}$	x
.0010	15,115	2.440 (+01)	5.833 (+12)	4.683 (−01)	1.245 (−11)	3.9824	11,714
.0016	15,319	3.561 (+01)	8.399 (+12)	5.302 (−01)	1.793 (−11)	3.9805	10,936
.0025	15,572	5.111 (+01)	1.186 (+13)	6.086 (−01)	2.533 (−11)	3.9787	10,171
.0040	15,859	7.230 (+01)	1.647 (+13)	7.078 (−01)	3.517 (−11)	3.9770	9,423
.0063	16,166	1.009 (+02)	2.256 (+13)	8.319 (−01)	4.812 (−11)	3.9753	8,686
.0100	16,478	1.391 (+02)	3.051 (+13)	9.866 (−01)	6.511 (−11)	3.9735	7,960
.0158	16,791	1.897 (+02)	4.083 (+13)	1.179 (+00)	8.713 (−11)	3.9713	7,242
.0251	17,109	2.562 (+02)	5.413 (+13)	1.416 (+00)	1.155 (−10)	3.9684	6,528
.0398	17,449	3.434 (+02)	7.111 (+13)	1.703 (+00)	1.518 (−10)	3.9648	5,815
.0631	17,838	4.572 (+02)	9.266 (+13)	2.043 (+00)	1.977 (−10)	3.9604	5,097
.1000	18,309	6.066 (+02)	1.198 (+14)	2.432 (+00)	2.554 (−10)	3.9555	4,363
.1585	18,893	8.039 (+02)	1.539 (+14)	2.865 (+00)	3.280 (−10)	3.9507	3,601
.2512	19,618	1.068 (+03)	1.969 (+14)	3.341 (+00)	4.198 (−10)	3.9461	2,797
.3981	20,505	1.426 (+03)	2.517 (+14)	3.856 (+00)	5.357 (−10)	3.9422	1,937
.6310	21,568	1.915 (+03)	3.215 (+14)	4.415 (+00)	6.836 (−10)	3.9390	1,009
1.000	22,810	2.591 (+03)	4.112 (+14)	5.029 (+00)	8.747 (−10)	3.9366	0
1.585	24,227	3.526 (+03)	5.269 (+14)	5.710 (+00)	1.121 (−09)	3.9347	−1,098
2.512	25,838	4.829 (+03)	6.764 (+14)	6.474 (+00)	1.439 (−09)	3.9328	−2,293
3.981	27,663	6.644 (+03)	8.695 (+14)	7.326 (+00)	1.849 (−09)	3.9306	−3,595
6.310	29,745	9.174 (+03)	1.117 (+15)	8.270 (+00)	2.375 (−09)	3.9276	−5,017
10.00	32,160	1.270 (+04)	1.432 (+15)	9.316 (+00)	3.036 (−09)	3.9231	−6,576
15.85	35,016	1.758 (+04)	1.828 (+15)	1.058 (+01)	3.845 (−09)	3.9158	−8,293
25.12	38,449	2.415 (+04)	2.312 (+15)	1.231 (+01)	4.757 (−09)	3.9041	−10,183
39.81	42,547	3.284 (+04)	2.884 (+15)	1.425 (+01)	5.754 (−09)	3.8938	−12,289
63.10	47,319	4.495 (+04)	3.577 (+15)	1.560 (+01)	7.023 (−09)	3.8937	−14,732
100.0	52,814	6.292 (+04)	4.498 (+15)	1.671 (+01)	8.780 (−09)	3.8999	−17,632
158.5	59,030	8.990 (+04)	5.757 (+15)	1.805 (+01)	1.121 (−08)	3.9075	−20,963

Table 4-7   Model Atmosphere. Main sequence, spectral type A0. (See Table 4-5.)

$$T_{eff} = 10,000°K, \quad \log g = 4.$$

τ_{5000}	T	P_g	N_e	κ_{5000}	ρ	$H^+/\Sigma H$	x
.0010	7,806	3.082 (+01)	6.259 (+12)	4.023 (−01)	4.770 (−11)	3.077 (−01)	−2,683
.0016	7,832	4.476 (+01)	8.133 (+12)	4.363 (−01)	7.102 (−11)	2.685 (−01)	−2,445
.0025	7,864	6.496 (+01)	1.057 (+13)	4.806 (−01)	1.052 (−10)	2.356 (−01)	−2,212
.0040	7,904	9.376 (+01)	1.376 (+13)	5.395 (−01)	1.541 (−10)	2.093 (−01)	−1,988
.0063	7,958	1.339 (+02)	1.797 (+13)	6.208 (−01)	2.218 (−10)	1.898 (−01)	−1,772
.0100	8,029	1.884 (+02)	2.361 (+13)	7.355 (−01)	3.124 (−10)	1.771 (−01)	−1,566
.0158	8,121	2.600 (+02)	3.129 (+13)	9.014 (−01)	4.283 (−10)	1.712 (−01)	−1,371
.0251	8,240	3.508 (+02)	4.190 (+13)	1.147 (+00)	5.691 (−10)	1.725 (−01)	−1,188
.0398	8,394	4.615 (+02)	5.694 (+13)	1.527 (+00)	7.287 (−10)	1.831 (−01)	−1,017
.0631	8,595	5.896 (+02)	7.876 (+13)	2.148 (+00)	8.927 (−10)	2.068 (−01)	−859
.1000	8,853	7.301 (+02)	1.105 (+14)	3.189 (+00)	1.040 (−09)	2.492 (−01)	−714
.1585	9,183	8.765 (+02)	1.560 (+14)	4.959 (+00)	1.143 (−09)	3.201 (−01)	−580
.2512	9,596	1.024 (+03)	2.175 (+14)	7.837 (+00)	1.186 (−09)	4.305 (−01)	−454
.3981	10,108	1.174 (+03)	2.917 (+14)	1.186 (+01)	1.173 (−09)	5.836 (−01)	−327
.6310	10,713	1.340 (+03)	3.663 (+14)	1.584 (+01)	1.152 (−09)	7.462 (−01)	−184
1.000	11,390	1.553 (+03)	4.356 (+14)	1.831 (+01)	1.180 (−09)	8.667 (−01)	0
1.585	12,148	1.862 (+03)	5.104 (+14)	1.943 (+01)	1.281 (−09)	9.355 (−01)	251
2.512	12,944	2.327 (+03)	6.099 (+14)	2.037 (+01)	1.479 (−09)	9.674 (−01)	590
3.981	13,803	3.026 (+03)	7.505 (+14)	2.168 (+01)	1.789 (−09)	9.827 (−01)	1,019
6.310	14,716	4.054 (+03)	9.489 (+14)	2.364 (+01)	2.235 (−09)	9.901 (−01)	1,532
10.00	15,674	5.531 (+03)	1.224 (+15)	2.639 (+01)	2.845 (−09)	9.940 (−01)	2,115
15.85	16,711	7.611 (+03)	1.596 (+15)	2.977 (+01)	3.638 (−09)	9.962 (−01)	2,759
25.12	17,853	1.053 (+04)	2.091 (+15)	3.370 (+01)	4.659 (−09)	9.975 (−01)	3,465
39.81	19,066	1.460 (+04)	2.739 (+15)	3.831 (+01)	5.993 (−09)	9.983 (−01)	4,232
63.10	20,392	2.027 (+04)	3.578 (+15)	4.342 (+01)	7.737 (−09)	9.988 (−01)	5,062

Table 4-8 Model Atmosphere. Main sequence, spectral type A9. (See Table 4-5.)

$$T_{eff} = 7500°K, \quad \log g = 4.$$

τ_{5000}	T	P_g	N_e	κ_{5000}	ρ	$H^+/\Sigma H$	x	F_c/F
.0010	5,898	6.847 (+02)	1.472 (+12)	2.276 (−02)	1.792 (−09)	1.790 (−03)	−1,360	.0000
.0016	5,921	9.189 (+02)	1.802 (+12)	2.715 (−02)	2.396 (−09)	1.633 (−03)	−1,247	.0000
.0025	5,949	1.229 (+03)	2.224 (+12)	3.270 (−02)	3.189 (−09)	1.510 (−03)	−1,135	.0000
.0040	5,986	1.633 (+03)	2.791 (+12)	3.995 (−02)	4.214 (−09)	1.431 (−03)	−1,025	.0000
.0063	6,033	2.154 (+03)	3.559 (+12)	4.949 (−02)	5.514 (−09)	1.394 (−03)	−918	.0000
.0100	6,087	2.818 (+03)	4.580 (+12)	6.179 (−02)	7.148 (−09)	1.385 (−03)	−812	.0000
.0158	6,148	3.657 (+03)	5.943 (+12)	7.769 (−02)	9.186 (−09)	1.401 (−03)	−709	.0000
.0251	6,221	4.708 (+03)	7.848 (+12)	9.907 (−02)	1.169 (−08)	1.459 (−03)	−608	.0000
.0398	6,312	6.000 (+03)	1.064 (+13)	1.291 (−01)	1.468 (−08)	1.585 (−03)	−510	.0000
.0631	6,425	7.552 (+03)	1.489 (+13)	1.724 (−01)	1.815 (−08)	1.806 (−03)	−415	.0000
.1000	6,562	9.372 (+03)	2.144 (+13)	2.358 (−01)	2.204 (−08)	2.160 (−03)	−324	.0000
.1585	6,741	1.144 (+04)	3.264 (+13)	3.379 (−01)	2.618 (−08)	2.796 (−03)	−238	.0000
.2512	7,002	1.363 (+04)	5.521 (+13)	5.312 (−01)	2.998 (−08)	4.180 (−03)	−160	.0000
.3981	7,365	1.573 (+04)	1.038 (+14)	9.275 (−01)	3.280 (−08)	7.262 (−03)	−93	.0000
.6310	7,846	1.752 (+04)	2.122 (+14)	1.816 (+00)	3.408 (−08)	1.442 (−02)	−40	.0000
1.000	8,510	1.888 (+04)	4.820 (+14)	4.328 (+00)	3.328 (−08)	3.375 (−02)	0	.0001
1.585	9,474	1.963 (+04)	1.217 (+15)	1.408 (+01)	2.944 (−08)	9.678 (−02)	24	.1099
2.512	10,095	2.007 (+04)	1.940 (+15)	2.794 (+01)	2.661 (−08)	1.708 (−01)	40	.5179
3.981	10,497	2.050 (+04)	2.500 (+15)	4.150 (+01)	2.486 (−08)	2.358 (−01)	56	.7406
6.310	10,841	2.097 (+04)	3.019 (+15)	5.614 (+01)	2.347 (−08)	3.016 (−01)	76	.8060
10.00	11,169	2.155 (+04)	3.533 (+15)	7.235 (+01)	2.229 (−08)	3.718 (−01)	101	.8820
15.85	11,514	2.226 (+04)	4.073 (+15)	9.090 (+01)	2.121 (−08)	4.506 (−01)	134	.8643
25.12	11,926	2.317 (+04)	4.678 (+15)	1.131 (+02)	2.006 (−08)	5.473 (−01)	178	.9016
39.81	12,445	2.434 (+04)	5.328 (+15)	1.371 (+02)	1.887 (−08)	6.626 (−01)	238	.8446
63.10	13,224	2.591 (+04)	5.985 (+15)	1.573 (+02)	1.752 (−08)	8.017 (−01)	324	.7893

Table 4-9 Model Atmosphere. Main sequence, spectral class G0. (See Table 4-5.)

$$T_{eff} = 6000°\text{K}, \quad \log g = 4.0.$$

τ_{5000}	T	P_g	N_e	κ_{5000}	ρ	$H^+/\Sigma H$	x	F_c/F
.0010	4,900	2.186 (+03)	3.005 (+11)	7.781 (−03)	6.898 (−09)	2.869 (−05)	−1,166	.0000
.0016	4,914	2.862 (+03)	3.757 (+11)	9.505 (−03)	9.007 (−09)	2.525 (−05)	−1,081	.0000
.0025	4,931	3.738 (+03)	4.712 (+11)	1.165 (−02)	1.172 (−08)	2.250 (−05)	−996	.0000
.0040	4,950	4.869 (+03)	5.926 (+11)	1.432 (−02)	1.521 (−08)	2.042 (−05)	−911	.0000
.0063	4,974	6.324 (+03)	7.483 (+11)	1.765 (−02)	1.966 (−08)	1.902 (−05)	−828	.0000
.0100	5,004	8.194 (+03)	9.485 (+11)	2.180 (−02)	2.533 (−08)	1.824 (−05)	−744	.0000
.0158	5,044	1.059 (+04)	1.214 (+12)	2.703 (−02)	3.247 (−08)	1.852 (−05)	−661	.0000
.0251	5,096	1.364 (+04)	1.571 (+12)	3.371 (−02)	4.140 (−08)	2.008 (−05)	−578	.0000
.0398	5,155	1.752 (+04)	2.042 (+12)	4.213 (−02)	5.256 (−08)	2.232 (−05)	−495	.0000
.0631	5,231	2.241 (+04)	2.711 (+12)	5.329 (−02)	6.624 (−08)	2.691 (−05)	−412	.0000
.1000	5,339	2.845 (+04)	3.753 (+12)	6.926 (−02)	8.242 (−08)	3.689 (−05)	−331	.0000
.1585	5,473	3.572 (+04)	5.412 (+12)	9.281 (−02)	1.009 (−07)	5.461 (−05)	−251	.0000
.2512	5,652	4.407 (+04)	8.454 (+12)	1.323 (−01)	1.206 (−07)	9.124 (−05)	−176	.0000
.3981	5,889	5.297 (+04)	1.471 (+13)	2.054 (−01)	1.391 (−07)	1.716 (−04)	−107	.0000
.6310	6,197	6.164 (+04)	2.883 (+13)	3.514 (−01)	1.538 (−07)	3.580 (−04)	−48	.0000
1.000	6,600	6.926 (+04)	6.417 (+13)	6.669 (−01)	1.632 (−07)	8.372 (−04)	0	.0000
1.585	7,119	7.536 (+04)	1.585 (+14)	1.389 (+00)	1.634 (−07)	2.168 (−03)	37	.0005
2.512	7,830	7.968 (+04)	4.485 (+14)	3.356 (+00)	1.564 (−07)	6.586 (−03)	64	.0856
3.981	8,455	8.263 (+04)	9.671 (+14)	6.857 (+00)	1.491 (−07)	1.505 (−02)	84	.4954
6.310	8,861	8.529 (+04)	1.509 (+15)	1.078 (+01)	1.456 (−07)	2.412 (−02)	102	.7649
10.00	9,179	8.812 (+04)	2.085 (+15)	1.530 (+01)	1.440 (−07)	3.376 (−02)	121	.8724
15.85	9,456	9.137 (+04)	2.723 (+15)	2.070 (+01)	1.436 (−07)	4.427 (−02)	144	.9437
25.12	9,710	9.524 (+04)	3.441 (+15)	2.722 (+01)	1.443 (−07)	5.572 (−02)	171	.9294
39.81	9,958	9.994 (+04)	4.286 (+15)	3.539 (+01)	1.461 (−07)	6.862 (−02)	203	.9560
63.10	10,205	1.057 (+05)	5.297 (+15)	4.579 (+01)	1.488 (−07)	8.328 (−02)	242	.9724

Table 4-10 Model Atmosphere. Main sequence, spectral class K2. (See Table 4-5.)

$T_{eff} = 5000°K$, $\log g = 4.0$.

τ_{5000}	T	P_g	N_e	κ_{5000}	ρ	$H^+/\Sigma H$	x	F_c/F
.0010	4,071	2.294 (+03)	1.556 (+11)	7.546 (−03)	8.720 (−09)	5.935 (−08)	−1,095	.0000
.0016	4,084	2.994 (+03)	1.942 (+11)	9.155 (−03)	1.134 (−08)	5.421 (−08)	−1,025	.0000
.0025	4,100	3.907 (+03)	2.429 (+11)	1.113 (−02)	1.475 (−08)	5.084 (−08)	−954	.0000
.0040	4,120	5.097 (+03)	3.045 (+11)	1.355 (−02)	1.915 (−08)	4.909 (−08)	−884	.0000
.0063	4,145	6.644 (+03)	3.836 (+11)	1.652 (−02)	2.482 (−08)	4.949 (−08)	−813	.0000
.0100	4,175	8.653 (+03)	4.853 (+11)	2.019 (−02)	3.210 (−08)	5.185 (−08)	−742	.0000
.0158	4,211	1.126 (+04)	6.175 (+11)	2.473 (−02)	4.140 (−08)	5.702 (−08)	−671	.0000
.0251	4,258	1.462 (+04)	7.948 (+11)	3.041 (−02)	5.318 (−08)	6.824 (−08)	−599	.0000
.0398	4,308	1.895 (+04)	1.024 (+12)	3.739 (−02)	6.814 (−08)	8.296 (−08)	−528	.0000
.0631	4,372	2.452 (+04)	1.337 (+12)	4.619 (−02)	8.689 (−08)	1.115 (−07)	−455	.0000
.1000	4,463	3.164 (+04)	1.788 (+12)	5.742 (−02)	1.099 (−07)	1.786 (−07)	−383	.0000
.1585	4,573	4.071 (+04)	2.422 (+12)	7.149 (−02)	1.379 (−07)	3.216 (−07)	−309	.0000
.2512	4,721	5.225 (+04)	3.359 (+12)	8.925 (−02)	1.714 (−07)	7.134 (−07)	−235	.0000
.3981	4,917	6.687 (+04)	4.791 (+12)	1.117 (−01)	2.106 (−07)	2.017 (−06)	−158	.0000
.6310	5,173	8.528 (+04)	7.142 (+12)	1.424 (−01)	2.552 (−07)	7.137 (−06)	−79	.0000
1.000	5,505	1.072 (+05)	1.213 (+13)	2.019 (−01)	3.013 (−07)	2.907 (−05)	0	.0000
1.585	5,924	1.291 (+05)	2.650 (+13)	3.612 (−01)	3.372 (−07)	1.126 (−04)	69	.0000
2.512	6,445	1.467 (+05)	7.245 (+13)	7.925 (−01)	3.518 (−07)	4.030 (−04)	119	.0051
3.981	7,049	1.587 (+05)	2.079 (+14)	1.833 (+00)	3.477 (−07)	1.309 (−03)	153	.1927
6.310	7,538	1.678 (+05)	4.411 (+14)	3.384 (+00)	3.433 (−07)	2.905 (−03)	180	.4789
10.00	7,916	1.763 (+05)	7.486 (+14)	5.287 (+00)	3.429 (−07)	4.998 (−03)	205	.6986
15.85	8,240	1.854 (+05)	1.140 (+15)	7.635 (+00)	3.456 (−07)	7.602 (−03)	231	.8157
25.12	8,534	1.956 (+05)	1.634 (+15)	1.058 (+01)	3.510 (−07)	1.077 (−02)	261	.8846
39.81	8,811	2.075 (+05)	2.258 (+15)	1.432 (+01)	3.593 (−07)	1.459 (−02)	294	.9276
63.10	9,080	2.214 (+05)	3.048 (+15)	1.914 (+01)	3.706 (−07)	1.913 (−02)	332	.9555

Table 4-11 Model Atmosphere. Giant, spectral type G5. (See Table 4-5.)

$$T_{eff} = 5000°K, \quad \log g = 2.0.$$

τ_{5000}	T	P_g	N_e	κ_{5000}	ρ	$\log g_{eff}$	x	F_c/F
.0010	4,065	1.315 (+02)	1.412 (+10)	1.130 (−03)	5.001 (−10)	1.9873	−115,125	.0000
.0016	4,082	1.789 (+02)	1.877 (+10)	1.333 (−03)	6.779 (−10)	1.9875	−107,004	.0000
.0025	4,096	2.422 (+02)	2.475 (+10)	1.592 (−03)	9.145 (−10)	1.9878	−98,994	.0000
.0040	4,118	3.260 (+02)	3.251 (+10)	1.913 (−03)	1.224 (−09)	1.9882	−91,107	.0000
.0063	4,146	4.362 (+02)	4.257 (+10)	2.310 (−03)	1.627 (−09)	1.9887	−83,328	.0000
.0100	4,181	5.805 (+02)	5.568 (+10)	2.799 (−03)	2.147 (−09)	1.9896	−75,633	.0000
.0158	4,222	7.690 (+02)	7.273 (+10)	3.401 (−03)	2.817 (−09)	1.9900	−67,995	.0000
.0251	4,272	1.015 (+03)	9.522 (+10)	4.139 (−03)	3.673 (−09)	1.9908	−60,385	.0000
.0398	4,333	1.334 (+03)	1.250 (+11)	5.043 (−03)	4.762 (−09)	1.9915	−52,765	.0000
.0631	4,406	1.750 (+03)	1.647 (+11)	6.146 (−03)	6.142 (−09)	1.9920	−45,104	.0000
.1000	4,499	2.291 (+03)	2.190 (+11)	7.487 (−03)	7.876 (−09)	1.9927	−37,353	.0000
.1585	4,617	2.994 (+03)	2.957 (+11)	9.134 (−03)	1.003 (−08)	1.9929	−29,471	.0000
.2512	4,784	3.902 (+03)	4.172 (+11)	1.133 (−02)	1.261 (−08)	1.9932	−21,421	.0000
.3981	4,963	5.036 (+03)	6.181 (+11)	1.480 (−02)	1.569 (−08)	1.9934	−13,388	.0000
.6310	5,251	6.300 (+03)	1.160 (+12)	2.320 (−02)	1.855 (−08)	1.9935	−6,006	.0000
1.000	5,581	7.482 (+03)	2.565 (+12)	4.277 (−02)	2.073 (−08)	1.9936	0	.0000
1.585	6,015	8.408 (+03)	6.954 (+12)	9.420 (−02)	2.160 (−08)	1.9936	4,365	.0000
2.512	6,560	9.040 (+03)	2.096 (+13)	2.309 (−01)	2.127 (−08)	1.9934	7,304	.0000
3.981	7,275	9.422 (+03)	7.003 (+13)	6.588 (−01)	1.988 (−08)	1.9927	9,161	.0106
6.310	7,977	9.630 (+03)	1.844 (+14)	1.734 (+00)	1.828 (−08)	1.9920	10,271	.6189
10.00	8,374	9.779 (+03)	2.956 (+14)	2.970 (+00)	1.743 (−08)	1.9918	11,146	.6808
15.85	8,633	9.931 (+03)	3.923 (+14)	4.203 (+00)	1.695 (−08)	1.9916	12,096	.8350
25.12	8,858	1.010 (+04)	4.942 (+14)	5.656 (+00)	1.658 (−08)	1.9916	13,219	.9005
39.81	9,068	1.030 (+04)	6.064 (+14)	7.427 (+00)	1.627 (−08)	1.9916	14,588	.9376
63.10	9,273	1.053 (+04)	7.330 (+14)	9.630 (+00)	1.599 (−08)	1.9917	16,282	.9603

Table 4-12 Model Atmosphere. Main sequence, spectral type K7. (See Table 4-5.)

$$T_{eff} = 4000°\text{K}, \quad \log g = 4.0.$$

τ_{5000}	T	P_g	N_e	κ_{5000}	ρ	$\log g_{eff}$	x	F_C/F
.0010	3,236	3.804 (+03)	3.901 (+10)	4.233 (−03)	1.867 (−08)	7.653 (−12)	−797	.0000
.0016	3,241	5.066 (+03)	4.830 (+10)	5.020 (−03)	2.501 (−08)	6.679 (−12)	−738	.0000
.0025	3,249	6.749 (+03)	6.036 (+10)	5.987 (−03)	3.350 (−08)	6.075 (−12)	−681	.0000
.0040	3,260	8.981 (+03)	7.580 (+10)	7.157 (−03)	4.486 (−08)	5.658 (−12)	−623	.0000
.0063	3,272	1.194 (+04)	9.575 (+10)	8.577 (−03)	6.002 (−08)	5.444 (−12)	−566	.0000
.0100	3,287	1.584 (+04)	1.215 (+11)	1.029 (−02)	8.019 (−08)	5.384 (−12)	−510	.0000
.0158	3,309	2.099 (+04)	1.560 (+11)	1.243 (−02)	1.067 (−07)	5.776 (−12)	−455	.0000
.0251	3,336	2.771 (+04)	2.020 (+11)	1.511 (−02)	1.410 (−07)	6.688 (−12)	−400	.0000
.0398	3,360	3.653 (+04)	2.594 (+11)	1.820 (−02)	1.868 (−07)	7.338 (−12)	−346	.0000
.0631	3,411	4.791 (+04)	3.488 (+11)	2.281 (−02)	2.417 (−07)	1.131 (−11)	−293	.0000
.1000	3,464	6.226 (+04)	4.666 (+11)	2.853 (−02)	3.095 (−07)	1.758 (−11)	−240	.0000
.1585	3,524	8.052 (+04)	6.293 (+11)	3.597 (−02)	3.929 (−07)	2.904 (−11)	−188	.0000
.2512	3,654	1.023 (+05)	9.575 (+11)	5.028 (−02)	4.704 (−07)	9.848 (−11)	−138	.0000
.3981	3,796	1.268 (+05)	1.477 (+12)	7.057 (−02)	5.496 (−07)	3.422 (−10)	−90	.0000
.6310	3,993	1.538 (+05)	2.494 (+12)	1.046 (−01)	6.196 (−07)	1.687 (−09)	−44	.0000
1.000	4,252	1.821 (+05)	4.517 (+12)	1.587 (−01)	6.764 (−07)	1.139 (−08)	0	.0000
1.585	4,587	2.122 (+05)	8.250 (+12)	2.311 (−01)	7.224 (−07)	1.051 (−07)	43	.0039
2.512	5,014	2.466 (+05)	1.429 (+13)	3.060 (−01)	7.634 (−07)	1.299 (−06)	89	.0200
3.981	5,548	2.881 (+05)	2.612 (+13)	4.184 (−01)	8.042 (−07)	1.703 (−05)	142	.0765
6.310	6,090	3.294 (+05)	6.173 (+13)	7.724 (−01)	8.369 (−07)	1.045 (−04)	192	.3599
10.00	6,514	3.641 (+05)	1.334 (+14)	1.406 (+00)	8.644 (−07)	2.877 (−04)	233	.5519
15.85	6,854	3.963 (+05)	2.447 (+14)	2.273 (+00)	8.939 (−07)	5.626 (−04)	270	.7333
25.12	7,160	4.290 (+05)	4.114 (+14)	3.443 (+00)	9.259 (−07)	9.573 (−04)	306	.8296
39.81	7,452	4.639 (+05)	6.561 (+14)	5.020 (+00)	9.615 (−07)	1.510 (−03)	343	.8904
63.10	7,738	5.024 (+05)	1.010 (+15)	7.145 (+00)	1.002 (−06)	2.268 (−03)	382	.9316

PROBLEMS

1. If T^4 is a linear function of τ, show that the structure of an atmosphere may be determined by integrating dP/dx and dT/dx directly without performing calculations involving τ.

2. Find the mean molecular weight of
   (a) pure hydrogen that is 50 per cent ionized;
   (b) a mixture of equal masses of hydrogen and helium, if the hydrogen is 50 per cent ionized and the helium is neutral;
   (c) a mixture of equal masses of hydrogen and helium, if the hydrogen is completely ionized and the helium is 50 per cent neutral and 50 percent ionized.

3. Defining an effective gravity g_{eff} from the relation $dP_g/d\bar{\tau} = -g_{\text{eff}}/\bar{\kappa}$, show that it can be expressed as in Table 4-5. Verify some of the values given for g_{eff} in Table 4-6.

4. Compare the contributions of radiation pressure to the total pressure at $\tau_{5000} = 10$ for atmospheres of various temperatures and surface gravities.

5. Refer to the model atmosphere of Table 4-7 at the level $\tau_{5000} = 10$.
   (a) Find the mean molecular weight μ.
   (b) Find the mean molecular weight μ_0 for the gas in the case that there is no ionization.
   (c) Making the good approximation that hydrogen supplies essentially all the electrons at $\tau_{5000} = 10$, verify the value tabulated for $H^+/\Sigma H$. Use the relation

$$1 + E = \frac{\mu_0}{\mu},$$

   where E is the average number of free electrons per nucleus of the gas.
   (d) Verify the tabulated value of N_e.

6. It is suggested in Section 3-1B that the peaks and valleys of the curve depicting the absorption coefficients in Fig. 4-5 be compared with those for the flux in Fig. 4-4. Why cannot this comparison be extended to the region of the higher values of $1/\lambda$ shown in the figures?

5

LINE ABSORPTION IN STELLAR ATMOSPHERES

This chapter deals with the formation of absorption lines, the mechanisms determining their contours, their strengths, and the information that may be derived from them. In Section 3-1, it is demonstrated that the spectral sequence is primarily a temperature sequence.

1 FORMATION OF ABSORPTION LINES

The radiation streaming toward the stellar atmosphere from the interior is nearly continuous in wavelength, since the temperature gradient in the interior is small and the matter is virtually enclosed and in equilibrium with the radiation. Under these conditions, the spectral distribution resembles that of black body radiation.* In the outer layers, on the other hand, the temperature gradient is appreciable, and the radiation field is considerably anisotropic. Atoms and ions capable of absorbing discrete frequencies will be encountered at the low temperatures, and more energy will be removed from the outward radiation in those frequencies than in the adjacent continuous spectrum.

Absorption of energy of some frequency ν_0 can take place if an atom or ion in the atmosphere contains two bound levels separated by an energy difference $h\nu_0$. The photon is then removed from the outgoing stream, and this diminishes the amount of radiation pouring from the star at this frequency. The photon may be re-emitted in a random direction a fraction of a second later; and, being thus turned back into the atmosphere, it is now likely to undergo further absorption. It may, perhaps, cause ejection of an electron formerly bound within some other atom or ion, and this electron may then interact with other particles, gaining or losing energy in the process. When the electron finally recombines with a third ion, the frequency of the emitted photon will, in general, be different from ν_0. The original photon at ν_0 has effectively been converted into another photon of arbitrary frequency.

* See the discussion in Chapter 2, Section 4-2C.

Energy is thus extracted at a discrete frequency and deposited into a continuous distribution or continuum. Thus, a dark line is formed in the continuous background.

Actually, spectral lines are not perfectly sharp, and radiation within a small range of frequencies near ν_0 will be absorbed. The mechanisms that produce this *line broadening* are discussed in Section 2.

Let us return to the moment when the photon of frequency ν_0 is absorbed by the atom or ion to raise a bound electron to a higher level. The electron will not remain in that level, but will either return to the original level or go to some other level, perhaps even to the continuum. When return to the level of origin occurs, the photon is simply scattered. On the other hand, when the reverse of the original transition is unlikely, true absorption takes place. The latter process applies especially to lines involving the uppermost levels. The frequent ionizations and re-combinations, as well as interchanges between bound levels, maintain the populations of the bound levels in equilibrium with the free electrons, and both can be characterized by the same temperature. In other words, the excitation temperature in the Boltzmann equation is the same as the kinetic temperature in the Maxwellian velocity distribution [eqs. (3-17) and (3-31)]. The same temperature, moreover, describes the ionization processes according to the Saha equation [eq. (3-25)]. Under these conditions, *local thermodynamic equilibrium* prevails. Lines of the higher series of hydrogen, such as the Brackett series, are examples of lines formed by true absorption, whereas Lyman α, corresponding to a transition between the levels $n = 1$ and $n = 2$, is formed by the scattering process.

In discussions of absorption lines, either of two models of the line-forming regions is often assumed. In the Schuster–Schwarzschild model, the absorption lines are considered to be produced in a shallow *reversing layer* that overlies the photosphere, while the photosphere itself radiates a continuous spectrum. This arrangement is analogous to a laboratory demonstration in which the continuous radiation produced by an incandescent bulb passes through a sodium vapor created by heating salt in a Bunsen flame. The sodium vapor scatters some of the energy in the D lines, in the yellow-orange region, so that a spectroscope placed in this beam shows dark lines against the bright background from the incandescent source. The Schuster–Schwarzschild model is reasonably good for lines due to particles that can exist only in the highest, coolest layers, such as molecules and neutral atoms having low ionization potentials. For ions requiring a higher temperature, a better approximation is that of the Eddington–Milne model, in which line absorption and continuous absorption take place in the same atmospheric layers, and the ratio of the absorption coefficient at any frequency within a spectral line to the absorption coefficient for the interpolated continuum at that frequency is taken to be constant with atmospheric depth. For a more refined calculation, one should find the line profile (Section 2) under the conditions of pressure and temperature prevailing at every level of the atmosphere and then take account of the transfer of the radiation for each frequency within the line.

2 LINE PROFILES*

The contour of a line on a graph of intensity or flux as a function of frequency or wavelength is called a *line profile*. We first give the equation for the line absorption coefficient as a function of frequency and then describe the mechanisms by which this profile is broadened. We shall *not* discuss the transfer problem for radiation within a line, which would enable us to combine the contributions from various depths to obtain the final line profile of the emergent radiation from the star.

2-1 THE LINE ABSORPTION COEFFICIENT. NATURAL BROADENING

An expression for the absorption coefficient as a function of frequency within the line can be obtained from classical electromagnetic theory. We do not give the details of this derivation, but merely quote some of the formulae.[†]

Consider a dipole formed by an atom[‡] and an electron that oscillates under the influence of an incident electromagnetic wave for which the electric vector lies along the z-axis. Equating the sum of the forces acting on the electron to the product of its mass and acceleration, we have[§]

$$m\ddot{z} = \underbrace{-m\gamma\dot{z}}_{\substack{\text{braking} \\ \text{(damping)} \\ \text{force}}} \underbrace{- m\omega_0^2 z}_{\substack{\text{restoring} \\ \text{force}}} \underbrace{- eE_0 e^{i\omega t}}_{\substack{\text{force produced} \\ \text{by incident} \\ \text{EM wave}}}, \qquad (5\text{-}1)$$

where

m = mass of the electron,

e = charge of the electron (absolute value),

---

* This section is not essential to the succeeding material.
† Consult L. H. Aller, 1963 (25), p. 161 et seq.; and R. v. d. R. Woolley and D. W. N. Stibbs, 1953 (26), p. 91 et seq.
‡ *Atom* here means the atom minus the oscillating electron; the electron is actually part of the atom.
§ The force due to the magnetic vector of the electromagnetic wave is negligible. Its magnitude is $(e/c)vH$, where v is the component of the velocity of the electron perpendicular to the direction of the magnetic vector of magnitude H. Since $H = E$ in a vacuum, it would be required that $v \sim c$ for the magnetic force to be comparable to the electric force eE.

$\omega_0 = 2\pi\nu_0$; ν_0 is the natural frequency of the electron,

$\omega = 2\pi\nu$; ν is the frequency of the incident electromagnetic wave,

E_0 = magnitude of the electric vector of the incident wave,

γ = damping constant (for *radiation damping*, i.e., *natural broadening*)

$$= \frac{2}{3} \frac{e^2}{c^3} \frac{\omega^2}{m} = \frac{8\pi^2}{3} \frac{e^2}{mc^3} \nu^2. \tag{5-2}$$

The expression for γ is related to the rate at which an accelerated charge loses energy. The electron is caused to oscillate by the incident wave if $\nu \approx \nu_0$, that is, if approximate resonance occurs.

With the help of other equations from electromagnetic theory, one gets finally

$$\kappa_\nu \rho = \frac{e^2}{mc} N \frac{\gamma/4\pi}{(\nu - \nu_0)^2 + (\gamma/4\pi)^2}, \tag{5-3}$$

where N = number of oscillators per cm^3 that can absorb at frequencies within the line centered on frequency ν_0.

The profile of the absorption line is closely related to the graph of κ_ν. For a thin atmospheric layer of thickness Δx between τ_1 and τ_2, where τ_2 corresponds to the higher layer, we have from eq. (2-16) that

$$I_\nu(\tau_2) = I_\nu(\tau_1)e^{-\kappa_\nu\rho\,\Delta x}$$

$$\approx I_\nu(\tau_1)(1 - \kappa_\nu\rho\,\Delta x)$$

$$I_\nu(\tau_2) - I_\nu(\tau_1) \approx -\kappa_\nu\rho\,\Delta x\,I_\nu(\tau_1).$$

Therefore, the decrease in the intensity at ν as the radiation traverses the layer is directly proportional to κ_ν. This results in a profile such as that in Fig. 5-1. The maximum depth of the profile occurs at $\nu = \nu_0$, for which the denominator in eq. (5-3) is simply $(\gamma/4\pi)^2$. Half the maximum depth is attained at

$$(\nu - \nu_0)^2 = \left(\frac{\gamma}{4\pi}\right)^2,$$

for which the denominator in eq. (5-3) has twice the value at the line center. Calling this interval $\Delta\nu_{1/2}$ or the *half-width* of the profile, we have

$$\Delta\nu_{1/2} = \frac{\gamma}{4\pi}. \tag{5-4}$$

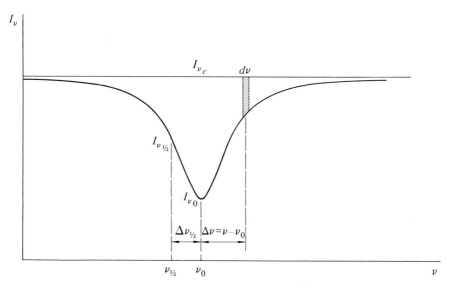

Fig. 5-1 Profile of a Naturally Broadened Line. At $\nu = \nu_{1/2}$, the profile reaches half its maximum depth. I_{ν_c} is the intensity of the continuum.

In terms of wavelength,

$$\lambda = \frac{c}{\nu}$$

$$\Delta\lambda_{1/2} = \frac{c}{\nu^2}\,\Delta\nu_{1/2},$$

where the sign may be neglected. Putting in γ from eq. (5-2), we find

$$\Delta\lambda_{1/2} = \frac{2\pi}{3}\frac{e^2}{mc^2}$$

$$= 0.000118 \text{ Å}.$$

This is very small and is the same for all lines. Twice this value gives the *total half-width* of the naturally broadened profile,

$$2\,\Delta\lambda_{1/2} = 0.00024 \text{ Å}. \tag{5-5}$$

We may ask what is the physical interpretation of the finite width of the naturally broadened profile. Classically, it means that an oscillating electron, like a mechanical oscillator, can respond to an imposed frequency slightly different from its resonant frequency. Quantum mechanically, the width of the line is a consequence of the finite width of the energy levels involved in the transition due to their finite lifetimes. The uncertainty principle, often stated in the form

$$\Delta(\text{position}) \cdot \Delta(\text{momentum}) \sim h,$$

can also be written as*

$$\Delta\mathscr{E} \cdot \Delta t \sim h, \qquad (5\text{-}6)$$

where $\Delta\mathscr{E}$ is the width of an energy level and Δt is its lifetime, that is, the length of time that an electron remains in the level.

Quantum mechanics requires that two modifications be made in the expression (5-3) for κ_ν. First, γ must be replaced by a new damping constant, $\Gamma_{\rm rad}$, defined below in terms of the Einstein transition probabilities. Second, N must be replaced by Nf, where f is called the *oscillator strength* or *f-value* and is the number of optically active electrons per absorbing atom. A certain fraction of the electrons that are optically active in a sample of matter will be engaged at any instant in making any one of the many possible transitions, or, equivalently, a certain fraction of the optical electrons in any one atom is engaged in making that transition. These fractions are proportional to the *f*-values and to factors involving the wavelength. If the *f*-values are taken to be negative for emission, their sum for all transitions from a given initial level equals the number of optical electrons (Thomas-Kuhn sum rule). Consider hydrogen in the ground state. Table 5-1 gives the oscillator strengths for discrete Lyman transitions and also for transitions to the

---

* Dimensionally, if we write x for position, m for mass, and v for velocity, we have

$$\Delta x \cdot \Delta mv \sim h$$

$$\frac{\Delta x}{v} \cdot \Delta mv^2 \sim h$$

$$\Delta t \cdot \Delta\mathscr{E} \sim h.$$

Table 5-1   Oscillator Strengths for Hydrogen. [From R. v. d. R. Woolley and D. W. N. Stibbs, 1953 (26).]*

FINAL LEVEL j \ INITIAL LEVEL i	$i = 1$ LYMAN	$i = 2$ BALMER	$i = 3$ PASCHEN
$j = 1$	—	−0.104	−0.0087
2	0.416	—	−0.284
3	0.0791	0.637	—
4	0.0290	0.119	0.841
5	0.0139	0.0443	0.150
6	0.0078	0.0212	0.0554
7	0.0048	0.0122	0.0269
8	0.0032	0.0080	0.0161
9 to ∞	0.0101	0.0237	0.0421
Contribution from lines	0.564	0.762	0.839
Contribution from transitions to continuum	0.436	0.238	0.161
$\sum_j f_{ij}$	1.000	1.000	1.000

* According to recent calculations by H. C. Goldwire, Jr., 1969 (232) and by D. H. Menzel, 1969 (233) for bound-bound transitions, some of the values given here for Balmer and Paschen lines should be revised.

continuum. The sum is equal to unity, since hydrogen has one electron. Similarly, the sum of the values for the Balmer and Paschen transitions equals unity, and we note that the f-values for the downward transitions are negative. For helium in the ground state, there are two electrons; and the sum of the oscillator strengths for all transitions from the ground state must therefore be 2. The quantum-mechanical formula for the absorption coefficient is then

$$\kappa_\nu \rho = \frac{e^2}{mc} Nf \frac{\Gamma_{\text{rad}}/4\pi}{(\nu - \nu_0)^2 + (\Gamma_{\text{rad}}/4\pi)^2}. \tag{5-7}$$

In this formula, one could add subscripts to denote the lower and upper energy levels, n and m, respectively, giving N_n, f_{nm}, Γ_{nm}.

The *Einstein transition coefficients* should be mentioned. They are defined for transitions between a lower level n and an upper level m:*

$N_m A_{mn} \, dt =$ number of atoms or ions in level m making a spontaneous downward radiative transition $m \to n$ during time dt;

$N_n B_{nm} I_{\nu_{nm}} \, dt =$ number of atoms or ions in level n making an upward radiative transition $n \to m$ during time dt when irradiated with intensity $I_{\nu_{nm}}$;

$N_m B_{mn} I_{\nu_{nm}} \, dt =$ number of atoms or ions in level m making an induced (stimulated) downward radiative transition during time dt when irradiated with intensity $I_{\nu_{nm}}$. (We do not distinguish between ν_{nm} and ν_{mn}.)

The last coefficient refers to a process in which the probability of *emission* of radiation at frequency ν_{nm} is enhanced by the irradiation. Since the induced photon goes in the same direction as the incident beam, the process amounts to a negative absorption.

We quote some useful relations involving these coefficients and Γ, γ, and f:

$$\frac{B_{mn}}{B_{nm}} \frac{g_m}{g_n} = 1 \tag{5-8}$$

$$A_{mn} = \frac{2h\nu^3}{c^2} B_{mn} \tag{5-9}$$

$$\Gamma_m = \sum_{n<m} A_{mn} + \sum_{n<m} B_{mn} I_{\nu_{mn}} + \sum_{n'>m} B_{mn'} I_{\nu_{mn'}} \tag{5-10}$$

$$\Gamma_{mn} = \Gamma_n + \Gamma_m \tag{5-11}$$

$$A_{mn} = 3 \frac{g_n}{g_m} f_{nm} \gamma \tag{5-12}$$

$$B_{nm} = \frac{\pi e^2}{mc} f_{nm} \frac{4\pi}{h\nu_{nm}}. \tag{5-13}$$

* The B-coefficients are sometimes defined in terms of energy density, u_ν: $u_\nu = 4\pi I_\nu/c$. Note also that the subscripts are written in the reverse order by some authors.

In eq. (5-10), the first two sums are taken over all levels below m, while the last sum is over all higher levels.*

2-2 DOPPLER BROADENING

The Doppler effect due to the thermal motions of atoms† provides another mechanism by which spectral lines are broadened. Consider a thin layer at some temperature T in the stellar atmosphere. At any instant, the absorbing atoms have a distribution of velocities along the line of sight to the observer. The atoms receding from the observer absorb wavelengths slightly longer than that of the line center, λ_0; and those approaching the observer absorb at slightly shorter wavelengths, as given by the (non-relativistic) Doppler formula

$$\frac{\Delta\lambda}{\lambda_0} = \frac{\Delta\nu}{\nu_0} = \frac{v_l}{c},$$

where v_l = velocity component along the line of sight to the observer. From eqs. (3-32) and (3-33), we have

$$\frac{N(v_l)\,dv_l}{N} = \frac{1}{\sqrt{\pi}}\exp\left[-(v_l^2/\alpha^2)\right]\frac{dv_l}{\alpha} \tag{5-14}$$

with

$$\alpha^2 = \frac{2kT}{m}. \tag{5-15}$$

If turbulence is present, we take

$$\alpha^2 = \frac{2kT}{m} + v_t^2,$$

where v_t is the most probable speed in the turbulent motions, which are assumed to follow a Maxwellian distribution.

In the thin layer under consideration, the intensity absorbed at any wavelength is proportional to the number of particles absorbing at that wavelength. In the notation of Fig. 5-1,

$$\frac{\text{intensity absorbed in narrow strip at } \Delta\nu}{\text{intensity absorbed over entire line}} = \frac{(I_{\nu_c} - I_\nu)\,d\nu}{\int_{\text{line}} (I_{\nu_c} - I_\nu)\,d\nu}$$

$$= \frac{N(v_l)\,dv_l}{N}$$

$$= \frac{1}{\sqrt{\pi}}\exp\left[-(v_l^2/\alpha^2)\right]\frac{dv_l}{\alpha}. \tag{5-16}$$

---

* The derivations of these relations are given, e.g., by L. H. Aller, 1963 (25).
† The discussion may, of course, be applied equally well to ions.

Let us now introduce the frequency shift $\Delta\nu_D$ corresponding to the most probable speed α:

$$\frac{\Delta\nu_D}{\nu_0} = \frac{\Delta\lambda_D}{\lambda_0} = \frac{\alpha}{c}.$$

Then

$$\frac{v_l}{\alpha} = \frac{\Delta\nu}{\Delta\nu_D}$$

and eq. (5-16) becomes

$$\frac{(I_{\nu_c} - I_\nu)\,d\nu}{\int_{\text{line}} (I_{\nu_c} - I_\nu)\,d\nu} = \frac{1}{\sqrt{\pi}} \exp\left[-(\Delta\nu/\Delta\nu_D)^2\right] \frac{d\nu}{\Delta\nu_D}.$$

Therefore

$$\frac{I_{\nu_c} - I_\nu}{\int_{\text{line}} (I_{\nu_c} - I_\nu)\,d\nu} = \frac{1}{\sqrt{\pi}} \exp\left[-(\Delta\nu/\Delta\nu_D)^2\right] \frac{1}{\Delta\nu_D}. \qquad (5\text{-}17)$$

At the line center, this expression has the value

$$\frac{1}{\sqrt{\pi}} \frac{1}{\Delta\nu_D}.$$

At $\Delta\nu_{1/2}$, that is, where the line reaches half its maximum depth, we have from eq. (5-17):

$$\frac{1}{2} = \frac{I_{\nu_c} - I_{\nu_{1/2}}}{I_{\nu_c} - I_{\nu_0}} = \exp\left[-(\Delta\nu_{1/2}/\Delta\nu_D)^2\right]$$

$$\left(\frac{\Delta\nu_{1/2}}{\Delta\nu_D}\right)^2 = \log_e 2,$$

and so the total half-width is

$$2\Delta\nu_{1/2} = \frac{2}{c}\sqrt{\frac{2kT}{m} \log_e 2}\,\nu_0 \qquad (5\text{-}18a)$$

or

$$2\Delta\lambda_{1/2} = \frac{2}{c}\sqrt{\frac{2kT}{m} \log_e 2}\,\lambda_0. \qquad (5\text{-}18b)$$

The half-width thus increases with temperature and decreases with the mass of the particle, as we should expect from considerations of the mobility of the particles. As a numerical example, we may cite the total half-width of $H\beta$ at the effective temperature of the Sun (5800°K), which is $2\Delta\lambda_{1/2} = 0.264$ Å. This half-width is about 1000 times greater than that due to natural broadening.

2-3 COLLISIONAL BROADENING

When the energy levels of the absorbing atoms or ions are perturbed by neighboring particles, there is, statistically, no longer a fixed separation between any two energy levels, and the spectral lines appear broadened. Two limiting cases may be considered: perturbations by discrete encounters and by the statistical effects of many particles. Nomenclature varies, and the term *collisional broadening* is sometimes restricted to broadening by discrete encounters, while *pressure broadening* sometimes refers to the statistical case only; both terms, however, may also be used in a general sense to include both types of interaction.

In the core of a line, discrete encounters tend to be more important than statistical effects, while the reverse is usually true in the wings, that is, at a relatively large distance from the line center. Some spectral lines, however, can be described almost entirely on the basis of one theory.

When an encounter takes place between any two particles separated momentarily by a distance r, the alteration in the energy levels of the perturbed particle produces a shift in the frequency of the spectral line. This shift can be represented by

$$\Delta \nu \propto r^{-n}.$$

A shift proportional to r^{-2} is produced when an optically active electron in a Coulomb field (such as the electron in H or He$^+$) is perturbed by an ion or electron. The shift is proportional to the first power of the electric field strength and is called the *first-order* or *linear Stark effect*. If the perturbed particle has an inner core of electrons, and the optical electron consequently experiences a non-Coulomb field, the passing ion or electron separates the nucleus from the center of the inner core and thereby creates a dipole moment. The resultant shift is proportional to r^{-4}, arising from the product of the imposed electric field strength (which varies as r^{-2}) and the dipole moment (which is proportional to this electric field strength). This is the *quadratic Stark effect*. A shift $\Delta \nu \propto r^{-3}$ is produced by resonance effects when neutral atoms of the same species interact. This is important for hydrogen (especially the line $H\alpha$) because of the large abundance of this element in most stars. For neutral atoms of different species, van der Waals forces result in a shift $\Delta \nu \propto r^{-6}$. In this case, hydrogen, because of its abundance, is important as the perturbing particle.

The effects of all the instantaneous shifts $\Delta \nu$ must be combined into a line profile. The absorption coefficient for collisional damping has the form of eq. (5-7) if Γ_{rad} for radiative damping is replaced by Γ_{coll}. This constant is sometimes tens of times larger than Γ_{rad}, resulting in a proportionately broader profile.

2-4 SIMULTANEOUS NATURAL, DOPPLER, AND COLLISIONAL BROADENING

The actual line profile may be broadened by all three effects simultaneously. The Doppler displacement of the central frequency ν_0 of the naturally broadened profile will be the same for all absorbing particles having the same velocity v_l but will be different from the displacement caused by particles having other velocities. Let us therefore introduce an absorption coefficient per absorbing particle, α_ν, such that

$$\kappa_\nu \rho = \int_N \alpha_\nu \, dN, \tag{5-19}$$

Fig. 5-2 The Line Absorption Coefficient per Ion for the K Line of Ca II at 3933 Å, for $T = 5700°$K. The core of the line is formed by Doppler broadening, the wings by radiation damping (*dashed curve*) or radiation plus collisional damping at $P = 7.2 \times 10^4$ dyne cm^{-2} (*solid curve*). The ordinate has been normalized to be zero at the line center. [After L. H. Aller, *Astrophysics: The Atmospheres of the Sun and Stars*, 2nd ed. Copyright © 1963, The Ronald Press Company, New York.]

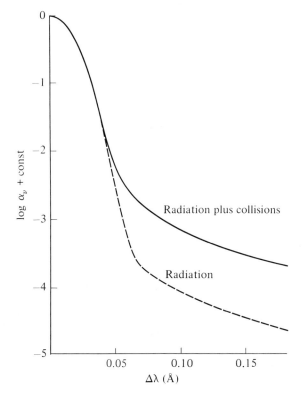

where N is the number of absorbing particles per cm^3. Then, since the central frequency is shifted by an amount

$$\Delta\nu_0 = \nu_0 \frac{v_l}{c}$$

and the radiative and collisional damping constants can be summed, we find

$$\alpha_\nu = \frac{\pi e^2}{mc} f \frac{\Gamma_{\rm rad} + \Gamma_{\rm coll}}{4\pi^2} \frac{1}{\{\nu - [\nu_0 + \nu_0(v_l/c)]\}^2 + [(\Gamma_{\rm rad} + \Gamma_{\rm coll})/4\pi]^2}. \quad (5\text{-}20)$$

The number of atoms having velocity v_l is given by eqs. (5-14) and (5-15), and, since

$$\kappa_\nu \rho = \int_{-\infty}^{+\infty} \alpha_\nu N(v_l)\, dv_l,$$

we get finally

$$\kappa_\nu \rho = \frac{\pi e^2}{mc} Nf \frac{\Gamma_{\rm rad} + \Gamma_{\rm coll}}{4\pi^2} \sqrt{\frac{m}{2\pi kT}} \times$$

$$\times \int_{-\infty}^{+\infty} \frac{\exp\left[-(mv_l^2/2kT)\right] dv_l}{[\nu - \nu_0(1 + v_l/c)]^2 + [(\Gamma_{\rm rad} + \Gamma_{\rm coll})/4\pi]^2}. \quad (5\text{-}21)$$

Figure 5-2 illustrates the contributions of the broadening mechanisms.

2-5 OTHER BROADENING MECHANISMS

A number of additional effects also cause lines to appear broadened. If more than one isotope of an element is present, the different masses will result in different particle velocities, and this will affect both the Doppler displacement and the collisional problem. Hyperfine splitting of energy levels may give the appearance of a broadened line, as may Zeeman splitting when magnetic fields are present. If the star is rotating or if there is an expanding shell of gas, different parts of the star will give systematically different Doppler shifts. The distortion of the profile caused by the instruments used in observing must also be considered.

2-6 COMPARISON OF OBSERVED AND CALCULATED LINE PROFILES

The general success of the theory in predicting the profiles of absorption lines is evident from Figs. 5-3 and 5-4. Profiles of the magnesium b$_1$ line and the sodium D$_2$ line in the solar spectrum are shown in Fig. 5-3 for the center of the solar disk and also for a place rather near to the solar limb. For Vega,

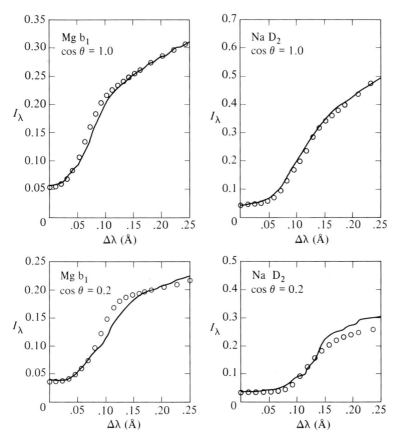

Fig. 5-3 Observed and Calculated Profiles of the Mg b_1 and Na D_2 Lines for the Solar Disk. The theoretical profiles (*dots*) are compared with the observations (*lines*) obtained by Curtis and White. The ordinates are normalized to unity in the continuum at $\cos \theta = 1$. [After R. G. Athay and R. C. Canfield, 1969 (237).]

of course, the observations in Fig. 5-4 refer to the light integrated over the entire disk. The Balmer lines Hα, Hβ, and Hγ, which are prominent in this A-type star, are in very good accord with the predicted profiles.* It is also apparent from these figures that perfect agreement has not yet been attained, and further improvements in the theory may be anticipated.†

---

* Tables of the emergent flux F_ν and of the detailed atmospheric structure of Vega are given in the reference from which Fig. 5-4 is taken.

† For further information on calculated and observed line profiles, see O. Gingerich, ed., 1969 (35), various papers and discussions.

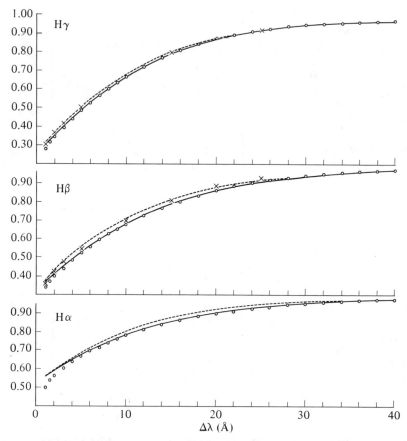

Fig. 5-4　Observed and Calculated Profiles of the Lines Hα, Hβ, and Hγ for Vega (α Lyrae). The theoretical profiles, as based on two different broadening theories (*solid* and *dashed lines*), are compared with the observations of Baschek and Oke (*crosses*) and Peterson (*dots*). [After R. Shild, D. M. Peterson, and J. B. Oke, 1971 (199u).]

3 LINE STRENGTHS

3-1 VARIATION WITH SPECTRAL TYPE

The spectral classification has been described in Chapter 1, Section 1-6. Lines of ions predominate in the early spectral classes, while lines of neutral atoms and even of molecules are characteristic of the later types. These differences are caused primarily by the differences in the effective temperatures. Atmospheric pressure plays a secondary role, while chemical abundances are generally so similar as to be important in classifying only a small minority of stars. We consider some examples to show more specifically how temperature controls the appearance of the spectrum.

A. First, let us note the behavior of some of the lines identified in Fig. 1-3: (i) Lines of He I (for example, 4026 Å and 4472 Å) appear only in the spectra of hot stars. These lines arise from an excited level and require a high temperature to raise the absorbing electron to this level before the appropriate photon can be absorbed. With increasing temperature, conditions become more favorable and the lines gain in strength until, in the O-type stars, the strengths decline as ionization sets in.

(ii) The H and K lines of Ca II are strongest in spectral classes G and K. Since an ion is responsible, the temperature must be high enough to maintain ionization to the extent of one electron but must not be so high as to result in further ionization.

(iii) The lines $H\beta$, $H\gamma$, and $H\delta$ are strongest in class A2. These are Balmer lines of hydrogen, arising from the level $n = 2$. The electron must therefore be raised to this level before absorption of a Balmer line can occur. Atmospheres earlier than A2, however, are so hot that hydrogen becomes ionized and is no longer capable of producing these lines.

B. As a second example, we can check whether the various levels of ionization occurring for different elements in any one spectral class are mutually consistent. In a first approximation, we may consider only the conditions at a representative level in the atmosphere, which we take as the level where $T = T_{\text{eff}}$. Then, since both the temperature and the electron pressure are common to all the constituents of the gas, the Saha equation (3-25) shows that the degree of ionization is determined by the ionization potential. (The effect of the partition functions may here be neglected.) Therefore, an ion of an element that has lost q electrons will occur simultaneously with an ion of another element that has lost s electrons if the qth ionization potential of the first is about the same as the sth ionization potential of the second (and the temperature is not high enough to activate the next stage of ionization). Table 5-2 lists some of the ions present in the various spectral classes, together with the ionization potential of the preceding stage that produced the given ion. We have enclosed H II in parentheses to indicate that hydrogen

Table 5-2 Ionization and Spectral Class. Each number is the ionization potential in electron volts for the *preceding* stage of ionization, which produces the ion designated.

SPECTRAL CLASS	ION AND IONIZATION POTENTIAL					
O	He II	C III	N III	O III	Si IV	
	25	24	30	35	33	
B	(H II)	C II	N II	O II	Si III	Fe III
	14	11	15	14	16	16
A–M	Mg II Ca II	Ti II	Cr II		Si II	Fe II
	8 6	7	7		8	8

first becomes significantly ionized in spectral class B although, of course, the bare proton cannot produce any spectral lines. Table 5-2 shows that a temperature increase is needed toward earlier spectral classes in order to activate the successively higher ionization potentials.

C. In the third example, we calculate for various temperatures the fraction of all hydrogen (atoms plus ions) that is capable of absorbing in the Balmer lines. We then compare the results with the observed strengths of the Balmer lines in the atmospheres of main-sequence stars for which the effective temperatures correspond to the temperatures on our list.

The fraction that we seek is the number of neutral atoms excited to the second level divided by the total number of hydrogen atoms and ions. In the notation of Chapter 3, this is

$$\frac{N_{I,2}}{N_I + N_{II}},$$

which can be expressed as the product of two terms, one concerned with excitation and the other with ionization:

$$\frac{N_{I,2}}{N_I + N_{II}} = \frac{N_{I,2}}{N_I}\frac{N_I}{N_I + N_{II}}. \tag{5-22}$$

These factors are computed from the Boltzmann and Saha equations and are already computed for several temperatures in Tables 3-3 and 3-5. Actually, Table 3-3 gives $N_{I,2}/N_{I,1}$, but the example in Section 2 of Chapter 3 shows that this is very nearly equal to $N_{I,2}/N_I$; that is, the vast majority of the atoms remain in the ground state at these temperatures. In Table 3-5, an electron pressure $P_e = 10$ dynes cm^{-2} was assumed, and we shall modify this table for $P_e = 100$ dynes cm^{-2}, which is more typical for the main sequence as a whole. We shall neglect the variation of P_e with spectral type, since the general results will not be seriously affected. Better values would be $P_e = 1000$ dyne cm^{-2} as representative of the atmospheres of the hottest stars, and $P_e = 1$ or 10 for the cooler stars.

The results are given in Fig. 5-5, which also shows the observed strengths of the Balmer lines. [The vertical scale of the latter curve has been expanded by a factor $\frac{5}{2}$, because theory shows that the strength of these lines is proportional to the $\frac{2}{5}$ power of the number of absorbing atoms (see Sections 3-2 and 3-3). It is only for weak lines that a direct proportion occurs.]

D. As a final example, we refer to Fig. 5-6, in which the strengths of lines of certain other atoms and ions are similarly plotted. In each case, a curve representing a higher degree of ionization is displaced toward the earlier spectral classes as compared with a curve for lower ionization.

The four examples we have given all verify the statement that changes in the temperature are the principal cause of the changes in the spectrum along the spectral sequence.

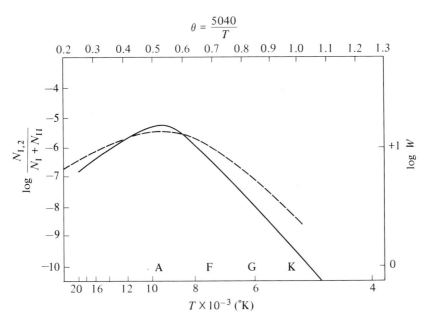

$$\theta = \frac{5040}{T}$$

Fig. 5-5 The Strengths of the Balmer Lines and the Number of Atoms Producing Them. The *solid curve* and the *left-hand ordinate* give the fraction of all hydrogen that is capable of absorbing the Balmer lines, $\log_{10} [N_{1,2}/(N_I + N_{II})]$ computed for constant $P_e = 100$ dyne cm^{-2}. The *dashed curve* and the *right-hand ordinate* give the observed strengths of these lines, expressed as log (equivalent width); see Sections 3-2 and 3-3. [Adapted from L. H. Aller, *Astrophsics: The Atmospheres of the Sun and Stars*, 1st ed. Copyright © 1953, The Ronald Press Company, New York.]

3-2 EQUIVALENT WIDTH

In the preceding discussions, we have spoken of line strength, meaning a combination of blackness (or depth of a line) and width, without being precise. We now define a measure of line strength that can be established numerically. Either intensity or flux can be used in this definition; however, since intensity cannot be observed for most stars (see Chapter 2, Section 1-1), we adopt the definition involving the flux. We define the *equivalent width* W_λ as the width in Ångströms that a line would have if it were completely black, if it had a rectangular profile, and if the energy subtracted by this equivalent line were the same as that subtracted by the actual line (Fig. 5-7). Thus,

$$\text{total energy in line} = W_\lambda \times (\text{height of continuum})$$

$$W_\lambda = \frac{\int_{\text{line}} (F_{\lambda_c} - F_\lambda) \, d\lambda}{F_{\lambda_c}}$$

$$= \int_{\text{line}} \left(1 - \frac{F_\lambda}{F_{\lambda_c}}\right) d\lambda. \qquad (5\text{-}23)$$

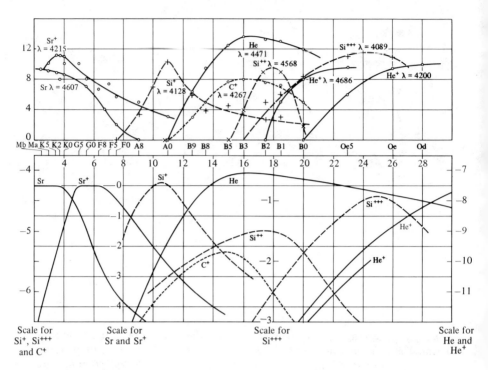

Fig. 5-6   The Strengths of Selected Lines along the Spectral Sequence.

Upper diagram: The variations of the observed intensities with spectral type. The abscissae are obtained from the Henry Draper Catalogue. The ordinates are expressed on an arbitrary scale.

Lower diagram: The computed values of the logarithms of the fractional concentrations, assuming $P_e = 131$ dyne cm^{-2}. The temperature scale is expressed in units of 10^3 °K and is adjusted to the abscissa of the upper diagram so as to obtain the best fit of the maxima of the corresponding curves. [After C. H. Payne, 1924, (231), p. 3.]

3-3 THE CURVE OF GROWTH*

The strength of an absorption line increases as the number of atoms or ions producing it increases, but the mathematical relationship is not always a simple one; a beam of radiation may encounter more particles that are capable of absorbing at a given frequency than there are photons in the beam at that frequency. A *curve of growth* is a graphical representation of the relationship, giving the logarithm of the equivalent width as a function of the logarithm of the number of absorbing atoms times the oscillator strength, that is, log W_λ vs. log N^*f. The quantity N^* may represent the number of

_____
* This section is not essential to the succeeding material.

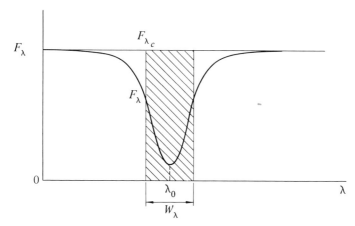

Fig. 5-7   The Equivalent Width of a Line. The equivalent width W_λ is the width of the rectangular profile for which the height is F_{λ_c} and the area is that of the spectral line. (I_λ may also be used to define the equivalent width.)

absorbing atoms above each cm^2 of the photosphere (if the Schuster–Schwarzschild model is assumed) or the number of absorbing atoms per gram of stellar matter. Actually, there may be multiplicative factors to W_λ or N^*f corresponding to the formula for W_λ in any given case, and the use of logarithms permits various such curves to be compared with a difference only in their zero points.

Fig. 5-8   Profiles of the K Line of Ca II at 3933 Å. Calculated for the Schuster–Schwarzschild model, with pure scattering and pure radiation damping. The number of ions producing the line is the number of ions above 1 cm^2 of the photosphere. In each case shown, the number of ions is taken as a multiple of 3.4×10^{11} ions, the factors being 1, 10, 10^2, 10^3, 10^4, 10^5, respectively, from the weakest to the strongest line. [After L. H. Aller, *Astrophysics: The Atmospheres of the Sun and Stars*, 2nd ed. Copyright © 1963, The Ronald Press Company, New York.]

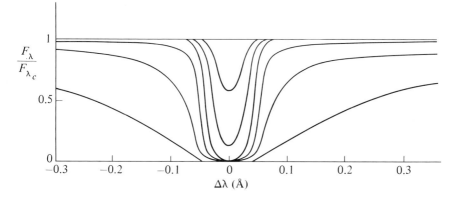

If we are able to control the number of atoms participating in a given transition, as in a laboratory source, or if we can calculate the line profile theoretically, we can obtain a curve of growth for a single spectral line. Figure 5-8 shows the theoretical profile of the K line of ionized calcium, at 3933 Å, for increasing numbers of absorbing ions. When the number of absorbers is small, the line is shallow and broadened principally by the Doppler effect. Since the peak of the Maxwellian distribution for velocity components is at zero velocity, the greatest absorption is at zero Doppler shift, corresponding to the center of the line. If the number of absorbers is increased but remains small by comparison with the number of photons, the energy absorbed at any wavelength within the line is increased in direct proportion to the number of absorbers. There is little augmentation of the width, and hence the area of the profile also increases proportionately, and $W_\lambda \propto N^*$. A further increase in the number of ions brings a slower increase in the depth of the line and in the equivalent width, since there are more ions than there are photons to be absorbed. When the line center at last becomes black, additional ions can have no further effect on the line center. By this time, however, there are many ions capable of absorbing at great distances from the line center, due to radiation and possibly collision damping, and broad wings are produced. For strong lines, $W_\lambda \propto \sqrt{N^* f (\Gamma_{\mathrm{rad}} + \Gamma_{\mathrm{coll}})}$. Figure 5-9 displays the variation of W_λ with N^*.

In the stellar atmosphere, N^* cannot be varied arbitrarily; but we can ob-

Fig. 5-9 The Curve of Growth. A curve of growth is plotted for the K line of Ca II. The *lower curve*, for pure radiation damping, corresponds to the profiles of Fig. 5-6. The *upper curve* includes collisional damping. [After L. H. Aller, *Astrophysics: The Atmospheres of the Sun and Stars*, 2nd ed. Copyright © 1963, The Ronald Press Company, New York.]

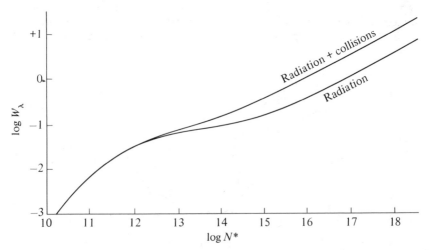

tain a curve of growth from the lines of a multiplet that have the same value of N^*, which is proportional to the number of atoms or ions in the lower level of the transition. Since these have different values of f, it is possible to determine N^* by plotting log W_λ against log f for the lines of the multiplet and overlaying these points upon a curve in which theoretically calculated or experimentally measured values of log W_λ are plotted against log N^*f. A comparison of the abscissae at once gives log N^*.

In this manner, the populations of the various excited states can be determined, and the Boltzmann equation then gives the excitation temperature. Similarly, when the numbers of ions in various stages of ionization have been found, the Saha equation determines the ionization temperature and also the electron pressure. The temperatures found from these equations will not necessarily agree with one another or with the effective temperature, because there may be departures from local thermodynamic equilibrium.

PROBLEMS

1. Show that eq. (5-3) reduces to the electron-scattering formula (which is independent of frequency) for $\nu \gg \nu_0$ and to the Rayleigh scattering formula (which depends on ν^3 or $1/\lambda^3$) for $\nu \ll \nu_0$.

2. What is the equivalent width of a line profile that is idealized as a triangle for which the base (at the continuum) extends for 2 Å and for which the apex is at a depth of one-half the intensity of the continuum?

3. Verify the general behavior of the curve for Si^+ in Fig. 5-6, making use of the model atmospheres of Chapter 4.

PART THREE

STELLAR INTERIORS

Direct observation of the conditions and processes in stellar interiors is not possible, and these must be deduced from the observable properties of stars and from physical laws. The observable properties include the absolute magnitudes and color indices of a substantially large number of stars, and the mass, radius, and luminosity of a small number of binary components and of the Sun. Additional checks on the theory are afforded by pulsating stars and by binary systems in which the line of aspides, that is, the major axis of the orbit, slowly rotates. These phenomena depend upon the internal conditions and hence hold clues for the theory of the interior. Recently it has become possible to measure the flux of neutrinos arriving at the Earth from the Sun, and this affords a test of our notions concerning the nuclear processes occurring in the deep interior. The interpretation of the data, however, is still doubtful. Information about the chemical composition of stellar atmospheres is provided spectroscopically, and it is presumed that the composition of much of the interior is like that of the atmosphere in the case of main-sequence stars. Giants, however, have already transmuted some of the atoms originally present in their deep interiors into different elements, and the spectroscopic data cannot give full information about the internal composition. Furthermore, it must be remembered that the amount of helium is difficult to measure, and therefore the parameters X, Y, and Z (respectively, the fractions by mass of hydrogen, helium, and all other elements collectively) are not really known. The value of X is apt to be in the range 60 to 90 per cent and Z only a few per cent or less.

The physical laws to be applied include various expressions of equilibrium and statements of various processes that will occur under given conditions. From these it is possible to compute *model stellar interiors*, which tabulate the pressure, temperature, density, mass, and net rate of energy flow as functions of distance from the stellar center, as well as specifying what processes are occurring at any layer. Depending on the specific problem, the chemical composition can either be assumed at the outset or determined as one of the results of the computed model.

In Chapter 6, we set forth the equations that are needed to calculate model interiors, but their detailed solution is explained in Part Four. Chapter 7 summarizes some of the results of such computations for various stages in the history of a star.

6

THE EQUATIONS FOR THE STELLAR INTERIOR

In this chapter, we derive the differential equations that govern the equilibrium of a fluid body that is held together by its own gravitation. It will be assumed that there is no rotation or magnetic field and that the star is spherically symmetrical. Furthermore, it will be supposed that any evolutionary changes occur so slowly that the star may be considered to be in equilibrium at any time.

1 THE MASS DISTRIBUTION AND THE PRESSURE GRADIENT

1-1 THE EQUATION OF CONTINUITY OF MASS

An immediate requirement is that the mass of any thin shell concentric with the stellar center must equal the volume of the shell multiplied by the density of the material it contains. If we let

r = distance from the stellar center,

M_r = mass contained in a sphere of radius r,

ρ = density at distance r from the center,

then the mass of the shell, whose thickness is dr, is

$$dM_r = 4\pi r^2 \rho \, dr.$$

This provides the first of our differential equations,

$$\frac{dM_r}{dr} = 4\pi r^2 \rho, \tag{6-1}$$

which is called the *equation of continuity of mass*. It cannot be solved without further information, because $\rho(r)$ is unknown.

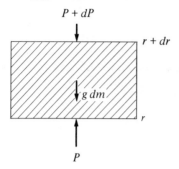

Fig. 6-1 The Forces on an Element of Matter. The element has mass dm, thickness dr, and cross-sectional area $d\sigma$ perpendicular to the plane of the figure. For equilibrium, the forces must be in balance.

1-2 THE EQUATION OF HYDROSTATIC EQUILIBRIUM

A second relation involving M_r and ρ is obtained from consideration of mechanical equilibrium. Consider, as in Fig. 6-1, an element of the thin shell of radius r, thickness dr, and area $d\sigma$ in a plane perpendicular to that of the figure. Then, if

P = pressure at distance r from the center

and

g = gravitational acceleration at distance r from the center ($g > 0$),

the requirement that the downward and upward forces on the element be in balance can be written as

$$(P + dP)\, d\sigma + g\, dm - P\, d\sigma = 0$$

or

$$dP\, d\sigma = -g\, dm.$$

The mass dm is the density multiplied by the volume,

$$dm = \rho\, dr\, d\sigma,$$

and the gravitational acceleration is

$$g = \frac{GM_r}{r^2},$$

where G is the gravitational constant. We shall demonstrate that the mass outside the sphere of radius r has no effect on computing g. The differential equation then becomes

$$\frac{dP}{dr} = -\frac{GM_r}{r^2}\, \rho. \tag{6-2}$$

This is called the *equation of hydrostatic equilibrium*.

We now show that we can neglect the mass exterior to radius r by considering the effect of an arbitrary thin shell at some radius larger than r. Let us draw a cone of two nappes (i.e., a double cone) with its apex at the position of an element of matter of mass dm and its axis in an arbitrary direction (see Fig. 6-2). Let the two nappes intersect the shell at distances D_1 and D_2 from dm, defining elements of mass dm_1 and dm_2. Then the gravitational forces exerted by these masses on dm are

$$F_1 = \frac{G\,dm_1}{D_1{}^2}\,dm$$

and

$$F_2 = \frac{G\,dm_2}{D_2{}^2}\,dm.$$

But dm_1 and dm_2 are proportional to the areas of the intersections of the cone and shell, hence

$$\frac{dm_1}{D_1{}^2} = \frac{dm_2}{D_2{}^2}$$

and

$$F_1 = F_2.$$

Since these act in opposite directions, there is no net force on dm. The remainder of the shell will similarly produce no net effect on dm, nor will any

Fig. 6-2   A Cone of Two Nappes Intersecting a Thin Spherical Shell. The apex of the cone is located at an element of matter for which the mass is dm, and the position interior to the shell is arbitrary. The volumes defined by the intersections of the cone and shell contain masses dm_1 and dm_2, and the distances of these elemental volumes from the apex, measured along the axis of the cone, are D_1 and D_2, respectively. The two masses exert equal and opposite forces on dm.

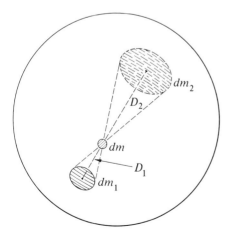

other shell of radius greater than r. It follows that only the mass M_r contributes to the gravitational acceleration at r.

1-3 THE MEAN MOLECULAR WEIGHT

Both the pressure and density appear in the equation of hydrostatic equilibrium (6-2). Under the conditions prevailing in many stellar interiors, the two are related by the perfect gas law, eq. (4-3):

$$P = \frac{k}{\mu H} \rho T.$$

Anticipating the result that the temperature in a stellar interior is high, we now obtain formulae for the mean molecular weight in the case that the material is completely ionized.

Since A_z is the average atomic mass per free particle, we may simply divide the total masses of all the particles in a sample of the material by the number of free particles in the sample. Each atom contributes one nucleus and z electrons, giving

$$\mu = \frac{\sum N_z A_z}{\sum N_z (1 + z)}.$$

The relation, however, can be more conveniently expressed in terms of the abundances of the various elements by mass rather than by number. Let us consider a sample of the stellar material and write

$$\frac{1}{\mu H} = \frac{\text{number of free particles in sample}}{\text{mass of sample}}.$$

Without losing generality, we may consider a single gram of the stellar matter. Then, if z = atomic number of an element, we have

$$\frac{1}{\mu H} = \text{number of free particles per gram of matter}$$

$$= \sum_z \frac{\text{number of free particles from atom } z}{\text{grams of element } z} \cdot \frac{\text{grams of element } z}{\text{gram of matter}}.$$

The last factor describes the chemical composition and may be denoted by

X_z = fraction (by mass) of element z in the stellar material.

The first factor may be expressed in terms of

n_z = number of nuclei of element z per gram of element z,

A_z = atomic weight of element z,

$A_z H$ = number of grams per nucleus z,

where H is the mass of 1 AMU.* Thus we have

$$\frac{1}{\mu} = \sum_z \frac{(1 + z)}{A_z} X_z \qquad \text{(complete ionization)}. \qquad (6\text{-}3)$$

Unless a star has already reached an advanced state of evolution, Z is only a few per cent or less. This fact permits us to make an approximation. The atomic weight of a heavy element (that is, of an element heavier than helium) is about twice the atomic number, and it is sufficient to set

$$\frac{1 + z}{A_z} \approx \frac{1}{2}$$

for $z > 2$. Following conventional notation, we may now write

$$Z = \sum_{z > 3} X_z = \text{fraction (by mass) of elements heavier than helium in the material,}$$

and also

$X =$ fraction (by mass) of hydrogen in the material,

$Y =$ fraction (by mass) of helium in the material.

Finally, rounding the values of A_z for hydrogen and helium to integers, we arrive at the simplified result

$$\mu = \frac{1}{2X + \frac{3}{4}Y + \frac{1}{2}Z} \qquad \text{(complete ionization)}. \qquad (6\text{-}4)$$

The value of H in the perfect gas law, when used with this expression for μ, should be that of the hydrogen atom if the gas consists predominantly of this element. We note also that μ has only a small range, between $\frac{1}{2}$ for pure hydrogen and 2 for pure heavy elements.

1-4 ESTIMATE OF THE PRESSURES AND TEMPERATURES IN THE SUN

The equation of hydrostatic equilibrium can be integrated in an approximate way to give an estimate of the pressures that may be expected in stellar interiors. Let us evaluate the pressure P_m at the mid-radius of the Sun, taking the integral of eq. (6-2) from the surface to the shell at one-half the

---

* If hydrogen is the principal constituent of the material and if its atomic weight is taken as 1 rather than as 1.008, then the perfect gas law will be more accurate if H is set equal to the mass of the hydrogen atom rather than 1 AMU.

total radius R. We shall assume that the density is constant throughout the Sun and therefore equal to its observed mean value. Then

$$M_r = \tfrac{4}{3}\pi r^3 \bar{\rho},$$

and

$$P_m - P_R = -G\tfrac{4}{3}\pi\bar{\rho}^2 \int_R^{(1/2)R} r\, dr$$

$$= \frac{\pi G}{2} \bar{\rho}^2 R^2.$$

Substituting

$$\bar{\rho} = 1.4 \text{ gm cm}^{-3},$$

$$R = 7 \times 10^{10} \text{ cm},$$

$$P_R = 0,$$

we find

$$P_m = 1 \times 10^{15} \text{ dyne cm}^{-2}$$

$$= 1 \times 10^9 \text{ atm.}$$

The Sun is composed chiefly of hydrogen, so the mean molecular weight may be taken as approximately $\tfrac{1}{2}$. The temperature T_m at $\tfrac{1}{2}R$ is then

$$T_m = \frac{\mu H}{k} \frac{P_m}{\bar{\rho}}$$

$$= 4 \times 10^6 \, ^\circ\text{K.}$$

The pressure and temperature computed in this simple way have given us, in this case, the correct order of magnitude for these quantities; one particular model solar interior has*

$$P_m = 0.6 \times 10^{15} \text{ dyne cm}^{-2}$$

$$T_m = 3 \times 10^6 \, ^\circ\text{K.}$$

Had we integrated between the surface and center, however, the discrepancies between our estimates and the values from the model would have been much greater.

1-5 THE LANE-EMDEN EQUATION

Let us examine the two differential equations obtained so far. They contain three dependent variables: P, M_r, and ρ. If we had one more equation containing only these quantities, and perhaps also the independent variable r, it would be possible to solve the system. The perfect gas law does not fulfill

---

* Model calculated by R. Weymann and tabulated by M. Schwarzschild, 1958 (50), p. 259.

our purpose, since it introduces the temperature; we should then have one more equation, but also one more dependent variable. A possibility is provided by the polytropic law

$$P = \mathcal{K}\rho^{\gamma}, \tag{6-5}$$

where $\mathcal{K}$ and γ are constants. This law can be used with high accuracy when convection is present in the deep interior or, with lower accuracy, for convection in the outer layers. Another way to obtain a relation of the form (6-5) under certain restricted conditions was given by Eddington, but it is now chiefly of historical interest. We shall describe his method in Chapter 10, Section 4. For the present, let us assume a law of the form (6-5) and discuss the solution based upon it.

The problem, then, is to solve the following system of three equations containing three unknowns:

$$\frac{dP}{dr} = -\frac{GM_r}{r^2}\rho$$

$$\frac{dM_r}{dr} = 4\pi r^2 \rho$$

$$P = \mathcal{K}\rho^{\gamma}.$$

It is convenient to combine these into a single equation of the second order. We begin by writing the first equation as

$$\frac{r^2}{\rho}\frac{dP}{dr} = -GM_r$$

and then differentiating with respect to r:

$$\frac{d}{dr}\left(\frac{r^2}{\rho}\frac{dP}{dr}\right) = -G\frac{dM_r}{dr}.$$

Substitution for dM_r/dr then gives

$$\frac{1}{r^2}\frac{d}{dr}\left(\frac{r^2}{\rho}\frac{dP}{dr}\right) = -4\pi G\rho.$$

Next we replace P by $\mathcal{K}\rho^{\gamma}$:

$$\frac{\mathcal{K}}{r^2}\frac{d}{dr}\left[\frac{r^2}{\rho}\frac{d(\rho^{\gamma})}{dr}\right] = -4\pi G\rho. \tag{6-6}$$

This contains only one dependent variable, ρ, and could be integrated numerically upon specification of the boundary conditions and the values of $\mathcal{K}$ and γ.

If the equations are valid for the stellar center, the appropriate boundary conditions are

$$\rho = \rho_c$$

and

$$\left.\frac{d\rho}{dr}\right|_c = 0, \tag{6-7}$$

where the subscript c denotes the center. The latter condition arises in the following way. At the center, the acceleration due to gravity,

$$g = \frac{GM_r}{r^2},$$

equals zero since a mass particle placed at the center would experience no acceleration. Thus, according to eq. (6-2),

$$\left.\frac{dP}{dr}\right|_c = 0,$$

and differentiation of eq. (6-5) gives

$$\frac{dP}{dr} = \mathcal{K}\gamma\rho^{\gamma-1}\frac{d\rho}{dr}.$$

Hence the gradient of the density must also be zero at the stellar center.

A separate solution would be required for each set of the parameters $\mathcal{K}$, γ, and ρ_c; but a transformation of the variables permits the solution to be standardized so that only γ, or rather $n = (\gamma - 1)^{-1}$, appears as a parameter. Let us introduce the *Emden variables*:

$$\xi = \frac{r}{\alpha} \tag{6-8}$$

$$\theta = \frac{T}{T_c}, \tag{6-9}$$

where α is at present unspecified and T_c is the central temperature. (We shall consider only those cases in which the polytropic solution is applicable at the center of the star.) The constant α will later be chosen in such a way that its dimensions are those of length, and ξ and θ will then be dimensionless quantities that are proportional to the radius and temperature, respectively, at any point.

To effect the change of variables, let us first express ρ as a function of ξ or θ. We have

$$\frac{\rho}{\rho_c} = \left(\frac{P}{P_c}\right)^{1/\gamma}$$

$$= \left(\frac{\rho T}{\rho_c T_c}\right)^{1/\gamma}$$

by the perfect gas law, if μ is constant. Then

$$\left(\frac{\rho}{\rho_c}\right)^{1-1/\gamma} = \left(\frac{T}{T_c}\right)^{1/\gamma} = \theta^{1/\gamma}$$

and

$$\rho = \rho_c \theta^{1/(\gamma-1)}.$$

If we now let*

$$n = \frac{1}{\gamma - 1},$$ (6-10)

we get

$$\rho = \rho_c \theta^n.$$ (6-11)

The new parameter n is called the *polytropic index*.
We note parenthetically that the perfect gas law yields

$$P = P_c \theta^{n+1}.$$ (6-11A)

Substituting the expression (11) into the differential equation (6-6) and also using

$$\gamma = 1 + \frac{1}{n},$$

we obtain

$$\frac{\mathscr{K}}{(\alpha\xi)^2} \frac{d}{d(\alpha\xi)} \left\{ \frac{(\alpha\xi)^2}{\rho_c \theta^n} \frac{d[(\rho_c \theta^n)^{1 + 1/n}]}{d(\alpha\xi)} \right\} = -4\pi G \rho_c \theta^n.$$

Then, since

$$\frac{d}{d\xi} \theta^{n+1} = (n + 1)\theta^n \frac{d\theta}{d\xi},$$

we find

$$\frac{(n+1)\mathscr{K}\rho_c^{(1/n)-1}}{4\pi G\alpha^2} \frac{1}{\xi^2} \frac{d}{d\xi}\left(\xi^2 \frac{d\theta}{d\xi}\right) = -\theta^n.$$ (6-12)

The scale factor α had been left unspecified. We may now define it at our convenience, and we do so in such a way as to make the constant factor in eq. (6-12) equal to unity:

$$\alpha = \left[\frac{(n+1)\mathscr{K}\rho_c^{(1/n)-1}}{4\pi G} \right]^{1/2},$$ (6-13)

which has dimensions of length. The differential equation then becomes

$$\frac{1}{\xi^2} \frac{d}{d\xi}\left(\xi^2 \frac{d\theta}{d\xi}\right) = -\theta^n.$$ (6-14)

This is the *Lane–Emden equation*. The boundary conditions at the center are

$$\theta = 1 \quad \text{and} \quad \frac{d\theta}{d\xi} = 0 \quad \text{at} \quad \xi = 0.$$ (6-15)

The Lane–Emden equation can be solved analytically for $n = 0$, 1, and 5. However, the solutions that will be of interest here require $n = 1.5$ or 3; and, for these, numerical integration is necessary. Published solutions for these

* See Section 4-4 for the general definition of n.

and other values of n are available. Tables for the cases $n = 1.5$ and 3 are given in Chapter 10, where their application to specific stellar models is illustrated.

We next show how to express the mass as a function of ξ. We have

$$M_r = \int_0^r 4\pi r^2 \rho \, dr$$

$$M(\xi) = \int_0^{\alpha\xi} 4\pi(\alpha\xi')^2 \rho_c \theta^n \, d(\alpha\xi')$$

$$= 4\pi\alpha^3 \rho_c \int_0^\xi \xi'^2 \theta^n \, d\xi',$$

where ξ' is used for the variable of integration.*

The integrand can be replaced by means of the Lane–Emden equation:

$$M(\xi) = 4\pi\alpha^3 \rho_c \int_0^\xi -\frac{d}{d\xi'}\left(\xi'^2 \frac{d\theta}{d\xi'}\right) d\xi'$$

$$= 4\pi\alpha^3 \rho_c \left[-\xi'^2 \frac{d\theta}{d\xi'}\right]_0^\xi$$

$$= 4\pi\alpha^3 \rho_c \left(-\xi^2 \frac{d\theta}{d\xi}\right). \qquad (6\text{-}16)$$

The function $(-\xi^2 \, d\theta/d\xi)$ is listed among the tabulated solutions.

In Chapter 10, it will be seen how the pressure, density, temperature, and mass distribution can be obtained as functions of radius within a polytropic region by scaling the tabulated quantities. It will also be shown how a first approximation to the values of these physical variables can be found throughout the entire star in certain cases.

2 THE RADIATIVE TEMPERATURE GRADIENT (RADIATIVE EQUILIBRIUM)

In those regions of a star in which the $P(\rho)$ relationship expressed in eq. (6-5) is not valid, an alternative law, such as the perfect gas law, must be used. In general, the temperature is thus introduced as an additional variable. The system of equations we have derived thus far,

$$\frac{dP}{dr} = -\frac{GM_r}{r^2} \rho$$

$$\frac{dM_r}{dr} = 4\pi r^2 \rho$$

$$P = \frac{k}{\mu H} \rho T,$$

---

* Note the change in the upper limit of the last equation. We have done more than merely take the constants outside the integral; we have changed the variable of integration, and the limits of the integral must be changed accordingly.

cannot be solved without a fourth equation involving the four dependent variables and the independent variable. We therefore seek another relation, which can be provided by an expression for the temperature gradient.

The equation for the temperature gradient depends upon the mode by which energy is transferred from the hotter to the cooler regions. In this section, we consider the case in which radiation alone transfers energy from one place to another, while in Section 4, the transfer of energy by convection will be discussed. In the present situation, then, we are concerned with *radiative equilibrium*: each element of matter re-radiates as much energy as it receives and adds to this whatever energy has been generated within the element.

First we demonstrate that conditions in the stellar interior permit the simplifying assumption of *local thermodynamic equilibrium*, in which a unique temperature characterizes the velocity distribution of the particles and the intensity of the radiation as a function of frequency. An important consequence of local thermodynamic equilibrium is that the radiation field approximates that of a black body, so that the intensity may, with caution, be replaced by the Planck function.

In strict thermodynamic equilibrium, the matter and radiation within a volume would behave as if enclosed in a container maintained at constant temperature. In such a container, all processes would reach equilibrium with one another and would proceed at rates determined by the prevailing temperature. In a stellar interior, there are no containing walls, but both particles and photons are much hampered in their movements. The distance over which a particle or photon is likely to travel before collision or absorption is small in comparison with the distance over which the temperature changes appreciably. Under these conditions, we have *local thermodynamic equilibrium*.

Let us make some very approximate calculations of the distances over which particles and photons may be expected to travel at the mid-radius of the Sun. First we find the likelihood that a particle will collide with another while moving through a distance of 1 cm. Consider the total target area within a 1-cm cube. If the gas consists entirely of ionized hydrogen, each nucleus and electron has a radius of 2×10^{-13} cm. Therefore,

$$\text{area per particle} = 10^{-25} \text{ cm}^2$$

and, since the density is about 1 gm cm^{-3},

$$\text{number of particles per cm}^3 \sim \frac{\rho}{H} = 10^{24} \text{ cm}^{-3}.$$

Then

$$\text{total target area (in 1 cm}^3) = \text{area per particle}$$
$$\times \text{ number of particles (in 1 cm}^3)$$

$$\sim 0.1 \text{ cm}^2.$$

This result means that, if the target areas were all projected onto the face of the cube, 0.1 of the 1 cm² area would be blocked. There is only a fair chance, therefore, that a nucleus or electron impinging upon this cube would suffer a collision. However, 10^2 such cubes, or a 1-meter column, would almost certainly be sufficient to halt the advance of the particle.

To answer the question whether the particles behave as if enclosed at constant temperature, we must know whether the temperature changes appreciably over the distance of 1 meter. At the mid-radius of the Sun, the temperature gradient is about the same as the mean value for the Sun, 10^{-3} °K m^{-1}. The latter value is found by dividing the central temperature by the total radius, since the surface temperature is approximately zero; this gives 2×10^7 °K$/7 \times 10^{10}$ cm. The temperature itself is of the order of 10^6 °K, hence the variation over 1 meter is negligible.*

To calculate how far a photon is likely to travel before being absorbed, we use eq. (2-15), taking mean values over frequency. With $\kappa \sim 1$ and $\rho \sim 1$, we find for a photon traveling radially that

$$\frac{dI}{I} \approx -dr.$$

Nearly all the radiation is absorbed if dr is 1 cm, a distance over which the temperature changes by only 10^{-5} °K. Hence both matter and radiation are, effectively, contained within a region at constant temperature, and local thermodynamic equilibrium prevails.

Let us now consider the equation of transfer, stated as eq. (2-24):

$$\frac{dI_\nu(\theta)}{dr} = j_\nu \rho \sec \theta - \kappa_\nu I_\nu(\theta) \rho \sec \theta. \tag{6-17}$$

The dependences on ν and θ are of no interest and can be eliminated by integration over these variables. To obtain integrals that can be readily interpreted, however, let us first multiply eq. (6-17) by $\cos^2 \theta / \kappa_\nu \rho$:

$$\frac{1}{\rho \kappa_\nu} \frac{d}{dr} I_\nu(\theta) \cos^2 \theta = \frac{j_\nu}{\kappa_\nu} \cos \theta - I_\nu(\theta) \cos \theta.$$

We now integrate over solid angle:

$$\frac{1}{\rho \kappa_\nu} \frac{d}{dr} \int_{\text{sphere}} I_\nu(\theta) \cos^2 \theta \, d\omega = \frac{j_\nu}{\kappa_\nu} \int_{\text{sphere}} \cos \theta \, d\omega - \int_{\text{sphere}} I_\nu \cos \theta \, d\omega. \tag{6-18}$$

The integral of $\cos \theta$ over a sphere is zero, hence the first term on the right vanishes. The second term on the right is the net flux F_ν. On the left of the

---

* Before proceeding, the reader should become familiar with Chapter 2, Sections 1-1, 1-3, 1-5, 2-1 (beginning), 2-2, and 3-1.

equation, we may set $I_\nu(\theta)$ equal to the Planck function $B_\nu(T)$. We then have

$$\frac{1}{\rho \kappa_\nu} \frac{d}{dr} B_\nu(T) \int_{\text{sphere}} \cos^2 \theta \, d\omega = -F_\nu. \tag{6-19}$$

Now the integral of $\cos^2 \theta$ over a sphere is $4\pi/3$, and if we write

$$\frac{d}{dr} B_\nu(T) = \frac{\partial B_\nu(T)}{\partial T} \frac{dT}{dr},$$

we find

$$\frac{4\pi}{3\rho \kappa_\nu} \frac{\partial B_\nu(T)}{\partial T} \frac{dT}{dr} = -F_\nu. \tag{6-20}$$

Integration over frequency then yields

$$\frac{4\pi}{3\rho} \frac{dT}{dr} \int_0^\infty \frac{1}{\kappa_\nu} \frac{\partial B_\nu(T)}{\partial T} = -F.$$

The net flux F may be expressed as

$$F = \frac{L_r}{4\pi r^2}, \tag{6-21}$$

where L_r is the net rate at which radiant energy flows across the sphere of radius r. Let us now define the *Rosseland mean absorption coefficient* $\bar\kappa$ from the relation

$$\frac{1}{\bar\kappa} \int_0^\infty \frac{\partial B_\nu(T)}{\partial T} \, d\nu = \int_0^\infty \frac{1}{\kappa_\nu} \frac{\partial B_\nu(T)}{\partial T} \, d\nu. \tag{6-22}$$

With the aid of eq. (1-9), we find

$$\int_0^\infty \frac{\partial B_\nu(T)}{\partial T} \, d\nu = \frac{d}{dT} B(T) = \frac{d}{dT} \left(\frac{\sigma}{\pi} T^4 \right)$$

$$= \frac{4\sigma}{\pi} T^3$$

$$= \frac{ac}{\pi} T^3, \tag{6-23}$$

where a is the radiation density constant. Therefore

$$\frac{dT}{dr} = -\frac{3}{4ac} \frac{\bar\kappa \rho}{T^3} \frac{L_r}{4\pi r^2}. \tag{6-24}$$

This is the final expression for the radiative temperature gradient. As may be expected, a large opacity (good insulation) permits a high temperature gradient to be maintained, while a high temperature gradient encourages a copious flow of energy, L_r.

Several remarks should be made concerning this derivation.

(i) The symbol L_r as introduced here describes the *radiative* energy flow, while in eq. (6-30) below, it refers to the *total* energy flow. This ambiguity is unfortunate but traditional. In practice, we shall not encounter any difficulty, because in our applications the flux will be carried either wholly by radiation or (almost) wholly by convection. The symbol L_r will therefore correctly denote the net amount of all energy transferred per second. We shall often call it the *net luminosity* at r.

(ii) In eq. (6-18), we replaced $I_\nu(\theta)$ by $B_\nu(T)$ on the left-hand side of the equation but not the right-hand side. On the left, $B_\nu(T)$ is multiplied by $\cos^2 \theta$ before integration, and the integrand is always positive. On the right, however, the factor $\cos \theta$ is negative for $\pi/2 \leqslant \theta \leqslant \pi$, and the integral of $B_\nu(T) \cos \theta$ would vanish. Thus there would be no *net* flux, and, consequently, no temperature gradient. In other words, $B_\nu(T)$ can be used to approximate the average intensity, but it cannot yield the *difference* of the outward and inward intensities.

(iii) The absorption coefficient κ_ν was transposed at the beginning of the derivation so as to be associated with $B_\nu(T)$ rather than the term that later yielded F_ν. The Rosseland mean coefficient that resulted from integration over frequency can be calculated for given ρ, T, and chemical composition without reference to a stellar interior. If, on the other hand, another function such as the flux F_ν had been used to define the mean, the numerical value of this weighting function would be unknown, and $\bar{\kappa}$ could not be evaluated.

(iv) It was tacitly assumed that j_ν is independent of θ. This is true for nuclear emission and spontaneous thermal emission but not for stimulated emission. If the latter is taken into account, the Rosseland mean coefficient contains the stimulated emission factor $(1 - e^{-h\nu/kT})$, for processes other than scattering:

$$\frac{1}{\bar{\kappa}} = \frac{\displaystyle\int_0^\infty \frac{1}{\kappa_\nu(1 - e^{-h\nu/kT})} \frac{\partial B_\nu(T)}{\partial T} \, d\nu}{\displaystyle\int_0^\infty \frac{\partial B_\nu(T)}{\partial T} \, d\nu}. \tag{6-25}$$

See Section 6-2A of Chapter 3.

(v) Equation (6-17) actually applies only to a plane-parallel stratification, while the curvature of the layers in a stellar *interior* is considerable. The correct expression for $dI_\nu(\theta)$ is

$$dI_\nu(\theta) = \frac{\partial I_\nu(\theta)}{\partial r} \, dr + \frac{\partial I_\nu(\theta)}{\partial \theta} \, d\theta. \tag{6-26}$$

In the derivation of dT/dr, however, the term arising from the variation with θ is approximately zero.*

---

* For an outline of the derivation taking into account the curvature of the layers, see M. Schwarzschild, 1958 (50), p. 38 et seq.

The opacity $\bar{\kappa}$ is discussed in Chapter 3, Sections 5 and 6. Tables 10-15 and 10-16 present some numerical data. Two relations that allow an approximate fit to tables giving $\bar{\kappa}$ as a function of ρ, T, and chemical composition at temperatures appropriate to a stellar interior are, from eqs. (3-58) and (3-59),

$$\bar{\kappa}_{bf} = 4.34 \times 10^{25} \frac{\bar{g}_{bf}}{t} Z(1 + X) \frac{\rho}{T^{3.5}} \qquad (6\text{-}27)$$

$$\bar{\kappa}_{ff} = 3.68 \times 10^{22} \bar{g}_{ff}(1 - Z)(1 + X) \frac{\rho}{T^{3.5}}, \qquad (6\text{-}28)$$

which are due to bound-free and free-free transitions, respectively. Bound-bound transitions can be important in the cooler regions, but no simple formula can be given. In addition, there is electron scattering, which is in any case independent of frequency. For this process, the coefficient is given by eq. (3-60):

$$\sigma_e = 0.20(1 + X). \qquad (6\text{-}29)$$

Equation (6-24) now provides an expression for the temperature gradient in radiative equilibrium. Unfortunately, by introducing L_r, we have momentarily been deflected from our original purpose of collecting enough equations to solve for the unknown variables. As we shall see, however, L_r can be expressed without involving any new independent variable.

3 THE GRADIENT OF THE NET LUMINOSITY (THERMAL EQUILIBRIUM)

If there are neither sources nor sinks of energy in the successive layers through which radiation is passing, then the same net amount of energy (integrated over frequency) must traverse each stratum per second. In this case, L_r must be constant. If, on the other hand, energy is being created in some shell, then this energy must be radiated away if conditions are to remain in equilibrium.

Consider Fig. 6-3 and let E_C be the energy created per second by nuclear reactions in the thin shell at radius r.* One-half of this energy flows outwards from the shell and one-half flows inwards. A net energy E per second, received from the layer below the shell, must necessarily leave the shell at its upper surface. Then the net energy flowing per second through the upper surface is $E + \frac{1}{2}E_C$, while that flowing through the lower surface per second is $E - \frac{1}{2}E_C$. The change in the net energy per second as it passes through the shell is therefore

$$dL_r = (E + \tfrac{1}{2}E_C) - (E - \tfrac{1}{2}E_C) = E_C.$$

---

* If there is gravitational contraction or expansion, this discussion and also eq. (6-30) require modification to account for the energy released or absorbed, respectively, in the process.

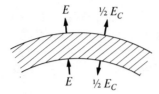

Fig. 6-3   The Net Rate of Energy Flow. In the absence of energy generation in a layer, the same net amount of energy E flows per second through the upper and lower boundaries. However, if energy E_C is created each second by nuclear reactions in the layer, then the net rate of energy flow through the upper surface is augmented by $\frac{1}{2}E_C$, while that through the lower surface is diminished by $\frac{1}{2}E_C$.

If we express the amount of energy E_C created per second as the energy ϵ created per second per gram multiplied by the number of grams in the shell, we get

$$dL_r = \epsilon \cdot dM_r$$

or

$$\frac{dL_r}{dr} = 4\pi r^2 \rho \epsilon \qquad (6\text{-}30)$$

by eq. (6-1). The energy-generation rate ϵ, often called the *energy-generation coefficient*, will later be expressed as a function of ρ, T, and the chemical composition (Section 5).

4 CONVECTION AND THE CONVECTIVE TEMPERATURE GRADIENT (CONVECTIVE EQUILIBRIUM)

There may be regions in a star where convection is maintained, bringing hot material upwards to cooler layers and thereby transferring energy outwards by mechanical means. The assumption of radiative equilibrium is no longer valid. The efficiency of convection as a means of transferring energy depends partly upon the number of particles that carry the energy and hence upon the density of the matter. In stellar atmospheres, where densities are low, radiation and convection together may carry the total flux. In stellar interiors, on the other hand, the densities may be high enough that convection accounts for virtually the entire flux.* It can be shown, furthermore, that in the deep interior and also in the outer regions of the star (but not too near the surface), the approximation that the temperature gradient equals the adiabatic gradient is a very good one.* In the discussions that follow, therefore, we shall make the assumptions that when convection occurs, it alone is

* See M. Schwarzschild, 1958 (50), p. 44 et seq.

responsible for essentially all the energy transfer and that adiabatic conditions prevail. Procedures that do not require these assumptions have been developed for convective envelopes, but they are not needed in the deep interior.

4-1 THE TRANSFER OF ENERGY BY CONVECTION

Let us first imagine a region in which a local density fluctuation causes some material to be buoyed upwards. We shall call this rising material a *convective element* or *cell*. As we shall see, the temperature inside the element remains higher than that of the immediate surroundings, and the particles comprising it therefore have a higher average kinetic energy than the particles in the surrounding material. This excess kinetic energy is released as the convective cell dissolves into the neighboring medium after traveling a distance, on the average, of one *mixing length l*. This length is usually expressed in terms of the *scale height H*, which is the distance over which the pressure or density, according to choice, varies by a factor of *e*. The mixing length is usually taken in the range 0.5 to 2.0 times the scale height:

$$0.5 \precsim l/H \precsim 2.0.$$

There must, of course, be descending material to compensate for that which is rising; and the descending matter, at lower temperature than its surroundings at any level, carries a deficiency of kinetic energy inwards. This has the same effect as transferring positive energy outwards, so that both inward and outward motions contribute to producing a flow of (positive) energy toward the surface of the star.

It should be stated that the theory of the convective process has not yet attained a high degree of sophistication, and even the qualitative description is not yet secure. Nevertheless, on the basis of the concepts we have described, we can obtain results that should be at least approximately correct.

In Section 4-2, we discuss the specific heats of a gas, in preparation for the derivation of the adiabatic gas law, the adiabatic temperature gradient, and the criterion for determining whether convection occurs in a given layer of the star.

4-2 SPECIFIC HEATS

The specific heat *C* of a gas is defined as the rate

$$C = \frac{dQ}{dT}$$

at which heat energy *dQ* must be added to the gas to produce a temperature change *dT*. In particular, we shall be concerned with the specific heats at constant pressure and at constant volume,

$$C_P = \frac{dQ}{dT}\Big|_P$$

$$C_V = \frac{dQ}{dT}\Big|_V.$$

As defined here, the specific heats depend upon the quantity of the gas, but our chief interest will lie in the ratio

$$\gamma = \frac{C_P}{C_V}. \tag{6-31}$$

Our goal in this section will be to obtain expressions for C_P and C_V and to evaluate γ numerically.

We make use of the first law of thermodynamics to relate the heat transferred to or from a system in terms of its physical properties:

$$dQ + dW_{on} = dU. \tag{6-32}$$

This expresses the fact that energy dQ imparted to a system in the form of heat, and mechanical work dW_{on} performed on the system, are transformed into an increase in the internal energy dU of the system. If we now transpose dW_{on} to the other side of the equation and let dW_{on} equal $-dW_{by}$, the negative work done *by* the system, we have

$$dQ = dU + dW_{by}. \tag{6-33}$$

The work performed by a convective cell during an expansion may be found by calculating the work done on a small area dA of the surface of the cell and then integrating over the entire surface. If the pressure inside the cell is P, and the walls are expanded through a distance dx, the work done on dA is

$$P\, dA\, dx.$$

Integration over the entire area of the cell yields

$$dW_{by} = PA\, dx$$

$$= P\, dV, \tag{6-34}$$

where dV is the change in the volume of the cell. Equation (6-33) can then be restated as

$$dQ = dU + P\, dV.$$

From this we find that

$$C_V = \frac{dU}{dT}. \tag{6-35}$$

The gases that we are concerned with are monatomic; that is, there are no molecules, although ions and electrons may be present. Therefore, there are no internal degrees of freedom, such as vibration of atoms within a molecule. For the time being, we confine our attention to the case where no energy is being consumed by ionization processes (the degree of ionization remaining fixed as the temperature varies).* The change in the internal energy then represents solely the change in the translatory energy of the particles. We have seen in eq. (3-40) that the mean kinetic energy per particle is $\frac{3}{2}kT$, and therefore the internal energy of a sample of gas containing N particles is

$$U = \tfrac{3}{2}kTN. \tag{6-36}$$

But

$$N = N_0 \sum_i \mathscr{N}_i = N_0 \mathscr{N},$$

where $\mathscr{N}_i$ is the number of moles of constituent i in the sample, $\mathscr{N}$ is the sum of these, and N_0 is Avogadro's number. Since N_0 can be written as the ratio of the gas constant $\mathscr{R}$ and Boltzmann's constant k, we have

$$U = \tfrac{3}{2}\mathscr{N}\mathscr{R}T,$$

which is a function of T only. From eq. (6-35), we then have

$$C_V = \tfrac{3}{2}\mathscr{N}\mathscr{R}. \tag{6-37}$$

The specific heat at constant pressure, C_P, is

$$C_P = \frac{dQ}{dT}\bigg|_P \tag{6-38}$$

$$= \frac{dU}{dT}\bigg|_P + P\frac{dV}{dT}\bigg|_P$$

$$= \tfrac{3}{2}\mathscr{N}\mathscr{R} + P\frac{dV}{dT}\bigg|_P .$$

The perfect gas law gives

$$P\frac{dV}{dT} + V\frac{dP}{dT} = \mathscr{N}\mathscr{R}, \tag{6-39}$$

hence

$$P\frac{dV}{dT}\bigg|_P = \mathscr{N}\mathscr{R}.$$

Therefore

$$C_P = \tfrac{5}{2}\mathscr{N}\mathscr{R}. \tag{6-40}$$

A useful relation between the two specific heats is

$$C_P = C_V + \mathscr{N}\mathscr{R}. \tag{6-41}$$

---

* More accurately, it is assumed that we are dealing with one of the nearly level portions of the ionization curve (cf. Fig. 3-4 or 3-5).

This relation shows that C_P is always greater than C_V; the process at constant pressure requires not only the heat necessary to produce the change in internal energy (temperature), but also the work to produce a change in volume.

The ratio of specific heats γ depends in part upon the condition of the gas. For a monatomic gas that is either completely ionized or completely neutral, eqs. (6-37) and (6-40) yield

$$\gamma = \tfrac{5}{3}. \tag{6-42}$$

If ionization processes are occurring in the gas, the energy required for ionization causes an increase in C_P and C_V. If the specific heats become very large, γ will approach unity:

$$\gamma = \frac{C_V + \mathcal{N}\mathcal{R}}{C_V}$$

$$\to 1.$$

4-3 THE ADIABATIC TEMPERATURE GRADIENT AND THE ADIABATIC GAS LAW

We now derive expressions for the temperature gradient and the gas law in the adiabatic case. Again we use the first law of thermodynamics, this time setting

$$dQ = 0$$

for an adiabatic process. Then

$$0 = dU + P \, dV$$

$$= \frac{dU}{dT} + P \frac{dV}{dT}$$

$$= C_V + \mathcal{N}\mathcal{R} - V\frac{dP}{dT}$$

by eqs. (6-35) and (6-39). Equation (6-41) gives

$$0 = C_P - V\frac{dP}{dT}. \tag{6-43}$$

But, by the perfect gas law,

$$V = \frac{\mathcal{N}\mathcal{R}T}{P}$$

$$= (C_P - C_V)\frac{T}{P},$$

so that eq. (6-43) yields

$$0 = C_P - (C_P - C_V)\frac{T}{P}\cdot\frac{dP}{dT}.$$

Separating the variables, we have

$$\frac{dT}{T} = \frac{C_P - C_V}{C_P}\frac{dP}{P}$$

$$= \left(1 - \frac{1}{\gamma}\right)\frac{dP}{P}, \tag{6-44}$$

and finally

$$\frac{d\log P}{d\log T} = \frac{d\ln P}{d\ln T} = \frac{\gamma}{\gamma - 1} \tag{6-45A}$$

$$= 2.5 \quad \text{if} \quad \gamma = \tfrac{5}{3}. \tag{6-45B}$$

The integrated form of this relation was already used in Section 1-5. Separation of the variables and integration from a pair of values (P_0, T_0) to any other pair (P, T), with primes denoting the variables of integration, gives

$$\int_{P_0}^{P} d\ln P' = \frac{\gamma}{\gamma - 1}\int_{T_0}^{T} d\ln T'$$

$$\ln P - \ln P_0 = \frac{\gamma}{\gamma - 1}\ln T - \frac{\gamma}{\gamma - 1}\ln T_0$$

$$\frac{P}{P_0} = \left(\frac{T}{T_0}\right)^{\gamma/(\gamma - 1)}$$

$$P = \mathcal{K}'T^{\gamma/(\gamma - 1)}, \tag{6-46}$$

where $\mathcal{K}'$ is a constant. It is useful to substitute ρ for T. From the perfect gas law, we get

$$\frac{P}{P_0} = \left(\frac{\rho_0}{P_0}\frac{P}{\rho}\right)^{\gamma/(\gamma - 1)},$$

if the mean molecular weight μ is constant. Rearranging this equation, we find

$$P^{1 - [\gamma/(\gamma - 1)]} = \text{const } \rho^{-[\gamma/(\gamma - 1)]}$$

$$P = \mathcal{K}\rho^{\gamma}, \tag{6-47}$$

where $\mathcal{K}$ is a constant. The feature to be noted is that this relation, called the *adiabatic gas law*, involves P and ρ but not T. We have already found in eq. (6-42) that $\gamma = \tfrac{5}{3}$ under the conditions of complete ionization in the deep interior, although in the regions near to the surface, the value is decreased.

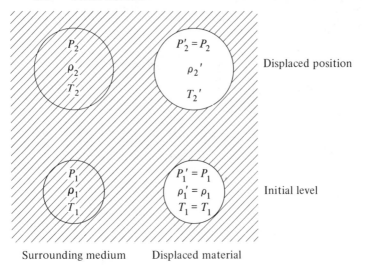

Surrounding medium   Displaced material

Fig. 6-4   The Criterion for Stability against Convection. A quantity of material displaced upwards continues to rise if its density is less than that of the surroundings. In this case, convection occurs. If the displaced material sinks back to its original position, the layer is stable against convection.

4-4 CONDITIONS FOR THE OCCURRENCE OF CONVECTION

We now seek a criterion by which we may determine whether radiative equilibrium prevails in a given layer. The fundamental question to be answered is whether an element of matter that has somehow been displaced vertically will continue to move in the same direction. If the motion is maintained, a convection current is produced; if the element returns to its original position, then the conditions are stable against convection, and radiative equilibrium is assured.*

The element in Fig. 6-4 will sink back to its initial position if it is heavier than a hypothetical element of the surrounding material having the same volume. Thus, if

$$\rho_2' > \rho_2, \tag{6-48}$$

the motion will be damped, and convection will be impossible.

It is more convenient to express the inequality in terms of the temperature gradient. Since the element will adjust its pressure to that of the surroundings, we have

$$P_2' = P_2,$$

---

* We are not discussing the case of degenerate matter, in which conduction is important.

which, together with the perfect gas law, leads to the requirement that

$$\rho_2 T_2 = \rho_2' T_2'.$$

Therefore, the inequality (6-48) requires that

$$T_2' < T_2$$

for stability against convection. If the temperature is decreasing in the outward direction,* the upward displacement of the element requires that

$$(T_1 - T_2') > (T_1 - T_2),$$

that is, the temperature in the moving element must decrease more rapidly than in the surroundings:

$$\left|\frac{dT}{dr}\right|_{\text{element}} > \left|\frac{dT}{dr}\right|_{\text{surroundings}}, \qquad (6\text{-}49\text{A})$$

or

$$\left.\frac{dT}{dr}\right|_{\text{element}} < \left.\frac{dT}{dr}\right|_{\text{surroundings}}. \qquad (6\text{-}49\text{B})$$

A third form of the stability criterion is expressed in terms of P rather than r. Since P decreases as r increases, the inequality (6-49B) can be written as

$$\left.\frac{dT}{dP}\right|_{\text{element}} > \left.\frac{dT}{dP}\right|_{\text{surroundings}};$$

or, taking the derivatives at level 1 and multiplying by P_1/T_1 (and then omitting the subscript), we have

$$\left.\frac{P}{T}\frac{dT}{dP}\right|_{\text{element}} > \left.\frac{P}{T}\frac{dT}{dP}\right|_{\text{surroundings}}.$$

This is the same as

$$\left.\frac{d\log T}{d\log P}\right|_{\text{element}} > \left.\frac{d\log T}{d\log P}\right|_{\text{surroundings}}.$$

The surroundings are in radiative equilibrium. If, then, no heat is transferred between the moving element and its surroundings, we can write (after inverting the derivatives and correspondingly changing the direction of the inequality)

$$\left.\frac{d\log P}{d\log T}\right|_{\text{adiabatic}} < \left.\frac{d\log P}{d\log T}\right|_{\text{radiative}}. \qquad (6\text{-}50)$$

---

* In unusual circumstances, such as those described in Section 4-3 of Chapter 7, the temperature may *increase* outwards. A similar argument, however, shows that in such a case eqs. (6-49B), (6-50), and (6-51B) remain valid.

Also, from eqs. (6-49A) and (6-49B),

$$\left|\frac{dT}{dr}\right|_{\text{adiabatic}} > \left|\frac{dT}{dr}\right|_{\text{radiative}} \tag{6-51A}$$

$$\frac{dT}{dr}\bigg|_{\text{adiabatic}} < \frac{dT}{dr}\bigg|_{\text{radiative}} . \tag{6-51B}$$

Equations (6-50) and (6-45A) give the result*

$$\frac{d\log P}{d\log T}\bigg|_{\text{radiative}} > \frac{\gamma}{\gamma - 1} . \tag{6-52}$$

If we introduce the parameter n defined by the relation

$$n + 1 = \frac{d\log P}{d\log T}, \tag{6-53}$$

we find from eq. (6-45A) that n is the same quantity that appears in eq. (6-10). We may also write the stability criterion as

$$(n + 1)_{\text{radiative}} > (n + 1)_{\text{adiabatic}}.$$

Of all the forms for expressing the condition for stability against convection, the one we shall find most useful is that of eq. (6-52), with γ set equal to $\frac{5}{3}$:

$$\frac{d\log P}{d\log T} > 2.5 \quad \text{(non-convective)}. \tag{6-54}$$

We now consider how convection may be induced. If the opacity of the stellar matter in some regions is high, radiation is hindered in its passage, and a numerically large radiative temperature gradient is encouraged between the two sides of a slab of the material. By eq. (6-51A), we may expect convection. Or, if a plentiful element (normally hydrogen or helium) is in a state of partial ionization, the ratio of specific heats γ is lowered. This, according to eq. (6-52), can also produce convection. These situations apply especially to a stellar atmosphere. In the central regions of a star, convection may occur as a result of the large radiative temperature gradient caused by nuclear reactions that are highly sensitive to temperature. The large gradient of the energy released per second by these reactions produces a steep gradient of the temperature and this, in turn, maintains convection. This may be clarified by considering eq. (6-24). The greater the sensitivity of the nuclear reactions to temperature, the greater the fraction of the total luminosity of the star that is generated very close to the center. The large value of L_r and,

---

* When radiation pressure is important, γ is replaced by Γ_2, where

$$\Gamma_2 = 1 + \frac{(4 - 3\beta)(\gamma - 1)}{\beta^2 + 3(\gamma - 1)(1 - \beta)(4 + \beta)}$$

with β = (gas pressure/total pressure). See S. Chandrasekhar, 1939 (53), p. 57.

all the more, of $L_r/4\pi r^2$ for given r near the center then induces a large temperature gradient according to eq. (6-24).

The principles we have derived in this section will be applied to the construction of stellar models in Chapter 10.

5 ENERGY GENERATION

For a region in radiative equilibrium in which L_r is not constant with r, an expression for ϵ, the energy generation coefficient introduced in eq. (6-30), must be available before the differential equations governing the structure can be solved. In this section, we consider the two important mechanisms that can generate energy, namely, nuclear reactions and gravitational contraction, and then give formulae for ϵ.

5-1 GRAVITATIONAL CONTRACTION

Historically, gravitational contraction was considered an energy source even before nuclear processes were understood. When the outward pressure in a star is not entirely adequate to overcome the crushing tendency of the gravitational forces, the star undergoes a contraction. This may be a very slow process, maintained over millions of years, while the star remains in quasi-equilibrium. In some cases, the entire star is affected, although it is also possible for the contraction to be limited to only part of the star. This can happen, for example, when a nuclear fuel in the central region of a star becomes exhausted and the production of nuclear energy consequently ceases. Each element of matter that is displaced inwards then has a smaller potential energy, and it is this fact that makes gravitational contraction a source of energy in stars. Since the total amount of energy in the universe must remain unchanged during the contraction, the decrease in potential energy must be compensated by an increase in other energy; either the kinetic energy of the gas can be raised, with an accompanying increase in the temperature, or the amount of radiant energy can be increased, providing a source of luminosity. We shall next investigate just how the energy is divided between these two possible forms.

We wish to learn, then, what increase in thermal energy corresponds to a given decrease in potential energy. If these are not numerically equal, the balance must consist of energy radiated away. We therefore must find expressions for the thermal energy, which we may call $\mathscr{T}$, and the gravitational potential energy Ω.

The potential energy per unit mass at distance r from the center is $-GM_r/r$; and, for a shell of mass dM_r, the potential energy is $-GM_r\,dM_r/r$. For the whole star, then,

$$\Omega = -\int_0^M \frac{GM_r}{r}\,dM_r. \tag{6-55}$$

Next we find an expression for $\mathscr{T}$. In eq. (3-40), we showed that the mean kinetic energy per particle of a perfect gas at temperature T is $\frac{3}{2}kT$. The total kinetic (thermal) energy within the star can then be found by summing over all particles in the star, taking account, of course, of the different temperatures of different particles:

$$\mathscr{T} = \int_{\text{star}} \tfrac{3}{2}kT \cdot dN, \tag{6-55A}$$

where dN is the number of particles in a thin shell at temperature T. This can be found as the mass of the shell divided by the average mass per particle:

$$dN = \frac{dM_r}{\mu H} = \frac{4\pi r^2 \rho \, dr}{\mu H}$$

by eq. (6-1), and thus

$$\mathscr{T} = \int_0^R \tfrac{3}{2}kT \frac{4\pi r^2 \rho \, dr}{\mu H}$$

$$= \frac{3}{2} \int_0^R 4\pi r^2 P \, dr. \tag{6-56}$$

Recollection of the equation of hydrostatic equilibrium, eq. (6-2),

$$\frac{dP}{dr} = -\frac{GM_r}{r^2} \rho, \tag{6-57}$$

suggests that a connection between Ω and $\mathscr{T}$ as expressed in eqs. (6-55) and (6-56) might be discovered if eq. (6-56) were integrated by parts to yield dP:

$$\mathscr{T} = \frac{3}{2} \left[\frac{4\pi}{3} r^3 P \right]_{\text{center}}^{\text{surface}} - \frac{3}{2} \int_{P_c}^0 \frac{4\pi}{3} r^3 \, dP.$$

At the surface, $P = 0$; and at the center, $r = 0$. Thus the term in brackets vanishes, while the integral may be rewritten with the aid of eq. (6-57) as

$$\mathscr{T} = \frac{3}{2} \int_0^R \frac{4\pi}{3} r^3 \frac{GM_r}{r^2} \rho \, dr$$

$$= \frac{1}{2} \int_0^M \frac{GM_r}{r} \, dM_r.$$

Therefore,

$$\mathscr{T} = -\tfrac{1}{2}\Omega$$

or

$$2\mathscr{T} + \Omega = 0. \tag{6-58}$$

This is the *virial theorem*.

For a change in potential energy resulting from a contraction,

$$-\Delta\Omega = 2\,\Delta\mathscr{T}. \tag{6-59}$$

That is, a decrease in potential energy $\Delta\Omega$ results not only in a heating by an amount $\Delta\mathscr{T}$, but requires the disposal of additional energy of an amount equal to $\Delta\mathscr{T}$; this is lost by the star in the form of radiant energy. In other words, half the energy made available by the contraction causes an increase in the temperature, while the other half is radiated away. This result would be modified if radiation pressure were taken into account or if the gas were not monatomic.

Now that we have demonstrated that contraction can be a source of luminosity, we must find how long it can continue to be effective. Let us calculate, for example, how long the Sun could have been radiating at its present rate if its energy were supplied entirely by gravitational contraction. Let us assume that, at an earlier time t_0, the Sun had a radius R_0. The potential energy at that time can be estimated from eq. (6-55), if we take an average, constant value of the integrand:

$$\Omega(R_0) \approx -\left(\frac{GM_r}{r}\right)_{av} M.$$

If we set

$$\left(\frac{GM_r}{r}\right)_{av} \approx G\frac{\tfrac{1}{2}M}{\tfrac{1}{2}R_0} = G\frac{M}{R_0},$$

then

$$\Omega(R_0) \approx -\frac{GM^2}{R_0}.$$

Similarly, the present value is approximately

$$\Omega(R_\odot) = -\frac{GM^2}{R_\odot}.$$

The change in gravitational potential energy, then, is

$$\Delta\Omega \approx -GM^2\left(\frac{1}{R_\odot} - \frac{1}{R_0}\right).$$

The radius R_0 is believed to have been greater than $R_\odot$, and we may take it to be infinity without incurring any appreciable error in $\Delta\Omega$. Assuming now that the solar luminosity has been nearly constant since time t_0,[*] we find the interval that has elapsed until the present time t_p by dividing the energy available for radiation, $-\tfrac{1}{2}\Delta\Omega$, by the rate at which the energy is expended:

$$t_p - t_0 \sim -\frac{\tfrac{1}{2}\Delta\Omega}{L_\odot}$$

$$\approx \frac{1}{2}\frac{GM^2}{R_\odot L_\odot}$$

$$\approx 2 \times 10^7 \text{ years.}$$

[*] In Chapter 7, we shall see that the solar luminosity was probably greater in the past, which only strengthens the final conclusion reached here.

Geological evidence, however, indicates that the terrestrial crust has an age of several billion years, and it is surely to be expected that the Sun is at least as old as the Earth. Even though we can place little credence in the precise time interval derived from this calculation, we cannot hope to extract another factor of 100 from a more careful analysis. We must conclude that, although gravitational contraction may play an important role during short phases of stellar evolution, another source must be responsible for most of the energy output of a star.

5-2 NUCLEAR PROCESSES

We next consider nuclear reactions that release energy. We must find what exothermic reactions can take place under the conditions existing in a stellar interior, and then we must determine which of these reactions will supply energy at a sufficient rate and for a sufficiently long time.

Let us consider the first question. If two nuclei are to interact, they must collide with sufficient kinetic energy to overcome the electrostatic repulsion between them. The Coulomb energy is

$$\frac{z_1' z_2' e^2}{d},$$

where z_1', z_2' are the effective nuclear charges when screening by electrons is taken into account, e is the electronic charge, and d is the separation of the nuclei. If there is to be a reaction, d must decrease to about one nuclear radius. This is about $1.1 \times 10^{-13} A^{1/3}$ cm, where A is the mass number of the nucleus. Then

$$\text{Coulomb energy} = 2.1 \times 10^{-6} \frac{z_1' z_2'}{A^{1/3}} \text{ erg}$$

$$= 2 \times 10^{-6} \text{ erg for a pair of H nuclei}$$

$$= 4 \times 10^{-4} \text{ erg for a pair of Fe nuclei.}$$

On the other hand, the average kinetic energy of a particle is $\frac{3}{2}kT$, and for a stellar interior at a temperature of 10 million degrees,

$$\text{mean kinetic energy per particle} = 2 \times 10^{-9} \text{ erg.}$$

This is only $1/1000$ of the energy needed by a proton to surmount the potential barrier of another proton. The Maxwellian distribution curve shows that only a very small fraction of particles have speeds $\sqrt{(1000)} \approx 30$ times greater than average, which is needed to give them a kinetic energy comparable to the Coulomb energy. However, the quantum-mechanical effect of "tunneling through" a potential barrier makes the situation considerably more favorable. The probability of penetration, which depends on the factor $e^{-z_1' z_2'}$, decreases rapidly with increasing atomic number of the interacting particles. Thus the lightest elements are the ones to be considered.

A. HYDROGEN AS A NUCLEAR FUEL

The collision of two hydrogen nuclei provides the lowest possible value of $z_1'z_2'$. This reaction does, in fact, form the starting point of the *proton-proton chain*, in which four hydrogen nuclei are eventually combined into a single helium nucleus. Another series of reactions, the carbon-nitrogen cycle (or the carbon-nitrogen-oxygen bi-cycle) also converts four nuclei of hydrogen into one of helium. Before listing these reactions in detail, let us see whether this source can produce energy for a sufficiently long time in the case of the Sun. We first compute the excess mass of four hydrogen atoms over that of a helium atom,* which is transformed into energy according to Einstein's relation

$$\Delta\mathscr{E} = \Delta mc^2. \tag{6-60}$$

We have

$$\text{mass of 4 H atoms} = 4\ (1.00750) = 4.03000\ \text{AMU}$$
$$\text{mass of 1 He atom} = \qquad\qquad 4.00130\ \text{AMU}$$
$$\Delta m = \overline{0.02870\ \text{AMU}.}$$

This yields an energy

$$\Delta\mathscr{E} = 4.283 \times 10^{-5}\ \text{erg}$$

$$= 26.73\ \text{MeV}.$$

The number of conversions of four H nuclei into one He nucleus needed per second to maintain the solar luminosity of 3.8×10^{33} erg sec^{-1} is

$$\frac{3.8 \times 10^{33}\ \text{erg sec}^{-1}}{4.28 \times 10^{-5}\ \text{erg conversion}^{-1}} = 0.89 \times 10^{38}\ \frac{\text{conversions}}{\text{sec}},$$

resulting in the destruction of 3.6×10^{38} H nuclei (atoms) per second. This must be compared with the number of H atoms in the Sun, which may be computed approximately as the mass of the Sun divided by the mass of a hydrogen atom:

$$\frac{2.0 \times 10^{33}\ \text{gm}}{1.7 \times 10^{-24}\ \text{gm}} = 1.2 \times 10^{57}\ \text{H atoms}.$$

---

* It is valid to use the masses of the atoms rather than the nuclei in this calculation, since two electrons from the surroundings are also converted in the actual reactions [see eq. (6-62), for example]. Thus we have

$$4\ \text{H (nuclei)} + 2\ e^- \rightarrow 1\ \text{He (nucleus)}$$

or, adding $2\ e^-$ to both sides of the reaction to get the equivalent of complete atoms,

$$4\ \text{H (nuclei)} + 4\ e^- \rightarrow 1\ \text{He (nucleus)} + 2\ e^-.$$

The Sun therefore depletes only 3×10^{-19} of its supply each second, and its present luminosity can be maintained for about $(3 \times 10^{-19})^{-1}$ seconds or 10^{11} years. At its present age of 4.5×10^9 years, the Sun has expended about 5 per cent of its hydrogen fuel.

B. THE PROTON-PROTON CHAIN*

We have seen that penetration of the potential barrier is most readily achieved when the colliding particles are both protons. The *proton-proton* (*p-p*) *chain* begins with this reaction, leading ultimately to the formation of He^4. In this first step [eq. (6-61) below], deuterium ($_1H^2$), a positron (β^+), and a neutrino (ν) are created. The positron meets one of the abundant negative electrons (β^-) in the stellar material, and the two are annihilated to form two γ-rays. When the deuteron combines with an H nucleus, He^3 is formed. The latter particle can next combine with another such nucleus formed previously, yielding a nucleus of ordinary He^4 and two H nuclei. Note that the first two reactions must take place twice in order to produce the two He^3 nuclei needed for the last reaction. A total of six H nuclei have therefore been consumed and transformed into one He^4 nucleus, two H nuclei, a neutrino, and energy. The reactions are listed below together with the available energy in MeV released at each step. The average additional energy carried off by the neutrino is set in parentheses.†

$$_1H^1 + {}_1H^1 \rightarrow {}_1H^2 + \beta^+ + \nu \quad 0.16\ (0.26) \qquad (6\text{-}61)$$

$$\beta^+ + \beta^- \rightarrow \gamma \quad 1.02 \qquad (6\text{-}62)$$

$$_1H^1 + {}_1H^2 \rightarrow {}_2He^3 + \gamma \quad 5.49 \qquad (6\text{-}63)$$

$$_2He^3 + {}_2He^3 \rightarrow {}_2He^4 + 2{}_1H^1 \quad 12.86 \qquad (6\text{-}64)$$

The available energy released is

$$2(0.16 + 1.02 + 5.49) + 12.86 = 26.20\ \text{MeV}.$$

The missing 0.53 MeV needed to give the total of 26.73 MeV found in Part A above has been carried off by the neutrinos. We count this 2 per cent of the

---

* Most of the numerical values in Sections B, C, and D are those quoted by D. D. Clayton, 1968 (51), Chapter 5, especially pp. 380 and 392. See also W. A. Fowler, G. R. Caughlan, and B. A. Zimmerman, 1967 (300); H. Reeves (L. H. Aller and D. B. McLaughlin, eds.), 1965 (58); J. N. Bahcall and R. M. May, 1968 (301) and 1969 (302); and J. N. Bahcall and C. P. Moeller, 1969 (303).
† The total energy released in a reaction, i.e., available energy plus neutrino loss, is known as the *Q-value*.

total as a loss to the star, because the neutrino will almost certainly pass through the star without interacting with any of its constituents.

When He^4 is already present in an amount comparable with that of hydrogen, and the temperature is in excess of 14×10^6 °K, another termination of the proton-proton chain will occur more frequently than eq. (6-64):

$$_2He^3 + {_2He^4} \rightarrow {_4Be^7} + \gamma \quad (1.59 \text{ MeV}). \tag{6-65}$$

The Be^7 then interacts either with an electron or a proton:

$$_4Be^7 + \beta^- \rightarrow {_3Li^7} + \nu \qquad 0.06 \,(0.80) \tag{6-66}$$

$$_3Li^7 + {_1H^1} \rightarrow 2{_2He^4} \qquad 17.35 \tag{6-67}$$

or

$$_4Be^7 + {_1H^1} \rightarrow {_5B^8} + \gamma \qquad 0.13 \tag{6-68}$$

$$_5B^8 \rightarrow {_4Be^8}* + \beta^+ + \nu \quad 10.78 \,(7.2) \tag{6-69}$$

$$_4Be^8* \rightarrow 2{_2He^4}. \qquad 0.095 \tag{6-70}$$

The asterisk represents an excited nucleus. The latter set of reactions appears more likely than the Li^7 chain for $T > 23 \times 10^6$ °K. At such temperatures, however, the CN cycle, to be discussed shortly, will predominate if the elements C and N are present in amounts comparable to those in the Sun. The reactions (6-61) to (6-63) need take place only once to produce the single He^3 nucleus required, and the net result is again the conversion of four H nuclei into one He^4 nucleus, with the production of energy.

We can better understand the amount of available energy produced by the various terminating reactions by examining Fig. 6-5. Plotted here is the energy-generation rate for the various branches of the *p-p* chain relative to the rate for the termination $He^3 + He^3$. This is the actual terminal reaction at temperatures around 10×10^6 °K, and, therefore, the ϵ-ratio here is unity. At lower temperatures, the *p-p* chain ends with reaction (6-63); but the participating reactions occur twice for each theoretical termination $He^3 + He^3$, and therefore the energy produced is

$$2(0.16 + 1.02 + 5.49) = 2(6.67) = 13.34 \text{ MeV}.$$

This is about one-half of the 26.20 MeV available upon completion of the chain through $He^3 + He^3$. At temperatures above 10×10^6 °K, there is a branching through the $He^3 + He^4$ reaction to the two chains involving Be^7, again requiring reactions (6-61) to (6-63) to take place only once. The rate would be twice that for the $He^3 + He^3$ termination were it not for the considerable neutrino losses. Above 20×10^6 °K,* the termination through

* This temperature depends upon the composition of the material. See Fig. 10-7.

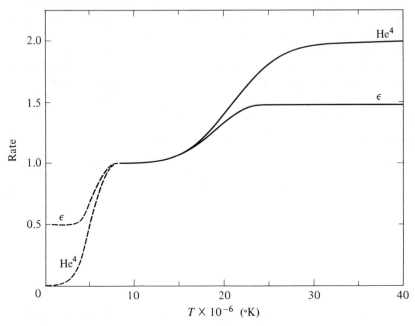

Fig. 6-5 The Energy-Generation Rate by the Proton-Proton Chain, and the Helium-4 Production Rate. In both cases, the rates are relative to the rate for the termination of the proton-proton chain through the $He^3 + He^3$ reaction. The dashed portions of the curves show qualitatively the conditions at low temperatures. The rates are calculated for a composition with $X = 0.70$ and $Y = 0.30$. The value of the cross-section factor $S_0(Be^7 + H^1)$, which enters the calculation of ϵ_{pp}, is taken as 0.04 keV barn. [Cross-section factors are not discussed in this book; see, e.g., D. D. Clayton, 1968 (51), p. 297 et seq. or H. Reeves (L. H. Aller and D. B. McLaughlin, eds.), 1965 (58).]

$_4Be^7 + _1H^1$ produces available energy of amount $(1.59 + 0.13 + 10.78 + 0.095 = 12.60$ MeV in addition to the 6.67 MeV from reactions (6-61) to (6-63). The sum of these, 19.27 MeV, must be counted twice and provides 38.54 MeV, or 1.44 of the amount available by completion of the chain through $He^3 + He^3$.

The relative rate at which He^4 is produced is also shown in Fig. 6-5. Again, the rate for the termination $He^3 + He^3$ is taken as unity, which is therefore the value near $T = 10 \times 10^6$ °K. The rate approaches zero at lower temperatures, since only the reactions (6-61) to (6-63) occur, and these produce no He^4. At higher temperatures, the relative rate approaches 2 as the B^8 chain predominates and creates a He^4 nucleus after each occurrence of the reactions (6-61) to (6-63), rather than after each two as required by the termination $He^3 + He^3$.

C. THE CN CYCLE AND THE CNO BI-CYCLE*

The reactions of the *CN cycle* are listed below, together with the available energy and, in parentheses, the additional energy carried by the neutrino. The energies are expressed in MeV.

$$_1H^1 + {}_6C^{12} \rightarrow {}_7N^{13} + \gamma \qquad\qquad 1.94 \qquad\qquad (6\text{-}71)$$
$$_7N^{13} \rightarrow {}_6C^{13} + \beta^+ + \nu \qquad\qquad 1.51\ (0.71)$$
$$_1H^1 + {}_6C^{13} \rightarrow {}_7N^{14} + \gamma \qquad\qquad 7.55 \qquad\qquad (6\text{-}72)$$
$$_1H^1 + {}_7N^{14} \rightarrow {}_8O^{15} + \gamma \qquad\qquad 7.29$$
$$_8O^{15} \rightarrow {}_7N^{15} + \beta^+ + \nu \qquad\qquad 1.76\ (1.00)$$
$$_1H^1 + {}_7N^{15} \rightarrow {}_6C^{12} + {}_2He^4 \qquad\qquad 4.96 \qquad\qquad (6\text{-}73)$$

$$25.01\ (1.71)$$

Again, four H nuclei have formed one He^4 nucleus. The C^{12} is used merely as a catalyst, being restored at the completion of the cycle. The neutrinos in this case dissipate, on the average, 6 per cent of the maximum energy.

At temperatures below 10×10^6 °K, only the first three reactions of the CN cycle take place. Accordingly, the available energy produced per cycle is

$$1.94 + 1.51 + 7.55 = 11.00 \text{ MeV},$$

or 44 per cent of that generated by a full cycle.

At temperatures greater than 17×10^6 °K, the last reaction in the CN cycle, (6-73), is sometimes replaced by

$$_1H^1 + {}_7N^{15} \rightarrow {}_8O^{16} + \gamma \qquad\qquad 12.13 \qquad\qquad (6\text{-}74)$$

$$_1H^1 + {}_8O^{16} \rightarrow {}_9F^{17} + \gamma \qquad\qquad 0.60$$

$$_9F^{17} \rightarrow {}_8O^{17} + \beta^+ + \nu \qquad\qquad 0.80\ (0.94)$$

$$\beta^+ + \beta^- \rightarrow \gamma \qquad\qquad 1.02$$

$$_1H^1 + {}_8O^{17} \rightarrow {}_7N^{14} + {}_2He^4 \qquad\qquad 1.19$$

Equation (6-74) occurs about thrice for every 1000 times that eq. (6-73) takes place. The full set of reactions, beginning with (6-71) and including the two branches that yield a He^4 nucleus, is called the *CNO bi-cycle*. In the events initiated by reaction (6-74), the original C^{12} is not replaced, but, rather, additional N^{14} is produced.

Once equilibrium is established in the CN cycle, about 98 or 99 per cent of the original C and N isotopes exist in the form of N^{14}. In equilibrium, all reactions proceed at the same rate per unit time and per unit volume. Hence a reaction that has a high rate *per reacting nucleus* will reach equilibrium by

* See footnote on p. 250 for references.

depleting its supply of available nuclei until the number of conversions per unit volume is the same as that for a slow reaction. A high conversion rate is then balanced by a small number of reactants, while a slow rate will be compensated by a large number of reactants. The conversion of N^{14} is the slowest step in the CN cycle, and therefore most of the C and N isotopes accumulate at this point in the form of N^{14}. The abundant isotope of oxygen, O^{16}, is also gradually transformed into N^{14} through the operation of the CNO bi-cycle, but a comparatively long time is required to establish an equilibrium abundance. For example, more than 10^8 years must elapse in the case that $T = 20 \times 10^6 \, °K$ and there are initially equal numbers of C^{12} and O^{16} nuclei.* The yield of energy in the O^{16} branch is negligibly small by comparison with that in the CN cycle itself for stars with normal relative abundances of carbon, nitrogen, and oxygen.

D. THE TRIPLE-ALPHA REACTION†

At temperatures near $10^8 \, °K$ or higher, He^4 nuclei are combined into C^{12} in two steps:

$$_2He^4 + {_2}He^4 \rightarrow {_4}Be^8 + \gamma \qquad -0.095 \qquad (6\text{-}75)$$

$$\left. \begin{array}{c} _4Be^8 + {_2}He^4 \rightarrow {_6}C^{12*} \\ _6C^{12*} \rightarrow {_6}C^{12} + \gamma \end{array} \right\} \qquad 7.37$$

The asterisk denotes an excited nucleus, which decays to the ground state with the emission of a γ-ray. The first reaction is slightly endothermic because Be^8 is more massive than $2He^4$.‡ The energy yield is $7.37 - 0.095 = 7.27$ MeV.

E. OTHER REACTIONS

The nuclear reactions already discussed are the most important ones for producing energy in stars. Once He^4 has been produced, the successive addition of α-particles leads to such reactions as

$$_6C^{12} + {_2}He^4 \rightarrow {_8}O^{16} + \gamma$$

$$_8O^{16} + {_2}He^4 \rightarrow {_{10}}Ne^{20} + \gamma$$

$$_{10}Ne^{20} + {_2}He^4 \rightarrow {_{12}}Mg^{24} + \gamma$$

. . . .

Reactions with neutrons, as well as other processes, also provide means by which successively heavier nuclei can be built.

---

* See G. R. Caughlan, 1965 (391) or D. D. Clayton, 1968 (51), p. 405.
† See footnote on p. 250 for references.
‡ Note that reaction (6-75) is the reverse of (6-70). The nucleus Be^8 is highly unstable.

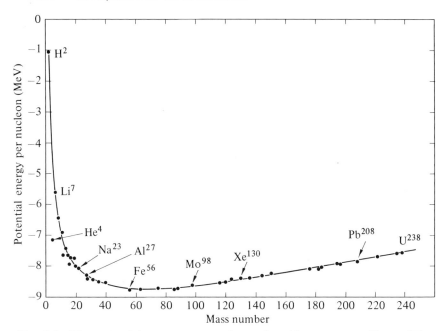

Fig. 6-6 The potential energy per nucleon of stable or near-stable nuclides relative to the state of complete separation. [M. R. Wehr and J. A. Richards, Jr., 1967 (398), p. 358.]

Energy is released in a nuclear reaction if the sum of the masses of the reacting particles is greater than the sum of the masses of the particles produced. The difference of these values, according to Einstein's relation, is converted into energy. Now the total mass of a nucleus is the sum of the masses of the constituent protons and neutrons plus the negative potential energy (expressed as an equivalent mass) that holds the nucleons together.* The potential energy per nucleon is plotted in Fig. 6-6 for various nuclei. Since the value becomes more negative with increasing mass number from 1 to 56 (with some exceptions), the trend is that these nuclei are progressively more stable and that energy is released in the formation of a heavier nucleus from lighter ones. Beyond Fe^{56}, fission rather than fusion tends to yield energy. For He^4, the potential energy is so near the minimum value that most of the energy that can be extracted by the fusion of nuclei has already been released in the conversion of H into He^4.

Nuclear reactions involving iron and other heavy elements can have important consequences for stellar structure. A core of iron and other

---

* The energy required to separate completely the particles composing the nucleus is called the *binding energy*; this positive number is just the negative of the potential energy.

elements of neighboring atomic number can result from successive reactions that build heavier elements from lighter ones. At very high temperatures, the iron-group nuclei can be disintegrated into He^4 nuclei plus neutrons. The tremendous energy that is absorbed by these reactions requires a rapid readjustment of the core and of the star as a whole. This mechanism may be a cause of supernova explosions.*

5-3 THE ENERGY-GENERATION RATE

The energy-generation rate ϵ is the amount of available energy (that is, with neutrino losses deducted) generated per gram of stellar matter per second. It may be expressed as the following sum over the individual reactions in a chain or cycle:

$$\epsilon = \sum \frac{\text{available energy generated}}{\text{reaction}} \times \frac{\text{reactions}}{cm^3\ sec} \times \frac{cm^3}{gm}. \qquad (6\text{-}76)$$

The first factor has been discussed in the preceding section. The last is simply ρ^{-1}. The second factor is the same for all the reactions of a series, if these proceed in equilibrium. This equality occurs even though the mean reaction times *per nucleus of one of the reactants* may vary by many orders of magnitude for the various steps in the series: if the mean reaction time per nucleus is very small, the reaction proceeds rapidly and the participating nuclei are depleted until there is such a low abundance of at least one of the elements involved that the mean reaction time *per cm^3* is the same as for a step in the series having a large mean reaction time per nucleus. Hence we may take ϵ as the product of the total energy available *per series* of reactions, the rate of any individual reaction per cm^3, and the reciprocal of the density. This expression may be used for the hydrogen and helium reactions discussed here.

The number of reactions per cm^3 per second depends upon the factors

$$\frac{\text{number of collisions}}{cm^3\ sec} \times \text{probability of penetration of potential barrier}$$

$$\times \text{ probability of transmutation per penetration.}$$

The last factor is included because the compound nucleus formed by the penetrating collision of two nuclei need not form the desired nucleus but may decay to produce other particles. Both the first and second factors depend on the kinetic energies of the particles and therefore on the temperature. The expressions include exponential terms. The first factor must evidently be proportional to the numbers of the reactants per cm^3, which, for either nuclear species in the reaction, can be written as the product of the fraction

* For further details of nucleosynthesis, see D. D. Clayton, 1968 (51), Chapter 7.

X_i (by mass) of the species i in the stellar material and the density of the stellar material:

$$\frac{\text{number of collisions}}{\text{cm}^3 \text{ sec}} \propto (X_1\rho)(X_2\rho).$$

Recalling that we had ρ^{-1} from the last factor in eq. (6-76), we see that

$$\epsilon \propto \rho X_1 X_2 \cdot \text{function } (T).$$

The density also enters in a more subtle way, through a factor describing the effectiveness of surrounding electrons in shielding the nuclear charges. The *electron screening factor*, also called the *electron shielding factor*, is given by the expression*

$$f_{a,b} = \exp (0.188 z_a z_b \zeta^{1/2} \rho^{1/2}/T_6^{3/2}),$$

or, in most cases, one may write

$$f_{a,b} \approx 1 + 0.188 z_a z_b \zeta^{1/2} \rho^{1/2}/T_6^{3/2},$$

where a and b identify the nuclei in the particular reaction for which the rate per cm^{-3} is calculated; also

$$T_n = T \times 10^{-n},$$

and

$$\zeta = \sum_z \frac{z^2 + z}{A_z} X_z$$

$$\approx \tfrac{1}{2}(3 + X) \text{ for small } Z.$$

Tables 10-13B and 10-14B give the values of $f_{1,1} = f_{pp}$ and $f_{1,7} = f_{\text{CN}}$ as functions of ρ and T.

The expression for the energy-generation rate by the *p-p* chain may now be written†:

$$\epsilon_{pp} = 2.36 \times 10^6 X^2 \rho T_6^{-2/3} \exp (-33.81/T_6^{1/3}) \psi f_{pp} \times$$

$$\times (1 + 0.0123 T_6^{1/3} + 0.0109 T_6^{2/3} + 0.00095 T_6) \quad \text{(6-77A)}$$

in erg $\text{gm}^{-1} \text{sec}^{-1}$. The last factor in eq. (6-77A) is a correction term. The quantity ψ takes into account the different effective energies released by the various branches of the chain and is 0.980 times the ratio of energy-generation

---

* Refer to D. D. Clayton, 1968 (51), pp. 357–361 for a discussion.
† The numerical values in the equations for ϵ_{pp} and ϵ_{CN} are based on the data summarized by D. D. Clayton, *op. cit.* This reference also derives the various factors in these equations. Note, however, that a number of misprints occur in the work.

rates shown in Fig. 6-5.* Graphs of $\psi(T)$ for several values of X are given in Fig. 10-7.

For the CN cycle, the rate is given by the expression

$$\epsilon_{\text{CN}} = 7.21 \times 10^{27} X X_{\text{CN}} \rho T^{-2/3} \exp\left(-152.31/T_6^{1/3}\right) f_{\text{CN}} \quad (6\text{-}77\text{B})$$

in erg gm^{-1} sec^{-1}, where X_{CN} is the abundance of N^{14}, comprising the N^{14} originally present and that which has been formed by conversion of C, O, and other N nuclei.

For ease in calculation, the temperature functions in eqs. (6-77A) and (6-77B) are sometimes reduced to the form T^{ν}, where ν is itself dependent on the temperature range under consideration. For the *p-p* chain, ν has in addition a slight dependence on the composition because ψ is a function of T and X. Tables 10-13A and 10-14A express ϵ_{pp} and ϵ_{CN} in the form

$$\epsilon = \epsilon_0 X_1 X_2 \rho T^{\nu} f_{a,b}. \quad (6\text{-}77\text{C})$$

For the *p-p* chain, $X_1 = X_2 = X$; for the CN cycle, $X_1 = X$ and $X_2 \approx X(\text{C} + \text{N})$ if nearly all carbon but no oxygen has been converted into N^{14}.

For the triple-alpha reaction, the energy-generation rate is highly dependent on the temperature. Near 10^8 °K, ϵ may be approximated by the expression

$$\epsilon_{3\alpha} \approx 4.4 \times 10^{-8} Y^3 \rho^2 T_8^{40} f_{3\alpha} \quad \text{erg gm}^{-1} \text{ sec}^{-1} \ (T \approx 10^8 \text{ °K}).$$

We have written this equation in terms of the total helium abundance Y rather than that of the reacting nuclide He^4, since nearly all the helium will occur in the form of this isotope.

6 BOUNDARY CONDITIONS. THE VOGT–RUSSELL THEOREM†

6-1 GENERAL CONSIDERATIONS

The equations required for the construction of homogeneous stellar models have now been assembled. Their solution requires the specification of numerical values for all the variables at the place in the star at which the integration is begun. For the purpose of this section, we shall limit our atten-

---

* The factor 0.980 is the fraction of the total energy of 26.73 MeV that is available upon completion of the *p-p* chain through the He^3 + He^3 branch. By excluding this factor from the definition of ψ and incorporating it instead into the coefficient of ϵ_{pp}, we are adopting the notation of D. D. Clayton, ref. (51). Some authors, e.g., H. Reeves in ref. (58), include the factor within ψ.

† See also J. P. Cox and R. T. Giuli, 1968 (52), Chapter 18 and pp. 622, 623. This reference also gives a more precise statement of the Vogt–Russell theorem than the one to be given here, as well as citing some cases in which it is invalid.

tion to integrations begun at the center and carried outwards.* The physical validity of the completed model will then depend on whether certain necessary conditions are fulfilled at the surface.

The boundary conditions required for any equilibrium model are

$$r = 0, \qquad M_r = 0, \qquad L_r = 0 \text{ (at the center)}$$

and

$$P = P_s \text{ (or } \rho = \rho_s\text{)}, \qquad T = T_s \text{ (at the surface),}$$

where the subscript s designates a value at (or very near) the surface.† The remaining quantities at the center, namely, P_c and T_c, must be assigned specific values; and the remaining quantities at the surface, namely, M, R, and L, will be automatically determined by the solution in an equilibrium model. The values of P_c, T_c, M, R, and L constrain the application of the model to a specific star, but they do not determine whether the model is physically meaningful.

As an example of a model that is not in equilibrium and hence not physically meaningful, consider one in which the integration is begun at the center with some definite values of P_c and T_c. One may find as the integration progresses that the temperature gradient becomes vanishingly small even though L_r is finite; yet in a nearly isothermal region the transfer of radiation is inhibited, and most of the energy liberated in the interior must remain within.‡ Consequently, the model cannot be in equilibrium. As another example, consider a solution carried inwards from the surface (although we shall not discuss such models further in this section). At each step of the integration, both r and M_r decrease from their values on the preceding line of the integration. The mathematical solution may yield a place at which the mass M_r has decreased to zero while the radius remains finite; all the matter in the star has been accounted for, but the center has not yet been reached. Alternatively, the radius may reach zero at finite mass, and the model cannot dispose of the remaining matter. We see from these examples that the values of the parameters P_c and T_c on the one hand and M, R, and L on the other hand are not entirely arbitrary, even within reasonable limits, unless we permit changes in the other parameters, namely X, Y, and Z; the latter values have tacitly been assumed to be fixed.

Let us now consider the way in which X, Y, and Z affect the calculation of a model. Specification of their values is necessary because they are contained in the formulae for μ, $\bar{\kappa}$, and ϵ. The question arises as to how the values are

---

* Examples of the traditional fitting method, in which integrations are begun both at the center and at the surface and carried to a common intermediate point, are presented in Part Four.

† The surface boundary conditions will be discussed later in more detail.

‡ A nearly isothermal region can exist if the matter is degenerate, for energy transfer then takes place by highly efficient electron conduction.

to be chosen. This depends upon the problem to be solved. Often it is desired to calculate a model, or perhaps an evolutionary sequence of models, for a given mass and population type. One then chooses X and Z (and automatically Y) appropriately for that type and considers these values to be given conditions. In an evolutionary sequence, the value of X applies to the initial, homogeneous model. This problem is fundamental in the sense that a real star also has a certain amount of matter of definite composition, and it must adjust its radius and luminosity to the values necessary for equilibrium. The uniqueness of R and L for given M, X, and Z will be discussed below. One may also wish to construct a homogeneous model having specified values of M, R, and L. If the model proves to have an envelope in radiative equilibrium, there is only one pair of values of X and Z that will permit the boundary conditions to be satisfied. This pair of values must be found by trial and error, by constructing models with various choices for X and Z until an equilibrium model is obtained. If the model proves to have a convective envelope, then the uncertainty in our knowledge of the conditions near the surface leaves some uncertainty as to which pair of values of X and Z is indeed the correct one. This will be discussed later.

We have implied that, for given M, the values assigned to X and Z uniquely determine the values of R and L. This, in essence, is the Vogt–Russell theorem, which we justify below. Conversely, for given M, the values of R and L uniquely determine X and Z. (For convective envelopes, in both cases, there is at least theoretically a unique solution, even if the theory is not yet sufficiently advanced to enable us to identify it among the solutions that are plausible.) The remainder of this section will be devoted to an intuitive demonstration of these statements. The conclusions drawn here will again be reached in Chapter 10, Section 5, on the basis of mathematical models applicable in certain cases. It should be mentioned that, in the general case, the Vogt–Russell theorem is not restricted to homogeneous stars.

6-2 QUALITATIVE DEMONSTRATION OF THE THEOREM

Let us consider an integration begun at the center. Two of the dependent variables, namely, the central pressure P_c and the central temperature T_c, may be chosen freely, while r, M_r, and L_r necessarily vanish. Let us perform an integration for some arbitrary, but specific, values of P_c and T_c. The boundary conditions at the starting point are therefore

$$r = 0, \qquad M_r = 0, \qquad L_r = 0, \qquad P = P_c, \qquad T = T_c.$$

We shall also take some definite values for X and Z.

As the integration progresses, it may become evident that the model is not physically valid. Let us then perform additional integrations, keeping X and Z unchanged but varying either P_c or T_c until we obtain a model that is not obviously deficient.

At each step of any integration, the compression of the matter becomes less because of the decreased weight of the overlying layers. Eventually, the density approaches zero. As a consequence, the pressure also approaches zero, while the mass M_r approaches a limiting value M. The boundary value of r defines the total radius R. The net luminosity L_r will already have reached a maximum value L, since nuclear processes will not occur at the low densities and temperatures of these layers. Near the surface, in the photospheric region, the equations appropriate to a stellar atmosphere should be used to obtain the physically correct boundary conditions. However, since both the pressure and temperature near the photosphere have such small values in comparison with those deeper in the envelope, little error will be made by substituting the *zero boundary conditions*

$$P = 0 \ (\text{or } \rho = 0), \qquad T = 0.$$

These will be assumed for the present.

Let us now consider an envelope in radiative equilibrium. For the integration we have performed, we test whether $T = 0$ at the place where the density becomes zero. For randomly chosen values of P_c and T_c, we cannot expect that ρ and T will approach zero simultaneously. If T has a value T_s that is not equal to zero, a new trial integration must be performed with a different choice for one of the central values. Let us retain P_c but vary T_c until the boundary condition $T_s = 0$ is fulfilled. This model will be in equilibrium, and it will have definite values of M, R, and L. Suppose that we now choose another value for P_c and calculate a new set of models, again seeking a value of T_c that will yield an equilibrium model. The new values of M, R, and L will be different from those of the first model.* For given values of X and Z, there is, in fact, a one-to-one correspondence between P_c (or T_c) on the one hand and the set M, R, L on the other. If an integration were now begun at the surface with these values of X, Z, and M, an equilibrium model would necessarily have the same values of R, L, P_c, and T_c as before. In fact, we should merely be repeating the same integration in the reverse direction. The conclusion we may draw in this case is that *the mass and the chemical composition uniquely determine the properties of the star*. This is the *Vogt–Russell theorem*, which we must now test for stars that have convective envelopes.

If the envelope is in convective equilibrium, and if the relation

$$P = \mathscr{K}' T^{2.5}$$

is employed throughout the envelope, then the surface temperature will automatically reach zero coincidentally with P. Hence, for a given value of P_c, the constraint upon T_c that was found for radiative envelopes does not

---

* After studying Chapter 10, Section 5, the reader may verify this statement by comparing eqs. (10-116), (10-117), (10-124), and (10-125), remembering that p_c, t_c, C, and D have definite numerical values.

exist in this case. For given values of X and Z, *both* P_c and T_c must be specified to determine a unique set of the values M, R, and L for an equilibrium model*; for example, a series of equilibrium models may be constructed having the same M but different R and L. Conversely, a specification of M, R, and L no longer determines X and Z uniquely, for various models may be constructed, which differ in the relative depth of the convective envelope.

The validity of the Vogt–Russell theorem can be restored if we consider the physical boundary conditions at the photosphere. Although each of the models for the given X, Z, and M satisfies the requirements for a model interior, only one of them yields an adequate description of the atmospheric layers. Let us therefore calculate model atmospheres, using, of course, the values of R and L appropriate to any particular model. Even if the envelope is convective, the uppermost layers are so tenuous that radiation escapes readily from them, and radiation rather than convection is the transfer mechanism. Thus the layers are in radiative equilibrium, and we may employ the theory developed in Chapter 2. On the basis of Eddington's first approximation, it is required that, for the layer having an optical depth τ equal to $\frac{2}{3}$, the temperature must equal the effective temperature as given by L and R.† The optical depth is a function of both temperature and density, and the required correlation places a constraint upon the atmospheric model. In the region below the photosphere, hydrogen is extensively ionized and convection results. The atmospheric calculation is carried through the superadiabatic layers, perhaps using the mixing-length theory, to the layers in which the convective transfer may be considered adiabatic. The values of P and T in this layer determine the constant $\mathscr{K}'$ in the relation

$$P = \mathscr{K}'T^{2.5},$$

and this value of $\mathscr{K}'$ will agree with that for the envelope of only one of the previously calculated models having the given M, R, and L.‡ Consequently, the Vogt–Russell theorem is upheld.

---

* Again referring to Chapter 10, Section 5, we may construct a series of models using Schwarzschild's variables with E as a parameter, such as the one in Table 10-10. Any one of these solutions will yield a model with the given X, Z, and P_c; but each will have a different T_c, M, R, and L. [Cf. eqs. (10-116), (10-117), (10-124), and (10-125), remembering that p_c, t_c, C, and D have definite numerical values for any given E.]

† The ambiguity as to whether the *radius of a star* refers to the outer surface or the base of the photosphere is not significant, since the photosphere occurs so very near the surface in the main-sequence stars we are considering.

We are also assuming here that radiative equilibrium prevails down to the level where $T = T_{\text{eff}}$, a condition met in all but the coolest main-sequence stars.

‡ Further information on surface conditions is given by M. Schwarzschild, 1958 (50), pp. 89–95, and J. P. Cox and R. T. Giuli, 1968 (52), Chapter 20.

Actually, the model in this case is not as well defined as may appear. The mixing-length theory, which is generally used, is only an approximation to the actual conditions; and, furthermore, the ratio l/H of mixing length to scale height is not well determined. Thus, there is a degree of uncertainty in the final results. For a model with specified M, X, and Z, one may construct several models having different relative depths of the convective envelope and also different values of R and L. Conversely, one may calculate various models with the same M, R, and L but different relative depths of the convective envelope and different X and Z. Observational data on radii and luminosities or chemical composition may suggest which solution is best.

The Vogt–Russell theorem may also be considered from another point of view. Let us carry the integration for the interior to a level at which the atmosphere may be considered to begin, i.e., to a place where the optical depth, as determined from a model atmosphere, is no longer extremely large. The numerical value of this optical depth is of no consequence. Let us denote by P_s and T_s the pressure and temperature at this place where the interior solution is terminated. The net luminosity and the mass will effectively have reached limiting values L and M, while r will change very little in the overlying strata and may be considered to define R. With these values of M, R, and L, we now calculate the surface gravity g and the effective temperature T_{eff}:

$$g = \frac{GM}{R^2}, \qquad \sigma T_{\text{eff}}^{\,4} = \frac{L}{4\pi R^2}.$$

For the same chemical composition as in the interior solution, we next calculate a model atmosphere having the values of g and T_{eff} just found, proceeding inwards until we arrive at the place where T has the value T_s. At this layer, we examine the fit between the atmosphere and interior. We are assured of the continuity of r, M_r, L_r, and T across the boundary between the solutions, and whether an equilibrium model has been found therefore depends on whether P as given by the atmosphere equals P_s as determined from the interior. We consequently find that there are three constraints upon the four differential equations for the interior:

$$M_r = 0 \text{ and } L_r = 0 \text{ at the center (defined by } r = 0)$$

and

$$P = P_s \text{ at the surface (defined by } T = T_s).$$

Since the differential equations admit four boundary conditions, one of the parameters, such as the total mass, may be chosen arbitrarily. Thus the structure is determined by the total mass and the given composition. If, instead, the zero boundary conditions are used in the radiative case, then $T = 0$ at the surface (defined by $\rho = 0$), and the conclusion remains unaltered. However, if the zero boundary conditions are used for a convective envelope based on the relation $P = \mathscr{K}'T^{2.5}$, then it is an automatic condition that $T = 0$ at $\rho = 0$, and one of the constraints upon the solution is removed. In this case, the mass and chemical composition alone do not determine the structure; an additional parameter must be specified. In actual stars, of course, the true physical conditions ensure the applicability of the Vogt–Russell theorem.

7 THE CALCULATION OF EVOLUTIONARY SEQUENCES

The process that generates the energy of a star may be nuclear trans-mutation, gravitational contraction, or both. Evolutionary sequences are obtained by calculating individual static models employing the usual differential equations, except perhaps for a modification in the expression for dL_r/dr. The time intervals taken to separate the models are sufficiently small that the changes may be followed with the required accuracy. The total mass and original chemical composition are prescribed, and an initial model is then calculated for some rather well-determined state, such as that of the zero-age main sequence. The next model is obtained for the given mass and the new chemical distribution, as we now explain.

Once any model of the sequence has been calculated, the distribution of the chemical elements in the next model can be predetermined. For the moment, we assume that there is no convection in the region of nuclear burning, and therefore mixing of the material does not occur. The expression for the change in the hydrogen content ΔX as a function of the time interval Δt between the successive models is easily obtained in a first approximation. We take ΔX to be proportional to ϵ, the amount of energy generated per second per gram of stellar material by the transmutation of hydrogen in the known model:

$$\Delta X \propto -\epsilon\,\Delta t; \qquad (6\text{-}78)$$

that is, for one gram of stellar material, the fraction of a gram of hydrogen consumed, ΔX, is proportional to the number of ergs of energy produced. The required proportionality factor is evidently the number of grams of hydrogen consumed per erg of energy produced, which can be expressed as

$$\frac{\text{grams of H consumed/cycle}}{\text{ergs/cycle}}.$$

For the conversion of hydrogen into helium, this ratio is given in Section 5-2A and yields the relation

$$\Delta X = -\frac{4m_{\text{H}}}{26.73\ \text{MeV} - \text{neutrino losses}}\,\epsilon\,\Delta t.$$

If more than one reaction or set of reactions is depleting the element, a separate term is written on the right-hand side for each of these.

A similar expression, of course, can be written for any other nuclear fuel that is being depleted and not replenished. If the element is at the same time being *created* by another nuclear reaction, a positive term must be added to the right-hand side of the equation.

In regions where convection is present, the new values of X must be averaged with respect to mass.

If there is rapid gravitational contraction, the energy released must be included in the expression for the energy balance:

$$\frac{dL_r}{dr} = 4\pi r^2 \rho(\epsilon_{\text{nucl}} + \epsilon_{\text{grav}}). \qquad (6\text{-}79)$$

The rate ϵ_{grav} is computed from the changes in the pressure and density distributions.*

8 DEGENERATE MATTER†

8-1 THE CONCEPT OF DEGENERACY

At high density or low temperature, the velocity distribution of particles departs from the Maxwellian law as a result of the operation of the uncertainty and exclusion principles. The electrons (or ions) may be considered to occupy a *phase space* having three co-ordinates for position and three for momentum. Since the simultaneous position and momentum of a particle are uncertain by the amounts Δx, Δy, Δz in position and Δp_x, Δp_y, Δp_z in momentum, where

$$\Delta x \, \Delta p_x \sim h$$

$$\Delta y \, \Delta p_y \sim h$$

$$\Delta z \, \Delta p_z \sim h$$

and h is Planck's constant, the phase space may be considered to be divided into cells of six-dimensional volume

$$(\Delta x \, \Delta y \, \Delta z)(\Delta p_x \, \Delta p_y \, \Delta p_z) \sim h^3.$$

According to the exclusion principle, no more than two electrons (or ions) can be placed into any cell. For a given number of electrons or ions, their density (and hence that of the matter) determines the available volume in physical space, and the temperature then determines the available volume in momentum space. Consequently, the density and temperature determine the proportion of filled cells and hence the degree of degeneracy.

Ions may remain non-degenerate even if degeneracy of the electrons exists,

---

* See M. Schwarzschild, 1958 (50), p. 36.

† This section may be omitted, although occasional references to degenerate matter will be made.

because the ionic masses are so much greater. In a non-degenerate gas, the average kinetic energies of the ions and electrons are equal. Thus, if m_e and $\langle v_{ex}^2 \rangle$ are the mass and the average value of the squares of the x-components of the electron velocities, and m_i and $\langle v_{ix}^2 \rangle$ are the same quantities for the ions, then

$$m_e \langle v_{ex}^2 \rangle = m_i \langle v_{ix}^2 \rangle.$$

The average momentum of the ions along the x-axis compared with that of the electrons is

$$\frac{m_i \langle v_{ix} \rangle}{m_e \langle v_{ex} \rangle} \sim \left(\frac{m_i}{m_e} \right)^{1/2}.$$

For a given physical volume, the ions occupy a phase space that is greater by the cube of this ratio, or a factor $(m_i/m_e)^{3/2}$. For helium, this is $(8000)^{3/2} = 7 \times 10^5$, which is also the ratio of the number of cells available to the ions and the number available to the electrons. For given density and temperature, then, the ions are much less degenerate than the electrons.

In the following sections, we shall consider electron degeneracy in non-relativistic cases.*

8-2 COMPLETE DEGENERACY

We now find the number of particles (electrons) $N_p \, dp$ per cm³ having a momentum in the range p to $p + dp$, in the case that all cells in phase space are filled. This result for complete degeneracy also sets an upper bound to N_p in the case of partial degeneracy. If the physical volume is 1 cm³ and the elemental volume in momentum space is expressed as $4\pi p^2 \, dp$, then the number of cells multiplied by two particles per cell is

$$N_p \, dp = 2 \times \frac{4\pi p^2 \, dp \times 1 \text{ cm}^2}{h^3}$$

and

$$N_p = \frac{8\pi}{h^3} p^2. \tag{6-80}$$

The total number of particles per cm³ is

$$N = \frac{8\pi}{h^3} \int p^2 \, dp, \tag{6-81}$$

where the upper limit must be some finite value p_0 if N is finite. Thus

$$N = \frac{8\pi}{3h^3} p_0^3. \tag{6-82}$$

* Relativistic effects are considered by S. Chandrasekhar, 1939 (53), Chapter X; and by J. P. Cox and R. T. Giuli, 1968 (52), Chapter 24.

All cells in phase space are filled, and the particles have momenta from zero to the maximum value p_0, which is called the *Fermi momentum.*

It is curious to note that degenerate matter can contract only if energy is *added* to it. If the volume is to become smaller, N must increase and so must p_0. Energy is therefore needed to raise some of the particles to a higher momentum. We may visualize the situation schematically by imagining a rectangle in which the sides represent, respectively, the total volume and the cube of the momentum $p_0{}^3$. The dimensions of the rectangle change as the maximum momentum and the volume available to the particles change, but the area of the rectangle, that is, the number of cells, must remain constant.

The partial pressure due to the degenerate electrons can be found from eq. (3-39)*:

$$P = \int_0^\infty mv^2 \cdot \tfrac{1}{3} N(v)\, dv$$

$$= \int_0^\infty \frac{p^2}{m} \cdot \frac{1}{3} N_p\, dp. \tag{6-83}$$

Thus we have in the present case

$$P = \frac{8\pi}{15mh^3} p_0{}^5$$

$$= \left(\frac{3}{8\pi}\right)^{2/3} \frac{h^2}{5m} N^{5/3}. \tag{6-84}$$

This may be expressed in terms of the density ρ. We shall use the symbol μ_e for the mean molecular weight *per free electron.* The value of μ_e for pure, ionized helium is 2. Then

$$N = \frac{\rho}{\mu_e H} \tag{6-85}$$

and

$$P = \left(\frac{3}{8\pi}\right)^{2/3} \frac{h^2}{5mH^{5/3}} \frac{1}{\mu_e{}^{5/3}} \rho^{5/3}. \tag{6-86}$$

The relation has the same form as the adiabatic gas law.

8-3 THE DISTRIBUTION OF MOMENTA

From statistical mechanics, it can be shown that the number of particles per unit volume having a momentum in the range p to $p + dp$ is given by the expression

$$N_p\, dp = \frac{8\pi}{h^3} \frac{p^2}{\exp\left[(p^2/2mkT) - \psi\right] + 1}\, dp. \tag{6-87}$$

* Note that N_p is a different function of p than is $N(v)$ of v and that $\int_0^\infty N(v)\, dv = \int_0^\infty N_p\, dp$.

This is the *Fermi–Dirac distribution* of momenta. The quantity $e^{-\psi}$ is a function of T and N, for which the value must be such that

$$\int_0^\infty N_p \, dp = N. \tag{6-88}$$

The behavior of $e^{-\psi}$ with T and N is complicated, but approximate relations that depend on the degree of degeneracy can be given. If the degree of degeneracy is not high, then $\psi \gtrsim 0$, and the distribution approaches that of the Maxwellian law. In this case,*

$$e^{-\psi} \approx \frac{2(2\pi mk)^{3/2}}{h^3} \frac{T^{3/2}}{N} \quad (\psi \gtrsim 0). \tag{6-89}$$

If $\psi \ll 0$, the denominator of eq. (6-87) approaches $\exp[(p^2/2mkT) - \psi]$, and the relation becomes

$$N_p \, dp = 4\pi \frac{N}{(2\pi mk)^{3/2}T^{3/2}} \exp[-(p^2/2mkT)] \, p^2 \, dp \tag{6-90}$$

or

$$\frac{N(v) \, dv}{N} = 4\pi \left(\frac{m}{2\pi k}\right)^{3/2} \frac{1}{T^{3/2}} \exp[-(mv^2/2kT)] \, v^2 \, dv.$$

This is identical with the Maxwellian law, eq. (3-38B). At the other extreme, $\psi \gg 0$, the denominator of eq. (6-87) approaches unity, and the distribution is approximately that of eq. (6-80) for the completely degenerate case. For moderate or high degeneracy,†

$$e^{-\psi} = e^{-\varphi/kT} \tag{6-91}$$

with

$$\varphi = \varphi_0 \left[1 - \frac{\pi^2}{12}\left(\frac{kT}{\varphi_0}\right)^2 - \frac{\pi^4}{80}\left(\frac{kT}{\varphi_0}\right)^4 + \cdots\right] \tag{6-92}$$

and

$$\varphi_0 = \frac{h^2}{8m}\left(\frac{3}{\pi} N\right)^{2/3}. \tag{6-93}$$

Figures 6-7 and 6-8 illustrate the distributions given by eq. (6-87), as well as the corresponding Maxwellian distributions, for various values of ψ, T, and N. We are now considering N to be the number of electrons per cm^3. The Maxwellian law does not take the exclusion principle into account and consequently predicts excessively high values of N_p at low momenta. Actually, the value of N_p cannot be greater than that indicated by the parabola representing N_p for the case of complete degeneracy.

---

* See J. E. Mayer and M. G. Mayer, 1940 (304), p. 114 et seq.
† Ibid., p. 378 et seq. Also see G. Joos (305), p. 633 et seq. for the case $\varphi = \varphi_0$. Usually, φ is denoted by the symbol μ.

In Fig. 6-7, the solid curves labeled $\psi = 0$, $\psi = 5$, and $\psi = 10$ are plotted for a common temperature of 10^6 °K. The value of N is then determined as the area under any curve, or, to varying degrees of accuracy, by eq. (6-89) or eqs. (6-91) to (6-93). As ψ increases at constant T, the material becomes more degenerate because of increasing density. For $\psi = 0$, there is fair agreement with the classical, Maxwellian distribution; but the departure of the Fermi–Dirac curves from the Maxwellian curves becomes more marked as ψ increases. When the matter is compressed, the states of low momentum become filled and the remaining electrons require higher momentum. Thus the peaks of the Fermi–Dirac curves are shifted toward the right as the density increases. The Maxwellian curves, on the other hand, differ only in their vertical scales, rising to a maximum at a value of p that is determined by the temperature alone. Figure 6-7 also shows the distributions for the same series of electron concentrations N when complete degeneracy is achieved by cooling the matter to a temperature $T = 0$. The areas under any of these curves must, of course, equal the areas under the curves for the same N in the partially degenerate and Maxwellian cases. If curves for $\psi \ll 0$ were to be shown, they would lie very near to the horizontal axis on the scale of this figure and would match very closely the corresponding Maxwellian curves.

Figure 6-8 depicts the distribution N_p at constant density but at different temperatures. Accordingly, the areas under all the curves are the same. Again, the solid curves refer to the Fermi–Dirac curves for $\psi = 0, 5, 10$, and ∞, corresponding to decreasing temperature, while the dashed curves show the Maxwellian distribution for the same pairs of N and T. As in Fig. 6-7, the solid and dashed curves are most nearly in coincidence for the case $\psi = 0$, in which the degeneracy is the least. If negative values of ψ were represented in Fig. 6-8, the Fermi–Dirac and Maxwellian curves would be in still closer agreement and would reach maximum values of N_p at still higher momentum. The areas under the curves would, of course, remain the same as for the other curves in the figure. Once again, we see that matter very nearly obeys the classical law if the density is so low or the temperature is so high that ψ is algebraically small; whereas, if ψ is large, the departures from the classical law are great. The limit of complete degeneracy, with $\psi = \infty$, can be achieved at finite concentration only if $T = 0$. The figure also shows that, as in the Maxwellian case, the temperature (at given density) is a measure of the spread of the momenta or speeds of the particles.

8-4 PRESSURE

We again make use of eq. (6-83) to derive the expression for the pressure. Accordingly, we may compare the pressures at the densities and temperatures assumed in Figs. 6-7 and 6-8 by multiplying each ordinate by p^2 and then finding the areas under the resulting curves. Figures 6-9 and 6-10 illustrate the graphs of $N_p \cdot p^2$.

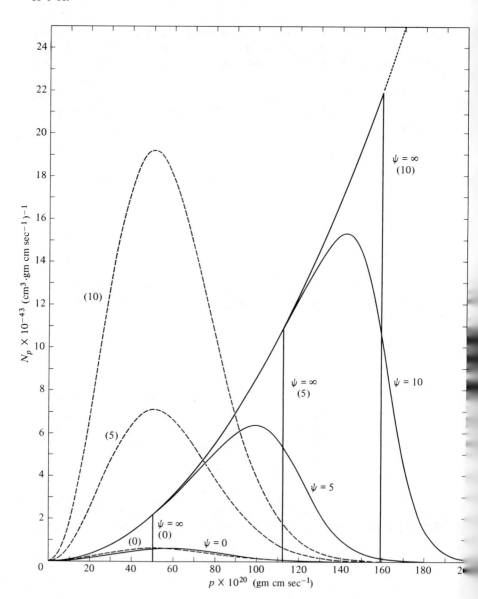

Fig. 6-7 The Distribution N_p for Electrons at Constant Temperatures $T = 10^6$ °K or 0°K.

The *solid curves* illustrate the Fermi–Dirac law for the cases $\psi = \infty$, 10, 5, and 0. The *dotted curve* is an extension of the parabola defining the upper boundary of all Fermi–Dirac distributions. The *dashed curves* show the Maxwellian law corresponding to the partially degenerate cases; each dashed curve is plotted for the same values of N and T as the solid curve for which the value of ψ equals the number in parentheses. The Maxwellian law does *not* give the correct distributions for these pairs of values of N and T.

In Fig. 6-7, the partially degenerate cases, with $\psi = 10$, 5, and 0, are plotted for $T = 10^6 \, °K$ and $N = 116 \times 10^{24}$, 42.8×10^{24}, and 3.7×10^{34}, respectively. For pure helium, the corresponding densities are 388, 143, and 12 gm cm^{-3}. Each completely degenerate case, with $\psi = \infty$ corresponding to $T = 0°K$, is plotted for a value of N that is the same as for the partially degenerate case with ψ equal to the number in parentheses.

In Fig. 6-8, the values of T are 0, 0.52×10^6, 1.00×10^6, and $5.2 \times 10^6 \, °K$ for the cases $\psi = \infty$, 10, 5, and 0, respectively. In all cases, $N = 42.8 \times 10^{24}$ cm^{-3}. Note that the solid curve for $\psi = 5$ and the corresponding dashed curve (5) are identical in Figs. 6-7 and 6-8.

Fig. 6-8 The Distribution N_p at a Constant Number of Electrons per Unit Volume $N = 42.8 \times 10^{24}$ cm^{-3}.

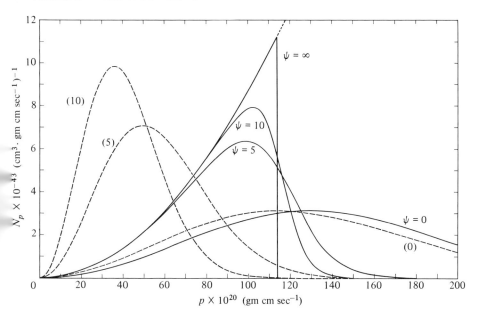

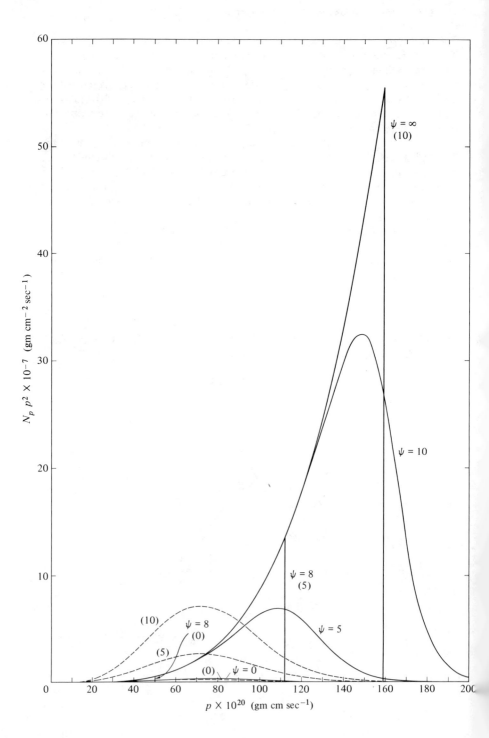

Fig. 6-9   The Distribution $N_p \cdot p^2$ for Electrons at Constant Temperatures of
10^6 °K or 0°K. The curves are obtained from Fig. 6-7 by multiplication of each
ordinate by p^2. The area under any curve is proportional to the electron pressure
at that temperature and density.

In Fig. 6-9, in which all curves are drawn either for the temperature
10^6 °K or 0°K, we see that the pressure increases with density. For the non-
degenerate (Maxwellian) case, the increase in P is proportional to the increase
in N or ρ. In degenerate matter, however, the area under the curve, and hence
the pressure, increases more rapidly. Therefore, at given density and temperature, degenerate matter exerts a higher pressure than does non-degenerate
matter.

In Fig. 6-10, which applies to constant density, the areas under the Maxwellian curves increase with temperature in such a way that P is proportional
to T. The areas under the Fermi–Dirac curves with large ψ, however, remain
nearly the same as the temperature is changed; and the greater the degree
of degeneracy, the less sensitive is the dependence on T. Thus the pressure of
highly degenerate matter is a function of density but is nearly independent of
temperature. For the case of complete degeneracy, we have already seen from
eq. (6-86) that P is a function of ρ alone.

Fig. 6-10   The Distribution $N_p \cdot p^2$ for a Constant Number of Electrons per
Unit Volume $N = 42.8 \times 10^{24}$ cm^{-3}. The curves are obtained from Fig. 6-8 by
multiplication of each ordinate by p^2. The area under any curve is proportional to
the electron pressure at that temperature and density. Note that the solid curve
for $\psi = 5$ and the corresponding dashed curve (5) are identical in Figs. 6-9 and
6-10.

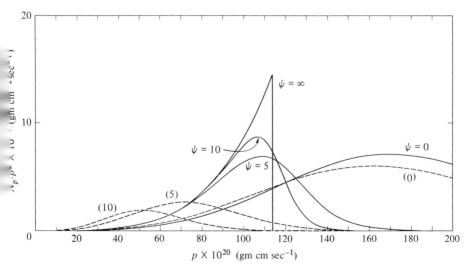

Let us now consider the situation quantitatively. From eqs. (6-83) and (6-87), we have

$$P = \frac{8\pi}{3mh^3} \int_0^\infty \frac{p^4 \, dp}{\exp\left[(p^2/2mkT) - \psi\right] + 1}.$$

To obtain the result in the usual form, we transform the variable from the momentum p to the energy divided by kT, which we shall denote by u:

$$u = \frac{1}{2}\frac{mv^2}{kT} = \frac{p^2}{2mkT}. \tag{6-94}$$

Then

$$P = \frac{8\pi}{3h^3}(2mkT)^{3/2}kT \int_0^\infty \frac{u^{3/2} \, du}{e^{u-\psi} + 1}.$$

The density can also be expressed in terms of u:

$$\frac{\rho}{\mu_e H} = N = \frac{4\pi}{h^3}(2mkT)^{3/2} \int_0^\infty \frac{u^{1/2} \, du}{e^{u-\psi} + 1}.$$

Upon introducing the Fermi–Dirac integrals, defined by

$$F_i(\psi) = \int_0^\infty \frac{u^i \, du}{e^{u-\psi} + 1}, \tag{6-95}$$

we obtain the expressions

$$P = \frac{4\pi}{h^3}(2mkT)^{3/2}kT[\tfrac{2}{3}F_{3/2}(\psi)] \tag{6-96}$$

and

$$\frac{\rho}{\mu_e H} = \frac{4\pi}{h^3}(2mkT)^{3/2}F_{1/2}(\psi). \tag{6-97}$$

The ratio of the pressure and the density is therefore

$$\frac{P}{\rho} = \frac{kT}{\mu_e H}\frac{\tfrac{2}{3}F_{3/2}(\psi)}{F_{1/2}(\psi)}, \tag{6-98}$$

which is nearly the same as the perfect gas law when

$$\frac{\tfrac{2}{3}F_{3/2}(\psi)}{F_{1/2}(\psi)} \approx 1.$$

This occurs, as we have already noted during the discussions of Figs. 6-9 and 6-10, when $\psi \ll 0$. The values of $\tfrac{2}{3}F_{3/2}(\psi)$ and $F_{1/2}(\psi)$ for various values of ψ are compared in Table 6-1. The last column of this table serves also to emphasize the fact that matter does not suddenly become degenerate at some density or temperature. Departures from the perfect gas law exist at *all* densities greater than zero and *all* temperatures less than infinity, and it is only a question of which significant figure in the pressure is affected.

Table 6-1   Values of the Fermi–Dirac Integrals. [From calculations by G. Wares, published by R. Härm and M. Schwarzschild, 1955 (306).]

ψ	$F_{1/2}(\psi)$	$\frac{2}{3}F_{3/2}(\psi)$	$\frac{2}{3}F_{3/2}(\psi)/F_{1/2}(\psi)$
−7	0.0008079	0.0008079	1.0000
−5	0.0059573	0.0059644	1.0012
−2	0.11459	0.11720	1.0228
0	0.67809	0.76854	1.1334
+2	2.5025	3.6915	1.4751
+3	3.9770	6.9025	1.7356
+5	7.8380	18.535	2.3648
+10	21.344	89.513	4.1938
+20	59.813	484.38	8.0982
+100	666.75	26683	40.019

Equation (6-96) must, of course, reduce to the perfect gas law when $\psi \ll 0$ and to eq. (6-86) when $\psi \gg 0$. If $\psi \ll 0$, we have

$$F_{3/2}(\psi) \approx e^{\psi} \int_{0}^{\infty} u^{3/2} e^{-u}\,du,$$

which we integrate by parts:

$$F_{3/2}(\psi) \approx e^{\psi}[-u^{3/2}e^{-u}]_{0}^{\infty} + \tfrac{3}{2}e^{\psi}\int_{0}^{\infty} u^{1/2}e^{-u}\,du.$$

The first term in this equation vanishes, and the second term is $(3/2)F_{1/2}(\psi)$ in this approximation. Hence we find from eq. (6-98) that

$$\frac{P}{\rho} = \frac{kT}{\mu_{e}H},$$

which is the perfect gas law.

If $\psi \gg 0$, the denominator of the integrand of $F_{3/2}(\psi)$ is approximately equal to unity for $u \ll \psi$ and increases rapidly to values much greater than unity for $u > \psi$. A graph of the integrand $u^{3/2}/(e^{u-\psi} + 1)$ would resemble the curves for large ψ in Figs. 6-9 and 6-10. Thus we may take

$$F_{3/2}(\psi) \approx \int_{0}^{\psi} u^{3/2}\,du$$

$$= \tfrac{2}{5}\psi^{5/2}.$$

Similarly,

$$F_{1/2}(\psi) = \int_{0}^{\psi} u^{1/2}\,du$$

$$= \tfrac{2}{3}\psi^{3/2}.$$

Thus we have from eqs. (6-96) and (6-97) that

$$P = \frac{4\pi}{h^3}(2mkT)^{3/2}kT \cdot \frac{2}{3} \cdot \frac{2}{5}\psi^{5/2}$$

and

$$\frac{\rho}{\mu_e H} = \frac{4\pi}{h^3}(2mkT)^{3/2} \cdot \frac{2}{3}\psi^{3/2},$$

from which we find that

$$P = \left(\frac{3}{8\pi}\right)^{2/3} \frac{h^2}{5mH^{5/3}} \frac{1}{\mu_e^{5/3}} \rho^{5/3}.$$

This agrees with eq. (6-86) for the case of complete degeneracy.

As we have determined at the beginning (Section 8-1), the ions normally obey the perfect gas law to a very good approximation even when the electrons are highly degenerate. The equation of state of the gas must be written with separate terms for the pressure due to ions, P_i, and that due to electrons, P_e; and for non-degeneracy of the ions, we have

$$P_{\text{gas}} = P_i + P_e$$

$$= \frac{k}{H}\rho T\left[\frac{1}{\mu_i} + \frac{1}{\mu_e}\frac{\frac{2}{3}F_{3/2}(\psi)}{F_{1/2}(\psi)}\right]. \tag{6-99}$$

If $\psi \gg 0$, the pressure due to the ions may be neglected if high accuracy is not required.

PROBLEMS

1. (a) Re-write the differential equations for stellar structure with M_r rather than r as the independent variable.
   (b) Explain why it may be more convenient to use the equations in this form when calculating an evolutionary sequence.

2. Refer to Table 7-25. Given the values of ρ_c, T_c, and the chemical composition (for which $Z = 0.02$), calculate
   (a) P_c;
   (b) P, ρ, and T at the outermost point tabulated for the convective core (indicated by italics in the column for T). Assume the polytropic relations.
   (c) Suggest reasons for any discrepancies between the answers to parts (a) and (b) and the published values.

3. Illustrate schematically the distribution of L_r inside a star in the following circumstances:
   (a) nuclear processes occur near the center;

(b) energy is liberated near the center while the remainder of the star undergoes gravitational contraction;

(c) nuclear transmutation and gravitational contraction proceed in the core, while expansion takes place outside the core;

(d) all the energy is produced by a thin shell at the edge of a central region exhausted of nuclear fuel.

(e) Compare the answers obtained above with the graphs of L_r in Figs. 7-10A, 7-5C, 7-28A, and 7-26A, respectively.

4. Suppose that a star contracts quasi-statically in such a way that the fraction of the total mass within any given fraction of the total radius remains unchanged. If the radius contracts to 90 per cent of its initial value, how will the temperatures be changed?

5. Calculate the relative values of ϵ_{pp} and ϵ_{CN} at the center of the Sun and at the center of a main-sequence star of mass 5 $M_\odot$. Use the data of Tables 7-25, 7-38, 10-13, and 10-14.

6. Is the distribution of masses along the main sequence related to the Vogt–Russell theorem?

7

STELLAR EVOLUTION

In the preceding chapter, we have described how a stellar model may be calculated. Such a model, however, can represent a star at only one epoch, for the continual emission of radiation from the surface requires that some process be taking place within the star to supply the outflowing energy. Evolution is a consequence of the fact that a star is shining.

Our knowledge of the course of stellar evolution has been increasing rapidly during the past decade, yet much remains unclear. The very early stages of star formation and the events following the red-giant stage are particularly obscure. Of great uncertainty is the question whether or not a loss of mass occurs during these phases; and, if so, whether the loss is abrupt or continuous, and how much of the stellar material is ejected.

The following pages describe the principal features of present ideas concerning stellar evolution. We shall trace the development of a star from the time it is a dense, self-gravitating cloud in the interstellar medium, through the pre–main-sequence, main-sequence, and giant stages. We shall mention some of the properties of post-giant stars and, finally, the structure of the white dwarfs, which are in the final phase of evolution. We shall point out some of the ways in which the stellar models depend upon the assumptions made in their construction; and we shall consider how well the theory accounts for the observations of actual stars.

Tabulated models for various masses and evolutionary stages are presented at the end of the chapter.

1 PROTOSTARS

Primitive stars in the process of formation are called *protostars*. There is little doubt that the stars have condensed from the interstellar medium of gas and dust particles (grains). The gas is principally hydrogen, which constitutes perhaps 60 to 70 per cent of the mass of the gas. Most of the remainder is helium, but there exists a few per cent of heavier elements. The composition of the grains is still uncertain. It has long been supposed that their surface, at least, may consist of ices of water, methane, and ammonia, while the core might be composed of heavier material including compounds of such elements as iron, silicon, magnesium, and oxygen. Recent observations, however, indicate that there is little ice in the grains.* An alternative hypothesis is that the grains are composed of graphite, possibly coated with solid hydrogen†; but again the theory encounters difficulties.‡ The size of a grain is of the order of 10^{-5} cm. The density of the grains, counted per unit volume of interstellar space, is about 10^{-26} gm cm^{-3}, while that of the gas is about 10^{-24} gm cm^{-3} or 1 atom per cm³. In nebulae, the densities may be as much as 10^4 times greater.

The relative abundances of the elements in the interstellar medium are similar to those found in Population I stars, and this fact is consistent with the hypothesis that the stars have condensed from this material. Population II stars, however, may contain as little as a hundredth of the proportion of heavier elements that is contained in Population I. It is supposed that Population II stars formed at earlier times in the history of the Galaxy, when the interstellar matter had not yet been enriched in heavier elements. This enrichment process is believed to be taking place continuously, as elements that have been synthesized in stellar interiors are by various processes released into space.§

The main-sequence O and B stars that are now observed tend to be found in close association with gas and dust. Dynamical considerations support the hypothesis that these stars have been formed comparatively recently from the surrounding material. Furthermore, the luminosities of these stars are so high that they would have exhausted their fuel supply if they had been formed less than 10^7 years ago.

Dark globules, sometimes found in nebulae, may be stars at an early stage of formation. There is also evidence that we might possibly be witnessing the collapse of protostars in the Orion Nebula.‖ The remarkable star FU Orionis, which became brighter by 5 or 6 magnitudes late in 1936 and has since maintained nearly that luminosity, may possibly be a star that has just passed through the final protostellar collapse.¶ During this stage, a shock wave is formed, and there is a sudden outpouring of energy. Recent observations in the infrared, however, shed doubt on the interpretation that protostars are being observed.

We now consider the course of events leading to the formation of a star. The process by which an interstellar cloud is concentrated until it is held together gravitationally to become a protostar is not known. In quantitative

* R. F. Knacke, D. D. Cudaback, and J. E. Gaustad, 1969 (308).

† N. C. Wickramasinghe and K. S. Krishna Swamy, 1969 (309).

‡ G. B. Field, 1969 (310).

§ Some aspects and problems of the chemical evolution of stars are discussed by I. R. King, 1971 (199zh).

‖ E. E. Becklin and G. Neugebauer, 1967 (311); and D. E. Kleinmann and F. J. Low, 1967 (312).

¶ G. H. Herbig (A. Beer and K. Aa. Strand, eds.), 1966 (313), p. 109 et seq.

work, it has simply been assumed that the number of atoms per cm^3 has somehow increased about a thousand-fold over that in a dense nebula. The two principal factors inhibiting the formation of a protostar are that the gas has a tendency to disperse before the density becomes high enough for self-gravitation to be effective, and that any initial angular momentum would cause excessively rapid rotation as the material contracts. Some mechanism must therefore be provided for gathering the material into a sufficiently small volume that self-gravitation may become effective, and the angular momentum must in some way be removed. For the sake of tractability, current theories neglect rotation, magnetic fields, and mass loss, although these may be important.

We shall now describe some calculations for a protostar of one solar mass.* The initial density is assumed to be $n = 10^8$ atomic mass units per cm^3 or $\rho = 1.7 \times 10^{-16}$ gm cm^{-3}, with a radius $R = 1.4 \times 10^{16}$ cm or 930 AU. An average temperature for the protostar may be defined as the total thermal energy divided by $\frac{3}{2}k \times$ number of particles in the protostar [cf. eq. (6-36)]. This value is taken initially to be 50°K, although this is probably too high. The opacity is provided chiefly by grains. The density and optical thickness are so low that photons escape readily from the protostar. As a consequence, most of the energy made available by the contraction is lost by radiation and does not raise the temperature of the gas in accordance with the virial theorem [see eq. (6-59)]. The pressure therefore remains much too low to support the gas against further compression, and a nearly free fall of the particles toward the center takes place.

During the first 5000 years, the density remains nearly uniform throughout the entire volume (while increasing with time), but then the material rapidly becomes highly concentrated toward the center. The initial and final configurations of this phase are described in Table 7-1 and are represented in the Hertzsprung–Russell diagram of Fig. 7-1.

* The remainder of this section describes some of the features of the investigations of J. E. Gaustad, 1963 (314); R. J. Gould, 1964 (315); S. E. Ananaba and J. E. Gaustad, 1968 (316); and P. Bodenheimer, 1968 (317).

Table 7-1   Early Stages of Protostellar Collapse ($M = 1\ M_\odot$). [After S. E. Ananaba and J. E. Gaustad, 1968 (316).]

TIME (YEARS)	R/R_0*	ρ† (gm cm^{-3})	n† (AMU cm^{-3})	T‡ (°K)	T_{eff} (°K)	$L/L_\odot$	$\mathcal{M}_{bol}$
0.0	1.0	1.7×10^{-16}	1.0×10^8	50	22	7.5	2.5
5040	0.079	3.4×10^{-13}	2.0×10^{11}	150	19	0.024	8.7

* R_0, the initial radius of the protostar, is 1.4×10^{16} cm = 930 AU.
† The density is uniform throughout each model.
‡ T is an average temperature defined as the total thermal energy divided by $\frac{3}{2}k \times$ number of particles in the protostar.

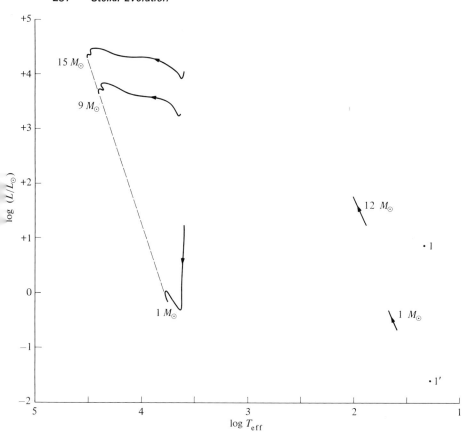

Fig. 7-1 Evolutionary Tracks of Protostars and Pre–Main-Sequence Stars in the Hertzsprung–Russell Diagram. At left are shown the tracks of pre–main-sequence stars with masses 15 $M_\odot$, 9 $M_\odot$, and 1 $M_\odot$, which are identical with those of Fig. 7-3A. The zero-age main sequence is represented by the *dashed line*. At right, the *dot labeled 1* is the initial model for a protostar of mass 1 $M_\odot$ and the *dot labeled 1′* represents the protostar 5000 years later. The *short lines* represent a later stage of evolution of protostars of mass 1 $M_\odot$ and 12 $M_\odot$. The time required to traverse the length of the short line is 18 years for a mass of 1 $M_\odot$ and 15 years for a mass of 12 $M_\odot$. The units of T_{eff} are degrees Kelvin. [The pre–main-sequence tracks are from I. Iben, Jr., 1965 (321). The dots are from S. E. Ananaba and J. E. Gaustad, 1968 (316). The short lines are from P. Bodenheimer, 1968 (317).]

The collapse is temporarily slowed in the central region when that part of the protostar becomes opaque, for the trapped photons interact with the particles to increase the average kinetic energy of the particles and hence the temperature and pressure of the gas. By this time, the grains have evaporated;

and the gas, chiefly in the form of H_2 molecules, is now responsible for the opacity. As the temperature rises above 1300°K, the dissociation of H_2 becomes a new means of diverting energy, and the rate of increase of the temperature is again inadequate to provide the necessary increase in gas pressure to prevent a rapid collapse.* When the dissociation of H_2 is nearly complete, the pressure near the center becomes large enough to produce a deceleration there for the second time, although the rate of contraction continues to be very high. The material farther out, in the zone where dissociation is still active, continues to collapse at an increasing rate. When that material reaches a supersonic velocity relative to the inner region, a shock front is formed. The calculations here described were not carried beyond this stage. The results are summarized in Table 7-2. The initial model in this series of calculations has somewhat different properties from those of Table 7-1; but for a general view of events, we may consider these models to represent a continuous sequence. Note that the time in Table 7-2 is counted from the epoch of the first model of that series, and that only 18 years are required for an increase in the central density by a factor of 10^{10}! The inner regions are contracting very rapidly, although the total radius remains approximately constant during this time.

A protostar of 12 solar masses has a similar history, except that the first deceleration does not occur. Results for this case are presented in Table 7-3. The tracks of the models with masses 1 $M_\odot$ and 12 $M_\odot$ are shown in Fig. 7-1.

* At higher temperatures, the ionization of hydrogen and helium has a similar effect.

Table 7-2 Intermediate Stages of Protostellar Collapse* ($M = 1\ M_\odot$). [After P. Bodenheimer, 1968 (317).]

TIME (YEARS)	ρ_c (gm cm^{-3})	$\rho_c/\bar{\rho}$	T_c (°K)	T_{eff} (°K)	$L/L_\odot$	$\mathscr{M}_{bol}$	FORM OF HYDROGEN
0.0	7.95 (-12)	6.9 (0)	42	39	0.21	6.4	H_2
11.071	2.85 (-11)	2.6 (1)	61	43	0.30	6.0	H_2
16.889	6.38 (-10)	5.9 (2)	185	46	0.44	5.6	H_2
17.720	4.46 (-9)	4.1 (3)	384	47	0.48	5.5	H_2
18.143	6.96 (-8)	6.4 (4)	1,120	47	0.48	5.5	H_2
18.298	1.11 (-6)	1.0 (6)	2,430	47	0.48	5.5	H_2, H
18.357	8.20 (-5)	7.5 (7)	4,090	47	0.48	5.5	H_2, H
18.363	7.56 (-4)	7.0 (8)	5,800	47	0.48	5.5	H, H_2
18.365	6.41 (-3)	5.9 (9)	10,400	47	0.48	5.5	H, H_2
18.366	2.33 (-2)	2.1 (10)	16,900	47	0.48	5.5	H, H^+
18.366	5.62 (-2)	5.2 (10)	26,400	47	0.48	5.5	H, H^+

* Values at the center are designated by the subscript c; $\bar{\rho}$ is the mean density.
A number in parentheses is the power of 10 by which a tabular entry must be multiplied.
The radius of the protostar remains approximately 7.6×10^{14} cm = 51 AU.

Table 7-3   Intermediate Stages of Protostellar Collapse* ($M = 12\ M_\odot$). [After P. Bodenheimer, 1968 (317).]

TIME (YEARS)	ρ_c (gm cm^{-3})	$\rho_c/\bar{\rho}$	T_c (°K)	T_{eff} (°K)	$L/L_\odot$	$\mathscr{M}_{\text{bol}}$	FORM OF HYDROGEN
0.0	7.66 (−12)	6.9 (0)	101	76	17	1.6	H$_2$
6.166	1.67 (−11)	1.5 (1)	124	95	44	0.6	H$_2$
11.877	9.47 (−11)	8.4 (1)	208	100	52	0.4	H$_2$
14.158	8.17 (−10)	7.2 (2)	435	102	58	0.3	H$_2$
15.019	1.47 (−8)	1.3 (4)	1,270	102	58	0.3	H$_2$
15.244	3.45 (−7)	3.0 (5)	2,450	102	58	0.3	H$_2$, H
15.308	2.71 (−5)	2.4 (7)	3,900	102	58	0.3	H$_2$, H
15.314	2.32 (−4)	2.0 (8)	5,300	102	58	0.3	H, H$_2$
15.317	1.92 (−3)	1.7 (9)	8,960	102	58	0.3	H, H$_2$
15.318	8.68 (−3)	7.6 (9)	17,000	102	58	0.3	H, H$^+$
15.319	2.70 (−2)	2.4 (10)	28,300	102	58	0.3	H, H$^+$

* Values at the center are designated by the subscript c; $\bar{\rho}$ is the mean density. A number in parentheses is the power of 10 by which a tabular entry must be multiplied. The radius of the protostar remains approximately 1.7×10^{15} cm = 120 AU.

If the mass of a protostar is only 0.1 $M_\odot$, the opacity is sufficiently high and the luminosity sufficiently low that dynamical collapse occurs only after dissociation of H$_2$ begins. Otherwise, a relatively slow contraction takes place, and the protostar remains in quasi-equilibrium. This process, called a *Helmholtz–Kelvin contraction*, was described in Chapter 6, Section 5-1.

The details of the last stages of protostellar evolution are still doubtful, and we proceed directly to the pre–main-sequence phase.

2 PRE–MAIN-SEQUENCE STARS

While protostars are characterized by rapid, nearly free-fall collapse of the material toward the center, the pre–main-sequence stage of evolution is governed by a slower contraction. Gravitation continues to bring the matter into a smaller volume, but it is now opposed by the gas pressure that has been increasing during the collapse phase. The configuration remains in quasi-equilibrium: the contraction is slow enough that a model describing the configuration at any moment may be calculated under the assumption that hydrostatic equilibrium prevails.

Before the importance of outer convective envelopes became clear, a calculation of the evolutionary tracks in the Hertzsprung–Russell diagram gave the results shown in Fig. 7-2.* The effects of the ionization of hydrogen

* L. G. Henyey, R. LeLevier, and R. D. Levée, 1955 (318).

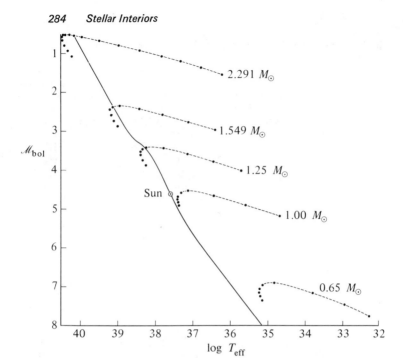

Fig. 7-2 Evolutionary Tracks of Pre–Main-Sequence Stars in the Hertzsprung–Russell Diagram. The solid line represents the main sequence. The masses of the models are indicated in the figure and the chemical composition is $X = 0.74$, $Y = 0.25$, and $Z = 0.01$. The units of T_{eff} are degrees Kelvin. [After L. G. Henyey, R. LeLevier, and R. D. Levée, 1955 (318).]

and helium were not considered, and, therefore, radiative equilibrium was assumed for the outer portions. As the radii of the models decrease with time, the luminosities increase gradually, and the tracks are directed toward the left and upwards in the diagram.

The tracks just described are considerably modified when the outer convection zone is taken into account.* Figures 7-3A and 7-3B present such results. The evolutionary path for the lower-mass stars is now initially downwards, rather than toward the left. Although the nearly vertical tracks for stars of low mass are now generally favored, the observations do not unequivocally prove their correctness; there is, in fact, some evidence in support of the nearly horizontal tracks.†

Another possibility exists if the inner regions of the protostar become opaque sooner than the outer parts, and the dividing photospheric surface gradually moves outwards with respect to mass as the contraction progresses.

---

* C. Hayashi, 1961 (319).
† See P. Bodenheimer, 1966 (320) for a brief review.

The evolutionary tracks, which depend upon the time required for the mass-accretion process, are shown in Fig. 7-4.

We shall now describe some of the details of the models calculated by Iben.* The tracks in the Hertzsprung–Russell diagram are shown in Fig. 7-3A, and the evolutionary times are given in Tables 7-4A and 7-4B. The abundances of hydrogen, helium, and heavier elements are assumed to be

$$X = 0.708, \qquad Y = 0.272, \qquad Z = 0.020.$$

The C^{12} abundance is initially taken to be higher than that which would exist if the nuclear reactions that create and destroy this isotope were in equilibrium, and the gradual depletion of C^{12} to an equilibrium abundance is studied. The initial model for each mass is chosen such that the central temperature is already high enough that hydrogen and helium are ionized throughout most of the model,† and yet the temperature is too low for energy generation by nuclear processes to be significant in comparison with that by gravitational contraction. For the model of one solar mass, the initial model has $\log (L/L_\odot) \sim 1.2$.

Some of the details of the evolution of a star of mass 1 $M_\odot$ are shown in Figs. 7-5A, 7-5B, and 7-5C. During the first 2×10^{14} seconds or 7×10^6 years, the radius and luminosity decrease in such a way that the effective temperature remains approximately constant at 4200°K ($\log T_{\text{eff}} = 3.62$). In Fig. 7-3A, the star follows the nearly vertical *Hayashi track* for a completely convective configuration of one solar mass. During this time, the ratio of central density to mean density remains nearly constant. Since the effective temperature is at first low, there is a deep convective envelope resulting from the ionization of hydrogen and helium (see Section 4-4 of Chapter 6). The convection, in fact, extends to the center during the first 10^6 years. Then a radiative core develops and increases in mass, eventually extending to the surface, as the opacities in the inner regions diminish with the increasing temperatures.

After the first 10^7 years ($\log t \approx 14.5$), nuclear reactions begin to contribute perceptibly to the luminosity. This marks the beginning of the rise in luminosity in Figs. 7-5A and 7-3A. Until that time, gravitational contraction supplies the luminosity at a net rate for the model designated by L_g.‡ When nuclear reactions become effective near the center, the energy they release

---

* The following discussion is drawn from the paper of I. Iben, Jr., 1965 (321).

† It was noted in the discussion of protostars that, under the prevailing conditions, the ionization of hydrogen and helium induces rapid collapse, rather than quasi-equilibrium contraction.

‡ The net rate L_g is the time rate of increase of the quantity: ($-$gravitational potential energy $-$ thermal energy). This may be compared with the result from eq. (6-59) for a monatomic gas, $\Delta\Omega = -2\,\Delta\mathscr{T}$; an amount of energy ΔE_{rad} must be lost by radiation such that $\Delta E_{\text{rad}} = \Delta\mathscr{T} = -\Delta\Omega - \Delta\mathscr{T}$.

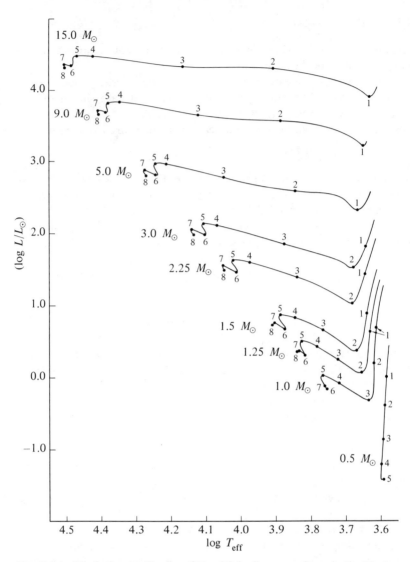

Fig. 7-3A Evolutionary Tracks of Pre–Main-Sequence Stars in the Hertzsprung-Russell Diagram. The mass, in units of the solar mass, is given at the left of each track. The small numbers correspond to the points in Table 7-4A, which give the time measured from the initial model for each mass. The units of T_{eff} are degrees Kelvin. [After I. Iben, Jr., 1965 (321).]

can *expand* the central regions and *increase* their potential energy. In this case, the central region makes a negative contribution to L_g. This occurs near $\log t \sim 15.0$, as indicated in Fig. 7-5B by the negative values of L_g/L and the diminished values of $\log \rho_c$ and $\log T_c$.* The nuclear processes taking place

---

* The subscript c designates the center.

Table 7-4A   Time t in Years Measured from the Initial Model for Each Mass. The last point for each mass represents the main sequence.* [From I. Iben, Jr., 1965 (321).]

POINT IN FIG. 7-3A	MASS OF MODEL (UNITS OF THE SOLAR MASS)								
	15	9	5	3	2.25	1.5	1.25	1.0	0.5
	10^4	10^5	10^5	10^6	10^6	10^7	10^7	10^7	10^8
1	0.067	0.014	0.294	0.034	0.079	0.023	0.045	0.012	0.003
2	0.377	0.015	1.069	0.208	0.594	0.236	0.396	0.106	0.018
3	0.935	0.364	2.001	0.763	1.883	0.580	0.880	0.891	0.087
4	2.203	0.699	2.860	1.135	2.505	0.758	1.115	1.821	0.309
5	2.657	0.792	3.137	1.250	2.818	0.862	1.404	2.529	1.550
6	3.984	1.019	3.880	1.465	3.319	1.043	1.755	3.418	—
7	4.585	1.915	4.559	1.741	3.993	1.339	2.796	5.016	—
8	6.170	1.505	5.759	2.514	5.855	1.821	2.954	—	—

* Each entry must be multiplied by 10^n as given at the head of each column.

are the conversion of H^1 into H^2 and then into He^3; and of C^{12} into N^{13}, C^{13}, and finally into N^{14} [see eqs. (6-61) to (6-63) and also (6-71) to (6-72)]. The nuclear reactions that would complete the full p-p chain and CN cycle do not operate efficiently at these low temperatures. The part of the luminosity generated by nuclear sources,

$$L_{\mathrm{nucl}} = \int_0^M \epsilon \, dM_r,$$

Table 7-4B   The Logarithm of the Time in Seconds, $\log t$, Measured From the Initial Models for Masses 1 $M_\odot$ and 15 $M_\odot$. [From data of I. Iben, Jr., 1965 (321).]

POINT IN FIG. 7-3A	MASS OF MODEL (UNITS OF THE SOLAR MASS)	
	15	1.0
1	10.33	12.57
2	11.07	13.52
3	11.47	14.45
4	11.84	14.76
5	11.92	14.90
6	12.10	15.03
7	12.16	15.20
8	12.29	—

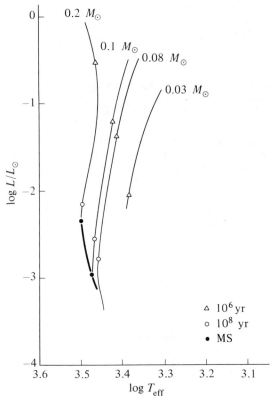

Fig. 7-3B Evolutionary Tracks of Pre–Main-Sequence Stars of Low Mass in the Hertzsprung–Russell Diagram. The masses, and the ages at two points on each track, are indicated. The heavy curve (*MS*) is the hydrogen-burning main sequence. The convective parameter is assumed to have the value $l/H = 1.0$. [Adapted from A. S. Grossman and H. C. Graboske, Jr., 1971 (400).]

together with the net contribution to the luminosity generated by the contraction process, L_g, must equal the total luminosity L:*

$$L_{nucl} + L_g = L.$$

As a result of the nuclear reactions taking place near the center, a convective core develops shortly before $\log t = 14.9$. At this time also, the radiative region that had been growing outwards from the center has reached the surface, and the model now has a radiative envelope and a convective core. However, as C^{12} is depleted toward its equilibrium abundance and the *p-p*

---

* Since part of L_{nucl} can be absorbed by the material and transformed into a negative contribution to L_g, the fraction of the luminosity that is *generated* by nuclear reactions is not necessarily the same as the fraction L_{nucl}^{out}/L of the luminosity *emitted* by the star; and L_g/L is not necessarily the same as L_g^{out}/L.

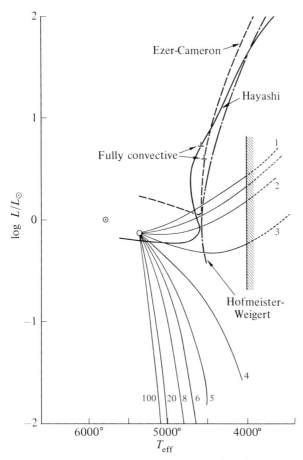

Fig. 7-4 Schematic Evolutionary Tracks of Pre–Main-Sequence Stars in the Hertzsprung–Russell Diagram. The units of T_{eff} are degrees Kelvin. The *numbered tracks* refer to models in which the photospheric surface moves outwards in time. The parameter is 4×10^8 years$/\tau_0$, where τ_0 is the time scale of the accretion; the mass M below the photosphere is assumed to increase at the rate $dM/dt = (\tau_0 M_0)^{-1} M^2$, where M_0 is the mass at $t = 0$. In this figure, $M_0 = M_\odot$. The terminal point of the tracks is the model calculated for the homogeneous Sun by R. L. Sears, 1959 (367). The *encircled dot* marks the position of the present Sun. The comparison tracks are those computed by D. Ezer and A. G. W. Cameron, 1963 (368); C. Hayashi, 1961 (319); and E. Hofmeister and A. Weigert (unpublished). The *vertical line* is the approximate minimum effective temperature of fully convective models. [After K. von Sengbusch and S. Temesvary (R. F. Stein and A. G. W. Cameron, eds.), 1966 (59), p. 212.]

chain becomes relatively more important, the temperature gradient near the center is reduced and convection is retarded. The convective core disappears at about $\log t = 15.3$. The waning of the luminosity along the initial downward track of Fig. 7-3A is reversed near point 3, at $\log t = 14.49$. Figure 7-5B

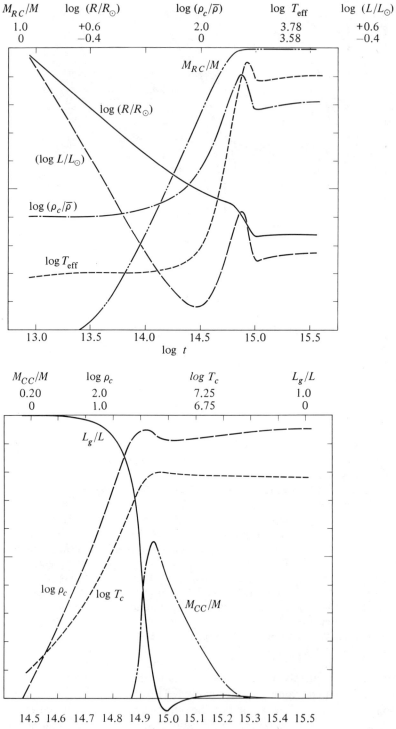

M_{RC}/M	$\log (R/R_\odot)$	$\log (\rho_c/\bar\rho)$	$\log T_{eff}$	$\log (L/L_\odot)$
1.0	+0.6	2.0	3.78	+0.6
0	−0.4	0	3.58	−0.4

M_{CC}/M	$\log \rho_c$	$\log T_c$	L_g/L
0.20	2.0	7.25	1.0
0	1.0	6.75	0

r	P	ρ	T	L_r
0.882 $R_\odot$	1.647×10^{17}	85.59	14.07×10^6	0.911 $L_\odot$
0	0	0	0	0

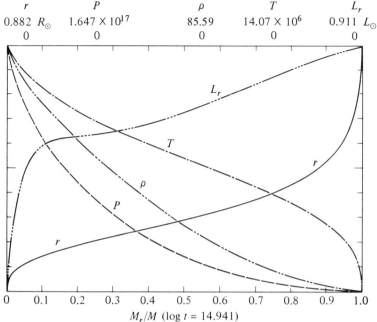

M_r/M (log $t = 14.941$)

Fig. 7-5A The Time Variation of Some Properties of a Pre–Main-Sequence Star of Mass 1 $M_\odot$. The abscissa is log t, where t is the time in seconds measured from the initial model of the series for this mass. The upper and lower limits of each ordinate are given. The ordinates are: M_{RC}/M, the fraction of the total mass contained in a radiative core; log $(R/R_\odot)$, where $R/R_\odot$ is the total radius relative to that of the Sun ($R_\odot = 6.96 \times 10^{10}$ cm); log $(\rho_c/\bar\rho)$, where ρ_c is the central density and $\bar\rho$ is the mean density; log $T_{\rm eff}$, where $T_{\rm eff}$ is the effective temperature in degrees Kelvin; and log $(L/L_\odot)$, where $L/L_\odot$ is the luminosity relative to that of the Sun ($L_\odot = 3.86 \times 10^{33}$ erg sec^{-1}). [After I. Iben, Jr., 1965 (321).]

Fig. 7-5B The Time Variation of Some Properties of a Pre–Main-Sequence Star of Mass 1 $M_\odot$. The abscissa is log t, where t is the time in seconds measured from the initial model of the series for this mass. The upper and lower limits of the scale for each curve are given. The ordinates are M_{CC}/M, the fraction of the mass contained in a convective core; log ρ_c, where ρ_c is the central density in gm cm^{-3}; log T_c, where T_c is the central temperature in degrees Kelvin; and L_g/L, the net fraction of the luminosity that is generated by gravitational contraction (but not necessarily the fraction of the *emitted* radiation that is due to gravitational contraction—see text). The value of L_g/L becomes negative near log $t = 15.0$: zero for this ordinate is on the horizontal axis. [Adapted from I. Iben, Jr., 1965 (321).]

Fig. 7-5C A Model of Mass 1 $M_\odot$ During the Pre–Main-Sequence Phase at Time log $t = 14.941$. The time is measured in seconds from the initial model of the series for this mass. The abscissa is the fractional mass M_r/M. The upper and lower limits of each ordinate are given. Each upper limit is the maximum value in the model. The ordinates are r, the radius in units of the solar radius ($R_\odot = 6.96 \times 10^{10}$ cm); P, the pressure in dyne cm^{-2}; ρ, the density in gm cm^{-3}; T, the temperature in degrees Kelvin; and L_r, the net luminosity in units of the solar luminosity ($L_\odot = 3.86 \times 10^{33}$ erg sec^{-1}). [Adapted from I. Iben, Jr., 1965 (321).]

291

reveals that at this time L_g/L begins to fall below unity, and therefore L_{nucl}/L rises from a value close to zero; the increasing central temperature and density have at last become high enough for nuclear reactions to begin making a contribution to the luminosity. At point 5 in Fig. 7-3A, the luminosity reaches a maximum and then declines as the stellar structure adjusts to the replacement of gravitational contraction by nuclear energy production, and the model settles toward a temporary C^{12}-burning main sequence. The supply of C^{12} is small, however, and the rapid depletion of the nuclear fuel leads to a slight further gravitational contraction before the central temperature and density become high enough for nuclear reactions, especially the *p-p* chain, to become the sole source of energy.

Fig. 7-6 The Time Variation of Some Properties of a Pre–Main-Sequence Star of Mass 15 $M_\odot$. The abscissa is log t, where t is the time in seconds measured from the initial model of the series for this mass. The upper and lower limits of each ordinate are given. The ordinates are M_{CC}/M, the fraction of the total mass contained in a convective core; log ρ_c, where ρ_c is the central density in gm cm^{-3}; log T_c, where T_c is the central temperature in degrees Kelvin; log $(L/L_\odot)$, where $L/L_\odot$ is the luminosity relative to the solar luminosity ($L_\odot = 3.86 \times 10^{33}$ erg sec^{-1}); and L_g/L, the net fraction of the luminosity that is generated by gravitational contraction (but not necessarily the fraction of the *emitted* radiation that is due to gravitational contraction—see text). [Adapted from I. Iben, Jr., 1965 (321).]

M_{CC}/M	log ρ_c	log T_c	log $(L/L_\odot)$	L_g/L
0.5	+0.9	7.6	4.55	1.0
0	−0.1	7.1	4.30	0

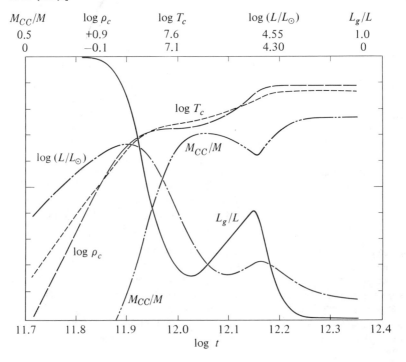

It is a matter of definition as to when the model may be said to have achieved main-sequence characteristics, but it will be considered here that the main sequence is reached at about $t = 5 \times 10^7$ years or $\log t = 15.2$, corresponding to point 7 in Fig. 7-3A. This model must yet evolve for 4.5×10^9 years, consuming much of the hydrogen in its inner regions, before the stage appropriate to the present Sun is reached.

The model of mass 15 $M_\odot$ undergoes a similar development, beginning with an initial structure possessing a small radiative core. Figure 7-6 shows the course of events beginning at a time somewhat preceding point 4 in Fig. 7-3A and continuing beyond point 8, which is taken to represent the main-sequence stage. During this time, the rising central temperature and density cause the onset of energy generation by reactions that convert C^{12} into N^{13}, and H^1 into He^3. This causes a decrease of L_g/L from unity, although the total luminosity L continues to rise. With nuclear sources now providing the flux near the center, the gravitational contraction there is temporarily retarded following $\log t = 11.9$, and the curve for $\log \rho_c$ therefore becomes nearly level. The curve for $\log T_c$ also rises more gradually. The slowing of the contraction results in a decrease in both the gravitational and total luminosity until the reduction of the C^{12} supply makes the nuclear source inadequate to maintain the structure. More rapid gravitational contraction then produces a rise in the luminosity, as well as in $\log \rho_c$ and $\log T_c$. The latter values finally become high enough for the full CN cycle (and also the CNO bi-cycle) to become effective, and the contraction is retarded. The ratio L_g/L decreases toward zero and L decreases to its main-sequence value.

The curve describing the mass of the convective core behaves rather like a mirror image to that of L_g/L. The contribution of gravitational contraction to the total energy output decreases when that due to nuclear processes increases; and the nuclear reactions promote a temperature gradient that is conducive to convection.

The track in Fig. 7-3A for a model with mass 0.5 $M_\odot$ displays only the initial, nearly vertical portion. The central temperature and density do not become high enough for C^{12}-burning to occur, although the conversion of H^1 into He^3 first reduces the rate of gravitational contraction and then produces an expansion of the core.

A comparison can be made with observations of actual stars in a (presumably) very young galactic cluster.* Figure 7-7 shows the Hertzsprung–Russell diagram for the stars of NGC 2264 and also the loci of models having the same age but different masses. Since the initial models for the various masses correspond to different epochs in the past, the ages have been standardized by measuring them from a time when the models would have had a theoretically infinite luminosity. Agreement between observation and theory can be achieved if one assumes that star formation in the cluster extended over

* This paragraph is based on the work of I. Iben, Jr., and R. J. Talbot, 1966 (322).

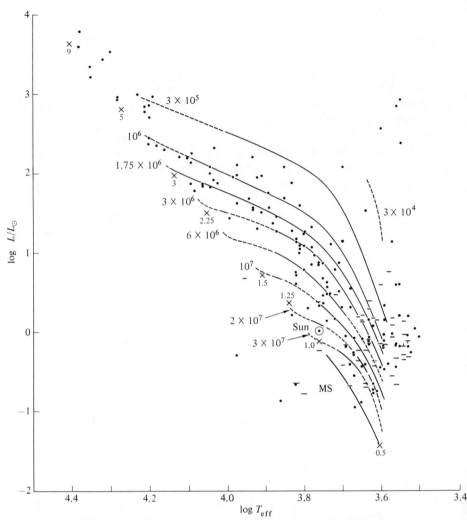

Fig. 7-7 Pre–Main-Sequence Models of Different Masses at the Same Age Compared with Observed Stars in the Galactic Cluster NGC 2264 in the Hertzsprung–Russell Diagram. *Dots* and *bars* refer to observations; bars represent stars showing Hα emission. Each point on a given locus corresponds to a different mass. The dashed portions of the loci are less accurate than the solid lines. The age in years, measured from the time when all models theoretically had infinite luminosity, is given beside each locus. The present position of the Sun is indicated by the *encircled dot*. The *crosses* are the zero-age main-sequence models of Fig. 7-3A, with the masses indicated. The lower end of the zero-age main sequence has been drawn as a solid line labeled *MS*. [Adapted from I. Iben, Jr., and R. J. Talbot, 1966 (322).]

an interval of time beginning more than 6.5×10^7 years ago, with the more massive stars tending to form later than those of lower mass.

It is important to realize that all stellar models depend upon the assumptions made in their construction. As an example of the effects of changing the parameters of the solution, Fig. 7-8 illustrates the sensitivity of the evolutionary track at one solar mass to a specific change in the metal content. This

Fig. 7-8 Comparison of Two Evolutionary Tracks of a Pre–Main-Sequence Star of One Solar Mass in the Hertzsprung–Russell Diagram. For the *solid curve*, it is assumed that the chemical composition includes a fraction 5.4×10^{-5}, by mass, of metals with ionization potential 7.5 eV. For the *dashed curve*, the fraction by mass of these elements is smaller by a factor of 10. [After I. Iben, Jr., 1965 (321).]

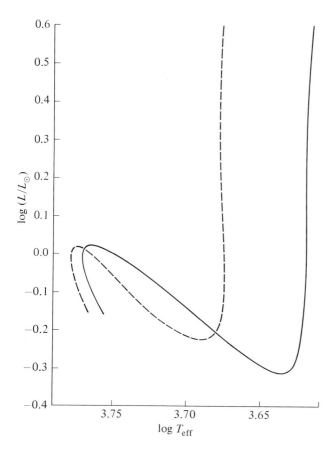

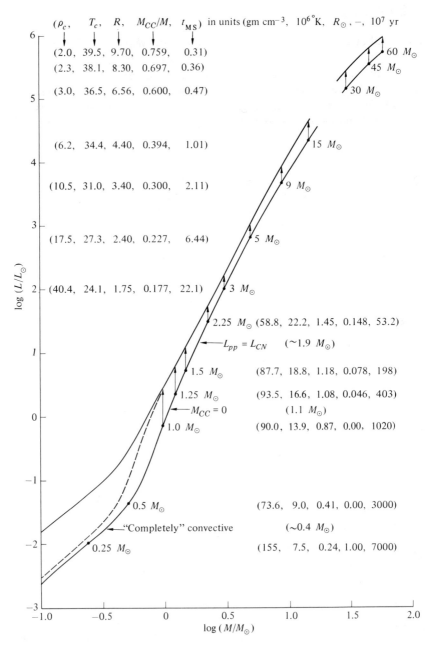

Fig. 7-9 The Theoretical Mass-Luminosity Relation. For $M \leqslant 15\ M_\odot$, the chemical composition is $X = 0.708$, $Y = 0.272$, $Z = 0.020$; for $M \geqslant 30\ M_\odot$, the chemical composition is $X = 0.70$, $Y = 0.27$, $Z = 0.03$. The *lower solid line* refers to the zero-age main sequence. The *upper solid curve* refers to the end of the main-sequence phase, the lower portion being an estimate. The *dashed curve* is an estimate for the locus of the low-mass models after 10^{10} years.

one parameter alone changes the effective temperature of a model by 600°K along the vertical portion of the track. Such differential effects between various possible solutions must be kept in mind when comparing different models representing the same star or when comparing theory with observations.

3 THE MAIN SEQUENCE

3-1 GENERAL DISCUSSION

The evolution described in the preceding sections requires 6×10^4 years for stars of 15 $M_\odot$ and 5×10^7 years for stars of 1 $M_\odot$. Less massive stars need still longer times to reach the main sequence and, in fact, some do not attain the main-sequence state at all. There is a limiting mass whose value is about 0.1 $M_\odot$, depending upon the composition.* Objects with smaller masses never develop sufficiently high central temperatures and densities for normal hydrogen-burning to begin. They contract until the matter becomes degenerate and eventually become completely degenerate black dwarfs.

As it arrives at the main sequence, a star is chemically homogeneous and becomes dependent upon nuclear sources for its supply of energy.† As the star gradually consumes the hydrogen near its center, converting it to helium, the structure changes very slowly and the star remains on the main sequence for an extended time. A star of one solar mass, for example, remains within the main-sequence band for 10^{10} years. The present age of the Sun is about one-half this. A star spends the major fraction of its lifetime in the main-sequence phase before it becomes a white dwarf; and it is for this reason that most stars are observed during this phase, that is, on the main sequence.

Some of the properties of main-sequence models are summarized in Fig. 7-9, which is a graph of the theoretical mass-luminosity relation for the

* S. S. Kumar, 1963 (323) and A. S. Grossman, 1970 (402).
† Actually, a slight amount of nuclear transmutation occurs prior to the main-sequence stage, as was described in Section 2, and the composition is not exactly uniform but is very nearly so.

The masses of the models are indicated. A key to the numerical entries is given at the top of the figure. The entries correspond to the mass indicated at the same horizontal level. The quantities given are the central density ρ_c, the central temperature T_c, the radius R, the maximum fraction M_{cc}/M of the mass contained in a convective core, and the time t_{MS} spent on the main sequence. [Adapted from I. Iben, Jr., 1967 (327). Data for masses 30 $M_\odot$, 45 $M_\odot$, and 60 $M_\odot$ are from R. Stothers, 1963 (324), 1964 (332), and 1966 (325).]

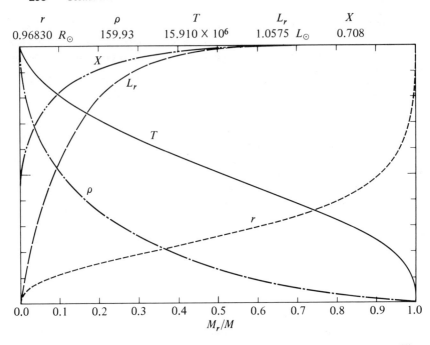

r	ρ	T	L_r	X
$0.96830\ R_\odot$	159.93	15.910×10^6	$1.0575\ L_\odot$	0.708

M_r/M

Fig. 7-10A A Model of Mass 1 $M_\odot$ during the Main-Sequence Phase at Time $t = 4.26990 \times 10^9$ Years. Radius r, density ρ, temperature T, net luminosity L_r, and hydrogen abundance X are shown as functions of fractional mass M_r/M. The lower limit of the ordinate is zero for all variables. The upper limits, given in the figure, are the total radius R (units of $R_\odot = 6.96 \times 10^{10}$ cm), central density ρ_c (gm cm^{-3}), central temperature T_c in degrees Kelvin, total luminosity L (units of $L_\odot = 3.86 \times 10^{33}$ erg sec^{-1}), and initial hydrogen abundance $X = 0.708$. The central pressure (not shown) is 2.5186×10^{17} dyne cm^{-2}. The time t is measured from the initial model calculated for the pre–main-sequence phase (see Section 2). [Adapted from I. Iben, Jr., 1967 (326).]

initial and terminal main-sequence structure.* The initial, or zero-age, main sequence is defined by a homogeneous chemical composition throughout the model (except for the very slight non-uniformity already noted). The termination of the main sequence is marked by the end of hydrogen-burning on a long time scale, as described below.

* Quantitative results depend upon the assumptions made in constructing the model in question (see Section 3-5 for some examples). All the models calculated by Iben and described in this chapter have the composition $X = 0.708$, $Y = 0.272$, $Z = 0.020$, while those of Stothers have $X = 0.70$, $Y = 0.27$, $Z = 0.03$. Iben's opacity coefficients do not include line absorption. (For the massive models considered by Stothers, electron scattering is the only important source of opacity; line absorption does not come into question.) We mention also that Iben's models have a ratio of mixing length to density scale-height l/H_d equal to $\frac{1}{2}$.

r	P	T	L_r	X
1.2681 $R_\odot$	13.146 × 10^{17}	19.097 × 10^6	2.1283 $L_\odot$	0.708

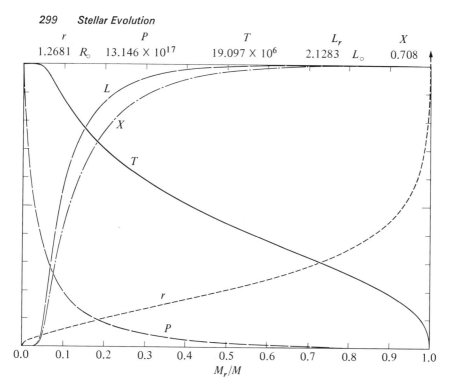

Fig. 7-10B A Model of Mass 1 $M_\odot$ during the Main-Sequence Phase at Time $t = 9.20150 \times 10^9$ Years. Radius r, pressure P, temperature T, net luminosity L_r, and hydrogen abundance X are shown as functions of fractional mass M_r/M. The lower limit of the ordinate is zero for all variables. The upper limits, given in the figure, are 1.2681 $R_\odot$ (with $R_\odot = 6.96 \times 10^{10}$ cm; however, the total radius is 1.3526 $R_\odot$), central pressure P_c (dyne cm^{-2}), central temperature T_c in degrees Kelvin, total luminosity L (units of $L_\odot = 3.86 \times 10^{33}$ erg sec^{-1}), and initial hydrogen abundance $X = 0.708$. The central density (not shown) is 1026.0 gm cm^{-3}. The time t is measured from the initial model calculated for the pre–main-sequence phase (see Section 2). [Adapted from I. Iben, Jr., 1967 (326).]

The central density decreases with increasing mass, except near 1 $M_\odot$, while the central temperature and the radius increase with mass.

The stars at the lower end of the main sequence have scarcely evolved from their zero-age structures during the 5 billion years that the Sun has been in existence, but those that are now at the upper end of the main sequence are only 3 to 5 million years old. Massive stars that formed at the same time as the Sun have already passed through much of their evolution.

Models with masses greater than 1.1 $M_\odot$ have convective cores, and the fraction of the mass contained in the core is an increasing function of the total mass of the model. This is due principally to the gradual replacement of the *p-p* chain as the main energy-producing mechanism by the CN (or CNO)

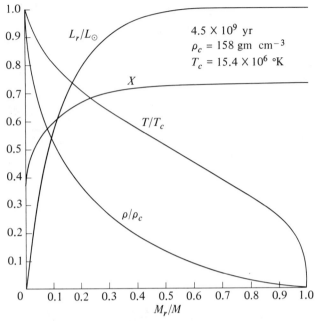

Fig. 7-11A A Model Solar Interior. Density relative to the central density ρ/ρ_c, temperature relative to central temperature T/T_c, net luminosity relative to total luminosity $L_r/L_\odot$, and hydrogen abundance X are shown as functions of fractional mass M_r/M. The chemical composition is $X = 0.730$, $Y = 0.245$, and $Z = 0.025$. The age is 4.5×10^9 years. [After S. Torres-Peimbert, E. Simpson, and R. K. Ulrich, 1969 (329).]

cycle, with its greater temperature sensitivity. The increasing influence of radiation pressure at higher masses also promotes convective instability.*

In the stars on the upper main sequence, the temperatures of the outer layers are so high that hydrogen becomes ionized very close to the surface. In stars with $T_{\mathrm{eff}} \gtrsim 8000°\mathrm{K}$ (log $T_{\mathrm{eff}} \gtrsim 3.9$), corresponding to spectral type late A or later, the ionization zone occurs well beneath the photosphere.† This has the consequence of inducing convection, not only in the layer of partial ionization but also in a region extending much farther into the star. The depth of the convective zone becomes greater as the mass of the model

---

* At the centers of the models of masses 30 $M_\odot$, 45 $M_\odot$, and 60 $M_\odot$, the fraction $1 - \beta$ of radiation pressure to total pressure is 0.23, 0.32, and 0.37, respectively. [R. Stothers, 1963 (324) and 1966 (325).]

† This statement may be verified for the model atmospheres of Chapter 4, if necessary with the aid of the ratios of Table 3-5 after correction of the ratios for the appropriate electron pressures [see eq. (3-29)]. The first ionization of helium (Table 3-6) also takes place in layers not far below the surface of early-type stars.

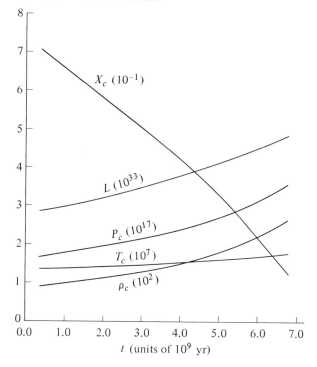

Fig. 7-11B The Evolution of the Sun during 7 Billion Years. Total luminosity L and central values of pressure P_c, temperature T_c, density ρ_c, and hydrogen abundance X_c are shown as functions of time t, which is measured from the initial (homogeneous) state for which the composition is $X = 0.730$, $Y = 0.245$, and $Z = 0.025$. The power of ten by which each value must be multiplied is indicated in parentheses. The values of P_c, ρ_c, and L are expressed in cgs units, and T_c is expressed in degrees Kelvin. [After S. Torres-Peimbert, E. Simpson, and R. K. Ulrich, 1969 (329).]

decreases, until the entire structure becomes convective at a mass of about $0.4\ M_\odot$.

3-2 MODELS OF ONE SOLAR MASS

A model of one solar mass* has a radiative region surrounded by a convective envelope. Figures 7-10A and 7-10B depict the structure at two epochs during the main-sequence evolution. In Fig. 7-10A, the central hydrogen has been reduced to approximately half its original value, while the energy-generation coefficient remains considerably high and L_r rises steeply from the center.†

---

* This discussion is based on the work of I. Iben, Jr., as described in 1967 (326) and (327). These references, especially the first, also describe the histories of several nuclear species during the course of the evolution.

† Note that $\epsilon = dL_r/dM_r$, which is proportional to the slope of the curve of L_r as a function of M_r/M.

In Fig. 7-10B, the supply of hydrogen has been exhausted in a small core, and energy production takes place in a thick shell surrounding the exhausted region. Since L_r inside the core is now equal to zero, the temperature gradient there is also zero, and this portion of the curve describing T in Fig. 7-10B is horizontal. As the nuclear reactions in the shell proceed, more mass is gradually included in the inert core until the *Schönberg–Chandrasekhar limit* is reached*; this is the maximum fraction of the total mass that can be maintained within an isothermal core, which is about 10 per cent in ordinary matter. However, under the conditions of partial degeneracy prevailing in the model described here, this is about 0.13. As more matter is incorporated into the core, the pressure becomes insufficient to support the overlying layers, and gravitational contraction of the core follows as a consequence. This results in further heating of the core and the establishment of a temperature gradient. Energy is released so rapidly by hydrogen-burning at the core boundary that the overlying layers are forced outwards, while at the same time the layers below are pushed inwards. The expanding material in the outer parts of the thick shell becomes cooler and less dense. Energy generation there is halted, but it is maintained in a narrowing shell just outside the exhausted core (note the rapid rise of L_r in Fig. 7-26A below, showing the structure at a time shortly after the model has left the main sequence). The beginning of the shell-narrowing may be considered to mark the termination of the main-sequence phase in a star of one solar mass. The corresponding part of the evolutionary track in Fig. 7-25 below is point 4.

Electron degeneracy becomes increasingly important with time. At the center of the model, degeneracy accounts for 0.017 of the total pressure at age zero and 0.075 of the total at 9.20×10^9 years, which is the epoch of Fig. 7-10B.

We now consider a model that has been calculated specifically to reproduce the characteristics of the present Sun.† Figure 7-11A shows some of the characteristics as a function of mass fraction. Figure 7-11B illustrates the evolution from the homogeneous phase to the present Sun, at a time 4.5×10^9 years after the initial main-sequence state, as well as the evolution during the next 2×10^9 years. The assumed composition is $X = 0.730$, $Y = 0.245$, and $Z = 0.025$. This value of Z is slightly higher than the maximum value 0.02 that allows at least marginal agreement between the theoretically predicted solar neutrino flux and the lower value actually observed.‡ According to this model, the present Sun has a central temperature of 15.4×10^6 °K and a central

---

* M. Schönberg and S. Chandrasekhar, 1942 (328).

† S. Torres-Peimbert, E. Simpson, and R. K. Ulrich, 1969 (329). For detailed listings of models for the homogeneous Sun and the present Sun as calculated by Z. Abraham, see Tables 7-37 and 7-38.

‡ If one adopts a recent revision in the solar iron abundance, increasing it by a factor of 10, the theory predicts a still higher neutrino flux, thereby enhancing the disagreement with the observations [W. D. Watson, 1969 (330)].

density of 158 gm cm^{-3}. The central hydrogen abundance has been reduced to $X = 0.376$.

3-3 A MODEL OF FIVE SOLAR MASSES*

In contrast with the conditions in a model of one solar mass, the central region of a model of 5 solar masses is convective, while the envelope is radiative. Because of the thorough mixing caused by the convection, the chemical composition is uniform in the core even though nuclear reactions

* This section is based on the work of I. Iben, Jr., 1966 (331) and 1967 (327). The first reference also describes in detail the abundances of various isotopes during the stellar evolution.

Fig. 7-12 A Model of Mass 5 $M_\odot$ during the Main-Sequence Phase at Time $t = 6.09931 \times 10^5$ Years. Radius r, pressure P, density ρ, temperature T, net luminosity L_r, and C^{12} abundance X_{12} are shown as functions of fractional mass M_r/M. The lower limit of the ordinate is zero for all variables. The upper limits, given in the figure, are 1.8466 $R_\odot$ (with $R_\odot = 6.96 \times 10^{10}$ cm; however, the total radius is 2.3970 $R_\odot$), central pressure P_c (dyne cm^{-2}), central density ρ_c (gm cm^{-3}), central temperature T_c (°K), total luminosity L (units of $L_\odot = 3.86 \times 10^{33}$ erg sec^{-1}), and initial abundance $X_{12} = 0.003610$. The time t is measured from the initial model calculated for the pre–main-sequence phase (see Section 2). [Adapted from I. Iben, Jr., 1966 (331).]

r	P	ρ	T	L_r	X_{12}
1.8466 $R_\odot$	0.80274 × 10^{17}	21.428	27.339 × 10^6	631.32 $L_\odot$	0.003610

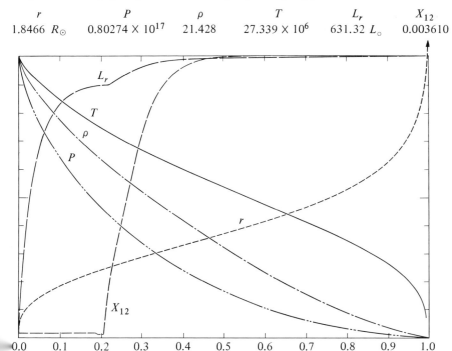

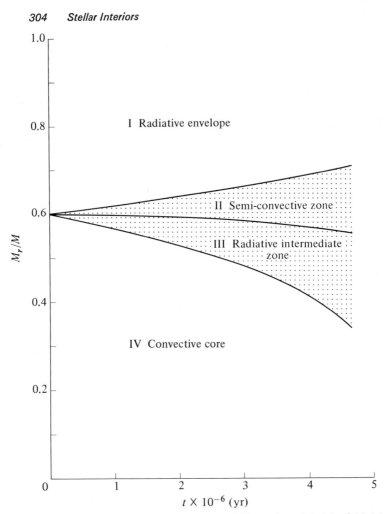

Fig. 7-13 The Evolution of the Structural Zones in a Model of 30 $M_\odot$ during Hydrogen-Burning. In the *dotted regions*, the hydrogen abundance varies continuously with mass. [After R. Stothers, 1963 (324).]

take place most rapidly at the center, where the temperature and density are highest. Figure 7-12 shows the structure of the model shortly after its arrival at the main sequence. The curves are qualitatively similar to those at the corresponding phase for the model of 1 $M_\odot$, somewhat preceding the phase depicted in Fig. 7-10A, except for an irregularity in L_r near $M_r/M = 0.2$.*

* The irregularity can be traced to the distribution of C^{12}. In the convective core, C^{12} has been reduced to an equilibrium abundance and is simply recycled in the CNO bi-cycle. Outside the core, however, this isotope is still higher in abundance (see Fig. 7-12) and the conversion of C^{12} to N^{14} provides additional energy, causing an increase in L_r beyond the convective core.

When the hydrogen abundance in the core has been reduced to 5 per cent, the entire model begins to contract. This event may be considered to define the termination of the main-sequence phase for stars of mass $\sim 3\ M_\odot$ or greater. For such stars, the end of the main sequence is designated as point 2 in Fig. 7-25.

3-4 A MODEL OF THIRTY SOLAR MASSES*

The surface temperature of a massive star is so high that the ionization of hydrogen takes place near the surface, and the outer convective zone may be neglected. The central temperature is so high that the CNO cycle is effective, and the high temperature sensitivity produces convection in a large core. In the zero-age model, the core contains 0.6 of the total mass, and the remainder of the star is in radiative equilibrium. Immediately afterwards, the structure becomes complex, as four distinct regions develop (Fig. 7-13): (I) a radiative envelope having the original homogeneous composition; (II) a semi-convective zone in which the gaseous motions are sufficient to modify the distribution of hydrogen but do not cause complete mixing and do not transfer a significant fraction of the total flux†; (III) a radiative zone with variable composition; (IV) a homogeneous convective core. The variation of the hydrogen abundance in successive models is shown in Fig. 7-14. The modified composition that is left behind as the convective region retreats is responsible for the continuous variation of X in zone III. The fraction of the total mass that is

Table 7-5   Evolutionary Models of a Star of Mass 30 $M_\odot$ during Hydrogen-Burning. This table is a partial listing from R. Stothers, 1963 (324). The original model numbers are retained.

	MODEL 0	MODEL 4
β_c *	0.768	0.578
$\log T_c$	7.562	7.649
$\log \rho_c$	0.482	0.650
$\log (L/L_\odot)$	5.148	5.426
$\log (R/R_\odot)$	0.817	1.118
$\log T_{\text{eff}}$	4.639	4.558
X_{core}	0.700	0.069
$t\ (10^6$ years$)$	0	4.67

* The quantity β is the ratio of gas pressure to total pressure.

* This discussion is based upon the work of R. Stothers, 1963 (324) and 1964 (332).
† See R. Stothers, 1963 (324) and also M. Schwarzschild and R. Härm, 1958 (334) for discussions of semi-convection. An alternative possibility to this treatment is suggested by R. J. Tayler, 1969 (335).

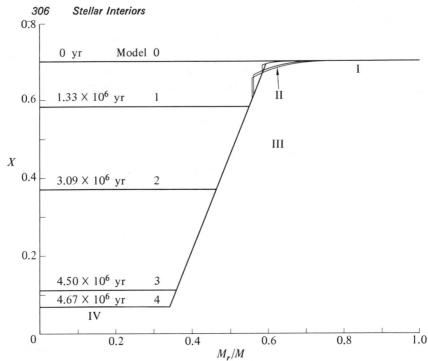

Fig. 7-14 The Depletion of Hydrogen in a Model of 30 $M_\odot$. The hydrogen abundance X is given as a function of fractional mass M_r/M. The numbers of the models and the corresponding times are given. The *Roman numerals* indicate the zones. [After R. Stothers, 1963 (324).]

contained in either of the intermediate regions increases with time at the expense of the core and envelope, in which the mass-fractions decrease.

Table 7-5 lists some of the characteristics of the models. The central temperature and density, for which the values are initially 36.5×10^6 °K and 3.03 gm cm^{-3}, increase with time. Radiation pressure constitutes 23 per cent of the total pressure at the center of the initial model, and this fraction increases with time.

When the hydrogen abundance of the core is depleted to $X = 0.03$, the nuclear-energy production is augmented by gravitational contraction, which supplies 0.1 per cent of the luminosity. The near-exhaustion of hydrogen in the core marks the termination of the main-sequence phase (point 2 in Fig. 7-25).

3-5 SENSITIVITY TO ASSUMPTIONS

The properties of stellar models depend upon the assumptions made in their construction. We shall now consider as examples the changes in the models resulting from differences in the hydrogen and helium abundances, energy-generation rate, opacity, and mixing length in the convective envelope, as well as the effects of stellar rotation.

Figure 7-15A shows the Hertzsprung–Russell diagram for various masses and chemical compositions. A model of given mass is shifted downwards and toward the right as X or Z increases, while the main sequence as a whole is shifted upwards as X or Z increases. Figure 7-15B is a similar diagram for several other compositions. Selecting the curves representative of Population I ($0.57 \gtrsim X \gtrsim 0.77$, $0.01 \gtrsim Z \gtrsim 0.03$), we find a range of 0.8 magnitude in $\mathscr{M}_{\text{bol}}$ for stars of one solar mass. A similar range exists for Population II.

The mass-luminosity diagram of Fig. 7-16 shows that the main sequence is displaced downwards with increasing X or Z. For Population I compositions, there is a range of 2.2 magnitudes in $\mathscr{M}_{\text{bol}}$ at one solar mass. Again, the range is comparable for Population II.

A change in the constant coefficient in the formula for the energy-generation rate has the effects shown in Table 7-6. Although one might expect the luminosity to be significantly affected, this quantity, in fact, remains the same. The reason is basically that the maintenance of hydrostatic equilibrium throughout the star requires that the temperature increase toward the center at a rate that produces the necessary pressures at various depths. In the presence of the temperature gradient, radiation then flows toward the surface in accordance with the equation of radiative equilibrium (6-24). If

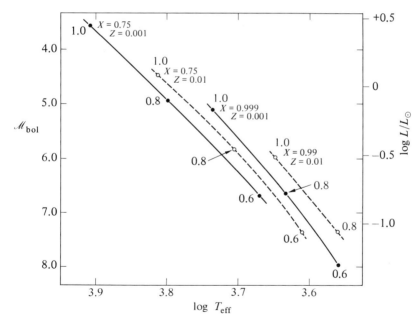

Fig. 7-15A   The Effect of Chemical Composition on the Main Sequence in the Hertzsprung–Russell Diagram. Each curve is calculated for a different chemical composition. The masses 0.6 $M_\odot$, 0.8 $M_\odot$, and 1.0 $M_\odot$ are indicated. [From P. Demarque, 1960 (369).]

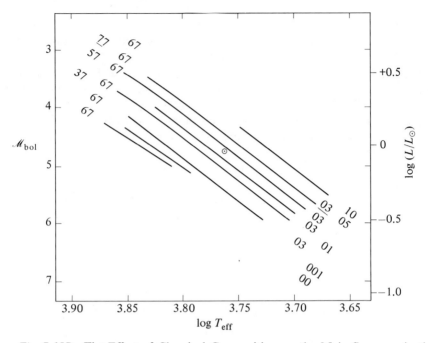

Fig. 7-15B The Effect of Chemical Composition on the Main Sequence in the Hertzsprung–Russell Diagram. Each curve is calculated for a different chemical composition. The value of X is indicated at the upper left, and the value of Z is indicated at the lower right of each curve. Decimal points have been omitted. The second curve from the top corresponds to two compositions ($X = 0.67, Z = 0.05$) and ($X = 0.77, Z = 0.03$); one pair of X, Z values has therefore been underlined. The *encircled dot* marks the position of the present Sun. [From P. Demarque, 1967 (370).]

the star is to remain in thermal equilibrium, exactly this luminosity must be generated within the star.* Thus, a change in the constant of the energy-generation formula must be compensated by adjustments in ρ and T to maintain the luminosity.

Figure 7-17 compares main sequences calculated with different opacity formulae and also with different values of the mixing length in models having convective envelopes. The opacities of Cox and Stewart include bound-bound (line) absorption, whereas those of Keller and Meyerott do not. Inclusion of line effects displaces individual models toward lower effective temperatures with little change in luminosity. The results of including recent opacity corrections are described in Section 3-6B.

A decrease in mixing length also reduces the effective temperature. The influence of the mixing length is important only at intermediate and late

---

* See M. Schwarzschild, 1958 (50), pp. 43, 44.

Table 7-6   Effects of a Change in the Energy Generation Rate.* [J. P. Cox and R. T. Giuli, 1961 (388).]

	QUANTITY					
	T_c	R	ρ_c	L	T_{eff}	$\mathcal{M}_{bol}$
Percentage Change†	∓8	±8	∓24	0	∓4	0

* The equation used is $\epsilon = A Y^3 \rho^2 T^{-3} e^{-B/T}$, where A and B are constants. The model considered is that of a star composed of pure helium.
† This is the percentage change resulting in the tabulated quantities when A is changed by a factor of ~ 20. The upper signs refer to an increase in A by this factor, and the lower signs refer to a decrease in A.

spectral types, where deep convective envelopes are present. In the later spectral types, the sensitivity to the choice of mixing length decreases, because the convection becomes more nearly adiabatic.

All the models described thus far have been calculated for non-rotating

Fig. 7-16 The Effect of Chemical Composition on the Theoretical Mass-Luminosity Relation for the Main Sequence. Each curve is calculated for a different chemical composition. The value of X is indicated at the upper right, and the value of Z is indicated at the lower left of each curve. Decimal points have been omitted. One of the curves corresponds to two compositions ($X = 0.67$, $Z = 0.01$) and ($X = 0.57$, $Z = 0.03$); one pair of X, Z values has therefore been underlined. The *encircled dot* marks the position of the present Sun. [From P. Demarque, 1967 (370).]

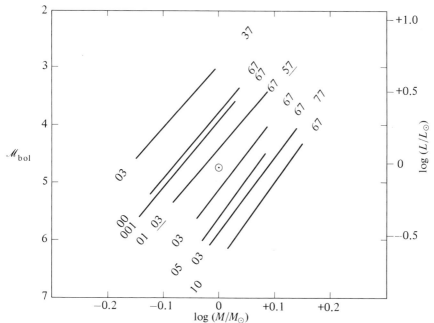

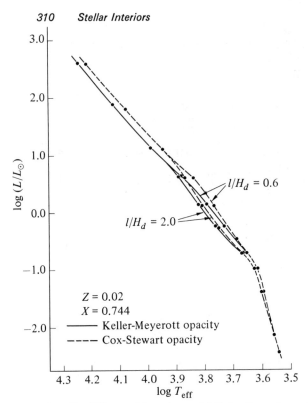

Fig. 7-17   The Effects of Opacity and Mixing Length on the Main Sequence in the Hertzsprung–Russell Diagram. The opacities calculated by A. N. Cox and J. N. Stewart, 1962 (372) include line absorption, whereas those of G. Keller and R. E. Meyerott, 1955 (373) do not. The quantity l/H_d is the ratio of the mixing length to the density scale-height. [After I. Iben, Jr., 1963 (376).]

stars. When rotation is included, the models have lower effective temperatures, while the absolute magnitude may either increase or decrease. The results depend in part upon the orientation of the rotational axis with respect to the observer.*

3-6 COMPARISON OF THEORY WITH OBSERVATIONS

A. THE UNCERTAINTIES IN THE COMPARED QUANTITIES

We shall compare the theoretical main-sequence models with observed stars in binary systems and in a galactic cluster. Before doing so, however, we should inquire as to the uncertainties in the quantities being compared.

The sensitivity of the models to various properties such as chemical com-

---

* A review is given by I. Iben, Jr., 1967 (327), pp. 599, 602. More details are given, for example, by J. W.-K. Mark, 1968 (336) and I. W. Roxburgh and P. A. Strittmatter, 1966 (199g).

position and mixing-length ratio has already been discussed, and we shall make allowance for reasonable variations in these parameters when constructing the theoretical main sequence. Other phenomena that have not been considered may also play a part in certain cases. Among these are possible magnetic fields and, of especial pertinence since we shall be

Fig. 7-18   A Schematic Distribution in the Plane of $\mathscr{M}_{\text{bol}}$ as a Function of log T_{eff}. This diagram for a hypothetical globular cluster and main sequence should be compared with Fig. 7-19.

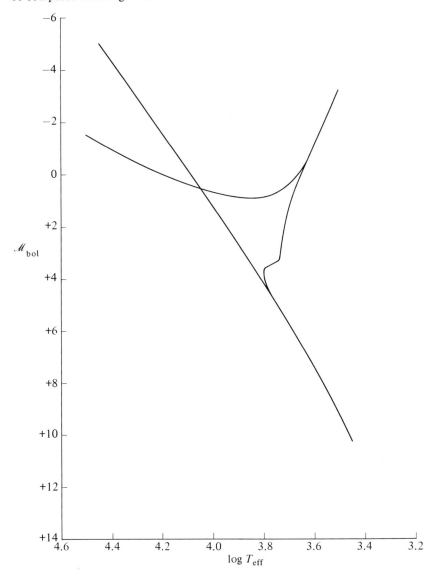

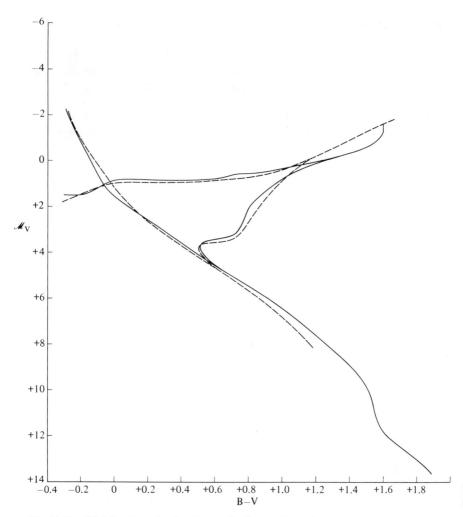

Fig. 7-19 Distributions in the Plane of $\mathcal{M}_V$ as a Function of B − V. Two transformations of Fig. 7-18 are shown. The *solid lines* are based on the table of D. C. Morton and T. F. Adams, 1968 (111) as modified by P. T. Bradley and D. C. Morton, 1969 (112) and D. M. Popper *et al.*, 1970 (136), and on the portions of the tables of H. L. Johnson, 1966 (113) for spectral classes G5 to M8. The *dashed lines* are based on the table given by D. L. Harris III (K. Aa. Strand, ed.), 1963 (1), with his revised effective temperatures. The table does not include the lower main sequence. The irregularity in the upper solid curve near B − V = +0.7 is caused by the difference in the zero points of the bolometric correction scales of the different tables.

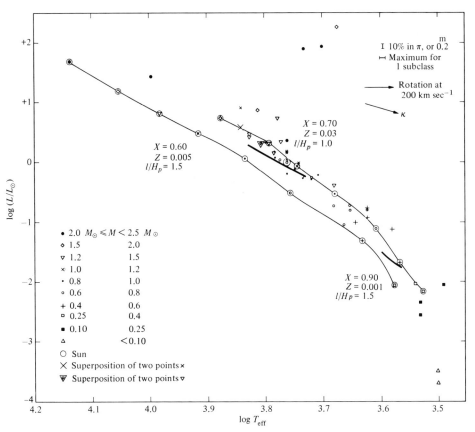

Fig. 7-20 Comparison of the Theoretical and Observed Hertzsprung–Russell Diagrams. Observational results from Fig. 1-14 are reproduced together with two theoretical initial main sequences having the compositions indicated; the lower curve is a composite for two compositions, joined at $\log T_{\text{eff}} \approx 3.6$. The lower envelope for Population I compositions lies between the curves drawn. The positions of theoretical models having the indicated masses (in units of the solar mass) are shown by the *encircled symbols*. The same symbols are used to denote observed masses of that value or greater, according to the key in the figure. Possible duplicity of some stars is not considered; consult Table 1-3. The *vertical segment* shows the displacement in $\log (L/L_{\odot})$ produced by an error of 10 per cent in the parallax or 0.2 mag in $\mathcal{M}_{\text{bol}}$. The *horizontal segment* shows the maximum displacement in $\log T_{\text{eff}}$ produced by an error of one subclass in spectral type. The *horizontal arrow* indicates the effect of stellar rotation with an equatorial velocity of 200 km sec^{-1}, averaged over aspect angle, according to the theory of I. W. Roxburgh and P. A. Strittmatter, 1966 (199g). The *oblique arrow* shows approximately the effect of including recent opacity corrections in the models for upper main-sequence stars of Population I. A smaller effect may be expected for cooler stars. The *upper* and *lower heavy arcs* indicate the positions of models having various Population I compositions and masses 1.0 $M_{\odot}$ and 0.4 $M_{\odot}$, respectively. [Curves from the results of H. Copeland, J. O. Jensen, and H. E. Jørgensen, 1970 (397).]

considering binary systems, the influence of a close companion. The latter may be of importance not only because of present perturbations between the components but also because of the effects of possible interactions during the past history.

The observations are also subject to error. The data for the binary systems that are listed in Tables 1-3 to 1-5 give some indication of the reliability of the observed quantities. For a galactic cluster, as for a binary system, one source of uncertainty is the distance. For the Hyades cluster, which is to be discussed here, various methods of determining the distance show discordances as great as 0.2 magnitude in the distance modulus or 0.08 in log L.* In addition, there are errors in the measurements of the apparent magnitude and color index of any individual star.

Finally, there is the question of the transformation between an observed quantity and the corresponding theoretical one. Most of the observed luminosities we shall be considering have been derived from apparent magnitudes and bolometric corrections with the use of eqs. (1-2A), (1-3), and (1-4). The observed effective temperatures are in many cases inferred from color indices. We must therefore be concerned with the reliability of the relations between these quantities. As a measure of reliability, we may compare the transformation of the schematic distribution of $\mathscr{M}_V$ with $B - V$ in Fig. 7-18 into the corresponding distribution of $\mathscr{M}_{bol}$ as a function of log T_{eff} in Fig. 7-19. This transformation has been performed twice, using alternatively the recent results of different investigators. The loci in Fig. 7-19 are not identical, and we may anticipate that further refinements in the transformations are yet to be made.

The conversion of $\mathscr{M}_{bol}$ into L introduces both $\mathscr{M}_{bol\odot}$ and $L_{\odot}$, and errors in these quantities also affect the comparison of observations and theory.

B. THE THEORETICAL MAIN SEQUENCE

Figures 7-20 to 7-23 show the Hertzsprung–Russell diagram, the mass-luminosity relation, and the mass-radius relation for observed binary systems, as well as the Hertzsprung–Russell diagram for the Hyades cluster. Also shown are the corresponding theoretical relations for the initial main sequence. In the investigation from which the curves were chosen,† the following values of the parameters $(X, Z, l/H_p)$ were considered: (0.70, 0.03, 1.0), (0.70, 0.03, 1.5), (0.70, 0.03, 2.0), (0.70, 0.02, 1.5), (0.60, 0.03, 1.5), (0.60, 0.005, 1.5), (0.90, 0.005, 1.5), and (0.90, 0.001, 1.5). In each diagram, the theoretical curves have been selected to produce the widest vertical range at any abscissa, and some of the curves are composites for two compositions.

___

* For a brief review of the problem of the distance modulus of the Hyades cluster, see W. F. van Altena, 1969 (107).
† H. Copeland, J. O. Jensen, and H. E. Jørgensen, 1970 (397).

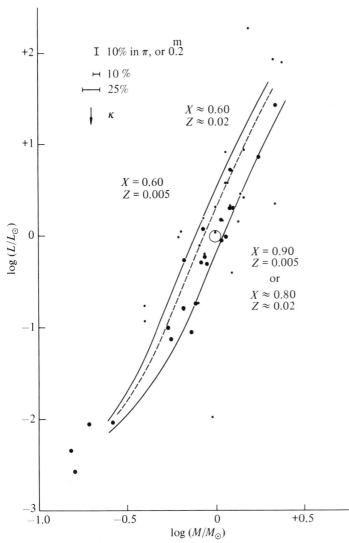

Fig. 7-21 Comparison of the Theoretical and Observed Mass-Luminosity Relations. Observational results from Fig. 1-12 are reproduced together with two theoretical initial main sequences having the compositions indicated. The *dashed line* has been interpolated. *Large dots* indicate higher reliability than *small dots*, but possible duplicity of some stars is not considered; consult Table 1-3. The *circle* represents the Sun. The *horizontal segments* show the displacements produced by errors of 10 and 25 per cent in the mass. The *vertical segment* shows the displacement produced by an error of 10 per cent in the parallax or an error of 0.2 mag in $\mathscr{M}_{bol}$. The *arrow* indicates approximately the effect of including recent opacity corrections in the models for upper main-sequence stars of Population I. A smaller effect may be anticipated for the lower main sequence. [Curves from the results of H. Copeland, J. O. Jensen, and H. E. Jørgensen, 1970 (397).]

The positions of the main-sequence curves are influenced by a number of effects. Although line absorption is included, recent corrections to the opacity* have not been incorporated. These cause a shift of the main sequence toward lower effective temperatures, especially for stars on the upper main sequence.† Changes in the abundances of individual heavy elements, such as iron, may alter the luminosity of a model by a significant amount, but such variations are not considered here. Stellar rotation, if sufficiently rapid, will also cause a shift to lower effective temperatures, while the luminosity that an observer would measure will be increased or decreased depending on the orientation of the rotational axis.‡ The short arrows in Figs. 7-20 to 7-23 indicate roughly the amount of the shift of the upper main sequence that may be expected from the opacity and rotation effects. It may also be noted that the downward bend of the curves in Figs. 7-20 and 7-23 below $\log T_{eff} \approx 3.6$ results from the inclusion in the calculations of the formation of the H_2 molecule at low temperatures.

C. DISCUSSION OF THE RESULTS

We may now compare the theory with the observations, bearing in mind the uncertainties that we have noted.

The agreement between the binary components and the theoretical sequences is fair. Figures 7-20 and 7-21 show that most of these stars can be approximated by the models, although discrepancies exist. The large radii or luminosities of some stars can be explained by evolution from the initial main sequence, an effect that is particularly apparent in Fig. 7-22. Failure of the observed points to be within the boundaries of the curves (and their extrapolations) may be due in other cases to any of the following causes: (1) the chemical compositions or mixing-length ratios appropriate to these stars are not included within the boundaries of these curves; (2) additional refinements are needed in the models; (3) additional refinements are needed in the transformations from observed to theoretical quantities; or (4) the observed values are not sufficiently accurate.

The main sequence of the Hyades cluster is compared with two theoretical curves in Fig. 7-23. Of the curves shown, the one for $X = 0.70$ and $Z = 0.03$ provides the better fit to the observations, and an interpolated curve would improve the agreement. Departure of the hottest stars from the theoretical

---

* T. R. Carson, D. F. Mayers, and D. W. N. Stibbs, 1968 (374); and W. D. Watson, 1969 (375) and 1969 (390).
† The shifts indicated in Figs. 7-20 to 7-22 are based on a preliminary calculation by E. Novotny, 1972 (401) for a model of 2.25 $M_\odot$ having $X = 0.596$ and $Z = 0.02$. The length of the arrow in Fig. 7-23, which applies to lower masses, is a rough estimate. Only the first and last of the corrections cited in the preceding footnote were included in the calculations.
‡ A diagram and short discussion are given by I. Iben, Jr., 1967 (327), pp. 559, 602.

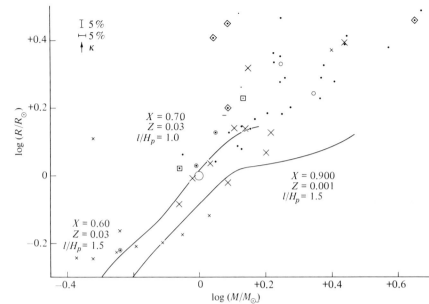

Fig. 7-22 Comparison of the Theoretical and Observed Mass-Radius Relations. Observational results from Fig. 1-13 are reproduced together with two theoretical initial main sequences having the compositions indicated; the upper curve is a composite for two compositions, joined at $\log (R/R_\odot) \approx -0.1$. The lower envelope for Population I models lies between the curves shown. *Large dots* indicate higher reliability than *small dots*. The W Ursae Majoris systems are represented by *large crosses* for the primary components and *small crosses* for the secondary components; reliability is not indicated. The *circle* designates the Sun. *Encircled dots* represent the superposition of two points. *Squares* and *diamonds* represent luminosity classes IV–V and IV, respectively; more luminous stars are not included in this figure. The *dash* indicates a star with an uncertain spectral classification. The *horizontal* and *vertical segments* show the displacements resulting from errors of 5 per cent in the mass or radius, respectively. The *arrow* shows approximately the effect of including recent opacity corrections in the upper main-sequence models of Population I. [Curves from the results of H. Copeland, J. O. Jensen and H. E. Jørgensen, 1970 (397).]

curve is explicable in terms of evolution away from the main sequence, while the overluminous and widely scattered stars at cooler temperatures apparently have not yet reached the main sequence. We cannot derive the hydrogen and heavy-element abundances of the Hyades on the basis of curve-fitting alone, for curves having different pairs of X and Z may have nearly the same locus; but spectroscopic observations indicate that the Hyades stars have a somewhat higher metal abundance than does the Sun.

In making a comparison of the Hyades stars with the theory, it should be

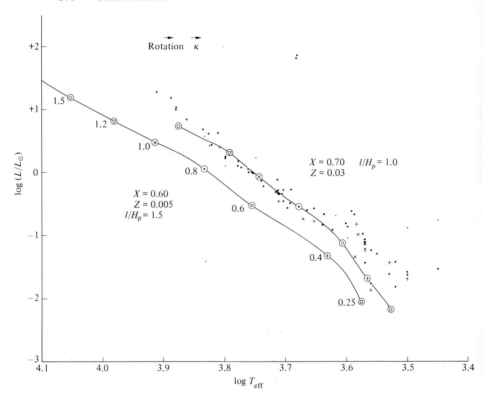

Fig. 7-23 Comparison of the Theoretical Hertzsprung–Russell Diagram with the Hyades Distribution. The observations of Fig. 1-17 have been transformed by use of Tables 1-1A and 1-1B, but the 18 stars lying below the main distribution in that figure are not shown here. Also, 16 of the 41 stars in Fig. 1-17 having $\log (L/L_\odot) > -0.10$ show spectroscopic or visual doubling and have been eliminated in the present figure. No correction has been applied for the differential distances of the stars. The *curves* are identical with those of Fig. 7-20. *Large dots* indicate a probability of membership in the cluster of 90 per cent or greater, *small dots* 80 to 89 per cent, and *crosses* 50 to 79 per cent in Table I of W. F. van Altena, 1969 (107). *Plus symbols* represent additional stars that are probable members, from van Altena's Table IIIA. The *underlined point* is the superposition of two large dots and one small one. The *arrows* give approximate shifts of the upper portions of the theoretical sequences, resulting from the inclusion of recent opacity corrections and of stellar rotation. The effect of rotation should be negligible for $\log T_{eff} \leqslant 3.8$, according to the theory of I. W. Roxburgh and P. A. Strittmatter, 1966 (199g) and the data of R. P. Kraft and M. H. Wrubel, 1965 (199h).

noted that the distance modulus is uncertain. The value $m - \mathcal{M} = +3.23$ magnitudes has been adopted here, but $+3.03$ magnitudes might also be correct. In latter case, the observed points would have to be lowered by 0.08 in $\log (L/L_\odot)$.

Our conclusion is that the theoretical results seem to be, on the whole, corroborated by observations of binary stars and the stars in the Hyades cluster.

4 EVOLUTION FROM THE MAIN SEQUENCE THROUGH THE RED-GIANT STAGE

4-1 GENERAL DISCUSSION*

Before commencing the description of stellar evolution beyond the main sequence, it may be well to clarify the meaning of the term *core*. Often, this term is used to denote the region in which hydrogen has been consumed. One may also speak of a convective core, a degenerate core, and so forth. Within a given model, more than one kind of core may be present. For example, there may be a central, degenerate domain within a region exhausted of hydrogen, and in this case there would be both a degenerate core and a hydrogen-exhausted (helium) core. The boundaries may or may not be the same. One must also be careful to distinguish between various kinds of change in the core; there may be a change in the radius of the core, which is an increase or decrease of the radius of the domain over which the specifying phenomenon applies; a physical expansion or contraction of the core, in which the material particles in the core move outwards or inwards; or a change in the mass of the core. For example, when a nuclear fuel in a convective core becomes depleted, the boundary of the convective region may recede toward the center. Both the radius and the mass of the convective core therefore decrease to zero, although there need be no physical motion of the material; the mass and the radius of the hydrogen-exhausted region may meanwhile remain unchanged. In a gravitationally contracting core, the matter moves toward the center and its density increases. If hydrogen is being consumed just outside the boundary of a helium core, the mass of the core increases as more helium is added to it. The entire region, including the boundary of the helium core, may be contracting at such a rate that the radius of the core remains constant as its mass increases.

We now turn to the description of the models. At the termination of the main-sequence phase, the hydrogen in the central region of a star has been exhausted, and it is the chemical inhomogeneity between the helium core and the hydrogen-rich envelope that causes the star to turn toward the giant branch. This effect can be seen from Fig. 7-24. The two tracks correspond to model sequences in which the initial conditions are the same; but in one case, there is no mixing between different layers, while in the other case, the entire star is assumed to be thoroughly mixed. The track for the homogeneous

---

* For a lecture on the special topic of globular cluster stars, see M. Schwarzschild, 1970 (399).

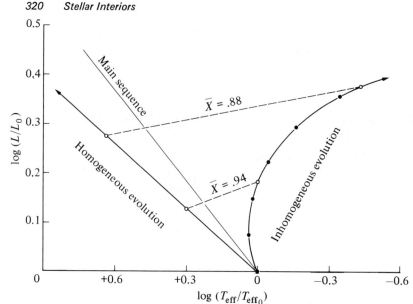

Fig. 7-24   The Effect of the Hydrogen Distribution on Evolutionary Tracks. The luminosity L and the effective temperature T_{eff} are expressed in terms of the corresponding quantities for the initial model. The track labeled *homogeneous evolution* is calculated on the assumption that all the stellar matter is thoroughly mixed (i.e., that X = constant with radius). The track labeled *inhomogeneous evolution* is calculated on the assumption that no mixing occurs (i.e., X is lower near the center). The *dashed lines* join models in which the average value X (with respect to mass) of the inhomogeneous model is the same as that of the homogeneous model. [From Martin Schwarzschild, *Structure and Evolution of the Stars* (Copyright © 1958 by Princeton University Press): Fig. 20.2, p. 172. Reprinted by permission of Princeton University Press.]

models leads below the main sequence, but that for the inhomogeneous models advances toward the giant region. According to the calculations presented in the previous discussions, the helium created by hydrogen-conversion does, in fact, remain in the inner region of the star, and therefore evolution into giant stars may be expected. This is borne out by the detailed calculations to be described in the following sections.

Fig. 7-25   Evolutionary Tracks in the Hertzsprung–Russell Diagram. The mass of each star is given at the left of the track. The composition is $X = 0.708$, $Y = 0.272$, and $Z = 0.020$ for all masses except 30 $M_\odot$, for which the composition is $X = 0.70$, $Y = 0.27$, $Z = 0.03$. *Dashed portions* of the curves are estimates. The *letters* along the tracks for 1 $M_\odot$ and 5 $M_\odot$ have the following significance: H_c = hydrogen-burning near the center; G = gravitational contraction of the entire star; H_{TS} = hydrogen-burning in a thick shell; H_S = hydrogen-burning in a thin shell; He = helium-burning near the center plus hydrogen-burning in a thin shell. The times required to reach the encircled points are given in Table 7-7.

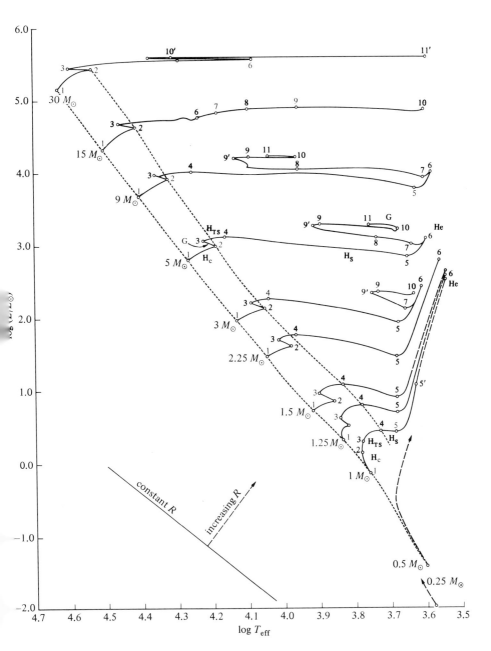

The *dotted lines* indicate the boundaries of the main sequence. The *line (lower left)* shows the slope of a path along which the radius remains constant. The track for 15 $M_\odot$ does not turn back as do the other tracks because the semi-convective zone was treated as fully convective [see R. Stothers and C.-W. Chin, 1968 (377)]. [Adapted from I. Iben, Jr., 1967 (327). The track for 30 $M_\odot$ is given by R. Stothers, 1966 (333).]

Table 7-7 Evolutionary Times. The times, expressed in years, refer to intervals between the points in Fig. 7-25.* [Adapted from I. Iben, Jr., 1967 (327).]

MASS ($M_\odot$) INTERVAL	1–2	2–3	3–4	4–5	5–6
30	4.80 (6)	8.64 (4)	←————	~1.0 (4) ————→	
15	1.010 (7)	2.270 (5)	←————	7.55 (4) ————→	
9	2.144 (7)	6.053 (5)	9.113 (4)	1.477 (5)	6.552 (4)
5	6.547 (7)	2.173 (6)	1.372 (6)	7.532 (5)	4.857 (5)
3	2.212 (8)	1.042 (7)	1.033 (7)	4.505 (6)	4.238 (6)
2.25	4.802 (8)	1.647 (7)	3.696 (7)	1.310 (7)	3.829 (7)
1.5	1.553 (9)	8.10 (7)	3.490 (8)	1.049 (8)	⩾2 (8)
1.25	2.803 (9)	1.824 (8)	1.045 (9)	1.463 (8)	⩾4 (8)
1.0	7 (9)	2 (9)	1.20 (9)	1.57 (8)	⩾1 (9)

MASS ($M_\odot$) INTERVAL	6–7	7–8	8–9	9–10$^{(\prime)}$	10$^{(\prime)}$–11$^{(\prime)}$
30	←————————	53.1 (4)	————————→		1.3 (4)
15	7.17 (5)	6.20 (5)	1.9 (5)	3.5 (4)	
9	4.90 (5)	9.50 (4)	3.28 (6)	1.55 (5)	2.86 (4)
5	6.05 (6)	1.02 (6)	9.00 (6)	9.30 (5)	7.69 (4)
3	2.51 (7)		4.08 (7)	6.00 (6)	

* A number in parentheses is the power of 10 by which an entry is to be multiplied.

The evolutionary tracks in the Hertzsprung–Russell diagram are shown for various masses in Fig. 7-25, and the evolutionary times are given in Table 7-7.* All tracks turn toward the right, although the effect is less marked in the stars of smaller mass as they leave the initial main sequence (points 1 in Fig. 7-25), since the change in composition with radius is gradual, rather than discontinuous as in a convective core.

As hydrogen is consumed in the central regions, the core contracts and hydrogen-burning in a shell commences. These changes can be understood by following the events in detail. The transformation of hydrogen into helium causes a gradual increase in the mean molecular weight, and, since the gas pressure is inversely proportional to the mean molecular weight, the gas pressure becomes inadequate to provide full support for the overlying layers. The matter in the central regions therefore becomes compressed. Not only is the density thus increased, but, by the virial theorem, the temperature is also raised. The contraction, however, is so slow that approximate equilibrium is maintained. The higher values of the temperature and density also increase the nuclear energy-generation rate despite the decreasing hydrogen abundance,

* The details of this discussion are based largely on the papers of Iben quoted in the following sections and also additional papers by him cited in these references.

and the luminosity of the star is not only maintained but increased. When the hydrogen abundance has decreased to a few per cent, stars of mass 1.25 $M_\odot$ and higher contract throughout their entire volume (points 2 to 3 in Fig. 7-25). The high energy-production rate persists even when the hydrogen abundance has fallen to a fraction of one per cent, although, with continuing depletion of fuel and diminishing rate of energy production, the central temperatures may no longer be maintained. When the hydrogen is almost exhausted in the core of a star of moderate mass, the temperatures near the center begin to decrease as nuclear processes can no longer replenish the energy that continues to radiate outwards from the hot core toward the cooler surroundings.* The temperatures throughout the cooling core tend to become more nearly uniform. The drop in core temperature leads to a drop in gas pressure, and the excess gravitational pressure rapidly forces the matter inwards (near point 3 in Fig. 7-25). The energy lost by radiation exceeds the gravitational energy gained by contraction, until energy balance is restored with the formation of a hydrogen-burning shell outside the core. In the layers just above the core, the densities and temperatures have been rising, until hydrogen has at last been ignited. Energy then flows both outwards and inwards, and the temperatures throughout the core gradually begin to increase once more.

As core contraction continues, the envelope expands.† The expansion in some stars is caused by the rapid production of energy in the shell, which causes the matter to be pushed away in both directions from the shell. The star quickly reaches the giant region of the Hertzsprung–Russell diagram.

---

* The term *moderate mass* in this statement means approximately the range $1\ M_\odot \gtrsim M \gtrsim 10\ M_\odot$. In stars of mass $1\ M_\odot$ and less, the absence of a convective core makes the hydrogen variation with radius more gradual, and the phases of core-burning and shell-formation are thus not clearly separated. The central temperature does not decrease but becomes approximately constant during this phase. For $M \gtrsim 10\ M_\odot$, the mass of the region in which hydrogen is depleted is so large that the Schönberg-Chandrasekhar limit is exceeded. Thus the central regions of massive stars contract strongly enough to maintain a temperature gradient in the core at all times, and the central temperature continues to increase even after the exhaustion of hydrogen.

† As we shall see from the detailed calculations described in Sections 4-2 to 4-4, it is usually true that envelope expansion accompanies core contraction, and also that envelope contraction accompanies core expansion. In stars that are not too massive (the upper limit lies between $5\ M_\odot$ and $9\ M_\odot$), the shell is positioned approximately at a node, and matter moves either away from it in both directions or toward it in both directions. The radius of the shell tends to remain fairly constant, since contraction or expansion would cause heating or cooling, respectively; and this would change the rate of energy output and the structure of the star. For further discussion, see R. F. Stein (R. F. Stein and A. G. W. Cameron, eds.), 1966 (59), p. 38 et seq., and J. P. Cox and R. T. Giuli, 1968 (52), pp. 998, 999, and 777–780.

The models now have deep convective envelopes, and the structure of such stars is strongly affected by the opacities very near the surface. These opacities depend upon the effective temperature, and it is found that, on the basis of present theory, no model can have an effective temperature below about 3000°K or 4000°K, depending on the assumptions made.* Thus, progress toward the right of the Hertzsprung–Russell diagram is halted at about the same effective temperature for all masses (see Fig. 7-25).

In stars of mass 3 $M_\odot$ or greater, the central temperature becomes high enough for ignition of the triple-alpha reaction (which converts helium to carbon) before the giant stage is reached. At the moderate densities of the central regions, this nuclear process gains importance in a gradual manner. On the other hand, in stars of mass greater than about 0.5 $M_\odot$ but less than about 2.5 or 3 $M_\odot$, the central regions become degenerate and the triple-alpha reaction begins with the violent *helium flash*, to be described later. Points 6 in Fig. 7-25 mark the beginning of significant helium-burning. Stars of low mass never achieve sufficiently high central temperatures for the helium flash to occur.†

Eventually, the core helium becomes depleted, and there is once more a transition to a gravitational contraction phase and the formation of a shell source outside the core. The helium shell-burning stage is the last for which detailed models have at present been computed in a continuous evolutionary sequence.

4-2 EVOLUTION OF MODELS OF APPROXIMATELY ONE SOLAR MASS

We now continue the discussion of the evolution of a model of one solar mass, begun in Section 3-2.‡

Figure 7-26A shows the structure at a time between the epochs corresponding to points 4 and 5 in Fig. 7-25, shortly after the main-sequence phase has been terminated. Since the nuclear energy is now produced in a fairly narrow shell, L_r rises steeply to a maximum value at about 20 per cent of the total mass. In the region exterior to a mass fraction of about 40 per cent, L_r *decreases* slightly because energy is being absorbed by the expanding envelope. In the core, the gravitational contraction continues to make a small positive contribution to L and to maintain a temperature gradient there. With the continuing compression, the central density has become so great (1.52 ×

---

* This is in contradiction to observations, which disclose the existence of cooler stars. D. L. Moss, 1968 (392) suggests how the models may be modified to lower the minimum theoretical temperature.
† C. Hayashi, R. Hōshi, and D. Sugimoto, 1962 (338).
‡ We continue to describe the work of Iben presented in the references cited in Section 3-2, supplemented by his article in 1965 (339).

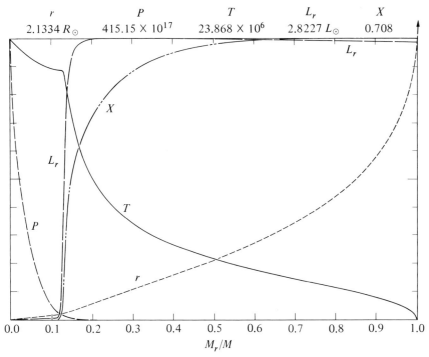

r	P	T	L_r	X
2.1334 $R_\odot$	415.15 × 10^{17}	23.868 × 10^6	2.8227 $L_\odot$	0.708

Fig. 7-26A   A Model of Mass 1 $M_\odot$ Shortly after Leaving the Main Sequence, at $t = 10.3059 \times 10^9$ Years. Radius r, pressure P, temperature T, net luminosity L_r, and hydrogen abundance X are shown as functions of fractional mass M_r/M. The lower limit of the ordinate is zero for all variables. The upper limits, given in the figure, are 2.1334 $R_\odot$ (with $R_\odot = 6.96 \times 10^{10}$ cm; however, the total radius is 2.2179 $R_\odot$), central pressure P_c (dyne cm^{-2}), central temperature T_c (°K), total luminosity L (units of $L_\odot = 3.86 \times 10^{33}$ erg sec^{-1}), and initial hydrogen abundance $X = 0.708$. The central density (not shown) is 15,214 gm cm^{-3}. The time is measured from the initial model calculated for the pre–main-sequence phase (see Section 2). [Adapted from I. Iben, Jr., 1967 (326).]

10^4 gm cm^{-3}) that electron degeneracy supplies 46 per cent of the total pressure. Convection occurs over the outer 6.31 per cent of the mass. The radius increases throughout the evolution.

At point 5' in Fig. 7-25, the model is well on the way toward the red-giant phase. Electron degeneracy at the center now accounts for 76 per cent of the total pressure. The temperature in the hydrogen-burning shell has become so high that the CN cycle yields more energy than the *p-p* chain, and the explosive rate of energy released by the nuclear reactions results in rapid expansion and cooling of the envelope. The consequent increase in the envelope opacities produces convection extending over the outer 71 per cent of the mass. In Fig. 7-26B, corresponding to point 5', the mixing caused by

r	P_g/P	ρ	T	L_r	X
$1\ R_\odot$	1	91171	27.351×10^6	$11.422\ L_\odot$	0.693

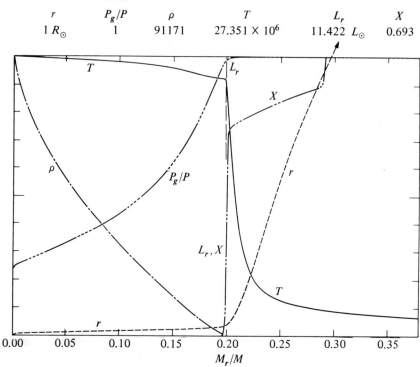

Fig. 7-26B A Model of Mass 1 $M_\odot$ during the Subgiant Stage at $t = 10.8747 \times 10^9$ Years. Radius r, ratio P_g/P of gas pressure computed from the perfect gas law to the actual pressure with degeneracy included, temperature T, net luminosity L_r, and hydrogen abundance X are shown as functions of fractional mass M_r/M in the range 0 to 0.38. The distribution of L_r is a step function rising from zero to maximum scale with the initial rise in X. The lower limit of the ordinate is zero for all variables. The upper limits, given in the figure, are 1 $R_\odot$ (with $R_\odot = 6.96 \times 10^{10}$ cm; however, the total radius is 6.1784 $R_\odot$), unity for the ratio of pressures, central density ρ_c (gm cm^{-3}), central temperature T_c (°K), total luminosity L (units of $L_\odot = 3.86 \times 10^{33}$ erg sec^{-1}), and hydrogen abundance $X = 0.693$. The central pressure (not shown) is 6552.2 dyne cm^{-2}. The time is measured from the initial model calculated for the pre–main-sequence phase (see Section 2). [Adapted from I. Iben, Jr., 1967 (326).]

the convection is responsible for the uniformity of the hydrogen abundance beyond a mass fraction of 29 per cent.

We continue our discussion by describing next the pioneering work that carried the calculations beyond the tip of the red-giant branch.* The assumed

---

* This discussion is based upon the first two of the following three papers: M. Schwarzschild and H. Selberg, 1962 (340); M. Schwarzschild and R. Härm, 1962 (341); R. Härm and M. Schwarzschild, 1964 (342). See also the more recent calculations of P. Demarque and J. G. Mengel, 1971 (404).

mass is somewhat higher, 1.3 $M_\odot$, and the original composition is $X = 0.900$, $Y = 0.099$, $Z = 0.001$. The results are summarized in Table 7-8. The initial model of this series, which is not given here, differs little from Model 2.* The initial model has 26 per cent of the total mass in a hydrogen-exhausted core, in which electrons are degenerate over the inner 24 per cent of the total stellar mass and non-degenerate over the remaining 2 per cent. Since a degenerate electron gas is highly conducting, the inner portion of the core is nearly isothermal (cf. log T_c and log T_b in Models 2 to 34). The Schönberg–Chandrasekhar limit is exceeded, and the core contracts gravitationally. The energy generated per second by the contraction has become significant in Model 2, where it contributes 0.0027 of the total luminosity (cf. log L_{rj} and log L). The chemical composition changes discontinuously at the boundary of the core, and a narrow hydrogen-burning shell supplies the greater part of the luminosity of the model. The envelope, which retains the original uniform composition, has an inner zone in radiative equilibrium and an outer part in convective equilibrium.

As the core continues to contract, the temperature rises, and helium-burning by means of the triple-alpha reaction commences. The release of this additional energy tends to heat the core further and to accelerate the rate of nuclear burning. If the core were composed of ordinary matter, the core would expand and cool, thereby reducing the nuclear burning rate to a level at which equilibrium between energy production and energy flow away from the core would be maintained. The electrons in the core, however, are highly degenerate and they supply the greater part of the total pressure (94 per cent in Model 21). Thus the pressure is very little influenced by a change in temperature, and a significant expansion cannot occur. (Note, however, that a slight expansion does proceed, following Model 21. This is indicated by the decreasing value of ρ_c.) As the helium burns, the energy released continues to heat the gas; and as the gas becomes hotter, the nuclear burning rate becomes ever greater. A thermal runaway ensues. Conditions change so rapidly that smaller and smaller time steps are required between the successive models computed. The interval between Models 1 and 2 is more than two million years, but the time step must be made shorter until the structure is changing so rapidly that consecutive models must be a second apart!† The central energy-generation rate at the peak of this *helium flash* exceeds 10^{14} erg gm^{-1} sec^{-1}, compared with ~ 10 erg gm^{-1} sec^{-1} at the center of the Sun. The luminosity of the core exceeds 10^{46} erg sec^{-1}, which is the luminosity of the entire Galaxy!† Such enormous energy outputs are also characteristic of

---

* The initial model is published in detail by M. Schwarzschild, 1958 (50), pp. 260, 261.

† A more refined computation indicates that conditions during the helium flash are actually a little less extreme. [R. Härm and M. Schwarzschild, 1966 (343).] Also see the more recent calculations of P. Demarque and J. G. Mengel, 1971 (404).

Table 7-8 An Evolutionary Sequence for the Helium Flash. This table is a partial listing from M. Schwarzschild and H. Selberg, 1962 (340) and M. Schwarzschild and R. Härm, 1962 (341). The original model numbers are retained.

Model No.	2	16	21	26	33	34	35	36	37	42
t (yr)	2.39×10^6	24.37×10^6								
t' (yr)			$-35{,}590$	-0.01080						
t' (sec)					-8.1	-1.6	0	$+43.2$	$+342.7$	$+1.522 \times 10^6$
Center:										
$\log P_c$	21.75	22.29	22.48	22.30	21.87	21.85	21.84	21.75	21.58	20.80
$\log T_c$	7.64	7.91	7.95	8.18	8.46	8.52	8.55	8.53	8.49	8.30
$\log \rho_c$	5.54	5.86	5.98	5.86	5.54	5.51	5.50	5.43	5.30	4.70
$\log \epsilon_c$			2.50	9.11	14.12	14.58	14.86	14.57	13.92	10.54
Bdy. of Deg. or Conv.:	(Deg.)	(Deg.)	(Deg.)	(Deg.)	(Deg.)	(Deg.)	—	(Conv.)	(Conv.)	(Conv.)
$\log r_b$	9.10	9.04	9.01	8.97	8.70	8.49	—	9.02	9.09	9.38
M_{rb}/M	0.25	0.37	0.40	0.33	0.06	0.01	—	0.25	0.28	0.37
$\log P_b$	19.56	20.19	20.35	20.92	21.63	21.76	—	20.86	20.57	19.15
$\log T_b$	7.64	7.90	7.95	8.18	8.46	8.52	—	8.17	8.09	7.64
$\log \rho_b$	4.13	4.48	4.60	4.95	5.38	5.45	—	4.89	4.69	3.71
$\log L_{rb}$	33.14	34.50	34.63	*	35.06	34.52	—	34.92	34.92	34.43
$\log L_{rbn}$					46.11	46.08	—	46.21	45.58	41.65
He-H Bdy.:										
$\log r_f$	9.25	9.27	9.27	9.34	9.41	9.41	9.41	9.42	9.44	9.56
M_{rf}/M	0.26	0.39	0.42	0.42	0.42	0.42	0.42	0.42	0.42	0.42
$\log P_f$	17.64	17.24	17.11	17.24	17.30	17.30	17.29	17.27	17.23	16.97
$\log T_f$	7.60	7.74	7.80	7.74	7.66	7.66	7.66	7.65	7.63	7.52
$\log \rho_{Hf}$			1.52	1.71	1.84	1.84	1.84	1.83	1.81	1.66
$\log \rho_{fe}$	1.85	1.31								
$\log L_{rff}$†	33.38	34.72	35.33	35.29	36.30	36.32	36.33	36.41	36.48	36.39
$\log L_{rfe}$†	33.38	34.72	37.38	37.00	36.64	36.64	36.64	36.62	36.59	36.39

Base of Conv.:

log r_k	11.05	11.29	11.35	11.47
M_{r_k}/M	0.29	0.40	0.43	0.47
log P_k	11.92	10.26	9.88	10.64
log T_k	6.16	5.98	5.95	5.89
log ρ_k	−2.42	−3.91	−4.25	−3.44
log L_{r_k}	35.95	37.12	37.38	36.39

Surface:

log R	12.18	12.92	13.08	12.48
$R/R_\odot$	22	120	170	43
log L	35.95	37.12	37.38	36.39
$L/L_\odot$	230	3,400	6,200	630
log T_{eff}	3.68	3.61	3.59	3.65
T_{eff} (°K)	4,800	4,100	3,900	4,400

The notation has the following meaning:

t is the time measured from Model 1, at an epoch just before energy release by gravitational contraction becomes significant;

t' is the time measured from the epoch at which the helium flash reaches its peak;

b indicates the boundary of the degenerate portions of Models 2 to 34 or of the convective portions of Models 36 to 42;

L_{rb} is the net luminosity at r_b and includes both nuclear and gravitational contributions;

L_{rbn} is the net luminosity at r_b contributed by helium reactions;

j indicates the boundary of the helium core and hydrogen-rich envelope;

i, e indicate, respectively, the interior and exterior surfaces of the core boundary;

c, k indicate, respectively, the center of the star and the inner surface of the convective envelope.

* To overcome computational difficulties, it was assumed that L_r in this model is constant in the non-degenerate portion of the helium core.

† In Models 2 and 16, the hydrogen-burning region is of finite extent and L_r is continuous across the core boundary. In Models 21 to 42, hydrogen-burning is assumed to be confined to an infinitesimally thin shell at the core boundary, and the energy released per second is given by the difference L_{rji} − L_{rje}.

supernovae, but the models do not represent such stars; the non-degenerate portion of the core blankets the luminosity so strongly that only a normal giant star is observable.

In the meantime, another phenomenon has been in progress. With the rising temperature and decreasing density, the degree of degeneracy becomes progressively lower. The outer portions of the core become, layer by layer, non-degenerate until, in Model 35, the center itself becomes non-degenerate. The restoration of ordinary properties to the matter results in expansion and cooling. The thermal runaway is halted. The readjustment of the pressure and temperature distributions then leaves the model in a state that is convectively unstable in the central portion of the helium core (Models 36 to 42).

The positions of Models 1 to 16, as well as 21 and 42, are shown in Fig. 7-27. The computation of the convective envelope was intended to be only approximate, and therefore the radii and luminosities (and hence the positions in the diagram) are also approximate. The hydrogen-rich envelopes were omitted in the construction of the other models, and therefore the characteristics at

Fig. 7-27   The Evolutionary Track of a Star of Mass 1.3 $M_\odot$ in the Hertzsprung–Russell Diagram, Preceding and Following the Helium Flash. The *dots* are the positions of individual models, with some of the model numbers indicated. The curve is a schematic representation of a globular cluster. [Adapted from M. Schwarzschild and H. Selberg, 1962 (340).]

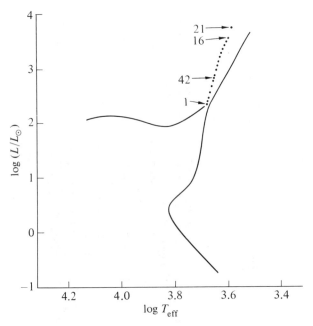

the surface are not known. Although the peak of the helium flash occurs in Model 35, the brightest exterior luminosity is attained by Model 21.*

The mass of the convective region that forms after the helium flash occurs becomes greater with time. Although calculations carried beyond Model 42 indicate that the convection will not penetrate into the hydrogen-rich envelope, certain effects that may be important were not considered in the investigation. Thus, a definite conclusion as to whether mixing occurs has not been reached, but the result found here has been supported by more recent investigations. If the convective core were eventually to extend into the convective envelope, the star would become completely mixed and would be expected to move rapidly toward the left in the Hertzsprung–Russell diagram, to a position corresponding to the left-hand end of the horizontal branch of a globular-cluster diagram (Fig. 7-27). Further evolution would then bring the star once more into the giant region.

Another investigation† has obtained models beyond the helium flash, for masses that are smaller than those in the preceding discussion. Such models are of interest in explaining the horizontal branch of globular clusters, and their description will be deferred.

We note one more point that is significant in connection with the late evolution of stars in the red-giant region. This applies not only to models of one solar mass but also, for example, to the model of 5 $M_\odot$ to be described later. After the helium in the core has been exhausted and a helium shell-burning phase begins, thermal instabilities lead to cyclic flashes in the shell, which is in this case non-degenerate.‡ These flashes cause a cyclic formation of a convective zone extending for some distance above the middle of the helium-burning shell. The calculations indicate that, after several cycles, this convective zone will reach the hydrogen-rich layers above. The probable mixing that ensues cannot cause the entire star to become chemically homogeneous because of the limited extent of the convective region, but the mixing might be important for certain processes in nucleosynthesis.

4-3 EVOLUTION OF A MODEL OF FIVE SOLAR MASSES

We shall now follow the development of the model whose main-sequence phase was described in Section 3-3.§

While the star is on the main sequence, uniformity of the core composition

---

* In stars that have approximately the metal abundance of the Sun, nitrogen-burning may trigger the helium flash at a lower temperature than that required for the triple-alpha reaction, thus terminating the red-giant branch sooner [P. P. Eggleton, 1968 (344)].

† P. Demarque and J. G. Mengel, 1971 (404). The models are a continuation of a previously computed sequence that follows the history of these stars.

‡ This phenomenon is described by M. Schwarzschild and R. Härm, 1967 (345).

§ The discussion is again drawn from the papers of I. Iben, Jr., cited in Section 3-3.

is maintained by convection, which in turn is maintained by the hydrogen-converting reactions near the center. Convection ceases when the central hydrogen abundance is nearly exhausted. As the nuclear fuel becomes depleted, gravitational contraction of the central regions makes an increasing contribution to the luminosity.

Figure 7-28A shows the structure at about point 3 in Fig. 7-25, just after the disappearance of the core. The value of X at the center is only 5.65×10^{-5}, yet hydrogen-burning there still supplies roughly half as much energy as does the gravitational contraction at the center. The much larger hydrogen abundance outside the former core region allows a rapid rise of L_r, and a shell source develops. The rate of energy-production in this shell is so high,

Fig. 7-28A A Model of Mass 5 $M_\odot$ Shortly after Leaving the Main Sequence, at $t = 6.82461 \times 10^7$ Years. Radius r, pressure P, density ρ, temperature T, net luminosity L_r, and hydrogen abundance X are shown as functions of fractional mass M_r/M. The lower limit of the ordinate is zero for all variables. The upper limits, given in the figure, are 2.9198 $R_\odot$ (with $R_\odot = 6.96 \times 10^{10}$ cm; however, the total radius is 3.9429 $R_\odot$), central pressure P_c (dyne cm^{-2}), central density ρ_c (gm cm^{-3}), central temperature T_c (°K), total luminosity L (units of $L_\odot = 3.86 \times 10^{33}$ erg sec^{-1}), and initial hydrogen abundance $X = 0.708$. The time is measured from the initial model calculated for the pre–main-sequence phase. [Adapted from I. Iben, Jr., 1966 (331).]

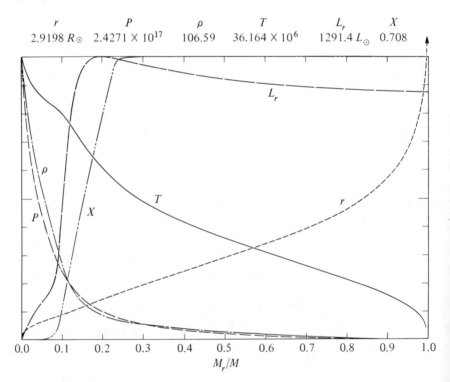

r	P	ρ	T	L_r	X
2.9198 $R_\odot$	2.4271 × 10^{17}	106.59	36.164 × 10^6	1291.4 $L_\odot$	0.708

M_r/M

in fact, that the mild explosiveness forces the material away in both directions, causing further compression of the central region and also expansion of the overlying layers. The expansion takes place at the expense of the radiative flux, part of which is converted into potential energy. Thus L_r decreases beyond mass fraction 0.2.

As the consumption of hydrogen near the center continues, nuclear energy-production there becomes ineffective and a nearly isothermal core develops. Hydrogen-burning now takes place only in the thick shell surrounding the core.

At about point 4 in Fig. 7-25, the mass of the core reaches the Schönberg–Chandrasekhar limit and a more rapid contraction of the core ensues. The temperatures and densities in the shell increase more rapidly, and an explosive rate of energy production is once more attained. The envelope is pushed outwards rapidly and the star quickly crosses the Hertzsprung gap.* To provide the required increase in the potential energy, the envelope absorbs part of the radiative flux that flows through it. This is supplemented by about an equal amount of energy derived from the thermal motions in the envelope. The blanketing of the nuclear energy flux by the envelope, together with a decrease in the energy output by the narrowing shell, causes a decrease in the luminosity. The temperatures in the envelope decrease during the expansion, and the resulting increase in the opacities induces the formation of a convective envelope that grows rapidly inwards from the surface region just before point 5 is reached. As the effective temperature continues to decrease, the principal opacity source in the outermost radiative region, the H^- ion, becomes ineffective as the supply of electrons is diminished by recombination with ions to form neutral atoms. The decrease in the opacity permits the escape of a larger radiative flux, and the luminosity rises. To maintain thermal balance, the star must provide the additional energy from its interior. This is accomplished partly by adjustments in the convective envelope that make the expansion adiabatic; thus the energy for the expansion is now supplied almost entirely by conversion of thermal energy within the layer itself, leaving the radiative flux nearly unchanged as it passes through the envelope. The remainder of the increased luminosity is supplied by an increase in the production rate in the shell, where the temperature now rises as the shell moves inwards. The path in the Hertzsprung–Russell diagram is nearly vertical and, as the convective envelope includes more and more of the stellar mass, approaches the Hayashi track.

Figure 7-28B illustrates the structure shortly after point 5 in Fig. 7-25 is reached. The convective envelope extends inwards to mass fraction 0.743. The net luminosity in this region is nearly constant with mass fraction, as discussed in the preceding paragraph. Near the center, energy production by

---

* The *Hertzsprung gap* is the region of the Hertzsprung–Russell diagram between the main sequence and the giant region; few stars occupy this gap.

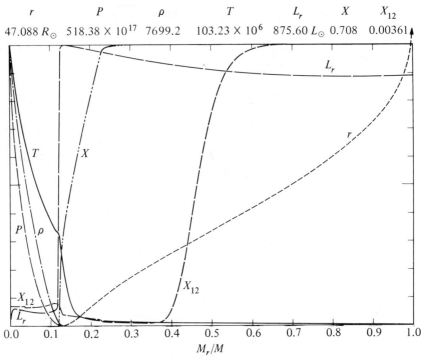

r	P	ρ	T	L_r	X	X_{12}
47.088 $R_\odot$	518.38 × 10^{17}	7699.2	103.23 × 10^6	875.60 $L_\odot$	0.708	0.00361

M_r/M

Fig. 7-28B   A Model of Mass 5 $M_\odot$ during the Giant Stage at $t = 7.03776 \times 10^7$ Years. Radius r, pressure P, density ρ, temperature T, net luminosity L_r, hydrogen abundance X, and carbon-12 abundance X_{12} are shown as functions of fractional mass M_r/M. The lower limit of the ordinate is zero for all variables. The upper limits, given in the figure, are 47.088 $R_\odot$ (with $R_\odot = 6.96 \times 10^{10}$ cm; however, the total radius is 51.328 $R_\odot$), central pressure P_c (dyne cm^{-2}), central density ρ_c (gm cm^{-3}), central temperature T_c (°K), total luminosity L (units of $L_\odot = 3.86 \times 10^{33}$ erg sec^{-1}), initial hydrogen abundance $X = 0.708$, and carbon-12 abundance $X_{12} = 0.003610$. The time is measured from the initial model calculated for the pre–main-sequence phase. [Adapted from I. Iben, Jr., 1966 (331).]

the reaction N^{14} (α, γ) F^{18} $(\beta^+\nu)$ O^{18} has been in progress since a short time preceding the development of the convective envelope and has by now become sufficiently rapid to cause an appreciable increase in L_r from the center and, indeed, to bring about convection in the inner 3 per cent of the stellar mass. The rapid outflow of energy also causes expansion of the central region; note the decline in L_r following the initial rise near the stellar center in Fig. 7-28B. The contraction of the core during the preceding evolution has raised the pressures and densities there to high values. Note also the sharp change in the slopes of these distributions at the position of the shell.

As N^{14} becomes consumed near the center, the contraction of the core is resumed. The temperature becomes so high (about 130 × 10^6 °K at the center) that the triple-alpha process becomes effective. This occurs at point 6 in Fig. 7-25. The sudden outpouring of energy from the new source causes expansion of the central region and slowing of the inward motion of the hydrogen-burning shell. This retards the rise of temperatures and densities in the shell and causes the total luminosity to decrease. The track in Fig. 7-25 therefore undergoes a sharp downward reversal at point 6.

The envelope now begins to contract and grow warmer. Opacities in the convective region decrease, and radiative equilibrium is once more established over a growing zone as the base of the convective envelope retreats toward the photosphere. With the lowering of the opacity, the radiative flux is increased. In order to provide the required additional energy, the inner regions

Fig. 7-28C   A Model of Mass 5 $M_\odot$ during the Giant Stage at $t = 7.73665 \times 10^7$ Years. Radius r, pressure P, density ρ, temperature T, net luminosity L_r, and helium-4 abundance X_4 are shown as functions of fractional mass M_r/M. The lower limit of the ordinate is zero for all variables. The upper limits, given in the figure, are 35.852 $R_\odot$ (with $R_\odot = 6.96 \times 10^{10}$ cm; however, the total radius is 50.612 $R_\odot$), central pressure P_c (dyne cm^{-2}), central density ρ_c (gm cm^{-3}), central temperature T_c (°K), total luminosity L (units of $L_\odot = 3.86 \times 10^{33}$ erg sec^{-1}), and helium-4 abundance $X_4 = 0.9763$. The time is measured from the initial model calculated for the pre–main-sequence phase (see Section 2). [Adapted from I. Iben, Jr., 1966 (331).]

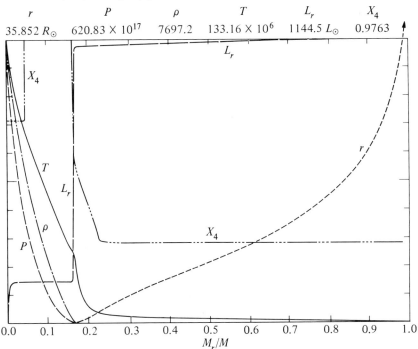

r	P	ρ	T	L_r	X_4
35.852 $R_\odot$	620.83 × 10^{17}	7697.2	133.16 × 10^6	1144.5 $L_\odot$	0.9763

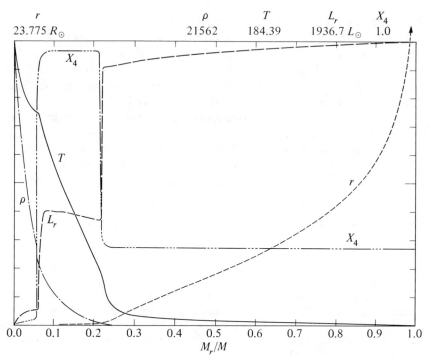

$$\begin{array}{ccccc}
r & \rho & T & L_r & X_4 \\
23.775\ R_\odot & 21562 & 184.39 & 1936.7\ L_\odot & 1.0
\end{array}$$

M_r/M

Fig. 7-28 D   A Model of Mass 5 $M_\odot$ during the Giant Stage at $t = 8.79060 \times 10^7$ Years. Radius r, density ρ, temperature T, net luminosity L_r, and helium-4 abundance X_4 are shown as functions of fractional mass M_r/M. The lower limit of the ordinate is zero for all variables. The upper limits, given in the figure, are 23.775 $R_\odot$ (with $R_\odot = 6.96 \times 10^{10}$ cm; however, the total radius is 44.141 $R_\odot$), central density ρ_c (gm cm^{-3}), central temperature T_c ($^\circ$K), total luminosity L (units of $L_\odot = 3.86 \times 10^{33}$ erg sec^{-1}), and helium-4 abundance $X_4 = 1.0$. The time is measured from the initial model calculated for the pre–main-sequence phase. [Adapted from I. Iben, Jr., 1966 (331).]

contract more rapidly, increasing the temperatures and densities in the shell and raising its energy-production rate. The luminosity once more begins to rise.

The structure illustrated in Fig. 7-28C occurs at a time between points 7 and 8, while the luminosity is rising. The variations of P, ρ, T, and r are qualitatively similar to those of Fig. 7-28B. On the other hand, L_r is now constant in the cooler parts of the core and increases in the contracting envelope.

The core has been expanding since reaching the top of the red-giant branch (point 6), but at an ever decreasing rate. The expansion is finally halted and reversed to a contraction between points 8 and 9'. Soon afterwards, the radius begins to increase, while the luminosity is slightly lowered by absorption of energy in the expanding envelope and reduced efficiency of the hydrogen-burning shell. The star moves toward point 10.*

As the helium content of the core becomes low, the luminosity is supplemented by gravitational contraction of the entire star and by helium-burning that has begun in a shell surrounding the core. The thin hydrogen-burning shell continues to be operative. The luminosity and effective temperature increase, and the evolutionary track again turns toward the left. Figure 7-28D shows the internal structure when the star reaches point 11. The locations of the two shells, in the vicinities of $M_r/M = 0.07$ and 0.22, are marked by rapid rises in the net luminosity. Within the inner core, which now consists principally of oxygen and possibly carbon, the release of energy is due to gravitational contraction and nuclear reactions. The mild explosiveness of the energy production in the helium shell causes an expansion of the region between the shells and a consequent decrease in L_r with mass fraction. Outside the hydrogen shell, the contraction of the envelope makes a positive contribution to the luminosity.

The series of models described here was terminated at point 11. However, other investigations of a star of 5 solar masses have carried the calculations

---

* The effective temperature at point 9′ is much higher than that calculated by E. Hofmeister, 1967 (346), using a different composition. See the solid curve in Fig. 7-37.

Fig. 7-29 The Evolutionary Track of a Star of Mass 5 $M_\odot$ in the Hertzsprung–Russell Diagram. The chemical composition is appropriate to extreme Population I. *Letters* indicating various points in the track correspond to those in Fig. 7-30. [After R. Kippenhahn, H.-C. Thomas, and A. Weigert, 1965 (347).]

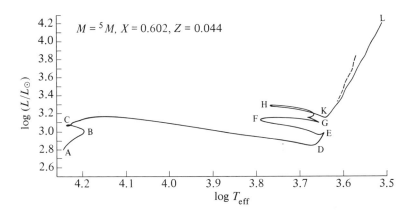

further.* Since the reaction $C^{12} + He^4 \rightarrow O^{16} + \gamma$ was not taken into account, the composition of the core at this stage is pure carbon. The helium-burning shell gains in efficiency and the envelope expands. This causes a decrease in the temperature at the hydrogen shell, which ceases to burn. The structure is now similar to that in the earlier, hydrogen shell-burning stage. Again a deep convective envelope is formed. The star reaches point K in Fig. 7-29, and the luminosity then rises rapidly.

* We next describe some results obtained by R. Kippenhahn, H.-C. Thomas, and A. Weigert, 1965 (347). The initial chemical composition is taken to be $X = 0.602$, $Y = 0.354$, $Z = 0.044$. The evolutionary track derived in this paper differs significantly from that obtained by E. Hofmeister, 1967 (346), who used improved calculations including line absorption in the opacities. The tracks are compared in Fig. 7-37.

Fig. 7-30 The Evolution of a Star of Mass 5 $M_\odot$. A vertical line drawn anywhere in this diagram would represent a single model (for approximately the inner half of the mass) at the time given in the abscissa. Note that the time scale is not uniform. Regions in convective equilibrium are indicated by *clouds*; other regions are in radiative equilibrium. Significant nuclear burning ($\epsilon > 10^3$ erg gm^{-1} sec^{-1}) is indicated by *black stripes*. *Dots* mark the regions in which the composition varies with fractional mass M_r/M; *wide spacing* is used for the transition from the initial hydrogen-rich composition to helium, *close spacing* for the transition from helium to carbon. [After R. Kippenhahn, H.-C. Thomas, and A. Weigert, 1965 (347).]

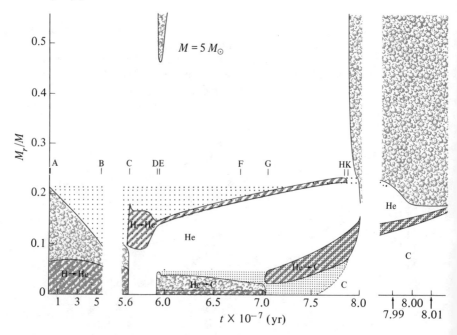

The subsequent internal evolution depends critically upon whether or not certain neutrino processes, which have been predicted, actually exist in nature. These processes convert photons into neutrinos in the presence of electrons.* The neutrinos, which do not interact with the stellar matter, then pass freely out of the star. If the neutrino flux is appreciable, this energy sink has important consequences for the evolution of the star in these later stages of its history.

In the case that such neutrino losses do not exist, a carbon-flash phenomenon occurs.† As in the star of 1.3 $M_\odot$, the high density at this stage of the evolution has produced electron degeneracy in the core. Thus the burning of nuclear fuel (in this case carbon) leads to an increase in temperature but does not cause the core to expand appreciably. The higher temperature still further promotes the carbon-burning, and a thermal runaway follows. This is halted only when the temperature becomes so high that the matter is no longer degenerate, and the resulting expansion cools the core. During this time, the temperatures and densities at the hydrogen-helium interface have been increasing, while the temperatures at the helium-burning shell have been decreasing. The hydrogen-burning shell is once more activated, while the helium-shell source becomes negligible. The evolution from the homogeneous main-sequence state to the onset of carbon-burning is summarized in Fig. 7-30. The variation of log $L/L_\odot$ during the later phases of evolution is shown in Fig. 7-31.

If the neutrino processes are assumed to exist, as appears likely, the internal events are very different, although there is little change at the surface‡ (Fig. 7-31). So much energy is carried out of the core by neutrinos that the central temperature decreases, although the fraction of the luminosity that is lost in this manner, L_ν/L, is only several per cent. The highest temperature in the model occurs at the boundary of the helium-exhausted core, and energy now flows *inwards* toward the center, as well as outwards from the core boundary. The central temperature is too low for the ignition of carbon. The unstable condition in the carbon flash is thus avoided, but another kind of instability appears: an excess of energy is trapped in the thin helium-burning shell, which raises its temperature. Since the triple-alpha reaction is highly sensitive to temperature, a thermal runaway occurs. The situation is finally

---

* For additional information on neutrino processes, see H. Reeves (L. H. Aller and D. B. McLaughlin, eds.), 1965 (58) and H.-Y. Chiu (R. F. Stein and A. G. W. Cameron, eds.), 1966 (59).

† This work has been carried out by R. Kippenhahn, H.-C. Thomas, and A. Weigert, 1966 (348). See the comments in the next footnote.

‡ The models of A. Weigert, 1966 (349) will now be described. This investigation, as well as that of the preceding paragraph, is a continuation of the work of R. Kippenhahn, H.-C. Thomas, and A. Weigert, 1965 (347). The same initial composition is therefore assumed in all three papers.

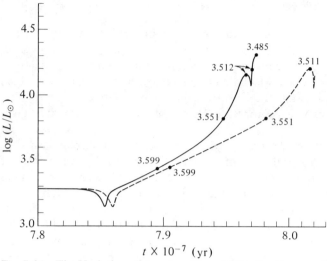

Fig. 7-31 The Variation of Luminosity and Effective Temperature with Time for a Model of Mass 5 $M_\odot$ in the Later Stages of Red-Giant Evolution. Neutrino processes were included in the calculation of the *solid curve* (hence there is no carbon flash). Neutrino processes were omitted in the calculation of the *dashed curve* (hence the carbon flash occurs). The *numbers* along the tracks give the logarithms of the effective temperatures at the points indicated. [After A. Weigert, 1966 (349).]

Fig. 7-32 The Evolutionary Track in the Hertzsprung–Russell Diagram of a Star of Mass 30 $M_\odot$. This track is the same as the top curve in Fig. 7-25. The models are designated as in Table 7-9, but only the first model for each phase is labeled. The *dots* indicate the remaining models. [After R. Stothers, 1966 (333).]

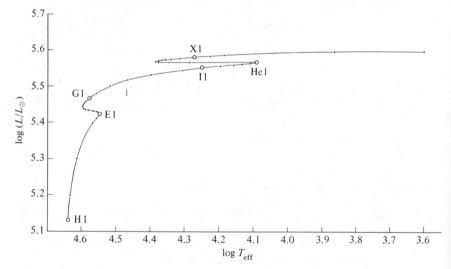

relieved by an expansion of the material; but this is followed by a contraction that restores the unstable conditions, and the pulsing is repeated with increasing amplitude at intervals of 4000 years. The model sequence was terminated after six cycles, and the course of the subsequent evolution is unknown.

4-4 EVOLUTION OF A MODEL OF THIRTY SOLAR MASSES*

We now describe the further evolution of the model discussed in Section 3-4. As hydrogen continues to be consumed and X falls below 0.03 in the convective core (beyond point 2 in Fig. 7-25 or point E1 in Fig. 7-32), gravitational contraction becomes increasingly important as an energy source (see

* This section is based on the investigations of R. Stothers, 1964 (332) and 1966 (333).

Fig. 7-33 The Evolution of the Structural Zones in a Model of Mass 30 $M_\odot$. The helium-burning stage, to which this diagram applies, is divided into three parts given by the three discontinuous intervals along the abscissa: in the first, $Y_{\text{core}} = 0.97$, and $0.061 \leqslant L_{\text{He}}/L \leqslant 0.331$; in the second, $0.97 \geqslant Y_{\text{core}} \geqslant 0.0129$ and $0.334 \geqslant L_{\text{He}}/L \geqslant 0.014$; in the third, Y_{core} and L_{He}/L continue to decrease. The ratio L_{He}/L is the fraction of the total luminosity that is produced by helium-burning. The *dashed line* represents the hydrogen-burning shell. *Dotted regions* are those in which the composition varies with the fractional mass M_r/M. The model numbers (at the top) are the same as in Table 7-9. [After R. Stothers, 1966 (333).]

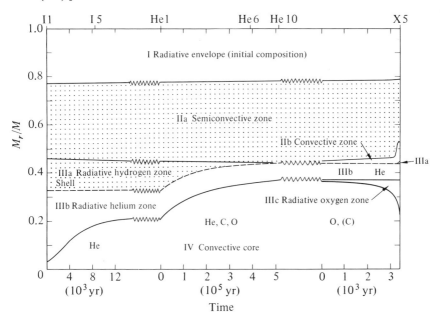

Table 7-9   Evolutionary Models of a Star of Mass 30 $M_\odot$.* This table is a partial listing from R. Stothers, 1964 (332) and 1966 (333). The original model designations are retained. These models continue the sequence begun in Table 7-5.

	E1	E2	E7	E10	G6
$(M_r/M)_s$	0.342	0.342	0.342	0.342	0.328
$\log(r_s/R_\odot)$	0.267	0.240	0.117	0.089	-0.142
$\log T_s$	7.436	7.458	7.571	7.589	7.683
$\log \rho_s$					
$(M_r/M)_{core}$	0.328	0.320	0.258	0.182	0.064
X_{core}	3.0×10^{-2}	9.5×10^{-3}	3.0×10^{-5}	4.9×10^{-8}	0
Y_{core}	0.94	0.96	0.97	0.97	0.97
$(X_C)_{core}$	~ 0	~ 0	~ 0	~ 0	~ 0
$\log T_c$	7.665	7.696	7.823	7.854	8.168
$\log \rho_c$	0.701	0.795	1.193	1.312	2.433
β_c	0.564	0.557	0.563	0.577	0.764
$L_{H,core}/L$	0.999	0.995	0.319	0.002	0.000
$L_{H,shell}/L$	0.000	0.001	0.141	0.249	0.575
L_{He}/L	0.000	0.000	0.000	0.000	0.000†
L_C/L	0.000	0.000	0.000	0.000	0.000
L_g/L	0.001	0.004	0.540	0.749	0.425
$\log(L/L_\odot)$	5.439	5.445	5.459	5.472	5.560
$\log(R/R_\odot)$	1.143	1.136	1.057	1.079	1.680
$\log T_{eff}$	4.548	4.554	4.596	4.589	4.310

* The subscript s designates the hydrogen-burning shell. The subscript c designates the center. The quantity X_C is the abundance by mass of carbon; β is the ratio of gas pressure to total pressure; and $L_{H,core}$, $L_{H,shell}$, L_{He}, L_C, and L_g are, respectively, the luminosity produced by hydrogen core-

Table 7-9). By the time X reaches the value 0.01 in the core, contraction already supplies 0.004 of the total luminosity. Meanwhile, the temperatures outside the core have risen sufficiently for the development of a hydrogen-burning shell within the radiative zone III (Fig. 7-33), and the shell at this time provides 0.001 of the total luminosity. The contraction process and the shell source contribute ever greater fractions of the total energy output as hydrogen is further consumed. When X in the core falls to about 10^{-7}, the hydrogen-burning core supplies only 0.002 of the total luminosity, while the shell contributes 0.249 and gravitational contraction 0.749 of the total. During this interval of hydrogen exhaustion, the luminosity increases slightly. The radius at first decreases by a small amount, since the entire star contracts. However, as the shell becomes important as an energy-producing region, the envelope expands, although the central region continues to contract (point 3 in Fig. 7-25). The expansion results from the relative increase in the contribu-

MODEL

I1	I5	He 1	He 6	He 10	X5
0.328	0.328	0.328	0.435	0.440	0.439
−1.968	−2.312	−2.346	−1.690	−1.860	−3.614
7.711	7.729	7.732	7.651	7.645	
0.656	0.680	0.694	0.265	0.093	
0.033	0.182	0.210	0.354	0.371	
0	0	0	0	0	0
0.97	0.97	0.970	0.188	0.0129	
~0	~0	0.000	0.575	0.332	
8.243	8.267	8.269	8.369	8.467	
2.699	2.732	2.733	2.858	3.136	
0.695	0.674	0.672	0.503	0.472	0.472
0.000	0.000	0.000	0.000	0.000	0.000
0.497	0.629	0.666	0.150	0.073	
0.061	0.297	0.334	0.443	0.014	
0.000	0.000	0.000	0.407	0.913	
0.442	0.074	0.000	0.000	0.000	
5.553	5.565	5.564	5.569	5.578	5.603
1.792	2.092	2.119	1.546	1.680	3.1
4.256	4.109	4.095	4.383	4.318	3.6

burning, hydrogen shell-burning, helium core-burning, carbon core-burning, and gravitational contraction.
† Although not explicitly included in this model, helium-burning already contributes 0.004 of the total luminosity.

tion of radiation pressure to the total pressure.* (In the model of 5 $M_\odot$, it will be remembered, the expansion of the envelope was caused by the somewhat explosive nature of the energy production in the shell.)

The relatively high value of the radiation pressure ($1 - \beta \approx 0.4$ near the center) is also responsible for the maintenance of convection in the core even after energy generation effectively ceases there. The mass-fraction contained within the core does, however, decrease and reaches a minimum value of 0.06.

The temperatures near the center have been rising steadily. When T_c exceeds approximately 150×10^6 °K, helium-burning by the triple-alpha reaction begins to contribute appreciably to the total luminosity (point 6 in Fig. 7-25 or point I1 in Fig. 7-32). The rate at which nuclear energy is produced

* Consult the first reference cited in the footnote on p. 341 for a more detailed explanation.

in the core increases with time, while gravitational contraction is correspondingly retarded (Models I1 and I5 in Table 7-9). Meanwhile, there is a continual increase in the mass fraction of the convective domain. When helium-burning accounts for 0.33 of the total luminosity, gravitational contraction is halted completely. At this time, the hydrogen-shell source still predominates, providing 0.67 of the total luminosity.

Helium is gradually consumed in the convective core, while the abundance X_C of carbon increases (Models He 1 to He 10 in Table 7-9). Since the temperatures are very high, part of the carbon created by the helium-conversion is transformed into oxygen by means of the reaction $C^{12} + He^4 \rightarrow O^{16} + \gamma$. The fractional luminosity due to carbon-burning increases to 0.91 between Models He 1 and He 10, while that due to helium-burning diminishes to 0.014 as Y decreases to 0.0129.

During the phase of helium-burning, the mass of the helium core has continued to increase as a result of continuing hydrogen-conversion in the shell at the edge of the core. Eventually, the shell reaches the semi-convective zone IIa (Model He 10 and Fig. 7-33). Since the hydrogen content of the material in this zone is higher than that of the radiative hydrogen zone IIIa, the fuel supply in the shell is augmented, and the active phase of hydrogen shell-burning is somewhat prolonged. A *fully* convective zone IIb develops in the layers just above the shell.

When helium becomes nearly exhausted in the core, falling below $Y = 0.01$, gravitational contraction again becomes important (Models He 10 to X5; points 10′ to 11′ in Fig. 7-25). Convection ceases to be effective in the outer parts of the core, where a radiative zone composed primarily of oxygen is left behind as the boundary of the convective region recedes to smaller masses. In the last model calculated, a small radiative region IIIa has developed between the shell and the fully convective zone IIb. The model sequence was terminated at this point.*

4-5 SENSITIVITY TO ASSUMPTIONS

We have already described the influence of certain parameters upon main-sequence models, and we now select a few examples to illustrate the effects upon models of subgiant and giant stars.

Figures 7-34A to 7-36 show the effects of changes in the chemical composition on evolutionary tracks in the Hertzsprung–Russell or color-magnitude diagram. A lower value of Z, for a fixed hydrogen or helium content, results in a higher luminosity at a given effective temperature. When Z is fixed, on the other hand, the track for the smaller value of Y (or higher value of X) is lower.

---

* The details of the evolution are modified when different assumptions are made. See R. Stothers and C.-W. Chin, 1968 (393).

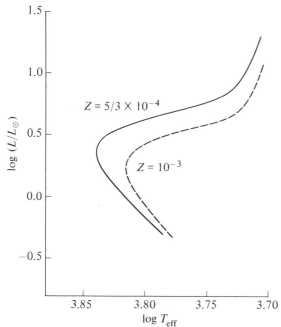

Fig. 7-34A The Effect of Metal Content Z on the Evolutionary Track for Population II in the Hertzsprung–Russell Diagram. The region of the turn-off from the main sequence is shown. The stellar mass is 0.7 $M_\odot$, and the hydrogen content is $X = 0.65$. [Adapted from M. Simoda and I. Iben, Jr., 1968 (378).]

Fig. 7-34B The Effect of Metal Content Z on the Evolutionary Track for Population II in the Color-Magnitude Diagram. The red-giant branch is shown. For all three tracks, the stellar mass is 1.2 $M_\odot$ and the helium content is $Y = 0$. [After P. Demarque and J. E. Geisler, 1963 (379).]

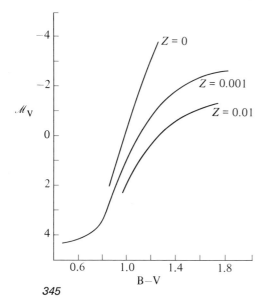

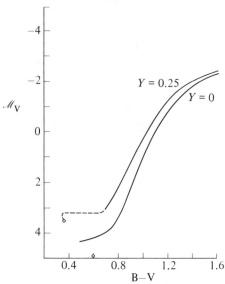

Fig. 7-35 The Effect of Hydrogen or Helium Content on the Evolutionary Track for Population II in the Color-Magnitude Diagram. For both tracks, the stellar mass is 1.2 $M_\odot$ and the metal content is $Z = 0.001$. The *dashed segment* is an estimate of the track followed from the main sequence. [After P. Demarque and J. E. Geisler, 1963 (379).]

A track for 5 $M_\odot$ and an extreme Population I composition is plotted in Fig. 7-37, together with a track calculated earlier. The later investigation incorporates the following improvements: new opacity tables were used, which take account of line absorption; improved formulae were used for energy generation by helium-burning; and a more accurate method was employed for calculating the chemical composition of the convective core during helium-burning. Since the onset of helium-burning occurs between points D and E, the portions of the tracks preceding this event differ only because of differences in the opacity.

Figure 7-38 illustrates the influence of a change in the value of the mixing length. The larger value causes the track to turn upward at a higher effective temperature.

We have already mentioned in the discussion of the 5 $M_\odot$ star the great changes produced in the case that neutrino losses are included in the computations. Drastic consequences also follow if matter is lost by the star during its evolution.* All these sensitivities of theoretical models must be kept in mind when a comparison is made with actual stars.

---

* Preliminary calculations including mass loss have been carried out by J. E. Forbes, 1968 (351) and by Y. Tanaka, 1966 (352).

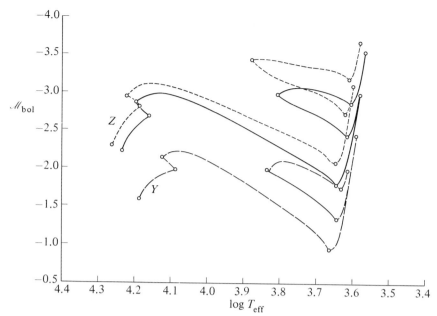

Fig. 7-36 The Effect of Chemical Composition on the Evolutionary Track for Population I in the Hertzsprung–Russell Diagram. The mass is 5 $M_\odot$. The unmarked, *solid curve* corresponds to the composition $X = 0.67$, $Y = 0.30$, and $Z = 0.03$. The *dashed curve*, labeled Y, represents a lower value of Y ($Y = 0.20$, $Z = 0.03$). The *dotted curve*, labeled Z, represents a lower value of Z ($Y = 0.30$, $Z = 0.015$). [After E. L. Hallgren and J. P. Cox, 1970 (350).]

Fig. 7-37 Comparison of Evolutionary Tracks in the Hertzsprung–Russell Diagram. The mass is 5 $M_\odot$, and the composition is $X = 0.602$, $Y = 0.354$, $Z = 0.044$. The *solid-line curve* supersedes the *dotted-line track* because it includes improvements in the calculations, as described in the text. [After E. Hofmeister, 1967 (346).]

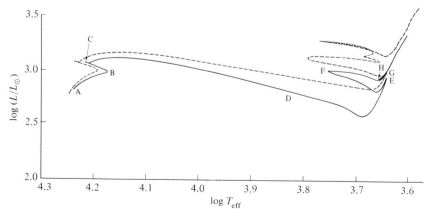

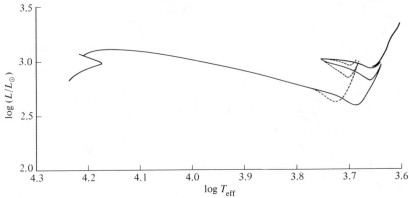

Fig. 7-38 Effect of Mixing Length upon Evolutionary Tracks. For the *solid curve*, the ratio l/H_p of mixing length to pressure scale-height is 1.5; for the *dotted curve*, the ratio is 2.1. The mass of the model is 5 $M_\odot$, and the chemical composition is $X = 0.602$, $Y = 0.354$, $Z = 0.044$. [After E. Hofmeister, 1967 (355).]

Fig. 7-39 The Color-Magnitude Diagram for the Globular Cluster M5. The curve is an estimated mean through the observed distribution of Fig. 1-19. The effective temperatures are approximate, since, strictly, T_{eff} is a function of both B − V and $\mathcal{M}_V$.

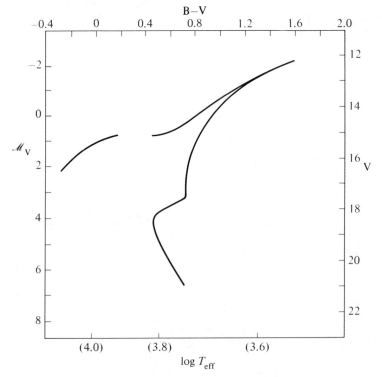

4-6 COMPARISON OF THEORY WITH OBSERVATIONS

For main-sequence models, we were able to make a direct comparison of models with observed binary components in the Hertzsprung–Russell diagram, the mass-luminosity diagram, and the mass-radius diagram. Very few reliable data are available for evolved stars, however, and detailed evolutionary sequences for a variety of masses and compositions have not yet been calculated. We therefore rely upon data pertaining to groups of stars, rather than individual stars, and determine how well the observations may be duplicated with the limited range of models available.

In making the comparisons, we must again bear in mind the uncertainties in the transformations between the theoretical and observed quantities, as indicated in Fig. 7-19.

Galactic and globular clusters are groups of stars that are especially well suited for comparison with theory, since the stars in any cluster may be expected to have nearly the same initial chemical composition and also similar ages; and, as we have seen, the composition, age, and mass of a star determine its other characteristics.

Fig. 7-40   The Color-Magnitude Diagram for the Galactic Cluster M67. The curve is an estimated mean through the observed distribution of Fig. 1-18. The effective temperatures are approximate, since, strictly, T_{eff} is a function of both B − V and $\mathcal{M}_V$.

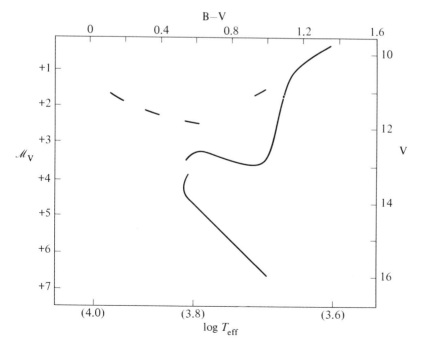

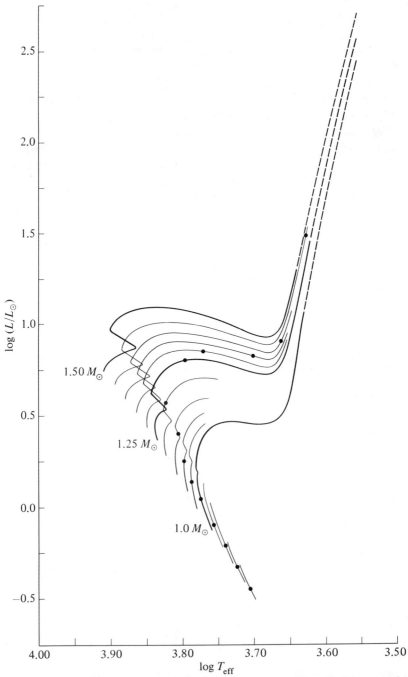

Fig. 7-41 The Theoretically Predicted Hertzsprung–Russell Diagram for a Population I Cluster at Age Approximately 4×10^9 Years. The composition is $X = 0.702$, $Y = 0.278$, $Z = 0.020$. The three *heavy lines* are the evolutionary tracks of stars of masses 1.0 $M_\odot$, 1.25 $M_\odot$, and 1.50 $M_\odot$ in Fig. 7-25. The *thin lines* are tracks interpolated at equal increments in mass. The *black dot* on each

A. THEORETICAL HERTZSPRUNG–RUSSELL AND COLOR-MAGNITUDE DIAGRAMS

A mean line through the main sequence and red-giant branch of a typical globular cluster or old galactic cluster (Figs. 7-39 and 7-40) immediately suggests comparison with the evolutionary tracks of the stars of lower mass in Fig. 7-25. For young clusters, the similarity is less apparent.

The evolutionary track of a star of given mass, however, is not what is actually given by the mean line in a color-magnitude diagram. The latter is rather the locus of stars of *different masses* at approximately the *same age*, not the locus of a star of given mass at different ages. We must construct a diagram that will give the required isochrone, using evolutionary tracks and a tabulation of the times taken to reach various points on any track. Figures 7-41 and 7-42 show some individual points on such isochrones based on the tracks of Fig. 7-25. Several evolutionary curves, at equal increments in mass, have been interpolated. On each curve, a dot has been placed at the point reached by the star at the assumed time, chosen as approximately 4×10^9 years in Fig. 7-41 and 2.5×10^8 years in Fig. 7-42. The chemical composition ($Z = 0.02$) and the low to moderate ages (less than the age of the Sun) make these diagrams appropriate for comparison with galactic, rather than with globular, clusters.

Although this procedure fixes the *locations* of stars in the theoretical Hertzsprung–Russell diagram, it is only partially adequate to determine the relative numbers of stars in the various portions of the figures. It is evident that the greatest number of stars is to be found on the lower main sequence, because the stars there are evolving slowly. Figure 7-42 indicates the paucity of stars in the space between the main sequence and the red-giant region, which results from the rapidity of the evolution during this phase. Quantitative results, however, can be obtained only if a separate track and dot are drawn for each star or, alternatively, if each dot is replaced by a number of dots equal or proportional to the number of stars having the given mass. This can be found from an expression given by Salpeter*:

$$N(M)\,dM = \text{const} \times M^{-1.35}\,dM;$$

$N(M)\,dM$ is the number of stars with masses in the range M to $M + dM$. The lower main sequence thus has a relative density of points that is even

---

* E. E. Salpeter, 1955 (353).

---

track shows the position of the star of the corresponding mass at time $\sim 4 \times 10^9$ years. The interpolations in this figure are not necessarily accurate and are intended only to illustrate the principles involved.

The distribution of dots should be compared qualitatively with diagram F of Fig. 7-43.

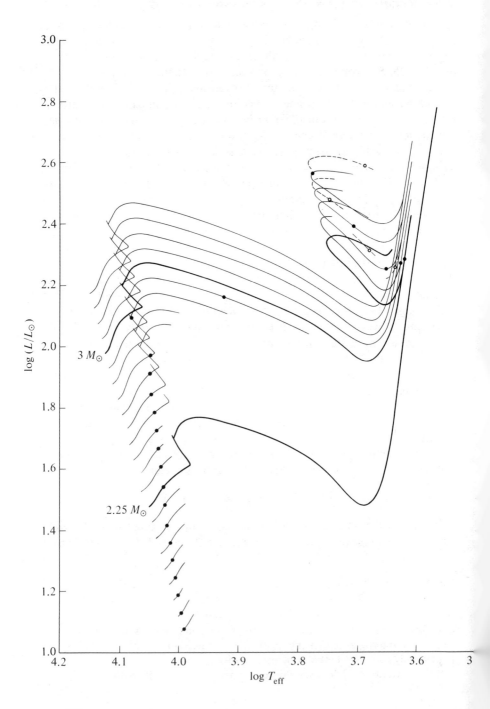

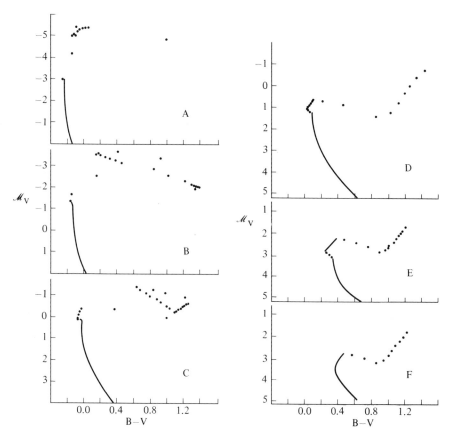

Fig. 7-43 Theoretically Predicted Color-Magnitude Diagrams for a Population I Cluster at Various Ages. The *solid lines* indicate a high density of points. The ages in units of 10^8 years are as follows: A 0.225; B 0.70; C 2.5; D 6; E 22.5; F 40. [After B. M. Schlesinger, 1969 (380).]

Fig. 7-42 The Theoretically Predicted Hertzsprung–Russell Diagram for a Population I Cluster at Age Approximately 2.5×10^8 Years. The composition is $X = 0.708$, $Y = 0.278$, $Z = 0.020$. The two *heavy lines* are the evolutionary tracks for stars of masses $2.25\ M_\odot$ and $3\ M_\odot$ in Fig. 7-25. The *thin lines* are tracks interpolated at equal increments in mass. The *black dot* on each track shows the position of the star of the corresponding mass at time $\sim 2.5 \times 10^8$ years. To make the locus of points more readily discernible, *white dots* have been placed on additional, dashed segments of evolutionary tracks. The interpolations in this figure are not necessarily accurate and are intended only to illustrate the principles involved.

This diagram should be compared qualitatively with diagram C of Fig. 7-43.

greater than indicated in Figs. 7-41 and 7-42, since the lower masses occur with the greatest frequency.

Figure 7-43 presents several theoretical distributions, which take into account the relative numbers of points at each mass. The number of points in certain regions of the diagrams is so large that a solid line, rather than individual points, had to be drawn. Diagrams C and F should be compared with Figs. 7-42 and 7-41, respectively. The same pair of ages and the same set of evolutionary tracks were assumed. In Fig. 7-43, however, the ordinate and abscissa are absolute visual magnitude and color index, rather than the logarithms of the luminosity and of effective temperature.

Some important results should be noted:

(a) The slower the evolution through a given phase, the greater the number of stars passing through that phase.

Fig. 7-44   The Hertzsprung-Russell Diagram of NGC 1866. The *dots* represent the non-variable stars in an annulus from 1.4 to 2.2 minutes of arc about the center of the cluster. The *crosses* represent Cepheid variables in this region. The three *encircled points* show the mean location of the lower main sequence, with *arrows* indicating the uncertainty; individual points on the lower main sequence are not shown. [After E. Meyer-Hofmeister, 1969 (354); original data from H. Arp and A. D. Thackeray, 1967 (381).]

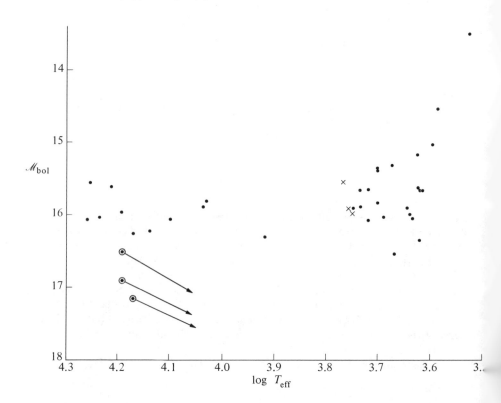

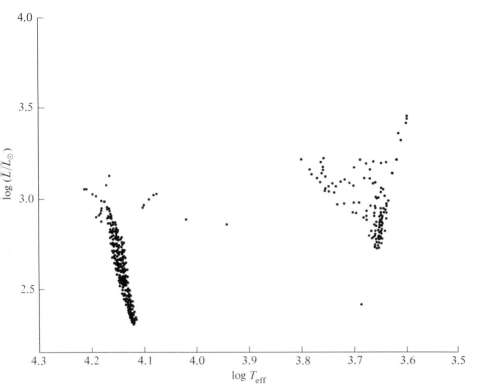

Fig. 7-45 The Theoretical Hertzsprung–Russell Diagram for an Extreme Population I Cluster at Age $(5.75 \pm 0.75) \times 10^7$ Years. The composition is $X = 0.602$, $Y = 0.354$, $Z = 0.044$. This diagram should be compared with Fig. 7-44. [After E. Meyer-Hofmeister, 1969 (354).]

(b) The turn-off from the main sequence occurs at lower mass with increasing age of the cluster.

(c) The brightest stars in a young cluster are blue; those in an old cluster are red.

(d) The distribution in young clusters shows large gaps, but in old clusters it is nearly continuous.

(e) The older the cluster, the less massive are the stars occupying the giant region; the more massive stars in the cluster have already proceeded to later stages of evolution.

(f) The older the cluster, the fainter are the brightest stars it contains.

(g) Except in the oldest cluster, the distribution shows a sudden turn to the left at the top of the main sequence. This is due to the similar deviation in the evolutionary tracks of stars of mass $1.25 \, M_\odot$ or greater, which are passing through the rapid contraction phase following the exhaustion of hydrogen in a convective core.

These theoretically deduced facts provide a basis for understanding and interpreting the features observed in actual clusters.

B. APPLICATION TO NGC 1866

We shall now consider one example of the comparison between theoretical and observed color-magnitude diagrams.* We choose NGC 1866 in the Large Magellanic Cloud, which is a relatively young cluster but which already contains a high proportion of red giants. The observations, transformed onto the plane of apparent bolometric magnitude as a function of $\log T_{\text{eff}}$, are shown in Fig. 7-44. The absolute magnitude was not used on account of the uncertainty in the distance to the cluster.

A theoretical diagram in good agreement with the observed points is shown in Fig. 7-45. An allowance has been made for an interval of star formation times, rather than assuming that all stars were formed at a single epoch. The age of the theoretical cluster is accordingly $(5.75 \pm 0.75) \times 10^7$ years. The chemical composition used to calculate the evolutionary tracks is $X = 0.602$, $Y = 0.345$, and $Z = 0.044$. The relevant masses range from 3.5 $M_\odot$ to 5.5 $M_\odot$, and Salpeter's mass distribution has been used to evaluate the relative numbers of points. As an additional result of the investigation, a matching of the two diagrams yields the distance modulus, which is 18.8 magnitudes.

C. CEPHEID VARIABLES

Observational tests of stellar models are also afforded by the Cepheid variables.† After a stellar model has been constructed, it is possible to test whether or not it is stable against pulsations; and, if it is unstable, the characteristics of the pulsation can be determined, within the limits of the pulsational theory assumed.

In most stars, any oscillations are rapidly damped out, and the star regains its stability. In some cases, however, a driving mechanism is present that is capable of sustaining the pulsations. The variability of the Cepheids is explained by a mechanism associated with the inner layers of the ionization zones of helium and hydrogen. During the phase of maximum compression during the pulsation, the increase in temperature causes an increase in the degree of ionization. The temperature in this region, however, does not rise by the amount that would be predicted from the degree of compression, since part of the energy released by the compression has been absorbed in the

---

* This study has been made by E. Meyer-Hofmeister, 1969 (354).
† These stars exhibit periodic light variations that are caused by pulsation. The period Π is related to the mean density $\bar{\rho}$ by the relation $\Pi^2\bar{\rho} = \text{const}$. There is also a relation between period and mean luminosity or absolute magnitude, such that Π increases nearly linearly with $\mathcal{M}$; however, the zero point is different for the two population types, and the Population I Cepheids are brighter by about one-and-a-half magnitudes. Actually, one must remember that the terms *Population I* and *Population II* are idealizations, and a gradation between the two populations exists.

ionization process. The flow of radiation to the exterior is also less than in the absence of ionization, because of the dependence of the net luminosity upon temperature. Thus a partial damming of the radiation takes place. The damming is enhanced by the increased opacity of the gas, and the excess pressure that is built up then pushes the layers outwards. At maximum expansion, the decrease in temperature causes recombination of the electrons and ions, the gas loses the energy of ionization, and the opacity decreases. The insufficiency of the gas pressure allows the material to fall back, whereupon the cycle is repeated. This mechanism depends upon *radiative* transfer of energy, but the convection in the rarefied atmospheres of these giant stars is inefficient, and radiation still carries the major part of the flux.*

There is, of course, an ionization zone in *all* stars; in order that pulsation may be maintained, it is necessary that the combination of temperatures and

* See J. P. Cox and R. T. Giuli, 1968 (52), Chapter 27, particularly pp. 1092–1095.

Fig. 7-46   The Theoretical Positions of Cepheid Variables in the Hertzsprung–Russell Diagram. The *black* and *white dots* mark the positions of maximum pulsational instability during each passage to or from the giant branch. The *dotted lines* indicate the approximate theoretical boundaries of the Cepheid instability strip for extreme Population I. The *arrowheads* and *numbers* on the track for the extreme Population I star of mass 9 $M_\odot$ show the direction and chronological order of each passage. [Adapted from E. Hofmeister, 1967 (346).]

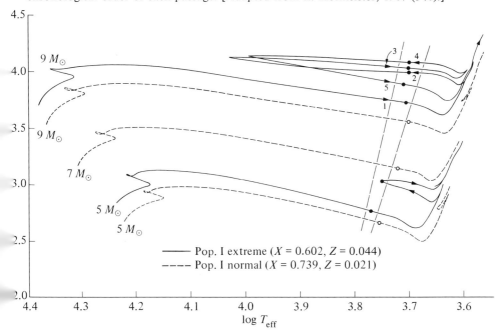

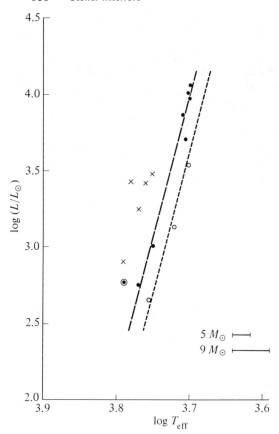

Fig. 7-47 Positions of Cepheid Variables in the Hertzsprung–Russell Diagram. The *dots* are identical with those of Fig. 7-46. The two *lines* represent means of the distributions for the extreme and normal Population I compositions. The *encircled dot* refers to a model with the extreme composition but a higher value of the mixing length. The *line segments* (*lower right*) indicate the approximate widths of the instability strip for masses 5 $M_\odot$ and 9 $M_\odot$. The *crosses* show the locations of observed galactic Cepheids from data of R. Kraft (K. Aa. Strand, ed.), 1963 (1), p. 438. [After E. Hofmeister, 1967 (382).]

densities within the effective ionization zone be favorable to the operation of the driving mechanism. After a stellar model has been computed, it can be determined whether the requirements for pulsation are fulfilled. There is actually a range of conditions that allows pulsation to occur, although in some cases the conditions may be optimum and in other cases just marginally effective. The stringency of the conditions accounts for the existence of the *Cepheid instability strip* (Fig. 7-46).

The pulsational characteristics of Population I models of masses 5 $M_\odot$,

7 $M_\odot$, and 9 $M_\odot$ have been compared with those of observed Cepheids.*
The dots on the evolutionary tracks in Fig. 7-46 mark the positions of optimum conditions for pulsation during each crossing of the instability strip.
Note that the tracks for stars of normal Population I composition do not pass
through the instability strip at all during the giant phase because of the short-
ness of the loops. There is a single crossing through the strip, which occurs
during the very rapid phase of gravitational contraction that brings the star
from the main sequence to the giant branch across the Hertzsprung gap. The
probability of *observing* a Cepheid variable at this phase of evolution is very
small. The properties of Cepheid variables can be explained only by evolutionary tracks having extended loops.

The points in Fig. 7-46 are shown again in Fig. 7-47, this time without the

* E. Hofmeister, 1967 (355). In addition to the comparisons cited here, this paper
also discusses period changes and the distribution of periods.

Fig. 7-48 The Period-Luminosity Relation for Cepheid Variables. The *dots*
and *squares* give the absolute visual magnitudes and periods of pulsation for the
models of maximum instability, for the extreme Population I composition
$X = 0.602$, $Y = 0.354$, $Z = 0.044$. (*Dots* refer to pulsation in the fundamental
mode, *squares* refer to pulsation in the first overtone.) The *crosses* and the *line*
show the observed period-luminosity relation according to R. Kraft, 1961 (394).
The ordinate for the observed points is the mean absolute visual magnitude.
[After E. Hofmeister, 1967 (382).]

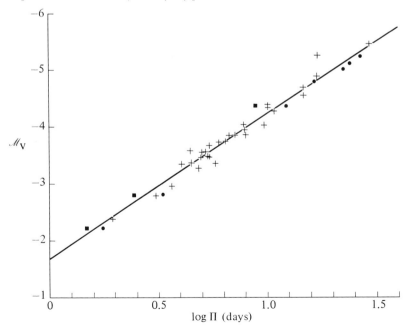

evolutionary tracks. The positions of some observed Cepheids are also shown. The models for the extreme Population I composition correspond better with the observations than do those for normal Population I. The calculation in which the higher value of mixing length is used shows the best agreement.

The period-luminosity relation can be predicted theoretically, with the results shown in Fig. 7-48. There is very good agreement between the observational points and the theoretical ones based on the extreme Population I composition. The mean line through the theoretical points for normal Population I (during the first crossing through the instability strip) would be lower by a few tenths of a magnitude.

The number of Cepheids relative to main-sequence stars in the solar neighborhood is known observationally and can be compared with the relative number determined from the lengths of time the models spend in these two phases. The best fit is obtained for the extreme Population I model with mass $9\ M_\odot$. Twice as many Cepheids are predicted as are observed, but this factor of two lies within the limits of the errors of the comparison.

5 EVOLUTION FOLLOWING THE RED-GIANT STAGE

5-1 GENERAL DISCUSSION

Relatively little is known about the events that take place within a star between the time that it leaves the region of the red giants in the Hertzsprung–Russell diagram and the time that it enters the domain of the small, subluminous stars below the main sequence. The observed objects that are believed to be presently in the post-giant phase of evolution include the central stars of planetary nebulae* and novae. Horizontal-branch stars are apparently in a phase of evolution that occurs between the red-giant stage already discussed and a subsequent return to the red-giant region.

White dwarf stars doubtless represent the final phase in the evolution of many stars. Figure 7-49 shows the positions of some of these classes of objects in a Hertzsprung–Russell diagram. Novae, in their quiet state, occupy a region in this diagram that lies generally between the nuclei of the planetary nebulae and the white dwarfs.† This fairly continuous distribution from the

---

* The central stars, often called *nuclei*, of planetary nebulae have ejected shells of gas (composed chiefly of hydrogen) that appear as greenish disks when viewed through a telescope. The nebulae derive their name from their resemblance to the planets Uranus and Neptune.

† We shall not discuss novae or supernovae. A review article is given by E. Schatzman (L. H. Aller and D. B. McLaughlin, eds.), 1965 (58), p. 327 et seq. A paper describing models that might lead to supernova explosions has been presented by G. Rakavy, G. Shaviv, and Z. Zinamon, 1967 (356). Also see D. D. Clayton, 1968 (51), pp. 544, 545; P. J. Brancazio and A. G. W. Cameron, eds., 1969 (73); and W. D. Arnett, 1971 (406).

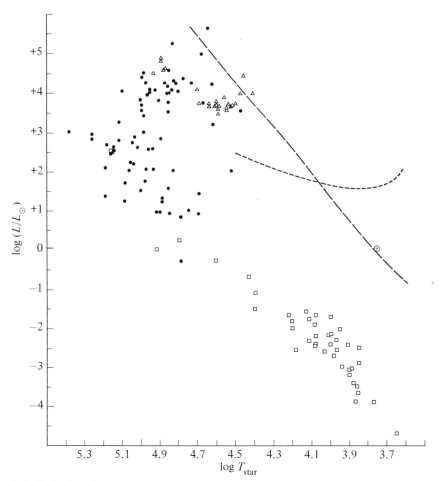

Fig. 7-49   The Hertzsprung–Russell Diagram of the Nuclei of Planetary Nebulae and White Dwarfs. Nuclei of planetary nebulae in the Magellanic Clouds are represented by *triangles*, other nuclei of planetary nebulae by *dots*. White dwarfs are represented by *squares*. The locations of the main sequence and, approximately, of the horizontal branch of a globular cluster are indicated by the *dashed* and *dotted curves*, respectively. The position of the Sun is represented by the *encircled point*. [Adapted from C. R. O'Dell (D. E. Osterbrock and C. R. O'Dell, eds.), 1968 (61), p. 369.]

red giants to the white dwarfs, however, is not necessarily an evolutionary sequence that is followed by all stars; for example, it is estimated that only 5 to 50 per cent of white dwarfs have evolved from the central stars of planetary nebulae.*

* V. Weidemann (D. E. Osterbrock and C. R. O'Dell, eds.), 1968 (61), p. 423; H. M. Van Horn, *op. cit.*, p. 426.

One of the difficulties that arises in attempting to trace the history past the red-giant phase is the uncertainty as to whether appreciable mass loss occurs. It is an observational fact that matter has been ejected from a nova or the nucleus of a planetary nebula; but there may be other phases when matter is lost by the star, either slowly or violently. Most giant M-type stars, in fact, are observed to be losing material continually at a slow rate, and the total amount lost over an extended time may be considerable. Large amounts of matter may be lost suddenly at stages when a star becomes unstable. One such possibility involves the transition to the white dwarf state, for the mass of such a star cannot exceed approximately 1.4 $M_\odot$ (see below); a star having a mass greater than this value may eject the excess. However, there is the alternative possibility that such a star will evolve not into a white dwarf but into a neutron star or a still denser collapsed star.*

Thermal instabilities are encountered in models that have passed through the red-giant branch and now possess a helium-burning shell. This complication has made it thus far impracticable to trace this evolution, as a tremendous number of models would be required. The short sequence of models for this phase that has been calculated produces a track that once more leads upwards along the red-giant branch. The details of the subsequent developments are still unknown.

The evolution of stars in close binary systems is further complicated by exchanges of matter between the components. When the more massive star reaches a critical size, it loses matter to its companion, which can eventually become the more massive of the two stars.†

5-2 STARS COMPOSED PRINCIPALLY OF HELIUM OR HELIUM-BURNING PRODUCTS

We have traced the evolution of the stars to a state in which they contain a core containing mainly helium, or a helium zone with an inner core of elements such as carbon and oxygen. The subsequent evolutionary phases are still not known in detail. Instabilities, possible mass loss, and the extent of mixing between inner and outer regions pose difficult questions, as we have seen. Some investigations have sought to bypass these complications by starting with a model that has already reached some specific phase of the later evolution, and we now describe some of these results.

If a composition of pure helium is assumed for simplicity, then stars of various masses lie on a main sequence lying to the left of the ordinary main sequence in the Hertzsprung–Russell diagram (Fig. 7-50). If a pure helium star originated from a giant phase of evolution, the hydrogen-rich envelope

---

* See J. P. Cox and R. T. Giuli, 1968 (52), p. 1007 et seq.

† For reports of some recent work, see M. Hack, ed., 1969 (62), Session IV.

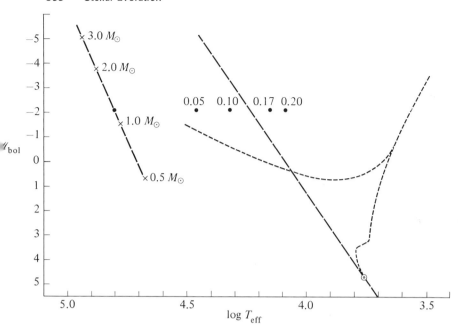

Fig. 7-50 The Positions of Helium Stars in the Hertzsprung–Russell Diagram. The pure helium stars form a main sequence that lies to the left of the ordinary main sequence; these sequences are shown by the two *dashed lines*. The *crosses* indicate various masses. The Sun is represented by the *encircled point*, and a schematic globular-cluster distribution by the *dotted curve*. The *dots* represent models with hydrogen envelopes, and the fractional mass $1 - M_r/M$ of the envelope is indicated by the number beside each dot; for these models, the mass is $1.2 \, M_\odot$. [Adapted from J. P. Cox and E. E. Salpeter, 1961 (357).]

then present must have been lost.* However, the retention of part of this envelope results in a structure that displaces the star considerably to the right in the Hertzsprung–Russell diagram (Fig. 7-50).† The evolution of models possessing substantial hydrogen envelopes will be considered in Section 5-3.

The evolutionary tracks of models that initially contain only helium and whose masses are $0.50 \, M_\odot$ and $0.70 \, M_\odot$ are shown in the Hertzsprung–Russell diagram of Fig. 7-51.‡ The tracks lead through the regions occupied by the nuclei of planetary nebulae and the white dwarfs (see below). Energy is supplied in these models by gravitational contraction and by helium- and carbon-burning.

---

* Such stars could also conceivably form from an interstellar cloud composed of helium (and heavier elements).
† J. P. Cox and E. E. Salpeter, 1961 (357).
‡ J. L'Ecuyer, 1966 (358).

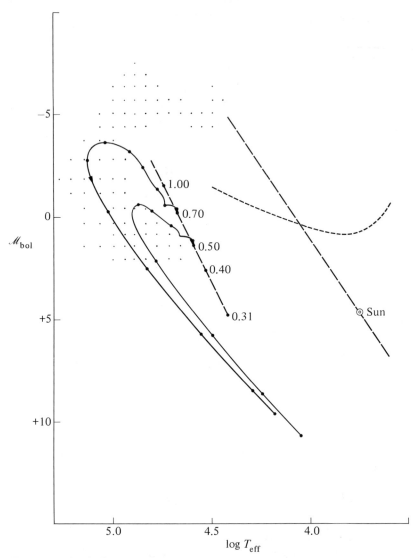

Fig. 7-51 Evolutionary Tracks in the Hertzsprung–Russell Diagram of Stars of Masses 0.5 $M_\odot$ and 0.7 $M_\odot$ Composed Initially of Pure Helium. The *dashed lines* represents the helium main sequence (at left) and the ordinary main sequence. The *dotted curve* indicates the approximate location of the horizontal branch of a globular cluster, and the *dotted region* shows schematically the positions of the nuclei of the planetary nebulae in Fig. 7-49. The Sun is represented by the *encircled point*. [Adapted from J. L'Ecuyer, 1966 (358).]

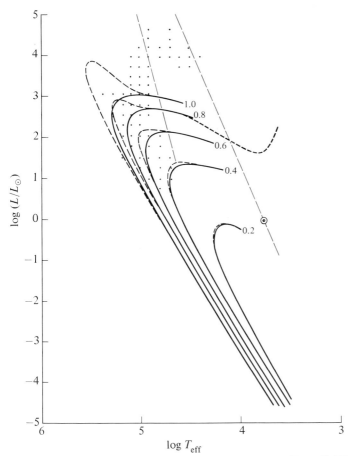

Fig. 7-52 Evolutionary Tracks in the Hertzsprung–Russell Diagram of Stars Composed of 80 Per Cent Oxygen and 20 Per Cent Carbon. The masses of the models, in units of the solar mass, are indicated by the numbers beside the tracks. The *dashed curves* represent sequences in which neutrino processes were included, and the *solid curves* indicate corresponding sequences with neutrino processes omitted. The *straight dashed lines* represent the helium main sequence (at left) and the ordinary main sequence. The *dotted curve* indicates the approximate location of the horizontal branch of a globular cluster, and the *dotted region* shows schematically the positions of the nuclei of the planetary nebulae in Fig. 7-49. The Sun is represented by the *encircled point*. [Adapted from S. C. Vila, 1967 (359).]

Models have also been constructed in which the composition is initially 80 per cent oxygen and 20 per cent carbon (by mass) in the core.* To simplify the computation near the surface, a thin envelope was attached, having $\log (M_r/M) = -10^{-4}$ and a composition of helium and heavy elements in the amounts $Y = 0.999$ and $Z = 0.001$. The energy is derived solely from gravitational contraction. Two sets of evolutionary tracks have been computed, depending upon whether neutrino processes do or do not occur (Fig. 7-52). These tracks also pass through the regions of the nuclei of planetary nebulae and the white dwarfs.

5-3 HORIZONTAL-BRANCH STARS†

It is not known whether a globular cluster star loses matter before reaching the horizontal branch. Some investigators have assumed that mass loss does

---

* S. C. Vila, 1967 (359).
† These are the stars occupying the region of the color-magnitude diagram that lies to the left of the red-giant branch. In Fig. 1-19, the horizontal branch lies at $V \sim 15$ or 16, and $-0.3 \gtrsim B - V \gtrsim +0.7$.

Fig. 7-53 Evolutionary Tracks in the Hertzsprung–Russell Diagram after the Helium-Flash Stage. The masses of the models and the initial composition are indicated in the figure. The *dashed lines* describe the rapid stages of evolution and the *solid lines* describe the slow stages. The solid lines pass through the region occupied by horizontal-branch stars. [P. Demarque and J. G. Mengel, 1971 (405).]

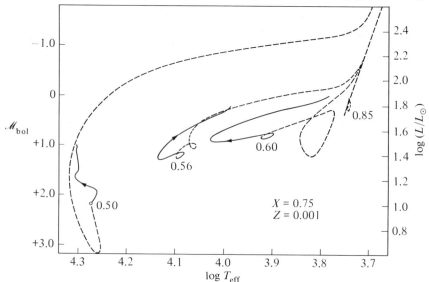

occur, while others have supposed that it does not. We shall describe a sequence of models for which the mass remains constant.*

The evolutionary tracks of several models representing horizontal-branch stars are shown in Fig. 7-53.† The history of these models has been traced in a continuous way from the main sequence without mass loss. The original composition is assumed to be characterized by $X = 0.75$ and $Z = 0.001$. By the time the present stage is reached, the helium-burning cores of these models have nearly equal masses of $0.465\ M_\odot$. Although the tracks cover a substantial area to the left of the red-giant branch, only a fairly narrow strip represents the main distribution of observable stars; other portions of the tracks are traversed so rapidly that they are only briefly occupied, and the stars are not likely to be detected in this phase. The tracks for the slower evolution fit the observed positions in the Hertzsprung–Russell diagram rather well.

5-4 NUCLEI OF PLANETARY NEBULAE

Most theories now assume that the nuclei of planetary nebulae originate directly from red giants, although this is not the only possibility.‡ The masses of these stars are uncertain, but typical values are probably in the range $0.5\ M_\odot$ to $1.2\ M_\odot$.§ Their cores probably contain elements such as C^{12} and O^{16}, which result from nuclear transformations; and they possibly have helium-rich envelopes, or hydrogen-rich envelopes of very small mass. Helium shell-burning may possibly be present. The models described in Section 5-2 account for some of the features exhibited by these stars, but problems still remain.‖

5-5 WHITE DWARF STARS

The gravitational contraction of a star during the phases of nuclear-fuel exhaustion leads ultimately to a state of very high compression. The white dwarf stars, which are in a final stage of evolution, therefore have extremely high densities, and the matter is highly degenerate except in the layers near the surface. Corresponding to the large values of the density, the values of the

---

* Models in which mass loss is assumed to have occurred have been calculated by V. Castellani, P. Giannone, and A. Renzini, 1969 (362). Observational aspects are discussed by E. B. Newell, 1970 (364).

† P. Demarque and J. G. Mengel, 1971 (405).

‡ See D. E. Osterbrock and C. R. O'Dell, eds., 1968 (61), particularly the papers and discussions relating to the Sixth Session; also G. S. Kutter, M. P. Savedoff, and D. W. Schuerman (M. Hack, ed.), 1969 (62), p. 311 et seq.

§ E. E. Salpeter (D. E. Osterbrock and C. R. O'Dell, eds.), 1968(61), p. 412.

‖ *Op. cit.*, various papers and discussions.

radius are very small. A typical white dwarf star has a mass of about 0.6 $M_\odot$ and a radius of about 0.01 $R_\odot$, which is the size of the Earth.

Since the matter is so highly degenerate, the equation of state is nearly independent of the temperature. The equations of hydrostatic equilibrium and of continuity of mass,

$$\frac{dP}{dr} = -G\frac{M_r}{r^2}\rho$$

and

$$\frac{dM_r}{dr} = 4\pi r^2 \rho,$$

together with the appropriate equation of state,* are sufficient to determine the structure in the case of complete degeneracy (since $T = \text{const} = 0$). The model will be little different if the actual temperature is taken into consideration, unless the mass is small (cf. Fig. 7-54). Apart from the chemical composition, then, the only parameter of the problem is the central density if it assumed that $T = 0$. An integration begun at the center then yields the total mass and the radius of the model, which are the values of M_r and r at the place where the pressure and density vanish.

Table 7-10 illustrates two important results: there is a one-to-one correspondence between mass and radius, and there exists a limiting mass.† The

* The equation of state is derived by S. Chandrasekhar, 1939 (53). It is expressed by the parametric equations (19) and (20) on p. 360 of this reference.
† For a physical explanation of these phenomena, see M. Schwarzschild, 1958 (50), pp. 233–235.

Table 7-10   The Physical Characteristics of Completely Degenerate Configurations. [Adapted for $\mu_e = 2$ from S. Chandrasekhar, 1939 (53), p. 427.]

M (units of $M_\odot$)	CENTRAL DENSITY ρ_c (gm cm^{-3})	MEAN DENSITY $\bar{\rho}$ (gm cm^{-3})	RADIUS $R \times 10^{-8}$ (cm)
1.44	∞	∞	0
1.38	1.93×10^9	3.70×10^7	2.06
1.33	6.74×10^8	1.57×10^7	2.72
1.22	1.63×10^8	5.08×10^6	3.84
1.08	5.30×10^7	2.10×10^6	4.96
0.88	1.57×10^7	7.9×10^5	6.4
0.74	7.00×10^6	4.04×10^5	7.6
0.61	3.60×10^6	2.29×10^5	8.6
0.50	1.96×10^6	1.34×10^5	9.6
0.40	1.07×10^6	7.7×10^4	10.8
0.22	2.46×10^5	1.92×10^4	14.0
0	0	0	∞

numerical values listed actually depend upon the mean molecular weight per electron, and hence upon the chemical composition. However, hydrogen cannot be expected to occur, except in the outermost layers. The validity of this assertion is not only suggested by the presumed history of these stars, but it is also demanded by considerations of their present state: even one per cent of hydrogen would cause an energy output by the proton-proton chain that would greatly exceed the low luminosities of these stars.* Furthermore, the densities are so high that pycnonuclear reactions would convert H^1 into He^4.† For helium or heavier elements, then, $\mu_e = 2$ irrespective of the precise composition of the material. More refined calculations that take account of electrostatic interactions between nuclei and electrons and of inverse β-decay

* See M. Schwarzschild, 1958 (50), pp. 239–240.
† L. Mestel (L. H. Aller and D. B. McLaughlin, eds.), 1965 (58), p. 304.

Fig. 7-54   The Mass-Radius Relation for White Dwarf Stars. The *black* and *white dots* represent observed points (respectively, the supposed upper and lower sequences in the observed distribution in the Hertzsprung-Russell diagram). *Parentheses* indicate uncertainty in the values, while *triangles* denote uncertainty in the spectral classification. The *solid curves* give the theoretical mass-radius relation of zero-temperature models as calculated by S. Chandrasekhar, 1939 (53), p. 427 for H and by T. Hamada and E. Salpeter, 1961 (385) for He, Mg, and Fe. The *dashed curve* is the mass-radius relation for stars with a neutron core, as calculated by Hamada and Salpeter. The two pairs of *crosses* refer to models of finite temperature as calculated by W. B. Hubbard and R. L. Wagner, 1970 (386). The upper cross at each mass refers to a helium model, and the lower cross refers to a magnesium model. [Adapted from Y. Terashita and S. Matsushima, 1969 (387).]

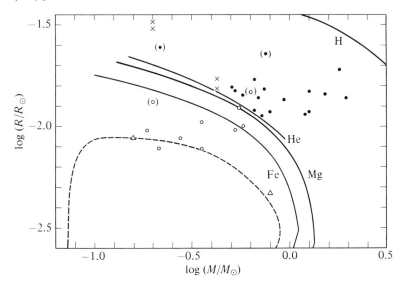

do, however, show a dependence on the identity of the elements present. Figure 7-54 shows the resulting mass-radius relations for several compositions.

Figure 7-54 also points out the present disagreement between theory and observations. Many of the observational points in this diagram indicate that large amounts of hydrogen must be present; yet we have already seen that this is not possible. On the other hand, these theoretical points did not allow for the possibility of internal magnetic fields, which can substantially increase the computed radii.*

Table 7-11 presents a theoretical model for a white dwarf star assumed to be composed of pure iron.† The densities are extremely high throughout the

---

* J. P. Ostriker and F. D. A. Hartw ck, 1968 (365).

† The mass and radius do not quite correspond to any point of the locus in Fig. 7-54, since somewhat different assumptions were made in the construction of this model. The choice of pure iron for the composition was made because this is the heaviest element that can be built from exothermic reactions; the actual composition may well be dominated by considerably lighter elements.

Table 7-11   A White-Dwarf Model of One Solar Mass with a Composition of Pure Iron.* [Calculated by S. C. Vila, unpubl. dissertation, Univ. of Rochester, 1965. This is Model 8 of M. P. Savedoff, H. M. Van Horn, and S. C. Vila, 1969 (389).]

$$M = M_\odot, \quad R = 6.099 \times 10^{-3} R_\odot, \quad L = 5.6707 \times 10^{-4} L_\odot.$$

$.r/R$	M_r/M	$\log P$	$\log T$	$\log \rho$	α	L_r/L	κ
0.000	0.000	25.217	7.071	7.948	0.00	0.000	0.40 (−6)
0.020,	0.000	25.217	7.071	7.947	0.00	0.000	0.40 (−6)
0.040	0.001	25.211	7.071	7.943	0.00	0.001	0.41 (−6)
0.060	0.003	25.201	7.071	7.935	0.00	0.003	0.42 (−6)
0.080	0.007	25.187	7.071	7.925	0.00	0.006	0.44 (−6)
0.100	0.013	25.169	7.070	7.912	0.00	0.012	0.46 (−6)
0.120	0.022	25.147	7.070	7.896	0.00	0.020	0.49 (−6)
0.140	0.034	25.122	7.070	7.877	0.00	0.032	0.52 (−6)
0.160	0.049	25.092	7.070	7.856	0.00	0.046	0.57 (−6)
0.180	0.068	25.060	7.070	7.832	0.00	0.063	0.62 (−6)
0.200	0.089	25.024	7.070	7.806	0.00	0.084	0.68 (−6)
0.220	0.114	24.985	7.070	7.777	0.00	0.107	0.76 (−6)
0.240	0.142	24.942	7.070	7.746	0.00	0.134	0.86 (−6)
0.260	0.173	24.898	7.070	7.713	0.00	0.163	0.97 (−6)
0.280	0.207	24.850	7.070	7.678	0.00	0.194	0.11 (−5)
0.300	0.241	24.799	7.070	7.640	0.00	0.228	0.13 (−5)
0.320	0.278	24.746	7.070	7.601	0.00	0.262	0.15 (−5)
0.340	0.316	24.690	7.070	7.561	0.00	0.299	0.17 (−5)
0.360	0.355	24.633	7.070	7.518	0.00	0.336	0.20 (−5)
0.380	0.395	24.573	7.070	7.477	0.00	0.374	0.24 (−5)
0.400	0.435	24.510	7.069	7.435	0.00	0.412	0.28 (−5)
0.420	0.476	24.446	7.069	7.391	0.00	0.450	0.34 (−5)
0.440	0.515	24.379	7.069	7.346	0.00	0.488	0.40 (−5)

Table 7-11 (*continued*)

r/R	M_r/M	$\log P$	$\log T$	$\log \rho$	α	L_r/L	κ
0.460	0.554	24.310	7.069	7.299	0.00	0.526	0.49 (-5)
0.480	0.593	24.237	7.069	7.250	0.00	0.563	0.60 (-5)
0.500	0.629	24.163	7.069	7.200	0.00	0.599	0.73 (-5)
0.520	0.666	24.086	7.068	7.148	0.01	0.635	0.91 (-5)
0.540	0.700	24.006	7.068	7.094	0.01	0.668	0.11 (-4)
0.560	0.732	23.923	7.068	7.038	0.01	0.700	0.14 (-4)
0.580	0.762	23.837	7.068	6.980	0.01	0.731	0.18 (-4)
0.600	0.791	23.749	7.068	6.920	0.01	0.760	0.23 (-4)
0.620	0.818	23.657	7.067	6.858	0.01	0.787	0.29 (-4)
0.640	0.842	23.562	7.067	6.794	0.01	0.812	0.38 (-4)
0.660	0.865	23.463	7.067	6.727	0.01	0.835	0.50 (-4)
0.680	0.885	23.360	7.066	6.657	0.01	0.856	0.67 (-4)
0.700	0.903	23.253	7.066	6.585	0.01	0.875	0.89 (-4)
0.720	0.920	23.141	7.066	6.509	0.01	0.893	0.12 (-3)
0.740	0.934	23.024	7.065	6.430	0.01	0.909	0.17 (-3)
0.760	0.947	22.900	7.065	6.347	0.01	0.924	0.24 (-3)
0.780	0.958	22.770	7.064	6.258	0.01	0.937	0.34 (-3)
0.800	0.967	22.631	7.063	6.165	0.02	0.948	0.49 (-3)
0.820	0.975	22.483	7.063	6.065	0.02	0.958	0.74 (-3)
0.840	0.981	22.323	7.062	5.963	0.02	0.967	0.11 (-2)
0.860	0.987	22.146	7.061	5.854	0.02	0.975	0.19 (-2)
0.880	0.991	21.943	7.059	5.730	0.03	0.982	0.32 (-2)
0.900	0.995	21.707	7.057	5.586	0.03	0.987	0.62 (-2)
0.920	0.997	21.422	7.055	5.412	0.04	0.992	0.13 (-1)
0.940	0.999	21.056	7.051	5.188	0.06	0.995	0.36 (-1)
0.960	1.000	20.536	7.045	4.872	0.09	0.998	0.15 (0)
0.980	1.000	19.586	7.026	4.290	0.21	1.000	0.19 ($+1$)
0.982	1.000	19.431	7.022	4.194	0.24	1.000	0.28 ($+1$)
0.984	1.000	19.252	7.017	4.080	0.27	1.000	0.45 ($+1$)
0.986	1.000	19.043	7.011	3.945	0.32	1.000	0.77 ($+1$)
0.988	1.000	18.792	7.001	3.782	0.38	1.000	0.15 ($+2$)
0.990	1.000	18.479	6.988	3.580	0.48	1.000	0.33 ($+2$)
0.992	1.000	18.071	6.965	3.286	0.60	1.000	0.90 ($+2$)
0.994	1.000	17.529	6.923	2.891	0.77	1.000	0.31 ($+3$)
0.996	1.000	16.759	6.828	2.275	0.88	1.000	0.13 ($+4$)
0.998	1.000	15.516	6.585	1.327	0.99	1.000	0.34 ($+4$)

* The quantity α is the ratio of the electron pressure as calculated from the perfect gas law to the actual electron pressure with degeneracy included ($\alpha = 1$ in non-degenerate matter, $\alpha \approx 0$ in highly degenerate matter).
  The opacity coefficient κ includes electron conduction. The number in parentheses is the power of 10 by which the entry must be multiplied.

interior; even at a fractional radius of 0.998, the value is approximately equal to the mean density of the Sun and is greater than that of water. The quantity α equals $(k\rho T/\mu_e H) \div P_e$, which is the ratio of the electron pressure computed from the perfect gas law to the actual electron pressure under conditions of degeneracy. Only in the uppermost region of the model, where

α approaches unity, does ordinary matter exist. We note further that the temperature remains nearly constant throughout the interior. This is due to the very low opacity of the degenerate matter, which therefore cannot maintain a large temperature gradient; a degenerate electron gas is highly conducting, and therefore energy is efficiently transferred outwards.

None of the luminosity is derived from nuclear sources and little from gravitational contraction. Nuclear fuels would most probably have been consumed in the interior during the preceding evolution, and any such fuel remaining in the higher regions would lead to an unstable structure.* Thus, the gradual cooling of the star is its last energy resource. It is principally the nuclei that provide the outflowing energy, for the electrons, being in a highly degenerate condition throughout most of the star, have already filled most of the available low-energy states and little further escape of energy from them is possible. The star continues to cool without appreciable reduction of radius, approaching a non-luminous, black dwarf state. The descent toward the lower right of the Hertzsprung–Russell diagram may be temporarily slowed by a transition from a gaseous state into a crystalline solid with the release of the latent heat of crystallization. This slowing of the evolution (if it exists) leads to an accumulation of white dwarfs along crystallizing sequences, analogous to the main sequence of non-degenerate stars.† The position of a crystallizing sequence depends upon the chemical composition.

---

* For further details, see M. Schwarzschild, 1958 (50), pp. 243–245; or L. Mestel (L. H. Aller and D. B. McLaughlin, eds.), 1965 (58), pp. 315–318.

† Whether or not such sequences have been observed is still a matter of controversy. According to E. M. Jones, 1970 (366), there is unpublished work by O. J. Eggen confirming the existence of two sequences. The theory is discussed by H. M. Van Horn, 1968 (395).

Table 7-12   Model Interior for 1 $M_\odot$ Prior to the Main-Sequence Phase, Preceding Point 1 in Fig. 7-3A.* [Calculated by I. Iben, Jr.; see ref. (321).]

1 $M_\odot$, $t = 1.35024 \times 10^{11}$ seconds $= 4.27 \times 10^3$ years.

$L = 14.512\,L_\odot$, $R = 8.095\,R_\odot$, $T_{\text{eff}} = 3967°$K.

$M_r/M_\odot$	$r/R_\odot$	$P \times 10^{-17}$	$T \times 10^{-6}$	$L_r/L_\odot$	ρ	X	He^4
0.0000	0.000	2.450 (-5)	*0.9903*	0.000 (0)	1.836 (-2)	0.708	0.272
0.0010	0.428	2.409 (-5)	*0.9836*	2.795 (-2)	1.818 (-2)	0.708	0.272
0.0027	0.593	2.371 (-5)	*0.9774*	7.323 (-2)	1.802 (-2)	0.708	0.272
0.0071	0.821	2.301 (-5)	*0.9657*	1.912 (-1)	1.772 (-2)	0.708	0.272
0.0185	1.141	2.169 (-5)	*0.9433*	4.955 (-1)	1.714 (-2)	0.708	0.272
0.0477	1.585	1.936 (-5)	*0.9014*	1.242 (0)	1.607 (-2)	0.708	0.272
0.0898	1.989	1.689 (-5)	*0.8537*	2.268 (0)	1.482 (-2)	0.708	0.272
0.1595	2.466	1.379 (-5)	*0.7874*	3.857 (0)	1.318 (-2)	0.708	0.272
0.2491	2.942	1.076 (-5)	*0.7130*	5.725 (0)	1.138 (-2)	0.708	0.272
0.3543	3.419	7.985 (-6)	*0.6331*	7.690 (0)	9.550 (-3)	0.708	0.272
0.4689	3.895	5.622 (-6)	*0.5503*	9.567 (0)	7.762 (-3)	0.708	0.272
0.5855	4.370	3.726 (-6)	*0.4670*	1.120 (1)	6.145 (-3)	0.708	0.272
0.6958	4.840	2.308 (-6)	*0.3859*	1.248 (1)	4.625 (-3)	0.708	0.272
0.7832	5.255	1.410 (-6)	*0.3172*	1.331 (1)	3.440 (-3)	0.708	0.272
0.8482	5.612	8.616 (-7)	*0.2609*	1.381 (1)	2.557 (-3)	0.708	0.272
0.8954	5.923	5.263 (-7)	*0.2149*	1.411 (1)	1.900 (-3)	0.708	0.272
0.9290	6.192	3.215 (-7)	*0.1774*	1.428 (1)	1.410 (-3)	0.708	0.272
0.9524	6.426	1.964 (-7)	*0.1473*	1.438 (1)	1.042 (-3)	0.708	0.272
0.9684	6.629	1.200 (-7)	*0.1235*	1.444 (1)	7.662 (-4)	0.708	0.272
0.9793	6.806	7.329 (-8)	*0.1045*	1.447 (1)	5.587 (-4)	0.708	0.272
0.9865	6.961	4.476 (-8)	*0.0889*	1.449 (1)	4.054 (-4)	0.708	0.272
0.9913	7.096	2.735 (-8)	*0.0753*	1.450 (1)	2.949 (-4)	0.708	0.272
0.9944	7.212	1.672 (-8)	*0.0633*	1.451 (1)	2.161 (-4)	0.708	0.272
0.9965	7.312	1.022 (-8)	*0.0533*	1.451 (1)	1.585 (-4)	0.708	0.272
0.9978	7.397	6.247 (-9)	*0.0454*	1.451 (1)	1.154 (-4)	0.708	0.272
0.9986	7.471	3.816 (-9)	*0.0395*	1.451 (1)	8.278 (-5)	0.708	0.272
0.9991	7.535	2.330 (-9)	*0.0349*	1.451 (1)	5.861 (-5)	0.708	0.272
0.9994	7.592	1.423 (-9)	*0.0312*	1.451 (1)	4.108 (-5)	0.708	0.272
0.9997	7.643	8.682 (-10)	*0.0281*	1.451 (1)	2.859 (-5)	0.708	0.272
0.9998	7.688	5.298 (-10)	*0.0255*	1.451 (1)	1.977 (-5)	0.708	0.272
0.9999	7.728	3.233 (-10)	*0.0233*	1.451 (1)	1.358 (-5)	0.708	0.272

At the center, $\epsilon_{\text{nucl}}/\epsilon_{\text{grav}} = 3.666 \times 10^{-13}$.

$$\int_0^M (L_r)_{\text{grav}}\, dM_r = 14.51\,L_\odot.$$

* The pressure P is expressed in dyne cm^{-2}, the temperature T in °K, and the density ρ in gm cm^{-3}. The adopted solar values are $M_\odot = 1.991 \times 10^{33}$ gm, $R_\odot = 6.960 \times 10^{10}$ cm, and $L_\odot = 3.86 \times 10^{33}$ erg sec^{-1}. The mass fractions of hydrogen and helium-4 are listed as X and He^4, respectively. Italics in the column for T indicate the presence of convection. A number in parentheses is the power of 10 by which the entry must be multiplied. The homogeneous composition of the initial models for these evolutionary sequences has $X = 0.708$ and $Z = 0.020$. Line absorption is not included in the opacity, and the ratio of mixing length to density scale-height is taken as 0.5; see ref. (321) for a more detailed description of the equations used, and, for Tables 7-15 to 7-36, see also the references cited there. Note that the conversion factor for time adopted by Iben is 1 year $= 3.16 \times 10^7$ seconds exactly.

Table 7-13   Model Interior for 1 $M_\odot$ Prior to the Main-Sequence Phase, at Point 3 in Fig. 7-3A. [Calculated by I. Iben, Jr.; see ref. (321) and note to Table 7-12.]

$1\ M_\odot$, $t = 2.81542 \times 10^{14}$ seconds $= 8.91 \times 10^6$ years,

$L = 0.4845\ L_\odot$, $R = 1.2606\ R_\odot$, $T_{\text{eff}} = 4297°\text{K}$.

$M_r/M_\odot$	$r/R_\odot$	$P \times 10^{-17}$	$T \times 10^{-6}$	$L_r/L_\odot$	ρ
0.0000	0.000	7.459 (-2)	6.050	0.000 (0)	9.102
0.0011	0.056	7.286 (-2)	6.017	1.538 (-3)	8.942
0.0015	0.062	7.247 (-2)	6.010	2.075 (-3)	8.909
0.0020	0.068	7.202 (-2)	6.001	2.782 (-3)	8.865
0.0028	0.076	7.138 (-2)	5.988	3.891 (-3)	8.806
0.0039	0.086	7.059 (-2)	5.973	5.425 (-3)	8.737
0.0053	0.095	6.974 (-2)	5.956	7.267 (-3)	8.653
0.0074	0.106	6.856 (-2)	5.932	1.015 (-2)	8.543
0.0115	0.123	6.660 (-2)	5.893	1.560 (-2)	8.370
0.0185	0.146	6.374 (-2)	5.833	2.496 (-2)	8.101
0.0302	0.173	5.987 (-2)	5.748	4.014 (-2)	7.737
0.0477	0.204	5.510 (-2)	5.639	6.244 (-2)	7.268
0.0694	0.234	5.019 (-2)	5.518	8.942 (-2)	6.763
0.1020	0.272	4.416 (-2)	5.356	1.282 (-1)	6.149
0.1364	0.305	3.887 (-2)	5.200	1.675 (-1)	5.582
0.2204	0.374	2.889 (-2)	4.853	2.558 (-1)	4.514
0.2951	0.429	2.227 (-2)	4.564	3.253 (-1)	3.688
0.3994	0.501	1.530 (-2)	4.169	4.081 (-1)	2.806
0.5156	0.582	9.724 (-3)	3.721	4.790 (-1)	2.008
0.5970	0.642	6.821 (-3)	3.383	5.120 (-1)	1.523
0.6537	0.687	5.187 (-3)	3.123	5.235 (-1)	1.256
0.7055	0.730	3.928 (-3)	2.847	5.211 (-1)	1.041
0.7511	0.771	2.985 (-3)	2.555	5.125 (-1)	0.881
0.7905	0.808	2.282 (-3)	2.295	5.057 (-1)	0.749
0.8246	0.842	1.748 (-3)	2.063	5.005 (-1)	0.639
0.8536	0.874	1.345 (-3)	1.858	4.966 (-1)	0.545
0.8784	0.904	1.036 (-3)	1.674	4.936 (-1)	0.466
0.8993	0.931	8.004 (-4)	1.510	4.913 (-1)	0.399
0.9170	0.957	6.186 (-4)	1.362	4.896 (-1)	0.342
0.9317	0.980	4.797 (-4)	1.230	4.883 (-1)	0.294
0.9440	1.002	3.719 (-4)	1.111	4.873 (-1)	0.252
0.9542	1.023	2.892 (-4)	1.005	4.865 (-1)	0.217
0.9684	1.056	1.840 (-4)	0.839	4.857 (-1)	0.168
0.9793	1.087	1.118 (-4)	0.661	4.851 (-1)	0.124
0.9865	1.114	6.816 (-5)	0.564	4.848 (-1)	0.092
0.9913	1.136	4.167 (-5)	0.464	4.847 (-1)	0.071
0.9944	1.155	2.552 (-5)	0.383	4.846 (-1)	0.053
0.9965	1.171	1.564 (-5)	0.317	4.845 (-1)	0.040
0.9978	1.184	9.587 (-6)	0.263	4.845 (-1)	0.029
0.9986	1.195	5.879 (-6)	0.219	4.845 (-1)	0.022
0.9991	1.204	3.606 (-6)	0.183	4.845 (-1)	0.016
0.9994	1.212	2.212 (-6)	0.154	4.845 (-1)	0.012
0.9997	1.219	1.357 (-6)	0.130	4.845 (-1)	0.009
0.9998	1.224	8.331 (-7)	0.110	4.845 (-1)	0.006
0.9999	1.229	5.113 (-7)	0.093	4.845 (-1)	0.005

At the center, $\epsilon_{\text{nucl}}/\epsilon_{\text{grav}} = 5.184 \times 10^{-3}$.

$$\int_0^M (L_r)_{\text{grav}}\, dM_r = 0.4838\ L_\odot.$$

Table 7-14 Model Interior for 1 $M_\odot$ Near Initial Main Sequence, Just Preceding Points 7 in Fig. 7-3A and 1 in Fig. 7-25. [Calculated by I. Iben, Jr.; see ref. (321) and note to Table 7-12.]

$$1 \ M_\odot, \quad t = 1.58093 \times 10^{15} \text{ seconds} = 5.00 \times 10^7 \text{ years,}$$

$$L = 0.7268 \ L_\odot, \quad R = 0.8653 \ R_\odot, \quad T_{\text{eff}} = 5740°\text{K.}$$

$M_r/M_\odot$	$r/R_\odot$	$P \times 10^{-17}$	$T \times 10^{-6}$	$L_r/L_\odot$	ρ	X	He^4
0.0000	0.0000	1.617 (0)	*1.390 (1)*	0.0000	8.515 (1)	0.706	0.273
0.0017	0.0302	1.573 (0)	*1.375 (1)*	0.0178	8.377 (1)	0.706	0.273
0.0033	0.0379	1.548 (0)	*1.366 (1)*	0.0324	8.299 (1)	0.706	0.273
0.0064	0.0478	1.508 (0)	*1.352 (1)*	0.0586	8.177 (1)	0.706	0.273
0.0126	0.0601	1.449 (0)	*1.330 (1)*	0.1011	7.986 (1)	0.706	0.273
0.0165	0.0659	1.416 (0)	1.319 (1)	0.1243	7.867 (1)	0.706	0.273
0.0215	0.0722	1.379 (0)	1.305 (1)	0.1545	7.745 (1)	0.706	0.273
0.0382	0.0884	1.274 (0)	1.267 (1)	0.2428	7.394 (1)	0.706	0.273
0.0714	0.1107	1.113 (0)	1.207 (1)	0.3774	6.808 (1)	0.707	0.273
0.1141	0.1319	9.510 (−1)	1.144 (1)	0.4994	6.108 (1)	0.707	0.272
0.2204	0.1720	6.587 (−1)	1.016 (1)	0.6532	4.855 (1)	0.708	0.272
0.3543	0.2139	4.102 (−1)	8.855 (0)	0.7037	3.501 (1)	0.708	0.272
0.5039	0.2598	2.250 (−1)	7.572 (0)	0.7212	2.228 (1)	0.708	0.272
0.5855	0.2869	1.532 (−1)	6.893 (0)	0.7247	1.673 (1)	0.708	0.272
0.6645	0.3162	9.922 (−2)	6.225 (0)	0.7262	1.205 (1)	0.708	0.272
0.7337	0.3463	6.284 (−2)	5.610 (0)	0.7268	8.486 (0)	0.708	0.272
0.7905	0.3758	3.979 (−2)	5.071 (0)	0.7270	5.949 (0)	0.708	0.272
0.8368	0.4051	2.514 (−2)	4.589 (0)	0.7271	4.161 (0)	0.708	0.272
0.8737	0.4341	1.593 (−2)	4.154 (0)	0.7271	2.912 (0)	0.708	0.272
0.9031	0.4630	1.010 (−2)	3.759 (0)	0.7270	2.042 (0)	0.708	0.272
0.9261	0.4913	6.434 (−3)	3.402 (0)	0.7270	1.437 (0)	0.708	0.272
0.9440	0.5193	4.108 (−3)	3.078 (0)	0.7270	1.015 (0)	0.708	0.272
0.9578	0.5466	2.642 (−3)	2.786 (0)	0.7270	7.205 (−1)	0.708	0.272
0.9684	0.5733	1.704 (−3)	2.520 (0)	0.7269	5.141 (−1)	0.708	0.272
0.9765	0.5990	1.108 (−3)	2.282 (0)	0.7269	3.688 (−1)	0.708	0.272
0.9826	0.6240	7.237 (−4)	2.066 (0)	0.7269	2.661 (−1)	0.708	0.272
0.9871	0.6477	4.768 (−4)	1.874 (0)	0.7269	1.932 (−1)	0.708	0.272
0.9905	0.6705	3.157 (−4)	1.696 (0)	0.7269	1.413 (−1)	0.708	0.272
0.9930	0.6920	2.112 (−4)	1.529 (0)	0.7269	1.046 (−1)	0.708	0.272
0.9949	0.7120	1.420 (−4)	1.362 (0)	0.7269	7.895 (−2)	0.708	0.272
0.9963	0.7301	9.654 (−5)	*1.178 (0)*	0.7269	6.185 (−2)	0.708	0.272
0.9973	0.7462	6.590 (−5)	*1.011 (0)*	0.7269	4.921 (−1)	0.708	0.272
0.9981	0.7603	4.536 (−5)	*8.711 (−1)*	0.7269	3.928 (−2)	0.708	0.272
0.9986	0.7727	3.130 (−5)	*7.510 (−1)*	0.7269	3.146 (−2)	0.708	0.272
0.9990	0.7836	2.173 (−5)	*6.492 (−1)*	0.7269	2.525 (−2)	0.708	0.272
0.9993	0.7932	1.511 (−5)	*5.614 (−1)*	0.7269	2.031 (−2)	0.708	0.272
0.9995	0.8016	1.057 (−5)	*4.867 (−1)*	0.7269	1.660 (−2)	0.708	0.272
0.9996	0.8090	7.388 (−6)	4.221 (−1)	0.7269	1.340 (−2)	0.708	0.272
0.9997	0.8153	5.189 (−6)	*3.669 (−1)*	0.7269	1.083 (−3)	0.708	0.272
0.9998	0.8210	3.642 (−6)	*3.190 (−1)*	0.7269	8.758 (−4)	0.708	0.272
0.9999	0.8265	2.444 (−6)	*2.727 (−1)*	0.7269	6.989 (−4)	0.708	0.272

At the center, $\epsilon_{\text{nucl}}/\epsilon_{\text{grav}} = 1.115 \times 10^2$.

$$\int_0^M (L_r)_{\text{grav}} \, dM_r = 1.004 \times 10^{-2} \ L_\odot.$$

Table 7-15 Model Interior for 1 $M_\odot$ during Main-Sequence Phase, Near Point 2 in Fig. 7-25. [Calculated by I. Iben, Jr.; see ref. (326) and note to Table 7-12.]

$$1\ M_\odot, \quad t = 2.13902 \times 10^{17} \text{ seconds} = 6.77 \times 10^9 \text{ years},$$

$$L = 1.3727\ L_\odot, \quad R = 1.0763\ R_\odot, \quad T_{\text{eff}} = 6034°K.$$

$M_r/M_\odot$	$r/R_\odot$	$P \times 10^{-17}$	$T \times 10^{-6}$	$L_r/L_\odot$	ρ	X	He^4
0.0000	0.0000	3.799 (0)	1.845 (1)	0.000	3.001 (2)	0.0457	0.930
0.0005	0.0130	3.697 (0)	1.831 (1)	0.006	2.906 (2)	0.0586	0.917
0.0007	0.0148	3.668 (0)	1.827 (1)	0.009	2.867 (2)	0.0640	0.911
0.0011	0.0175	3.618 (0)	1.820 (1)	0.015	2.807 (2)	0.0726	0.903
0.0018	0.0208	3.551 (0)	1.810 (1)	0.025	2.725 (2)	0.0842	0.891
0.0030	0.0247	3.461 (0)	1.797 (1)	0.041	2.621 (2)	0.100	0.875
0.0048	0.0293	3.344 (0)	1.778 (1)	0.067	2.486 (2)	0.122	0.854
0.0078	0.0351	3.189 (0)	1.751 (1)	0.107	2.320 (2)	0.151	0.824
0.0126	0.0419	2.993 (0)	1.716 (1)	0.165	2.123 (2)	0.188	0.788
0.0215	0.0516	2.715 (0)	1.665 (1)	0.258	1.872 (2)	0.240	0.736
0.0344	0.0625	2.415 (0)	1.606 (1)	0.375	1.619 (2)	0.298	0.679
0.0477	0.0717	2.174 (0)	1.555 (1)	0.483	1.428 (2)	0.346	0.630
0.0661	0.0828	1.912 (0)	1.495 (1)	0.614	1.238 (2)	0.402	0.575
0.0873	0.0941	1.674 (0)	1.436 (1)	0.741	1.073 (2)	0.452	0.525
0.1179	0.1085	1.407 (0)	1.362 (1)	0.885	9.086 (1)	0.508	0.470
0.1637	0.1278	1.111 (0)	1.270 (1)	1.041	7.337 (1)	0.567	0.411
0.2230	0.1505	8.363 (−1)	1.170 (1)	1.172	5.764 (1)	0.617	0.361
0.2794	0.1708	6.453 (−1)	1.088 (1)	1.251	4.625 (1)	0.648	0.330
0.2990	0.1777	5.900 (−1)	1.062 (1)	1.271	4.278 (1)	0.656	0.322
0.3215	0.1856	5.323 (−1)	1.032 (1)	1.290	3.955 (1)	0.664	0.314
0.3488	0.1951	4.697 (−1)	9.984 (0)	1.310	3.587 (1)	0.673	0.306
0.3994	0.2127	3.712 (−1)	9.386 (0)	1.335	3.023 (1)	0.684	0.294
0.5156	0.2548	2.088 (−1)	8.121 (0)	1.364	2.001 (1)	0.699	0.278
0.5970	0.2872	1.328 (−1)	7.282 (0)	1.371	1.385 (1)	0.703	0.273
0.6537	0.3123	9.318 (−2)	6.703 (0)	1.372	1.058 (1)	0.705	0.272
0.7055	0.3381	6.473 (−2)	6.166 (0)	1.373	7.987 (0)	0.707	0.272
0.7511	0.3639	4.498 (−2)	5.681 (0)	1.373	6.030 (0)	0.707	0.272
0.7905	0.3894	3.139 (−2)	5.246 (0)	1.373	4.555 (0)	0.708	0.272
0.8246	0.4151	2.191 (−2)	4.849 (0)	1.373	3.443 (0)	0.708	0.272
0.8536	0.4406	1.537 (−2)	4.487 (0)	1.373	2.608 (0)	0.708	0.272
0.8784	0.4663	1.078 (−2)	4.151 (0)	1.373	1.980 (0)	0.708	0.272
0.8993	0.4917	7.606 (−3)	3.843 (0)	1.373	1.507 (0)	0.708	0.272
0.9170	0.5172	5.370 (−3)	3.557 (0)	1.373	1.151 (0)	0.708	0.272
0.9317	0.5423	3.814 (−3)	3.294 (0)	1.373	8.813 (−1)	0.708	0.272
0.9440	0.5674	2.711 (−3)	3.050 (0)	1.373	6.773 (−1)	0.708	0.272
0.9542	0.5920	1.939 (−3)	2.826 (0)	1.373	5.222 (−1)	0.708	0.272
0.9628	0.6164	1.389 (−3)	2.618 (0)	1.373	4.040 (−1)	0.708	0.272
0.9697	0.6402	1.001 (−3)	2.428 (0)	1.373	3.136 (−1)	0.708	0.272
0.9775	0.6730	6.343 (−4)	2.184 (0)	1.373	2.268 (−1)	0.708	0.272
0.9853	0.7180	3.352 (−4)	1.886 (0)	1.373	1.387 (−1)	0.708	0.272
0.9905	0.7607	1.796 (−4)	1.634 (0)	1.373	8.571 (−2)	0.708	0.272
0.9939	0.8010	9.751 (−5)	1.421 (0)	1.373	5.345 (−2)	0.708	0.272
0.9961	0.8389	5.365 (−5)	1.245 (0)	1.373	3.356 (−2)	0.708	0.272
0.9975	0.8742	2.993 (−5)	1.092 (0)	1.373	2.130 (−2)	0.708	0.272
0.9985	0.9066	1.695 (−5)	9.413 (−1)	1.373	1.393 (−2)	0.708	0.272
0.9990	0.9322	1.032 (−5)	7.823 (−1)	1.373	1.013 (−2)	0.708	0.272
0.9994	0.9561	6.008 (−6)	6.306 (−1)	1.373	7.315 (−3)	0.708	0.272
0.9996	0.9760	3.537 (−6)	5.104 (−1)	1.373	5.318 (−3)	0.708	0.272
0.9998	0.9922	2.100 (−6)	4.147 (−1)	1.373	3.920 (−3)	0.708	0.272
0.9998	1.0057	1.255 (−6)	3.378 (−1)	1.373	2.875 (−3)	0.708	0.272
0.9999	1.0158	7.919 (−7)	2.813 (−1)	1.373	2.146 (−3)	0.708	0.272

At the center, $\epsilon_{\text{nucl}}/\epsilon_{\text{grav}} = 9.796 \times 10^3$.

$$\int_0^M (L_r)_{\text{grav}}\, dM_r = -9.758 \times 10^{-4}\ L_\odot.$$

Table 7-16 Model Interior for 1 $M_\odot$ during Main-Sequence Phase, following Point 3 in Fig. 7.25. [Calculated by I. Iben, Jr.; see ref. (326) and note to Table 7-12.]

$$1\ M_\odot, \quad t = 3.12935 \times 10^{17} \text{ seconds} = 9.90 \times 10^9 \text{ years,}$$

$$L = 2.644\ L_\odot, \quad R = 1.6262\ R_\odot, \quad T_{\text{eff}} = 5783°K.$$

$M_r/M_\odot$	$r/R_\odot$	$P \times 10^{-17}$	$T \times 10^{-6}$	$L_r/L_\odot$	ρ	X	He^4
0.0000	0.0000	4.183 (1)	2.002 (1)	0.000 (0)	2.779 (3)	0.000	0.975
0.0004	0.0057	4.013 (1)	2.001 (1)	1.374 (-5)	2.692 (3)	0.000	0.975
0.0011	0.0084	3.833 (1)	1.999 (1)	4.201 (-5)	2.594 (3)	0.000	0.975
0.0031	0.0120	3.510 (1)	1.997 (1)	1.183 (-4)	2.416 (3)	0.000	0.975
0.0082	0.0170	2.970 (1)	1.994 (1)	3.137 (-4)	2.122 (3)	0.000	0.975
0.0226	0.0255	2.054 (1)	1.989 (1)	8.723 (-4)	1.568 (3)	0.889 (-11)	0.975
0.0407	0.0334	1.375 (1)	1.986 (1)	1.561 (-3)	1.070 (3)	0.705 (-7)	0.975
0.0618	0.0418	8.834 (0)	1.983 (1)	3.030 (-3)	6.971 (2)	0.640 (-4)	0.975
0.0704	0.0452	7.407 (0)	1.982 (1)	8.232 (-3)	5.864 (2)	0.599 (-3)	0.975
0.0786	0.0484	6.271 (0)	1.980 (1)	3.621 (-2)	4.992 (2)	0.386 (-2)	0.971
0.0840	0.0507	5.609 (0)	1.976 (1)	9.834 (-2)	4.413 (2)	0.117 (-1)	0.964
0.0900	0.0532	4.973 (0)	1.966 (1)	2.540 (-1)	3.837 (2)	0.324 (-1)	0.943
0.0966	0.0563	4.354 (0)	1.946 (1)	5.722 (-1)	3.187 (2)	0.782 (-1)	0.898
0.1032	0.0596	3.825 (0)	1.913 (1)	9.718 (-1)	2.613 (2)	0.141 (0)	0.835
0.1078	0.0620	3.505 (0)	1.885 (1)	1.226 (0)	2.284 (2)	0.184 (0)	0.792
0.1161	0.0666	3.018 (0)	1.829 (1)	1.571 (0)	1.889 (2)	0.250 (0)	0.726
0.1259	0.0723	2.560 (0)	1.762 (1)	1.826 (0)	1.557 (2)	0.308 (0)	0.669
0.1372	0.0790	2.149 (0)	1.688 (1)	2.013 (0)	1.294 (2)	0.358 (0)	0.619
0.1489	0.0859	1.823 (0)	1.619 (1)	2.147 (0)	1.097 (2)	0.400 (0)	0.577
0.1720	0.0994	1.369 (0)	1.503 (1)	2.317 (0)	8.414 (1)	0.463 (0)	0.514
0.1978	0.1141	1.037 (0)	1.395 (1)	2.429 (0)	6.536 (1)	0.514 (0)	0.463
0.2348	0.1346	7.333 (-1)	1.272 (1)	2.522 (0)	4.974 (1)	0.567 (0)	0.410
0.2872	0.1628	4.782 (-1)	1.135 (1)	2.589 (0)	3.439 (1)	0.617 (0)	0.361
0.3269	0.1838	3.561 (-1)	1.051 (1)	2.616 (0)	2.670 (1)	0.643 (0)	0.336
0.3406	0.1910	3.230 (-1)	1.025 (1)	2.622 (0)	2.451 (1)	0.650 (0)	0.329
0.3543	0.1983	2.931 (-1)	9.995 (0)	2.627 (0)	2.269 (1)	0.656 (0)	0.322
0.3824	0.2133	2.412 (-1)	9.510 (0)	2.635 (0)	1.962 (1)	0.667 (0)	0.311
0.4224	0.2349	1.836 (-1)	8.879 (0)	2.642 (0)	1.610 (1)	0.679 (0)	0.299
0.4806	0.2673	1.238 (-1)	8.056 (0)	2.646 (0)	1.187 (1)	0.691 (0)	0.287
0.5390	0.3018	8.257 (-2)	7.306 (0)	2.647 (0)	8.695 (0)	0.697 (0)	0.279
0.5970	0.3389	5.423 (-2)	6.616 (0)	2.648 (0)	6.298 (0)	0.701 (0)	0.273
0.6537	0.3791	3.489 (-2)	5.974 (0)	2.647 (0)	4.491 (0)	0.704	0.272
0.7055	0.4209	2.240 (-2)	5.401 (0)	2.647 (0)	3.183 (0)	0.706	0.272
0.7511	0.4631	1.452 (-2)	4.899 (0)	2.646 (0)	2.274 (0)	0.707	0.272
0.7905	0.5053	9.525 (-3)	4.457 (0)	2.646 (0)	1.637 (0)	0.707	0.272
0.8246	0.5481	6.290 (-3)	4.059 (0)	2.645 (0)	1.187 (0)	0.708	0.272
0.8536	0.5908	4.199 (-3)	3.703 (0)	2.645 (0)	8.674 (-1)	0.708	0.272
0.8784	0.6340	2.818 (-3)	3.381 (0)	2.645 (0)	6.379 (-1)	0.708	0.272
0.8993	0.6768	1.910 (-3)	3.092 (0)	2.645 (0)	4.721 (-1)	0.708	0.272
0.9170	0.7199	1.301 (-3)	2.828 (0)	2.644 (0)	3.516 (-1)	0.708	0.272
0.9317	0.7625	8.942 (-4)	2.591 (0)	2.644 (0)	2.634 (-1)	0.708	0.272
0.9440	0.8050	6.170 (-4)	2.375 (0)	2.644 (0)	1.984 (-1)	0.708	0.272
0.9542	0.8469	4.295 (-4)	2.182 (0)	2.644 (0)	1.501 (-1)	0.708	0.272
0.9628	0.8885	2.999 (-4)	2.006 (0)	2.644 (0)	1.141 (-1)	0.708	0.272
0.9697	0.9293	2.112 (-4)	1.850 (0)	2.644 (0)	8.701 (-2)	0.708	0.272
0.9755	0.9697	1.491 (-4)	1.707 (0)	2.644 (0)	6.664 (-2)	0.708	0.272
0.9801	1.0091	1.062 (-4)	1.578 (0)	2.644 (0)	5.123 (-2)	0.708	0.272

Table 7-16 (*continued*)

$M_r/M_\odot$	$r/R_\odot$	$P \times 10^{-17}$	$T \times 10^{-6}$	$L_r/L_\odot$	ρ	X	He^4
0.9840	1.0481	7.576 (−5)	1.460 (0)	2.644 (0)	3.953 (−2)	0.708	0.272
0.9871	1.0859	5.449 (−5)	1.356 (0)	2.644 (0)	3.058 (−2)	0.708	0.272
0.9905	1.1377	3.455 (−5)	1.227 (0)	2.644 (0)	2.201 (−2)	0.708	0.272
0.9939	1.2083	1.840 (−5)	1.066 (0)	2.644 (0)	1.344 (−2)	0.708	0.272
0.9961	1.2739	1.003 (−5)	9.147 (−1)	2.644 (0)	8.506 (−3)	0.708	0.272
0.9975	1.3319	5.604 (−6)	7.401 (−1)	2.644 (0)	5.826 (−3)	0.707	0.272
0.9985	1.3803	3.194 (−6)	5.916 (−1)	2.644 (0)	4.150 (−3)	0.707	0.272
0.9990	1.4166	1.954 (−6)	4.864 (−1)	2.644 (0)	3.111 (−3)	0.707	0.272
0.9994	1.4504	1.144 (−6)	3.929(−1)	2.644 (0)	2.254 (−3)	0.707	0.272
0.9996	1.4783	6.758 (−7)	3.186 (−1)	2.644 (0)	1.642 (−3)	0.707	0.272
0.9998	1.5015	4.023 (−7)	2.592 (−1)	2.644 (0)	1.202 (−3)	0.707	0.272
0.9998	1.5206	2.409 (−7)	2.115 (−1)	2.644 (0)	8.822 (−4)	0.707	0.272
0.9999	1.5351	1.522 (−7)	1.766 (−1)	2.644 (0)	6.582 (−4)	0.707	0.272

At the center, $\epsilon_{\text{nucl}}/\epsilon_{\text{grav}} = 0$.

$$\int_0^M (L_r)_{\text{grav}} \, dM_r = -6.346 \times 10^{-3} \, L_\odot.$$

Table 7-17   Model Interior for 1 $M_\odot$ during Subgiant Phase, at Point 5 in Fig. 7-25. [Calculated by I. Iben, Jr.; see ref. (326) and note to Table 7-12.]

1 $M_\odot$, $t = 3.27165 \times 10^{17}$ seconds $= 1.04 \times 10^{10}$ years,

$L = 2.771 \, L_\odot$, $R = 2.350 \, R_\odot$, $T_{\text{eff}} = 4868°$K.

$M_r/M_\odot$	$r/R_\odot$	$P \times 10^{-17}$	$T \times 10^{-6}$	$L_r/L_\odot$	ρ	X	He^4
0.0000	0.0000	6.100 (2)	2.442 (1)	0.000	1.978 (4)	0.000	0.975
0.0004	0.0030	5.868 (2)	2.437 (1)	0.000	1.931 (4)	0.000	0.975
0.0011	0.0043	5.619 (2)	2.432 (1)	0.000	1.878 (4)	0.000	0.975
0.0031	0.0062	5.166 (2)	2.422 (1)	0.000	1.779 (4)	0.000	0.975
0.0082	0.0087	4.395 (2)	2.403 (1)	0.001	1.604 (4)	0.000	0.975
0.0226	0.0129	3.029 (2)	2.356 (1)	0.002	1.268 (4)	0.000	0.975
0.0375	0.0160	2.113 (2)	2.312 (1)	0.003	9.688 (3)	0.000	0.975
0.0571	0.0197	1.291 (2)	2.254 (1)	0.005	6.723 (3)	0.000	0.975
0.0752	0.0231	7.747 (1)	2.206 (1)	0.007	4.574 (3)	0.000	0.975
0.0873	0.0257	5.242 (1)	2.178 (1)	0.009	3.295 (3)	0.000	0.975
0.0979	0.0282	3.558 (1)	2.159 (1)	0.011	2.376 (3)	0.000	0.975
0.1115	0.0321	1.992 (1)	2.142 (1)	0.013	1.456 (3)	0.000	0.975
0.1209	0.0356	1.239 (1)	2.135 (1)	0.015	9.303 (2)	0.000	0.975
0.1270	0.0384	8.763 (0)	2.131 (1)	0.036	6.464 (2)	0.001	0.974
0.1298	0.0399	7.370 (0)	2.127 (1)	0.115	5.441 (2)	0.007	0.968
0.1327	0.0416	6.154 (0)	2.114 (1)	0.408	4.432 (2)	0.033	0.942

Table 7-17 (*continued*)

$M_r/M_\odot$	$r/R_\odot$	$P \times 10^{-17}$	$T \times 10^{-6}$	$L_r/L_\odot$	ρ	X	He⁴
0.1349	0.0431	5.303 (0)	2.091 (1)	0.904	3.562 (2)	0.083	0.892
0.1364	0.0442	4.826 (0)	2.069 (1)	1.287	3.092 (2)	0.126	0.850
0.1378	0.0454	4.391 (0)	2.042 (1)	1.651	2.692 (2)	0.170	0.806
0.1401	0.0474	3.778 (0)	1.989 (1)	2.092	2.230 (2)	0.231	0.746
0.1429	0.0503	3.142 (0)	1.917 (1)	2.400	1.807 (2)	0.284	0.693
0.1489	0.0570	2.172 (0)	1.768 (1)	2.638	1.289 (2)	0.344	0.633
0.1563	0.0658	1.451 (0)	1.613 (1)	2.726	9.287 (1)	0.385	0.592
0.1678	0.0805	8.471 (−1)	1.423 (1)	2.775	5.786 (1)	0.429	0.548
0.1782	0.0942	5.647 (−1)	1.293 (1)	2.792	4.102 (1)	0.460	0.517
0.1933	0.1144	3.467 (−1)	1.150 (1)	2.802	2.767 (1)	0.496	0.482
0.2142	0.1426	2.023 (−1)	1.010 (1)	2.806	1.758 (1)	0.533	0.444
0.2402	0.1776	1.192 (−1)	8.870 (0)	2.805	1.159 (1)	0.569	0.408
0.2680	0.2146	7.544 (−2)	7.926 (0)	2.803	7.964 (0)	0.598	0.379
0.2951	0.2504	5.174 (−2)	7.222 (0)	2.801	5.929 (0)	0.621	0.357
0.3269	0.2923	3.511 (−2)	6.564 (0)	2.798	4.279 (0)	0.641	0.336
0.3406	0.3103	3.014 (−2)	6.322 (0)	2.797	3.743 (0)	0.649	0.329
0.3543	0.3285	2.602 (−2)	6.097 (0)	2.796	3.330 (0)	0.655	0.323
0.3824	0.3658	1.959 (−2)	5.688 (0)	2.794	2.693 (0)	0.667	0.312
0.4224	0.4196	1.344 (−2)	5.188 (0)	2.790	2.047 (0)	0.678	0.299
0.4806	0.5002	8.068 (−3)	4.583 (0)	2.786	1.376 (0)	0.690	0.287
0.5390	0.5856	4.937 (−3)	4.065 (0)	2.782	9.423 (−1)	0.697	0.279
0.5970	0.6766	3.045 (−3)	3.612 (0)	2.779	6.516 (−1)	0.701	0.273
0.6537	0.7736	1.878 (−3)	3.208 (0)	2.776	4.518 (−1)	0.704	0.272
0.7055	0.8724	1.180 (−3)	2.860 (0)	2.774	3.169 (−1)	0.706	0.272
0.7511	0.9698	7.612 (−4)	2.565 (0)	2.773	2.276 (−1)	0.707	0.272
0.7905	1.0644	5.047 (−4)	2.313 (0)	2.772	1.669 (−1)	0.707	0.272
0.8246	1.1572	3.412 (−4)	2.091 (0)	2.771	1.247 (−1)	0.708	0.272
0.8536	1.2464	2.359 (−4)	1.894 (0)	2.770	9.487 (−2)	0.708	0.272
0.8784	1.3324	1.658 (−4)	1.704 (0)	2.770	7.395 (−2)	0.708	0.272
0.8993	1.4126	1.187 (−4)	*1.504 (0)*	2.770	5.972 (−2)	0.708	0.272
0.9232	1.5148	7.583 (−5)	*1.258 (0)*	2.771	4.561 (−2)	0.708	0.272
0.9462	1.6295	4.398 (−5)	*1.013 (0)*	2.771	3.283 (−2)	0.708	0.272
0.9628	1.7290	2.607 (−5)	*8.219 (−1)*	2.771	2.441 (−2)	0.708	0.272
0.9744	1.8146	1.576 (−5)	*6.723 (−1)*	2.771	1.802 (−2)	0.708	0.272
0.9826	1.8887	9.636 (−6)	*5.523 (−1)*	2.771	1.340 (−2)	0.708	0.272
0.9887	1.9584	5.654 (−6)	*4.466 (−1)*	2.771	9.832 (−3)	0.708	0.272
0.9927	2.0170	3.350 (−6)	*3.627 (−1)*	2.771	7.174 (−3)	0.708	0.272
0.9954	2.0664	1.999 (−6)	*2.956 (−1)*	2.771	5.258 (−3)	0.708	0.272
0.9971	2.1079	1.200 (−6)	*2.418 (−1)*	2.771	3.864 (−3)	0.708	0.272
0.9981	2.1428	7.231 (−7)	*1.986 (−1)*	2.771	2.843 (−3)	0.708	0.272
0.9988	2.1693	4.602 (−7)	*1.674 (−1)*	2.771	2.157 (−3)	0.708	0.272
0.9992	2.1944	2.789 (−7)	*1.394 (−1)*	2.771	1.581 (−3)	0.708	0.272
0.9995	2.2155	1.694 (−7)	*1.173 (−1)*	2.771	1.153 (−3)	0.708	0.272
0.9997	2.2335	1.030 (−7)	9.935 (−2)	2.771	8.370 (−4)	0.708	0.272
0.9998	2.2487	6.277 (−8)	8.403 (−2)	2.771	6.085 (−4)	0.708	0.272
0.9999	2.2615	3.828 (−8)	7.070 (−2)	2.771	4.447 (−4)	0.708	0.272

At the center, $\epsilon_{\mathrm{nucl}}/\epsilon_{\mathrm{grav}} = 0$.

$$\int_0^M (L_r)_{\mathrm{grav}} \, dM_r = -2.425 \times 10^{-2} \, L_\odot.$$

Table 7-18   Model Interior for 1 $M_\odot$ during Subgiant Phase, at Point 5′ in Fig. 7-25. [Calculated by I. Iben, Jr.; see ref. (326) and note to Table 7-12.]

1 $M_\odot$, $t = 3.43640 \times 10^{17}$ seconds $= 1.09 \times 10^{10}$ years,

$L = 11.412\, L_\odot$, $R = 6.178\, R_\odot$, $T_{eff} = 4276°K$.

$M_r/M_\odot$	$r/R_\odot$	$P \times 10^{-17}$	$T \times 10^{-6}$	$L_r/L_\odot$	ρ	X	He^4
0.0000	0.0000	6.552 (3)	2.735 (1)	0.000	9.117 (4)	0.000	0.975
0.0007	0.0022	6.284 (3)	2.734 (1)	1.378 (-5)	8.893 (4)	0.000	0.975
0.0056	0.0045	5.492 (3)	2.730 (1)	1.171 (-4)	8.271 (4)	0.000	0.975
0.0407	0.0094	3.045 (3)	2.713 (1)	9.998 (-4)	5.980 (4)	0.000	0.975
0.0979	0.0141	1.183 (3)	2.677 (1)	3.171 (-3)	3.213 (4)	0.000	0.975
0.1412	0.0177	4.341 (2)	2.625 (1)	6.208 (-3)	1.642 (4)	0.000	0.975
0.1678	0.0209	1.590 (2)	2.570 (1)	9.964 (-3)	7.768 (3)	0.000	0.975
0.1850	0.0243	4.982 (1)	2.532 (1)	1.524 (-2)	3.018 (3)	0.000	0.975
0.1930	0.0275	1.822 (1)	2.520 (1)	2.043 (-2)	1.185 (3)	0.000	0.975
0.1971	0.0305	8.012 (0)	2.516 (1)	4.443 (-2)	5.101 (2)	0.001	0.975
0.1979	0.0314	6.446 (0)	2.514 (1)	3.531 (-1)	4.060 (2)	0.010	0.965
0.1984	0.0320	5.519 (0)	2.506 (1)	1.426 (0)	3.246 (2)	0.053	0.923
0.1986	0.0324	5.113 (0)	2.497 (1)	2.536 (0)	2.819 (2)	0.102	0.874
0.1989	0.0328	4.727 (0)	2.483 (1)	4.078 (0)	2.388 (2)	0.172	0.804
0.1991	0.0333	4.361 (0)	2.463 (1)	5.821 (0)	2.017 (2)	0.251	0.726
0.1994	0.0340	3.969 (0)	2.431 (1)	7.654 (0)	1.708 (2)	0.336	0.641
0.1999	0.0353	3.355 (0)	2.360 (1)	9.772 (0)	1.342 (2)	0.432	0.545
0.2009	0.0383	2.383 (0)	2.196 (1)	1.110 (1)	9.957 (1)	0.494	0.484
0.2045	0.0531	6.679 (-1)	1.658 (1)	1.140 (1)	3.775 (1)	0.516	0.461
0.2084	0.0754	1.781 (-1)	1.239 (1)	1.142 (1)	1.334 (1)	0.524	0.454
0.2120	0.1023	5.984 (-2)	9.767 (0)	1.142 (1)	5.477 (0)	0.530	0.447
0.2171	0.1525	1.585 (-2)	7.315 (0)	1.142 (1)	1.976 (0)	0.538	0.440
0.2223	0.2130	5.794 (-3)	5.870 (0)	1.142 (1)	8.768 (-1)	0.545	0.432
0.2304	0.3163	1.996 (-3)	4.612 (0)	1.142 (1)	3.857 (-1)	0.557	0.421
0.2457	0.5073	6.636 (-4)	3.527 (0)	1.142 (1)	1.638 (-1)	0.576	0.402
0.2776	0.8374	2.414 (-4)	2.645 (0)	1.142 (1)	7.599 (-2)	0.607	0.371
0.2904	0.9498	1.899 (-4)	2.428 (0)	1.142 (1)	6.092 (-2)	0.647	0.330
0.2921	0.9640	1.848 (-4)	2.402 (0)	1.142 (1)	5.827 (-2)	0.680	0.298
0.2928	0.9705	1.825 (-4)	2.390 (0)	1.142 (1)	5.714 (-2)	0.693	0.284
0.3352	1.2925	1.075 (-4)	1.939 (0)	1.142 (1)	4.253 (-2)	0.693	0.284
0.4514	1.9524	4.490 (-5)	1.372 (0)	1.142 (1)	2.592 (-2)	0.693	0.284
0.6462	2.8622	1.450 (-5)	8.753 (-1)	1.141 (1)	1.299 (-2)	0.693	0.284
0.7832	3.5271	5.799 (-6)	6.075 (-1)	1.141 (1)	7.436 (-3)	0.693	0.284
0.8690	4.0231	2.610 (-6)	4.419 (-1)	1.141 (1)	4.633 (-3)	0.693	0.284
0.9290	4.4704	1.097 (-6)	3.130 (-1)	1.141 (1)	2.797 (-3)	0.693	0.284
0.9684	4.8958	3.856 (-7)	2.071 (-1)	1.141 (1)	1.462 (-3)	0.693	0.284
0.9887	5.2601	1.134 (-7)	1.305 (-1)	1.141 (1)	7.145 (-4)	0.693	0.284
0.9968	5.5485	2.778 (-8)	8.199 (-2)	1.141 (1)	2.874 (-4)	0.693	0.284
0.9990	5.7213	8.009 (-9)	5.319 (-2)	1.141 (1)	1.299 (-4)	0.693	0.284
0.9997	5.8333	2.438 (-9)	3.715 (-2)	1.141 (1)	5.926 (-5)	0.693	0.284
0.9999	5 9167	7.067 (-10)	2.806 (-2)	1.141 (1)	2.380 (-5)	0.693	0.284

At the center, $\epsilon_{nucl}/\epsilon_{grav} = 0$.

$$\int_0^M (L_r)_{grav}\, dM_r = 2.996 \times 10^{-2}\, L_\odot.$$

Table 7-19   Model Interior for 1.25 $M_\odot$ during the Main-Sequence Phase, at Approximately Point 1 in Fig. 7-25. [Calculated by I. Iben, Jr.; see ref. (326) and note to Table 7-12.]

$$1.25 \ M_\odot, \quad t = 9.62796 \times 10^{14} \text{ seconds} = 3.05 \times 10^7 \text{ years,}$$

$$L = 2.296 \ L_\odot, \quad R = 1.0855 \ R_\odot, \quad T_{\text{eff}} = 6833°\text{K.}$$

$M_r/M_\odot$	$r/R_\odot$	$P \times 10^{-17}$	$T \times 10^{-6}$	$L_r/L_\odot$	ρ	X	He⁴
0.0000	0.0000	2.055 (0)	*1.638 (1)*	0.000	9.207 (1)	0.705	0.274
0.0015	0.0282	2.010 (0)	*1.624 (1)*	2.900 (−2)	9.086 (1)	0.705	0.274
0.0018	0.0305	2.002 (0)	*1.621 (1)*	3.585 (−2)	9.064 (1)	0.705	0.274
0.0023	0.0331	1.993 (0)	*1.618 (1)*	4.476 (−2)	9.040 (1)	0.705	0.274
0.0036	0.0383	1.972 (0)	1.612 (1)	6.737 (−2)	8.988 (1)	0.705	0.274
0.0059	0.0451	1.941 (0)	1.602 (1)	1.064 (−1)	8.904 (1)	0.705	0.274
0.0095	0.0531	1.899 (0)	1.588 (1)	1.649 (−1)	8.788 (1)	0.706	0.274
0.0147	0.0617	1.847 (0)	1.571 (1)	2.435 (1)	8.369 (1)	0.706	0.274
0.0212	0.0699	1.792 (0)	1.554 (1)	3.335 (1)	8.482 (1)	0.706	0.274
0.0318	0.0804	1.714 (0)	1.529 (1)	4.653 (1)	8.258 (1)	0.706	0.273
0.0505	0.0947	1.598 (0)	1.491 (1)	6.668 (1)	7.908 (1)	0.706	0.273
0.0762	0.1098	1.466 (0)	1.448 (1)	9.004 (1)	7.470 (1)	0.706	0.273
0.1210	0.1303	1.279 (0)	1.384 (1)	1.237 (0)	6.845 (1)	0.707	0.273
0.1550	0.1433	1.159 (0)	1.342 (1)	1.455 (0)	6.380 (1)	0.707	0.273
0.1788	0.1516	1.084 (0)	1.313 (1)	1.588 (0)	6.060 (1)	0.707	0.273
0.2245	0.1663	9.544 (−1)	1.262 (1)	1.798 (0)	5.636 (1)	0.707	0.272
0.3519	0.2022	6.702 (−1)	1.134 (1)	2.114 (0)	4.423 (1)	0.708	0.272
0.4638	0.2311	4.842 (−1)	1.035 (1)	2.207 (0)	3.531 (1)	0.708	0.272
0.5606	0.2560	3.574 (−1)	9.543 (0)	2.241 (0)	2.797 (1)	0.708	0.272
0.6839	0.2892	2.318 (−1)	8.557 (0)	2.265 (0)	2.068 (1)	0.708	0.272
0.7691	0.3142	1.645 (−1)	7.877 (0)	2.274 (0)	1.571 (1)	0.708	0.272
0.8282	0.3333	1.258 (−1)	7.395 (0)	2.279 (0)	1.283 (1)	0.708	0.272
0.8851	0.3534	9.421 (−2)	6.919 (0)	2.283 (0)	1.029 (1)	0.708	0.272
0.9391	0.3749	6.897 (−2)	6.447 (0)	2.286 (0)	8.110 (0)	0.708	0.272
0.9883	0.3971	4.974 (−2)	5.993 (0)	2.288 (0)	6.296 (0)	0.708	0.272
1.0309	0.4193	3.579 (−2)	5.574 (0)	2.290 (0)	4.878 (0)	0.708	0.272
1.0671	0.4413	2.580 (−2)	5.190 (0)	2.291 (0)	3.776 (0)	0.708	0.272
1.0982	0.4633	1.857 (−2)	4.834 (0)	2.292 (0)	2.922 (0)	0.708	0.272
1.1243	0.4850	1.341 (−2)	4.504 (0)	2.293 (0)	2.262 (0)	0.708	0.272
1.1464	0.5068	9.672 (−3)	4.195 (0)	2.294 (0)	1.754 (0)	0.708	0.272
1.1648	0.5282	7.004 (−3)	3.908 (0)	2.294 (0)	1.362 (0)	0.708	0.272
1.1802	0.5495	5.069 (−3)	3.638 (0)	2.295 (0)	1.060 (0)	0.708	0.272
1.1929	0.5704	3.686 (−3)	3.389 (0)	2.295 (0)	8.265 (−1)	0.708	0.272
1.2036	0.5911	2.679 (−3)	3.155 (0)	2.295 (0)	6.460 (−1)	0.708	0.272
1.2122	0.6113	1.957 (−3)	2.938 (0)	2.296 (0)	5.061 (−1)	0.708	0.272
1.2194	0.6313	1.430 (−3)	2.735 (0)	2.296 (0)	3.975 (−1)	0.708	0.272
1.2253	0.6506	1.049 (−3)	2.548 (0)	2.296 (0)	3.129 (−1)	0.708	0.272
1.2301	0.6697	7.704 (−4)	2.372 (0)	2.296 (0)	2.469 (−1)	0.708	0.272
1.2339	0.6881	5.683 (−4)	2.211 (0)	2.296 (0)	1.952 (−1)	0.708	0.272
1.2371	0.7061	4.192 (−4)	2.060 (0)	2.296 (0)	1.546 (−1)	0.708	0.272
1.2397	0.7235	3.107 (−4)	1.923 (0)	2.296 (0)	1.226 (−1)	0.708	0.272
1.2417	0.7404	2.302 (−4)	1.796 (0)	2.296 (0)	9.743 (−2)	0.708	0.272
1.2434	0.7567	1.714 (−4)	1.678 (0)	2.296 (0)	7.753 (−2)	0.708	0.272
1.2447	0.7726	1.276 (−4)	1.569 (0)	2.296 (0)	6.179 (−2)	0.708	0.272
1.2458	0.7879	9.359 (−5)	1.468 (0)	2.296 (0)	4.929 (−2)	0.708	0.272
1.2467	0.8027	7.126 (−5)	1.376 (0)	2.296 (0)	3.934 (−2)	0.708	0.272
1.2473	0.8169	5.347 (−5)	1.292 (0)	2.296 (0)	3.139 (−2)	0.708	0.272
1.2479	0.8308	4.008 (−5)	1.216 (0)	2.296 (0)	2.503 (−2)	0.708	0.272
1.2483	0.8441	3.017 (−5)	1.146 (0)	2.296 (0)	1.997 (−2)	0.708	0.272
1.2487	0.8571	2.269 (−5)	1.079 (0)	2.296 (0)	1.597 (−2)	0.708	0.272
1.2490	0.8695	1.714 (−5)	1.017 (0)	2.296 (0)	1.278 (−2)	0.708	0.272

At the center, $\epsilon_{\text{nucl}}/\epsilon_{\text{grav}} = -2.154 \times 10^3$.

$$\int_0^M (L_r)_{\text{grav}} \, dM_r = 0.04874 \ L_\odot.$$

Table 7-20 Model Interior for 1.5 $M_\odot$ during the Main-Sequence Phase, at Approximately Point 1 in Fig. 7-25. [Calculated by I. Iben, Jr.; see ref. (326) and note to Table 7-12.]

$$1.5\ M_\odot, \quad t = 5.80606 \times 10^{14}\ \text{seconds} = 1.85 \times 10^7\ \text{years}.$$

$$L = 5.418\ L_\odot, \quad R = 1.1826\ R_\odot, \quad T_{eff} = 8114°\text{K}.$$

$M_r/M_\odot$	$r/R_\odot$	$P \times 10^{-17}$	$T \times 10^{-6}$	$L_r/L_\odot$	ρ	X	He^4
0.0000	0.0000	2.202 (0)	1.859 (1)	0.000	8.714 (1)	0.705	0.274
0.0021	0.0323	2.148 (0)	1.841 (1)	1.345 (−1)	8.590 (1)	0.705	0.274
0.0034	0.0381	2.128 (0)	1.834 (1)	2.079 (−1)	8.543 (1)	0.705	0.274
0.0054	0.0447	2.100 (0)	1.824 (1)	3.168 (−1)	8.478 (1)	0.705	0.274
0.0089	0.0528	2.062 (0)	1.811 (1)	4.805 (−1)	8.389 (1)	0.705	0.274
0.0141	0.0617	2.013 (0)	1.794 (1)	6.988 (−1)	8.269 (1)	0.705	0.274
0.0235	0.0736	1.939 (0)	1.767 (1)	1.029 (0)	8.095 (1)	0.705	0.274
0.0415	0.0895	1.823 (0)	1.724 (1)	1.500 (0)	7.818 (1)	0.705	0.274
0.0539	0.0982	1.755 (0)	1.698 (1)	1.746 (0)	7.617 (1)	0.705	0.274
0.0637	0.1041	1.706 (0)	1.679 (1)	1.912 (0)	7.489 (1)	0.706	0.274
0.0785	0.1122	1.637 (0)	1.652 (1)	2.176 (0)	7.315 (1)	0.706	0.273
0.1452	0.1405	1.382 (0)	1.553 (1)	3.041 (0)	6.628 (1)	0.706	0.273
0.2403	0.1708	1.106 (0)	1.444 (1)	3.909 (0)	5.720 (1)	0.707	0.272
0.3578	0.2018	8.463 (−1)	1.330 (1)	4.745 (0)	4.842 (1)	0.708	0.272
0.5277	0.2416	5.670 (−1)	1.183 (1)	5.216 (0)	3.605 (1)	0.708	0.272
0.6502	0.2695	4.150 (−1)	1.086 (1)	5.313 (0)	2.886 (1)	0.708	0.272
0.7759	0.2991	2.914 (−1)	9.911 (0)	5.357 (0)	2.230 (1)	0.708	0.272
0.9007	0.3307	1.953 (−1)	8.980 (0)	5.381 (0)	1.658 (1)	0.708	0.272
1.0210	0.3652	1.240 (−1)	8.063 (0)	5.395 (0)	1.179 (1)	0.708	0.272
1.0893	0.3876	9.163 (−2)	7.520 (0)	5.400 (0)	9.192 (0)	0.708	0.272
1.1432	0.4073	6.996 (−2)	7.074 (0)	5.404 (0)	7.474 (0)	0.708	0.272
1.1940	0.4282	5.241 (−2)	6.630 (0)	5.406 (0)	5.987 (0)	0.708	0.272
1.2412	0.4504	3.851 (−2)	6.193 (0)	5.409 (0)	4.718 (0)	0.708	0.272
1.2842	0.4737	2.779 (−2)	5.765 (0)	5.411 (0)	3.664 (0)	0.708	0.272
1.3207	0.4968	2.007 (−2)	5.370 (0)	5.412 (0)	2.839 (0)	0.708	0.272
1.3517	0.5199	1.447 (−2)	5.003 (0)	5.414 (0)	2.201 (0)	0.708	0.272
1.3777	0.5428	1.047 (−2)	4.664 (0)	5.415 (0)	1.707 (0)	0.708	0.272
1.3996	0.5656	7.574 (−3)	4.345 (0)	5.415 (0)	1.326 (0)	0.708	0.272
1.4177	0.5880	5.499 (−3)	4.050 (0)	5.416 (0)	1.032 (0)	0.708	0.272
1.4328	0.6103	3.992 (−3)	3.773 (0)	5.416 (0)	8.048 (−1)	0.708	0.272
1.4453	0.6321	2.911 (−3)	3.516 (0)	5.417 (0)	6.290 (−1)	0.708	0.272
1.4556	0.6536	2.122 (−3)	3.274 (0)	5.417 (0)	4.928 (−1)	0.708	0.272
1.4640	0.6746	1.555 (−3)	3.051 (0)	5.417 (0)	3.871 (−1)	0.708	0.272
1.4709	0.6953	1.140 (−3)	2.842 (0)	5.417 (0)	3.048 (−1)	0.708	0.272
1.4765	0.7153	8.391 (−4)	2.648 (0)	5.418 (0)	2.406 (−1)	0.708	0.272
1.4811	0.7349	6.179 (−4)	2.466 (0)	5.418 (0)	1.903 (−1)	0.708	0.272
1.4848	0.7539	4.572 (−4)	2.299 (0)	5.418 (0)	1.509 (−1)	0.708	0.272
1.4879	0.7724	3.383 (−4)	2.143 (0)	5.418 (0)	1.199 (−1)	0.708	0.272
1.4903	0.7901	2.516 (−4)	2.001 (0)	5.418 (0)	9.537 (−2)	0.708	0.272
1.4922	0.8075	1.870 (−4)	1.869 (0)	5.418 (0)	7.597 (−2)	0.708	0.272
1.4938	0.8241	1.397 (−4)	1.748 (0)	5.418 (0)	6.061 (−2)	0.708	0.272
1.4951	0.8402	1.043 (−4)	1.634 (0)	5.418 (0)	4.844 (−2)	0.708	0.272
1.4961	0.8557	7.819 (−5)	1.530 (0)	5.418 (0)	3.875 (−2)	0.708	0.272
1.4969	0.8707	5.859 (−5)	1.433 (0)	5.418 (0)	3.103 (−2)	0.708	0.272
1.4975	0.8851	4.409 (−5)	1.345 (0)	5.418 (0)	2.485 (−2)	0.708	0.272
1.4980	0.8990	3.314 (−5)	1.265 (0)	5.418 (0)	1.989 (−2)	0.708	0.272
1.4984	0.9124	2.502 (−5)	1.192 (0)	5.418 (0)	1.591 (−2)	0.708	0.272
1.4988	0.9254	1.887 (−5)	1.123 (0)	5.418 (0)	1.275 (−2)	0.708	0.272

At the center, $\epsilon_{nucl}/\epsilon_{grav} = -612.0$.

$$\int_0^M (L_r)_{grav}\, dM_r = 0.05098\ L_\odot.$$

Table 7-21   Model Interior for 2.25 $M_\odot$ during the Main-Sequence Phase, Just Following Point 1 in Fig. 7-25. [Calculated by I. Iben, Jr.; see ref. (326a) and note to Table 7-12.]

2.25 $M_\odot$, $t = 1.99068 \times 10^{14}$ seconds $= 6.30 \times 10^{6}$ years.

$L = 30.21\ L_\odot$, $R = 1.4559\ R_\odot$, $T_{\text{eff}} = 11{,}237°$K.

$M_r/M_\odot$	$r/R_\odot$	$P \times 10^{-17}$	$T \times 10^{-6}$	$L_r/L_\odot$	ρ	X	He⁴
0.0000	0.0000	1.770 (0)	2.216 (1)	0.000	5.893 (1)	0.705	0.274
0.0018	0.0352	1.740 (0)	2.202 (1)	7.926 (−1)	5.835 (1)	0.705	0.274
0.0026	0.0398	1.732 (0)	2.198 (1)	1.112 (0)	5.820 (1)	0.705	0.274
0.0043	0.0470	1.718 (0)	2.190 (1)	1.741 (0)	5.792 (1)	0.705	0.274
0.0070	0.0554	1.698 (0)	2.180 (1)	2.691 (0)	5.754 (1)	0.705	0.274
0.0113	0.0652	1.672 (0)	2.167 (1)	4.070 (0)	5.701 (1)	0.705	0.274
0.0185	0.0769	1.635 (0)	2.148 (1)	6.072 (0)	5.628 (1)	0.705	0.274
0.0285	0.0891	1.592 (0)	2.125 (1)	8.452 (0)	5.540 (1)	0.705	0.274
0.0462	0.1052	1.526 (0)	2.090 (1)	1.178 (1)	5.406 (1)	0.705	0.274
0.1031	0.1393	1.365 (0)	1.999 (1)	1.820 (1)	5.090 (1)	0.705	0.274
0.2072	0.1794	1.148 (0)	1.867 (1)	2.292 (1)	4.620 (1)	0.705	0.274
0.2668	0.1973	1.048 (0)	1.800 (1)	2.406 (1)	4.325 (1)	0.705	0.274
0.3289	0.2138	9.554 (−1)	1.736 (1)	2.497 (1)	4.086 (1)	0.707	0.272
0.4419	0.2405	8.095 (−1)	1.636 (1)	2.619 (1)	3.671 (1)	0.707	0.272
0.4963	0.2524	7.474 (−1)	1.592 (1)	2.689 (1)	3.482 (1)	0.707	0.272
0.5725	0.2682	6.679 (−1)	1.535 (1)	2.787 (1)	3.236 (1)	0.708	0.272
0.6530	0.2843	5.920 (−1)	1.478 (1)	2.871 (1)	2.981 (1)	0.708	0.272
0.8238	0.3172	4.537 (−1)	1.365 (1)	2.964 (1)	2.521 (1)	0.708	0.272
1.0452	0.3595	3.115 (−1)	1.229 (1)	2.998 (1)	1.934 (1)	0.708	0.272
1.2662	0.4040	2.029 (−1)	1.099 (1)	3.008 (1)	1.390 (1)	0.708	0.272
1.3870	0.4304	1.553 (−1)	1.029 (1)	3.012 (1)	1.140 (1)	0.708	0.272
1.5043	0.4583	1.162 (−1)	9.589 (0)	3.014 (1)	9.168 (0)	0.708	0.272
1.6159	0.4878	8.486 (−2)	8.904 (0)	3.015 (1)	7.229 (0)	0.708	0.272
1.7142	0.5171	6.173 (−2)	8.273 (0)	3.017 (1)	5.659 (0)	0.708	0.272
1.7998	0.5462	4.476 (−2)	7.690 (0)	3.017 (1)	4.420 (0)	0.708	0.272
1.8731	0.5750	3.250 (−2)	7.157 (0)	3.018 (1)	3.446 (0)	0.708	0.272
1.9361	0.6037	2.354 (−2)	6.662 (0)	3.019 (1)	2.684 (0)	0.708	0.272
1.9893	0.6320	1.708 (−2)	6.208 (0)	3.019 (1)	2.089 (0)	0.708	0.272
2.0346	0.6603	1.238 (−2)	5.786 (0)	3.019 (1)	1.626 (0)	0.708	0.272
2.0724	0.6882	8.999 (−3)	5.396 (0)	3.020 (1)	1.266 (0)	0.708	0.272
2.1043	0.7161	6.534 (−3)	5.031 (0)	3.020 (1)	9.869 (−1)	0.708	0.272
2.1306	0.7434	4.763 (−3)	4.692 (0)	3.020 (1)	7.705 (−1)	0.708	0.272
2.1527	0.7705	3.470 (−3)	4.374 (0)	3.020 (1)	6.027 (−1)	0.708	0.272
2.1707	0.7970	2.540 (−3)	4.079 (0)	3.020 (1)	4.723 (−1)	0.708	0.272
2.1857	0.8233	1.858 (−3)	3.802 (0)	3.020 (1)	3.711 (−1)	0.708	0.272
2.1979	0.8487	1.366 (−3)	3.545 (0)	3.020 (1)	2.922 (−1)	0.708	0.272
2.2080	0.8738	1.004 (−3)	3.304 (0)	3.020 (1)	2.306 (−1)	0.708	0.272
2.2161	0.8981	7.417 (−4)	3.081 (0)	3.020 (1)	1.824 (−1)	0.708	0.272
2.2227	0.9219	5.478 (−4)	2.871 (0)	3.020 (1)	1.447 (−1)	0.708	0.272
2.2281	0.9447	4.066 (−4)	2.677 (0)	3.020 (1)	1.150 (−1)	0.708	0.272
2.2325	0.9671	3.017 (−4)	2.495 (0)	3.021 (1)	9.164 (−2)	0.708	0.272
2.2360	0.9885	2.250 (−4)	2.328 (0)	3.021 (1)	7.316 (−2)	0.708	0.272
2.2388	1.0093	1.677 (−4)	2.172 (0)	3.021 (1)	5.851 (−2)	0.708	0.272
2.2411	1.0292	1.256 (−4)	2.030 (0)	3.021 (1)	4.685 (−2)	0.708	0.272
2.2429	1.0486	9.405 (−5)	1.898 (0)	3.021 (1)	3.754 (−2)	0.708	0.272
2.2443	1.0671	7.073 (−5)	1.776 (0)	3.021 (1)	3.012 (−2)	0.708	0.272
2.2455	1.0850	5.315 (−5)	1.663 (0)	3.021 (1)	2.421 (−2)	0.708	0.272
2.2464	1.1020	4.011 (−5)	1.558 (0)	3.021 (1)	1.947 (−2)	0.708	0.272
2.2471	1.1186	3.024 (−5)	1.460 (0)	3.021 (1)	1.568 (−2)	0.708	0.272

At the center, $\epsilon_{\text{nuol}}/\epsilon_{\text{grav}} = -1.531 \times 10^{3}$.

$$\int_0^M (L_r)_{\text{grav}}\, dM_r = 0.06324\ L_\odot.$$

Table 7-22 Model Interior for 3 $M_\odot$ during Initial Main-Sequence Phase, at Point 1 in Fig. 7-25. [Calculated by I. Iben, Jr.; see ref. (339) and note to Table 7-12.]

3 $M_\odot$, $t = 7.76905 \times 10^{13}$ seconds $= 2.46 \times 10^6$ years.

$L = 94.95\ L_\odot$, $R = 1.7381\ R_\odot$, $T_{\text{eff}} = 13{,}694°\text{K}$.

$M_r/M_\odot$	$r/R_\odot$	$P \times 10^{-17}$	$T \times 10^{-6}$	$L_r/L_\odot$	ρ
0.0000	0.0000	1.350 (0)	2.408 (1)	0.000	4.133 (1)
0.0025	0.0442	1.328 (0)	2.392 (1)	2.701 (0)	4.092 (1)
0.0040	0.0515	1.320 (0)	2.387 (1)	4.078 (0)	4.078 (1)
0.0065	0.0606	1.308 (0)	2.378 (1)	6.356 (0)	4.057 (1)
0.0104	0.0712	1.293 (0)	2.367 (1)	9.729 (0)	4.028 (1)
0.0170	0.0840	1.271 (0)	2.351 (1)	1.478 (1)	3.989 (1)
0.0275	0.0988	1.242 (0)	2.330 (1)	2.177 (1)	3.935 (1)
0.0464	0.1182	1.197 (0)	2.297 (1)	3.212 (1)	3.856 (1)
0.0935	0.1507	1.110 (0)	2.230 (1)	4.974 (1)	3.698 (1)
0.1751	0.1882	9.949 (−1)	2.135 (1)	6.604 (1)	3.473 (1)
0.3614	0.2457	7.996 (−1)	1.959 (1)	7.885 (1)	3.025 (1)
0.4195	0.2602	7.500 (−1)	1.910 (1)	8.029 (1)	2.910 (1)
0.5037	0.2795	6.844 (−1)	1.843 (1)	8.172 (1)	2.753 (1)
0.5849	0.2967	6.269 (−1)	1.784 (1)	8.310 (1)	2.599 (1)
0.6621	0.3122	5.767 (−1)	1.733 (1)	8.531 (1)	2.467 (1)
0.7226	0.3239	5.399 (−1)	1.694 (1)	8.717 (1)	2.362 (1)
0.8084	0.3400	4.914 (−1)	1.642 (1)	8.956 (1)	2.226 (1)
0.9794	0.3707	4.054 (−1)	1.544 (1)	9.258 (1)	1.972 (1)
1.3963	0.4435	2.428 (−1)	1.330 (1)	9.435 (1)	1.380 (1)
1.6346	0.4868	1.733 (−1)	1.215 (1)	9.454 (1)	1.082 (1)
1.8608	0.5314	1.202 (−1)	1.107 (1)	9.464 (1)	8.277 (0)
2.0856	0.5812	7.838 (−2)	9.972 (0)	9.472 (1)	6.018 (0)
2.2933	0.6356	4.834 (−2)	8.898 (0)	9.478 (1)	4.182 (0)
2.4784	0.6957	2.793 (−2)	7.848 (0)	9.484 (1)	2.757 (0)
2.5920	0.7419	1.819 (−2)	7.128 (0)	9.487 (1)	1.935 (0)
2.6617	0.7760	1.323 (−2)	6.640 (0)	9.488 (1)	1.511 (0)
2.7202	0.8095	9.638 (−3)	6.192 (0)	9.490 (1)	1.180 (0)
2.7698	0.8430	7.014 (−3)	5.774 (0)	9.491 (1)	9.217 (−1)
2.8109	0.8759	5.121 (−3)	5.388 (0)	9.492 (1)	7.205 (−1)
2.8454	0.9086	3.736 (−3)	5.024 (0)	9.493 (1)	5.640 (−1)
2.8837	0.9532	2.417 (−3)	4.557 (0)	9.493 (1)	4.122 (−1)
2.9202	1.0091	1.385 (−3)	4.018 (0)	9.494 (1)	2.676 (−1)
2.9479	1.0686	7.530 (−4)	3.493 (0)	9.494 (1)	1.672 (−1)
2.9663	1.1248	4.133 (−4)	3.036 (0)	9.495 (1)	1.055 (−1)
2.9783	1.1777	2.289 (−4)	2.640 (0)	9.495 (1)	6.711 (−2)
2.9862	1.2269	1.279 (−4)	2.297 (0)	9.495 (1)	4.305 (−2)
2.9912	1.2725	7.207 (−5)	2.005 (0)	9.495 (1)	2.778 (−2)
2.9945	1.3146	4.091 (−5)	1.757 (0)	9.495 (1)	1.798 (−2)
2.9965	1.3534	2.337 (−5)	1.543 (0)	9.495 (1)	1.169 (−2)
2.9978	1.3891	1.342 (−5)	1.359 (0)	9.495 (1)	7.618 (−3)

At the center, $\epsilon_{\text{nucl}}/\epsilon_{\text{grav}} = -1.301 \times 10^3$.

$$\int_0^M (L_r)_{\text{grav}}\, dM_r = 0.1948\ L_\odot.$$

Table 7-23 Model Interior for 5 $M_\odot$ Prior to the Main-Sequence Phase, Preceding Point 1 in Fig. 7-3A. [Calculated by I. Iben, Jr.; see ref. (321) and note to Table 7-12.]

$$5\ M_\odot, \quad t = 2.71201 \times 10^{10} \text{ seconds} = 8.58 \times 10^2 \text{ years},$$

$$L = 365.9\ L_\odot, \quad R = 35.23\ R_\odot, \quad T_{\text{eff}} = 4261°\text{K}.$$

$M_r/M_\odot$	$r/R_\odot$	$P \times 10^{-17}$	$T \times 10^{-6}$	$L_r/L_\odot$	ρ	X	He^4
0.0000	0.000	1.800 (−6)	1.043 (0)	0.000	1.261 (−3)	0.708	0.272
0.0048	1.752 (0)	1.767 (−6)	1.038 (0)	6.728 (−1)	1.245 (−3)	0.708	0.272
0.0126	2.425 (0)	1.738 (−6)	1.034 (0)	1.764 (0)	1.230 (−3)	0.708	0.272
0.0331	3.364 (0)	1.683 (−6)	1.025 (0)	4.615 (0)	1.203 (−3)	0.708	0.272
0.0860	4.670 (0)	1.582 (−6)	1.009 (0)	1.189 (1)	1.152 (−3)	0.708	0.272
0.1849	6.108 (0)	1.446 (−6)	9.861 (−1)	2.520 (1)	1.079 (−3)	0.708	0.272
0.3318	7.545 (0)	1.293 (−6)	9.575 (−1)	4.446 (1)	9.959 (−4)	0.708	0.272
0.5286	8.983 (0)	1.133 (−6)	9.239 (−1)	6.936 (1)	9.056 (−4)	0.708	0.272
0.6787	9.896 (0)	1.031 (−6)	8.999 (−1)	8.772 (1)	8.469 (−4)	0.708	0.272
0.9515	1.133 (1)	8.751 (−7)	8.577 (−1)	1.196 (2)	7.552 (−4)	0.708	0.272
1.2636	1.277 (1)	7.288 (−7)	8.091 (−1)	1.533 (2)	6.677 (−4)	0.708	0.272
1.6089	1.421 (1)	5.949 (−7)	*7.510 (−1)*	1.857 (2)	5.881 (−4)	0.708	0.272
1.9802	1.566 (1)	4.748 (−7)	*6.885 (−1)*	2.170 (2)	5.137 (−4)	0.708	0.272
2.3666	1.710 (1)	3.701 (−7)	*6.251 (−1)*	2.467 (2)	4.423 (−4)	0.708	0.272
2.7569	1.854 (1)	2.810 (−7)	*5.616 (−1)*	2.739 (2)	3.749 (−4)	0.708	0.272
3.1396	1.998 (1)	2.072 (−7)	*4.987 (−1)*	2.977 (2)	3.145 (−4)	0.708	0.272
3.5049	2.141 (1)	1.477 (−7)	*4.367 (−1)*	3.176 (2)	2.569 (−4)	0.708	0.272
3.8429	2.286 (1)	1.012 (−7)	*3.763 (−1)*	3.336 (2)	2.050 (−4)	0.708	0.272
4.1442	2.430 (1)	6.609 (−8)	*3.181 (−1)*	3.457 (2)	1.591 (−4)	0.708	0.272
4.4001	2.573 (1)	4.092 (−8)	*2.631 (−1)*	3.543 (2)	1.195 (−4)	0.708	0.272
4.5899	2.700 (1)	2.502 (−8)	*2.165 (−1)*	3.594 (2)	8.889 (−5)	0.708	0.272
4.7236	2.811 (1)	1.529 (−8)	*1.781 (−1)*	3.624 (2)	6.610 (−5)	0.708	0.272
4.8161	2.906 (1)	9.349 (−9)	*1.465 (−1)*	3.640 (2)	4.915 (−5)	0.708	0.272
4.8790	2.989 (1)	5.716 (−9)	*1.207 (−1)*	3.649 (2)	3.652 (−5)	0.708	0.272
4.9211	3.059 (1)	3.494 (−9)	*1.000 (−1)*	3.654 (2)	2.705 (−5)	0.708	0.272
4.9490	3.120 (1)	2.135 (−9)	8.404 (−2)	3.657 (2)	1.982 (−5)	0.708	0.272
4.9673	3.173 (1)	1.304 (−9)	7.218 (−2)	3.658 (2)	1.427 (−5)	0.708	0.272
4.9792	3.219 (1)	7.962 (−10)	6.269 (−2)	3.659 (2)	1.016 (−5)	0.708	0.272
4.9868	3.260 (1)	4.865 (−10)	5.385 (−2)	3.659 (2)	7.274 (−6)	0.708	0.272

At the center, $\epsilon_{\text{nucl}}/\epsilon_{\text{grav}} = 8.251 \times 10^{-15}$.

$$\int_0^M (L_r)_{\text{grav}}\, dM_r = 365.9\ L_\odot.$$

Table 7-24   Model Interior for 5 $M_\odot$ Prior to the Main-Sequence Phase, at Point 3 in Fig. 7-3A. [Calculated by I. Iben, Jr.; see ref. (321) and note to Table 7-12.]

$$5\ M_\odot, \quad t = 6.32213 \times 10^{12} \text{ seconds} = 2.00 \times 10^5 \text{ years.}$$

$$L = 583.1\ L_\odot, \quad R = 6.450\ R_\odot, \quad T_{\text{eff}} = 11{,}190°\text{K.}$$

$M_r/M_\odot$	$r/R_\odot$	$P \times 10^{-17}$	$T \times 10^{-6}$	$L_r/L_\odot$	ρ	X	He^4
0.0000	0.0000	3.286 (-2)	1.056 (1)	0.000	2.288 (0)	0.708	0.272
0.0050	0.1457	3.211 (-2)	1.050 (1)	1.040 (0)	2.249 (0)	0.708	0.272
0.0070	0.1635	3.192 (-2)	1.049 (1)	1.459 (0)	2.240 (0)	0.708	0.272
0.0094	0.1806	3.172 (-2)	1.047 (1)	1.957 (0)	2.229 (0)	0.708	0.272
0.0132	0.2025	3.144 (-2)	1.045 (1)	2.739 (0)	2.214 (0)	0.708	0.272
0.0185	0.2268	3.109 (-2)	1.042 (1)	3.821 (0)	2.197 (0)	0.708	0.272
0.0248	0.2507	3.071 (-2)	1.039 (1)	5.121 (0)	2.176 (0)	0.708	0.272
0.0348	0.2813	3.018 (-2)	1.034 (1)	7.156 (0)	2.148 (0)	0.708	0.272
0.0486	0.3156	2.954 (-2)	1.029 (1)	9.968 (0)	2.116 (0)	0.708	0.272
0.0716	0.3607	2.860 (-2)	1.021 (1)	1.460 (1)	2.067 (0)	0.708	0.272
0.1111	0.4208	2.723 (-2)	1.009 (1)	2.251 (1)	1.993 (0)	0.708	0.272
0.1614	0.4806	2.576 (-2)	9.956 (0)	3.245 (1)	1.911 (0)	0.708	0.272
0.2240	0.5412	2.419 (-2)	9.805 (0)	4.466 (1)	1.823 (0)	0.708	0.272
0.2984	0.6018	2.256 (-2)	9.642 (0)	5.895 (1)	1.730 (0)	0.708	0.272
0.4440	0.7001	1.989 (-2)	9.355 (0)	8.625 (1)	1.584 (0)	0.708	0.272
0.6787	0.8296	1.647 (-2)	8.942 (0)	1.287 (2)	1.377 (0)	0.708	0.272
0.9515	0.9578	1.336 (-2)	8.506 (0)	1.757 (2)	1.175 (0)	0.708	0.272
1.3302	1.1174	1.003 (-2)	7.946 (0)	2.372 (2)	9.458 (-1)	0.708	0.272
1.6819	1.2576	7.633 (-3)	7.451 (0)	2.904 (2)	7.700 (-1)	0.708	0.272
2.0566	1.4057	5.628 (-3)	6.937 (0)	3.431 (2)	6.113 (-1)	0.708	0.272
2.4448	1.5637	4.008 (-3)	6.408 (0)	3.932 (2)	4.726 (-1)	0.708	0.272
2.8344	1.7330	2.750 (-3)	5.869 (0)	4.387 (2)	3.551 (-1)	0.708	0.272
3.2143	1.9156	1.812 (-3)	5.322 (0)	4.776 (2)	2.588 (-1)	0.708	0.272
3.5750	2.1144	1.140 (-3)	4.766 (0)	5.092 (2)	1.824 (-1)	0.708	0.272
3.7780	2.2428	8.415 (-4)	4.433 (0)	5.248 (2)	1.422 (-1)	0.708	0.272
3.9373	2.3552	6.435 (-4)	4.156 (0)	5.360 (2)	1.161 (-1)	0.708	0.272
4.0872	2.4736	4.842 (-4)	3.881 (0)	5.456 (2)	9.369 (-2)	0.708	0.272
4.2262	2.5978	3.584 (-4)	3.609 (0)	5.537 (2)	7.465 (-2)	0.708	0.272
4.3539	2.7286	2.603 (-4)	3.339 (0)	5.604 (2)	5.870 (-2)	0.708	0.272
4.4636	2.8587	1.889 (-4)	3.087 (0)	5.657 (2)	4.601 (-2)	0.708	0.272
4.5569	2.9875	1.370 (-4)	2.853 (0)	5.696 (2)	3.613 (-2)	0.708	0.272
4.6349	3.1132	9.976 (-5)	2.639 (0)	5.726 (2)	2.841 (-2)	0.708	0.272
4.7006	3.2374	7.262 (-5)	2.441 (0)	5.749 (2)	2.238 (-2)	0.708	0.272
4.7549	3.3582	5.309 (-5)	2.260 (0)	5.767 (2)	1.765 (-2)	0.708	0.272
4.8003	3.4773	3.880 (-5)	2.094 (0)	5.782 (2)	1.393 (-2)	0.708	0.272
4.8375	3.5928	2.848 (-5)	1.945 (0)	5.793 (2)	1.100 (-2)	0.708	0.272
4.8683	3.7066	2.089 (-5)	1.807 (0)	5.802 (2)	8.688 (-3)	0.708	0.272
4.8934	3.8167	1.540 (-5)	1.681 (0)	5.809 (2)	6.873 (-3)	0.708	0.272
4.9140	3.9249	1.134 (-5)	1.565 (0)	5.814 (2)	5.445 (-3)	0.708	0.272
4.9307	4.0294	8.393 (-6)	1.458 (0)	5.818 (2)	4.316 (-3)	0.708	0.272
4.9444	4.1319	6.206 (-6)	1.361 (0)	5.821 (2)	3.423 (-3)	0.708	0.272
4.9553	4.2308	4.609 (-6)	1.273 (0)	5.824 (2)	2.713 (-3)	0.708	0.272
4.9643	4.3279	3.421 (-6)	1.193 (0)	5.826 (2)	2.149 (-3)	0.708	0.272
4.9714	4.4215	2.549 (-6)	1.119 (0)	5.827 (2)	1.705 (-3)	0.708	0.272
4.9772	4.5133	1.899 (-6)	1.049 (0)	5.828 (2)	1.355 (-3)	0.708	0.272
4.9818	4.6014	1.421 (-6)	9.847 (-1)	5.829 (2)	1.078 (-3)	0.708	0.272
4.9856	4.6875	1.063 (-6)	9.239 (-1)	5.830 (2)	8.597 (-4)	0.708	0.272
4.9885	4.7698	7.983 (-7)	8.675 (-1)	5.830 (2)	6.866 (-4)	0.708	0.272
4.9909	4.8500	5.994 (-7)	8.143 (-1)	5.831 (2)	5.493 (-4)	0.708	0.272

At the center, $\epsilon_{\text{nucl}}/\epsilon_{\text{grav}} = 1.373 \times 10^{-4}$.

$$\int_0^M (L_r)_{\text{grav}}\, dM_r = 583.0\ L_\odot.$$

Table 7-25 Model Interior for 5 $M_\odot$ during the Main-Sequence Phase, Following Point 1 in Fig. 7-25. [Calculated by I. Iben, Jr.; see ref. (331) and note to Table 7-12.]

$$5\ M_\odot, \quad t = 7.82849 \times 10^{13}\ \text{seconds} = 2.48 \times 10^6\ \text{years},$$

$$L = 626.0\ L_\odot, \quad R = 2.422\ R_\odot, \quad T_{\text{eff}} = 18{,}588°\text{K}.$$

$M_r/M_\odot$	$r/R_\odot$	$P \times 10^{-17}$	$T \times 10^{-6}$	$L_r/L_\odot$	ρ	X	He^4
0.0000	0.0000	7.728 (−1)	2.723 (1)	0.000	2.086 (1)	0.696	0.284
0.0037	0.0633	7.610 (−1)	2.708 (1)	1.683 (1)	2.067 (1)	0.696	0.284
0.0058	0.0733	7.570 (−1)	2.702 (1)	2.521 (1)	2.061 (1)	0.696	0.284
0.0094	0.0864	7.510 (−1)	2.694 (1)	3.950 (1)	2.051 (1)	0.696	0.284
0.0153	0.1015	7.429 (−1)	2.683 (1)	6.087 (1)	2.038 (1)	0.696	0.284
0.0248	0.1196	7.316 (−1)	2.667 (1)	9.331 (1)	2.020 (1)	0.696	0.284
0.0401	0.1407	7.164 (−1)	2.646 (1)	1.391 (2)	1.995 (1)	0.696	0.284
0.0653	0.1661	6.953 (−1)	2.616 (1)	2.031 (2)	1.960 (1)	0.696	0.284
0.1068	0.1968	6.663 (−1)	2.574 (1)	2.865 (2)	1.911 (1)	0.696	0.284
0.1763	0.2343	6.263 (−1)	2.514 (1)	3.854 (2)	1.843 (1)	0.696	0.284
0.2984	0.2824	5.692 (−1)	2.423 (1)	4.892 (2)	1.744 (1)	0.696	0.284
0.5436	0.3519	4.800 (−1)	2.270 (1)	5.773 (2)	1.588 (1)	0.696	0.284
0.9747	0.4414	3.638 (−1)	2.040 (1)	6.141 (2)	1.332 (1)	0.696	0.284
1.1674	0.4753	3.219 (−1)	1.946 (1)	6.179 (2)	1.229 (1)	0.707	0.272
1.3651	0.5082	2.835 (−1)	1.856 (1)	6.196 (2)	1.130 (1)	0.707	0.272
1.8296	0.5807	2.078 (−1)	1.672 (1)	6.234 (2)	9.305 (0)	0.708	0.272
2.2110	0.6387	1.578 (−1)	1.536 (1)	6.259 (2)	7.712 (0)	0.708	0.272
2.6011	0.6992	1.156 (−1)	1.405 (1)	6.265 (2)	6.200 (0)	0.708	0.272
2.9881	0.7629	8.145 (−2)	1.278 (1)	6.265 (2)	4.821 (0)	0.708	0.272
3.3615	0.8309	5.492 (−2)	1.155 (1)	6.264 (2)	3.614 (9)	0.708	0.272
3.7116	0.9045	3.518 (−2)	1.035 (1)	6.263 (2)	2.597 (0)	0.708	0.272
3.9373	0.9600	2.489 (−2)	9.523 (0)	6.262 (2)	1.963 (0)	0.708	0.272
4.0872	1.0021	1.905 (−2)	8.942 (0)	6.262 (2)	1.602 (0)	0.708	0.272
4.2262	1.0464	1.432 (−2)	8.370 (0)	6.262 (2)	1.289 (0)	0.708	0.272
4.3539	1.0931	1.056 (−2)	7.805 (0)	6.261 (2)	1.021 (0)	0.708	0.272
4.4636	1.1398	7.758 (−3)	7.277 (0)	6.261 (2)	8.035 (−1)	0.708	0.272
4.5569	1.1864	5.688 (−3)	6.786 (0)	6.261 (2)	6.323 (−1)	0.708	0.272
4.6349	1.2321	4.181 (−3)	6.333 (0)	6.261 (2)	4.974 (−1)	0.708	0.272
4.7006	1.2775	3.068 (−3)	5.910 (0)	6.261 (2)	3.914 (−1)	0.708	0.272
4.7549	1.3220	2.259 (−3)	5.518 (0)	6.260 (2)	3.082 (−1)	0.708	0.272
4.8003	1.3661	1.662 (−3)	5.148 (0)	6.260 (2)	2.431 (−1)	0.708	0.272
4.8375	1.4091	1.227 (−3)	4.802 (0)	6.260 (2)	1.921 (−1)	0.708	0.272
4.8683	1.4514	9.053 (−4)	4.477 (0)	6.260 (2)	1.522 (−1)	0.708	0.272
4.8934	1.4924	6.710 (−4)	4.176 (0)	6.260 (2)	1.207 (−1)	0.708	0.272
4.9140	1.5327	4.970 (−4)	3.894 (0)	6.260 (2)	9.598 (−2)	0.708	0.272
4.9307	1.5715	3.699 (−4)	3.632 (0)	6.260 (2)	7.646 (−2)	0.708	0.272
4.9444	1.6094	2.751 (−4)	3.386 (0)	6.260 (2)	6.105 (−2)	0.708	0.272
4.9553	1.6458	2.056 (−4)	3.158 (0)	6.260 (2)	4.883 (−2)	0.708	0.272
4.9643	1.6813	1.535 (−4)	2.944 (0)	6.260 (2)	3.915 (−2)	0.708	0.272
4.9714	1.7151	1.152 (−4)	2.746 (0)	6.260 (2)	3.144 (−2)	0.708	0.272
4.9772	1.7480	8.635 (−5)	2.561 (0)	6.260 (2)	2.530 (−2)	0.708	0.272
4.9818	1.7793	6.504 (−5)	2.390 (0)	6.260 (2)	2.039 (−2)	0.708	0.272
4.9856	1.8095	4.896 (−5)	2.231 (0)	6.260 (2)	1.646 (−2)	0.708	0.272
4.9885	1.8383	3.702 (−5)	2.086 (0)	6.260 (2)	1.329 (−2)	0.708	0.272
4.9909	1.8660	2.798 (−5)	1.952 (0)	6.260 (2)	1.074 (−2)	0.708	0.272

At the center, $\epsilon_{\text{nucl}}/\epsilon_{\text{grav}} = -5.381 \times 10^3$.

$$\int_0^M (L_r)_{\text{grav}}\, dM_r = -2.215\ L_\odot.$$

Table 7-26   Model Interior for 5 $M_\odot$ during Main-Sequence Phase, Following Point 2 in Fig. 7-25. [Calculated by I. Iben, Jr.; see ref. (331) and note to Table 7-12.]

$$5\ M_\odot, \quad t = 2.10126 \times 10^{15} \text{ seconds} = 6.65 \times 10^7 \text{ years},$$

$$L = 1009.4\ L_\odot, \quad R = 4.331\ R_\odot, \quad T_{\text{eff}} = 15{,}664°\text{K}.$$

$M_r/M_\odot$	$r/R_\odot$	$P \times 10^{-17}$	$T \times 10^{-6}$	$L_r/L_\odot$	ρ	X	He^4
0.000	0.000	6.982 (−1)	3.296 (1)	0.000	3.080 (1)	0.040	0.936
0.002	0.043	6.864 (−1)	3.276 (1)	2.751 (1)	3.048 (1)	0.040	0.936
0.002	0.047	6.839 (−1)	3.271 (1)	3.568 (1)	3.042 (1)	0.040	0.936
0.003	0.052	6.810 (−1)	3.266 (1)	4.618 (1)	3.034 (1)	0.040	0.936
0.005	0.060	6.756 (−1)	3.257 (1)	6.759 (1)	3.020 (1)	0.040	0.936
0.007	0.069	6.682 (−1)	3.244 (1)	9.982 (1)	3.000 (1)	0.040	0.936
0.011	0.081	6.569 (−1)	3.224 (1)	1.530 (2)	2.969 (1)	0.040	0.936
0.019	0.096	6.417 (−1)	3.197 (1)	2.282 (2)	2.928 (1)	0.040	0.936
0.030	0.113	6.207 (−1)	3.159 (1)	3.332 (2)	2.870 (1)	0.040	0.936
0.049	0.133	5.927 (−1)	3.107 (1)	4.653 (2)	2.791 (1)	0.040	0.936
0.079	0.158	5.550 (−1)	3.034 (1)	6.198 (2)	2.684 (1)	0.040	0.936
0.128	0.187	5.049 (−1)	2.931 (1)	7.755 (2)	2.537 (1)	0.040	0.936
0.298	0.257	3.779 (−1)	2.637 (1)	9.603 (2)	2.174 (1)	0.040	0.936
0.398	0.289	3.220 (−1)	2.485 (1)	9.850 (2)	1.924 (1)	0.040	0.936
0.478	0.312	2.835 (−1)	2.373 (1)	9.929 (2)	1.705 (1)	0.070	0.907
0.521	0.324	2.648 (−1)	2.316 (1)	9.968 (2)	1.524 (1)	0.124	0.853
0.592	0.346	2.367 (−1)	2.226 (1)	1.002 (3)	1.281 (1)	0.197	0.780
0.660	0.367	2.129 (−1)	2.146 (1)	1.005 (3)	1.100 (1)	0.263	0.715
0.722	0.387	1.940 (−1)	2.079 (1)	1.007 (3)	9.739 (0)	0.316	0.663
0.771	0.403	1.804 (−1)	2.028 (1)	1.008 (3)	8.880 (0)	0.362	0.617
0.816	0.418	1.693 (−1)	1.984 (1)	1.009 (3)	8.038 (0)	0.416	0.564
0.873	0.437	1.564 (−1)	1.931 (1)	1.009 (3)	7.354 (0)	0.455	0.524
0.924	0.455	1.460 (−1)	1.886 (1)	1.009 (3)	6.739 (0)	0.502	0.478
0.975	0.472	1.366 (−1)	1.844 (1)	1.010 (3)	6.183 (0)	0.549	0.431
1.065	0.503	1.219 (−1)	1.773 (1)	1.010 (3)	5.491 (0)	0.610	0.370
1.130	0.526	1.127 (−1)	1.726 (1)	1.010 (3)	4.909 (0)	0.672	0.308
1.264	0.571	9.682 (−2)	1.638 (1)	1.010 (3)	4.417 (0)	0.705	0.275
1.610	0.680	6.760 (−2)	1.456 (1)	1.010 (3)	3.480 (0)	0.707	0.273
1.980	0.788	4.692 (−2)	1.302 (1)	1.010 (3)	2.709 (0)	0.707	0.272
2.367	0.899	3.194 (−2)	1.165 (1)	1.010 (3)	2.065 (0)	0.707	0.272

Table 7-26 (*continued*)

$M_r/M_\odot$	$r/R_\odot$	$P \times 10^{-17}$	$T \times 10^{-6}$	$L_r/L_\odot$	ρ	X	He^4
2.757	1.015	2.115 (−2)	1.042 (1)	1.010 (3)	1.535 (0)	0.708	0.272
3.140	1.138	1.353 (−2)	9.278 (0)	1.010 (3)	1.107 (0)	0.708	0.272
3.469	1.257	8.736 (−3)	8.317 (0)	1.010 (3)	7.843 (−1)	0.708	0.272
3.644	1.327	6.730 (−3)	7.805 (0)	1.010 (3)	6.447 (−1)	0.708	0.272
3.810	1.401	5.118 (−3)	7.308 (0)	1.010 (3)	5.240 (−1)	0.708	0.272
3.968	1.479	3.833 (−3)	6.824 (0)	1.010 (3)	4.209 (−1)	0.708	0.272
4.116	1.561	2.827 (−3)	6.354 (0)	1.010 (3)	3.337 (−1)	0.708	0.272
4.253	1.648	2.046 (−3)	5.892 (0)	1.009 (3)	2.608 (−1)	0.708	0.272
4.377	1.739	1.459 (−3)	5.447 (0)	1.009 (3)	2.012 (−1)	0.708	0.272
4.484	1.830	1.039 (−3)	5.030 (0)	1.009 (3)	1.552 (−1)	0.708	0.272
4.573	1.920	7.437 (−4)	4.647 (0)	1.009 (3)	1.201 (−1)	0.708	0.272
4.649	2.010	5.326 (−4)	4.292 (0)	1.009 (3)	9.312 (−2)	0.708	0.272
4.712	2.097	3.835 (−4)	3.968 (0)	1.009 (3)	7.242 (−2)	0.708	0.272
4.765	2.184	2.764 (−4)	3.668 (0)	1.009 (3)	5.648 (−2)	0.708	0.272
4.808	2.268	2.003 (−4)	3.394 (0)	1.009 (3)	4.418 (−2)	0.708	0.272
4.844	2.351	1.453 (−4)	3.139 (0)	1.009 (3)	3.465 (−2)	0.708	0.272
4.874	2.431	1.059 (−4)	2.906 (0)	1.009 (3)	2.726 (−2)	0.708	0.272
4.898	2.510	7.732 (−5)	2.691 (0)	1.009 (3)	2.151 (−2)	0.708	0.272
4.918	2.586	5.675 (−5)	2.494 (0)	1.009 (3)	1.701 (−2)	0.708	0.272
4.934	2.661	4.166 (−5)	2.312 (0)	1.009 (3)	1.348 (−2)	0.708	0.272
4.947	2.732	3.075 (−5)	2.147 (0)	1.009 (3)	1.070 (−2)	0.708	0.272
4.957	2.802	2.269 (−5)	1.996 (0)	1.009 (3)	8.501 (−3)	0.708	0.272
4.966	2.869	1.683 (−5)	1.859 (0)	1.009 (3)	6.759 (−3)	0.708	0.272
4.973	2.934	1.248 (−5)	1.732 (0)	1.009 (3)	5.384 (−3)	0.708	0.272
4.978	2.997	9.305 (−6)	1.616 (0)	1.009 (3)	4.295 (−3)	0.708	0.272
4.983	3.057	6.933 (−6)	1.508 (0)	1.009 (3)	3.431 (−3)	0.708	0.272
4.986	3.115	5.191 (−6)	1.410 (0)	1.009 (3)	2.743 (−3)	0.708	0.272
4.989	3.171	3.885 (−6)	1.320 (0)	1.009 (3)	2.194 (−3)	0.708	0.272

At the center, $\epsilon_{\text{nuol}}/\epsilon_{\text{grav}} = -7.107 \times 10^5$.

$$\int_0^M (L_r)_{\text{grav}} \, dM_r = -1.058 \, L_\odot.$$

Table 7-27   Model Interior for 5 $M_\odot$ Following Main-Sequence Phase, Near Point 4 in Fig. 7-25. [Calculated by I. Iben, Jr.; see ref. (331) and note to Table 7-12.]

5 $M_\odot$, $t = 2.19982 \times 10^{15}$ seconds = 6.96×10^7 years,

$L = 1299.3\,L_\odot$, $R = 5.819\,R_\odot$, $T_{\text{eff}} = 14{,}395°K$.

$M_r/M_\odot$	$r/R_\odot$	$P \times 10^{-17}$	$T \times 10^{-6}$	$L_r/L_\odot$	ρ	X	He^4
0.000	0.000	3.343 (1)	3.995 (1)	0.000	1.306 (3)	0.000	0.976
0.001	0.010	3.225 (1)	3.974 (1)	4.437 ($-$2)	1.269 (3)	0.000	0.976
0.002	0.014	3.135 (1)	3.958 (1)	1.065 ($-$1)	1.241 (3)	0.000	0.976
0.006	0.019	2.963 (1)	3.926 (1)	2.725 ($-$1)	1.187 (3)	0.000	0.976
0.014	0.026	2.685 (1)	3.873 (1)	6.612 ($-$1)	1.100 (3)	0.000	0.976
0.038	0.037	2.139 (1)	3.760 (1)	1.869 (0)	9.211 (2)	0.000	0.976
0.083	0.051	1.526 (1)	3.618 (1)	4.179 (0)	6.840 (2)	0.000	0.976
0.123	0.061	1.152 (1)	3.521 (1)	6.381 (0)	5.332 (2)	0.000	0.976
0.164	0.071	8.780 (0)	3.445 (1)	8.648 (0)	4.175 (2)	0.000	0.976
0.215	0.083	6.243 (0)	3.371 (1)	1.155 (1)	3.063 (2)	0.000	0.976
0.268	0.095	4.384 (0)	3.316 (1)	1.449 (1)	2.172 (2)	0.000	0.976
0.329	0.111	2.937 (0)	3.273 (1)	1.766 (1)	1.503 (2)	0.000	0.976
0.382	0.126	2.059 (0)	3.247 (1)	2.117 (1)	1.042 (2)	0.000	0.976
0.445	0.146	1.347 (0)	3.222 (1)	4.229 (1)	6.853 (1)	0.001	0.975
0.480	0.158	1.070 (0)	3.202 (1)	1.029 (2)	5.353 (1)	0.006	0.970
0.506	0.167	9.094 ($-$1)	3.175 (1)	2.172 (2)	4.458 (1)	0.018	0.959
0.536	0.179	7.523 ($-$1)	3.122 (1)	4.424 (2)	3.612 (1)	0.039	0.937
0.568	0.193	6.201 ($-$1)	3.038 (1)	7.314 (2)	2.884 (1)	0.081	0.896
0.598	0.207	5.212 ($-$1)	2.938 (1)	9.804 (2)	2.317 (1)	0.131	0.846
0.628	0.222	4.426 ($-$1)	2.830 (1)	1.148 (3)	1.919 (1)	0.178	0.800
0.660	0.238	3.762 ($-$1)	2.714 (1)	1.253 (3)	1.612 (1)	0.231	0.747
0.705	0.263	3.056 ($-$1)	2.563 (1)	1.321 (3)	1.289 (1)	0.283	0.695
0.747	0.285	2.574 ($-$1)	2.440 (1)	1.345 (3)	1.081 (1)	0.332	0.646
0.805	0.317	2.078 ($-$1)	2.291 (1)	1.358 (3)	8.844 (0)	0.388	0.591
0.850	0.341	1.790 ($-$1)	2.190 (1)	1.361 (3)	7.535 (0)	0.437	0.543
0.902	0.370	1.531 ($-$1)	2.089 (1)	1.362 (3)	6.460 (0)	0.481	0.498
0.956	0.398	1.327 ($-$1)	1.999 (1)	1.362 (3)	5.600 (0)	0.529	0.451
1.031	0.438	1.107 ($-$1)	1.889 (1)	1.360 (3)	4.756 (0)	0.580	0.400
1.108	0.478	9.375 ($-$2)	1.792 (1)	1.359 (3)	4.001 (0)	0.650	0.330
1.148	0.499	8.675 ($-$2)	1.748 (1)	1.358 (3)	3.647 (0)	0.698	0.282

Table 7-27 (*continued*)

$M_r/M_\odot$	$r/R_\odot$	$P \times 10^{-17}$	$T \times 10^{-6}$	$L_r/L_\odot$	ρ	X	He⁴
1.331	0.589	6.323 (−2)	1.578 (1)	1.353 (3)	2.962 (0)	0.705	0.274
1.610	0.711	4.246 (−2)	1.392 (1)	1.347 (3)	2.294 (0)	0.706	0.273
1.980	0.861	2.664 (−2)	1.211 (1)	1.339 (3)	1.657 (0)	0.707	0.272
2.367	1.013	1.677 (−2)	1.062 (1)	1.331 (3)	1.191 (0)	0.707	0.272
2.757	1.172	1.040 (−2)	9.332 (0)	1.324 (3)	8.430 (−1)	0.708	0.272
3.026	1.289	7.335 (−3)	8.523 (0)	1.320 (3)	6.398 (−1)	0.708	0.272
3.214	1.376	5.660 (−3)	7.979 (0)	1.317 (3)	5.278 (−1)	0.708	0.272
3.398	1.468	4.326 (−3)	7.462 (0)	1.314 (3)	4.318 (−1)	0.708	0.272
3.575	1.563	3.269 (−3)	6.966 (0)	1.312 (3)	3.499 (−1)	0.708	0.272
3.745	1.663	2.442 (−3)	6.491 (0)	1.310 (3)	2.807 (−1)	0.708	0.272
3.906	1.768	1.800 (−3)	6.032 (0)	1.308 (3)	2.229 (−1)	0.708	0.272
4.058	1.880	1.308 (−3)	5.590 (0)	1.306 (3)	1.749 (−1)	0.708	0.272
4.199	1.997	9.351 (−4)	5.158 (0)	1.305 (3)	1.357 (−1)	0.708	0.272
4.329	2.122	6.577 (−4)	4.738 (0)	1.303 (3)	1.039 (−1)	0.708	0.272
4.443	2.249	4.598 (−4)	4.345 (0)	1.302 (3)	7.928 (−2)	0.708	0.272
4.539	2.374	3.238 (−4)	3.990 (0)	1.302 (3)	6.069 (−2)	0.708	0.272
4.621	2.498	2.284 (−4)	3.665 (0)	1.301 (3)	4.664 (−2)	0.708	0.272
4.688	2.619	1.623 (−4)	3.371 (0)	1.301 (3)	3.597 (−2)	0.708	0.272
4.745	2.740	1.155 (−4)	3.100 (0)	1.300 (3)	2.784 (−2)	0.708	0.272
4.792	2.856	8.285 (−5)	2.856 (0)	1.300 (3)	2.164 (−2)	0.708	0.272
4.830	2.971	5.953 (−5)	2.632 (0)	1.300 (3)	1.687 (−2)	0.708	0.272
4.863	3.084	4.288 (−5)	2.427 (0)	1.300 (3)	1.319 (−2)	0.708	0.272
4.889	3.193	3.107 (−5)	2.242 (0)	1.300 (3)	1.034 (−2)	0.708	0.272
4.910	3.301	2.254 (−5)	2.073 (0)	1.300 (3)	8.114 (−3)	0.708	0.272
4.928	3.404	1.645 (−5)	1.922 (0)	1.299 (3)	6.375 (−3)	0.708	0.272
4.942	3.506	1.201 (−5)	1.784 (0)	1.299 (3)	5.018 (−3)	0.708	0.272
4.953	3.603	8.815 (−6)	1.657 (0)	1.299 (3)	3.958 (−3)	0.708	0.272
4.963	3.699	6.472 (−6)	1.541 (0)	1.299 (3)	3.128 (−3)	0.708	0.272
4.970	3.791	4.776 (−6)	1.435 (0)	1.299 (3)	2.475 (−3)	0.708	0.272
4.976	3.881	3.525 (−6)	1.338 (0)	1.229 (3)	1.959 (−3)	0.708	0.272
4.981	3.967	2.615 (−6)	1.252 (0)	1.299 (3)	1.551 (−3)	0.708	0.272
4.985	4.051	1.939 (−6)	1.172 (0)	1.299 (3)	1.229 (−3)	0.708	0.272
4.988	4.132	1.446 (−6)	1.099 (0)	1.299 (3)	9.751 (−4)	0.708	0.272
4.990	4.211	1.078 (−6)	1.029 (0)	1.299 (3)	7.755 (−4)	0.708	0.272

At the center, $\epsilon_{\text{nucl}}/\epsilon_{\text{grav}} = 0$.

$$\int_0^M (L_r)_{\text{grav}} \, dM_r = -45.37 \, L_\odot.$$

Table 7-28   Model Interior for 5 $M_\odot$ during Subgiant Phase, at Point 5 in Fig. 7-25. [Calculated by I. Iben, Jr.; see ref. (331) and note to Table 7-12.]

$$5\ M_\odot, \quad t = 2.22282 \times 10^{15}\ \text{seconds} = 7.03 \times 10^7\ \text{years},$$

$$L = 698.5\ L_\odot, \quad R = 43.61\ R_\odot, \quad T_{\text{eff}} = 4502°\text{K}.$$

$M_r/M_\odot$	$r/R_\odot$	$P \times 10^{-17}$	$T \times 10^{-6}$	$L_r/L_\odot$	ρ	X	He^4
0.0000	0.000	5.447 (2)	1.033 (2)	0.000	8.064 (3)	0.000	0.975
0.0016	6.551 (−3)	5.259 (2)	1.019 (2)	1.236 (1)	7.913 (3)	0.000	0.975
0.0122	1.311 (−2)	4.730 (2)	9.775 (1)	4.920 (1)	7.493 (3)	0.000	0.975
0.0911	2.701 (−2)	2.977 (2)	8.144 (1)	5.876 (1)	5.853 (3)	0.000	0.975
0.1613	3.404 (−2)	2.075 (2)	7.062 (1)	4.779 (1)	4.566 (3)	0.000	0.975
0.1803	3.572 (−2)	1.878 (2)	6.788 (1)	4.507 (1)	4.245 (3)	0.000	0.975
0.1813	3.580 (−2)	1.868 (2)	6.774 (1)	4.493 (1)	4.232 (3)	0.000	0.976
0.2040	3.774 (−2)	1.654 (2)	6.472 (1)	4.190 (1)	3.959 (3)	0.000	0.976
0.2516	4.169 (−2)	1.262 (2)	5.938 (1)	3.725 (1)	3.440 (3)	0.000	0.976
0.3285	4.822 (−2)	7.681 (1)	5.247 (1)	3.581 (1)	2.359 (3)	0.000	0.976
0.4063	5.577 (−2)	4.116 (1)	4.628 (1)	4.022 (1)	1.480 (3)	0.000	0.976
0.4644	6.285 (−2)	2.253 (1)	4.184 (1)	4.560 (1)	8.913 (2)	0.000	0.976
0.5108	7.036 (−2)	1.204 (1)	3.854 (1)	5.074 (1)	5.325 (2)	0.000	0.976
0.5409	7.697 (−2)	7.154 (0)	3.670 (1)	5.452 (1)	3.254 (2)	0.000	0.976
0.5737	8.728 (−2)	3.451 (0)	3.514 (1)	5.920 (1)	1.689 (2)	0.000	0.976
0.5947	9.722 (−2)	1.896 (0)	3.438 (1)	9.804 (1)	9.135 (1)	0.003	0.973
0.6053	1.040 (−1)	1.338 (0)	3.364 (1)	3.176 (2)	6.167 (1)	0.030	0.947
0.6090	1.068 (−1)	1.172 (0)	3.314 (1)	4.590 (2)	5.232 (1)	0.049	0.927
0.6128	1.100 (−1)	1.023 (0)	3.249 (1)	6.038 (2)	4.493 (1)	0.072	0.905
0.6188	1.157 (−1)	8.167 (−1)	3.117 (1)	7.828 (2)	3.599 (1)	0.107	0.870
0.6308	1.292 (−1)	5.115 (−1)	2.810 (1)	9.212 (2)	2.391 (1)	0.157	0.821
0.6479	1.532 (−1)	2.567 (−1)	2.387 (1)	9.458 (2)	1.353 (1)	0.204	0.774
0.6629	1.794 (−1)	1.378 (−1)	2.058 (1)	9.481 (2)	8.027 (0)	0.226	0.752
0.6761	2.067 (−1)	7.958 (−2)	1.806 (1)	9.490 (2)	5.085 (0)	0.243	0.735
0.6864	2.314 (−1)	5.168 (−2)	1.631 (1)	9.495 (2)	3.594 (0)	0.258	0.721
0.7009	2.711 (−1)	2.842 (−2)	1.417 (1)	9.497 (2)	2.306 (0)	0.276	0.702
0.7216	3.397 (−1)	1.239 (−2)	1.166 (1)	9.495 (2)	1.183 (0)	0.300	0.678
0.7424	4.237 (−1)	5.658 (−3)	9.715 (0)	9.485 (2)	6.266 (−1)	0.326	0.653
0.7631	5.238 (−1)	2.754 (−3)	8.216 (0)	9.470 (2)	3.483 (−1)	0.349	0.630
0.7838	6.384 (−1)	1.445 (−3)	7.071 (0)	9.450 (2)	2.059 (−1)	0.372	0.606

Table 7-28 (*continued*)

$M_r/M_\odot$	$r/R_\odot$	$P \times 10^{-17}$	$T \times 10^{-6}$	$L_r/L_\odot$	ρ	X	He⁴
0.8045	7.663 (−1)	8.200 (−4)	6.191 (0)	9.426 (2)	1.300 (−1)	0.388	0.591
0.8328	9.579 (−1)	4.264 (−4)	5.293 (0)	9.391 (2)	7.663 (−2)	0.424	0.555
0.8612	1.161 (0)	2.503 (−4)	4.633 (0)	9.356 (2)	4.987 (−2)	0.445	0.534
0.9023	1.463 (0)	1.358 (−4)	3.960 (0)	9.306 (2)	3.068 (−2)	0.481	0.498
0.9556	1.859 (0)	7.514 (−5)	3.383 (0)	9.243 (2)	1.881 (−2)	0.529	0.451
1.0196	2.326 (0)	4.463 (−5)	2.931 (0)	9.169 (2)	1.300 (−2)	0.565	0.415
1.0984	2.880 (0)	2.785 (−5)	2.563 (0)	9.081 (2)	8.402 (−3)	0.637	0.343
1.1378	3.150 (0)	2.304 (−5)	2.425 (0)	9.038 (2)	6.963 (−3)	0.690	0.290
1.2665	3.981 (0)	1.423 (−5)	2.102 (0)	8.899 (2)	5.056 (−3)	0.704	0.275
1.4335	4.939 (0)	9.006 (−6)	1.838 (0)	8.728 (2)	3.639 (−3)	0.706	0.274
1.7549	6.579 (0)	4.672 (−6)	1.516 (0)	8.432 (2)	2.339 (−3)	0.707	0.273
2.1338	8.379 (0)	2.498 (−6)	1.273 (0)	8.119 (2)	1.487 (−3)	0.707	0.272
2.5229	1.023 (1)	1.389 (−6)	1.091 (0)	7.824 (2)	9.634 (−4)	0.708	0.272
2.9115	1.219 (1)	7.770 (−7)	9.410 (−1)	7.569 (2)	6.255 (−4)	0.708	0.272
3.2883	1.430 (1)	4.298 (−7)	8.118 (−1)	7.359 (2)	4.017 (−4)	0.708	0.272
3.6439	1.661 (1)	2.319 (−7)	6.981 (−1)	7.193 (2)	2.527 (−4)	0.708	0.272
3.9682	1.914 (1)	1.211 (−7)	5.968 (−1)	7.070 (2)	1.548 (−4)	0.708	0.272
4.2530	2.194 (1)	6.085 (−8)	5.055 (−1)	6.986 (2)	9.203 (−5)	0.708	0.272
4.4838	2.488 (1)	3.009 (−8)	4.229 (−1)	6.944 (2)	5.456 (−5)	0.708	0.272
4.6492	2.761 (1)	1.559 (−8)	*3.436 (−1)*	6.942 (2)	3.453 (−5)	0.708	0.272
4.7648	2.998 (1)	8.412 (−9)	*2.721 (−1)*	6.961 (2)	2.363 (−5)	0.708	0.272
4.8440	3.200 (1)	4.686 (−9)	*2.173 (−1)*	6.972 (2)	1.652 (−5)	0.708	0.272
4.8977	3.374 (1)	2.662 (−9)	*1.745 (−1)*	6.978 (2)	1.171 (−5)	0.708	0.272
4.9336	3.521 (1)	1.536 (−9)	*1.408 (−1)*	6.982 (2)	8.389 (−6)	0.708	0.272
4.9572	3.645 (1)	8.976 (−10)	*1.140 (−1)*	6.983 (2)	6.058 (−6)	0.708	0.272
4.9727	3.751 (1)	5.291 (−10)	9.282 (−2)	6.984 (2)	4.395 (−6)	0.708	0.272
4.9826	3.840 (1)	3.140 (−10)	7.646 (−2)	6.985 (2)	3.182 (−6)	0.708	0.272
4.9890	3.916 (1)	1.874 (−10)	6.485 (−2)	6.985 (2)	2.265 (−6)	0.708	0.272

At the center, $\epsilon_{\text{nucl}}/\epsilon_{\text{grav}} = -45.42$.

$$\int_0^M (L_r)_{\text{grav}} \, dM_r = -254.1 \, L_\odot.$$

Table 7-29   Model Interior for 5 $M_\odot$ during Giant Phase, Just Preceding Point 6 in Fig. 7-25.
[Calculated by I. Iben, Jr.; see ref. (331) and note to Table 7-12.]

5 $M_\odot$, $t = 2.23797 \times 10^{15}$ seconds $= 7.08 \times 10^7$ years,

$L = 1231.5 L_\odot$, $R = 73.80 R_\odot$, $T_{eff} = 3988°K$.

$M_r/M_\odot$	$r/R_\odot$	$P \times 10^{-17}$	$T \times 10^{-6}$	$L_r/L_\odot$	ρ	X	He^4
0.0000	0.000	1.038 (3)	*1.240* (2)	0.000	1.269 (4)	0.000	0.968
0.0026	6.635 (−3)	9.901 (2)	*1.217* (2)	2.102 (1)	1.238 (4)	0.000	0.968
0.0192	1.317 (−2)	8.623 (2)	*1.153* (2)	6.000 (1)	1.148 (4)	0.000	0.968
0.1386	2.733 (−2)	4.623 (2)	*9.018* (1)	5.771 (1)	8.233 (3)	0.000	0.968
0.1734	3.002 (−2)	3.904 (2)	*8.435* (1)	5.475 (1)	7.126 (3)	0.000	0.968
0.1767	3.026 (−2)	3.841 (2)	*8.381* (1)	5.447 (1)	6.977 (3)	0.000	0.968
0.1805	3.054 (−2)	3.771 (2)	*8.320* (1)	5.417 (1)	6.889 (3)	0.000	0.971
0.1806	3.055 (−2)	3.768 (2)	8.318 (1)	5.416 (1)	6.880 (3)	0.000	0.975
0.1813	3.060 (−2)	3.755 (2)	8.306 (1)	5.411 (1)	6.865 (3)	0.000	0.976
0.2129	3.285 (−2)	3.205 (2)	7.825 (1)	5.204 (1)	6.294 (3)	0.000	0.976
0.3004	3.886 (−2)	1.981 (2)	6.718 (1)	4.839 (1)	4.820 (3)	0.000	0.976
0.4063	4.665 (−2)	9.581 (1)	5.579 (1)	4.901 (1)	2.791 (3)	0.000	0.976
0.4644	5.181 (−2)	5.678 (1)	4.977 (1)	5.088 (1)	1.847 (3)	0.000	0.976
0.5208	5.819 (−2)	2.904 (1)	4.397 (1)	5.328 (1)	1.103 (3)	0.000	0.976
0.5610	6.451 (−2)	1.504 (1)	4.008 (1)	5.531 (1)	6.308 (2)	0.000	0.976
0.5917	7.162 (−2)	7.481 (0)	3.757 (1)	5.720 (1)	3.425 (2)	0.000	0.976
0.6128	7.907 (−2)	3.881 (0)	3.627 (1)	5.889 (1)	1.800 (2)	0.000	0.976
0.6278	8.716 (−2)	2.093 (0)	3.560 (1)	6.583 (1)	9.997 (1)	0.001	0.976
0.6361	9.351 (−2)	1.382 (0)	3.511 (1)	2.286 (2)	6.105 (1)	0.024	0.953
0.6395	9.683 (−2)	1.145 (0)	3.460 (1)	4.712 (2)	4.762 (1)	0.063	0.913
0.6419	9.953 (−2)	9.977 (−1)	3.402 (1)	6.863 (2)	4.004 (1)	0.101	0.876
0.6449	1.034 (−1)	8.337 (−1)	3.302 (1)	9.250 (2)	3.286 (1)	0.145	0.832
0.6509	1.127 (−1)	5.745 (−1)	3.051 (1)	1.161 (3)	2.306 (1)	0.197	0.781
0.6584	1.264 (−1)	3.546 (−1)	2.723 (1)	1.220 (3)	1.547 (1)	0.218	0.759
0.6659	1.425 (−1)	2.155 (−1)	2.417 (1)	1.227 (3)	1.045 (1)	0.230	0.748
0.6740	1.627 (−1)	1.241 (−1)	2.118 (1)	1.228 (3)	6.890 (0)	0.240	0.737
0.6844	1.943 (−1)	5.960 (−2)	1.780 (1)	1.229 (3)	3.877 (0)	0.255	0.723
0.6947	2.339 (−1)	2.787 (−2)	1.488 (1)	1.229 (3)	2.136 (0)	0.268	0.710
0.7051	2.837 (−1)	1.273 (−2)	1.239 (1)	1.230 (3)	1.154 (0)	0.281	0.697
0.7154	3.464 (−1)	5.717 (−3)	1.029 (1)	1.230 (3)	6.143 (−1)	0.293	0.685

Table 7-29 (*continued*)

$M_r/M_\odot$	$r/R_\odot$	$P \times 10^{-17}$	$T \times 10^{-6}$	$L_r/L_\odot$	ρ	X	He^4
0.7258	4.254 (−1)	2.551 (−3)	8.548 (0)	1.230 (3)	3.248 (−1)	0.305	0.673
0.7361	5.240 (−1)	1.148 (−3)	7.118 (0)	1.231 (3)	1.723 (−1)	0.317	0.661
0.7465	6.453 (−1)	5.304 (−4)	5.960 (0)	1.231 (3)	9.299 (−2)	0.332	0.647
0.7569	7.910 (−1)	2.563 (−4)	5.022 (0)	1.231 (3)	5.209 (−2)	0.345	0.633
0.7672	9.596 (−1)	1.312 (−4)	4.267 (0)	1.231 (3)	3.096 (−2)	0.352	0.627
0.7776	1.150 (0)	7.126 (−5)	3.671 (0)	1.231 (3)	1.922 (−2)	0.363	0.615
0.7879	1.360 (0)	4.112 (−5)	3.199 (0)	1.231 (3)	1.247 (−2)	0.378	0.600
0.8004	1.634 (0)	2.295 (−5)	2.760 (0)	1.231 (3)	8.274 (−3)	0.386	0.593
0.8158	2.003 (0)	1.230 (−5)	2.354 (0)	1.231 (3)	4.918 (−3)	0.411	0.568
0.8328	2.436 (0)	6.953 (−6)	2.038 (0)	1.231 (3)	3.265 (−3)	0.424	0.555
0.8612	3.190 (0)	3.305 (−6)	1.692 (0)	1.231 (3)	1.797 (−3)	0.445	0.534
0.8895	3.960 (0)	1.893 (−6)	1.472 (0)	1.231 (3)	1.145 (−3)	0.465	0.514
0.9237	4.889 (0)	1.144 (−6)	1.299 (0)	1.231 (3)	7.568 (−4)	0.501	0.479
0.9747	6.233 (0)	6.715 (−7)	1.139 (0)	1.232 (3)	4.906 (−4)	0.548	0.431
1.0653	8.432 (0)	3.691 (−7)	9.735 (−1)	1.232 (3)	3.018 (−4)	0.609	0.371
1.1304	9.885 (0)	2.766 (−7)	8.981 (−1)	1.232 (3)	2.230 (−4)	0.672	0.308
1.2351	1.202 (1)	1.984 (−7)	8.141 (−1)	1.232 (3)	1.828 (−4)	0.703	0.276
1.3985	1.483 (1)	1.381 (−7)	7.238 (−1)	1.232 (3)	1.366 (−4)	0.707	0.273
1.6956	1.903 (1)	8.705 (−8)	*6.140 (−1)*	1.232 (3)	1.069 (−4)	0.708	0.272
2.1434	2.428 (1)	5.137 (−8)	*5.068 (−1)*	1.232 (3)	7.599 (−5)	0.708	0.272
2.6791	2.984 (1)	2.945 (−8)	*4.124 (−1)*	1.232 (3)	5.413 (−5)	0.708	0.272
3.4337	3.753 (1)	1.295 (−8)	*3.024 (−1)*	1.231 (3)	3.329 (−5)	0.708	0.272
3.9682	4.354 (1)	6.264 (−9)	*2.287 (−1)*	1.231 (3)	2.088 (−5)	0.708	0.272
4.2530	4.726 (1)	3.776 (−9)	*1.879 (−1)*	1.231 (3)	1.541 (−5)	0.708	0.272
4.4838	5.081 (1)	2.200 (−9)	*1.521 (−1)*	1.231 (3)	1.112 (−5)	0.708	0.272
4.6492	5.389 (1)	1.293 (−9)	*1.234 (−1)*	1.231 (3)	8.063 (−6)	0.708	0.272
4.7648	5.655 (1)	7.653 (−10)	*1.005 (−1)*	1.231 (3)	5.869 (−6)	0.708	0.272
4.8440	5.884 (1)	4.561 (−10)	*8.254 (−1)*	1.231 (3)	4.274 (−6)	0.708	0.272
4.8977	6.083 (1)	2.721 (−10)	*6.926 (−1)*	1.231 (3)	3.069 (−6)	0.708	0.272

At the center, $\epsilon_{\text{nucl}}/\epsilon_{\text{grav}} = -94.10$.

$$\int_0^M (L)_{\text{grav}} \, dM_r = -4.524 \, L_\odot.$$

Table 7-30 Model Interior for 5 $M_\odot$ during Giant Phase, at Point 9' in Fig. 7-25. [Calculated by I. Iben, Jr.; see ref. (331) and note to Table 7-12.]

$$5\ M_\odot,\quad t = 2.69398 \times 10^{15}\ \text{seconds} = 8.53 \times 10^7\ \text{years},$$
$$L = 1854.6\ L_\odot,\quad R = 20.94\ R_\odot,\quad T_{\text{eff}} = 8294°\text{K}.$$

$M_r/M_\odot$	$r/R_\odot$	$P \times 10^{-17}$	$T \times 10^{-6}$	$L_r/L_\odot$	ρ	X	He^4
0.0000	0.000	5.427 (2)	1.540 (2)	0.000	6.654 (3)	0.000	0.213
0.0026	8.216 (−3)	5.227 (2)	1.519 (2)	5.809 (1)	6.512 (3)	0.000	0.213
0.0137	1.447 (−2)	4.828 (2)	1.475 (2)	2.033 (2)	6.252 (3)	0.000	0.213
0.0630	2.472 (−2)	3.856 (2)	1.356 (2)	3.853 (2)	5.494 (3)	0.000	0.213
0.2074	3.905 (−2)	2.302 (2)	1.116 (2)	4.218 (2)	4.125 (3)	0.000	0.213
0.2725	4.389 (−2)	1.829 (2)	1.022 (2)	4.219 (2)	3.464 (3)	0.000	0.213
0.2895	4.509 (−2)	1.720 (2)	9.982 (1)	4.219 (2)	3.298 (3)	0.000	0.213
0.2904	4.515 (−2)	1.714 (2)	9.970 (1)	4.219 (2)	3.259 (3)	0.000	0.283
0.2908	4.519 (−2)	1.711 (2)	9.964 (1)	4.219 (2)	2.996 (3)	0.000	0.581
0.2929	4.535 (−2)	1.699 (2)	9.935 (1)	4.219 (2)	2.775 (3)	0.000	0.866
0.3369	4.899 (−2)	1.447 (2)	9.361 (1)	4.219 (2)	2.445 (3)	0.000	0.972
0.3563	5.054 (−2)	1.349 (2)	9.128 (1)	4.223 (2)	2.330 (3)	0.000	0.973
0.3685	5.149 (−2)	1.290 (2)	8.988 (1)	4.227 (2)	2.265 (3)	0.000	0.974
0.3883	5.304 (−2)	1.200 (2)	8.765 (1)	4.233 (2)	2.166 (3)	0.000	0.975
0.4454	5.742 (−2)	9.705 (1)	8.166 (1)	4.237 (2)	1.920 (3)	0.000	0.976
0.6038	6.967 (−2)	5.066 (1)	6.710 (1)	4.234 (2)	1.243 (3)	0.000	0.976
0.7180	7.957 (−2)	2.853 (1)	5.748 (1)	4.232 (2)	8.174 (2)	0.000	0.976
0.8109	8.924 (−2)	1.581 (1)	4.980 (1)	4.232 (2)	5.344 (2)	0.000	0.976
0.8817	9.859 (−2)	8.799 (0)	4.392 (1)	4.234 (2)	3.369 (2)	0.000	0.976
0.9301	1.069 (−1)	5.234 (0)	3.996 (1)	4.235 (2)	2.196 (2)	0.000	0.976
0.9749	1.174 (−1)	2.775 (0)	3.654 (1)	4.239 (2)	1.294 (2)	0.000	0.976
1.0013	1.260 (−1)	1.694 (0)	3.476 (1)	4.242 (2)	8.121 (1)	0.000	0.976
1.0220	1.353 (−1)	1.043 (0)	3.358 (1)	4.703 (2)	4.877 (1)	0.013	0.963
1.0266	1.379 (−1)	9.229 (−1)	3.331 (1)	5.639 (2)	4.084 (1)	0.047	0.929
1.0287	1.393 (−1)	8.703 (−1)	3.317 (1)	6.445 (2)	3.652 (1)	0.080	0.897
1.0304	1.405 (−1)	8.281 (−1)	3.303 (1)	7.332 (2)	3.307 (1)	0.118	0.859
1.0322	1.418 (−1)	7.872 (−1)	3.287 (1)	8.388 (2)	2.971 (1)	0.162	0.815
1.0339	1.433 (−1)	7.479 (−1)	3.268 (1)	9.557 (2)	2.660 (1)	0.212	0.765
1.0357	1.449 (−1)	7.101 (−1)	3.247 (1)	1.077 (3)	2.385 (1)	0.265	0.713
1.0374	1.466 (−1)	6.740 (−1)	3.223 (1)	1.195 (3)	2.149 (1)	0.316	0.662
1.0392	1.485 (−1)	6.395 (−1)	3.196 (1)	1.306 (3)	1.951 (1)	0.364	0.615
1.0427	1.526 (−1)	5.752 (−1)	3.136 (1)	1.491 (3)	1.658 (1)	0.445	0.535
1.0478	1.593 (−1)	4.942 (−1)	3.039 (1)	1.664 (3)	1.383 (1)	0.521	0.459
1.0595	1.763 (−1)	3.539 (−1)	2.812 (1)	1.812 (3)	1.019 (1)	0.589	0.391
1.0886	2.238 (−1)	1.696 (−1)	2.346 (1)	1.852 (3)	5.791 (0)	0.623	0.357
1.1132	2.673 (−1)	1.008 (−1)	2.062 (1)	1.854 (3)	3.763 (0)	0.653	0.327
1.1384	3.140 (−1)	6.431 (−2)	1.842 (1)	1.854 (3)	2.612 (0)	0.687	0.293
1.1695	3.732 (−1)	4.068 (−2)	1.639 (1)	1.854 (3)	1.842 (0)	0.699	0.280
1.2062	4.425 (−1)	2.624 (−2)	1.465 (1)	1.854 (3)	1.319 (0)	0.701	0.278
1.2900	5.957 (−1)	1.254 (−2)	1.209 (1)	1.854 (3)	7.843 (−1)	0.704	0.275
1.3983	7.833 (−1)	6.481 (−3)	1.017 (1)	1.854 (3)	4.747 (−1)	0.707	0.273
1.5078	9.631 (−1)	3.960 (−3)	8.930 (0)	1.855 (3)	3.270 (−1)	0.708	0.272
1.6652	1.208 (0)	2.297 (−3)	7.728 (0)	1.855 (3)	2.200 (−1)	0.708	0.272
1.8558	1.490 (0)	1.365 (−3)	6.730 (0)	1.855 (3)	1.506 (−1)	0.708	0.272
2.0724	1.802 (0)	8.343 (−4)	5.906 (0)	1.855 (3)	1.050 (−1)	0.708	0.272
2.3407	2.185 (0)	4.905 (−4)	5.125 (0)	1.855 (3)	7.189 (−2)	0.708	0.272
2.6205	2.591 (0)	2.954 (−4)	4.468 (0)	1.855 (3)	4.923 (−2)	0.708	0.272
2.9871	3.149 (0)	1.558 (−4)	3.761 (0)	1.855 (3)	3.133 (−2)	0.708	0.272
3.3610	3.778 (0)	7.982 (−5)	3.145 (0)	1.855 (3)	1.925 (−2)	0.708	0.272
3.7103	4.459 (0)	4.031 (−5)	2.623 (0)	1.855 (3)	1.168 (−2)	0.708	0.272
4.0277	5.209 (0)	1.960 (−5)	2.173 (0)	1.855 (3)	6.900 (−3)	0.708	0.272
4.3047	6.051 (0)	8.999 (−6)	1.788 (0)	1.855 (3)	3.871 (−3)	0.708	0.272
4.5216	6.946 (0)	4.048 (−6)	1.472 (0)	1.855 (3)	2.113 (−3)	0.708	0.272
4.6758	7.840 (0)	1.867 (−6)	1.229 (0)	1.855 (3)	1.167 (−3)	0.708	0.272
4.7816	8.719 (0)	8.913 (−7)	1.041 (0)	1.855 (3)	6.502 (−4)	0.708	0.272
4.8555	9.605 (0)	4.299 (−7)	8.833 (−1)	1.855 (3)	3.691 (−4)	0.708	0.272
4.9051	1.047 (1)	2.124 (−7)	7.533 (−1)	1.855 (3)	2.128 (−4)	0.708	0.272

At the center, $\epsilon_{\text{nucl}}/\epsilon_{\text{grav}} = -4.495 \times 10^3$.

$$\int_0^M (L_r)_{\text{grav}}\, dM_r = 0.8197\ L_\odot.$$

Table 7-31 Model·Interior for 5 $M_\odot$ during Giant Phase, at Point 11 in Fig. 7-25. [Calculated by I. Iben, Jr.; see ref. (331) and note to Table 7-12.]

$$5\ M_\odot, \quad t = 2.77783 \times 10^{15}\ \text{seconds} = 8.79 \times 10^7\ \text{years},$$

$$L = 1936.7\ L_\odot, \quad R = 44.14\ R_\odot, \quad T_{\text{eff}} = 5775°\text{K}.$$

$M_r/M_\odot$	$r/R_\odot$	$P \times 10^{-17}$	$T \times 10^{-6}$	$L_r/L_\odot$	ρ	X	He^4
0.0000	0.000	2.029 (3)	*1.844* (2)	0.000	2.156 (4)	0.000	0.005
0.0037	6.295 (−3)	1.907 (3)	1.801 (2)	5.335 (0)	2.080 (4)	0.000	0.005
0.0158	1.031 (−2)	1.718 (3)	1.736 (2)	1.875 (1)	1.965 (4)	0.000	0.005
0.1799	2.619 (−2)	7.314 (2)	1.446 (2)	9.412 (1)	1.068 (4)	0.000	0.009
0.3017	3.419 (−2)	4.110 (2)	1.373 (2)	1.004 (2)	6.125 (3)	0.000	0.034
0.3021	3.422 (−2)	4.101 (2)	1.373 (2)	1.004 (2)	5.180 (3)	0.000	0.547
0.3108	3.493 (−2)	3.934 (2)	1.368 (2)	2.328 (2)	4.731 (3)	0.000	0.772
0.3224	3.588 (−2)	3.725 (2)	1.356 (2)	4.161 (2)	4.422 (3)	0.000	0.843
0.3347	3.690 (−2)	3.517 (2)	1.337 (2)	5.647 (2)	4.192 (3)	0.000	0.887
0.3470	3.792 (−2)	3.325 (2)	1.315 (2)	6.615 (2)	3.999 (3)	0.000	0.921
0.3859	4.105 (−2)	2.798 (2)	1.240 (2)	7.681 (2)	3.597 (3)	0.000	0.962
0.5415	5.277 (−2)	1.437 (2)	9.932 (1)	7.658 (2)	2.287 (3)	0.000	0.973
0.5664	5.462 (−2)	1.288 (2)	9.597 (1)	7.674 (2)	2.119 (3)	0.000	0.974
0.5975	5.696 (−2)	1.120 (2)	9.190 (1)	7.673 (2)	1.936 (3)	0.000	0.976
0.7760	7.148 (−2)	4.504 (1)	7.057 (1)	7.412 (2)	1.093 (3)	0.000	0.976
0.9202	8.698 (−2)	1.597 (1)	5.406 (1)	7.215 (2)	5.026 (2)	0.000	0.976
1.0168	1.032 (−1)	5.222 (0)	4.234 (1)	7.107 (2)	2.098 (2)	0.000	0.976
1.0718	1.198 (−1)	1.733 (0)	3.555 (1)	7.062 (2)	8.224 (1)	0.000	0.976
1.0907	1.295 (−1)	9.635 (−1)	3.346 (1)	7.820 (2)	4.324 (1)	0.037	0.939
1.0935	1.315 (−1)	8.699 (−1)	3.312 (1)	8.974 (2)	3.540 (1)	0.105	0.872
1.0956	1.333 (−1)	8.010 (−1)	3.281 (1)	1.036 (3)	2.943 (1)	0.187	0.790
1.0978	1.355 (−1)	7.359 (−1)	3.243 (1)	1.194 (3)	2.428 (1)	0.285	0.693
1.1000	1.379 (−1)	6.750 (−1)	3.198 (1)	1.347 (3)	2.034 (1)	0.380	0.599
1.1021	1.408 (−1)	6.185 (−1)	3.148 (1)	1.473 (3)	1.746 (1)	0.460	0.519
1.1046	1.443 (−1)	5.593 (−1)	3.084 (1)	1.580 (3)	1.523 (1)	0.528	0.452
1.1095	1.522 (−1)	4.576 (−1)	2.949 (1)	1.694 (3)	1.230 (1)	0.603	0.376
1.1304	1.919 (−1)	2.035 (−1)	2.426 (1)	1.763 (3)	6.500 (0)	0.671	0.309
1.1695	2.829 (−1)	5.704 (−2)	1.776 (1)	1.766 (3)	2.394 (0)	0.699	0.281
1.2137	4.034 (−1)	1.894 (−2)	1.356 (1)	1.769 (3)	1.064 (0)	0.702	0.278
1.2698	5.732 (−1)	6.749 (−3)	1.054 (1)	1.775 (3)	4.798 (−1)	0.704	0.276
1.3431	8.081 (−1)	2.603 (−3)	8.355 (0)	1.784 (3)	2.319 (−1)	0.706	0.274
1.4640	1.200 (0)	9.251 (−4)	6.471 (0)	1.797 (3)	1.075 (−1)	0.707	0.272
1.6348	1.737 (0)	3.650 (−4)	5.105 (0)	1.813 (3)	5.341 (−2)	0.708	0.272
1.8984	2.519 (0)	1.428 (−4)	3.969 (0)	1.832 (3)	2.685 (−2)	0.708	0.272
2.2110	3.408 (0)	6.376 (−5)	3.180 (0)	1.851 (3)	1.489 (−2)	0.708	0.272
2.6205	4.578 (0)	2.678 (−5)	2.502 (0)	1.870 (3)	7.984 (−3)	0.708	0.272
3.1386	6.185 (0)	9.680 (−6)	1.905 (0)	1.890 (3)	3.864 (−3)	0.708	0.272
3.6433	8.092 (0)	3.356 (−6)	1.454 (0)	1.907 (3)	1.762 (−3)	0.708	0.272
4.0872	1.037 (1)	1.083 (−6)	1.112 (0)	1.921 (3)	7.480 (−4)	0.708	0.272
4.4434	1.316 (1)	3.161 (−7)	8.372 (−1)	1.929 (3)	2.898 (−4)	0.708	0.272
4.6758	1.614 (1)	9.604 (−8)	6.368 (−1)	1.934 (3)	1.150 (−4)	0.708	0.272
4.8146	1.912 (1)	3.174 (−8)	4.937 (−1)	1.936 (3)	4.855 (−5)	0.708	0.272
4.8970	2.209 (1)	1.099 (−8)	3.862 (−1)	1.936 (3)	2.150 (−5)	0.708	0.272

At the center, $\epsilon_{\text{nucl}}/\epsilon_{\text{grav}} = 0.8536.$

$$\int_0^M (L_r)_{\text{grav}}\, dM_r = 131.5\ L_\odot.$$

Table 7-32 Model Interior for 9 $M_\odot$ during the Main-Sequence Phase. This is a homogeneous model and is not part of an evolutionary sequence. (Calculated by I. Iben, Jr.)

$$9 \ M_\odot, \quad X = 0.708, \quad Z = 0.02,$$

$$L = 4450 \ L_\odot, \quad R = 3.405 \ R_\odot, \quad T_{\text{eff}} = 25,600°K.$$

$M_r/M_\odot$	$r/R_\odot$	$P \times 10^{-17}$	$T \times 10^{-6}$	$L_r/L_\odot$
0.000	0.0000	4.655 (−1)	3.111 (1)	0.000
7.259 (−5)	2.133 (−2)	4.651 (−1)	3.110 (1)	1.200 (0)
5.031 (−4)	4.069 (−2)	4.642 (−1)	3.108 (1)	8.243 (0)
3.487 (−3)	7.765 (−2)	4.609 (−1)	3.100 (1)	5.566 (1)
2.415 (−2)	1.485 (−1)	4.492 (−1)	3.072 (1)	3.513 (2)
1.668 (−1)	2.862 (−1)	4.077 (−1)	2.968 (1)	1.744 (3)
8.052 (−1)	5.000 (−1)	3.106 (−1)	2.693 (1)	3.878 (3)
2.682 (0)	8.059 (−1)	1.616 (−1)	2.123 (1)	4.440 (3)
5.045 (0)	1.107 (0)	6.195 (−2)	1.562 (1)	4.449 (3)
6.668 (0)	1.354 (0)	2.348 (−2)	1.206 (1)	4.450 (3)
7.683 (0)	1.579 (0)	8.868 (−3)	9.483 (0)	4.450 (3)
8.284 (0)	1.790 (0)	3.349 (−3)	7.556 (0)	4.450 (3)
8.625 (0)	1.990 (0)	1.267 (−3)	6.047 (0)	4.450 (3)
8.811 (0)	2.180 (0)	4.807 (−4)	4.828 (0)	4.450 (3)
8.908 (0)	2.355 (0)	1.829 (−4)	3.833 (0)	4.450 (3)
8.957 (0)	2.514 (0)	6.970 (−5)	3.031 (0)	4.450 (3)
8.980 (0)	2.655 (0)	2.661 (−5)	2.390 (0)	4.450 (3)
8.991 (0)	2.777 (0)	1.017 (−5)	1.892 (0)	4.450 (3)
8.996 (0)	2.883 (0)	3.894 (−6)	1.506 (0)	4.450 (3)
8.998 (0)	2.973 (0)	1.494 (−6)	1.210 (0)	4.450 (3)
8.999 (0)	3.049 (0)	5.755 (−7)	9.778 (−1)	4.450 (3)
9.000 (0)	3.114 (0)	2.226 (−7)	7.901 (−1)	4.450 (3)
9.000 (0)	3.169 (0)	8.651 (−8)	6.380 (−1)	4.450 (3)
9.000 (0)	3.214 (0)	3.377 (−8)	5.149 (−1)	4.450 (3)
9.000 (0)	3.252 (0)	1.324 (−8)	4.154 (−1)	4.450 (3)
9.000 (0)	3.283 (0)	5.214 (−9)	3.346 (−1)	4.450 (3)
9.000 (0)	3.308 (0)	2.061 (−9)	2.692 (−1)	4.450 (3)
9.000 (0)	3.328 (0)	8.177 (−10)	2.163 (−1)	4.450 (3)
9.000 (0)	3.345 (0)	3.254 (−10)	1.735 (−1)	4.450 (3)
9.000 (0)	3.359 (0)	1.299 (−10)	1.390 (−1)	4.450 (3)
9.000 (0)	3.369 (0)	5.194 (−11)	1.113 (−1)	4.450 (3)
9.000 (0)	3.378 (0)	2.081 (−11)	8.971 (−2)	4.450 (3)
9.000 (0)	3.385 (0)	8.401 (−12)	7.444 (−2)	4.450 (3)
9.000 (0)	3.391 (0)	3.446 (−12)	6.204 (−2)	4.450 (3)
9.000 (0)	3.396 (0)	1.423 (−12)	4.848 (−2)	4.450 (3)
9.000 (0)	3.400 (0)	5.815 (−13)	3.778 (−2)	4.450 (3)
9.000 (0)	3.403 (0)	2.358 (−13)	3.005 (−2)	4.450 (3)
9.000 (0)	3.405 (0)	1.147 (−13)	2.575 (−2)	4.450 (3)
9.000 (0)	3.405 (0)	9.595 (−14)	2.494 (−2)	4.450 (3)
9.000 (0)	3.408 (0)	2.903 (−14)	2.204 (−2)	4.450 (3)
9.000 (0)	3.412 (0)	8.680 (−15)	2.151 (−2)	4.450 (3)

Table 7-32 (*continued*)

ρ	ϵ	κ	e^ψ *	P_g/P
1.054 (1)	3.206 (4)	3.435 (−1)		
1.054 (1)	3.192 (4)	3.435 (−1)	5.698 (−3)	9.493 (−1)
1.052 (1)	3.154 (4)	3.435 (−1)	5.697 (−3)	9.494 (−1)
1.048 (1)	3.022 (4)	3.436 (−1)	5.693 (−3)	9.495 (−1)
1.031 (1)	2.580 (4)	3.441 (−1)	5.679 (−3)	9.500 (−1)
9.705 (0)	1.422 (4)	3.457 (−1)	5.630 (−3)	9.520 (−1)
8.194 (0)	2.550 (3)	3.509 (−1)	5.500 (−3)	9.573 (−1)
5.469 (0)	3.622 (1)	3.696 (−1)	5.245 (−3)	9.683 (−1)
2.871 (0)	8.352 (−1)	4.067 (−1)	4.360 (−3)	9.757 (−1)
1.413 (0)	1.188 (−1)	4.474 (−1)	3.166 (−3)	9.773 (−1)
6.774 (−1)	1.916 (−2)	4.935 (−1)	2.172 (−3)	9.769 (−1)
3.210 (−1)	2.980 (−3)	5.472 (−1)	1.449 (−3)	9.755 (−1)
1.514 (−1)	2.218 (−4)	6.121 (−1)	9.553 (−4)	9.734 (−1)
7.181 (−2)	2.746 (−5)	6.924 (−1)	6.348 (−4)	9.715 (−1)
3.436 (−2)	3.096 (−6)	7.453 (−1)	4.293 (−4)	9.702 (−1)
1.655 (−2)	3.004 (−7)	7.833 (−1)	2.941 (−4)	9.695 (−1)
8.011 (−3)	2.483 (−8)	7.988 (−1)	2.034 (−4)	9.691 (−1)
3.864 (−3)	1.807 (−9)	7.954 (−1)	1.392 (−4)	9.682 (−1)
1.856 (−3)	1.164 (−10)	8.225 (−1)	9.417 (−5)	9.667 (−1)
8.839 (−4)	6.867 (−12)	8.432 (−1)	6.230 (−5)	9.639 (−1)
4.195 (−4)	3.643 (−13)	9.400 (−1)	4.069 (−5)	9.600 (−1)
2.000 (−4)	1.628 (−14)	1.043 (0)	2.671 (−5)	9.559 (−1)
9.580 (−5)	6.040 (−16)	1.150 (0)	1.763 (−5)	9.517 (−1)
4.613 (−5)	1.831 (−17)	1.259 (0)	1.171 (−5)	9.475 (−1)
2.245 (−5)	0.000	1.372 (0)	7.864 (−6)	9.433 (−1)
1.094 (−5)	0.000	1.482 (0)	5.305 (−6)	9.394 (−1)
5.357 (−6)	0.000	1.586 (0)	3.598 (−6)	9.358 (−1)
2.636 (−6)	0.000	1.683 (0)	2.458 (−6)	9.325 (−1)
1.303 (−6)	0.000	1.770 (0)	1.691 (−6)	9.297 (−1)
6.476 (−7)	0.000	1.845 (0)	1.171 (−6)	9.274 (−1)
3.230 (−7)	0.000	1.901 (0)	8.160 (−7)	9.256 (−1)
1.598 (−7)	0.000	1.786 (0)	5.578 (−7)	9.215 (−1)
7.661 (−8)	0.000	1.909 (0)	3.538 (−7)	9.079 (−1)
3.705 (−8)	0.000	2.638 (0)	2.249 (−7)	8.916 (−1)
1.992 (−8)	0.000	2.946 (0)	1.750 (−7)	9.021 (−1)
1.088 (−8)	0.000	2.481 (0)	1.389 (−7)	9.117 (−1)
5.591 (−9)	0.000	2.164 (0)	1.006 (−7)	9.128 (−1)
3.143 (−9)	0.000	1.895 (0)	7.134 (−8)	9.034 (−1)
2.698 (−9)	0.000	1.806 (0)	6.425 (−8)	8.984 (−1)
8.179 (−10)	0.000	9.792 (−1)	2.345 (−8)	7.952 (−1)
1.191 (−10)	0.000	4.034 (−1)	3.540 (−9)	3.781 (−1)

* The quantity e^ψ measures the degree of degeneracy, higher values indicating greater degeneracy. See eq. (6-89).

Table 7-33 Model Interior for 15 $M_\odot$ Prior to the Main-Sequence Phase, Preceding Point 1 in Fig. 7-3A. [Calculated by I. Iben, Jr.; see ref. (321) and note to Table 7-12.]

15 $M_\odot$, $t = 1.26094 \times 10^9$ seconds $= 3.99 \times 10^1$ years,

$L = 10{,}694\,L_\odot$, $R = 210.9\,R_\odot$, $T_{eff} = 4050°$K.

$M_r/M_\odot$	$r/R_\odot$	$P \times 10^{-17}$	$T \times 10^{-6}$	$L_r/L_\odot$	ρ
0.000	0.000	1.726 (-8)	0.4951	0.000	2.362 (-5)
1.359 (-2)	9.345 (0)	1.693 (-8)	0.4927	1.701 (1)	2.331 (-5)
3.575 (-2)	1.294 (1)	1.664 (-8)	0.4906	4.461 (1)	2.302 (-5)
9.399 (-2)	1.796 (1)	1.609 (-8)	0.4864	1.167 (2)	2.249 (-5)
2.468 (-1)	2.501 (1)	1.507 (-8)	0.4784	3.033 (2)	2.148 (-5)
6.076 (-1)	3.437 (1)	1.340 (-8)	0.4644	7.337 (2)	1.976 (-5)
1.187 (0)	4.396 (1)	1.148 (-8)	0.4466	1.401 (3)	1.765 (-5)
1.977 (0)	5.354 (1)	9.531 (-9)	0.4260	2.272 (3)	1.540 (-5)
2.950 (0)	6.313 (1)	7.688 (-9)	0.4032	3.292 (3)	1.316 (-5)
4.068 (0)	7.270 (1)	6.040 (-9)	0.3789	4.392 (3)	1.110 (-5)
5.280 (0)	8.230 (1)	4.631 (-9)	0.3533	5.512 (3)	9.153 (-6)
6.534 (0)	9.190 (1)	3.474 (-9)	0.3266	6.587 (3)	7.453 (-6)
7.466 (0)	9.902 (1)	2.769 (-9)	0.3059	7.330 (3)	6.366 (-6)
8.699 (0)	1.086 (2)	1.997 (-9)	0.2752	8.242 (3)	5.144 (-6)
9.884 (0)	1.182 (2)	1.398 (-9)	0.2435	9.030 (3)	4.117 (-6)
1.099 (1)	1.278 (2)	9.453 (-10)	0.2125	9.665 (3)	3.228 (-6)
1.198 (1)	1.375 (2)	6.131 (-10)	0.1823	1.014 (4)	2.471 (-6)
1.283 (1)	1.469 (2)	3.819 (-10)	0.1537	1.046 (4)	1.845 (-6)
1.347 (1)	1.554 (2)	2.362 (-10)	0.1289	1.063 (4)	1.371 (-6)
1.394 (1)	1.630 (2)	1.456 (-10)	0.1076	1.071 (4)	1.019 (-6)
1.428 (1)	1.697 (2)	8.950 (-11)	0.0896	1.074 (4)	7.562 (-7)
1.452 (1)	1.756 (2)	5.491 (-11)	0.0746	1.074 (4)	5.605 (-7)
1.468 (1)	1.808 (2)	3.363 (-11)	0.0627	1.072 (4)	4.116 (-7)
1.479 (1)	1.853 (2)	2.056 (-11)	0.0543	1.070 (4)	2.945 (-7)

At the center, $\epsilon_{nucl}/\epsilon_{grav} = 2.357 \times 10^{-21}$.

$$\int_0^M (L_r)_{grav}\, dM_r = 1.069 \times 10^4\, L_\odot.$$

Table 7-34 Model Interior for 15 $M_\odot$ Prior to the Main-Sequence Phase, at Point 3 in Fig. 7-3A.
[Calculated by I. Iben, Jr.; see ref. (321) and note to Table 7-12.]

$$15\ M_\odot, \quad t = 2.95424 \times 10^{11} \text{ seconds} = 9.35 \times 10^3 \text{ years},$$

$$L = 20,220\ L_\odot, \quad R = 22.01\ R_\odot, \quad T_{\text{eff}} = 14,699°\text{K}.$$

$M_r/M_\odot$	$r/R_\odot$	$P \times 10^{-17}$	$T \times 10^{-6}$	$L_r/L_\odot$	ρ	X	He^4
0.000	0.000	1.217 (−3)	7.836 (0)	0.000	1.064 (−1)	0.708	0.272
1.737 (−2)	6.138 (−1)	1.188 (−3)	7.787 (0)	4.353 (1)	1.045 (−1)	0.708	0.272
2.428 (−2)	6.873 (−1)	1.181 (−3)	7.775 (0)	6.075 (1)	1.041 (−1)	0.708	0.272
3.261 (−2)	7.593 (−1)	1.173 (−3)	7.761 (0)	8.146 (1)	1.036 (−1)	0.708	0.272
4.569 (−2)	8.511 (−1)	1.162 (−3)	7.742 (0)	1.139 (2)	1.029 (−1)	0.708	0.272
6.386 (−2)	9.534 (−1)	1.149 (−3)	7.719 (0)	1.589 (2)	1.021 (−1)	0.708	0.272
8.573 (−2)	1.054 (0)	1.135 (−3)	7.693 (0)	2.129 (2)	1.011 (−1)	0.708	0.272
1.201 (−1)	1.182 (0)	1.115 (−3)	7.657 (0)	2.973 (2)	9.984 (−2)	0.708	0.272
1.678 (−1)	1.326 (0)	1.090 (−3)	7.613 (0)	4.137 (2)	9.835 (−2)	0.708	0.272
2.730 (−1)	1.570 (0)	1.044 (−3)	7.526 (0)	6.685 (2)	9.539 (−2)	0.708	0.272
4.361 (−1)	1.851 (0)	9.841 (−4)	7.412 (0)	1.058 (3)	9.144 (−2)	0.708	0.272
6.569 (−1)	2.144 (0)	9.170 (−4)	7.276 (0)	1.575 (3)	8.690 (−2)	0.708	0.272
9.293 (−1)	2.435 (0)	8.471 (−4)	7.127 (0)	2.199 (3)	8.202 (−2)	0.708	0.272
1.258 (0)	2.728 (0)	7.750 (−4)	6.963 (0)	2.934 (3)	7.690 (−2)	0.708	0.272
1.803 (0)	3.138 (0)	6.748 (−4)	6.716 (0)	4.133 (3)	7.004 (−2)	0.708	0.272
2.743 (0)	3.728 (0)	5.381 (−4)	6.332 (0)	6.035 (3)	5.943 (−2)	0.708	0.272
3.835 (0)	4.325 (0)	4.158 (−4)	5.922 (0)	8.100 (3)	4.926 (−2)	0.708	0.272
5.033 (0)	4.930 (0)	3.119 (−4)	5.496 (0)	1.015 (4)	3.994 (−2)	0.708	0.272
6.283 (0)	5.545 (0)	2.274 (−4)	5.061 (0)	1.205 (4)	3.172 (−2)	0.708	0.272
7.466 (0)	6.138 (0)	1.644 (−4)	4.648 (0)	1.367 (4)	2.506 (−2)	0.708	0.272
8.699 (0)	6.789 (0)	1.129 (−4)	4.214 (0)	1.521 (4)	1.906 (−2)	0.708	0.272
9.884 (0)	7.477 (0)	7.452 (−5)	3.782 (0)	1.652 (4)	1.408 (−2)	0.708	0.272
1.099 (1)	8.209 (0)	4.698 (−5)	3.354 (0)	1.759 (4)	1.006 (−2)	0.708	0.272
1.160 (1)	8.673 (0)	3.475 (−5)	3.102 (0)	1.812 (4)	7.916 (−3)	0.708	0.272
1.207 (1)	9.075 (0)	2.661 (−5)	2.895 (0)	1.850 (4)	6.506 (−3)	0.708	0.272
1.251 (1)	9.492 (0)	2.006 (−5)	2.691 (0)	1.883 (4)	5.286 (−3)	0.708	0.272
1.290 (1)	9.905 (0)	1.508 (−5)	2.501 (0)	1.910 (4)	4.278 (−3)	0.708	0.272
1.323 (1)	1.031 (1)	1.130 (−5)	2.323 (0)	1.933 (4)	3.456 (−3)	0.708	0.272
1.352 (1)	1.072 (1)	8.475 (−6)	2.160 (0)	1.951 (4)	2.786 (−3)	0.708	0.272
1.377 (1)	1.112 (1)	6.335 (−6)	2.009 (0)	1.967 (4)	2.241 (−3)	0.708	0.272
1.398 (1)	1.151 (1)	4.740 (−6)	1.871 (0)	1.980 (4)	1.799 (−3)	0.708	0.272
1.416 (1)	1.189 (1)	3.538 (−6)	1.742 (0)	1.990 (4)	1.442 (−3)	0.708	0.272
1.431 (1)	1.227 (1)	2.645 (−6)	1.623 (0)	1.998 (4)	1.156 (−3)	0.708	0.272
1.443 (1)	1.265 (1)	1.973 (−6)	1.512 (0)	2.004 (4)	9.258 (−4)	0.708	0.272
1.453 (1)	1.301 (1)	1.476 (−6)	1.411 (0)	2.009 (4)	7.409 (−4)	0.708	0.272
1.462 (1)	1.337 (1)	1.101 (−6)	1.317 (0)	2.013 (4)	5.922 (−4)	0.708	0.272
1.469 (1)	1.372 (1)	8.243 (−7)	1.232 (0)	2.017 (4)	4.726 (−4)	0.708	0.272
1.475 (1)	1.407 (1)	6.158 (−7)	1.153 (0)	2.019 (4)	3.770 (−4)	0.708	0.272
1.480 (1)	1.440 (1)	4.616 (−7)	1.079 (0)	2.021 (4)	3.010 (−4)	0.708	0.272

At the center, $\epsilon_{\text{nucl}}/\epsilon_{\text{grav}} = 1.237 \times 10^{-7}$.

$$\int_0^M (L_r)_{\text{grav}}\, dM_r = 2.022 \times 10^4\ L_\odot.$$

Table 7-35 Model Interior for 15 $M_\odot$ during the Main-Sequence Phase, at Point 1 in Fig. 7-3A. [Calculated by I. Iben, Jr.; see ref. (321) and note to Table 7-12.]

$$15\ M_\odot, \quad t = 4.36787 \times 10^{12} \text{ seconds} = 1.38 \times 10^5 \text{ years},$$

$$L = 20,820\ L_\odot, \quad R = 4.648\ R_\odot, \quad T_{eff} = 32,220°\text{K}.$$

$M_r/M_\odot$	$r/R_\odot$	$P \times 10^{-17}$	$T \times 10^{-6}$	$L_r/L_\odot$	ρ	X	He^4
0.000	0.0000	3.130 (−1)	3.408 (1)	0.000	6.0994	0.704	0.276
1.449 (−2)	0.1498	3.074 (−1)	3.389 (1)	5.460 (2)	6.0301	0.704	0.276
2.214 (−2)	0.1727	3.056 (−1)	3.382 (1)	8.094 (2)	6.0084	0.704	0.276
3.575 (−2)	0.2029	3.028 (−1)	3.372 (1)	1.259 (3)	5.9740	0.704	0.276
5.824 (−2)	0.2392	2.989 (−1)	3.358 (1)	1.960 (3)	5.9266	0.704	0.276
9.399 (−2)	0.2813	2.937 (−1)	3.339 (1)	2.988 (3)	5.8615	0.704	0.276
1.530 (−1)	0.3320	2.864 (−1)	3.312 (1)	4.504 (3)	5.7721	0.704	0.276
2.468 (−1)	0.3910	2.768 (−1)	3.276 (1)	6.559 (3)	5.6494	0.704	0.276
3.812 (−1)	0.4545	2.651 (−1)	3.230 (1)	8.956 (3)	5.5009	0.704	0.276
6.837 (−1)	0.5582	2.437 (−1)	3.143 (1)	1.280 (4)	5.2285	0.704	0.276
1.155 (0)	0.6743	2.174 (−1)	3.028 (1)	1.631 (4)	4.8631	0.704	0.276
2.158 (0)	0.8533	1.747 (−1)	2.818 (1)	1.940 (4)	4.3044	0.704	0.276
4.127 (0)	1.1120	1.164 (−1)	2.461 (1)	2.059 (4)	3.3345	0.704	0.276
5.350 (0)	1.2498	8.972 (−2)	2.254 (1)	2.067 (4)	2.7885	0.704	0.276
5.780 (0)	1.2965	8.155 (−2)	2.182 (1)	2.068 (4)	2.5920	0.704	0.276
6.283 (0)	1.3506	7.268 (−2)	2.098 (1)	2.074 (4)	2.4462	0.708	0.272
7.466 (0)	1.4778	5.441 (−2)	1.912 (1)	2.082 (4)	2.0269	0.708	0.272
8.699 (0)	1.6148	3.872 (−2)	1.726 (1)	2.083 (4)	1.6104	0.708	0.272
9.884 (0)	1.7573	2.643 (−2)	1.549 (1)	2.083 (4)	1.2339	0.708	0.272
1.099 (1)	1.9074	1.721 (−2)	1.379 (1)	2.083 (4)	0.9079	0.708	0.272
1.189 (1)	2.0512	1.116 (−2)	1.232 (1)	2.082 (4)	0.6496	0.708	0.272
1.234 (1)	2.1357	8.571 (−3)	1.153 (1)	2.082 (4)	0.5345	0.708	0.272
1.275 (1)	2.2208	6.532 (−3)	1.077 (1)	2.082 (4)	0.4358	0.708	0.272
1.311 (1)	2.3056	4.955 (−3)	1.007 (1)	2.082 (4)	0.3541	0.708	0.272
1.341 (1)	2.3891	3.755 (−3)	9.413 (0)	2.082 (4)	0.2868	0.708	0.272
1.368 (1)	2.4721	2.835 (−3)	8.799 (0)	2.082 (4)	0.2317	0.708	0.272
1.390 (1)	2.5537	2.140 (−3)	8.229 (0)	2.082 (4)	0.1868	0.708	0.272
1.409 (1)	2.6348	1.611 (−3)	7.695 (0)	2.082 (4)	0.1503	0.708	0.272
1.425 (1)	2.7142	1.213 (−3)	7.200 (0)	2.082 (4)	0.1208	0.708	0.272
1.438 (1)	2.7929	9.119 (−4)	6.734 (0)	2.082 (4)	0.0971	0.708	0.272
1.449 (1)	2.8696	6.867 (−4)	6.302 (0)	2.082 (4)	0.0780	0.708	0.272
1.459 (1)	2.9453	5.161 (−4)	5.895 (0)	2.082 (4)	0.0626	0.708	0.272
1.466 (1)	3.0189	3.889 (−4)	5.515 (0)	2.082 (4)	0.0503	0.708	0.272
1.473 (1)	3.0912	2.926 (−4)	5.155 (0)	2.082 (4)	0.0405	0.708	0.272
1.478 (1)	3.1610	2.208 (−4)	4.817 (0)	2.082 (4)	0.0327	0.708	0.272

At the center, $\epsilon_{nuol}/\epsilon_{grav} = -3.144 \times 10^3$.

$$\int_0^M (L_r)_{grav}\, dM_r = -96.60\ L_\odot.$$

Table 7-36   Model Interior for 15 $M_\odot$ in Terminal Main-Sequence Phase, at Point 2 in Fig. 7-25. [Calculated by I. Iben, Jr.; see ref. (331a) and note to Table 7-12.]

$$15\ M_\odot, \quad t = 3.23598 \times 10^{14} \text{ seconds} = 1.02 \times 10^7 \text{ years},$$

$$L = 41{,}780\ L_\odot, \quad R = 9.991\ R_\odot, \quad T_{\text{eff}} = 26{,}160^\circ\text{K}.$$

$M_r/M_\odot$	$r/R_\odot$	$P \times 10^{-17}$	$T \times 10^{-6}$	$L_r/L_\odot$	ρ	X	He^4
0.000	0.0000	3.268 (−1)	4.199 (1)	0.000	9.106 (0)	0.032	0.943
8.535 (−3)	0.1098	3.200 (−1)	4.174 (1)	1.081 (3)	8.981 (0)	0.032	0.943
1.123 (−2)	0.1205	3.187 (−1)	4.169 (1)	1.395 (3)	8.956 (0)	0.032	0.943
1.548 (−2)	0.1342	3.167 (−1)	4.162 (1)	1.879 (3)	8.922 (0)	0.032	0.943
2.428 (−2)	0.1563	3.133 (−1)	4.148 (1)	2.843 (3)	8.860 (0)	0.032	0.943
3.956 (−2)	0.1843	3.082 (−1)	4.129 (1)	4.416 (3)	8.767 (0)	0.032	0.943
6.386 (−2)	0.2169	3.014 (−1)	4.103 (1)	6.708 (3)	8.640 (0)	0.032	0.943
1.040 (−1)	0.2563	2.919 (−1)	4.065 (1)	1.006 (4)	8.466 (0)	0.032	0.943
1.678 (−1)	0.3024	2.794 (−1)	4.014 (1)	1.454 (4)	8.227 (0)	0.032	0.943
2.730 (−1)	0.3587	2.623 (−1)	3.942 (1)	2.035 (4)	7.902 (0)	0.032	0.943
4.769 (−1)	0.4380	2.357 (−1)	3.823 (1)	2.800 (4)	7.372 (0)	0.032	0.943
7.598 (−1)	0.5205	2.064 (−1)	3.679 (1)	3.414 (4)	6.781 (0)	0.032	0.943
1.460 (0)	0.6726	1.528 (−1)	3.372 (1)	3.997 (4)	5.608 (0)	0.032	0.943
2.350 (0)	0.8259	1.049 (−1)	3.021 (1)	4.151 (4)	4.399 (0)	0.032	0.943
2.824 (0)	0.9009	8.512 (−2)	2.840 (1)	4.168 (4)	3.768 (0)	0.032	0.943
3.167 (0)	0.9546	7.268 (−2)	2.712 (1)	4.173 (4)	3.221 (0)	0.070	0.906
3.359 (0)	0.9871	6.632 (−2)	2.641 (1)	4.176 (4)	2.797 (0)	0.123	0.853
3.594 (0)	1.0296	5.922 (−2)	2.555 (1)	4.178 (4)	2.410 (0)	0.177	0.800
3.823 (0)	1.0734	5.300 (−2)	2.474 (1)	4.180 (4)	2.087 (0)	0.233	0.745
4.127 (0)	1.1356	4.569 (−2)	2.370 (1)	4.181 (4)	1.761 (0)	0.293	0.685
4.388 (0)	1.1923	4.025 (−2)	2.284 (1)	4.182 (4)	1.502 (0)	0.357	0.621
4.727 (0)	1.2697	3.421 (−2)	2.177 (1)	4.182 (4)	1.271 (0)	0.425	0.554
4.853 (0)	1.2999	3.222 (−2)	2.139 (1)	4.182 (4)	1.125 (0)	0.497	0.482
4.910 (0)	1.3146	3.136 (−2)	2.121 (1)	4.182 (4)	1.036 (0)	0.571	0.409
5.330 (0)	1.4238	2.585 (−2)	2.000 (1)	4.182 (4)	9.281 (−1)	0.571	0.409
5.683 (0)	1.5141	2.211 (−2)	1.907 (1)	4.182 (4)	7.705 (−1)	0.664	0.316
5.846 (0)	1.5580	2.059 (−2)	1.866 (1)	4.182 (4)	7.352 (−1)	0.664	0.316
6.298 (0)	1.6783	1.699 (−2)	1.759 (1)	4.181 (4)	6.274 (−1)	0.694	0.285
6.921 (0)	1.8446	1.314 (−2)	1.626 (1)	4.181 (4)	5.302 (−1)	0.707	0.272
7.590 (0)	2.0219	1.001 (−2)	1.498 (1)	4.181 (4)	4.411 (−1)	0.707	0.272
8.210 (0)	2.1873	7.764 (−3)	1.391 (1)	4.180 (4)	3.708 (−1)	0.708	0.272
8.820 (0)	2.3542	6.006 (−3)	1.293 (1)	4.180 (4)	3.102 (−1)	0.708	0.272
9.418 (0)	2.5243	4.619 (−3)	1.202 (1)	4.180 (4)	2.579 (−1)	0.708	0.272
9.998 (0)	2.6983	3.528 (−3)	1.117 (1)	4.179 (4)	2.128 (−1)	0.708	0.272
1.056 (1)	2.8777	2.671 (−3)	1.037 (1)	4.179 (4)	1.741 (−1)	0.708	0.272
1.109 (1)	3.0629	2.002 (−3)	9.612 (0)	4.179 (4)	1.412 (−1)	0.708	0.272
1.160 (1)	3.2557	1.482 (−3)	8.895 (0)	4.179 (4)	1.132 (−1)	0.708	0.272
1.207 (1)	3.4566	1.084 (−3)	8.215 (0)	4.178 (4)	8.976 (−2)	0.708	0.272
1.251 (1)	3.6666	7.810 (−4)	7.568 (0)	4.178 (4)	7.032 (−2)	0.708	0.272
1.290 (1)	3.8764	5.631 (−4)	6.980 (0)	4.178 (4)	5.492 (−2)	0.708	0.272
1.323 (1)	4.0866	4.057 (−4)	6.440 (0)	4.178 (4)	4.289 (−2)	0.708	0.272
1.352 (1)	4.2945	2.934 (−4)	5.949 (0)	4.178 (4)	3.351 (−2)	0.708	0.272
1.377 (1)	4.5023	2.121 (−4)	5.495 (0)	4.178 (4)	2.622 (−2)	0.708	0.272
1.398 (1)	4.7068	1.539 (−4)	5.077 (0)	4.178 (4)	2.056 (−2)	0.708	0.272
1.416 (1)	4.9100	1.117 (−4)	4.687 (0)	4.178 (4)	1.617 (−2)	0.708	0.272
1.431 (1)	5.1085	8.146 (−5)	4.332 (0)	4.178 (4)	1.275 (−2)	0.708	0.272
1.443 (1)	5.3046	5.941 (−5)	4.003 (0)	4.178 (4)	1.007 (−2)	0.708	0.272
1.453 (1)	5.4952	4.354 (−5)	3.703 (0)	4.178 (4)	7.966 (−3)	0.708	0.272
1.462 (1)	5.6827	3.192 (−5)	3.426 (0)	4.178 (4)	6.319 (−3)	0.708	0.272
1.469 (1)	5.8639	2.351 (−5)	3.172 (0)	4.178 (4)	5.023 (−3)	0.708	0.272
1.475 (1)	6.0413	1.732 (−5)	2.937 (0)	4.178 (4)	4.001 (−3)	0.708	0.272
1.480 (1)	6.2120	1.282 (−5)	2.722 (0)	4.178 (4)	3.193 (−3)	0.708	0.272

At the center, $\epsilon_{\text{nucl}}/\epsilon_{\text{grav}} = -1.550 \times 10^4$.

$$\int_0^M (L_r)_{\text{grav}}\, dM_r = -75.94\ L_\odot.$$

Table 7-37   Model Interior for the Initial Sun.* (Calculated by Z. Abraham, 1970, private communication.)

$$1\ M_\odot,\quad X = 0.7203,\quad Z = 0.02,$$

$$L = 0.7242\ L_\odot,\quad R = 0.9480\ R_\odot,\quad T_{\text{eff}} = 5479°\text{K}.$$

$M_r/M_\odot$	$r/R_\odot$	$P \times 10^{-17}$	$T \times 10^{-6}$	$L_r/L_\odot$
0.000	0.000	1.676 (0)	1.338 (1)	0.000
1.218 (−4)	1.237 (−2)	1.668 (0)	1.336 (1)	8.978 (−4)
1.558 (−4)	1.343 (−2)	1.666 (0)	1.335 (1)	1.146 (−3)
1.992 (−4)	1.459 (−2)	1.665 (0)	1.335 (1)	1.462 (−3)
2.549 (−4)	1.584 (−2)	1.662 (0)	1.334 (1)	1.866 (−3)
3.261 (−4)	1.720 (−2)	1.660 (0)	1.333 (1)	2.381 (−3)
4.173 (−4)	1.867 (−2)	1.657 (0)	1.332 (1)	3.039 (−3)
5.342 (−4)	2.028 (−2)	1.654 (0)	1.331 (1)	3.878 (−3)
6.841 (−4)	2.203 (−2)	1.650 (0)	1.330 (1)	4.949 (−3)
8.765 (−4)	2.394 (−2)	1.645 (0)	1.329 (1)	6.315 (−3)
1.124 (−3)	2.602 (−2)	1.639 (0)	1.327 (1)	8.059 (−3)
1.442 (−3)	2.829 (−2)	1.632 (0)	1.325 (1)	1.028 (−2)
1.852 (−3)	3.077 (−2)	1.624 (0)	1.323 (1)	1.312 (−2)
2.381 (−3)	3.348 (−2)	1.615 (0)	1.320 (1)	1.674 (−2)
3.065 (−3)	3.646 (−2)	1.604 (0)	1.317 (1)	2.136 (−2)
3.953 (−3)	3.972 (−2)	1.591 (0)	1.313 (1)	2.725 (−2)
5.108 (−3)	4.332 (−2)	1.575 (0)	1.308 (1)	3.476 (−2)
6.617 (−3)	4.729 (−2)	1.557 (0)	1.303 (1)	4.433 (−2)
8.594 (−3)	5.170 (−2)	1.534 (0)	1.296 (1)	5.654 (−2)
1.120 (−2)	5.659 (−2)	1.508 (0)	1.288 (1)	7.210 (−2)
1.466 (−2)	6.207 (−2)	1.476 (0)	1.278 (1)	9.192 (−2)
1.928 (−2)	6.824 (−2)	1.437 (0)	1.266 (1)	1.172 (−1)
2.552 (−2)	7.524 (−2)	1.390 (0)	1.252 (1)	1.493 (−1)
3.405 (−2)	8.328 (−2)	1.333 (0)	1.234 (1)	1.902 (−1)
4.598 (−2)	9.269 (−2)	1.262 (0)	1.211 (1)	2.421 (−1)
6.320 (−2)	1.040 (−1)	1.173 (0)	1.181 (1)	3.079 (−1)
8.947 (−2)	1.184 (−1)	1.057 (0)	1.141 (1)	3.908 (−1)
1.325 (−1)	1.377 (−1)	8.996 (−1)	1.083 (1)	4.926 (−1)
1.825 (−1)	1.569 (−1)	7.508 (−1)	1.024 (1)	5.744 (−1)
2.325 (−1)	1.740 (−1)	6.272 (−1)	9.695 (0)	6.302 (−1)

Table 7-37 (*continued*)

$M_r/M_\odot$	$r/R_\odot$	$P \times 10^{-17}$	$T \times 10^{-6}$	$L_r/L_\odot$
2.825 (−1)	1.901 (−1)	5.224 (−1)	9.191 (0)	6.684 (−1)
3.356 (−1)	2.069 (−1)	4.262 (−1)	8.744 (0)	6.964 (−1)
3.856 (−1)	2.224 (−1)	3.501 (−1)	8.312 (0)	7.078 (−1)
4.356 (−1)	2.380 (−1)	2.846 (−1)	7.898 (0)	7.142 (−1)
4.856 (−1)	2.541 (−1)	2.282 (−1)	7.494 (0)	7.182 (−1)
5.356 (−1)	2.709 (−1)	1.800 (−1)	7.096 (0)	7.207 (−1)
5.836 (−1)	2.880 (−1)	1.405 (−1)	6.718 (0)	7.222 (−1)
6.274 (−1)	3.049 (−1)	1.097 (−1)	6.372 (0)	7.231 (−1)
6.673 (−1)	3.216 (−1)	8.560 (−2)	6.055 (0)	7.236 (−1)
7.035 (−1)	3.383 (−1)	6.683 (−2)	5.766 (0)	7.239 (−1)
7.363 (−1)	3.549 (−1)	5.218 (−2)	5.498 (0)	7.240 (−1)
7.658 (−1)	3.717 (−1)	4.074 (−2)	5.246 (0)	7.241 (−1)
7.925 (−1)	3.885 (−1)	3.181 (−2)	5.007 (0)	7.241 (−1)
8.165 (−1)	4.054 (−1)	2.484 (−2)	4.778 (0)	7.242 (−1)
8.380 (−1)	4.225 (−1)	1.940 (−2)	4.557 (0)	7.242 (−1)
8.573 (−1)	4.398 (−1)	1.515 (−2)	4.345 (0)	7.242 (−1)
8.746 (−1)	4.572 (−1)	1.183 (−2)	4.144 (0)	7.242 (−1)
8.900 (−1)	4.748 (−1)	9.240 (−3)	3.954 (0)	7.242 (−1)
9.038 (−1)	4.925 (−1)	7.217 (−3)	3.771 (0)	7.242 (−1)
9.160 (−1)	5.105 (−1)	5.637 (−3)	3.594 (0)	7.242 (−1)
9.269 (−1)	5.286 (−1)	4.403 (−3)	3.422 (0)	7.242 (−1)
9.366 (−1)	5.469 (−1)	3.440 (−3)	3.257 (0)	7.242 (−1)
9.451 (−1)	5.653 (−1)	2.687 (−3)	3.102 (0)	7.242 (−1)
9.526 (−1)	5.838 (−1)	2.099 (−3)	2.955 (0)	7.242 (−1)
9.593 (−1)	6.025 (−1)	1.640 (−3)	2.814 (0)	7.242 (−1)
9.651 (−1)	6.213 (−1)	1.281 (−3)	2.677 (0)	7.242 (−1)
9.702 (−1)	6.402 (−1)	1.001 (−3)	2.543 (0)	7.242 (−1)
9.747 (−1)	6.591 (−1)	7.824 (−4)	2.407 (0)	7.242 (−1)
9.786 (−1)	6.779 (−1)	6.114 (−4)	2.263 (0)	7.242 (−1)
9.820 (−1)	6.964 (−1)	4.779 (−4)	2.090 (0)	7.242 (−1)
9.849 (−1)	7.141 (−1)	3.736 (−4)	1.895 (0)	7.242 (−1)
9.874 (−1)	7.308 (−1)	2.921 (−4)	1.718 (0)	7.242 (−1)
9.895 (−1)	7.467 (−1)	2.284 (−4)	1.557 (0)	7.242 (−1)

* The pressure P is expressed in dyne cm^{-2}, the temperature T in °K, and the density ρ in gm cm^{-3}. The adopted solar values are $M_\odot = 1.991 \times 10^{33}$ gm, $R_\odot = 6.960 \times 10^{10}$ cm, and $L_\odot = 3.86 \times 10^{33}$ erg sec^{-1}. The mass fractions of hydrogen and helium-4 are listed in Table 7-38 as X and He⁴, respectively. Italics in the column for T indicate the presence of convection. The opacities are based on the tables of W. D. Watson, 1970 (207) and include line absorption. The ratio of mixing length to density scale-height in the convective envelope of Table 7-38 is 0.5.

Table 7-38 Model Interior for the Present Sun. (Calculated by Z. Abraham, 1970, private communication; see note to Table 7-37.)

$$1\ M_\odot, \quad t = 1.43300 \times 10^{17}\ \text{seconds} = 4.53 \times 10^9\ \text{years},$$

$$L = 1.0046\ L_\odot, \quad R = 1.0304\ R_\odot, \quad T_{\text{eff}} = 5704°\text{K}.$$

$M_r/M_\odot$	$r/R_\odot$	$P \times 10^{-17}$	$T \times 10^{-6}$	$L_r/L_\odot$	ρ	X	He^4
0.000	0.000	2.564 (0)	1.560 (1)	0.000	1.624 (2)	0.360	0.618
9.211 (−4)	2.005 (−2)	2.493 (0)	1.545 (1)	8.335 (−3)	1.579 (2)	0.374	0.604
1.305 (−3)	2.258 (−2)	2.475 (0)	1.540 (1)	1.168 (−2)	1.565 (2)	0.377	0.600
1.852 (−3)	2.544 (−2)	2.452 (0)	1.535 (1)	1.639 (−2)	1.549 (2)	0.382	0.596
2.634 (−3)	2.870 (−2)	2.423 (0)	1.529 (1)	2.304 (−2)	1.528 (2)	0.387	0.590
3.757 (−3)	3.243 (−2)	2.386 (0)	1.521 (1)	3.241 (−2)	1.503 (2)	0.395	0.583
5.378 (−3)	3.672 (−2)	2.340 (0)	1.511 (1)	4.564 (−2)	1.471 (2)	0.404	0.574
7.738 (−3)	4.169 (−2)	2.282 (0)	1.498 (1)	6.433 (−2)	1.432 (2)	0.415	0.563
1.120 (−2)	4.751 (−2)	2.209 (0)	1.481 (1)	9.070 (−2)	1.384 (2)	0.429	0.549
1.634 (−2)	5.441 (−2)	2.115 (0)	1.460 (1)	1.279 (−1)	1.323 (2)	0.447	0.531
2.411 (−2)	6.271 (−2)	1.997 (0)	1.432 (1)	1.804 (−1)	1.249 (2)	0.469	0.509
3.612 (−2)	7.297 (−2)	1.846 (0)	1.396 (1)	2.544 (−1)	1.157 (2)	0.496	0.482
5.735 (−2)	8.729 (−2)	1.633 (0)	1.342 (1)	3.678 (−1)	1.032 (2)	0.534	0.444
9.467 (−2)	1.071 (−1)	1.352 (0)	1.266 (1)	5.268 (−1)	8.783 (1)	0.582	0.397
1.625 (−1)	1.356 (−1)	9.956 (−1)	1.154 (1)	7.238 (−1)	6.836 (1)	0.637	0.342
2.025 (−1)	1.504 (−1)	8.392 (−1)	1.099 (1)	8.015 (−1)	5.835 (1)	0.658	0.321
2.200 (−1)	1.566 (−1)	7.795 (−1)	1.076 (1)	8.290 (−1)	5.503 (1)	0.666	0.314
2.375 (−1)	1.627 (−1)	7.242 (−1)	1.054 (1)	8.532 (−1)	5.194 (1)	0.671	0.308
2.550 (−1)	1.686 (−1)	6.728 (−1)	1.033 (1)	8.743 (−1)	4.904 (1)	0.678	0.301
2.725 (−1)	1.745 (−1)	6.250 (−1)	1.012 (1)	8.928 (−1)	4.631 (1)	0.683	0.296
3.156 (−1)	1.888 (−1)	5.204 (−1)	9.626 (0)	9.289 (−1)	4.074 (1)	0.694	0.286
4.256 (−1)	2.251 (−1)	3.192 (−1)	8.499 (0)	9.795 (−1)	2.858 (1)	0.709	0.270
5.256 (−1)	2.601 (−1)	1.947 (−1)	7.573 (0)	9.978 (−1)	1.921 (1)	0.715	0.262
5.926 (−1)	2.861 (−1)	1.339 (−1)	6.971 (0)	1.003 (0)	1.435 (1)	0.717	0.260
6.518 (−1)	3.117 (−1)	9.219 (−2)	6.442 (0)	1.004 (0)	1.070 (1)	0.719	0.260
7.034 (−1)	3.372 (−1)	6.369 (−2)	5.980 (0)	1.004 (0)	7.967 (0)	0.719	0.260
7.484 (−1)	3.629 (−1)	4.404 (−2)	5.570 (0)	1.005 (0)	5.921 (0)	0.720	0.260
7.873 (−1)	3.887 (−1)	3.053 (−2)	5.196 (0)	1.005 (0)	4.400 (0)	0.720	0.260
8.210 (−1)	4.151 (−1)	2.117 (−2)	4.844 (0)	1.005 (0)	3.276 (0)	0.720	0.260
8.498 (−1)	4.417 (−1)	1.472 (−2)	4.514 (0)	1.005 (0)	2.443 (0)	0.720	0.260
8.746 (−1)	4.689 (−1)	1.023 (−2)	4.207 (0)	1.005 (0)	1.824 (0)	0.720	0.260
8.957 (−1)	4.965 (−1)	7.121 (−3)	3.922 (0)	1.005 (0)	1.361 (0)	0.720	0.260
9.137 (−1)	5.246 (−1)	4.962 (−3)	3.652 (0)	1.005 (0)	1.019 (0)	0.720	0.260
9.289 (−1)	5.531 (−1)	3.460 (−3)	3.398 (0)	1.005 (0)	7.640 (−1)	0.720	0.260
9.418 (−1)	5.820 (−1)	2.416 (−3)	3.165 (0)	1.005 (0)	5.726 (−1)	0.720	0.260
9.526 (−1)	6.114 (−1)	1.687 (−3)	2.950 (0)	1.005 (0)	4.290 (−1)	0.720	0.260
9.617 (−1)	6.411 (−1)	1.180 (−3)	2.750 (0)	1.005 (0)	3.217 (−1)	0.720	0.260
9.692 (−1)	6.713 (−1)	8.249 (−4)	2.558 (0)	1.005 (0)	2.419 (−1)	0.720	0.260
9.755 (−1)	7.016 (−1)	5.781 (−4)	2.369 (0)	1.005 (0)	1.828 (−1)	0.720	0.260
9.807 (−1)	7.317 (−1)	4.051 (−4)	2.157 (0)	1.005 (0)	1.406 (−1)	0.720	0.260
9.849 (−1)	7.605 (−1)	2.848 (−4)	1.886 (0)	1.005 (0)	1.127 (−1)	0.720	0.260
9.899 (−1)	8.016 (−1)	1.638 (−4)	1.513 (0)	1.005 (0)	8.214 (−2)	0.720	0.260

At the center, $\epsilon_{\text{nucl}}/\epsilon_{\text{grav}} = 1.011 \times 10^5$, and $P_{\text{gas}}/P = 0.9994$.

PROBLEMS

1. Why is the virial theorem not generally applicable to protostars?

2. Might the pre–main-sequence model for a star of one solar mass in Table 7-12 be expected to obey the polytropic law for index $n = 1.5$? Test the answer by checking several entries in the table.

3. Refer to Table 7-32 for the internal structure of a main-sequence star of mass 9 $M_\odot$.
   (a) Calculate roughly the main-sequence lifetime. Compare the answer with the value given in Fig. 7-9.
   (b) What is the principal source of opacity near the center?
   (c) Verify the values given for P_g/P near the center.

4. What fraction of the total pressure at the center of the Sun is due to degeneracy?

5. Correlate the distributions of X, He^4, and L_r in Fig. 7-28D and Table 7-31 for a giant star of mass 5 $M_\odot$. Identify the principal chemical elements and sources of energy in the various regions of the model.

6. During the course of its evolution, a star of mass 5 $M_\odot$ crosses the Hertzsprung gap toward the left on its way to the main sequence and later follows a similar path toward the right into the giant region. Compare the structures at the midpoints of the two crossings.

7. Find a simple, approximate expression for the energy-generation rate as a function of M_r for the white dwarf described in Table 7-11. Relate this expression to the principal mechanism by which the energy is produced.

PART FOUR

THE CALCULATION
OF MODEL
ATMOSPHERES AND
INTERIORS

In Part Four, the equations obtained in Chapters 4 and 6 are applied to the construction of a model solar atmosphere and a number of model stellar interiors. Since most of these require numerical integration, we discuss this procedure in general terms in Chapter 8. Chapter 9 illustrates in detail the computation of a model atmosphere for the Sun, while Chapter 10 is concerned with the construction of model interiors.

8

NUMERICAL INTEGRATION

1 DERIVATION OF A FORMULA FOR NUMERICAL INTEGRATION

The differential equations for the stellar atmosphere and interior have the form

$$\frac{dv}{dz} = f(z, v, w, \cdots), \qquad (8\text{-}1)$$

where z is the independent variable, v is a dependent variable, and the quantities $w, \cdots$ represent any additional dependent variables or functions of the dependent variables, such as the opacity coefficient. In the atmospheric case, only one equation of the form (8-1) is considered at a time. The calculation of a stellar interior, however, requires that several such equations be solved simultaneously.

To illustrate the principle of numerical integration, we consider first a method in which the dependent variables are expressed in Taylor series that are truncated after the term that includes the first derivative. The expansion for the variable v is made about the point v_0, which corresponds to z_0 and f_0. It is assumed that z_0, v_0, and f_0 are known, and we wish to find v_1 and f_1 at some value z_1 close to z_0. We have

$$v_1 \approx v_0 + (z_1 - z_0)f_0.$$

If there are several simultaneous differential equations, each of the dependent variables is evaluated from a similar expansion. The procedure is repeated for successive values of z, which are normally taken at equal intervals. If we let h denote the common interval and let the subscript i designate values on any line i of the integration, we may write

$$h = z_{i+1} - z_i \qquad (8\text{-}2)$$

and

$$v_{i+1} \approx v_i + hf_i. \qquad (8\text{-}3)$$

The formula (8-3) has the disadvantage that it is inaccurate unless the interval h is very small or the function v is nearly linear with z, for only then are the second and higher derivatives negligible. If additional terms were retained in eq. (8-3) to improve the accuracy, we might find that the higher derivatives

of v were difficult or impossible to calculate; for example, we should encounter terms requiring the numerical value of the derivative of the opacity
coefficient. We shall therefore derive a method based on the *differences* of
successive tabular entries of the function $f = dv/dz$, rather than the derivatives.* The format of this calculation is illustrated in Table 8-1, where we
have set

$$^1\Delta_i = hf_i - hf_{i-1}$$

$$^2\Delta_i = {}^1\Delta_i - {}^1\Delta_{i-1}$$

$$^3\Delta_i = {}^2\Delta_i - {}^2\Delta_{i-1}$$

$$^4\Delta_i = {}^3\Delta_i - {}^3\Delta_{i-1}.$$

$$\vdots \qquad\qquad \vdots$$

We shall find an expression of the form

$$v_{i+1} = v_i + hf_i + a_1{}^1\Delta_i + a_2{}^2\Delta_i + a_3{}^3\Delta_i + \cdots, \tag{8-4}$$

where $a_1, a_2, a_3, \cdots$ are constants. Again, it is necessary to know initially the
values of $v, f, {}^1\Delta, {}^2\Delta, {}^3\Delta, \cdots$ at some value of z, which we may call z_0. The
initial values and other quantities required to calculate them are indicated by
bold-faced type in Table 8-1.

Since each new line that has been calculated assumes the role of the initial
line for the computation of the following level of the integration, we shall
simplify the notation by using the subscript 0 for the last known line of
integration and the subscript 1 for the next line to be found.

To derive eq. (8-4), including the numerical values of the coefficients, we

* The Runge–Kutta method, which is widely used, is not discussed in this book.
See H.-Y. Chiu, 1968 (63), p. 454, and J. B. Scarborough, 1966 (76), p. 358 et seq.

Table 8-1   Format for Numerical Integration Using Differences
of $hf = h(dv/dz)$.

z	v	hf	$^1\Delta$	$^2\Delta$	$^3\Delta$	$^4\Delta$
$\vdots$						
z_{-4}	v_{-4}	hf_{-4}				
z_{-3}	v_{-3}	hf_{-3}	$^1\Delta_{-3}$			
z_{-2}	v_{-2}	hf_{-2}	$^1\Delta_{-2}$	$^2\Delta_{-2}$		
z_{-1}	v_{-1}	hf_{-1}	$^1\Delta_{-1}$	$^2\Delta_{-1}$	$^3\Delta_{-1}$	
z_0	v_0	hf_0	$^1\Delta_0$	$^2\Delta_0$	$^3\Delta_0$	$^4\Delta_0$
z_1	v_1	hf_1	$^1\Delta_1$	$^2\Delta_1$	$^3\Delta_1$	$^4\Delta_1$
z_2	v_2	hf_2	$^1\Delta_2$	$^2\Delta_2$	$^3\Delta_2$	$^4\Delta_2$
z_3	v_3	hf_3	$^1\Delta_3$	$^2\Delta_3$	$^3\Delta_3$	$^4\Delta_3$
$\vdots$	$\vdots$	$\vdots$	$\vdots$	$\vdots$	$\vdots$	$\vdots$

represent the function hf by a polynomial φ. The degree n of this polynomial must be at least as great as the order of the highest difference desired. Then

$$\varphi = c_0 + c_1(z - z_0) + c_2(z - z_0)(z - z_{-1}) +$$
$$+ c_3(z - z_0)(z - z_{-1})(z - z_{-2}) + \cdots +$$
$$+ c_n(z - z_0)(z - z_{-1}) \cdots (z - z_{-n}).$$

We shall require that φ be equal to hf at the points $z_0, z_{-1}, z_{-2}, \cdots, z_{-n}$. From this condition, we can evaluate the coefficients as follows.

At $z = z_0$,

$$hf_0 = \varphi(z_0) = c_0$$
$$\therefore c_0 = hf_0.$$

At $z = z_{-1}$,

$$hf_{-1} = \varphi(z_{-1}) = c_0 + c_1(z_{-1} - z_0)$$

$$c_1 = \frac{hf_{-1} - c_0}{z_{-1} - z_0}$$

$$= \frac{hf_{-1} - hf_0}{-h}$$

$$\therefore c_1 = \frac{{}^1\Delta_0}{h}.$$

At $z = z_{-2}$,

$$hf_{-2} = \varphi(z_{-2}) = c_0 + c_1(z_{-2} - z_0) + c_2(z_{-2} - z_0)(z_{-2} - z_{-1})$$

$$= hf_0 + \frac{{}^1\Delta_0}{h}(-2h) + c_2(-2h)(-h)$$

$$c_2 = \frac{hf_{-2} - hf_0 + 2\,{}^1\Delta_0}{2h^2}$$

$$= \frac{hf_{-2} - hf_0 + 2(hf_0 - hf_{-1})}{2h^2}$$

$$= \frac{(hf_0 - hf_{-1}) - (hf_{-1} - hf_{-2})}{2h^2}$$

$$= \frac{{}^1\Delta_0 - {}^1\Delta_{-1}}{2h^2}$$

$$\therefore c_2 = \frac{{}^2\Delta_0}{2h^2}.$$

At $z = z_{-3}$,

$$hf_{-3} = \varphi(z_{-3}) = c_0 + c_1(z_{-3} - z_0) + c_2(z_{-3} - z_0)(z_{-3} - z_{-1}) +$$
$$+ c_3(z_{-3} - z_0)(z_{-3} - z_{-1})(z_{-3} - z_{-2})$$

$$= hf_0 + \frac{{}^1\Delta_0}{h}(-3h) + \frac{{}^2\Delta_0}{2h^2}(-3h)(-2h) + c_3(-3h)(-2h)(-h)$$

$$c_3 = \frac{hf_{-3} - hf_0 + 3\,{}^1\Delta_0 - 3^2\Delta_0}{-3!\,h^3}.$$

Since

$$^2\Delta_0 = {}^1\Delta_0 - {}^1\Delta_{-1}$$
$$= {}^1\Delta_0 - (hf_{-1} - hf_{-2}),$$

we have

$$c_3 = \frac{hf_{-3} - hf_0 + 3\,{}^1\Delta_0 - 3\,{}^1\Delta_0 + 3(hf_{-1} - hf_{-2})}{-3!\,h^3}$$

$$= \frac{-(hf_0 - hf_{-1}) + (hf_{-1} - hf_{-2}) - (hf_{-2} - hf_{-3}) + (hf_{-1} - hf_{-2})}{-3!\,h^3}$$

$$= \frac{-({}^1\Delta_0 - {}^1\Delta_{-1}) - ({}^1\Delta_{-2} - {}^1\Delta_{-1})}{-3!\,h^3}$$

$$= \frac{-({}^2\Delta_0 - {}^2\Delta_{-1})}{-3!\,h^3}$$

$$\therefore\ c_3 = \frac{{}^3\Delta_0}{3!\,h^3}.$$

In general,

$$c_n = \frac{{}^n\Delta_0}{n!\,h^n}.$$

Thus

$$h\frac{dv}{dz} = hf = \varphi = hf_0 + \frac{{}^1\Delta_0}{h}(z - z_0) + \frac{{}^2\Delta_0}{2h^2}(z - z_0)(z - z_{-1}) +$$

$$+ \frac{{}^3\Delta_0}{3!\,h^3}(z - z_0)(z - z_{-1})(z - z_{-2}) + \cdots. \qquad (8\text{-}5)$$

This is Newton's formula for backward interpolation. To find v_{+1}, we must integrate this equation, giving

$$h(v_{+1} - v_0) = \int_{z_0}^{z_1} \left(h\frac{dv}{dz}\right) dz$$

$$= \int_{z_0}^{z_1} \left[hf_0 + \frac{{}^1\Delta_0}{h}(z - z_0) + \frac{{}^2\Delta_0}{2h^2}(z - z_0)(z - z_{-1}) + \right.$$

$$\left. + \frac{{}^3\Delta_0}{3!\,h^3}(z - z_0)(z - z_{-1})(z - z_{-2}) + \cdots \right] dz.$$

A transformation of the variable of integration will simplify the result. Let

$$u = \frac{z - z_0}{h},$$

$$du = \frac{dz}{h}.$$

The upper and lower limits of the integral then become

$$u_1 = 1$$
$$u_0 = 0,$$

while

$$z - z_{-1} = (z - z_0) + (z_0 - z_{-1})$$
$$= hu + h$$
$$= h(u + 1)$$

and

$$z - z_{-2} = (z - z_0) + (z_0 - z_{-1}) + (z_{-1} - z_{-2})$$
$$= hu + h + h$$
$$= h(u + 2).$$

Therefore,

$$h(v_{+1} - v_0) = \int_0^1 \left[hf_0 + {}^1\Delta_0 u + \frac{{}^2\Delta_0}{2} u(u + 1) + \right.$$

$$\left. + \frac{{}^3\Delta_0}{3!} u(u + 1)(u + 2) + \cdots \right] h \, du$$

$$= h^2 f_0 u |_0^1 + \tfrac{1}{2} h \, {}^1\Delta_0 u^2 |_0^1 + \frac{{}^2\Delta_0}{2} h[\tfrac{1}{3}u^3 + \tfrac{1}{2}u^2]_0^1 +$$

$$+ \frac{{}^3\Delta_0}{3!} h[\tfrac{1}{4}u^4 + u^3 + u^2]_0^1 + \cdots$$

$$= h^2 f_0 + \tfrac{1}{2} h \, {}^1\Delta_0 + \tfrac{5}{12} h \, {}^2\Delta_0 + \tfrac{3}{8} h \, {}^3\Delta_0 + \cdots$$

or

$$v_{+1} = v_0 + hf_0 + \tfrac{1}{2}{}^1\Delta_0 + \tfrac{5}{12}{}^2\Delta_0 + \tfrac{3}{8}{}^3\Delta_0 + \cdots$$
$$= v_0 + hf_0 + 0.5 {}^1\Delta_0 + 0.41667 {}^2\Delta_0 + 0.3750 {}^3\Delta_0 + 0.3486 {}^4\Delta_0 +$$
$$+ 0.3299 {}^4\Delta_0 + \cdots. \tag{8-6}$$

This is the equation we have sought.

A similar derivation, using z_{+1}, z_0, z_{-1}, z_{-2}, $\cdots$ and the (unknown) derivative and differences at z_{+1} yields

$$v_{+1} = v_0 + hf_{+1} - \tfrac{1}{2}{}^1\Delta_{+1} - \tfrac{1}{12}{}^2\Delta_{+1} - \tfrac{1}{24}{}^3\Delta_{+1} - \tfrac{19}{720}{}^4\Delta_{+1} - \cdots$$
$$= v_0 + hf_{+1} - 0.5 {}^1\Delta_{+1} - 0.08333 {}^2\Delta_{+1} - 0.04167 {}^3\Delta_{+1} -$$
$$- 0.02639 {}^4\Delta_{+1} - 0.01875 {}^5\Delta_{+1} - \cdots. \tag{8-7}$$

The latter formula has the advantage of faster convergence, so that fewer terms are needed; and rounding errors, which accumulate in the higher differences, have less influence on the result. The obvious disadvantage is that the derivative and differences at z_{+1} are unknown. Hence it is necessary to estimate hf_{+1}, compute the differences $^1\Delta_{+1}, \, ^2\Delta_{+1}, \, ^3\Delta_{+1}, \cdots$, then calculate v_{+1} from formula (8-7), and finally calculate hf_{+1} using this value of v_{+1}. If the estimated and calculated values of hf_{+1} do not agree, a new estimate must be made and the cycle repeated.

2 GENERAL CONSIDERATIONS

We now make several remarks concerning numerical integrations:

(i) If the function f were indeed a polynomial, say of degree n, then all differences beyond the nth would vanish (assuming there were no rounding errors). The integration formulae (8-6) and (8-7) would then be exactly correct if all terms involving $^{n+1}\Delta$ and higher were neglected, since these would all be zero.* When f is not a polynomial, one must truncate either of the formulae after retaining enough terms that the remainder does not affect the computed value to the desired number of significant figures.

(ii) If an error of one unit occurs in a particular value of hf, the error is compounded in successive differences as shown in Table 8-2. Thus, in the fourth difference, an error of 6 units accumulates. The number of differences retained should not be so large that errors due to rounding and numerical approximation seriously affect the result. Rather than carry a large number of differences, it is better to use a smaller interval. If necessary, the interval can be halved after the integration is under way. On the other hand, if the differences become very small, the interval can be doubled.

---

* If f were a polynomial, one could, of course, integrate analytically.

Table 8-2   Cumulative Effect of Rounding Errors. An error $+e$ in hf_0 accumulates in successive differences.

hf	$^1\Delta$	$^2\Delta$	$^3\Delta$	$^4\Delta$
$\vdots$	$\vdots$	$\vdots$	$\vdots$	$\vdots$
hf_{-2}	$^1\Delta_{-2}$	$^2\Delta_{-2}$	$^3\Delta_{-2}$	$^4\Delta_{-2}$
hf_{-1}	$^1\Delta_{-1}$	$^2\Delta_{-1}$	$^3\Delta_{-1}$	$^4\Delta_{-1}$
$hf_0 + e$	$^1\Delta_0 + e$	$^2\Delta_0 + e$	$^3\Delta_0 + e$	$^4\Delta_0 + e$
hf_1	$^1\Delta_1 - e$	$^2\Delta_1 - 2e$	$^3\Delta_1 - 3e$	$^4\Delta_1 - 4e$
hf_2	$^1\Delta_2$	$^2\Delta_2 + e$	$^3\Delta_2 - 3e$	$^4\Delta_2 - 6e$
hf_3	$^1\Delta_3$	$^2\Delta_3$	$^3\Delta_3 - e$	$^4\Delta_3 - 4e$
hf_4	$^1\Delta_4$	$^2\Delta_4$	$^3\Delta_4$	$^4\Delta_4 + e$
hf_5	$^1\Delta_5$	$^2\Delta_5$	$^3\Delta_5$	$^4\Delta_5$
$\vdots$	$\vdots$	$\vdots$	$\vdots$	$\vdots$

If any difference oscillates between positive and negative values or between large and small values on succeeding lines, then this column of differences, as well as all higher ones, is not meaningful and should be discarded.

(iii) It is important that any function that enters into hf, such as the absorption coefficient, should vary smoothly with successive lines of the integration. Otherwise, oscillations will appear in the differences.

(iv) A numerical integration can be reversed in direction. The values of hf should be written in the reverse order, and a new table of differences formed.

We are now ready to proceed with the calculation of model atmospheres and interiors.

PROBLEMS

1. Integrate the differential equation $dy/dx = 15x^2$ numerically. Obtain the starting values analytically, beginning at $x = 0$ and using an interval of 0.1. Continue by numerical integration to $x = 0.5$, and then compare the results with values of y obtained analytically.

2. Derive the integration formula (8-7).

9

A MODEL SOLAR ATMOSPHERE

1 STATEMENT OF THE PROBLEM

We are to find $T(\bar{\tau})$, $P(\bar{\tau})$, $\rho(\bar{\tau})$, and $x(\bar{\tau})$ in the range $0.05 \leqslant \bar{\tau} \leqslant 2.00$ for the solar atmosphere. The following data are given*:

$$T_{\mathrm{eff}} = 5800^{\circ}\mathrm{K},$$

$$g = 2.741 \times 10^4 \text{ cm sec}^{-1}.$$

These two required parameters can of course be calculated from the observed quantities

$$M = 1.991 \times 10^{33} \text{ gm},$$

$$R = 6.960 \times 10^{10} \text{ cm},$$

$$L = 3.91 \times 10^{33} \text{ erg sec}^{-1}.$$

We shall assume that the chemical composition is given by Table 3-7.

The temperatures at all desired optical depths may be found immediately, from a formula for $T(\bar{\tau})$. An analytical approximation that is valid in a small interval in $\bar{\tau}$ provides starting values for the integration of $dP/d\bar{\tau}$. After the tabulation of P as a function of $\bar{\tau}$ has been obtained, the supplementary integration of $dx/d \log P$ establishes the correspondence between x and P, and hence also $\bar{\tau}$. Other quantities, such as the density and electron pressure, can also be tabulated.

2 CALCULATION OF $T(\bar{\tau})$

We shall calculate $T(\bar{\tau})$ on the basis of Eddington's first approximation†:

$$T^4 = \tfrac{1}{2}T_{\mathrm{eff}}{}^4(1 + \tfrac{3}{2}\bar{\tau}) \qquad\qquad (2\text{-}51)\ (9\text{-}1)$$

$$T = 4879(1 + \tfrac{3}{2}\bar{\tau})^{1/4}.$$

* The values of L and hence T_{eff} are not the most recent ones available. See Chapter 1, Section 1-2.

† In addition to the consecutive number of an equation in this and the following chapters, we also state the original location in this book; for example eq. (9-1) in this chapter was derived in Chapter 2, where it was listed as eq. (2-51).

Table 9-1 $T(\bar{\tau})$ and $\theta(\bar{\tau})$.

$\bar{\tau}$	$T\,(°\text{K})$	$\theta = \dfrac{5040}{T}$	$\bar{\tau}$	$T\,(°\text{K})$	$\theta = \dfrac{5040}{T}$
0.050	4967.9	1.0145	0.55	5670.7	0.8888
0.075	5010.7	1.0058	0.60	5728.1	0.8799
0.100	5052.4	0.9975	0.65	5783.8	0.8714
0.125	5093.1	0.9896	0.70	5838.0	0.8633
0.150	5132.8	0.9819	0.75	5890.6	0.8556
0.175	5171.7	0.9745	0.80	5941.9	0.8482
0.200	5209.6	0.9674	0.85	5991.9	0.8411
0.225	5246.8	0.9606	0.90	6040.7	0.8343
0.250	5283.2	0.9540	0.95	6088.4	0.8278
0.275	5318.9	0.9476	1.00	6134.9	0.8215
0.300	5353.8	0.9414			
0.325	5388.1	0.9354	1.10	6224.9	0.8097
0.350	5421.7	0.9296	1.20	6311.2	0.7986
0.375	5454.8	0.9240	1.30	6394.1	0.7882
0.400	5487.2	0.9185	1.40	6473.8	0.7785
0.425	5519.1	0.9132	1.50	6550.8	0.7694
0.450	5550.4	0.9080	1.60	6625.1	0.7607
0.475	5581.2	0.9030	1.70	6697.0	0.7526
0.500	5611.5	0.8982	1.80	6766.6	0.7448
			1.90	6834.2	0.7375
			2.00	6899.8	0.7305

Since the opacity is given in terms of θ rather than T, we also need the values of

$$\theta = \frac{5040}{T}. \qquad\qquad (3\text{-}21)\ (9\text{-}2)$$

Both T and θ are listed in Table 9-1.

3 STARTING VALUES

The basic differential equation is

$$\frac{dP}{d\bar{\tau}} = \frac{g}{\bar{\kappa}}. \qquad\qquad (4\text{-}5)\ (9\text{-}3)$$

To begin the integration, we require several values of $g/\bar{\kappa}$, and hence of P, at equal intervals of $\bar{\tau}$. These may be found from an analytical expression obtained by integrating eq. (9-3), with $\bar{\kappa}$ given by a formula valid in some limited portion of the atmosphere.

To obtain such a formula for $\bar{\kappa}$, we examine the curves giving $\log \bar{\kappa}(\log P_g, \theta)$ in Fig. 3-13 or $\bar{\kappa}(P_g, \theta)$ in Fig. 9-1 or Figs. 9-2A to 9-2G. In the latter two, the ranges of P_g and θ have been chosen as approximately those appropriate to the solar atmosphere, as determined from published models. It is immaterial at what place in the atmosphere the calculation is begun, and we may choose

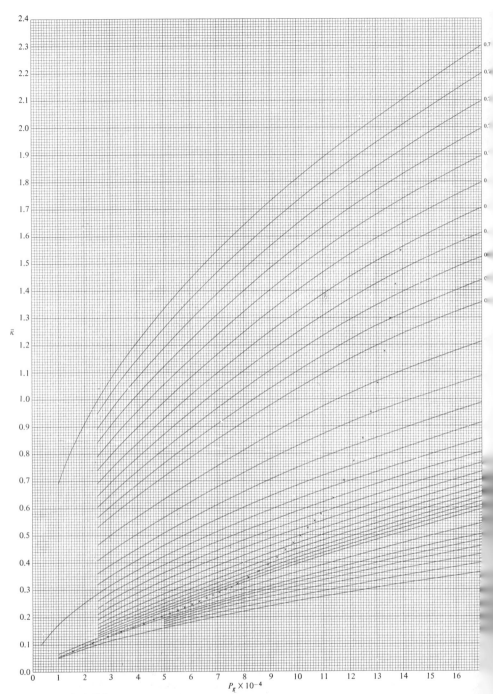

Fig. 9-1 The Variation of $\bar{\kappa}$ in the Solar Atmosphere. The *crosses* indicate the values of $\bar{\kappa}(P_g, \theta)$ at the tabulated points in the model solar atmosphere calculated in this chapter. The curves are identical with those of Figs. 9-2A to 9-2G.

this to obtain the most convenient formula. Published models show that, for θ between 0.9 and 1.0 (somewhat higher in the atmosphere than the level $\theta_{\text{eff}} = 0.87$), the range of P_g may be taken as 4 to 5. This corresponds to a portion of Fig. 3-13 where $\log \bar{\kappa}$ is nearly independent of θ. In this region,

$$\log \bar{\kappa} = -4.40 + 0.8 \log P \qquad \begin{cases} 0.9 \gtrsim \theta \gtrsim 1.0 \\ 4 \gtrsim \log P \gtrsim 5. \end{cases} \qquad (9\text{-}4)$$

We have replaced P_g by P, since radiation pressure is negligible.

The adequacy of this formula can be tested after the starting values have been computed and x as a function of $\bar{\tau}$ has also been found. It is necessary, first of all, that $\log P$ as given by the model should have values in the range 4 to 5 for θ between 0.9 and 1.0. Furthermore, the integral of $\bar{\kappa}\rho \, dx$ over the range of the starting values should equal $\Delta\bar{\tau}$ as given by the tabulated independent variable. Suppose, for example, that the starting values of the pressure as derived by use of the approximate relation (9-4) were too small for the given temperatures and optical depths. Then $\bar{\kappa}$ would also be too small, as would ρ, which is computed from the perfect gas law. Hence $\int \bar{\kappa}\rho \, dx$ would be less than the tabulated interval $\Delta\bar{\tau}$. In this model, $\int \bar{\kappa}\rho \, dx$ over the range of the starting values $(0.200 \leqslant \bar{\tau} \leqslant 0.300)$ is 0.0903, rather than 0.1000. The 10 per cent error is tolerable for our purpose.

We therefore adopt the approximate formula

$$\bar{\kappa} = 10^{-4.40}P^{0.8} \qquad (9\text{-}5)$$

for computing the starting values. Substitution into eq. (9-3) then gives

$$\frac{dP}{d\bar{\tau}} = 10^{4.40}g\,\frac{1}{P^{0.8}}.$$

Separating the variables and integrating, we have

$$\frac{1}{1.8}P^{1.8} = 10^{4.40}g\bar{\tau} + \text{const.}$$

The value of the constant is zero, since the vanishing of the density at the surface requires that $P = 0$ at $\bar{\tau} = 0.$* Then

$$P^{1.8} = 1.8 \times 10^{4.40}g\bar{\tau}$$

$$= 1.239 \times 10^9\bar{\tau}. \qquad (9\text{-}6)$$

This relation is used to calculate P for $\bar{\tau} = 0.200$ to 0.300 in Tables 9-2 and 9-3. Since the integration is to proceed in the direction of smaller, as well as larger, optical depths, two separate tables are prepared. The values of

---

* In evaluating the constant at the surface, we are tacitly assuming that the formula adopted for $\bar{\kappa}$ is valid in the entire region between optical depth equal to $\bar{\tau}$ and optical depth equal to zero. Reference to Fig. 9-1 shows that the approximation remains a good one at small P in the relevant range of temperature.

$h \, dP/d\bar{\tau} = hg/\bar{\kappa}$ can then be found, with $\bar{\kappa}$ (still for the starting values) either calculated from eq. (9-5) or read from Figs. 9-2A to 9-2G. Since the formula for $\bar{\kappa}$ is only an approximation to $\bar{\kappa}$ as read from the curves, we cannot expect the two values to agree precisely. The latter will be adopted. The differences of $h \, dP/d\bar{\tau}$ can now be found, and the information needed to begin the integration will be complete.

4 NUMERICAL INTEGRATION FOR $P(\bar{\tau})$

The value of P at the next level is to be determined by numerical integration of the differential equation

$$\frac{dP}{d\bar{\tau}} = \frac{g}{\bar{\kappa}}.$$

We illustrate by computing the entries at $\bar{\tau} = 0.175$ in Table 9-3.
   (i) Using eq. (8-6),

$$v_{+1} = v_0 + hf_0 + 0.5\,{}^1\!\Delta_0 + 0.417\,{}^2\!\Delta_0 + 0.375\,{}^3\!\Delta_0 + \cdots,$$

we have

$$P_{+1} = [4.607 - 0.359 + 0.5(-0.020) + 0.417(-0.003)] \times 10^4$$
$$= 4.237 \times 10^4.$$

With this value of P and the corresponding θ, we find $\bar{\kappa} = 0.175$ from Figs. 9-2A to 9-2G. Thus

$$\left(h\frac{dP}{d\bar{\tau}} \right)_{+1} = h\frac{g}{\bar{\kappa}} = -0.025 \times \frac{2.741 \times 10^4}{0.175}$$
$$= -0.392 \times 10^4$$

and

$${}^1\!\Delta_{+1} = -0.033$$
$${}^2\!\Delta_{+1} = -0.013$$
$${}^3\!\Delta_{+1} = -0.010.$$

Figs. 9-2A to 9-2G   The Rosseland Mean Absorption Coefficient $\bar{\kappa}$ as a Function of Gas Pressure P_g, with $\theta = 5040/T$ as Parameter. The composition assumed has $X = 0.56$, $Y = 0.41$, $Z = 0.03$ and is listed in detail in Table 3-6. The curves for $\theta = 0.70, 0.80, 0.90, 1.00,$ and 1.10 are taken from Fig. 3-13 [due to E. Vitense, 1951 (203)], which gives log $\bar{\kappa}$ as a function of log P_g, with θ as parameter. The remaining curves have been interpolated, and a value read from one of these curves may differ from the value that would be predicted by the theory employed in the calculation of the curves of Fig. 3-13; nevertheless, an internal consistency within two units of the third significant figure may be expected when successive values of $\bar{\kappa}$ are read from these curves during the computation of a model atmosphere.

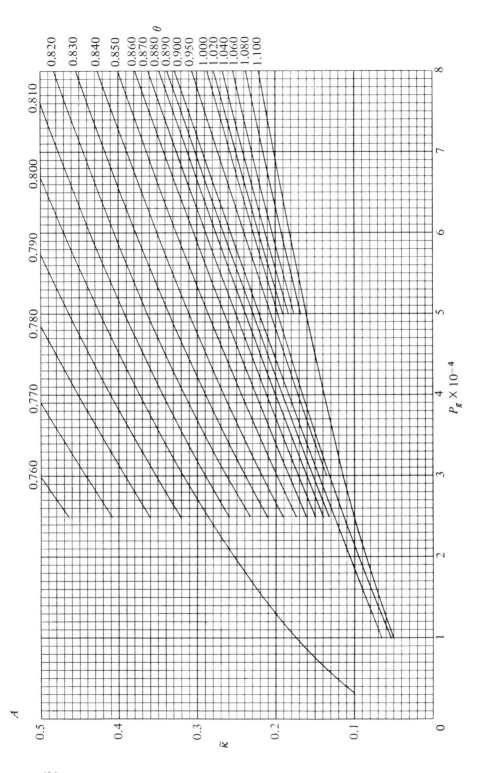

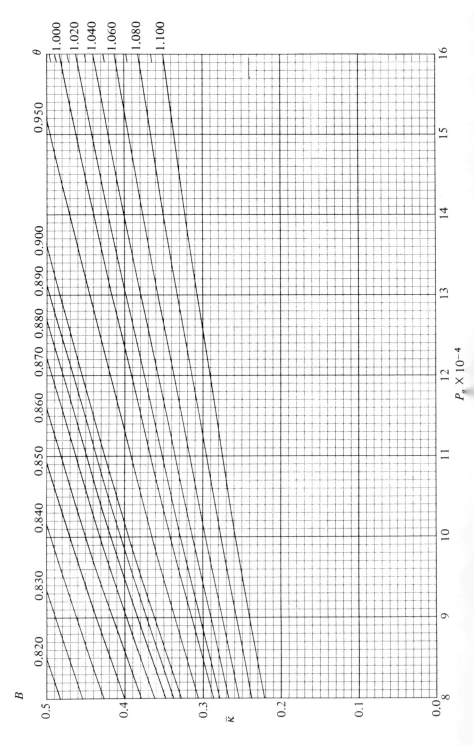

424

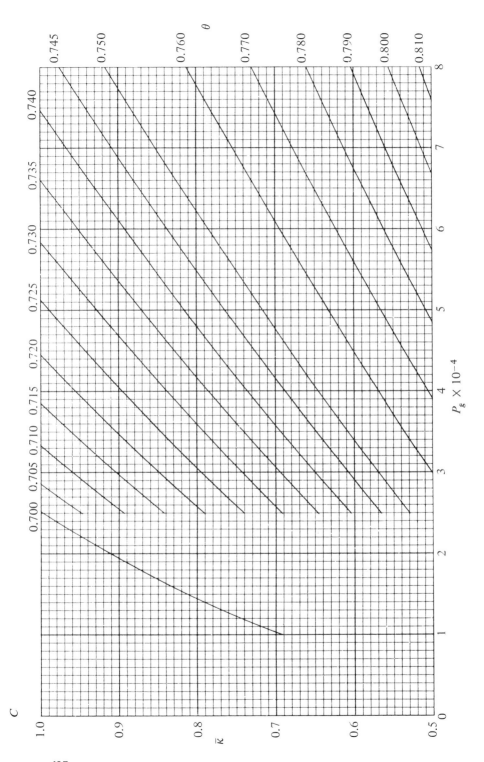

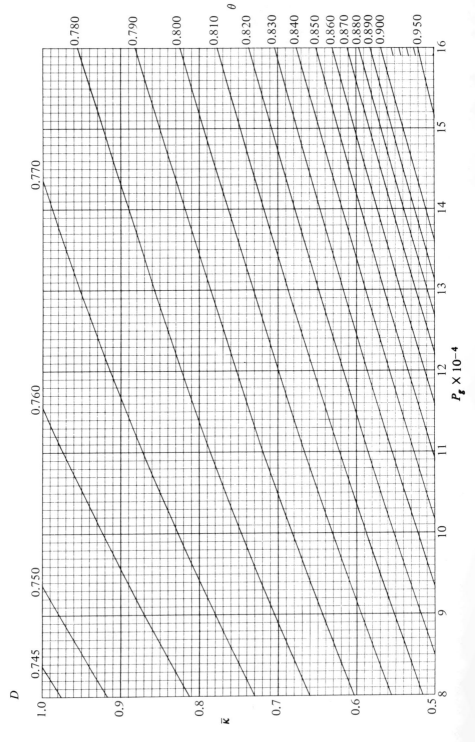

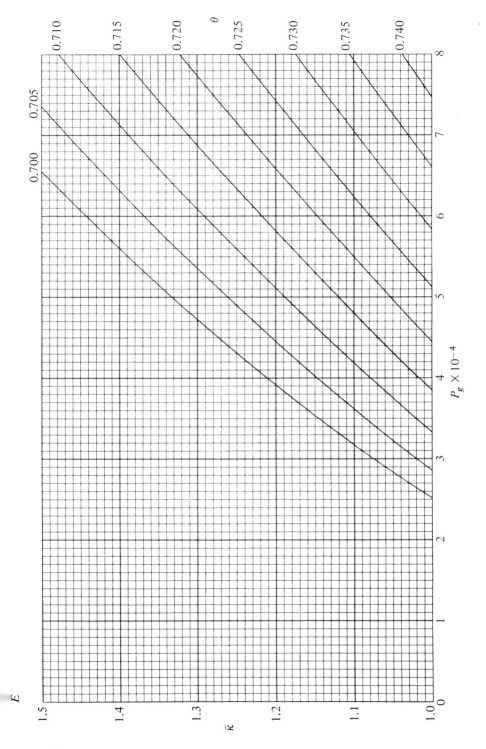

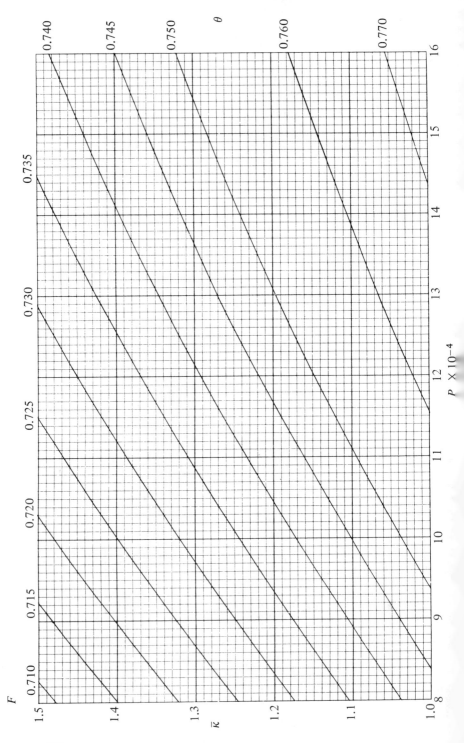

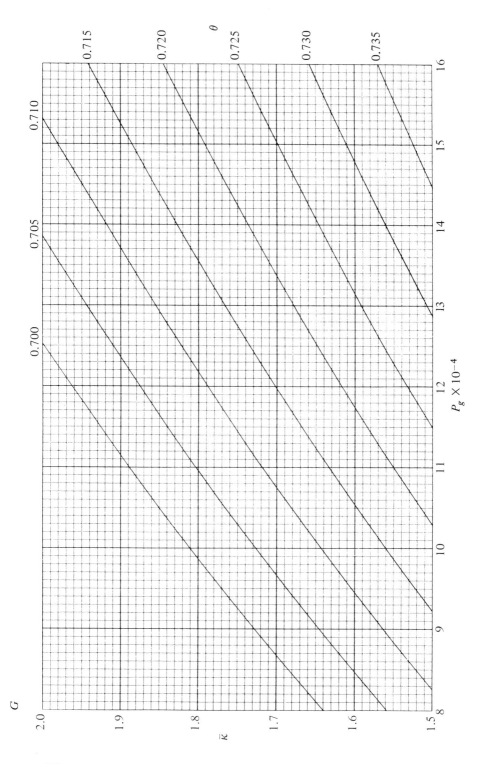

This line of the integration is now complete and we are ready to proceed to $\bar{\tau} = 0.150$. This method was used to compute Tables 9-2, 9-3, and 9-4.

Table 9-2   Integration of $dP/d\bar{\tau}$ (Inwards).

$\bar{\tau}$	P (dyne cm^{-2})	$h\dfrac{dP}{d\bar{\tau}} = h\dfrac{g}{\kappa}$	$^1\Delta$	$^2\Delta$	$^3\Delta$
0.200	4.607×10^4	0.359×10^4			*
0.225	4.919	0.339	-0.020×10^4		
0.250	5.216	0.322	-0.017	$+0.003 \times 10^4$	
0.275	5.499	0.305	-0.017	0.000	-0.003×10^4
0.300	5.772	0.290	-0.015	$+0.002$	$+0.002$
0.325	6.055	0.277	-0.013	$+0.002$	0.000
0.350	6.326	0.266	-0.011	$+0.002$	0.000
0.375	6.587	0.255	-0.011	0.000	-0.002
0.400	6.837	0.245	-0.010	$+0.001$	-0.001
0.425	7.077	0.235	-0.010	0.000	-0.001
0.450	7.307	0.228	-0.007	$+0.003$	-0.003
0.475	7.533	0.221	-0.007	0.000	-0.003
0.500	7.750				
Continue at double interval:					
0.30		0.580			
0.35		0.532	-0.048		
0.40		0.490	-0.042	$+0.006$	
0.45		0.456	-0.034	$+0.008$	$+0.002$
0.50	7.750	0.425	-0.031	$+0.003$	-0.005
0.55	8.161	0.397	-0.028	$+0.003$	0.000
0.60	8.545	0.372	-0.025	$+0.003$	0.000
0.65	8.906	0.351	-0.021	$+0.004$	$+0.001$
0.70	9.248	0.328	-0.023	-0.002	-0.006
0.75	9.564	0.308	-0.020	$+0.003$	$+0.005$
0.80	9.863	0.291	-0.017	$+0.003$	0.000
0.85	10.147	0.275	-0.016	$+0.001$	-0.002
0.90	10.414	0.261	-0.014	$+0.002$	$+0.001$
0.95	10.669	0.248	-0.013	$+0.001$	-0.001
1.00	10.911				
Continue at double the preceding interval:					
0.60		0.744			
0.70		0.656	-0.088		
0.80		0.582	-0.074	$+0.014$	
0.90		0.522	-0.060	$+0.014$	0.000
1.00	10.911	0.475	-0.047	$+0.013$	-0.001
1.10	11.368	0.431	-0.044	$+0.003$	-0.010
1.20	11.778	0.392	-0.039	$+0.005$	$+0.002$
1.30	12.153	0.356	-0.036	$+0.003$	-0.002
1.40	12.492	0.321	-0.035	$+0.001$	-0.002
1.50	12.796	0.289	-0.032	$+0.003$	$+0.002$
1.60	13.070	0.259	-0.030	$+0.002$	-0.001
1.70	13.315	0.233	-0.026	$+0.004$	$+0.002$
1.80	13.537	0.211	-0.022	$+0.004$	0.000
1.90	13.739	0.193	-0.018	$+0.004$	0.000
2.00	13.925				

* The third differences were not used in the integration.

A Model Solar Atmosphere

Table 9-3 Integration of $dP/d\bar\tau$ (Outwards).

$\bar\tau$	$P\times10^{-4}$ (dyne cm^{-2})	$h\dfrac{dP}{d\bar\tau}\times10^{-4}$	$^1\Delta\times10^{-4}$	$^2\Delta\times10^{-4}$	$^3\Delta\times10^{-4}$	$^4\Delta\times10^{-4}$	$^5\Delta\times10^{-4}$	$^6\Delta\times10^{-4}$
0.300		−0.290						
0.275		−0.305	−0.015					
0.250		−0.322	−0.017	−0.002				
0.255		−0.339	−0.017	0.000	+0.002*			
0.200	4.607	−0.359	−0.020	−0.003	−0.003*			
0.175	4.237	−0.392	−0.033	−0.013	−0.010			
0.150	3.819	−0.426	−0.034	−0.001	+0.012*			
0.125	3.376	−0.469	−0.043	−0.009	−0.008			
0.100	2.878	−0.535	−0.066	−0.023	−0.014	−0.006		
0.075	2.293	−0.653	−0.118	−0.052	−0.029	−0.015	−0.009	
0.050	1.541	−0.902	−0.249	−0.131	−0.079	−0.050	−0.035	−0.026

* These differences were not used in the integration.

Table 9-4 $\bar\kappa(\bar\tau)$ and Differences.

$\bar\tau$	$\bar\kappa$ (cm^2 gm^{-1})	$^1\Delta\,(\bar\kappa)$ ($h=0.025$)	$^1\Delta\,(\bar\kappa)$ ($h=0.050$)	$\bar\tau$	$\bar\kappa$ (cm^2 gm^{-1})	$^1\Delta\,(\bar\kappa)$ ($h=0.050$)	$^1\Delta\,(\bar\kappa)$ ($h=0.10$)	$^2\Delta\,(\bar\kappa)$ ($h=0.10$)
0.050	0.076			0.55	0.345	0.023		
0.075	0.105	0.029		0.60	0.368	0.023		
0.100	0.128	0.023		0.65	0.391	0.023		
0.125	0.146	0.018		0.70	0.418	0.027		
0.150	0.161	0.015		0.75	0.445	0.027		
0.175	0.175	0.014		0.80	0.471	0.026	0.053	
0.200	0.191	0.016		0.85	0.498	0.027		
0.225	0.202	0.011		0.90	0.526	0.028	0.055	0.002
0.250	0.213	0.011	0.022	0.95	0.552	0.026		
0.275	0.225	0.012		1.00	0.577	0.025	0.051	−0.004
0.300	0.236	0.011	0.023					
0.325	0.247	0.011		1.10	0.636		0.059	0.008
0.350	0.258	0.011	0.022	1.20	0.700		0.064	0.005
0.375	0.269	0.011		1.30	0.771		0.071	0.006
0.400	0.280	0.011	0.022	1.40	0.855		0.084	0.013
0.425	0.291	0.011		1.50	0.950		0.095	0.009
0.450	0.301	0.010	0.021	1.60	1.060		0.110	0.015
0.475	0.310	0.009		1.70	1.177		0.117	0.007
0.500	0.322	0.012	0.021	1.80	1.298		0.121	0.004
				1.90	1.423		0.125	0.004
				2.00	1.549		0.126	0.001

(ii) Alternatively, the entries at $\bar\tau=0.175$ can be found by use of eq. (8-7),

$$v_{+1}=v_0+hf_{+1}-0.5\,^1\Delta_{+1}-0.0833\,^2\Delta_{+1}-0.0417\,^3\Delta_{+1}+\cdots.$$

We must first estimate hf_{+1} and the differences. If we assume

$$^3\Delta_{+1}=0,$$

then

$$^2\Delta_{+1} = -0.003$$
$$^1\Delta_{+1} = -0.023$$
$$hf_{+1} = -0.382.$$

With these values, the first estimate for P is

$$P_{+1} = [4.607 - 0.382 - 0.5(-0.023) - 0.0833(-0.003)] \times 10^4$$
$$= 4.237 \times 10^4.$$

To check the validity of this result, we obtain $\bar{\kappa} = 0.175$ from the figure and then calculate

$$hf_{+1} = -0.025 \frac{2.741 \times 10^4}{0.175}$$
$$= -0.392$$
$$^1\Delta_{+1} = -0.033$$
$$^2\Delta_{+1} = -0.013$$
$$^3\Delta_{+1} = -0.010.$$

We then find

$$P_{+1} = [4.607 - 0.392 - 0.5(-0.033) - 0.0833(-0.013) -$$
$$- 0.0417(-0.010)] \times 10^4$$
$$= 4.233 \times 10^4.$$

This second estimate for P again yields $\bar{\kappa} = 0.175$ and, consequently, the same values of hf_{+1}, $^1\Delta_{+1}$, $^2\Delta_{+1}$, $^3\Delta_{+1}$ as did the first estimate. The line at $\bar{\tau} = 0.175$ would then differ from that given in Table 9-3 only in the value of P, which would be taken as 4.233. This discrepancy of four units in the fourth significant figure is tolerable, since $\bar{\kappa}$ can be read to an accuracy no better than three figures.

In Table 9-4, we have entered the values of $\bar{\kappa}$ and $^1\Delta(\bar{\kappa})$ as each line of the integration was performed. This serves as a check on the regularity of the variation of $\bar{\kappa}$. Small fluctuations must be expected because of inaccuracies in the curves. The progression of $\bar{\kappa}$ is shown in Fig. 9-1.

For continuing the integration of $dP/d\bar{\tau}$ toward the surface (Table 9-3), a smaller interval would be required. The integration could not be carried all the way to $\bar{\tau} = 0$, because the approach of $\bar{\kappa}$ toward zero would cause $dP/d\bar{\tau}$ to increase toward infinity.*

---

* That the absorption coefficient approaches zero at low pressure can be seen from Fig. 9-1 or Fig. 9-2A. It may be understood by considering Fig. 3-12D. From the shapes of the curves for the total coefficient, we see that H^- is the principal opacity source. The overlapping of the curves implies that $\kappa_\nu(H^-)$ is proportional to P_e; the H atom must first attract an electron to become H^-. Thus κ_ν or $\bar{\kappa}$ approaches zero with P_e, which in turn approaches zero with P or ρ.

5 NUMERICAL INTEGRATION FOR $x(\log P)$ OR $x(\bar{\tau})$

After we have obtained a tabulation of P as a function of $\bar{\tau}$, we can perform another numerical integration to find the variation of the geometrical depth x with P or $\bar{\tau}$. The differential equation to be solved is

$$\frac{dx}{d \log_{10} P} = -\log_e 10 \frac{k}{\mu H} \frac{1}{g} T \qquad (4\text{-}7)\ (9\text{-}7)$$

$$= -4.605 \times 10^3 T;$$

or, for layers not too near the surface, we may use instead the relation

$$\frac{dx}{d\bar{\tau}} = -\frac{1}{\bar{\kappa}\rho} = -\frac{k}{\mu H} \frac{T}{\bar{\kappa} P}.$$

We consider first the integration of $dx/d \log P$.

The mean molecular weight μ may be calculated as if no ionization had occurred. Hydrogen is almost completely neutral, as can be seen from Fig. 3-4. Although the electron pressure assumed for that graph has the constant value of 10 dyne cm^{-2}, the Saha equation shows that the higher electron pressures prevailing throughout most of our model (Table 9-6) will lower the degree of ionization below that shown. Similarly, Fig. 3-5 demonstrates that helium is neutral. The metals, on the other hand, have low ionization potentials, and a considerable fraction of them may be ionized. Since their abundance is low, however, we shall incur only a small error if we assume them also to be neutral. Thus we may use the expression

$$\mu = \frac{\sum_z N_z A_z}{\sum_z N_z}. \qquad (4\text{-}4)\ (9\text{-}8)$$

For the composition assumed in this model,

$$\mu = \frac{44,760}{29,750} = 1.505.$$

We can now immediately calculate the entire column of values of $h\, dx/d \log_{10} P$, since T can be obtained for given $\log P$ by interpolation for $\bar{\tau}$ against P in Table 9-2 or 9-3 and then interpolation for T against this value of $\bar{\tau}$ in Table 9-1. The differences are then computed. It remains only to establish the zero point of x, which can be chosen arbitrarily since eq. (9-7) does not depend on the magnitude of x. The obvious assignment would be $x = 0$ at the surface of the star; but here, $\log P = -\infty$, and we have chosen instead to set $x = 0$ at $\bar{\tau} = 0.05$. The results of the integration are given in Table 9-5A. The values of x in Table 9-6 have been found by interpolation.

For $\bar{\tau} \geqslant 0.60$, the direct integration yielding x as a function of $\bar{\tau}$ is shown in Table 9-5B. Again, the entire columns of $h\, dx/d\bar{\tau}$, $^1\Delta$, $^2\Delta$, $\cdots$ can be calculated at once. The value $x = -178$ km has been assigned at $\bar{\tau} = 0.60$ to

Table 9-5A   Integration of $dx/(d \log P)$.

$\log P$	$P \times 10^{-4}$ (dyne cm^{-2})	$\bar{\tau}$	$-x$ (km)	$-h\dfrac{dx}{d\log P}$	$-^1\Delta$	$-^2\Delta$
4.1878	1.541	0.0500	0	5.72		
4.2128	1.632	0.0525	5.72	5.72	0.00	
4.2378	1.729	0.0555	11.44	5.73	0.01	
4.2628	1.831	0.0585	17.17	5.74	0.01	
4.2878	1.940	0.0620	22.92	5.74	0.00	
4.3128	2.055	0.0660	28.66	5.75	0.01	
4.3378	2.177	0.0705	34.41	5.76	0.01	
4.3628	2.306	0.0755	40.18	5.77	0.01	
4.3878	2.442	0.0815	45.95	5.78	0.01	
4.4128	2.587	0.0875	51.74	5.79	0.01	
4.4378	2.740	0.0945	57.53	5.81	0.02	
4.4628	2.903	0.1015	63.35	5.82	0.01	
4.4878	3.075	0.1100	69.17	5.84	0.02	
4.5128	3.257	0.1195	75.02	5.85	0.01	
4.5378	3.450	0.1295	80.87	5.87	0.02	
4.5628	3.654	0.1405	86.75	5.89	0.02	
4.5878	3.871	0.1525	92.65	5.91	0.02	
4.6128	4.100	0.1670	98.57	5.94	0.03	
4.6378	4.343	0.1825	104.52	5.97	0.03	
4.6628	4.600	0.2000	110.51	6.00	0.03	
4.6878	4.873	0.2210	116.52	6.03	0.03	
4.7128	5.162	0.2455	122.57	6.07	0.04	
4.7378	5.468	0.2725	128.66	6.12	0.05	
4.7628	5.792	0.3010	134.80	6.16	0.04	
4.7878	6.135	0.3320	140.98	6.21	0.05	
4.8128	6.498	0.3660	147.21	6.27	0.06	
4.8378	6.883	0.4050	153.51	6.32	0.05	
4.8628	7.291	0.4490	159.85	6.39	0.07	
4.8878	7.723	0.4975	166.28	6.46	0.07	
4.9128	8.181	5.525	172.77	6.53	0.07	
4.9378	8.666	0.6160	179.34	6.61	0.08	
4.9628	9.179	0.6905	185.99	6.71	0.10	
4.9878	9.723	0.7770	192.75	6.81	0.10	
5.0128	10.299	0.8785	199.61	6.93	0.12	0.02
5.0378	10.909	1.0000	206.61	7.06	0.13	0.01
5.0628	11.556	1.1435	213.74	7.21	0.15	0.02
5.0878	12.241	1.3245	221.03	7.38	0.17	0.02
5.1128	12.966	1.5590	228.50	7.59	0.19	0.02
5.1378	13.734	1.9000	236.19	7.87	0.28	0.09
5.1628	14.548		244.24			

agree with Table 9-5A, for ease of comparison of the two tables. The geometrical depths corresponding to smaller optical depths have not been calculated in Table 9-5B because the differences are excessively large in that region.

Table 9-5B   Integration of $dx/d\bar{\tau}$.*

$\bar{\tau}$	$-x$ (km)	$-h\dfrac{dx}{d\bar{\tau}}$	$-^1\Delta$	$-^2\Delta$	$-^3\Delta$
0.10		+75.1			
0.20		32.5	−42.6		
0.30		21.5	−11.0	+31.6	
0.40		15.7	−5.8	5.2	−26.4
0.50		12.3	−3.4	2.4	−2.8
0.60	178	10.0	−2.3	1.1	−1.3
0.70	186.8	8.3	−1.7	0.6	−0.5
0.80	194.3	7.0	−1.3	0.4	−0.2
0.90	200.8	6.0	−1.0	0.3	−0.1
1.00	206.4	5.3	−0.7	0.3	
1.10	211.4	4.7	−0.6	0.1	
1.20	215.9	4.2	−0.5	0.1	
1.30	219.9	3.7	−0.5	0.0	
1.40	223.3	3.3	−0.4	0.1	
1.50	226.5	3.0	−0.3	0.1	
1.60	229.4	2.6	−0.4	0.1	
1.70	231.7	2.3	−0.3	0.1	
1.80	233.9	2.1	−0.2	0.1	
1.90	235.9	+1.9	−0.2	+0.0	
2.00	237.7				

* This alternative integration for x as a function of τ has been performed only for $\bar{\tau} \geqslant 0.6$ because the differences at smaller optical depth are large. The value of x at $\bar{\tau} = 0.60$ is taken from Table 9-5A to permit a direct comparison of Tables 9-5A and 9-5B.

6 THE DENSITY AND ELECTRON PRESSURE

The density at any level can be computed from the perfect gas law,

$$\rho = \frac{\mu H}{k}\frac{P}{T},\qquad\qquad (4\text{-}3)\ (9\text{-}9)$$

since μ, P, and T are now known for all values of $\bar{\tau}$ or x. The values are given in Table 9-6.

Although we have not shown explicitly how to calculate the electron pressure P_e, approximate values, if desired, can be obtained from Fig. 3-14 as functions of P and θ.* Values of the electron pressure obtained in this manner are also listed in Table 9-6.

* See Chapter 3, Section 7, for a method of calculating P_e.

Table 9-6   Model Solar Atmosphere.

$T_{eff} = 5{,}802°K$, $g = 2.741 \times 10^4$ cm sec^{-2}; $X = 0.56$, $Y = 0.41$, $Z = 0.03$.

$\bar{\tau}$	$-x$ (km)	T (°K)	θ	$P \times 10^{-4}$ (dyne cm^{-2})	$\rho \times 10^8$ (gm cm^{-3})	$\bar{\kappa}$ (cm^2 gm^{-1})	P_e (dyne cm^{-2})	(P_e/P) $\times 10^4$
0.05	0	4,968	1.0145	1.54	5.7	0.076	2.5	1.6
0.10	62	5,052	0.9975	2.88	10.4	0.128	4.5	1.6
0.15	91	5,133	0.9819	3.82	13.6	0.161	6.2	1.6
0.20	111	5,210	0.9674	4.61	16.1	0.191	7.7	1.7
0.25	124	5,283	0.9540	5.22	18.0	0.213	9.1	1.7
0.30	134	5,354	0.9414	5.77	19.7	0.236	10	1.8
0.35	144	5,422	0.9296	6.33	21.3	0.258	12	1.9
0.40	153	5,487	0.9185	6.84	22.7	0.280	13	2.0
0.45	160	5,550	0.9080	7.31	24.0	0.301	15	2.0
0.50	167	5,612	0.8982	7.75	25.2	0.322	17	2.2
0.55	172	5,671	0.8888	8.16	26.2	0.345	19	2.3
0.60	178	5,728	0.8799	8.55	27.2	0.368	21	2.4
0.65	183	5,784	0.8714	8.91	28.1	0.391	23	2.6
0.70	187	5,838	0.8633	9.25	28.9	0.418	25	2.7
0.75	191	5,891	0.8556	9.56	29.6	0.445	28	2.9
0.80	194	5,942	0.8482	9.86	30.3	0.471	29	3.0
0.85	198	5,992	0.8411	10.15	30.9	0.498	32	3.1
0.90	201	6,041	0.8343	10.41	31.5	0.526	35	3.3
0.95	204	6,088	0.8278	10.67	32.0	0.552	37	3.5
1.00	207	6,135	0.8215	10.91	32.5	0.577	40	3.7
1.10	212	6,225	0.8097	11.37	33.3	0.636	46	4.1
1.20	216	6,311	0.7986	11.78	34.0	0.700	55	4.7
1.30	220	6,394	0.7882	12.15	34.7	0.771	64	5.2
1.40	224	6,474	0.7785	12.49	35.2	0.855	72	5.8
1.50	227	6,551	0.7694	12.80	35.6	0.950	83	6.5
1.60	230	6,625	0.7607	13.07	36.0	1.060	95	7.2
1.70	232	6,697	0.7526	13.32	36.3	1.177	110	8.2
1.80	234	6,767	0.7448	13.54	36.5	1.298	120	9.1
1.90	236	6,834	0.7375	13.74	36.7	1.423	140	10
2.00	238	6,900	0.7305	13.92	36.8	1.549	160	11

7 A TEST FOR CONVECTION

A test can be applied at each level to determine whether radiative equilibrium is maintained. For simplicity, we shall assume that convective processes, if present, occur adiabatically. In this case,

$$\frac{d \log P}{d \log T} > \frac{\gamma}{\gamma - 1} \quad \text{if non-convective.} \qquad \text{(6-52) (9-10)}$$

Since hydrogen and helium are almost completely neutral, we may take

$$\gamma = \tfrac{5}{3}. \qquad \text{(6-42) (9-11)}$$

Then

$$\frac{d \log P}{d \log T} > 2.5 \quad \text{if non-convective.} \qquad \text{(6-54) (9-12)}$$

For purposes of calculation, we may write this inequality as

$$\frac{d \ln P}{d \ln T} = \frac{1}{P} h \frac{dP}{d\bar{\tau}} \bigg/ \frac{1}{T} h \frac{dT}{d\bar{\tau}} > 2.5.$$

Differentiation of eq. (9-1) yields

$$\frac{dT}{d\bar{\tau}} = \frac{3}{16} T_{\text{eff}}^{4} \frac{1}{T^3}.$$

Therefore, the criterion becomes

$$\frac{16}{3} \frac{g}{\bar{\kappa}P} \left(\frac{T}{T_{\text{eff}}} \right)^4 > 2.5. \qquad (9\text{-}13)$$

The left-hand side of this expression has the value 2.68 at $\bar{\tau} = 1.10$ and 2.48 at $\bar{\tau} = 1.20$. Hence, convection begins just above $\bar{\tau} = 1.20$. Calculation of the radiative and convective fluxes, however, would show that radiation still predominates as an energy transfer mechanism.

The solar atmosphere calculated in this section is summarized in Table 9-6. The differences between this model and that of Table 4-2 are comparable to those between various published solutions.

PROBLEMS

1. Refer to Table 4-9 for the atmosphere of a main-sequence star of spectral class G0. For the layers in which convection transfers nearly all the energy, compare the values given for the pressure with those obtained from the adiabatic gas law.

2. Refer to Table 4-6 for the atmosphere of a main-sequence star of spectral class B0.5. Assuming the opacity coefficient to have the constant value $\bar{\kappa} = 1$ and the effective gravity to have the constant value g, integrate $dP/d\bar{\tau}$ analytically. Compare several values of P for $0.001 \leqslant \bar{\tau} \leqslant 1.000$ with those given in the table.

10

MODEL STELLAR INTERIORS

This chapter is devoted to details of the construction of several types of model interiors. It is not necessary that the entire chapter be studied from beginning to end; rather, those parts may be selected that are of especial interest.

Section 1 contains a summary of the equations and a description of a method of solution. Sections 2 and 3 apply these principles to the calculation of two examples, called Models A and B, respectively. Polytropic solutions are discussed in Section 4. Although the latter have restricted utility in the present day, their simplicity affords a measure of insight that makes their consideration worthwhile. The specific examples are based on Models A and B. The chapter closes with Section 5 on Schwarzschild's transformation, which, although no longer widely used, nevertheless illuminates the subject.

All tables containing fundamental data (such as energy-generation rates and Emden functions) that are needed for constructing these and similar models are collected at the end of the chapter.

1 MODEL INTERIORS OBTAINED BY NUMERICAL INTEGRATION

Sections 2 and 3 will illustrate in detail the construction of model interiors, considering alternatively radiative and convective equilibrium. In this section, we summarize the equations to be used and show how they may be solved. We also obtain formulae from which starting values for the integrations can be obtained. Only homogeneous models will be considered, and the equation of state will be represented by the perfect gas law. Wherever convection occurs, conditions will be treated as if adiabatic.

We shall be concerned mainly with the physical variables r, P, T, M_r, and L_r. However, an alternative solution with transformed variables will be given in Section 2, and the necessary equations will be presented there. The transformed solution is more efficient to calculate in the absence of a modern type of automatic or desk calculator.

1-1 THE DIFFERENTIAL EQUATIONS

A. THE EQUATIONS IN GENERAL FORM

The differential equations that may be used for both radiative and convective equilibrium are

$$\frac{dM_r}{dr} = 4\pi r^2 \rho \qquad\qquad (6\text{-}1)\ (10\text{-}1)$$

$$\frac{dP}{dr} = -\frac{GM_r}{r^2}\rho \qquad\qquad (6\text{-}2)\ (10\text{-}2)$$

$$\frac{dL_r}{dr} = 4\pi r^2 \rho\epsilon. \qquad\qquad (6\text{-}30)\ (10\text{-}3)$$

The temperature gradient is

$$\frac{dT}{dr} = -\frac{3}{16\pi ac}\frac{\bar{\kappa}\rho}{T^3}\frac{L_r}{r^2} \quad \text{(radiative)} \qquad (6\text{-}24)\ (10\text{-}4)$$

$$\frac{dT}{dr} = 0.4\frac{T}{P}\frac{dP}{dr} \qquad \text{(convective)} \qquad (6\text{-}45\text{B})\ (10\text{-}5)$$

$$= -0.4\frac{T}{P}\frac{GM_r}{r^2}\rho. \qquad\qquad (10\text{-}6)$$

The density may be eliminated from the equations by the use of the perfect gas law, which is valid both in the radiative and in the convective case:

$$\rho = \frac{\mu H}{k}\frac{P}{T}. \qquad\qquad (4\text{-}3)\ (10\text{-}7)$$

In adiabatic convective equilibrium, we can also use the adiabatic gas law,

$$P = \mathcal{K}\rho^\gamma, \qquad\qquad (6\text{-}47)\ (10\text{-}8)$$

which is equivalent to

$$P = \mathcal{K}'T^{\gamma/(\gamma-1)}. \qquad\qquad (6\text{-}46)\ (10\text{-}9)$$

If ionization is complete,

$$\gamma = \tfrac{5}{3}.$$

The quantities μ, $\bar{\kappa}$, and ϵ appearing in these equations must be expressed in terms of the dependent variables and the composition parameters.

B. THE EQUATIONS IN THE FORMS OF THE PRESENT EXAMPLES

We shall adopt the following formulae to express the mean molecular weight, the opacity coefficient, and the energy-generation rate:

$$\mu = \frac{1}{2X + \frac{3}{4}Y + \frac{1}{2}Z} \qquad (6\text{-}4)\ (10\text{-}10)$$

$$\bar{\kappa} = \bar{\kappa}_{bf} = \frac{4.34 \times 10^{25}}{t/\bar{g}_{bf}} Z(1 + X)\frac{\rho}{T^{3.5}} \qquad (3\text{-}58)\ (10\text{-}11)$$

$$\epsilon = \epsilon_0 X_1 X_2 \rho T^\nu. \qquad (6\text{-}77C)\ (10\text{-}12)$$

The ratio $t/\bar{g}_{bf}$ in the opacity law will be held constant. With these substitutions, the differential equations can be written in the following forms.

Radiative case

$$\frac{dM_r}{dr} = 4\pi \frac{H}{k} \mu \frac{P}{T} r^2 \qquad (10\text{-}13)$$

$$\frac{dP}{dr} = -\frac{GH}{k} \mu \frac{P}{T} \frac{M_r}{r^2} \qquad (10\text{-}14)$$

$$\frac{dT}{dr} = -\frac{3}{16\pi ac} \frac{4.34 \times 10^{25}}{t/\bar{g}_{bf}} \left(\frac{H}{k}\right)^2 Z(1 + X)\mu^2 \frac{P^2}{T^{8.5}} \frac{L_r}{r^2}. \qquad (10\text{-}15)$$

If appreciable energy production is taking place at radius r,

$$\frac{dL_r}{dr} = 4\pi \left(\frac{H}{k}\right)^2 \epsilon_0 X_1 X_2 \mu^2 P^2 T^{\nu-2} r^2; \qquad (10\text{-}16)$$

otherwise, this equation is eliminated and L_r is set equal to L in eq. (10-15). These equations must all be solved simultaneously.

Convective case (I)

$$\frac{dM_r}{dr} = 4\pi \frac{H}{k} \mu \frac{P}{T} r^2 \qquad (10\text{-}17)$$

$$\frac{dP}{dr} = -\frac{GH}{k} \mu \frac{P}{T} \frac{M_r}{r^2} \qquad (10\text{-}18)$$

$$\frac{dT}{dr} = -0.4 \frac{GH}{k} \mu \frac{M_r}{r^2}. \qquad (10\text{-}19)$$

If appreciable energy is being produced,

$$\frac{dL_r}{dr} = 4\pi \left(\frac{H}{k}\right)^2 \epsilon_0 X_1 X_2 \mu^2 P^2 T^{\nu-2} r^2. \qquad (10\text{-}20)$$

Since L_r is not required in eqs. (10-17) to (10-19), we can integrate eq. (10-20) separately after P and T have been tabulated.

Convective case (II)

The adiabatic relation between P and T may be used in place of the differential equation (10-18) for the calculation of P. In this case, we have

$$\frac{dM_r}{dr} = 4\pi \frac{H}{k} \mathscr{K}' \mu T^{1.5} r^2 \tag{10-21}$$

and

$$\frac{dT}{dr} = -0.4 \frac{GH}{k} \mu \frac{M_r}{r^2}, \tag{10-22}$$

which must be solved simultaneously. Then P is found from

$$P = \mathscr{K}' T^{2.5}, \tag{10-23}$$

and the integration for L_r is performed using eq. (10-20) after P and T have been established.

1-2 STARTING VALUES

We must be able to calculate starting values both at the center and at the surface, as it is often not possible to integrate through the entire model in one direction. The factor r^{-2} appearing in some of the derivatives causes difficulty near the center unless it is properly compensated by another variable, making it possible for all derivatives to approach zero simultaneously toward the center. Similarly, the factor $T^{-8.5}$ may become very large near the surface of radiative envelopes. Thus we should be prepared to start the solution analytically both at the surface and at the center and to integrate in both directions. The solutions must then be fitted at an intermediate point. A method introduced by L. G. Henyey and his collaborators, which uses difference equations rather than differential equations, overcomes this complication but is more difficult to apply.*

A. INTEGRATIONS FROM THE SURFACE

Near the stellar surface, the mass M_r decreases slowly from the total mass M, while the net luminosity L_r is equal to the value of L since nuclear energy production is insignificant at such low temperatures. The near constancy of these variables makes possible the derivation of an analytical solution. It is also necessary, however, that the opacity coefficient be expressed in a form that leads to a relation between P and T that can be integrated analytically. We shall adopt Kramers' law as given by eq. (10-11).

---

* For a description of this and a similar method developed by A. N. Cox and R. R. Brownlee, see R. L. Sears and R. R. Brownlee (L. H. Aller and D. B. McLaughlin, eds.), 1965 (58), p. 603 et seq. Also see H.-Y. Chiu, 1968 (63), pp. 456 to 460.

Radiative case

If eq. (10-14) is divided by eq. (10-15), with M_r set equal to M and L_r set equal to L, we find

$$\frac{dP}{dT} = \left[\frac{16\pi acGk}{3H}\frac{M}{L}\frac{t/\bar{g}_{bf}}{4.34 \times 10^{25}}\frac{1}{\mu Z(1 + X)}\right]\frac{T^{7.5}}{P}. \quad (10\text{-}24)$$

Let us denote the factor in brackets by A:

$$A = \frac{16\pi acGk}{3 \times 4.34 \times 10^{25}H}\frac{M}{L}\frac{t/\bar{g}_{bf}}{\mu Z(1 + X)}. \quad (10\text{-}25)$$

Separating the variables and integrating, we get

$$\tfrac{1}{2}P^2\Big|_{P_s}^{P} = \frac{A}{8.5}T^{8.5}\Big|_{T_s}^{T}. \quad (10\text{-}26)$$

It will be adequate for our purpose to use the zero boundary conditions

$$P_s = 0 \quad \text{and} \quad T_s = 0 \quad \text{at } r = R, \quad (10\text{-}27)$$

in which case

$$P^2 = \frac{A}{4.25}T^{8.5}. \quad (10\text{-}28)$$

This relation can now be used in eq. (10-15), which can be expressed as

$$\frac{dT}{dr} = -\frac{GH}{Ak}M\mu\frac{P^2}{T^{8.5}r^2}, \quad (10\text{-}29)$$

giving

$$\frac{dT}{dr} = -\frac{GH}{4.25k}M\mu\frac{1}{r^2} \quad (10\text{-}30)$$

$$T\Big|_{T_s}^{T} = \frac{GH}{4.25k}M\mu\frac{1}{r}\Big|_{R}^{r} \quad (10\text{-}31)$$

or

$$T = \frac{GH}{4.25k}M\mu\left(\frac{1}{r} - \frac{1}{R}\right). \quad (10\text{-}32)$$

From this formula, T can be calculated for several successive values of r. Then P is given by eq. (10-28). Since this approximation is valid only if $M_r = M$, the value of $h\, dM_r/dr$ must be computed to test if this condition is fulfilled to the required accuracy. The derivatives and differences of P and T, as well as of M_r, must then be calculated.

Convective case

Integration of eq. (10-19) with constant M and the zero boundary condition gives

$$T = 0.4\frac{GH}{k}M\mu\left(\frac{1}{r} - \frac{1}{R}\right). \quad (10\text{-}33)$$

The values of T are found for several successive values of r near the surface, and the derivatives and differences are also computed. The derivatives and differences of M_r are computed simultaneously as a check that M_r is still approximately equal to M.

No starting values are needed for P, since this is determined from the relation

$$P = \mathscr{K}'T^{2.5}. \tag{10-34}$$

If the value of $\mathscr{K}'$ has not been calculated from an integration through the interior regions, it must be assumed as a trial parameter.

B. INTEGRATIONS FROM THE CENTER

To obtain starting values for the dependent variables when the integration is begun at the stellar center, we shall use Taylor expansions with just enough terms to allow departure from the values at the center. We must therefore evaluate successively each of the following terms for any variable v:

$$v = v_c + \frac{dv}{dr}\bigg|_c r + \frac{1}{2}\frac{d^2v}{dr^2}\bigg|_c r^2 + \frac{1}{3\cdot2}\frac{d^3v}{dr^3}\bigg|_c r^3 + \cdots, \tag{10-35}$$

where the subscript c denotes a value at the center.

For the mass, we have from eq. (10-1) at $r = 0$:

$$\frac{dM_r}{dr}\bigg|_c = 4\pi[r^2\rho]_c = 0$$

$$\frac{d^2M_r}{dr^2}\bigg|_c = 4\pi\left[2r\rho + r^2\frac{d\rho}{dr}\right]_c = 0$$

$$\frac{d^3M_r}{dr^3} = 4\pi\left[2\rho + 4r\frac{d\rho}{dr} + r^2\frac{d^2\rho}{dr^2}\right]_c$$

$$= 8\pi\rho_c.$$

Therefore

$$M_r = \tfrac{4}{3}\pi\rho_c r^3. \tag{10-36}$$

This is the same result we should have obtained by setting

$$M_r = \text{density} \times \text{volume},$$

taking r sufficiently small that the average value of ρ within the sphere is equal to ρ_c to the required accuracy.

For the pressure, we have from eq. (10-2) and the preceding results for M_r that

$$\frac{dP}{dr}\bigg|_c = -\left[\frac{GM_r}{r^2}\rho\right]_c = -[G\tfrac{4}{3}\pi\rho^2 r]_c = 0$$

$$\frac{d^2P}{dr^2}\bigg|_c = -\tfrac{4}{3}\pi G\left[2\rho\frac{d\rho}{dr}r + \rho^2\right]_c$$

$$= -\tfrac{4}{3}\pi G\rho_c^2.$$

Hence

$$P = P_c - \tfrac{2}{3}\pi G \rho_c^2 r^2. \tag{10-37}$$

For the net luminosity, we find from eq. (10-3) that

$$\left.\frac{dL_r}{dr}\right|_c = 4\pi[r^2\rho\epsilon]_c = 0$$

$$\left.\frac{d^2L_r}{dr^2}\right|_c = 4\pi\left[2r\rho\epsilon + r^2\frac{d\rho}{dr}\epsilon + r^2\rho\frac{d\epsilon}{dr}\right]_c = 0$$

$$\left.\frac{d^3L_r}{dr^3}\right|_c = 4\pi[2\rho\epsilon + \text{terms proportional to } r \text{ or } r^2]_c$$

$$= 8\pi\rho_c\epsilon_c$$

and

$$L_r = \tfrac{4}{3}\pi\rho_c\epsilon_c r^3. \tag{10-38}$$

The temperature in the radiative case is calculated from eq. (10-4) and the result for L_r:

$$\left.\frac{dT}{dr}\right|_c = -\frac{3}{16\pi ac}\left[\frac{\bar\kappa\rho}{T^3}\frac{L_r}{r^2}\right]_c = -\frac{3}{16\pi ac}\left[\frac{4\pi}{3}\frac{\bar\kappa\rho^2\epsilon}{T^3}r\right]_c = 0$$

$$\left.\frac{d^2T}{dr^2}\right|_c = -\frac{3}{16\pi ac}\left[\frac{\bar\kappa\rho}{T^3}\frac{d}{dr}\left(\frac{L_r}{r^2}\right) + \frac{L_r}{r^2}\frac{d}{dr}\left(\frac{\bar\kappa\rho}{T^3}\right)\right]_c$$

$$= -\frac{3}{16\pi ac}\left[\frac{\bar\kappa\rho}{T^3}\left(\frac{1}{r^2}\frac{dL_r}{dr} - \frac{2L_r}{r^3}\right)\right]_c$$

$$= -\frac{1}{4ac}\frac{\bar\kappa_c\rho_c^2\epsilon_c}{T_c^3}.$$

Hence

$$T = T_c - \frac{1}{8ac}\frac{\bar\kappa_c\rho_c^2\epsilon_c}{T_c^3}r^2. \tag{10-39}$$

In the convective case, using eq. (10-5) and the expressions for P and its derivatives, we get

$$\left.\frac{dT}{dr}\right|_c = \frac{2}{5}\left[\frac{T}{P}\frac{dP}{dr}\right]_c = 0$$

$$\left.\frac{d^2T}{dr^2}\right|_c = \frac{2}{5}\left[\frac{1}{P}\frac{dT}{dr}\frac{dP}{dr} - \frac{1}{P^2}\left(\frac{dP}{dr}\right)^2 + \frac{T}{P}\frac{d^2P}{dr^2}\right]_c$$

$$= -\frac{2}{5}\cdot\frac{4}{3}\pi G\rho_c^2\frac{T_c}{P_c}$$

and

$$T = T_c - \frac{4}{15}\pi G\rho_c^2\frac{T_c}{P_c}r^2. \tag{10-40}$$

C. SUMMARY OF FORMULAE

Near the surface, with zero boundary conditions, we have:

Radiative case

$$T = \frac{GH}{4.25k} \mu M \left(\frac{1}{r} - \frac{1}{R} \right) \qquad \text{(10-32) (10-41)}$$

$$P = \left[\frac{1}{4.25} \frac{16\pi acGk}{3H} \frac{t/\bar{g}_{bf}}{4.34 \times 10^{25}} \frac{1}{\mu Z(1 + X)} \frac{M}{L} \right]^{1/2} T^{4.25}, \qquad \text{(10-28) (10-42)}$$

based on Kramers' law for $\bar{\kappa}_{bf}$ with a constant ratio $(t/\bar{g}_{bf})$. This ratio must be estimated in advance and later checked for consistency with ρ and T. The values of X, Z, M, R, and L must either be given or estimated.

Convective case

$$T = 0.4 \frac{GM}{k} \mu M \left(\frac{1}{r} - \frac{1}{R} \right) \qquad \text{(10-33) (10-43)}$$

with $T = 0$ at the surface; and, since adiabatic conditions are assumed,

$$P = \mathscr{K}' T^{2.5}.$$

The values of X, Z, M, R, and $\mathscr{K}'$ must be given or estimated. Although L is not required in these two equations, a definite value must also be assigned to this quantity before a complete model can be constructed. These details will become clearer from the illustrative examples.

Near the center,

$$M_r = \tfrac{4}{3}\pi \rho_c r^3 \qquad \text{(10-36) (10-44)}$$

$$P = P_c - \tfrac{2}{3}\pi G \rho_c^2 r^2 \qquad \text{(10-37) (10-45)}$$

$$L_r = \tfrac{4}{3}\pi \rho_c \epsilon_c r^3 \qquad \text{(10-38) (10-46)}$$

$$T = T_c - \frac{1}{8ac} \frac{\bar{\kappa}_c \rho_c^2 \epsilon_c}{T_c^3} r^2 \quad \text{(radiative)} \qquad \text{(10-39) (10-47)}$$

$$T = T_c - \frac{4}{15} \pi G \rho_c^2 \frac{T_c}{P_c} r^2 \quad \text{(convective).} \qquad \text{(10-40) (10-48)}$$

It should be noted that the derivation of these equations has not required the specification of the formulae to be used for $\bar{\kappa}$, ϵ, or the equation of state; hence they are valid under a variety of conditions. In numerical evaluation of the starting values, any two of the quantities P_c, T_c, or ρ_c, as well as X and Z, must be known or estimated.

1-3 INTEGRATION PROCEDURE

We now consider the procedure for advancing to the next line of integration, when all the information on a given line is known.

The most direct method would be to use the integration formula (8-6) to calculate the values of M_r, P, L_r, and T on the new line and then to calculate all the derivatives and differences. However, to avoid the need of using a small interval to keep errors in the differences from becoming significant, we shall proceed according to the method described below. Formula (8-6) will be used only to obtain preliminary values for some of the variables, which will later be checked.

A. RADIATIVE CASE

We consider first the case of radiative equilibrium, using Table 10-7 as an illustration. All variables will be expressed in the units adopted in the table.

Suppose that all the values at $r = 0.3$ are known, and the next line, at $r = 0.4$, is desired.

(i) The integration formula (8-6),

$$v_{+1} = v_0 + hf_0 + 0.5\,^1\Delta_0 + 0.4167\,^2\Delta_0 + 0.375\,^3\Delta_0 + \cdots,$$

can be used to estimate P and T at $r = 0.4$:

$$P_{est} = 146 - 7 + 0.5(-2)$$

$$= 138$$

and

$$T_{est} = 1.167 - 0.022 + 0.5(-0.007)$$

$$= 1.1415,$$

which we shall take as

$$T_{est} = 1.141.$$

(ii) These values are used to calculate M_r at $r = 0.4$ from the derivative and differences (using the numerical coefficient appropriate to this particular case and these particular units):

$$h\frac{dM_r}{dr} = 0.009260h\,\frac{P}{T}r^2$$

$$= 0.009260 \times 0.1 \times \frac{138}{1.141} \times 0.4^2$$

$$= 0.018;$$

then

$$^1\Delta_{+1} = 0.018 - 0.010$$

$$= 0.008$$

$$^2\Delta_{+1} = 0.008 - 0.005$$

$$= 0.003,$$

and, from the integration formula (8-7),

$$v_{+1} = v_0 + hf_{+1} - 0.5\,^1\Delta_{+1} - 0.0833\,^2\Delta_{+1} - 0.0417\,^3\Delta_{+1} + \cdots,$$

we get

$$M_r = 0.10 + 0.018 - 0.5(0.008) - 0.0833(0.003)$$
$$= 0.024.$$

(iii) A partial check of P_{est} is made, using P_{est} itself, T_{est}, and M_r as just found, in the equation

$$h\frac{dP}{dr} = -4.914h\frac{P}{T}\frac{M_r}{r^2}$$

$$= -4.914 \times 0.1 \times \frac{138}{1.141} \times \frac{0.024}{0.4^2}$$

$$= -9.$$

Then

$$^1\Delta_{+1} = -9 - (-7)$$
$$= -2,$$

and integration formula (8-7) yields

$$P_{\text{calc}} = 146 - 9 - 0.5(-2)$$
$$= 138,$$

which agrees with the estimated value. If a discrepancy had been found, it would be necessary to repeat steps (ii) and (iii) with an adjusted value of P_{est}.

(iv) If energy is being produced, L_r is now found with the aid of its derivative, using P_{calc} and T_{est}:

$$h\frac{dL_r}{dr} = 0.0003537hP^2T^2r^2 \qquad (\nu = 4)$$

$$= 0.0003537 \times 0.1 \times 138^2 \times 1.41^2 \times 0.4^2$$

$$= 0.140.$$

Then

$$^1\Delta_{+1} = 0.140 - 0.092$$
$$= +0.048$$
$$^2\Delta_{+1} = 0.048 - 0.046$$
$$= +0.002$$
$$^3\Delta_{+1} = 0.002 - 0.012$$
$$= -0.010$$

and integration formula (8-7) gives

$$L_r = 0.101 + 0.140 - 0.5(0.048) - 0.0833(+0.002) - 0.0417(-0.010)$$
$$= 0.217.$$

(v) Next, T_{calc} is similarly calculated, using P_{calc}, T_{calc}, and L_r:

$$h\frac{dT}{dr} = -0.00003374h\,\frac{P^2}{T^{8.5}}\frac{L_r}{r^2}$$

$$= -0.00003374 \times 0.1\,\frac{138^2}{1.141^{8.5}}\frac{0.217}{0.4^2}$$

$$= -0.028.$$

Then

$$^1\Delta_{+1} = -0.028 - (-0.022)$$

$$= -0.006,$$

and integration formula (8-7) gives

$$T_{\text{calc}} = 1.167 - 0.028 - 0.5(-0.006)$$

$$= 1.142.$$

This differs from the estimated value, and so we should repeat steps (ii) to (v) using P_{calc} and T_{calc} (or an adjusted value) in place of the original estimates. Since we have kept an additional significant figure in T (to allow for rounding errors when T is raised to the power 8.5 in $h\,dT/dr$), a change of one or two units in T will usually not produce any change in the other quantities. We find in this case that no adjustment is needed in M_r and P, but the integration for L_r is altered to the values in Table 10-7. The integration for T is found to be self-consistent.

B. CONVECTIVE CASE

(I) If it has been decided to perform the integration for P, we proceed as in the radiative case except that the convective temperature gradient must be used, and step (iv) is postponed until P and T are firmly established. In fact, the integration for L_r may be delayed until the rest of the model has been computed. This has been done on lines $r = 0.9$ to 1.2 of Table 10-7.

(II) If P is not being integrated, as on lines $r = 1.4$ to 2.6 of Table 10-8A, an estimate for T on the new line is used to compute

$$h\frac{dM_r}{dr}, \qquad ^1\Delta_{+1}, \qquad ^2\Delta_{+1}, \cdots; \qquad M_r$$

as in step (ii); however, we now use eq. (10-21) to find $h\,dM_r/dr$. In this example, $\mathscr{K}'$ was determined as the ratio $P/T^{2.5}$ appropriate to the place in the core solution at which the convective envelope was reached. With this value of $\mathscr{K}'$, we have

$$h\frac{dM_r}{dr} = 0.9057hT^{1.5}r^2.$$

The resulting value of M_r is then substituted into the equation

$$h\frac{dT}{dr} = -1.965h\frac{M_r}{r^2}.$$

The differences $^1\Delta_{+1}, {}^2\Delta_{+1}, \cdots$ are computed, and T_{calc} is found from the integration formula. If the computed value disagrees with the estimated one, iteration is required. Then P can be found from the relation

$$P = \mathscr{K}'T^{2.5},$$

and L_r can be integrated independently.

We are now ready to proceed to the illustrative examples.

2 MODEL A: RADIATIVE ENVELOPE AND CONVECTIVE CORE

2-1 STATEMENT OF THE PROBLEM

The object of this example is to illustrate the construction of a homogeneous model having a radiative envelope and a convective core. We shall prescribe definite values for the mass, radius, and luminosity that represent an upper main-sequence (A-type) star and may therefore be expected to yield the desired structure*:

$$M = 2.5\ M_\odot = 4.962 \times 10^{33}\ \text{gm},$$

$$R = 1.59\ R_\odot = 11.05 \times 10^{10}\ \text{cm},$$

$$L = 21.2\ L_\odot = 80.14 \times 10^{33}\ \text{erg sec}^{-1}.$$

Definite values are required for X, Y, and Z in order that numerical calculations may be performed, and we shall assume the trial values

$$X = 0.90, \qquad Y = 0.09, \qquad Z = 0.01 \qquad (\mu = 0.5340).$$

The validity of this choice will be considered in Section 2-4.

The integration will begin at the surface, where all the parameters M, R, L, X, and Z are known. In Sections 2-2 and 2-3, we shall illustrate two of the possible methods for calculating the radiative envelope and three of the possible methods by which the solution for the radiative envelope may be fitted to a convective core.

To solve the differential equations, we need $\bar{\kappa}$ and ϵ. Since high accuracy is not needed for our illustration, we shall consider only bound-free transitions for the opacity and use Kramers' law with a constant ratio of guillotine factor to Gaunt factor,

$$t/\bar{g}_{\text{bf}} = 3.162 \quad \text{or} \quad \log t/\bar{g}_{\text{bf}} = 0.5000.$$

---

* The older values for the Sun are used here: $M_\odot = 1.985 \times 10^{33}$ gm, $R_\odot = 6.951 \times 10^{10}$ cm, and $L_\odot = 3.78 \times 10^{33}$ erg sec^{-1}.

Then

$$\bar{\kappa} = \bar{\kappa}_{bf} = \frac{4.34 \times 10^{25}}{3.162} Z(1 + X) \frac{\rho}{T^{3.5}}.$$

The suitability of this value of $t/\bar{g}$ can be judged only after the calculation for the radiative region has been completed. We may then compare it with the values given in Table 10-15.

It will be seen as the integration progresses that the temperature in the radiative envelope remains low, and we may make the approximation that no energy is generated there. This has the advantage of eliminating the integration for L_r and reducing the problem to the solution of only three, rather than four, simultaneous differential equations. In the core, however, the integration for L_r is required, and we must have an expression for the energy-generation rate ϵ. This can be chosen from Tables 10-13 and 10-14 for the expected temperatures, which we estimate to be around $1.5 \times 10^7 \,°K$ near the center.* At this low temperature, the contribution of the CN cycle may be neglected (see Table 10-3 below). The formula for ϵ_{pp} may be obtained from Table 10-13A, although the relation used in the calculations presented here is

$$\epsilon = \epsilon_{pp} = 0.100X^2\rho T_7{}^4 \qquad (10\text{-}48A)$$

for all temperatures. Actually, a homogeneous model of this mass and composition should lie on the upper main sequence, and it would therefore be expected that a high central temperature would cause the CN cycle to predominate over the *p-p* chain. As we shall see, our model is not a physically possible one but must rather be considered an unsuccessful trial solution.

Two independent computations of the entire model will be presented. The physical variables r, P, T, M_r, and L_r are employed in Section 2-2, where both envelope and core are obtained by numerical integration. This method is generally preferable. If computing facilities are very limited, however, one may prefer a transformation that eliminates successive multiplications and divisions; Section 2-3 illustrates the use of logarithmic variables for the envelope and published tables of Emden functions for the core. Of course, other variables or combinations of variables may also be used.

2-2 CALCULATION WITH PHYSICAL VARIABLES†

A. THE RADIATIVE ENVELOPE

Near the surface, we have from eq. (10-42) that

$$P = 26.296T^{4.25},$$

---

* This particular choice of T_c is made here for approximate agreement with the results of Section 2-3.

† We continue to express all variables in the units employed in Tables 10-1 and 10-2.

Table 10-1A Model A: Radiative Envelope $(L_r = L)$.*

$$M = 4.962 \times 10^{33} \text{ gm}, \quad R = 11.05 \times 10^{10} \text{ cm}, \quad L = 80.14 \times 10^{33} \text{ erg sec}^{-1};$$

$$X = 0.90, \quad Y = 0.09, \quad Z = 0.01.$$

r	M_r	$h\dfrac{dM_r}{dr}$	$^1\Delta$	$^2\Delta$	P	$h\dfrac{dP}{dr}$	$^1\Delta$	$^2\Delta$	$^3\Delta$	T	$h\dfrac{dT}{dr}$	$^1\Delta$	$n+1$
9.6					0.00031	20				0.0690	109		
9.4					0.00058	35	15			0.0801	114	5	
9.2					0.00103	57	22	7 ⁻		0.0918	120	6	
9.0					0.00174	88	31	9	2	0.1040	123	3	
8.8					0.00285	135	47	16	7	0.1167	130	7	
8.6	4.96	− 0			0.00451	201	66	19	3	0.1300	136	6	4.26
8.4	4.95	− 1			0.00695	292	91	25	6	0.1439	143	7	
8.2	4.94	− 1			0.0105	42	13	4	2	0.1586	150	7	
8.0	4.93	− 1			0.0156	60	18	5	1	0.1740	158	8	
7.8	4.92	− 1			0.0227	83	23	5	0	0.1902	165	7	
7.6	4.91	− 1			0.0325	115	32	9	4	0.2071	173	8	
7.4	4.90	− 2			0.0461	158	43	11	2	0.2249	182	9	
7.2	4.88	− 2			0.0647	216	58	15	4	0.2436	192	10	
7.0	4.86	− 3			0.0899	292	76	18	3	0.2633	203	11	4.21
6.8	4.83	− 3			0.124	39	10	2	0	0.2842	214	11	
6.6	4.80	− 4			0.170	53	14	4	2	0.3062	226	12	
6.4	4.76	− 5			0.232	71	18	4	0	0.3295	240	14	
6.2	4.71	− 6			0.314	94	23	5	1	0.3542	254	14	
6.0	4.65	− 6			0.422	124	30	7	2	0.3803	267	13	
5.8	4.58	− 8	− 2		0.565	163	39	9	2	0.4078	283	16	
5.6	4.49	− 9	− 1		0.752	213	50	11	2	0.4369	300	17	
5.4	4.40	− 10	− 1		0.996	277	64	14	3	0.4677	317	17	4.10
5.2	4.29	− 12	− 2		1.31	36	8	2	1	0.500	33	1	
5.0	4.16	− 13	− 1		1.72	46	10	2	0	0.534	36	3	
4.8	4.02	− 15	− 2		2.24	59	13	3	1	0.571	37	1	
4.6	3.86	− 16	− 1		2.91	75	16	3	0	0.609	40	3	
4.4	3.69	− 18	− 2		3.76	95	20	4	1	0.650	41	1	
4.2	3.50	− 20	− 2		4.83	120	25	5	1	0.692	44	3	
4.0	3.29	− 22	− 2		6.17	149	29	4		0.737	46	2	3.84
3.8	3.07	− 23	− 1		7.83	183	34	5		0.784	49	3	
3.6	2.83	− 25	− 2		9.86	223	40	6		0.834	51	2	
3.4	2.57	− 26	− 1		12.3	27	5	1		0.886	53	2	
3.2	2.31	− 27	⁻ 1		15.3	32	5	0		0.940	56	3	
3.0	2.03	− 28	− 1		18.8	37	5	0		0.997	59	3	3.32
2.8	1.75	− 27	+ 1		22.7	41	4	− 1		1.056	60	1	3.20
2.6	1.48	− 27	0		27.0	46	5	+ 1		1.117	61	1	3.08
2.4	1.22	− 25	+ 2		31.8	49	3	− 2		1.179	63	2	2.90
2.2	0.978	− 233	+ 17	0	36.8	52	3	0		1.243	64	1	2.72
2.0	0.756	− 209	+ 24	+ 7	42.0	52	0	− 3		1.308	66	2	2.49

Interpolated boundary of convective core, at $n + 1 = 2.50$: $r = 2.01$, $M_r = 0.764$, $P = 41.7$, $T = 1.305$, $P/T^{2.5} = 21.43$.

* The units in which the variables are expressed are: $r(10^{10} \text{ cm})$, $P(10^{15} \text{ dyne cm}^{-2})$, $T(10^7 \text{ °K})$, $M_r (10^{33} \text{ gm})$. The derivatives and differences are given in units of the last place of the corresponding variables. An extra digit, which contains a zero-point error, has been retained in the integration for M_r on lines $r \leqslant 2.2$ in order to minimize rounding errors, particularly in the construction of Table 10-2A.

and from eq. (10-41) that

$$T = 5.0402\left(\frac{1}{r} - \frac{1}{11.052}\right).$$

After T and P have been computed from these formulae, we calculate the derivatives (see below) and differences to complete the lines set in bold-faced type in Table 10-1A. The values of M_r have been obtained by numerical integration, starting with the boundary value. This is adequate since the mass changes so slowly near the surface.

The derivatives are computed throughout the radiative region from eqs. (10-13) to (10-15), and also (10-16) if L_r is variable. For comparison, the envelope has been computed twice: in Table 10-1A, L_r is considered to be constant; while in Table 10-1B, the differential equation for L_r is integrated. We have in either case that

$$h\frac{dM_r}{dr} = 0.008135h\frac{P}{T}r^2 \qquad (10\text{-}49)$$

and

$$h\frac{dP}{dr} = -4.317h\frac{P}{T}\frac{M_r}{r^2}.$$

Also, in Table 10-1A,

$$h\frac{dT}{dr} = -0.007289h\frac{P^2}{T^{8.5}r^2},$$

Table 10-1B   Radiative Envelope (L_r Variable).* This is a continuation of Table 10-1A, replacing lines for $r < 4.0$.

r	M_r	$h\dfrac{dM_r}{dr}$	$^1\Delta$	$^2\Delta$	P	$h\dfrac{dP}{dr}$	$^1\Delta$	$^2\Delta$	L_r	$h\dfrac{dL_r}{dr}$	$^1\Delta$	T	$h\dfrac{dT}{dr}$	$^1\Delta$	$n+1$
3.8	3.07	−23	−1		7.83	183	34	5	80.1	0		0.784	49	3	
3.6	2.83	−25	−2		9.86	223	40	6	80.1	−1.	−1	0.834	51	2	
3.4	2.57	−26	−1		12.3	27	5	1	80.0	−1	0	0.886	53	2	
3.2	2.31	−27	−1		15.3	32	5	0	79.9	−2	−1	0.940	56	3	
3.0	2.03	−28	−1		18.8	37	5	0	79.6	−3	−1	0.997	58	2	3.34
2.8	1.75	−27	+1		22.7	41	4	−1	79.3	−4	−1	1.056	60	2	3.23
2.6	1.48	−27	0		27.0	46	5	+1	78.7	−5	−1	1.116	61	1	3.11
2.4	1.22	−25	+2		31.8	49	3	−2	78.1	−7	−2	1.178	62	1	2.95
2.2	0.978	−234	+16	0	36.8	52	3	0	77.3	−9	−2	1.240	63	2	2.76
2.0	0.755	−210	+24	+8	42.1	53	1	−2	76.3	−10	−1	1.304	64	1	2.53
1.8	0.558	−183	+27	+3	47.4	51	−2	−3	75.2	−12	−2	1.369	66	2	2.26

Interpolated boundary of convective core, at $n + 1 = 2.50$: $r = 1.975$, $M_r = 0.730$, $P = 42.7$, $L_r = 76.2$, $T = 1.311$.

* The units are the same as in Table 10-1A.

or, in Table 10-1B,

$$h \frac{dL_r}{dr} = 0.0004266 h P^2 T^2 r^2 \qquad (10\text{-}50)$$

$$h \frac{dT}{dr} = -0.00009096 h \frac{P^2}{T^{8.5}} \frac{L_r}{r^2}.$$

The method described in Section 1-3A was followed in performing the integrations.

The test for convection is given by the inequality (6-54). We therefore compute

$$n + 1 = \frac{d \log P}{d \log T} = \frac{T \, h \, dP/dr}{P \, h \, dT/dr}$$

on various lines of the integration and compare the value with 2.5. Convection is found to begin at about $r = 2.0$. Interpolation to locate more precisely the radius at which the value is 2.50 yields:

If $L_r = L$ (Table 10-1A):

$$r = 2.01$$
$$M_r = 0.76$$
$$P = 41.7$$
$$T = 1.305$$
$$L = 80.1. \qquad (10\text{-}51)$$

If L_r is variable (Table 10-1B):

$$r = 1.98$$
$$M_r = 0.73$$
$$P = 42.7$$
$$T = 1.311$$
$$L_r = 76.2.$$

B. THE CONVECTIVE CORE

We may continue inwards into the convective core, now integrating only the differential equations for M_r and T. This has been done in Table 10-2A for the case $L_r = L$ in the envelope. Equation (10-49) for dM_r/dr is reduced to dependence on T and r by substituting for P the expression

$$P = 21.43 T^{2.5}, \qquad (10\text{-}52)$$

Table 10-2A   Model A: Convective Core (Continued from Radiative Envelope, Table 10-1A).*

r	M_r	$h\dfrac{dM_r}{dr}$	$^1\Delta$	$^2\Delta$	T	$h\dfrac{dT}{dr}$	$^1\Delta$	$^2\Delta$	P
2.0	0.756	−209	+24	+7	1.308	66	2		42.0
1.8	0.560	−182	+27	+3	1.372	60	−6	−8	47.2
1.6	0.392	−153	+29	+2	1.429	53	−7	−1	52.3
1.4	0.254	−123	+30	+1	1.478	45	−8	−1	56.9
1.2	0.146	−94	+29	−1	1.518	35	−10	−2	60.8
1.0	0.066	−67	+27	−2	1.547	23	−12	−2	63.8
0.8	0.011	−44	+23	−4	1.562	6	−17	−5	65.3

* The units are the same as in Table 10-1A.

in which the constant has been determined as $P/T^{2.5}$ at the interpolated core boundary. Then the equation

$$h\frac{dM_r}{dr} = 0.1744hT^{1.5}r^2 \qquad (10\text{-}53)$$

permits the calculation of M_r. Simultaneously, we find T by integrating eq. (10-22):

$$h\frac{dT}{dr} = -1.727h\frac{M_r}{r^2}. \qquad (10\text{-}54)$$

Then P is found from eq. (10-52), and L_r is determined from a separate integration of eq. (10-50).

By the time $r = 0.8$ is reached in Table 10-2A, the mass is about to become negative. Clearly, this is not an equilibrium model. We shall return later to the consideration of possible changes that might be made to obtain an equilibrium structure.

Alternatively, we can begin an integration from the center, using eqs. (10-53), (10-54), and (10-52) to get M_r, T, and P. The central density is determined when T_c is specified, since P_c is related to T_c through eq. (10-52), and μ has the same value as in the envelope. Let us take the estimate

$$T_c = 1.61.$$

Then

$$\rho_c = 28.34 \text{ gm cm}^{-3},$$

and the starting values of M_r and T can be computed from eqs. (10-44) and (10-48):

$$M_r = 0.1187r^3$$

and

$$T = 1.61 - 0.1025r^2.$$

The integration for L_r is independent of those for T and M_r. Starting values are obtained from eq. (10-46):

$$L_r = 1.830r^3,$$

since

$$\epsilon_c = 15.42.$$

The derivative is again given by eq. (10-50). If ρ and ϵ have been tabulated (as in Table 10-3), we may also use eq. (10-3), which becomes

$$h\frac{dL_r}{dr} = 0.01257h\rho\epsilon r^2.$$

Table 10-2B contains the results of these calculations.

Table 10-2B   Model A: Convective Core (Begun at Center).*

$$T_c = 1.610, \quad P = 21.43T^{2.5}.$$

r	M_r	$h\dfrac{dM_r}{dr}$	$^1\Delta$	$^2\Delta$	$^3\Delta$	T	$h\dfrac{dT}{dr}$	$^1\Delta$	P	L_r	$h\dfrac{dL_r}{dr}$	$^1\Delta$	$^2\Delta$	$^3\Delta$
0.0	0.0000	0				1.610			70.48	0.00	0			
0.1	0.0001	4	4			1.609	-2		70.37	0.00	1	1		
0.2	0.0010	14	10	6		1.606	-4	-2	70.05	0.02	2	1	0	
0.3	0.0032	32	18	8		1.601	-6	-2	69.50	0.05	5	3	2	
0.4	0.0076	56	24	6		1.594	-8	-2	68.75	0.12	8	3	0	
0.5	0.0147	87	31	7		1.585	-10	-2	67.78	0.22	12	4	1	
0.6	0.0252	124	37	6		1.574	-12	-2	66.61	0.36	17	5	1	
Continue at double interval:														
0.0										0				
0.2		28					-8			4	4			
0.4		112	84				-16	-8		16	12	8		
0.6	0.0252	248	136	52		1.574	-24	-8	66.61	0.36	34	18	6	-2
0.8	0.0587	429	181	45	-7	1.546	-32	-8	63.69	0.80	53	19	1	-5
1.0	0.1122	647	218	37	-8	1.510	-39	-7	60.04	1.41	70	17	-2	-3
1.2	0.189	89	24	2		1.468	-45	-6	55.95	2.18	83	13	-4	-2
1.4	0.291	116	27	3		1.420	-51	-6	51.49	3.04	89	6	-7	-3
1.6	0.421	143	27	0	-3	1.366	-57	-6	46.74	3.94	89	0	-6	$+1$
1.8	0.577	169	26	-1	-1	1.306	-62	-5	41.77	4.80	82	-7	-7	-1
2.0	0.758	193	24	-2	-1	1.242	-65	-3	36.84	5.57	71	-11	-4	$+3$
2.2	0.962	215	22	-2	0	1.175	-69	-4	32.07	6.22	59	-12	-1	$+3$

* The units are the same as in Table 10-1A.

Table 10-3   Values of ρ, $\bar{\kappa}$, ϵ for Model A (Envelope and Core of Tables 10-1A, 10-1B, and 10-2B).

$r \times 10^{-10}$	ρ	$\bar{\kappa}$	ϵ
10.0	0.000879	2.99	
9.0	0.01086	2.47	
8.0	0.0580	2.18	
7.0	0.221	1.95	
6.0	0.718	1.75	
5.0	2.09	1.55	
4.0	5.42	1.30	
3.0	12.2	1.02	0.98
2.0	19.20		3.70
1.8	20.70		4.88
1.6	22.15		6.25
1.4	23.47		7.73
1.2	24.67		9.28
1.0	25.74		10.84
0.8	26.67		12.34
0.6	27.40		13.62
0.4	27.68		14.60
0.2	28.24		15.22
0.0	28.34		15.42

$$\bar{\kappa} = \bar{\kappa}_{bf} = \frac{4.34 \times 10^{25}}{3.162} \, 0.01(1.90) \frac{\rho}{T^{3.5}}$$

$$\epsilon = \epsilon_{pp} = 0.100 \times 10^{-28}(0.90)^2 \rho T^4.$$

At $r = 0$, $\epsilon_{CN} = 0.77$ for $X_{CN} = 0.35Z$; however, ϵ_{CN} has been neglected.

We must now find the values of M_r, P, T, and L_r at the boundary of the convective core. We had determined from the envelope solutions that $r = 2.01$ if $L_r = L$, while $r = 1.98$ if L_r is variable. Hence we interpolate for these values of the radius. We find
at $r = 2.01$:

$$M_r = 0.769,$$

$$P = 36.5,$$

$$T = 1.238,$$

$$L_r = 5.60;$$

at $r = 1.98$:

$$M_r = 0.740,$$

$$P = 37.3,$$

$$T = 1.248,$$

$$L_r = 5.50.$$

These numbers do not agree precisely with those in eqs. (10-51). The discrepancy in L_r is especially large.

Comments will be made on these results in Section 2-4.

2-3 CALCULATION WITH LOGARITHMIC VARIABLES IN THE ENVELOPE AND EMDEN VARIABLES IN THE CORE

A. THE RADIATIVE ENVELOPE

Define the following variables*:

$$y = \log r \qquad (10\text{-}55)$$

$$\eta = \log M_r$$

$$\psi = \log P$$

$$\lambda = \log L_r$$

$$\tau = \log T.$$

The equation of continuity of mass (10-13) becomes

$$\frac{d \log M_r}{d \log r} = \frac{r}{M_r} \frac{dM_r}{dr} = \frac{4\pi H}{k} \mu \frac{P}{TM_r} r^3, \qquad (10\text{-}56)$$

and therefore

$$\log \left(\frac{d\eta}{dy}\right) = \log \frac{4\pi H}{k} + \log \mu + \psi - \tau - \eta + 3y. \qquad (10\text{-}57)$$

The equation of hydrostatic equilibrium (10-14) becomes

$$\frac{d \log P}{d \log r} = \frac{r}{P} \frac{dP}{dr} = -\frac{GH}{k} \mu \frac{M_r}{Tr}, \qquad (10\text{-}58)$$

and

$$\log \left(-\frac{d\psi}{dy}\right) = \log \frac{GH}{k} + \log \mu + \eta - \tau - y. \qquad (10\text{-}59)$$

The equation for the radiative temperature gradient (10-15) is transformed into

$$\frac{d \log T}{d \log r} = \frac{r}{T} \frac{dT}{dr} = -\frac{3}{16\pi ac} \frac{4.34 \times 10^{25}}{t/\bar{g}_{\text{bf}}} \left(\frac{H}{k}\right)^2 Z(1 + X)\mu^2 \frac{P^2 L_r}{T^{9.5} r},$$

hence

$$\log \left(-\frac{d\tau}{dy}\right) = \log \left[\frac{3}{16\pi ac} 4.34 \times 10^{25} \left(\frac{H}{k}\right)^2\right] +$$

$$+ \log \left[\frac{Z(1 + X)\mu^2}{t/\bar{g}_{\text{bf}}}\right] + 2\psi - 9.5\tau + \lambda - y.$$

* The notation adopted here is not standard.

A similar transformation can be made for the derivative of L_r, although it is not needed here since we shall set $L_r = L$. From eq. (10-16), we have

$$\frac{d \log L_r}{d \log r} = \frac{r}{L_r} \frac{dL_r}{dr} = 4\pi \left(\frac{H}{k}\right)^2 \epsilon_0 X_1 X_2 \mu^2 \frac{P^2 T^{\nu-2}}{L_r} r^3$$

and

$$\log \left(\frac{d\lambda}{dy}\right) = \log \left[4\pi \left(\frac{H}{k}\right)^2\right] + \log (\epsilon_0 X_1 X_2 \mu^2) + 2\psi + (\nu - 2)\tau - \lambda + 3y.$$

In this example, which was presented in Section 2-1, the equations become:

$$\log \left(\frac{d\eta}{dy}\right) = -7.0896 + \psi - \tau - \eta + 3y \qquad (10\text{-}60)$$

$$\log \left(-\frac{d\psi}{dy}\right) = -15.3648 + \eta - \tau - y \qquad (10\text{-}61)$$

$$\log \left(-\frac{d\tau}{dy}\right) = +44.3626 + 2\psi - 9.5\tau - y, \qquad (10\text{-}62)$$

with the surface values

$$y_0 = 11.0436$$

$$\eta_0 = 33.6957$$

$$\lambda_0 = 34.9038.$$

Starting values near the surface are needed, and these can be obtained by taking logarithms in eqs. (10-42) and (10-41):

$$\psi = \frac{1}{2} \log \left[\frac{1}{4.25} \frac{16\pi acGk}{3H} \frac{t/\bar{g}_{bf}}{4.34 \times 10^{25}} \frac{1}{\mu Z(1+X)} \frac{M}{L}\right] + 4.25\tau \qquad (10\text{-}63)$$

and

$$\tau = \log \left(\frac{GH}{4.25k} \mu M\right) + \log \left(\frac{1}{10^y} - \frac{1}{10^{y_0}}\right). \qquad (10\text{-}64)$$

Evaluation of the coefficients gives

$$\psi = -13.3300 + 4.25\tau \qquad (10\text{-}65)$$

$$\tau = 17.7026 + \log (10^{-y} - 10^{-11.0436}). \qquad (10\text{-}66)$$

These expressions have been used to calculate ψ, τ, $\log (-h \, d\eta/dy)$, $\log (h \, d\psi/dy)$, and $\log (h \, d\tau/dy)$ for $y = 10.95$ to 10.92 in Table 10-4. After taking the appropriate antilogarithms, we calculate the differences $^1\Delta$, $^2\Delta, \cdots$. This completes the computation of the starting values.

The integration is continued until the value of

$$n + 1 = \frac{d \log P}{d \log T} = \frac{d\psi/dy}{d\tau/dy} \qquad (10\text{-}67)$$

decreases to 2.5; according to the inequality (6-54), this marks the beginning of the convective region. In this example, we shall not perform an integration for the core but rather attach a solution that has already been computed in terms of the Emden variables. The fitting is to take place at the interpolated position at which convection begins. At this interface,

$$y = 10.298,$$

$$\eta = 32.875,$$

$$\psi = 16.628,$$

$$\tau = 7.118$$

or

$$r = 1.986 \times 10^{10},$$

$$M_r = 0.750 \times 10^{33},$$

$$P = 42.5 \times 10^{15},$$

$$T = 1.312 \times 10^{7},$$

$$\rho = 21.0.$$

Ideally, these values should be identical with those given in eqs. (10-51) for the boundary of the core in Table 10-1A. Errors due to rounding and different numerical procedures, however, have produced small discrepancies between the corresponding values. In particular, $n + 1$ in the present case reaches 2.50 at a slightly smaller radius, and there is the additional systematic effect of comparing the models at different values of r.

B. THE CONVECTIVE CORE

Table 10-11 lists the polytropic solution for the index $n = 1.5$. In Section 4 of Chapter 6, we have shown that this solution is applicable to a convective core. The range of the tabulation, however, extends from the center to the surface of the star, and we must therefore locate the tabulated or interpolated line of entries that corresponds to the boundary of the core in our model. This is accomplished with the aid of the functions U and V, defined below, which are ratios whose values are independent of the particular set of variables in which they are expressed. Either U or V at the core boundary can be evaluated from the envelope solution in terms of the logarithmic variables; and the radius ξ at which U or V has the same value in Table 10-11 must then be the boundary of the core.

We now define U and V. Since we desire quantities that are dimensionless and also readily calculable, we may take ratios of the form

$$(v_2/v_1) \frac{dv_1}{dr} \bigg/ \frac{dv_2}{dr},$$

Table 10-4   Radiative Envelope Using Logarithmic Variables.*

y	$\log\left(-h\dfrac{d\eta}{dy}\right)$	η	$h\dfrac{d\eta}{dy}$	$^1\Delta$	$^2\Delta$	$\log\left(h\dfrac{d\psi}{dy}\right)$	ψ	$h\dfrac{d\psi}{dy}$
10.95	**$\bar{4}.37$**	**33.696**	**0**			**$\bar{1}.341$**	**12.341**	**219**
10.94	**$\bar{4}.50$**	**33.696**	**0**			**$\bar{1}.301$**	**12.551**	**200**
10.93	**$\bar{4}.61$**	**33.696**	**0**			**$\bar{1}.266$**	**12.743**	**184**
10.92	**$\bar{4}.72$**	**33.696**	**-1**			**$\bar{1}.234$**	**12.921**	**171**
10.91	$\bar{4}.82$	33.695	-1			$\bar{1}.204$	13.087	160
10.90	$\bar{4}.91$	33.694	-1			$\bar{1}.176$	13.242	150
10.89	$\bar{4}.99$	33.693	-1			$\bar{1}.151$	13.387	142
10.88	$\bar{3}.07$	33.692	-1			$\bar{1}.128$	13.526	134
10.87	$\bar{3}.14$	33.691	-1			$\bar{1}.106$	13.656	128
10.86	$\bar{3}.20$	33.690	-2			$\bar{1}.086$	13.782	122
Continue at double interval:								
10.94								
10.92								342
10.90			-2					300
10.88			-2					268
10.86		33.690	-3				13.782	244
10.84	$\bar{3}.62$	33.687	-4	-1		$\bar{1}.348$	14.015	223
10.82	$\bar{3}.73$	33.682	-5	-1		$\bar{1}.313$	14.229	206
10.80	$\bar{3}.83$	33.677	-7	-2		$\bar{1}.281$	14.427	191
10.78	$\bar{3}.92$	33.669	-8	-1		$\bar{1}.249$	14.611	177
10.76	$\bar{2}.00$	33.660	-10	-2		$\bar{1}.218$	14.782	165
10.74	$\bar{2}.067$	33.649	-12	-2		$\bar{1}.189$	14.941	154
10.72	$\bar{2}.133$	33.636	-14	-2		$\bar{1}.160$	15.090	144
10.70	$\bar{2}.193$	33.621	-16	-2		$\bar{1}.131$	15.229	135
Continue at double interval:								
10.82			-11					411
10.78			-17	-6				355
10.74			-23	-6				309
10.70		33.621	-31	-8	-2		15.229	270
10.66	$\bar{2}.600$	33.585	-40	-9	-1	$\bar{1}.373$	15.482	236
10.62	$\bar{2}.689$	33.540	-49	-9	0	$\bar{1}.312$	15.702	205
10.58	$\bar{2}.764$	33.486	-58	-9	0	$\bar{1}.248$	15.893	177
10.54	$\bar{2}.826$	33.424	-67	-9	0	$\bar{1}.182$	16.057	152
10.50	$\bar{2}.880$	33.352	-76	-9	0	$\bar{1}.111$	16.198	129
10.46	$\bar{2}.924$	33.272	-84	-8	$+1$	$\bar{1}.036$	16.317	109
10.42	$\bar{2}.961$	33.184	-91	-7	$+1$	$\bar{2}.957$	16.417	91
10.38	$\bar{2}.991$	33.090	-98	-7	0	$\bar{2}.876$	16.500	75
10.34	$\bar{1}.016$	32.989	-104	-6	$+1$	$\bar{2}.791$	16.568	62
10.30	$\bar{1}.037$	32.822	-109	-5	$+1$	$\bar{2}.702$	16.624	50
10.26	$\bar{1}.054$	32.771	-113	-4	$+1$	$\bar{2}.612$	16.669	41

Interpolated boundary of convective core, at $n + 1 = 2.50$:

$$y = 10.298, \quad \eta = 32.875, \quad \psi = 16.628, \quad \tau = 7.118.$$

$^1\Delta$	$^2\Delta$	$^3\Delta$	$\log\left(h\dfrac{d\tau}{dy}\right)$	τ	$h\dfrac{d\tau}{dy}$	$^1\Delta$	$^2\Delta$	$n+1$
			$\bar{2}.715$	6.040	52			4.23
-19			$\bar{2}.670$	6.090	47	-5		
-16	$+3$		$\bar{2}.636$	6.135	43	-4		
-13	$+3$		$\bar{2}.603$	6.177	40	-3		
-11	$+2$		$\bar{2}.575$	6.216	38	-2		
-10	$+1$		$\bar{2}.543$	6.253	35	-3		4.30
-8	$+2$		$\bar{2}.520$	6.287	33	-2		
-8	0		$\bar{2}.504$	6.319	32	-1		
-6	$+2$		$\bar{2}.480$	6.350	30	-2		
-6	0		$\bar{2}.466$	6.379	29	-1		
					94			
					80	-14		
-42					70	-10	$+4$	
-32	$+10$				64	-6	$+4$	
-24	$+8$	-2		6.379	58	-6	0	
-21	$+3$	-5	$\bar{2}.721$	6.434	53	-5	$+1$	
-17	$+4$	$+1$	$\bar{2}.694$	6.485	49	-4	$+1$	
-15	$+2$	-2	$\bar{2}.664$	6.532	46	-3	$+1$	4.14
-14	$+1$	-1	$\bar{2}.634$	6.576	43	-3	0	
-12	$+2$	$+1$	$\bar{2}.597$	6.618	40	-3	0	
-11	$+1$	-1	$\bar{2}.574$	6.656	37	-3	0	
-10	$+1$	0	$\bar{2}.550$	6.692	35	-2	$+1$	
-9	$+1$	0	$\bar{2}.525$	6.726	33	-2	0	4.04
					99			
-56					86	-13		
-46	$+10$				75	-11	$+2$	
-39	$+7$	-3		6.726	67	-8	$+3$	
-34	$+5$	-2	$\bar{2}.773$	6.789	59	-8	0	
-31	$+3$	-2	$\bar{2}.721$	6.845	53	-6	$+2$	
-28	$+3$	0	$\bar{2}.668$	6.895	47	-6	0	
-25	$+3$	0	$\bar{2}.618$	6.939	41	-6	0	
-23	$+2$	-1	$\bar{2}.570$	6.978	37	-4	$+2$	3.48
-20	$+3$	$+1$	$\bar{2}.515$	7.013	33	-4	0	
-18	$+2$	-1	$\bar{2}.461$	7.044	29	-4	0	3.13
-16	$+2$	0	$\bar{2}.410$	7.071	26	-3	$+1$	2.92
-13	$+3$	$+1$	$\bar{2}.358$	7.095	23	-3	0	2.71
-12	$+1$	-2	$\bar{2}.301$	7.117	20	-2	$+1$	2.52
-9	$+3$	$+2$	$\bar{2}.251$	7.136	18	-2	0	2.30

* The derivatives and differences are expressed in units of the last place of the corresponding variables.

where v_1 and v_2 are variables whose derivatives have been tabulated in the process of numerical integration. If we set $v_2 = r$ and $v_1 = M_r$, we can define

$$U = \frac{r}{M_r} \frac{dM_r}{dr} \tag{10-68}$$

$$= \frac{d \log M_r}{d \log r} \tag{10-69}$$

$$= \frac{d\eta}{dy}; \tag{10-70}$$

and if instead we set $v_1 = P$, we can define

$$V = -\frac{r}{P} \frac{dP}{dr} \tag{10-71}$$

$$= -\frac{d \log P}{d \log r} \tag{10-72}$$

$$= -\frac{d\psi}{dy}. \tag{10-73}$$

The function $(n + 1)$ in eq. (6-53) is also of this form, with $v_1 = P$ and $v_2 = T$:

$$n + 1 = \frac{d \log P}{d \log T} \tag{10-74}$$

$$= \frac{d\psi}{d\tau}. \tag{10-75}$$

In terms of the Emden variables, we have from eqs. (6-8), (6-11), (6-16), and (6-11A) that

$$U = \frac{\alpha\xi}{-4\pi\alpha^3 \rho_c \xi^2 \dfrac{d\theta}{d\xi}} 4\pi(\alpha\xi)^2(\rho_c \theta^n)$$

$$= -\frac{\xi\theta^n}{\dfrac{d\theta}{d\xi}}, \tag{10-76}$$

$$V = -\frac{\alpha\xi}{P_c \theta^{n+1}} \frac{d(P_c \theta^{n+1})}{d(\alpha\xi)}$$

$$= -(n + 1)\frac{\xi}{\theta} \frac{d\theta}{d\xi}. \tag{10-77}$$

Both U and V may be interpreted physically. If we arrange the factors, we have

$$U = \frac{r}{M_r} 4\pi r^2 \rho$$

$$= 3 \frac{\rho}{M_r / \frac{4}{3}\pi r^3}$$

$$= 3 \frac{\text{local density}}{\text{mean density within sphere of radius } r}$$

Fig. 10-1 The U, V Plane for Two Radiative Envelopes and the Polytropic Solution for the Index $n = 1.5$. The radiative envelopes are those of Model A (Tables 10-1A for $r \geqslant 0.4$ and 10-1B) and of Kushwaha (Table 10-6). The equilibrium model of Kushwaha becomes convective just at the point at which the U, V curve meets that of the polytrope. The model of Tables 10-1A and 10-1B is not in equilibrium, and its termination point in the U, V plane does not coincide with the polytropic curve.

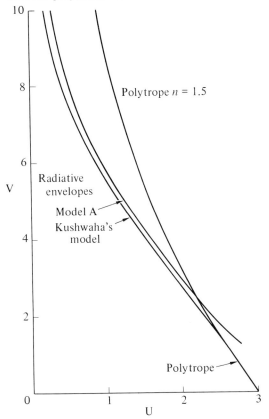

and

$$V = \frac{r}{P} \frac{GM_r}{r^2} \rho$$

$$= \frac{3}{2} \frac{GM_r/r}{\frac{3}{2}kT/\mu H}$$

$$= \frac{3}{2} \frac{|\text{local gravitational potential energy/gram}|}{\text{local internal energy/gram}},$$

according to the discussion at the beginning of Section 5-1 in Chapter 6. The value of U is three at the center and zero at the surface, while V is zero

Fig. 10-2 The U, V Plane for Adiabatic Convective Envelopes and a Radiative Core. The radiative core is that of Table 10-7. The envelopes are labeled with their values of E [see eq. (10-126)]. The relative depth of the convective envelope is governed by the value of E, which is 45.48 for a completely convective model that is identical with the polytrope of index $n = 1.5$ (cf. Fig. 10-1). The radiative core solution shown is continuous with that of the interpolated envelope for which $E = 45.44$.

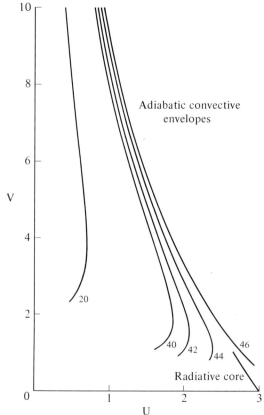

at the center and infinite at the surface (with the boundary condition $T = 0$). The variations of U and V within selected models, including the present one, are shown in Figs. 10-1 and 10-2. More will be said about these figures later.

We can now join the core and envelope in our example at their common interface. At the boundary of the envelope, we find

$$U = 2.725,$$
$$V = 1.250.$$

For these values, Table 10-11 gives, respectively,

$$\xi_U = 0.964,$$
$$\xi_V = 1.205.$$

The lack of coincidence of these two values of ξ already discloses the fact that the model is not in equilibrium*; nevertheless, to complete the example, let us attach a convective core at each of the two values.

The constants in the transformations that define ξ and θ, eqs. (6-8) and (6-9), are evaluated from r and T at the core boundary. Designating by subscripts U and V the quantities pertinent to the fitting points ξ_U and ξ_V, respectively, we find

$$\alpha = \frac{r}{\xi}: \quad \alpha_U = \frac{1.986 \times 10^{10}}{0.964} = 2.060 \times 10^{10} \text{ cm} \qquad (10\text{-}78)$$

$$\alpha_V = \frac{1.986 \times 10^{10}}{1.205} = 1.648 \times 10^{10} \text{ cm}$$

and

$$T_c = \frac{T}{\theta}: \quad T_{cU} = \frac{1.312 \times 10^7}{0.855} = 1.535 \times 10^7 \text{ °K} \qquad (10\text{-}79)$$

$$T_{cV} = \frac{1.312 \times 10^7}{0.782} = 1.678 \times 10^7 \text{ °K.}$$

By requiring continuity of the pressure at the boundary, we have from eq. (6-11A) that

$$P_c = \frac{P}{\theta^{n+1}}: \quad P_{cU} = \frac{42.5 \times 10^{15}}{0.677} = 62.8 \times 10^{15} \text{ dyne cm}^{-2} \qquad (10\text{-}80)$$

$$P_{cV} = \frac{42.5 \times 10^{15}}{0.541} = 78.6 \times 10^{15} \text{ dyne cm}^{-2}.$$

Alternatively, we could have obtained P_c from eq. (6-46),

$$P_{c'} = \mathscr{K}'T_c^{2.5},$$

* The impossibility of achieving a proper fit between the core and envelope is demonstrated also in Fig. 10-1 by the fact that U and V at the boundary of the envelope do not lie on the curve for the polytrope with $n = 1.5$.

with the constant $\mathcal{K}'$ evaluated as $P/T^{2.5}$ at the interpolated core boundary. Note also that the relation (6-11), together with the requirement of continuity of the density,* gives

$$\rho_c = \frac{\rho}{\theta^n}: \quad \rho_{cU} = \frac{21.0}{0.791} = 26.5 \text{ gm cm}^{-3} \tag{10-81}$$

$$\rho_{cV} = \frac{21.0}{0.692} = 30.3 \text{ gm cm}^{-3},$$

and these values necessarily agree with those computed from the perfect gas law, using P_c and T_c.

The mass at the core boundary is found from eq. (6-16):

$$M_\xi = 4\pi\alpha^3 \rho_c \left(-\xi^2 \frac{d\theta}{d\xi} \right) \tag{10-82}$$

$$M_{\xi U} = 4\pi(2.060 \times 10^{10})^3 26.5(0.261) = 0.761 \times 10^{33} \text{ gm}$$

$$M_{\xi V} = 4\pi(1.648 \times 10^{10})^3 30.3(0.470) = 0.802 \times 10^{33} \text{ gm}.$$

The envelope solution, on the other hand, gave $M_r = 0.750 \times 10^{33}$ gm. Although we have imposed equality between the envelope and core values of r, T, P (or ρ) at either of the two assumed fitting points, this was possible because the constants α, T_c, P_c (or ρ_c) are free parameters that could be specified accordingly; but we do not have an additional disposable constant to ensure equality of M_r and M_ξ. Hence we cannot, in general, expect these to agree.

Integration through the core for L_r gives the total energy produced per second, since we have assumed that none is produced in the envelope. From eqs. (10-3) and (10-48A), we have

$$L_\xi = 4\pi\alpha^3 \rho_c{}^2 T_c{}^4 \epsilon_0 X^2 \int_0^{\xi_{max}} \xi^2 \theta^{2n+4} \, d\xi \tag{10-83}$$

$$L_{\xi U} = 4\pi(2.060 \times 10^{10})^3(26.5)^2(1.535 \times 10^7)^4(10.0 \times 10^{-30}) \times$$

$$\times (0.90)^2(1.623 \times 0.1)$$

$$= 5.65 \times 10^{33} \text{ erg sec}^{-1},$$

$$L_{\xi V} = 4\pi(1.648 \times 10^{10})^3(30.3)^2(1.678 \times 10^7)^4(10.0 \times 10^{-30}) \times$$

$$\times (0.90)^2(2.323 \times 0.1)$$

$$= 7.72 \times 10^{33} \text{ erg sec}^{-1}.$$

* The density could be discontinuous if a corresponding discontinuity in μ maintained continuity of the *pressure* across the boundary.

Table 10-5 $\int \xi^2 \theta^7 \, d\xi$ for L_ξ.*

ξ	$\xi^2\theta^7$	$^1\Delta$	$^2\Delta$	$^3\Delta$	$\dfrac{1}{h}\int \xi^2\theta^7\,d\xi$
0.0	0.000				0.000
0.1	0.010	10			0.005
0.2	0.038	28	18		0.028
0.3	0.081	43	15	−3	0.086
0.4	0.133	52	9	−6	0.192
0.5	0.187	54	2	−7	0.353
0.6	0.236	49	−5	−7	0.565
0.7	0.276	40	−9	−4	0.822
0.8	0.302	26	−14	−5	1.112
0.9	0.313	11	−15	−1	1.421
1.0	0.308	−5	−16	−1	1.733
1.1	0.290	−18	−13	+3	2.033
1.2	0.262	−28	−10	+3	2.310
1.3	0.227	−35	−7	+3	2.555

* The differences are expressed in units of 0.001.

The integration occurring here is shown in Table 10-5. Again there is disagreement between the envelope and core solutions, since these values of L are not the same as that assumed for the envelope. These difficulties are discussed in Section 2-4.

2-4 DISCUSSION OF THE RESULTS

The model that we have calculated is not in equilibrium, and we now inquire as to how it may be corrected. If we are confident that we have used the best possible representations of the opacity and energy-generation rate, then the only recourse is to vary one or more of the free parameters X and Z and, if we integrate the core solution from the center, T_c.* In the present example, however, we have oversimplified the expression for $\bar{\kappa}$. Free-free transitions, bound-bound transitions, and electron scattering do make contributions, and $t/\bar{g}_{bf}$ is not really constant. The energy-generation rate, on the other hand, cannot be much improved.

* Actually, T_c need not enter the problem as a free parameter. As we have seen in Table 10-2A, it is possible to continue the integration inwards from the envelope. Thus, if the gradients of M_r, P, T, and L_r had approached zero simultaneously as r approached zero, an equilibrium model would have been obtained. Since T would have attained some definite value T_c at the center, it is the values chosen for X and Z that determine whether or not there exists the possibility of matching a core solution to the envelope.

Table 10-6   Kushwaha's Model. [See R. S. Kushwaha, 1957 (500). From Martin Schwarzschild, *Structure and Evolution of the Stars* (copyright © 1958 by Princeton University Press): Table 28.2, p. 255. Reprinted by permission of Princeton University Press.]

$$\frac{M}{M_\odot} = 2.5, \quad \frac{L}{L_\odot} = 21.2, \quad \frac{R}{R_\odot} = 1.59.$$

r/R	$\dfrac{M_r}{M}$	$\dfrac{L_r}{L}$	$\log P$	$\log T$	$\log \rho$	$\bar{\kappa}$	U	V	$n+1$
0.00	0.000	0.000	17.166	7.297	+1.684	Conv.	3.000	0.000	2.500
0.02	0.000	0.020	17.161	7.295	1.681	Conv.	2.992	0.022	2.500
0.04	0.003	0.122	17.147	7.289	1.672	Conv.	2.969	0.087	2.500
0.06	0.011	0.317	17.123	7.280	1.658	Conv.	2.930	0.195	2.500
0.08	0.027	0.551	17.090	7.267	1.638	Conv.	2.876	0.348	2.500
0.10	0.050	0.757	17.048	7.250	1.613	Conv.	2.808	0.547	2.500
0.12	0.083	0.887	16.995	7.229	1.581	Conv.	2.724	0.792	2.500
0.14	0.125	0.957	16.933	7.204	1.544	Conv.	2.627	1.087	2.500
0.16	0.177	1.000	16.860	7.172	1.499	0.955	2.515	1.433	2.589
0.18	0.236	1.000	16.777	7.142	1.446	1.03	2.377	1.823	2.892
0.20	0.300	1.000	16.685	7.112	1.384	1.10	2.218	2.243	3.156
0.22	0.368	1.000	16.583	7.080	1.313	1.18	2.047	2.685	3.383
0.24	0.436	1.000	16.473	7.049	1.235	1.25	1.871	3.139	3.577
0.26	0.503	1.000	16.356	7.017	1.150	1.33	1.695	3.598	3.740
0.28	0.567	1.000	16.233	6.984	1.059	1.42	1.525	4.056	3.878
0.30	0.627	1.000	16.105	6.952	0.963	1.49	1.362	4.507	3.994
0.32	0.681	1.000	15.972	6.919	0.863	1.58	1.209	4.951	4.091
0.34	0.729	1.000	15.836	6.886	0.760	1.66	1.068	5.385	4.172
0.36	0.772	1.000	15.697	6.853	0.654	1.75	0.938	5.811	4.240
0.38	0.810	1.000	15.556	6.820	0.546	1.83	0.820	6.230	4.297
0.40	0.843	1.000	15.412	6.787	0.436	1.92	0.713	6.645	4.345
0.42	0.870	1.000	15.268	6.754	0.324	2.01	0.618	7.055	4.386
0.44	0.894	1.000	15.120	6.720	+0.210	2.11	0.533	7.470	4.420
0.46	0.914	1.000	14.972	6.687	+0.096	2.20	0.457	7.888	4.448
0.48	0.931	1.000	14.823	6.654	−0.020	2.29	0.391	8.313	4.472
0.50	0.944	1.000	14.672	6.620	−0.138	2.39	0.332	8.754	4.492
0.52	0.956	1.000	14.519	6.586	−0.257	2.50	0.281	9.212	4.508
0.54	0.965	1.000	14.364	6.551	−0.377	2.63	0.236	9.693	4.523
0.56	0.973	1.000	14.207	6.517	−0.500	2.73	0.197	10.20	4.534
0.58	0.979	1.000	14.048	6.482	−0.624	2.85	0.163	10.74	4.544
0.60	0.984	1.000	13.884	6.446	−0.751	2.99	0.134	11.34	4.553
0.62	0.988	1.000	13.719	6.410	−0.881	3.12	0.110	11.98	4.559
0.64	0.991	1.000	13.549	6.372	−1.014	3.28	0.089	12.68	4.565
0.66	0.993	1.000	13.376	6.334	−1.149	3.45	0.071	13.45	4.570
0.68	0.995	1.000	13.195	6.295	−1.290	3.61	0.056	14.33	4.574
0.70	0.996	1.000	13.009	6.254	−1.435	3.81	0.044	15.31	4.578
0.72	0.997	1.000	12.816	6.212	−1.586	4.02	0.033	16.42	4.581
0.74	0.998	1.000	12.613	6.168	−1.745	4.24	0.025	17.68	4.584
0.76	0.999	1.000	12.400	6.121	−1.912	4.52	0.019	19.18	4.586
0.78	0.999	1.000	12.173	6.072	−2.089	4.80	0.013	20.93	4.588
0.80	1.000	1.000	11.932	6.019	−2.278	5.16	0.009	23.04	4.590
0.82	1.000	1.000	11.672	5.963	−2.481	5.53	0.006	25.60	4.591
0.84	1.000	1.000	11.387	5.901	−2.704	6.00	0.004	28.82	4.593
0.86	1.000	1.000	11.073	5.832	−2.950	6.60	0.003	32.94	4.594
0.88	1.000	1.000	10.718	5.755	−3.228	7.29	0.001	38.44	4.596
0.90	1.000	1.000	10.310	5.666	−3.548	8.22	0.001	46.04	4.598
0.92	1.000	1.000	9.816	5.559	−3.934	9.48	0.000	57.69	4.598
0.94	1.000	1.000	9.196	5.424	−4.420	11.38	0.000	76.93	4.598
0.96	1.000	1.000	8.342	5.238	−5.089	14.71	0.000	124.1	4.598
0.98	1.000	1.000	6.908	4.926	−6.212	22.69	0.000	225.3	4.598
1.00	1.000	1.000	—	—	—	—	0.000	∞	4.598

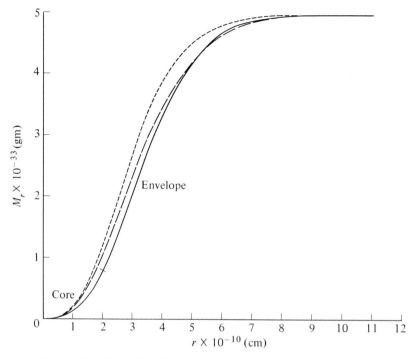

Fig. 10-3A   The Mass Distribution in Models with a Radiative Envelope and a Convective Core. Model A (Tables 10-1A, 10-1B, and 10-2B) is indicated by the *solid curve*, and Kushwaha's model (Table 10-6) is indicated by the *dotted curve*. For comparison, a polytrope of index $n = 3$ is represented by the *dashed curve*. All models have $M = 2.5\ M_{\odot}$ and $R = 1.59\ R_{\odot}$.

An equilibrium model for the same values of M, R, L, X, and Z as in our model was obtained by Kushwaha* with

$$\bar{\kappa} = 1.4\left[\frac{4.34 \times 10^{25}}{t/\bar{g}_{bf}}\,Z(1 + X)\frac{\rho}{T^{3.5}} + 0.19(1 + X)\right],$$

where

$$t/\bar{g}_{bf} = 2.82[\rho(1 + X)]^{0.2}$$

and

$$\epsilon = \epsilon_{CN} = 0.08\,X X_{CN}\rho T_7^{16}.$$

The opacity includes the contribution of electron scattering, which is simply added to the Kramers' expression for bound-free absorption. The empirical factor 1.4 improves the agreement of this formula with tables of more accurately computed values of $\bar{\kappa}$, but the tables do not include line absorption

---

* R. S. Kushwaha, 1957 (500).

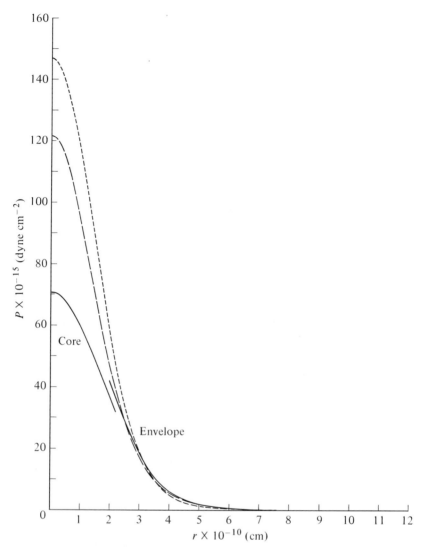

Fig. 10-3B   The Pressure Distribution in Models with a Radiative Envelope and a Convective Core. The models and their representations are the same as in Fig. 10-3A. Model A is not in equilibrium, and there is consequently a discontinuity between the envelope and the core.

or more recent corrections. The coefficient 0.19 used here for electron scattering should rather have been 0.20. Only the CN cycle is considered an energy-production mechanism, since it is more effective than the *p-p* chain at the higher core temperatures of this model. The expression adopted, however, gives ϵ_{CN} too large by an order of magnitude as compared with the modern

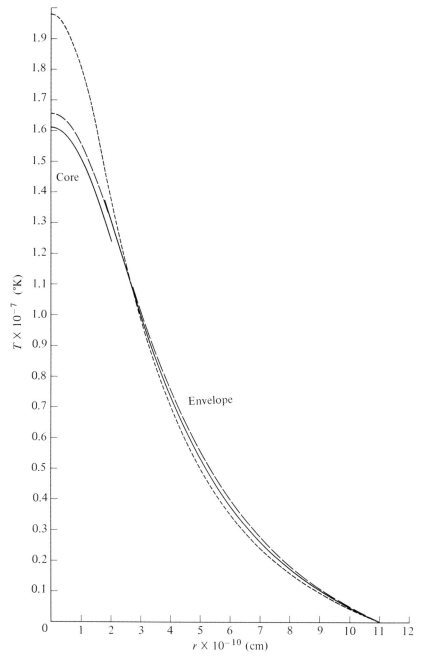

Fig. 10-3C The Temperature Distribution in Models with a Radiative Envelope and a Convective Core. The models and their representations are the same as in Fig. 10-3A.

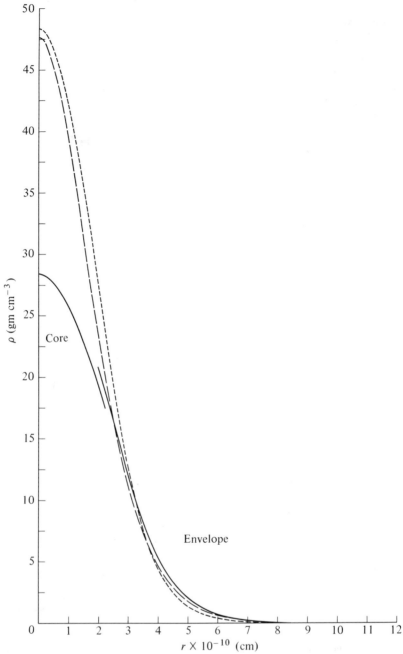

Fig. 10-3D The Density Distribution in Models with a Radiative Envelope and a Convective Core. The models and their representations are the same as in Fig. 10-3A.

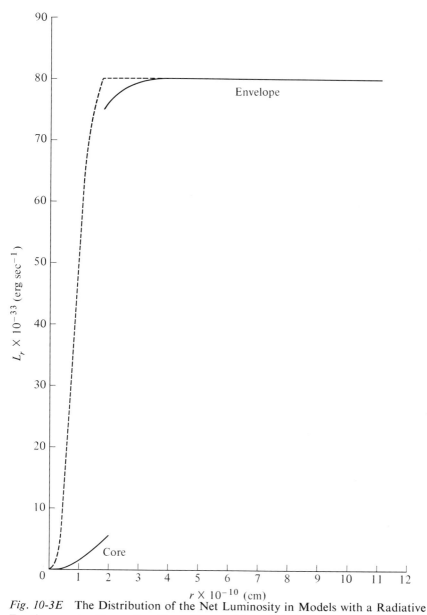

Fig. 10-3E The Distribution of the Net Luminosity in Models with a Radiative Envelope and a Convective Core. The models and their representations are the same as in Fig. 10-3A.

values calculated from eq. (6-77B) or Table 10-14A. Radiation pressure is taken into account, but its influence is very small. At the core boundary, for example, it constitutes only 0.0017 of the total pressure.

Kushwaha's model is presented in Table 10-6 and is shown in Figs. 10-3A to 10-3E, together with the present solution for variable L_r from Tables

10-1A (for $r \geqslant 0.4$), 10-1B, and 10-2B. The polytropic solution for $n = 3$ is also illustrated (see Section 4-2).

3 MODEL B : CONVECTIVE ENVELOPE AND RADIATIVE CORE

3-1 STATEMENT OF THE PROBLEM

The object of this example is to illustrate the construction of a homogeneous model having a convective envelope and a radiative core. We shall attempt to construct a model for a star similar to the initial, homogeneous Sun, since the latter is known to have the desired structure. Let us choose the values

$$M = M_\odot = 1.991 \times 10^{33} \text{ gm,}$$

$$X = 0.72, \qquad Y = 0.26, \qquad Z = 0.02 \qquad (\mu = 0.6079).$$

The envelope will be assumed to have a polytropic index $n = 1.5$ throughout. The boundary conditions at the surface will be taken as

$$P = T = 0 \quad \text{at} \quad r = R.$$

If we were to begin the calculation at the surface, we should have to assume values for R, L, and $\mathscr{K}'$. On the other hand, if we begin at the center, we need only to assume the two values P_c and T_c. We choose the latter course, but with the understanding that we have lost control of the total mass of the model; the value of M_r for which the density goes to zero will not necessarily be the prescribed mass 1 $M_\odot$. This approach has the advantage that an equilibrium model can be attained with a single integration (even though it may have the wrong mass).* The result of the calculation performed here will, in fact, be a model having a mass of 0.6 $M_\odot$. It must therefore be regarded as an unsuccessful first trial at obtaining the desired model of solar mass, although it will fulfill our immediate purpose of demonstrating the calculation of a radiative core and a convective envelope.

The central pressure and temperature will be taken as

$$P_c = 157 \times 10^{15} \text{ dyne cm}^{-2}, \qquad T_c = 1.200 \times 10^7 \text{ °K.}$$

Not all values that seem reasonable estimates prove to be satisfactory boundary values. Some combinations of P_c and T_c may lead to convection already at the center, while others result in a model that is entirely radiative. Still others produce a density that increases with radius, a condition that would occur only under unusual circumstances.† The central values selected here yield a model of the desired type.

---

* See Chapter 6, Section 6.
† See J. P. Cox and R. T. Giuli, 1968 (52), p. 601.

3-2 THE RADIATIVE CORE

We must first obtain explicit formulae for $\bar{\kappa}$ and ϵ that are appropriate to the pressures and temperatures to be encountered. The density corresponding to P_c and T_c is

$$\rho_c = 96.41 \text{ gm cm}^{-3}.$$

We shall assume that the opacity is given by Kramers' law for bound-free transitions,

$$\bar{\kappa} = \bar{\kappa}_{\text{bf}} = \frac{4.34 \times 10^{25}}{t/\bar{g}_{\text{bf}}} Z(1 + X) \frac{\rho}{T^{3.5}},$$

and a value must be assigned to $t/\bar{g}_{\text{bf}}$. Consulting Table 10-15, we adopt the constant value

$$\frac{t}{\bar{g}_{\text{bf}}} = 20.$$

A calculation of $\bar{\kappa}_{\text{ff}}$ and σ_e reveals that these are considerably less than $\bar{\kappa}_{\text{bf}}$, hence we are justified in ignoring them in this illustrative example.

The expression for the energy-generation rate ϵ may be obtained from Table 10-13A, although the model calculated here uses the relation

$$\epsilon = \epsilon_{pp} = 0.100X^2\rho T_7{}^4$$

for all temperatures. The CN cycle is inefficient at these low temperatures and is neglected (see Table 10-9 below).

We now compute starting values for M_r, P, L_r, and T from eqs. (10-44) to (10-47)*:

$$M_r = 0.4038r^3$$
$$P = 157 - 129.8r^2$$
$$L_r = 4.185r^3$$
$$T = 1.2 - 0.3695r^2.$$

The derivatives are computed from eqs. (10-13) to (10-16):

$$h\frac{dM_r}{dr} = 0.009260h\frac{P}{T}r^2 \qquad (10\text{-}84)$$

$$h\frac{dP}{dr} = -4.914h\frac{P}{T}\frac{M_r}{r^2} \qquad (10\text{-}85)$$

$$h\frac{dL_r}{dr} = 0.0003537hP^2T^2r^2 \qquad (10\text{-}86)$$

$$h\frac{dT}{dr} = -0.00003374h\frac{P^2}{T^{8.5}}\frac{L_r}{r^2}. \qquad (10\text{-}87)$$

* All variables will be expressed in the units adopted in Tables 10-7 and 10-8.

Table 10-7   Model B: Radiative Core and Continuation into Convective Envelope.*
$P_c = 157$, $T_c = 1.200$, $X = 0.72$, $Y = 0.26$, $Z = 0.02$.

r	M_r	$h\dfrac{dM_r}{dr}$	$^1\Delta$	$^2\Delta$	P	$h\dfrac{dP}{dr}$	$^1\Delta$	$^2\Delta$
0.0	**0.000**	**0**			**157**	**0**		
0.1	**0.000**	**1**	**1**		**156**	**−3**	**−3**	
0.2	**0.003**	**5**	**4**	**3**	**152**	**−5**	**−2**	
0.3	0.010	10	5	1	146	−7	−2	
0.4	0.024	18	8	3	138	−9	−2	
0.5	0.046	27	9	1	128	−10	−1	
0.6	0.078	36	9	0	117	−12	−2	
0.7	0.119	46	10	1	105	−12	0	
0.8	0.170	56	10	0	92.8	−124	−04	

Continuation into convective envelope (L_r is integrated independently):

0.9	0.231	65	9	−1	80.4	−122	+2	+6
1.0	0.300	73	8	−1	68.5	−116	+6	+4
1.1	0.376	79	6	−2	57.2	−108	+8	+2
1.2	0.458	84	5	−1	46.9	−98	+10	+2

When the starting values are being calculated, the *formulae* for M_r and L_r should be substituted into the expressions (10-85) and (10-87), respectively, since M_r and L_r retain only one or two significant digits. The differences $^1\Delta$, $^2\Delta$, $\cdots$, are then calculated, completing the data set in bold-faced type in Table 10-7.

The integration now proceeds as described in Section 1-3A. A test can be made after each line has been completed to check whether radiative equilibrium is maintained. We use the inequality (6-53) and calculate

$$n + 1 = \frac{d \log P}{d \log T} = \frac{T \, h \, dP/dr}{P \, h \, dT/dr}.$$

When the value decreases to 2.5, the integration must be continued with a convective temperature gradient. We may assume to sufficient accuracy that the core boundary in Table 10-7 occurs at $r = 0.8$.

3-3 THE CONVECTIVE ENVELOPE

A set of published solutions using transformed variables is available for adiabatic envelopes,* but we shall obtain the solution anew for the specific model of this section.

* Computed by D. E. Osterbrock and published by R. Härm and M. Schwarzschild, 1955 (306).

Table 10-7 (*continued*)

L_r	$h\dfrac{dL_r}{dr}$	$^1\Delta$	$^2\Delta$	$^3\Delta$	T	$h\dfrac{dT}{dr}$	$^1\Delta$	$n+1$
0.000	0				1.200	0		2.69
0.004	12	12			1.196	−8	−8	2.64
0.033	46	34	22		1.185	−15	−7	
0.101	92	46	12	−10	1.167	−22	−7	
0.218	141	49	3	−9	1.142	−28	−6	
0.380	179	38	−11	−14	1.110	−35	−7	
0.571	200	21	−19	−8	1.072	−41	−6	
0.774	202	2	−19	0	1.028	−46	−5	2.57
0.969	186	−16	−18	+1	0.979	−53	−7	2.48
1.141	158	−28	−12	+6	0.925	−56	−3	
1.283	125	−33	−5	+7	0.867	−59	−3	
1.391	91	−34	−1	+4	0.807	−61	−2	
1.466	62	−29	+5	+6	0.745	−63	−2	

* The units in which the variables are expressed are: r (10^{10} cm), P (10^{15} dyne cm^{-2}), T (10^7 °K), M_r (10^{33} gm), L_r (10^{33} erg sec^{-1}). The derivatives and differences are expressed in units of the last place of the corresponding variables. An extra digit, which contains a zero-point error, has been retained in the integration for P on lines $r \geqslant 0.8$ to minimize rounding errors.

We may discontinue the integrations for P and L_r. After the integration for T has been completed, we can find P from the relation

$$P = \mathscr{K}'T^{2.5},$$

with $\mathscr{K}'$ determined as the ratio $P/T^{2.5}$ at $r = 0.8$. However, to help eliminate rounding errors and also to emphasize the essential similarity of the convective and radiative regions, we continue the integration for P as far as line $r = 1.2$ in Table 10-7 (cf. Section 1-3B). The derivative $h\,dT/dr$ is now computed from eq. (10-19),

$$h\frac{dT}{dr} = -1.965h\frac{M_r}{r^2}.$$

The integration for L_r may be postponed until the other integrations have been completed. In this case, the entire column of $h\,dL_r/dr$ and the differences can be calculated at one time, and L_r can then be found by integrating continuously from one line to the next.

When the line $r = 1.2$ is reached, the average value of $\mathscr{K}'$ for lines $r = 0.8$ to 1.2 is found:

$$\mathscr{K}' = (P/T^{2.5})_{av} = 97.8.$$

This value is used for the computation of P in the remainder of the model, given in Table 10-8A. (See Section 1-3B, second method.) The value of

Table 10-8A   Model B: Convective Envelope Continued from Radiative Core of Table 10-7, Using $P = 97.8T^{2.5}$.*

r	M_r	$h\frac{dM_r}{dr}$	$^1\Delta$	$^2\Delta$	$^3\Delta$	T	$h\frac{dT}{dr}$	$^1\Delta$	$^2\Delta$	P	L_r	$h\frac{dL_r}{dr}$	$^1\Delta$	$^2\Delta$	$^2\Delta$
0.4												28			
0.6												40	+12		
0.8		112					−106					37	−3	−15	
1.0		146	34				−118	−12				25	−12	−9	+6
1.2	0.458	168	22	−12		0.745	−125	−7	+5	46.9	1.47	12	−13	−1	+8
1.4	0.630	173	5	−17	−5	0.619	−126	−1	+6	29.5	1.55	5	−7	+6	+7
1.6	0.798	161	−12	−17	0	0.494	−123	+3	+4	16.8	1.58	1	−4	+3	−3
1.8	0.947	135	−26	−14	+3	0.375	−115	+8	+5	8.42	1.58	0	−1	+3	0
2.0	1.065	99	−36	−10	+4	0.265	−105	+10	+2	3.54	1.58	0	0	+1	−2
2.2	1.144	59	−40	−4	+6	0.166	−93	+12	+2	1.10	1.58	0	0	0	−1
2.4	1.184	23	−36	+4	+8	0.079	−81	+12	0	0.172	1.58	0	0	0	0
2.6	1.194	0	−23	+13	+9	0.004	−69	+12	0						0

* The units are the same as in Table 10-7.

$h\,dM_r/dr$ may now be found from

$$h\frac{dM_r}{dr} = 0.9057hT^{1.5}r^2,\tag{10-88}$$

where P/T in eq. (10-84) has been replaced by $\mathcal{K}'T^{1.5}$.

Toward the end of the table, L_r clearly approaches a constant value, but it is not obvious just where r, M_r, and T reach their surface values. Extrapolation suggests that the surface may occur at

$$M_r = 1.194$$

and

$$r = 2.61.$$

An integration using these values is begun near the surface and carried inwards (Table 10-8B). Starting values for the temperature are given by eq. (10-41):

$$T = 2.347\left(\frac{1}{r} - \frac{1}{2.61}\right).$$

On lines other than $r = R$, the value of M_r is obtained by numerical integration. Since M_r changes so slowly near the surface, no significant error is caused by the lack of $^1\Delta$ on the first line. Equation (10-88) is used for $h\,dM_r/dr$. As before, P is computed from the relation

$$P = 97.8T^{2.5}.$$

A comparison of Tables 10-8A and 10-8B shows agreement within the limits of the rounding errors.

Table 10-8B   Model B: Convective Envelope from Surface.*

$M = 1.194 \times 10^{33}$ gm, $R = 2.61 \times 10^{10}$ cm, $L = 1.58 \times 10^{33}$ erg sec^{-1};

$X = 0.72$, $Y = 0.26$, $Z = 0.02$; $P = 97.8T^{2.5}$.

r	M_r	$h\dfrac{dM_r}{dr}$	$^1\Delta$	$^2\Delta$	T	$h\dfrac{dT}{dr}$	$^1\Delta$	$^2\Delta$	P
2.60	1.194	0			0.0035	174			0.00007
2.55	1.194	−1	−1		0.0212	180	6		0.00678
2.50	1.192	−2	−1		0.0396	187	7		0.0305
2.45	1.189	−4	−2		0.0587	195	8		0.0817
2.40	1.184	−6	−2		0.0786	202	7		0.1694
Continue at double interval:									
2.6		0				348			
2.5		−4	−4			374	26		
2.4	1.184	−11	−7	−3	0.0786	404	30	4	
2.3	1.169	−20	−9	−2	0.1205	434	30	0	0.493
2.2	1.144				0.1654	464	30	0	1.088

* The units are the same as in Table 10-7.

Table 10-9   Values of ρ, $\bar{\kappa}$, ϵ for Model B (Core and Envelope of Tables 10-7, 10-8A, and 10-8B).

$r \times 10^{-10}$	ρ	$\bar{\kappa}$	ϵ
0.0	96.41	1.202	10.36
0.1	96.12	1.213	10.20
0.2	94.52	1.232	9.66
0.3	92.19	1.268	8.86
0.4	89.05	1.321	7.85
0.5	84.97	1.392	6.69
0.6	80.42	1.488	5.51
0.7	75.27	1.613	4.36
0.8	69.77		3.32
1.0	58.22		1.71
1.2	46.39		0.74
1.4	35.12		0.27
1.6	25.06		0.08
1.8	16.55		0.02
2.0	9.84		0.00
2.2	4.88		
2.4	1.60		
2.6	0.02		

$$\bar{\kappa} = \frac{4.34 \times 10^{25}}{20}\, 0.02(1.72)\, \frac{\rho}{T^{3.5}}$$

$$\epsilon = \epsilon_{pp} = 0.100 \times 10^{-28}(0.72)^2 \rho T^4$$

At $r = 0$, $\epsilon_{CN} = 0.012$ for $X_{CN} = 0.29Z$; ϵ_{CN} has been neglected.

The values of ρ, $\bar{\kappa}$, and ϵ are listed in Table 10-9. The structure is illustrated in Figs. 10-4A to 10-4E.

3-4 DISCUSSION OF THE RESULTS

It is clear that the model we have obtained is much less massive than was intended. To pursue the original aim of constructing a model for a star of *one* solar mass, we should have to vary P_c and T_c until this total mass resulted, as well as a radius and luminosity appropriate to the main sequence. Another approach to the problem, of course, is to start the integration at the surface, using the prescribed mass and estimated values for the radius, luminosity, and parameter $\mathcal{K}'$.

Having obtained a model of 0.6 $M_\odot$ by our present calculation, we may inquire as to its position in the Hertzsprung–Russell diagram. The effective temperature is found from L and R, and the position relative to observed visual binary components is plotted in Fig. 10-5. We see that the model lies

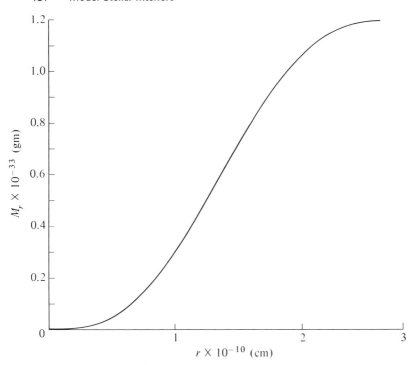

Fig. 10-4A The Mass Distribution in the Model with a Convective Envelope and a Radiative Core. Model B (Tables 10-7, 10-8A, and 10-8B) is represented, which has $M = 0.6 \, M_\odot$ and $R = 0.375 \, R_\odot$. This curve is nearly indistinguishable from that of the polytrope of index $n = 1.5$ that has the same mass and radius.

well to the left of the main sequence in this plane, although it accords rather well with the mass-luminosity relation shown in Fig. 10-6. To obtain a model with the radius and luminosity appropriate to a star on the main sequence having the same mass and chemical composition, it would be necessary to change P_c and T_c (see Chapter 6, Section 6). In a more realistic model, more accurate expressions for $\bar{\kappa}$ and ϵ would be required. Calculations of the degree of ionization of the material and of departure from the perfect gas law due to degeneracy should be included. It should also be remembered that the radius of the model depends on the theory used for the convective layers near the surface and that we have used the simplest equations and boundary conditions. Furthermore, the formation of H_2 molecules influences the model significantly at low temperatures.*

Our model may be compared with a more accurate one for the same mass

* See the models of H. Copeland, J. O. Jensen, and H. E. Jørgensen, 1970 (397).

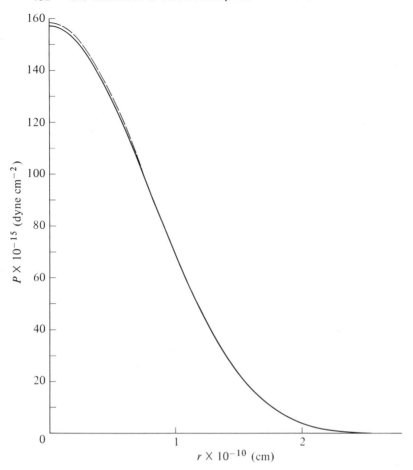

Fig. 10-4B   The Pressure Distribution in the Model with a Convective Envelope and a Radiative Core. The *solid curve* represents Model B (Tables 10-7, 10-8A, and 10-8B). For comparison, the distribution for the polytrope of index $n = 1.5$ that has the same mass and radius is indicated by the *dashed curve* in the region where the curves are distinguishable.

that includes the refinements mentioned above.* The composition, with $X = 0.70$ and $Z = 0.02$, is similar to that used here. The ratio of mixing length to scale height is 1.5. The surface and central characteristics are as follows:

	$R/R_\odot$	$L/L_\odot$	T_{eff} (°K)	T_c (°K)	ρ_c (gm cm^{-3})
Model B:	0.375	0.40	7500	1.20×10^7	96.4
Copeland *et al.*:	0.569	0.095	4270	0.99×10^7	91.2

* The model has been calculated by H. Copeland, J. O. Jensen, and H. E. Jørgensen, 1970 (397).

The more accurate model has a lower central temperature and density and hence also a lower central pressure. Its surface characteristics place it on the lower main sequence.

It may appear that we have calculated a model suitable to a subdwarf star. This is not the case, however. Some of these stars lie to the left of the main sequence as a consequence of their low metal abundance, which is characteristic of Population II stars. In the atmospheres of these subdwarfs, there is relatively little blocking of the radiation in the ultraviolet and blue regions by the numerous metallic lines that would be present at these wavelengths in the spectra of Population I stars. Thus there is a higher percentage of light emitted in these short wavelength regions than in the case of a Population I star of the same luminosity. After correction of the magnitudes and colors for the comparative *lack* of a blanketing effect, these subdwarf stars are found to lie near to the Population I main sequence. Other subluminous stars, such

Fig. 10-4C The Temperature Distribution in the Model with a Convective Envelope and a Radiative Core. The curves have the same meanings as in Fig. 10-4B.

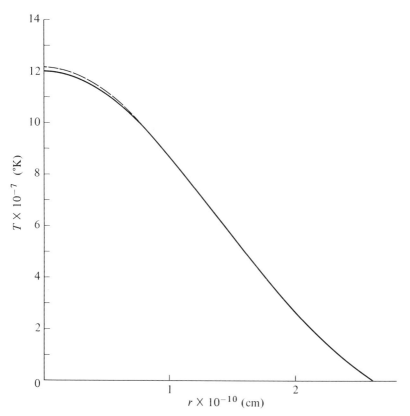

$r \times 10^{-10}$ (cm)

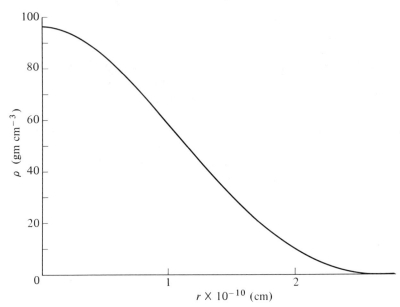

Fig. 10-4D   The Density Distribution in the Model with a Convective Envelope and a Radiative Core. Model B (Tables 10-7, 10-8A, and 10-8B) is represented. This curve is nearly indistinguishable from that of the polytrope of index $n = 1.5$ with same mass and radius.

as those found in the Hyades cluster, apparently have a structure different from that of main-sequence stars.

One more point must be mentioned. If we had begun the computation at the surface, testing $d \log P / d \log T$ against the value 2.5, we should have obtained the result that the surface layers are in radiative equilibrium. Indeed, models for the Sun were previously constructed with radiative envelopes and convective cores, although it is now believed that the reverse structure is correct. To show that there is an extensive convection zone just below the relatively thin layer in radiative equilibrium requires consideration of the ionization of hydrogen. This we omit here.

4 POLYTROPIC MODEL INTERIORS OBTAINED FROM PUBLISHED TABLES

4-1 GENERAL DISCUSSION

Let us now consider some approximate solutions that can be obtained simply by applying scaling factors to the existing tabulated solutions of the Lane–Emden equation, derived in Section 1-5 of Chapter 6. Although models that represent stars as completely polytropic, from center to surface, have been largely superseded by more accurate ones based on numerical integration, it is nevertheless instructive to compute polytropic models because of their simplicity. We shall obtain models that may be compared with Models A and B of Sections 2 and 3, respectively.

Eddington, several decades ago, manipulated the relation between pressure and density into a polytropic form by means of the following considerations.*

* See A. S. Eddington, 1926 (54), p. 116 et seq.

Fig. 10-4E   The Distribution of the Net Luminosity in the Model with a Convective Envelope and a Radiative Core. Model B (Tables 10-7, 10-8A, and 10-8B) is represented.

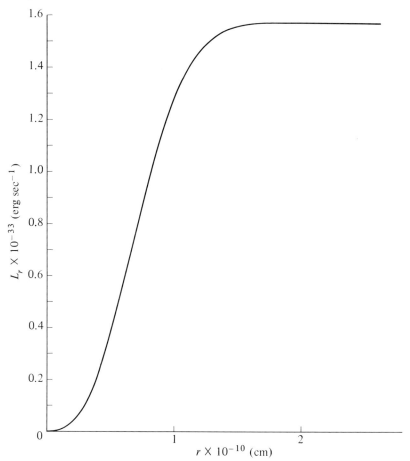

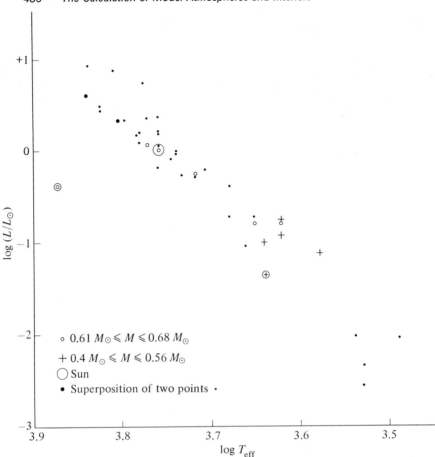

Fig. 10-5   The Hertzsprung–Russell Diagram. The observational results of Fig. 1-14 are reproduced together with Model B (Tables 10-7, 10-8A, and 10-8B), which is represented by the *encircled dot*, and the transformed model of Section 5-4, which is represented by the *encircled plus sign*. The *large circle* represents the Sun.

Let

$$P_g = \text{gas pressure}$$

$$P_{rad} = \text{radiation pressure}$$

$$P = P_g + P_{rad}$$

$$\beta = \frac{P_g}{P}.$$

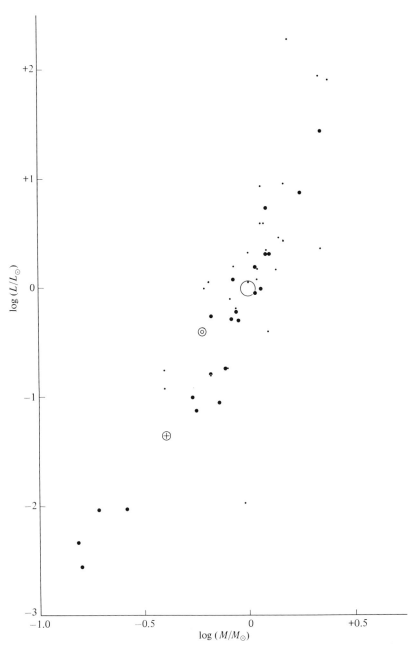

Fig. 10-6 The Mass-Luminosity Relation. Observational results from Fig. 1-12 are reproduced together with Model B, represented by the *encircled dot*, and the transformed model of Section 5-4, represented by the *encircled plus sign*. The *large circle* represents the Sun.

In eq. (2-11), we may with good approximation replace $I_\nu(\theta)$ by $B_\nu(T)$. If we then integrate over frequency, we find

$$P_{\text{rad}} = \frac{1}{c} \int_{\text{sphere}} \int_0^\infty B_\nu(T) \, d\nu \, \cos^2 \theta \, d\omega$$

$$= \frac{1}{c} \cdot \frac{\sigma}{\pi} T^4 \cdot \frac{4\pi}{3},$$

using eq. (1-9). Then

$$P_{\text{rad}} = \tfrac{1}{3} a T^4 = (1 - \beta) P. \tag{10-89}$$

Also

$$P_g = \frac{k}{\mu H} \rho T = \beta P. \tag{10-90}$$

Eliminating T by raising eq. (10-90) to the fourth power and dividing by eq. (10-89), we find

$$P = \left[\frac{3}{a} \left(\frac{k}{H} \right)^4 \frac{1 - \beta}{(\mu\beta)^4} \right]^{1/3} \rho^{4/3}. \tag{10-91}$$

This relation has the form of eq. (6-5),

$$P = \mathcal{K} \rho^\gamma. \tag{10-92}$$

Note that this derivation does not require the interpretation of the exponent of ρ as a ratio of specific heats. The value of β is constant under conditions of radiative equilibrium if the combination of variables $\kappa L_r / M_r$, which is proportional to the local opacity multiplied by the average energy-generation rate within the sphere, remains constant throughout the star.* This was a reasonable assumption in Eddington's time, although it is now known that $\kappa L_r / M_r$, and hence β and $\mathcal{K}$, are variable within a star. Nevertheless, we shall proceed with Eddington's assumption of the constancy of β and, making the further assumption that μ is constant, consider eq. (10-92) with constant $\mathcal{K}$ to be valid throughout the interior. We shall thus consider a polytropic model of index

$$n = \frac{1}{\gamma - 1} = 3,$$

which will then be compared with more refined calculations.

A second example, for the index $n = 1.5$ appropriate to convective equilibrium, will also be given.

---

* See L. H. Aller, 1954 (55), pp. 55–58.

The polytropic solutions needed for the two illustrations are given in Tables 10-11 and 10-12. The various columns have the following significance:

$$\xi = \frac{r}{\alpha} \qquad \text{(6-8) (10-93)}$$

$$\frac{\xi}{\xi_0} = \frac{r}{R} \qquad \text{(10-94)}$$

$$\theta = \frac{T}{T_c} \qquad \text{(6-9) (10-95)}$$

$$\frac{d\theta}{d\xi} = \frac{\alpha}{T_c}\frac{dT}{dr}$$

$$\theta^n = \frac{\rho}{\rho_c} \qquad \text{(6-11) (10-96)}$$

$$\theta^{n+1} = \frac{P}{P_c} \qquad \text{(6-11A) (10-97)}$$

$$-\xi^2\frac{d\theta}{d\xi} = \frac{M_\xi}{4\pi\alpha^3\rho_c}. \qquad \text{(6-16) (10-98)}$$

The functions U and V were discussed in Section 2-3B. It should be noted that the surface of the star is reached when θ decreases to zero, at a value of ξ designated by ξ_0.

4-2 A MODEL WITH $n = 3$ (COMPARE WITH MODEL A)

We now find the polytropic solution with index $n = 3$ that corresponds to Model A of Section 2. The given quantities are

$$M = 2.5\ M_\odot = 4.962 \times 10^{33}\ \text{gm},$$

$$R = 1.59\ R_\odot = 11.05 \times 10^{10}\ \text{cm}.$$

Then, from eq. (10-93),

$$\alpha = \frac{R}{\xi_0} = \frac{11.05 \times 10^{10}}{6.89685} \qquad \text{(10-99)}$$

$$= 1.6022 \times 10^{10}\ \text{cm},$$

and from eq. (10-98),

$$\rho_c = \frac{M}{4\pi\alpha^3[-\xi^2(d\theta/d\xi)]_{\xi_0}} \qquad \text{(10-100)}$$

$$= \frac{4.962 \times 10^{33}}{4\pi(1.6022 \times 10^{10})^3 2.0182}$$

$$= 47.57\ \text{gm cm}^{-3}.$$

With these constants, we can now find $\mathcal{K}$ from eq. (6-13):

$$\mathcal{K} = \frac{4\pi G\alpha^2}{(n + 1)\rho_c^{(1/n) - 1}} \tag{10-101}$$

$$= \frac{4\pi(6.668 \times 10^{-8})(1.6022 \times 10^{10})^2}{4(47.57)^{-2/3}}$$

$$= 0.7060 \times 10^{15}$$

in cgs units. Also,

$$P_c = \mathcal{K}\rho_c^{1 + 1/n} \tag{6-5) (10-102}$$

$$= 121.7 \times 10^{15} \text{ dyne cm}^{-2}$$

and

$$T_c = \frac{\mu H}{k}\frac{P_c}{\rho_c} \quad (\mu = 0.5340 \text{ as in Section 2})$$

$$= 1.656 \times 10^7 \text{ °K}.$$

Then, for any point in the model,

$$\rho = \rho_c\theta^n \tag{10-103}$$

$$P = P_c\theta^{n + 1} \tag{10-104}$$

$$T = T_c\theta \tag{10-105}$$

$$M_\xi = M\frac{[-\xi^2(d\theta/d\xi)]}{[-\xi^2(d\theta/d\xi)]_{\xi_0}}. \tag{10-106}$$

Figures 10-3A to 10-3D compare the polytrope with Model A and also with the solution obtained by Kushwaha (Table 10-6). It should be noted that Model A does not have a proper fit of the core and envelope. The function L_r cannot be obtained without numerical integration and is therefore not considered here. The agreement between the polytropic solution and that of Kushwaha is sufficiently good for the polytrope to be considered a first approximation to the more refined model. For small values of the radius, where the differences are greatest, the polytrope is closer to Kushwaha's solution than is Model A.

A polytropic solution offers a considerable simplification over the calculation of the general radiative case. No knowledge of the opacity $\bar{\kappa}$ or the energy-generation coefficient ϵ is required. In fact, one does not even need to state that the star is shining! If information about the luminosity or the distribution of energy sources is required, however, an integration for L_ξ can be performed in terms of the Emden variables as in eq. (10-83).

4-3 A MODEL WITH $n = 1.5$ (COMPARE WITH MODEL B)

In Model B of Section 3, the quantities given initially are the central pressure and temperature,

$$P_c = 157 \times 10^{15} \text{ dyne cm}^{-2},$$

$$T_c = 1.20 \times 10^7 \text{ °K},$$

although we could as well base a polytropic solution on the derived total mass and radius. Since Model B is convective over most of its radius, we choose $n = 1.5$ as the polytropic index, rather than $n = 3$. The appropriate Emden functions are given in Table 10-12.

Equations (10-103), (10-104), and (10-105) again give ρ, P, and T for any radius ξ in the star, with ρ_c computed from P_c and T_c:

$$\rho_c = 96.41 \text{ gm cm}^{-3} \quad (\mu = 0.6079 \text{ as in Section 3}).$$

Equation (10-102) then gives

$$\mathscr{K} = 0.7745 \times 10^{14}$$

and eq. (10-101) shows that

$$\alpha = 0.7099 \times 10^{10} \text{ cm}.$$

With this value, r may be calculated for any given ξ according to eq. (10-93). Also, using eqs. (10-99) and (10-100), we find

$$R = 2.59 \times 10^{10} \text{ cm} = 0.372 \, R_\odot$$

$$M = 1.176 \times 10^{33} \text{ gm} = 0.591 \, M_\odot.$$

These values are in close agreement with the mass and radius of Model B,

$$R = 2.61 \times 10^{10} \text{ cm} = 0.375 \, R_\odot$$

$$M = 1.194 \times 10^{33} \text{ gm} = 0.600 \, M_\odot.$$

For a graphical comparison of the polytropic solution and the numerical integration, let us use the mass and radius of Model B, thereby allowing both solutions to be plotted as functions of a common radius. We find

$$\alpha = \frac{R}{\xi_0}$$

$$= 0.71433 \times 10^{10} \text{ cm,}$$

$$\rho_c = \frac{M}{4\pi\alpha^3[-\xi^2(d\theta/d\xi)]_{\xi_0}}$$

$$= 96.04 \text{ gm cm}^{-3},$$

$$\mathcal{K} = \frac{4\pi G\alpha^2}{(n+1)\rho_c^{(1/n)-1}}$$

$$= 0.7842 \times 10^{14},$$

$$P_c = \mathcal{K}\rho_c^{1+1/n}$$

$$= 158.4 \times 10^{15} \text{ dyne cm}^{-2},$$

$$T_c = \frac{\mu H}{k}\frac{P_c}{\rho_c}$$

$$= 1.215 \times 10^7 \text{ °K.}$$

Again, ρ, P, T, and M_r are found as functions of r from eqs. (10-93) and (10-103) to (10-106). Figures 10-4A to 10-4D display the results. The polytrope is seen to be a very good approximation in this case.

5 SCHWARZSCHILD'S TRANSFORMATION

Under certain conditions, an equilibrium model having given values of M, R, L, X, and Z can be transformed into another equilibrium model that has different values for these parameters. The variables P, T, ρ, M_r, and L_r in the new model are related to those in the original model at the same fractional radius by constant scale factors. Thus, for example, ρ/ρ_c as a function of r/R would be identical for the two cases. Two models related in this way are said to be *homologous*. The polytropes of given index n are examples of a homologous family.

Schwarzschild has shown how integrations can be performed using dimensionless variables, from which the individual properties of any given star have been removed. Once an equilibrium solution has been obtained by fitting a core and envelope that have been integrated in terms of the dimensionless variables, a stellar model is obtained by determining the appropriate scale factors. We shall now give Schwarzschild's transformation equations and describe the procedures for obtaining models of upper and lower main-sequence stars. A numerical illustration will then be given, in which Model B of Section 3 will be transformed into one of smaller mass.

5-1 THE EQUATIONS

Let us scale r and M_r in proportion to their maximum values,

$$r = Rx$$

$$M_r = Mq,$$

letting x and q be new variables in place of r and M_r. Let us also set

$$P = Qp$$

$$T = St,$$

where p and t are new variables replacing P and T, while Q and S are constants. Then, by eq. (10-13),

$$\frac{M}{R}\frac{dq}{dx} = 4\pi \frac{H}{k}\mu\frac{Qp}{St}R^2x^2, \tag{10-107}$$

and by eq. (10-14),

$$\frac{Q}{R}\frac{dp}{dx} = -\frac{GH}{k}\mu\frac{Qp}{St}\frac{Mq}{R^2x^2}. \tag{10-108}$$

We can define Q and S in such a way as to eliminate the constants in these two equations, yielding

$$\frac{dq}{dx} = \frac{p}{t}x^2$$

and

$$\frac{dp}{dx} = -\frac{p}{t}\frac{q}{x^2}.$$

The expressions for Q and S are obtained by equating the constant factors on either side in eqs. (10-107) and (10-108):

$$\frac{M}{R} = \frac{4\pi H}{k}\mu\frac{Q}{S}R^2 \tag{10-109}$$

and

$$\frac{Q}{R} = \frac{GH}{k}\mu\frac{Q}{S}\frac{M}{R^2}. \tag{10-110}$$

The last relation gives immediately

$$S = \frac{GH}{k}\mu\frac{M}{R};$$

and then from eq. (10-109), we find

$$Q = \frac{G}{4\pi}\frac{M^2}{R^4}.$$

With the constants Q and S determined, we can investigate the form taken by eq. (10-17), which is valid in the convective case:

$$\frac{S}{R}\frac{dt}{dx} = 0.4 \frac{St}{Qp}\frac{Q}{R}\frac{dp}{dx}$$

$$\frac{dt}{dx} = 0.4 \frac{t}{p}\frac{dp}{dx}.$$

The coefficient consists only of the factor present in the original equation, since the transformation constants are canceled in logarithmic differentiation.

Upon integration, the last equation yields

$$\log p = 2.5 \log t + \text{const}$$

or

$$p = Et^{2.5} \tag{10-111}$$

with zero boundary conditions. This replaces eq. (10-9). Transformation back to the original variables permits a determination of E:

$$\frac{4\pi R^4}{GM^2} P = E\left(\frac{k}{GH}\frac{R}{\mu M}\right)^{2.5} T^{2.5};$$

but

$$P = \mathscr{K}'T^{2.5} \tag{10-112}$$

according to eq. (10-9), and therefore

$$E = 4\pi G^{1.5}\left(\frac{H}{k}\right)^{2.5} \mu^{2.5}\mathscr{K}'M^{0.5}R^{1.5}.$$

If we now define a new variable f from the relation

$$L_r = Lf,$$

the remaining differential equations will contain constant coefficients. Writing $\bar{\kappa}$ in the form

$$\bar{\kappa} = \kappa_0 \frac{\rho}{T^{3.5}}, \qquad \kappa_0 = \frac{4.34 \times 10^{25}}{t/\bar{g}_{bf}} Z(1 + X),$$

we have from eq. (10-15) for the radiative temperature gradient:

$$\frac{S}{R}\frac{dt}{dx} = -\frac{3}{16\pi ac}\left(\frac{H}{k}\right)^2 \mu^2 \kappa_0 \frac{(Qp)^2 Lf}{(St)^{8.5}(Rx)^2}$$

or

$$\frac{dt}{dx} = -C\frac{p^2}{t^{8.5}}\frac{f}{x^2},$$

where

$$C = \frac{3}{4ac}\left(\frac{1}{4\pi}\right)^3\left(\frac{k}{GH}\right)^{7.5}\frac{\kappa_0}{\mu^{7.5}}\frac{LR^{0.5}}{M^{5.5}}.$$

Similarly, eq. (10-16) [using eq. (10-12)] yields

$$\frac{L}{R}\frac{df}{dx} = 4\pi\left(\frac{H}{k}\right)^2 \epsilon_0 X_1 X_2 \mu^2 (Qp)^2 (St)^{\nu-2}(Rx)^2$$

or

$$\frac{df}{dx} = Dp^2 t^{\nu-2} x^2,$$

with

$$D = \frac{1}{4\pi}\left(\frac{GH}{k}\right)^\nu \mu^\nu \epsilon_0 X_1 X_2 \frac{M^{\nu+2}}{LR^{\nu+3}}.$$

We now summarize the transformed equations and variables*:

$$x = \frac{r}{R} \tag{10-113}$$

$$q = \frac{M_r}{M} \tag{10-114}$$

$$f = \frac{L_r}{L} \tag{10-115}$$

$$p = P\left/\frac{GM^2}{4\pi R^4}\right. \tag{10-116}$$

$$t = T\left/\frac{GH}{k}\mu\frac{M}{R}\right. \tag{10-117}$$

$$\frac{dq}{dx} = \frac{p}{t}x^2 \tag{10-118}$$

$$\frac{dp}{dx} = -\frac{p}{t}\frac{q}{x^2} \tag{10-119}$$

$$\frac{df}{dx} = Dp^2 t^{\nu-2}x^2 \tag{10-120}$$

$$\frac{dt}{dx} = -C\frac{p^2}{t^{8.5}}\frac{f}{x^2} \quad \text{(radiative)} \tag{10-121}$$

$$\frac{dt}{dx} = 0.4\frac{t}{p}\frac{dp}{dx} \tag{10-122}$$

which is equivalent to

$$p = Et^{2.5} \tag{10-123}$$

(convective)

* We are still assuming that the composition is homogeneous throughout; that bound-free transitions are the only source of opacity, with $t/\bar{g}_{bf} = $ const; and that radiation pressure and degeneracy are negligible. For a relaxation of some of these restrictions, see M. Schwarzschild, 1958 (50).

$$C = \frac{3}{4ac}\left(\frac{1}{4\pi}\right)^3\left(\frac{k}{GH}\right)^{7.5}\frac{\kappa_0}{\mu^{7.5}}\frac{LR^{0.5}}{M^{5.5}} \tag{10-124}$$

$$D = \frac{1}{4\pi}\left(\frac{GH}{k}\right)^{\nu}\mu^{\nu}\epsilon_0 X_1 X_2 \frac{M^{\nu+2}}{LR^{\nu+3}} \tag{10-125}$$

$$E = 4\pi G^{1.5}\left(\frac{H}{k}\right)^{2.5}\mu^{2.5}\mathscr{K}' M^{0.5} R^{1.5}. \tag{10-126}$$

Equation (10-124) may be considered to represent a theoretical mass-luminosity law, since R varies slowly along the main sequence and enters this relation with only a small power.

5-2 APPLICATION TO THE UPPER MAIN SEQUENCE

We now outline the method of solving these equations to obtain a model for a star on the upper main sequence.*

Separate integrations for the radiative envelope and the convective core are fitted together by means of the homology variables U, V, and $n + 1$ (cf. Section 2-3 B). For the core, there is a unique solution that is represented by a single curve in the U, V plane; this is the polytropic solution for $n = 1.5$ (Table 10-11, Fig. 10-1).

For the envelope, integration of eqs. (10-118), (10-119), and (10-121) is required. We shall set $f = 1$ in the envelope, assuming that energy is generated only in the core. The existence of the coefficient C in eq. (10-121) requires that a number of trial solutions be made with various values for C, until one is obtained such that $n + 1$ reaches 2.5 simultaneously as the U, V curve representing that solution touches the curve for the convective core (see Fig. 10-1). This matching in the U, V plane is a necessary, but not sufficient, condition for an equilibrium model. The boundary conditions introduce no new parameters, since these may be taken as

$$x = 1: \quad q = 1, \quad p = 0, \quad t = 0.$$

Equation (10-124), together with the numerical value found for C, provides one constraint upon the values of M, R, L, X, and Z. The evaluation of D, together with eq. (10-125), will yield a second constraint.

To determine D, we integrate eq. (10-120) in the core, which requires the assignment of a value to ν. In selecting a value, we must estimate the temperatures near the center and check the suitability of our choice from Tables 10-13 and 10-14 after the specific stellar model has been completed. It may then be necessary to make a new estimate of the appropriate value of ν and to repeat the calculation. The value of f at the core boundary is unity, since

---

* See M. Schwarzschild, 1958 (50), p. 121 et seq. Also see R. S. Kushwaha, 1957 (500).

all energy is assumed to be generated in the core. Designating values at the core boundary by the subscript b, we have

$$f_b = 1 = D \int_0^{x_b} p^2 t^{\nu-2} x^2 \, dx. \tag{10-127}$$

The integral depends upon the central values p_c and t_c, and it would appear that we have lost the advantage of using dimensionless variables in place of the physical variables that required a choice of only T_c (cf. Section 2-2). This difficulty can be overcome by making an additional transformation to the Emden variables. From eqs. (10-93), (10-95), (10-97), (10-113), (10-116), and (10-117) we find

$$\frac{x}{x_b} = \frac{r}{r_b} = \frac{\xi}{\xi_b} \tag{10-128}$$

$$\frac{p}{p_b} = \frac{P}{P_b} = \frac{\theta^{2.5}}{\theta_b^{2.5}} \tag{10-129}$$

$$\frac{t}{t_b} = \frac{T}{T_b} = \frac{\theta}{\theta_b}, \tag{10-130}$$

allowing eq. (10-127) to be written as

$$1 = D \frac{p_b^2 t_b^{\nu-2}}{\theta_b^{\nu+3}} \left(\frac{x_b}{\xi_b}\right)^3 \int_0^{\xi_b} \theta^{\nu+3} \xi^2 \, d\xi.$$

The boundary conditions at the center become

$$\xi_c = 0, \qquad \theta_c = 1,$$

and the integral itself is now a definite number that does not depend on any unknown parameters. The values of x_b, p_b, and t_b are known from the envelope solution, while ξ_b and θ_b are found from Table 10-11 as the values corresponding to U (or V) as calculated for the terminal point of the envelope. The value of D is then determined. We note that eqs. (10-128) to (10-130) may also be used to find x, p, and t in the core, while q can be obtained from a similar transformation, with the aid of eq. (10-98):

$$\frac{q}{q_b} = \frac{M_r}{M_{rb}} = \frac{\left(-\xi^2 \dfrac{d\theta}{d\xi}\right)}{\left(-\xi^2 \dfrac{d\theta}{d\xi}\right)_b}.$$

With C and D evaluated, we can now solve from eqs. (10-124) and (10-125) for any two of the quantities M, R, L, X, and Z if the other three are given; this result confirms the Vogt–Russell theorem. Finally, eqs. (10-113) to (10-117) permit transformation back to the physical variables. The parameters κ_0, ϵ_0, and ν must be consistent with the values of P and T obtained, and a repetition of the model calculation may be necessary.

We recapitulate the assumptions that have been made in calculating the dimensionless solution in this section: the composition is uniform throughout the model; radiation pressure is negligible; the opacity coefficient in the envelope is given by Kramers' law for bound-free transitions with constant $t/\bar{g}_{bf}$; energy production in the envelope is negligible; energy production in the core proceeds at a rate $\epsilon = \epsilon_0 X_1 X_2 \rho T^\nu$, where $\epsilon_0 X_1 X_2$ and ν are constants; the temperature and pressure are related by the adiabatic gas law in the core and by the perfect gas law in the envelope; the temperature and pressure vanish at the surface; and the values of κ_0, ϵ_0, and ν must be consistent with the conditions occurring in the model. *With these restrictions, all models having radiative envelopes and convective cores can be obtained from the dimensionless solution just calculated.*

5-3 APPLICATION TO THE LOWER MAIN SEQUENCE

We next outline Schwarzschild's procedure for deriving a model for a star on the lower main sequence that has an adiabatic convective envelope and a radiative core.*

For the envelope, the solution of eqs. (10-118), (10-119), and (10-123) yields p, t, and q as functions of x. The boundary conditions at the surface are

$$x = 1: \qquad q = 1, \qquad p = 0, \qquad t = 0.$$

To each value of the parameter E, there corresponds only one core solution with the characteristics described below. The value of E determines the fractional depth of the envelope, such that E is zero for a model in which the depth of the convective layers is zero (i.e., for a radiative envelope), while E is 45.48 for a model in which the convective region extends from the surface to the center. Solutions for various values of E are available as published tables.† The presence of $\mathscr{K}'$ as a factor in E introduces an uncertainty in the final model because, in the outer regions of the star, it depends upon the poorly determined value of the mixing length. For this reason, a number of models with different values of E are often computed in a given case. The calculation of $f(x)$ will be described later.

For the core, the simultaneous solution of eqs. (10-118) to (10-121) is required. The boundary conditions at the center are

$$x = 0: \qquad q = 0, \qquad p = p_c, \qquad f = 0, \qquad t = t_c.$$

* M. Schwarzschild, 1958 (50), p. 131 et seq. Also see D. E. Osterbrock, 1953 (501).
† Computed by D. E. Osterbrock and published by R. Härm and M. Schwarzschild, 1955 (306).

To eliminate the dependence on t_c, let us introduce a new set of variables for the core, designated by asterisks. Let these be related to the previous variables by means of constants with subscript 0:

$$x^* = \frac{x}{x_0}, \qquad q^* = \frac{q}{q_0}, \qquad p^* = \frac{p}{p_0}, \qquad t^* = \frac{t}{t_0}, \qquad f^* = \frac{f}{f_0}. \qquad (10\text{-}131)$$

Then the differential equations become

$$\frac{q_0}{x_0}\frac{dq^*}{dx^*} = \frac{p_0 p^*}{t_0 t^*}x_0^2 x^{*2}$$

$$\frac{p_0}{x_0}\frac{dp^*}{dx^*} = -\frac{p_0 p^*}{t_0 t^*}\frac{q_0 q^*}{x_0^2 x^{*2}}$$

$$\frac{t_0}{x_0}\frac{dt^*}{dx^*} = -C\frac{p_0^2 p^{*2}}{t_0^{8.5}t^{*8.5}}\frac{f_0 f^*}{x_0^2 x^{*2}}$$

$$\frac{f_0}{x_0}\frac{df^*}{dx^*} = Dp_0^2 p^{*2} t_0^{\nu-2} t^{*\nu-2} x_0^2 x^{*2}.$$

We can eliminate the constant coefficients in these differential equations by taking

$$\frac{p_0 x_0^3}{q_0 t_0} = 1, \qquad \frac{q_0}{t_0 x_0} = 1, \qquad C\frac{p_0^2 f_0}{t_0^{9.5}x_0} = 1, \qquad D\frac{p_0^2 t_0^{\nu-2} x_0^3}{f_0} = 1. \qquad (10\text{-}132)$$

Since these are only four conditions on the five new constants, we may choose one of them arbitrarily. Let us set

$$t_0 = t_c.$$

Then

$$\frac{dq^*}{dx^*} = \frac{p^*}{t^*}x^{*2}$$

$$\frac{dp^*}{dx^*} = -\frac{p^*}{t^*}\frac{q^*}{x^{*2}}$$

$$\frac{dt^*}{dx^*} = -\frac{p^{*2}}{t^{*8.5}}\frac{f^*}{x^{*2}}$$

$$\frac{df^*}{dx^*} = p^{*2}t^{*\nu-2}x^{*2},$$

with the boundary conditions at the center

$$x^* = 0: \qquad q^* = 0, \qquad p^* = p_c^*, \qquad f^* = 0, \qquad t^* = 1.$$

The value of p_c^* is not specified and remains as a free parameter. With this transformation, then, the core solution requires (for a given value of ν) only a single family of solutions, depending on p_c^*.

A matching of the core and envelope again takes place in the U, V plane; a core solution is attached to the envelope that has the same U, V pair at the point where $n + 1$ becomes 2.5 in the core (see Fig. 10-2). Each value of p_c^* thus corresponds to one value of E.

For any matching pair of core and envelope solutions, the fitting conditions at the interface now determine the five constants introduced in eqs. (10-131). The core solution has been performed in terms of x^*, q^*, p^*, f^*, and t^*, while the envelope has been integrated in terms of x, q, p, and t. Substitution of these values into the first four of eqs. (10-131) now allows the determination of x_0, q_0, p_0, and t_0. To find f_0, we must integrate eq. (10-120) in the envelope, giving

$$f|_{f_b}^1 = 1 - f_b = D \int_{x_b}^1 p^2 t^{\nu-2} x^2 \, dx, \qquad (10\text{-}133)$$

where the subscript b represents the boundary of the core and envelope. The quadrature leaves both f_b and D undetermined, but an iterative procedure can be used to find these quantities and also f_0. An initial guess for D gives a value for f_b from eq. (10-133), and the last equation of eqs. (10-131) then yields f_0. A new value of D is then computed from the last equation of eqs. (10-132), and the cycle is repeated if necessary. With the constants x_0, q_0, p_0, f_0, and t_0 known, it is now possible to express the core variables in terms of x, q, p, f, and t.

The value of C can be found from the third equation of eqs. (10-132), and, as for the upper main sequence, C and D together now provide two conditions for determining any two of the quantities M, R, L, X, and Z if three of these are given*; this result would confirm the Vogt–Russell theorem if the value of E (or p_c^*) could somehow be prescribed in any given case (see Section 6 of Chapter 6). The physical variables may then be found from eqs. (10-113) to (10-117).

We now summarize the assumptions that have been made: the composition is homogeneous throughout the model; radiation pressure is negligible; the opacity coefficient is given by Kramers' law for bound-free transitions with constant $t/\bar{g}_{bf}$; the energy-generation rate is expressed in the form $\epsilon = \epsilon_0 X_1 X_2 \rho T^\nu$, where $\epsilon_0 X_1 X_2$ and ν are constants; the temperature and pressure are related by the adiabatic gas law in the envelope and by the perfect gas law in the core; the temperature and pressure vanish at the surface; and the values of κ_0, ϵ_0, and ν must be consistent with the temperatures and pressures occurring in the final model. *With these restrictions, all models having a radiative core and convective envelope with the prescribed value of E (or p_c^*) can be obtained from the dimensionless solution just calculated.*

---

* See M. Schwarzschild, 1958 (50), p. 135 for the technique of determining X and Z for given values of M, R, and L.

5-4 A TRANSFORMED MODEL

In Section 3, we obtained a model for a homogeneous star of normal composition but found that our choices of P_c and T_c placed it below the main sequence. The great depth of the convective envelope indicates that the basic structure might be more appropriate to a later-type star. Since such a star would be less luminous, it would also be less massive; and we shall therefore transform our model to another having only $\frac{2}{3}$ of the original mass, or $0.4\ M_\odot$. We shall assume that X, Z, κ_0, ϵ_0, and ν remain unchanged.

The individual characteristics of any particular model are contained, as we have seen, in eqs. (10-124), (10-125), and (10-126). Let us use unprimed symbols for the original model and primed symbols for the new one. Since C has the same value in both cases, we have from eq. (10-124) that

$$\frac{(L'/L)(R'/R)^{0.5}}{(M'/M)^{5.5}} = 1,$$

and similarly from eq. (10-125) that

$$\frac{(M'/M)^6}{(L'/L)(R'/R)^7} = 1 \qquad (\nu = 4).$$

Solution of these equations with $M'/M = \frac{2}{3}$ yields

$$R'/R = 0.9694$$

$$L'/L = 0.1091.$$

From eqs. (10-116) and (10-117), we then find

$$\frac{P'}{P} = \frac{(M'/M)^2}{(R'/R)^4} = 0.5033$$

$$\frac{T'}{T} = \frac{M'/M}{R'/R} = 0.6877.$$

In particular, we find from Table 10-7 that

$$P_c' = 0.5033 P_c = 79.0 \times 10^{15}\ \text{dyne cm}^{-2}$$

$$T_c' = 0.6877 T_c = 0.825 \times 10^7\ {}^\circ\text{K}$$

$$\rho_c' = 70.6\ \text{gm cm}^{-3}$$

$$P_b' = 0.5033 P_b = 46.7\ \text{dyne cm}^{-2}$$

$$T_b' = 0.6877 T_b = 0.673 \times 10^7\ {}^\circ\text{K}$$

$$\rho_b' = 51.1\ \text{gm cm}^{-3}.$$

With these values of T and ρ, Table 10-15 shows that the assumption

$$\frac{t}{g_{\text{bf}}} = 20$$

is still adequate. Tables 10-13A and 10-13B indicate that ϵ should now be computed from the formula

$$\epsilon = 0.0866 \times 1.09 X^2 \rho T_7{}^5$$

$$= 0.0944 X^2 \rho T_7{}^5;$$

thus the assumed expression yields values that are about 30 per cent too high at the center.

The positions of Model B and the transformed model are compared in the Hertzsprung–Russell diagram of Fig. 10-5 and the mass-luminosity diagram of Fig. 10-6. As expected, the transformed model is a considerable improvement. A realistic model, however, would have to include the theoretical refinements mentioned in the discussion of Model B.

In Table 10-10, we have listed some of the dimensionless parameters of these models. While data pertaining to Model B have been used, those of the transformed model would be equally valid.

Table 10-10 Dimensionless Quantities for the Schwarzschild Transformation of Model B.* The original values of X, Y, Z, κ_0, ϵ_0, and ν are retained.

$$E = 4\pi G^{1.5}\left(\frac{H}{k}\right)^{2.5} \mu^{2.5} \mathscr{K}' M^{0.5} R^{1.5}$$

$$= 4\pi G^{1.5}\left(\frac{H}{k}\right)^{2.5} 0.6079^{2.5}\frac{0.9781}{\sqrt{10}}(1.194 \times 10^{33})^{0.5}(2.61 \times 10^{10})^{1.5}$$

$$= 45.44$$

$$U_b = \frac{r_b}{M_{rb}}\frac{dM_r}{dr}\bigg|_b = \frac{0.80 \times 10^{10}}{0.170 \times 10^{33}}\left(\frac{0.056 \times 10^{33}}{0.1 \times 10^{10}}\right)$$

$$= 2.64$$

$$V_b = -\frac{r_b}{P_b}\frac{dP}{dr}\bigg|_b = -\frac{0.80 \times 10^{10}}{92.7 \times 10^{15}}\left(-\frac{12.4 \times 10^{15}}{0.1 \times 10^{10}}\right)$$

$$= 1.07$$

$$x_b = \frac{r_b}{R} = \frac{0.80 \times 10^{10}}{2.61 \times 10^{10}}$$

$$= 0.307$$

$$q_b = \frac{M_{rb}}{M} = \frac{0.170 \times 10^{33}}{1.194 \times 10^{33}}$$

$$= 0.142$$

$$p_b = P_b\bigg/\frac{GM^2}{4\pi R^4} = 92.7 \times 10^{15}\bigg/\frac{G}{4\pi}\frac{(1.194 \times 10^{33})^2}{(2.61 \times 10^{10})^4}$$

$$= 569$$

Table 10-10 (*continued*)

$$t_b = T_b \bigg/ \frac{GH}{k} \mu \frac{M}{R} = 0.979 \times 10^7 \bigg/ \frac{GH}{k} 0.6079 \frac{1.194 \times 10^{33}}{2.61 \times 10^{10}}$$

$$= 0.436$$

$$f_0 = \frac{L_{rb}}{L} = \frac{0.969 \times 10^{33}}{1.58 \times 10^{33}}$$

$$= 0.613$$

$$p_c = P_c \bigg/ \frac{GM^2}{4\pi R^4} = 157 \times 10^{15} \bigg/ \frac{G}{4\pi} \frac{(1.194 \times 10^{33})^2}{(2.61 \times 10^{10})^4}$$

$$= 963$$

$$t_c = T_c \bigg/ \frac{GH}{k} \mu \frac{M}{R} = 1.20 \times 10^7 \bigg/ \frac{GH}{k} 0.6079 \frac{1.194 \times 10^{33}}{2.61 \times 10^{10}}$$

$$= 0.534$$

$$C = \frac{3}{4ac} \left(\frac{1}{4\pi}\right)^3 \left(\frac{k}{GH}\right)^{7.5} \frac{\kappa_0}{\mu^{7.5}} \frac{LR^{0.5}}{M^{5.5}}$$

$$= \frac{3}{4ac} \left(\frac{1}{4\pi}\right)^3 \left(\frac{k}{GH}\right)^{7.5} \frac{4.34 \times 10^{25}}{20} \frac{0.02(1.72)}{0.6079^{7.5}} \frac{1.58 \times 10^{33}(2.61 \times 10^{10})^{0.5}}{(1.194 \times 10^{33})^{5.5}}$$

$$= 2.47 \times 10^{-6}$$

$$D = \frac{1}{4\pi} \left(\frac{GH}{k}\right)^v \mu^v \epsilon_0 X_1 X_2 \frac{M^{v+2}}{LR^{v+3}}$$

$$= \frac{1}{4\pi} \left(\frac{GH}{k}\right)^4 0.6079^4 (10.0 \times 10^{-30})(0.72)^2 \frac{(1.194 \times 10^{33})^6}{1.58 \times 10^{33}(2.61 \times 10^{10})^7}$$

$$= 5.34$$

$$(n+1)_c = \left(\frac{T}{P}\frac{dP}{dr}\bigg/\frac{dT}{dr}\right)_c = \left(\frac{T_7}{P_{15}}\right)_c \left(-4.914 \frac{P_{15}M_{r33}}{T_7 r_{10}^2}\right)_c \left(-0.00003374 \frac{P_{15}^2 L_{r33}}{T_7^{8.5} r_{10}^2}\right)_c^{-1}$$

$$= \left(\frac{T_7}{P_{15}}\right)_c \left(-4.914 \frac{P_{15}}{T_7} 0.4038 r_{10}\right)_c \left(-0.00003374 \frac{P_{15}^2}{T_7^{8.5}} 4.185 r_{10}\right)_c^{-1}$$

$$= \left(\frac{4.914 \times 0.4038}{0.00003374 \times 4.185} \frac{T_7^{8.5}}{P_{15}^2}\right)_c = \left(\frac{4.914 \times 0.4038}{0.00003374 \times 4.185} \frac{1.20^{8.5}}{157^2}\right)$$

$$= 2.69$$

---

* The units for the variables in the expression for $(n+1)_c$ are the same as in Section 3; here, however, the scaling factors have been explicitly indicated by numerical subscripts. For example, $T_7 = T \times 10^{-7}$.

Table 10-11   Emden Functions* ($n = 1.5$). [Adapted from The Royal Society, British Assoc. for the Adv. of Sci., 1932 (77).]

ξ	$\dfrac{\xi}{\xi_0}$	θ	$-\dfrac{d\theta}{d\xi}$	θ^n	θ^{n+1}	$-\xi^2\dfrac{d\theta}{d\xi}$	U	V
0.0	0	1	0	1	1	0	3	0
0.1	0.0274	0.9983	0.0333	0.9975	0.9958	$0.0^3 33$	2.997	0.0083
0.2	0.0547	0.9934	0.0663	0.9900	0.9835	0.0026	2.988	0.0333
0.3	0.0821	0.9851	0.0987	0.9777	0.9632	0.0089	2.973	0.0751
0.4	0.1095	0.9737	0.1302	0.9607	0.9354	0.0208	2.952	0.1337
0.5	0.1368	0.9591	0.1605	0.9393	0.9009	0.0401	2.925	0.2092
0.6	0.1642	0.9416	0.1895	0.9137	0.8603	0.0682	2.893	0.3019
0.7	0.1916	0.9213	0.2169	0.8842	0.8146	0.1063	2.854	0.4119
0.8	0.2190	0.8983	0.2424	0.8514	0.7648	0.1551	2.810	0.5397
0.9	0.2463	0.8728	0.2659	0.8155	0.7118	0.2154	2.760	0.6854
1.0	0.2737	0.8452	0.2873	0.7770	0.6567	0.2873	2.705	0.8497
1.1	0.3011	0.8155	0.3064	0.7364	0.6005	0.3707	2.644	1.033
1.2	0.3284	0.7840	0.3231	0.6941	0.5442	0.4653	2.578	1.236
1.3	0.3558	0.7509	0.3375	0.6507	0.4886	0.5703	2.507	1.461
1.4	0.3832	0.7166	0.3494	0.6066	0.4346	0.6849	2.430	1.707
1.5	0.4105	0.6811	0.3590	0.5621	0.3829	0.8077	2.349	1.976
1.6	0.4379	0.6448	0.3661	0.5178	0.3339	0.9373	2.263	2.271
1.7	0.4653	0.6080	0.3710	0.4740	0.2882	1.0722	2.172	2.594
1.8	0.4926	0.5707	0.3737	0.4312	0.2461	1.2107	2.077	2.946
1.9	0.5200	0.5333	0.3742	0.3895	0.2077	1.3510	1.977	3.333
2.0	0.5474	0.4959	0.3728	0.3492	0.1732	1.491	1.874	3.759
2.1	0.5748	0.4588	0.3696	0.3108	0.1426	1.630	1.766	4.229
2.2	0.6021	0.4221	0.3646	0.2742	0.1157	1.765	1.654	4.752
2.3	0.6295	0.3859	0.3582	0.2397	0.0925	1.895	1.539	5.337
2.4	0.6569	0.3505	0.3504	0.2075	0.0727	2.018	1.421	5.998
2.5	0.6842	0.3159	0.3413	0.1775	0.0561	2.133	1.300	6.753
2.6	0.7116	0.2823	0.3313	0.1499	0.0423	2.240	1.177	7.630
2.7	0.7390	0.2497	0.3204	0.1247	0.0311	2.336	1.051	8.663
2.8	0.7663	0.2182	0.3088	0.1019	0.0222	2.421	0.924	9.908
2.9	0.7937	0.1879	0.2967	0.0815	0.0153	2.496	0.796	11.449
3.0	0.8211	0.1589	0.2843	0.0633	0.0101	2.558	0.668	13.42
3.1	0.8484	0.1311	0.2715	0.0474	0.0062	2.610	0.542	16:06
3.2	0.8758	0.1046	0.2588	0.0338	0.0035	2.650	0.418	19.80
3.3	0.9032	0.0793	0.2460	0.0223	0.0018	2.679	0.300	25.59
3.4	0.9305	0.0553	0.2334	0.0130	$0.0^3 72$	2.699	0.190	35.85
3.5	0.9579	0.0326	0.2212	0.0059	$0.0^3 19$	2.710	0.093	59.34
3.6	0.9853	0.0111	0.2094	0.0012	$0.0^4 13$	2.714	0.020	169.92
ξ_0	1	0	0.2033	0	0	2.7141	0	∞

$\xi_0 = 3.65375$

* The notation $0.0^x XX$ signifies that x zeroes follow the decimal point.

Table 10-12   Emden Functions* ($n = 3$). [Adapted from The Royal Society, British Assoc. for the Adv. of Sci., 1932 (77).]

ξ	$\dfrac{\xi}{\xi_0}$	θ	$-\dfrac{d\theta}{d\xi}$	θ^n	θ^{n+1}	$-\xi^2\dfrac{d\theta}{d\xi}$	U	V
0.0	0	1	0	1	1	0	3	0
0.1	0.0145	0.9983	0.0332	0.9950	0.9934	0.0003	2.994	0.0133
0.2	0.0290	0.9934	0.0659	0.9802	0.9737	0.0026	2.976	0.0530
0.3	0.0435	0.9852	0.0974	0.9562	0.9421	0.0088	2.947	0.1186
0.4	0.0580	0.9740	0.1272	0.9239	0.8998	0.0203	2.906	0.2089
0.5	0.0725	0.9598	0.1548	0.8843	0.8488	0.0387	2.856	0.3226
0.6	0.0870	0.9431	0.1800	0.8388	0.7910	0.0648	2.795	0.4582
0.7	0.1015	0.9239	0.2025	0.7887	0.7287	0.0992	2.726	0.6137
0.8	0.1160	0.9027	0.2220	0.7355	0.6639	0.1421	2.650	0.7871
0.9	0.1305	0.8796	0.2386	0.6806	0.5986	0.1932	2.567	0.9764
1.0	0.1450	0.8551	0.2521	0.6251	0.5345	0.2521	2.479	1.1795
1.1	0.1595	0.8293	0.2628	0.5703	0.4730	0.3180	2.387	1.3943
1.2	0.1740	0.8026	0.2707	0.5170	0.4149	0.3898	2.292	1.6189
1.3	0.1885	0.7752	0.2760	0.4659	0.3612	0.4665	2.194	1.8515
1.4	0.2030	0.7475	0.2790	0.4176	0.3121	0.5469	2.095	2.0904
1.5	0.2175	0.7195	0.2799	0.3725	0.2680	0.6298	1.996	2.334
1.6	0.2320	0.6915	0.2790	0.3307	0.2287	0.7141	1.897	2.582
1.7	0.2465	0.6638	0.2764	0.2924	0.1941	0.7988	1.799	2.832
1.8	0.2610	0.6363	0.2725	0.2576	0.1639	0.8829	1.702	3.083
1.9	0.2755	0.6093	0.2674	0.2262	0.1378	0.9655	1.607	3.336
2.0	0.2900	0.5829	0.2615	0.1980	0.1154	1.0460	1.514	3.589
2.1	0.3045	0.5570	0.2548	0.1728	0.0963	1.1237	1.424	3.843
2.2	0.3190	0.5319	0.2476	0.1505	0.0800	1.1983	1.337	4.096
2.3	0.3335	0.5075	0.2399	0.1307	0.0663	1.2693	1.253	4.349
2.4	0.3480	0.4839	0.2320	0.1133	0.0548	1.3365	1.172	4.603
2.5	0.3625	0.4611	0.2240	0.0981	0.0452	1.400	1.094	4.857
2.6	0.3770	0.4391	0.2158	0.0847	0.0372	1.459	1.020	5.112
2.7	0.3915	0.4180	0.2077	0.0730	0.0305	1.514	0.949	5.368
2.8	0.4060	0.3976	0.1997	0.0628	0.0250	1.566	0.881	5.625
2.9	0.4205	0.3780	0.1918	0.0540	0.0204	1.613	0.817	5.885
3.0	0.4350	0.3592	0.1840	0.0464	0.0167	1.656	0.756	6.148
3.1	0.4495	0.3412	0.1765	0.0397	0.0136	1.696	0.698	6.415
3.2	0.4640	0.3239	0.1692	0.0340	0.0110	1.733	0.643	6.687
3.3	0.4785	0.3073	0.1622	0.0290	0.0089	1.766	0.591	6.965
3.4	0.4930	0.2915	0.1554	0.0248	0.0072	1.796	0.542	7.250
3.5	0.5075	0.2763	0.1488	0.0211	0.0058	1.823	0.496	7.543
3.6	0.5220	0.2617	0.1426	0.0179	0.0047	1.848	0.452	7.846
3.7	0.5365	0.2477	0.1366	0.0152	0.0038	1.870	0.412	8.160
3.8	0.5510	0.2344	0.1309	0.0129	0.0030	1.890	0.374	8.487
3.9	0.5655	0.2216	0.1254	0.0109	0.0024	1.907	0.338	8.828
4.0	0.5800	0.2093	0.1202	0.0092	0.0019	1.923	0.305	9.187
4.1	0.5945	0.1975	0.1152	0.0077	0.0015	1.936	0.274	9.565
4.2	0.6090	0.1862	0.1105	0.0065	0.0012	1.949	0.246	9.965
4.3	0.6235	0.1754	0.1060	0.0054	0.0009	1.959	0.219	10.390
4.4	0.6380	0.1650	0.1017	0.0045	0.0007	1.969	0.194	10.844

Table 10-12 (continued)

ξ	$\dfrac{\xi}{\xi_0}$	θ	$-\dfrac{d\theta}{d\xi}$	θ^n	θ^{n+1}	$-\xi^2\dfrac{d\theta}{d\xi}$	U	V
4.5	0.6525	0.1551	0.0976	0.0037	0.0006	1.977	0.172	11.331
4.6	0.6670	0.1455	0.0938	0.0031	0.0004	1.984	0.151	11.856
4.7	0.6815	0.1363	0.0901	0.0025	0.0003	1.990	0.132	12.424
4.8	0.6960	0.1275	0.0866	0.0021	0.0003	1.995	0.115	13.041
4.9	0.7105	0.1190	0.0833	0.0017	0.0002	1.999	0.099	13.717
5.0	0.7250	0.1108	0.0801	0.0014	0.0^315	2.003	0.0849	14.46
5.1	0.7395	0.1030	0.0771	0.0011	0.0^311	2.006	0.0722	15.28
5.2	0.7540	0.0954	0.0743	0.0^387	0.0^483	2.009	0.0607	16.20
5.3	0.7685	0.0881	0.0716	0.0^368	0.0^460	2.011	0.0506	17.23
5.4	0.7830	0.0811	0.0690	0.0^353	0.0^443	2.013	0.0417	18.39
5.5	0.7975	0.0743	0.0666	0.0^341	0.0^430	2.014	0.0339	19.72
5.6	0.8120	0.0677	0.0643	0.0^331	0.0^421	2.015	0.0271	21.25
5.7	0.8265	0.0614	0.0621	0.0^323	0.0^414	2.016	0.0213	23.03
5.8	0.8410	0.0553	0.0600	0.0^317	0.0^594	2.017	0.0164	25.14
5.9	0.8555	0.0494	0.0579	0.0^312	0.0^560	2.017	0.0123	27.66
6.0	0.8700	0.0437	0.0560	0.0^484	0.0^537	2.018	0.0^290	30.75
6.1	0.8845	0.0382	0.0542	0.0^456	0.0^521	2.018	0.0^263	34.61
6.2	0.8990	0.0329	0.0525	0.0^436	0.0^512	2.018	0.0^242	39.58
6.3	0.9135	0.0277	0.0508	0.0^421	0.0^659	2.018	0.0^226	46.22
6.4	0.9280	0.0227	0.0493	0.0^412	0.0^627	2.018	0.0^215	55.52
6.5	0.9425	0.0179	0.0478	0.0^557	0.0^610	2.018	0.0^378	69.52
6.6	0.9570	0.0132	0.0463	0.0^523	0.0^730	2.018	0.0^332	92.93
6.7	0.9715	0.0086	0.0450	0.0^664	0.0^855	2.018	0.0^495	140.14
6.8	0.9860	0.0042	0.0436	0.0^772	0.0^930	2.018	0.0^411	284.85
ξ_0	1	0	0.0424	0	0	2.0182	0	∞

$\xi_0 = 6.89685$

* The notation $0.0^x XX$ signifies that x zeros follow the decimal point.

Table 10-13A   Energy Generation by the Proton-Proton Chain.
The table gives the values of ϵ_0 and ν in the formula

$$\epsilon_{pp} = \epsilon_0 X^2 \rho T_7{}^\nu \cdot f_{pp},*$$

where

$$T_7 = T \times 10^{-7} \; (^\circ K).$$

T_7	ϵ_0	ν	T_7	ϵ_0	ν
0.807	0.0866	5	2.363	0.179	3.5
1.115	0.0839	4.5	3.147	0.291	3
1.612	0.0813	4.5	5.201	0.580	2.5
2.162	0.119	4			

The values given reproduce the formula

$$\epsilon_{pp} = 2.36 \times 10^6 X^2 \rho T_6{}^{-2/3} e^{-33.81/T_6{}^{1/3}} \psi f_{pp} \cdot$$

$$\cdot (1 + 0.0123 T_6{}^{1/3} + 0.0109 T_6{}^{2/3} + 0.00095 T_6) \quad (6\text{-}77A)$$

with a maximum error of 5 per cent (if the correction below is applied) for any temperature within the range of the table. The electron screening factor f_{pp} is evaluated in Table 10-13B.

* The values of ϵ_0 have been calculated for $\psi = 0.70$. For other compositions, therefore, ϵ_0 as given above should be multiplied by $\psi(X)/\psi(0.70)$ as determined from Fig. 10-7.

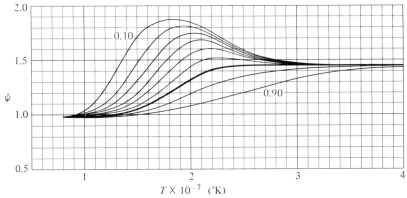

Fig. 10-7 The Function ψ in the Energy-Generation Coefficient ϵ_{pp}. This function expresses the relative efficiencies of the various terminal reactions of the *p-p* chain occurring at various temperatures and compositions. The values of X appropriate to the curves are, respectively, 0.10, 0.20, 0.30, 0.40, 0.50, 0.60, 0.70, 0.80, and 0.90; the first and last of these are labeled in the figure. The curve for $X = 0.70$ is emphasized. The value of Z is assumed to be zero or small, as in normal stars. The cross-section factor $S_0(\mathrm{Be}^7 + \mathrm{H}^1)$ is taken as 0.04 keV barn.

Table 10-13B Electron Screening Factors for the Proton-Proton Chain. The table gives f_{pp}.* The density is expressed in gm cm^{-3} and the temperature in units of 10^7 °K.

ρ \ T_7	0.8	1	2	3	4	5
1	1.01	1.01	1.00	1.00	1.00	1.00
10	1.04	1.03	1.01	1.00	1.00	1.00
20	1.05	1.04	1.01	1.01	1.00	1.00
40	1.07	1.05	1.02	1.01	1.01	1.00
60	1.09	1.06	1.02	1.01	1.01	1.01
80	1.11	1.08	1.03	1.01	1.01	1.01
100	1.12	1.08	1.03	1.02	1.01	1.01
200		1.04	1.02	1.01	1.01
400		1.06	1.03	1.02	1.01
600			1.04	1.03	1.02
800				1.03	1.02
1000				1.03	1.02

* The values of f_{pp} are calculated for a composition with $X = 0.70$ and $Y = 0.30$ but may be used for other compositions with small Z. For $X = 0.10$, for example, f_{pp} differs from the value given by 1 per cent at most.

Table 10-14A   Energy Generation by the Carbon-Nitrogen Cycle.*
The table gives the values of ϵ_0 and ν in the formula

$$\epsilon_{CN} = \epsilon_0 X X_{CN} \rho T_7{}^\nu f_{CN} \qquad (T_7 < 5)$$

or

$$\epsilon_{CN} = \epsilon_0 X X_{CN} \rho T_8{}^\nu f_{CN} \qquad (T_8 > 0.5),$$

where

$$T_n = T \times 10^{-n} \; (^\circ K).$$

T_7	ϵ_0	ν	T_8	ϵ_0	ν
0.987	2.83 (-4)	23	0.5126	4.83 ($+12$)	13
1.124	2.92 (-4)	22	0.6439	2.77 ($+12$)	12
1.483	5.33 (-4)	20	0.8240	2.02 ($+12$)	11
1.721	8.55 (-4)	19			
2.012	1.60 (-3)	18			
2.373	3.48 (-3)	17			
2.827	9.01 (-3)	16			
3.403	2.80 (-2)	15			
4.148	1.05 (-1)	14			

The values given reproduce the formula

$$\epsilon_{CN} = 7.21 \times 10^{27} X X_{CN} \rho T_6{}^{-2/3} e^{-152.31/T_6{}^{1/3}} f_{CN}$$

(6-77B)

with a maximum error of 10 per cent for $T_7 \leqslant 1.4$ and 3 per cent for $T_7 \geqslant 1.5$. The electron screening factor f_{CN} is evaluated in Table 10-14B.

* A number in parentheses is the power of 10 by which the entry is to be multiplied.

Table 10-14B   Electron Screening Factors for the Carbon-Nitrogen Cycle. The table gives f_{CN}.* The density is expressed in gm cm^{-3} and the temperature in units of $10^7 \; ^\circ K$.

ρ \ T_7	1	1.25	1.5	2	3	4	5	8
1	1.06	1.04	1.03	1.02	1.01	1.01	1.01	1.00
10	1.20	1.14	1.10	1.07	1.04	1.02	1.02	1.01
20	1.29	1.20	1.15	1.09	1.05	1.03	1.02	1.01
40	1.43	1.29	1.22	1.13	1.07	1.05	1.03	1.02
60	1.55	1.37	1.27	1.17	1.09	1.06	1.04	1.02
80	1.66	1.44	1.32	1.20	1.10	1.07	1.05	1.02
100	1.76	1.50	1.36	1.22	1.12	1.07	1.05	1.03
200			1.55	1.33	1.17	1.11	1.07	1.04
400					1.24	1.15	1.11	1.05
600					1.31	1.19	1.13	1.06
800						1.22	1.15	1.07
1000						1.25	1.17	1.08
2000								1.12

* The values of f_{CN} are calculated for a composition with $X = 0.70$ and $Y = 0.30$ but may be used also for other compositions with small Z. The maximum error for other compositions occurs for the largest value of f_{CN}. For $X = 0.10$, for example, the value $f_{CN} = 1.76$ should be diminished by 5 per cent.

Table 10-15 $\text{Log}_{10}\,(t/\bar{g}_{bf})$ for the Russell Mixture. The relative abundances by mass are

$$Fe:(K + Ca):Si:(Na + Mg):O = 2:1:1:4:8.$$

[P. M. Morse, 1940 (503).]

$\log T$	$\log \rho(1 + X)$												
	−2.0	−1.5	−1.0	−0.5	0.0	0.5	1.0	1.5	2.0	2.5	3.0	3.5	4.0
5.6	0.10	0.28	0.56	0.88	1.23	1.62	2.02	2.46	2.92	3.43	3.98	4.55	5.14
5.7	0.09	0.17	0.44	0.76	1.09	1.48	1.90	2.34	2.80	3.30	3.83	4.41	5.00
5.8	0.13	0.17	0.36	0.67	1.01	1.38	1.78	2.21	2.66	3.16	3.69	4.27	4.86
5.9	0.23	0.27	0.38	0.65	0.98	1.30	1.68	2.09	2.54	3.03	3.56	4.13	4.72
6.0	0.32	0.35	0.42	0.63	0.92	1.22	1.58	1.98	2.41	2.90	3.42	4.00	4.58
6.1	0.27	0.30	0.35	0.55	0.81	1.12	1.47	1.85	2.27	2.76	3.28	3.86	4.44
6.2	0.21	0.23	0.28	0.45	0.69	0.98	1.32	1.71	2.13	2.61	3.14	3.72	4.30
6.3	0.20	0.22	0.26	0.37	0.56	0.84	1.18	1.57	2.00	2.47	3.00	3.58	4.16
6.4	0.17	0.19	0.22	0.28	0.42	0.70	1.04	1.43	1.85	2.33	2.86	3.44	4.02
6.5	0.11	0.13	0.15	0.20	0.32	0.58	0.92	1.28	1.71	2.19	2.72	3.30	3.88
6.6	0.10	0.12	0.14	0.19	0.28	0.50	0.81	1.17	1.58	2.05	2.58	3.16	3.74
6.7	0.13	0.15	0.17	0.21	0.28	0.45	0.72	1.07	1.47	1.92	2.44	3.02	3.60
6.8	0.22	0.23	0.25	0.27	0.33	0.47	0.70	1.01	1.38	1.82	2.32	2.88	3.46
6.9	0.31	0.32	0.34	0.37	0.43	0.53	0.72	0.99	1.32	1.73	2.21	2.75	3.32
7.0	0.41	0.42	0.45	0.49	0.54	0.62	0.77	1.00	1.30	1.67	2.11	2.63	3.19
7.1	0.49	0.50	0.52	0.54	0.58	0.65	0.77	0.98	1.25	1.61	2.02	2.52	3.07
7.2	0.56	0.56	0.57	0.58	0.60	0.64	0.73	0.92	1.18	1.52	1.93	2.42	2.95
7.3	0.63	0.63	0.64	0.65	0.67	0.69	0.74	0.87	1.06	1.41	1.83	2.32	2.84
7.4	0.75	0.75	0.75	0.76	0.77	0.79	0.83	0.91	1.05	1.36	1.76	2.25	2.74
7.5	0.90	0.90	0.90	0.91	0.93	0.95	0.98	1.04	1.16	1.40	1.75	2.19	2.66
7.6	1.10	1.10	1.10	1.10	1.11	1.13	1.16	1.21	1.31	1.53	1.82	2.19	2.61
7.7	1.33	1.33	1.33	1.33	1.34	1.36	1.38	1.42	1.52	1.69	1.93	2.23	2.58
7.8	1.59	1.59	1.59	1.59	1.59	1.60	1.62	1.66	1.73	1.86	2.04	2.29	2.58
7.9	1.81	1.81	1.81	1.81	1.81	1.82	1.83	1.85	1.90	2.00	2.14	2.35	2.69
8.0	2.00	2.00	2.00	2.00	2.00	2.00	2.01	2.03	2.06	2.12	2.24	2.41	2.62
8.1	2.14	2.14	2.14	2.14	2.14	2.14	2.14	2.16	2.18	2.23	2.33	2.46	2.65
8.2	2.27	2.27	2.27	2.27	2.27	2.27	2.27	2.28	2.29	2.34	2.41	2.52	2.68
8.3	2.36	2.36	2.36	2.36	2.36	2.36	2.36	2.36	2.37	2.41	2.47	2.56	2.71
8.4	2.44	2.44	2.44	2.44	2.44	2.44	2.44	2.44	2.45	2.47	2.52	2.60	2.74

Table 10-16 Rosseland Mean Absorption Coefficients (cm² gm⁻¹).* $X = 0.80$, $Y = 0.19$, $Z = 0.01$. (For heavier elements, the mass fractions X_z are: $X_6 = 0.00141$, $X_7 = 0.00046$, $X_8 = 0.00420$, $X_{10} = 0.00298$, $X_{11} = 0.00001$, $X_{12} = 0.00018$, $X_{13} = 0.00001$, $X_{14} = 0.00026$, $X_{18} = 0.00039$, $X_{26} = 0.00008$.) [A. N. Cox and J. N. Stewart, 1970 (205).]

$\log \rho$ / T	−1	0	1	2	3	4
1.00 (09)					1.20 (−01)	1.20 (−01)
5.00 (08)				1.74 (−01)	1.74 (−01)	1.74 (−01)
2.00 (08)			2.47 (−01)	2.47 (−01)	2.48 (−01)	2.52 (−01)
1.00 (08)		2.92 (−01)	2.93 (−01)	2.96 (−01)	3.13 (−01)	3.90 (−01)
5.00 (07)	3.22 (−01)	3.23 (−01)	3.27 (−01)	3.50 (−01)	4.52 (−01)	8.49 (−01)

$\log \rho$ / T	−6	−5	−4	−3	−2	−1
2.00 (07)					3.43 (−01)	3.45 (−01)
1.00 (07)				3.51 (−01)	3.54 (−01)	3.72 (−01)
5.00 (06)			3.55 (−01)	3.60 (−01)	3.96 (−01)	6.31 (−01)
2.00 (06)		3.60 (−01)	3.83 (−01)	5.24 (−01)	1.65 (00)	1.05 (01)
1.00 (06)	3.62 (−01)	3.88 (−01)	5.09 (−01)	1.62 (00)	1.26 (01)	5.13 (01)

$\log \rho$ / T	−11	−10	−9	−8	−7	−6
5.00 (05)					3.63 (−01)	3.89 (−01)
2.00 (05)				3.76 (−01)	5.06 (−01)	1.56 (00)
1.00 (05)				6.32 (−01)	2.24 (00)	1.85 (01)
7.00 (04)			4.65 (−01)	1.06 (00)	7.26 (00)	8.60 (01)
5.00 (04)			7.32 (−01)	3.52 (00)	3.48 (01)	3.64 (02)
3.00 (04)		5.75 (−01)	1.29 (00)	8.18 (00)	9.28 (01)	1.15 (03)
2.00 (04)		6.73 (−01)	2.71 (00)	2.53 (01)	2.84 (02)	2.66 (03)
1.50 (04)		1.22 (00)	7.86 (00)	7.99 (01)	6.31 (02)	2.19 (03)
1.20 (04)		2.70 (00)	2.22 (01)	1.28 (02)	3.38 (02)	6.08 (02)
1.00 (04)		4.81 (00)	1.92 (01)	4.10 (01)	6.98 (01)	1.27 (02)
9.00 (03)	1.09 (00)	3.52 (00)	7.37 (00)	1.26 (01)	2.28 (01)	4.51 (01)
8.00 (03)	7.50 (−01)	1.11 (00)	1.63 (00)	2.84 (00)	5.96 (00)	1.45 (01)
7.00 (03)	1.70 (−01)	1.59 (−01)	2.43 (−01)	5.33 (−01)	1.35 (00)	3.72 (00)

$\log \rho$ / T	−16	−15	−14	−13	−12	−11
6.00 (03)					3.61 (−02)	1.68 (−02)
5.00 (03)					2.44 (−03)	1.20 (−03)
4.00 (03)					9.81 (−05)	6.66 (−05)
3.00 (03)					2.27 (−05)	2.50 (−05)
2.50 (03)					1.54 (−05)	1.66 (−05)
1.50 (03)					1.48 (−06)	1.25 (−06)

* A number in parentheses is the power of 10 by which an entry must be multiplied. The density ρ is expressed in gm cm⁻³ and the temperature T in °K.

5	6	7	8	9
1.20 (−01)	1.20 (−01)	1.20 (−01)	1.49 (−01)	2.60 (00)
1.76 (−01)	1.80 (−01)	2.01 (−01)	8.25 (−01)	5.68 (03)
2.69 (−01)	3.03 (−01)	9.80 (−01)	4.92 (02)	
6.28 (−01)	2.04 (00)	7.83 (01)		
2.03 (00)	2.76 (01)			

0	1	2	3	4	5
3.57 (−01)	4.19 (−01)	6.40 (−01)	1.58 (00)	4.81 (00)	4.03 (01)
4.84 (−01)	8.59 (−01)	2.09 (00)	8.43 (00)	3.91 (01)	
1.59 (00)	3.93 (00)	1.38 (01)	5.87 (01)		
2.89 (01)	6.02 (01)	2.39 (02)			
1.32 (02)	4.75 (02)				

−5	−4	−3	−2	−1	0
5.86 (−01)	2.37 (00)	1.86 (01)	7.75 (01)	1.75 (02)	6.74 (02)
1.32 (01)	1.47 (02)	7.52 (02)	1.93 (03)	2.39 (03)	
2.34 (02)	2.77 (03)	1.60 (04)	2.75 (04)	1.85 (04)	
1.05 (03)	8.82 (03)	3.82 (04)	4.22 (04)		
3.82 (03)	2.93 (04)	1.23 (05)	9.80 (04)		
1.19 (04)	7.61 (04)	2.71 (05)			
1.26 (04)	3.02 (04)	5.76 (04)			
4.42 (03)	8.14 (03)	1.71 (04)			
1.09 (03)	2.24 (03)	5.21 (03)			
2.63 (02)	6.35 (02)	1.58 (03)			
1.11 (02)	3.00 (02)				
3.94 (01)	1.13 (02)				
1.11 (01)	3.37 (01)				

−10	−9	−8	−7	−6	−5
1.11 (−02)	2.37 (−02)	6.95 (−02)	2.25 (−01)	7.47 (−01)	2.66 (00)
1.29 (−03)	2.93 (−03)	9.11 (−03)	3.73 (−02)	1.81 (−01)	7.05 (−01)
1.04 (−04)	4.70 (−04)	2.57 (−03)	1.12 (−02)	4.18 (−02)	1.25 (−01)
3.57 (−05)	7.01 (−05)	2.47 (−04)	1.02 (−03)	3.61 (−03)	9.16 (−03)
2.24 (−05)	3.55 (−05)	6.68 (−05)	1.40 (−04)	2.99 (−04)	6.52 (−04)
1.43 (−06)	1.87 (−06)	2.56 (−06)	3.55 (−06)	4.92 (−06)	6.71 (−06)

PROBLEMS

1. Show that the surface of Model B can be located in the outward integration without ambiguity if a smaller interval is used. (Repeat the calculation of Table 10-8A for $r > 2.4$ with $h = 0.02$. To start this integration, interpolate for M_r and T on lines $r = 2.34$, 2.36, and 2.38 and find the derivatives and differences on these lines and also at $r = 2.40$. The interpolation can be performed by the use of eq. (8-5): $\varphi = \varphi_0 + (^1\Delta_0/h)(z - z_0) + (^2\Delta_0/2h^2)(z - z_0)(z - z_{-1}) + \cdots .$)

2. (a) Determine a polytropic representation for the interior of a star having the same central pressure and central temperature as that of Section 5-4.
   (b) Compare the total masses and radii of the two models.

3. (a) Obtain a polytropic representation for the initial Sun.
   (b) Why is the agreement with Table 7-37 so much poorer than that between Model A and Kushwaha's model?

4. (a) Test the adequacy of the theoretical mass-luminosity law in Section 5 [that is, test the constancy of C in eq. (10-124)] for the models of Fig. 7-9.
   (b) Explain why the law can be applied only over short segments of the main sequence.

5. (a) Use Schwarzschild's transformation to obtain a model of mass $0.3\,M_\odot$.
   (b) Test the validity of the expressions used for κ and ϵ.

APPENDIX

TERM PROJECTS

1. (a) Calculate $P(\bar\tau)$ for a model atmosphere having $T_{\text{eff}} = 6000°\text{K}$, $g = 10^4$ cm sec^{-2}, and the chemical composition of Table 3-7. The approximate formula

$$\bar\kappa = 10^{-4.484}P^{0.808}$$

may be used in the range $0.92 \gtrsim \theta \gtrsim 1.0$ and $1 \times 10^4 \gtrsim P \gtrsim 4 \times 10^4$.
(b) Calculate $x(\bar\tau)$ for this atmosphere.
(c) Compare the results of parts (a) and (b) with those of Table 4-9.
(d) Test the adequacy of the approximate formula used in part (a).

2. (Short project.) Calculate a model solar atmosphere with the same given conditions and assumptions as used in Chapter 9, but integrate directly in terms of the depth x rather than the optical depth τ (cf. Problem 1 of Chapter 4).
(a) Derive expressions for dP/dx and dT/dx.
(b) To obtain starting values, interpolate in Table 9-6 to find P and T at $-x = 100$, 110, 120, and 130 km. Then evaluate the derivatives and differences.
(c) Proceed with the numerical integration.
(d) Compare the results with those of Table 9-6.

3. (a) Calculate a model interior having the same mass, radius, and luminosity as Model A, namely,

$$M = 4.962 \times 10^{33} \text{ gm}, \qquad R = 11.05 \times 10^{10} \text{ cm},$$

$$L = 80.14 \times 10^{33} \text{ erg sec}^{-1},$$

but with different parameters for the composition, energy-generation law, or opacity law. For example, choose any of the following compositions:

$X = 0.90,$	$Z = 0.015$	$X = 0.85,$	$Z = 0.02$
$X = 0.85,$	$Z = 0.015$	$X = 0.80,$	$Z = 0.02$
	$X = 0.90,$	$Z = 0.01.$	

(Not all reasonable values for the parameters lead to a model with a convective core; and if a convective core is obtained, it may have $U > 3$

513

at its outer boundary. The compositions above, together with the same opacity law (including $t/\bar{g}$ value) as in Model A, yield convective cores with $U < 3$ at the boundary).

(b) Test the adequacy of the assumptions made.

4. (a) Perform a numerical integration to obtain the transformed model of Section 5-4, which has

$$M = 0.796 \times 10^{33} \text{ gm,}$$

$$R = 2.53 \times 10^{10} \text{ cm,}$$

$$L = 0.1724 \times 10^{33} \text{ erg sec}^{-1},$$

$$X = 0.72, \qquad Z = 0.02.$$

Use the same energy-generation and opacity laws as for Model B.

(b) Compare the results with those of Section 5-4.

APPENDIX

TABLE OF CONSTANTS

Table of Constants*

QUANTITY	SYMBOL	VALUE	LOG (VALUE)
Solar mass	$M_\odot$	1.991×10^{33} gm	33.2991
Solar radius	$R_\odot$	6.960×10^{10} cm	10.8426
Solar luminosity	$L_\odot$	3.82×10^{33} erg sec^{-1}	33.582
Solar effective temperature	$T_{\text{eff}\odot}$	5770°K	3.7612
Astronomical unit	AU	149597892.9 ± 5.0 km	8.174925477
Speed of light	c	2.9979250×10^{10} cm sec^{-1}	10.47682076
Planck's constant	h	6.626196×10^{-27} erg sec	-26.1787357
Gravitational constant	G	6.6732×10^{-8} dyne cm^2 gm^{-2}	-7.17567
Charge of electron	e	4.803250×10^{-10} esu	-9.3184648
Boltzmann's constant	k	1.380622×10^{-16} erg °K^{-1}	-15.859925
Stefan–Boltzmann constant	σ	5.66961×10^{-5} erg sec^{-1} cm^{-2} °K^{-4}	-4.246447
Radiation pressure constant	$a = 4\sigma/c$	7.56471×10^{-15} erg cm^{-3} °K^{-4}	-14.121208
Mass of electron	m_e	9.109558×10^{-28} gm	-27.0405027
Mass of H atom	m_{H}	1.67333×10^{-24} gm	-23.776418
Atomic mass unit (C^{12} scale)	AMU	1.660531×10^{-24} gm	-23.7797530
1 AMU $\times c^2$		931.4812 MeV	2.9691741
Avogadro's number	N_0	6.022170×10^{23} mole^{-1}	23.7797530
Gas constant	$\mathscr{R}$	8.31434×10^7 erg mole^{-1} °K^{-1}	7.919828
Electron volt	eV	$1.6021917 \times 10^{-12}$ erg	-11.79528552

* Except for m_{H}, the values of the physical (as distinguished from the astronomical) constants are those given by B. N. Taylor, W. H. Parker, and D. N. Langenberg, 1969 (199c). The value of m_{H} is that given by C. W. Allen, 1963 (10). The value of the astronomical unit is that found by W. G. Melbourne, D. O. Muhleman, and D. A. O'Handley, 1968 (199d).

SELECTED BIBLIOGRAPHY

This bibliography consists of two parts: general references (principally books) and specialized references (principally journal articles). In the first part, a superscript 1, 2, 3, or 4 prefixing the number of the reference indicates that the work is also pertinent to Part One, Two, Three, or Four, respectively. In the second part, the following abbreviations have been adopted for the names of journals:

Ann. d'Ap.	*Annales d'Astrophysique*
Ann. Rev.	*Annual Review of Astronomy and Astrophysics*
A.J.	*Astronomical Journal*
Astron. Ap.	*Astronomy and Astrophysics*
Ap. J.	*Astrophysical Journal*
Ap. Sp. Sci.	*Astrophysics and Space Science*
J. Obs.	*Journal des Observateurs*
Mém. Soc. Roy. Sci. Liège	*Mémoires de la Société Royale des Sciences (Liège)*
M.N.R.A.S.	*Monthly Notices of the Royal Astronomical Society*
Prog. Theo. Phys.	*Progress of Theoretical Physics*
P.A.S.J.	*Publications of the Astronomical Society of Japan*
P.A.S.P.	*Publications of the Astronomical Society of the Pacific*
Sol. Phys.	*Solar Physics*
Z.f.Ap.	*Zeitschrift für Astrophysik*

The journal *Astronomy and Astrophysics* merges and replaces the following publications, beginning January 1969: *Ann. d'Ap., Bull. of the Astr. Institutes of the Netherlands, Bulletin Astronomique, J. Obs., Z.f.Ap.*

GENERAL REFERENCES
PART ONE—OBSERVATIONAL DATA

1. K. Aa. Strand, ed. (1963). *Basic Astronomical Data; Stars and Stellar Systems*, Vol. III. Univ. of Chicago Press, Chicago.
[2,3]2. J. A. Hynek, ed. (1951). *Astrophysics*. McGraw-Hill, New York.
[2]3. J. Dufay (1964). *Introduction to Astrophysics: The Stars*. (Transl. from the French by O. Gingerich.) Dover, New York.
4. P. van de Kamp (1967). *Principles of Astrometry*. W. H. Freeman, San Francisco.

2,35. J. C. Brandt (1966). *The Physics and Astronomy of the Sun and Stars.* McGraw-Hill, New York.

2,36. T. L. Swihart (1968). *Astrophysics and Stellar Astronomy.* Wiley, New York.

2,37. G. O. Abell (1969). *Exploration of the Universe,* 2nd ed. Holt, Rinehart and Winston, New York.

2,38. L. Motz and A. Duveen (1966). *Essentials of Astronomy.* Wadsworth, Belmont, California.

9. L. Binnendijk (1960). *Properties of Double Stars.* Univ. of Pennsylvania Press, Philadelphia.

2,310. C. W. Allen (1963). *Astrophysical Quantities,* 2nd ed. Athlone, London.

2,311. Landolt-Börnstein *Numerical Data and Functional Relationships in Science and Technology,* * New Series (1965) (K. H. Hellwege, ed.-in-chief), Vol. I: *Astronomy and Astrophysics.* Springer-Verlag, Berlin.

2,312. A. Unsöld (1969). *The New Cosmos.* (Transl. from the German by W. H. McCrea.) Springer-Verlag, New York.

2,313. H.-Y. Chiu, R. L. Warasila, and J. L. Remo, eds. (1969). *Stellar Astronomy:* Proceedings of the Summer Inst. for Observational Astronomy, State Univ. of New York at Stony Brook, 1967. Gordon and Breach, New York.

PART TWO—STELLAR ATMOSPHERES

25. L. H. Aller (1963). *Astrophysics: The Atmospheres of the Sun and Stars,* 2nd ed. (1st ed., 1953). Ronald, New York.

26. R. v. d. R. Woolley and D. W. N. Stibbs (1953). *The Outer Layers of a Star.* The Clarendon Press, Oxford.

27. A. Unsöld (1968). *Physik der Sternatmosphären mit besonderer Berücksichtigung der Sonne,* rev. 2nd ed. Springer-Verlag, Berlin.

28. S. Chandrasekhar (1950). *Radiative Transfer.* The Clarendon Press, Oxford. Reprinted by Dover, New York (1960).

29. V. Kourganoff with the collab. of I. W. Busbridge (1952). *Basic Methods in Transfer Problems.* The Clarendon Press, Oxford. Reprinted by Dover, New York (1963).

330. V. A. Ambartsumyan, ed. (1958). *Theoretical Astrophysics.* (Transl. from the Russian by J. B. Sykes.) Pergamon, London.

31. J. C. Pecker and E. Schatzman (1959). *Astrophysique Générale.* Masson, Paris.

1,332. S. Flügge, ed. (1958). *Handbuch der Physik,* Vol. L.† Springer-Verlag, Berlin.

33. D. H. Menzel, ed. (1966). *Selected Papers on the Transfer of Radiation.* Dover, New York.

34. G. P. Kuiper, ed. (1953). *The Sun; The Solar System,* Vol. I. Univ. of Chicago Press, Chicago.

35. O. Gingerich, ed. (1969). *Theory and Observation of Normal Stellar Atmospheres:* Proceedings of the Third Harvard–Smithsonian Conference on Stellar Atmospheres. M.I.T. Press, Cambridge, Mass.

36. J. L. Greenstein, ed. (1960). *Stellar Atmospheres; Stars and Stellar Systems,* Vol. VI. Univ. of Chicago Press, Chicago.

37. V. V. Sobolev (1963). *A Treatise on Radiative Transfer.* (Transl. from the Russian by S. I. Gaposchkin.) D. Van Nostrand, Princeton.

38. H. Zirin (1966). *The Solar Atmosphere.* Blaisdell, Waltham, Mass.

* English and German.

† Articles are in English, German, or French.

[3]39. J. C. Brandt and P. W. Hodge (1964). *Solar System Astrophysics.* McGraw-Hill, New York.

[3]40. A. A. Mikhailov, ed. (1969). *Physics of Stars and Stellar Systems*: A Course in Astrophysics and Stellar Astronomy, Vol. 2. (Transl. by Z. Lerman.) Israel Program Sci. Transl., Jerusalem.

41. D. Mihalas (1970). *Stellar Atmospheres.* Freeman, San Francisco.

PART THREE—STELLAR INTERIORS

[2,4]50. M. Schwarzschild (1958). *Structure and Evolution of the Stars.* Princeton Univ. Press, Princeton.

[2,4]51. D. D. Clayton (1968). *Principles of Stellar Evolution and Nucleosynthesis.* McGraw-Hill, New York.

[2,4]52. J. P. Cox in collab. with R. T. Giuli (1968). *Principles of Stellar Structure,* 2 vols. Gordon and Breach, New York.

[4]53. S. Chandrasekhar (1939). *An Introduction to the Study of Stellar Structure.* Univ. of Chicago Press, Chicago. Reprinted by Dover, New York (1957).

[2,4]54. A. S. Eddington (1926). *The Internal Constitution of the Stars.* Cambridge Univ. Press, Cambridge. Reprinted by Dover, New York (1959).

[4]55. L. H. Aller (1954). *Astrophysics: Nuclear Transformations, Stellar Interiors, and Nebulae.* Ronald, New York.

[2,4]56. D. H. Menzel, P. L. Bhatnagar, and H. K. Sen (1963). *Stellar Interiors.* Wiley, New York.

[2]57. D. A. Frank-Kamenetskii (1962). *Physical Processes in Stellar Interiors.* (Transl. from the Russian.) Publ. for the Natl. Sci. Found. and N.A.S.A. by the Israel Program for Sci. Transl., Jerusalem.

[2,4]58. L. H. Aller and D. B. McLaughlin, eds. (1965). *Stellar Structure; Stars and Stellar Systems,* Vol. VIII. Univ. of Chicago Press, Chicago.

59. R. F. Stein and A. G. W. Cameron, eds. (1966). *Stellar Evolution*: Proceedings of a Sympos. held Nov. 1963 sponsored by the Inst. for Space Studies of the Goddard Space Flight Center, N.A.S.A. Plenum, New York.

[1]60. S. Flügge, ed. (1958). *Handbuch der Physik,* Vol. LI.* Springer-Verlag, Berlin.

61. D. E. Osterbrock and C. R. O'Dell, eds. (1968). *Planetary Nebulae*: Internatl. Astr. Union Sympos. No. 34. D. Reidel, Dordrecht, Holland.

62. M. Hack, ed. (1969). *Mass Loss from Stars*: Proceedings of the Second Trieste Colloq. on Astrophysics, 1968. Springer-Verlag, New York.

[1,2,4]63. H.-Y. Chiu (1968). *Stellar Physics.* Blaisdell, Waltham, Mass.

64. S. S. Kumar, ed. (1969). *Low-Luminosity Stars*: Proceedings of the Sympos. on Low-Luminosity Stars, U. of Virginia, 1968. Gordon and Breach, New York.

65. E. Schatzman (1958). *White Dwarfs.* Interscience, New York.

66. L. Gratton, ed. (1963). *Star Evolution*: Proceedings of the Internatl. School of Physics "Enrico Fermi," Course XXVIII. Academic Press, New York.

67. R. C. Cameron (1968). *Introduction to Space Science,* 2nd ed. (W. N. Hess and G. W. Mead, eds.), Ch. 21. Gordon and Breach, New York.

68. H. Reeves (1968). *Stellar Evolution and Nucleosynthesis.* Gordon and Breach, New York.

69. E. Langer, M. Herz, and J. P. Cox (1966). *Recent Work on Stellar Interiors: A Bibliography of Material Published between 1958 and Mid-1966.* (Report No. 88 of the Joint Inst. for Lab. Astrophysics of the Univ. of Colorado and Natl. Bureau of Standards.)

* Articles are in English, German, or French.

[1,2]70. M. Hack, ed. (1966). *Colloquium on Late-Type Stars*: Proceedings of the Colloq. held in Trieste, 1966. Osservatorio Astronomico, Trieste.

71. Institut d'Astrophysique (1970). *Évolution Stellaire Avant la Séquence Principale**: Communications Présentées au Seizième Colloque International d'Astrophysique Tenu a Liège 1969 (Extrait des Mémoires in-8° Soc. Roy. Sci. Liège, 5ième Série, Tome XIX). Institut d'Astrophysique, Cointe-Ougrée, Belgium.

72. P. J. Brancazio and A. G. W. Cameron, eds. (1969). *Supernovae and their Remnants*: Proceedings of the Conference on Supernovae, Goddard Inst. for Space Studies, N.A.S.A., 1967. Gordon and Breach, New York.

73. Institut d'Astrophysique (1959). *Modèles d'Étoiles et Évolution Stellaire*†: Communications Présentées au Neuvième Colloque International d'Astrophysique Tenu a Liège 1959 (Extrait des Mémoires in-8° Soc. Roy. Sci. Liège, 5ième Série, Tome III). Institut d'Astrophysique, Cointe-Ougrée, Belgium.

[1,2,4]74. L. Motz (1970). *Astrophysics and Stellar Structure*. Ginn, Waltham, Mass.

PART FOUR—THE CALCULATIONS OF MODEL ATMOSPHERES AND INTERIORS

75. B. Alder, S. Fernbach, and M. Rotenberg (1967). *Methods in Computational Physics*, Vol. 7. Academic Press, New York.

76. J. B. Scarborough (1966). *Numerical Mathematical Analysis*, 6th ed. Johns Hopkins, Baltimore.

77. The Royal Society, British Association for the Advancement of Science (1932). *Mathematical Tables*, Vol. II.

SPECIALIZED REFERENCES

PART ONE—OBSERVATIONAL DATA

100. F. K. Richtmyer and E. H. Kennard (1947). *Introduction to Modern Physics*, 4th ed. McGraw-Hill, New York.

101. H. L. Johnson (1965). *Communic. Lunar and Planet. Lab.* No. 53, **3**, 73.

102. F. B. Wood (1946). *Princeton Univ. Contrib.* No. 21.

103. R. F. Sanford (1951). *Ap. J.* **113**, 299.

105. M. F. Walker (1956). *Ap. J. Suppl.* **2**, 365.

106. R. L. Wildey (1964). *Ap. J. Suppl.* **8**, 439.

107. W. F. van Altena (1969). *A.J.* **74**, 2.

108. H. L. Johnson and A. R. Sandage (1955). *Ap. J.* **121**, 616.

109. O. J. Eggen and A. R. Sandage (1964). *Ap. J.* **140**, 130.

110. H. Arp (1962). *Ap. J.* **135**, 311.

111. D. C. Morton and T. F. Adams (1968). *Ap. J.* **151**, 611.

112. P. T. Bradley and D. C. Morton (1969). *Ap. J.* **156**, 687.

113. H. L. Johnson (1966). *Ann. Rev.* **4**, 193.

114. D. L. Lambert (1967). *Nature* **215**, 43.

115. K. W. Ogilvie and T. D. Wilkerson (1969). *Sol. Phys.* **8**, 435.

116. N. Durgaprasad, C. E. Fichtel, D. E. Guss, and D. V. Reames (1968). *Ap. J.* **154**, 307.

117. I. Iben, Jr. (1968). *Physical Review Letters* **21**, 1208.

118. C. A. Rouse (1969). *Astron. Ap.* **3**, 122.

118a. O. Engvold, O. Kjeldseth Moe, and P. Maltby (1970). *Astron. Ap.* **9**, 79.

119. N. Grevesse (1968). *Sol. Phys.* **5**, 159.

* Articles are in English or French.
† Articles are in English.

120. O. Engvold (1970). *Sol. Phys.* **11**, 183.
121. D. L. Lambert (1968). *M.N.R.A.S.* **138**, 143.
122. D. L. Lambert (1967). *Observatory* **87**, 228.
123. D. L. Lambert and B. Warner (1968). *M.N.R.A.S.* **138**, 181.
124. D. L. Lambert and B. Warner (1968). *M.N.R.A.S.* **140**, 197.
125. D. L. Lambert and B. Warner (1968). *M.N.R.A.S.* **138**, 213.
126. D. L. Lambert, E. A. Mallia, and J. Brault (1971). *Sol. Phys.* **19**, 289.
127. B. Warner (1968). *M.N.R.A.S.* **138**, 229.
128. B. Warner (1969). *Observatory* **89**, 107.
129. N. Grevesse and J. P. Swings (1971). *Astron. Ap.* **13**, 329.
129a. H. Holweger and K. B. Oertel (1971). *Astron. Ap.* **10**, 434.
130. M. Kock and J. Richter (1968). *Z. f. Ap.* **69**, 180.
131. D. L. Lambert, E. A. Mallia, and B. Warner (1969). *M.N.R.A.S.* **142**, 71.
132. D. L. Lambert and E. A. Mallia (1968). *M.N.R.A.S.* **140**, 13.
133. T. K. Krueger, L. H. Aller, J. Ross, and S. J. Czyzak (1968). *Ap. J.* **152**, 765.
133a. G. Bachmann, K. Pflug, and J. Staude (1970). *Sol. Phys.* **15**, 113.
134. R. B. King, G. M. Lawrence, and J. K. Link (1965). *Ap. J.* **142**, 386.
134a. Ø. Hauge (1969). *Sol. Phys.* **10**, 315.
135. N. Grevesse and G. Blanquet (1969). *Sol. Phys.* **8**, 5.
135a. H. Holweger (1971). *Astron. Ap.* **10**, 128.
136. D. M. Popper, H. E. Jørgensen, D. C. Morton, and D. S. Leckrone (1970). *Ap. J.* (*Letters*) **161**, L57.
137. D. Labs and H. Neckel (1968). *Z. f. Ap.* **69**, 1.
138. E. G. Laue and A. J. Drummond (1968). *Science* **161**, 888.
139. Goddard Space Flight Center (1968). Rept. No. X-322-68-304.
139a. N. Grevesse and J. P. Swings (1970). *Sol. Phys.* **13**, 19.
140. O. J. Eggen (1965). *A.J.* **70**, 19.
140a. R. L. Wildey, E. M. Burbidge, A. R. Sandage, and G. R. Burbidge (1962). *Ap. J.* **135**, 94.
141. C. E. Worley (1969). *A.J.* **74**, 764.
141a. O. J. Eggen (1963). *Ap. J. Suppl.* **8**, 125.
142. A. P. Cowley, W. A. Hiltner, and A. N. Witt (1967). *A.J.* **72**, 1334.
142a. H. L. Johnson, R. I. Mitchell, B. Iriarte, and W. Z. Wiśniewski (1966). *Communic. Lunar and Planetary Lab.* No. 63, **4**, Part 3.
143. C. E. Worley (1963). *Publ. U.S. Naval Obs.*, 2nd Ser., Vol. XVIII, Part III.
144. D. Hoffleit (1964). *Catalogue of Bright Stars*, 3rd rev. ed. Yale Univ. Obs., New Haven.
145. A. Cowley, C. Cowley, M. Jaschek, and C. Jaschek (1969). *A.J.* **74**, 375.
146. K. Aa. Strand (1969). *A.J.* **74**, 760.
147. A. Slettebak (1963). *Ap. J.* **138**, 118.
148. D. F. Gray (1967). *Ap. J.* **149**, 317.
149. W. J. Luyten (1949). *Ap. J.* **109**, 532.
150. A. H. Joy and M. L. Humason (1949). *P.A.S.P.* **61**, 133.
151. W. J. Luyten (1971) reported by P. van de Kamp (1971). *Ann. Rev.* **9**, 103.
152. P. van de Kamp and C.-Y. Yang (1967). *A.J.* **72**, 848.
153. P. Couteau and P. Laques (1965). *J. Obs.* **48**, 33.
154. O. J. Eggen and J. L. Greenstein (1965). *Ap. J.* **141**, 83.
154a. W. H. van den Bos (1926). *Bulletin Astron. Institutes Netherlands* **3**, 128.
155. P. van de Kamp (1959). *A.J.* **64**, 236.
156. D. M. Popper (1954). *Ap. J.* **120**, 316.
156a. P. W. Merrill (1922). *Ap. J.* **56**, 40.
157. S. L. Lippincott (1955). *A.J.* **60**, 379.

158. R. Hanbury Brown, J. Davis, L. R. Allen, and J. M. Rome (1967). *M.N.R.A.S.* **137**, 393.
158a. K. Nariai and D. A. Klinglesmith (1969). *Theory and Observation of Normal Stellar Atmospheres* (O. Gingerich, ed.), p. 315. M.I.T. Press, Cambridge, Mass.
159. I. W. Lindenblad (1970). *A.J.* **75**, 841.
160. W. H. van den Bos (1960). *J. Obs.* **43**, 145.
160a. J. R. W. Heintze (1968). *Bulletin Astron. Institutes Netherlands* **20**, 1.
161. K. Aa. Strand (1951). *Ap. J.* **113**, 1.
162. R. Grossenbacher and W. S. Mesrobian (1969). *A.J.* **74**, 951.
163. N. G. Roman (1950). *Ap. J.* **112**, 554.
164. R. v. d. R. Woolley and L. S. T. Symms (1937). *M.N.R.A.S.* **97**, 445.
165. C. Gasteyer (1954). *A.J.* **59**, 243.
166. D. F. Gray (1965). *A.J.* **70**, 304.
166a. G. S. Mumford III (1956). *A.J.* **61**, 213.
167. P. Couteau (1962). *J. Obs.* **45**, 37.
168. W. H. van den Bos (1938). *Union Obs. Circular* No. 99, p. 448.
169. W. H. van den Bos (1945). *A.J.* **51**, 198.
170. D. F. Gray (1968). *A.J.* **73**, 769.
171. K. Aa. Strand (1937). *Annals Leiden Obs.* **18**, 77.
172. F. Pavel (1949). *Astronomische Nachrichten* **277**, 156.
173. P. van de Kamp and J. L. Warren (1969). *A.J.* **74**, 241.
174. K. Aa. Strand (1955). *A.J.* **60**, 42.
175. K. Aa. Strand (1937). *Annals Leiden Obs.* **18**, 90.
175a. K. Aa. Strand (1943). *P.A.S.P.* **55**, 28.
176. W. D. Heintz (1969). *A.J.* **74**, 768.
177. E. Silbernagel (1929). *Astronomische Nachrichten* **234**, 441.
178. P. Baize (1949). *J. Obs.* **32**, 53.
179. O. J. Eggen (1967). *Ann. Rev.* **5**, 105 (p. 131).
180. P. Baize (1952). *l'Astronomie* **66**, 76.
180a. P. Baize (1946). *J. Obs.* **29**, 17.
181. D. F. Gray (1964). *A.J.* **69**, 406.
182. R. L. Duncombe and J. Ashbrook (1952). *A.J.* **57**, 92.
183. A. R. Upgren (1962). *A.J.* **67**, 539.
184. R. G. Hall, Jr. (1949). *A.J.* **54**, 106.
185. K. Aa. Strand (1937). *Annals Leiden Obs.*, **18**, 136.
186. J. Ames and M.-T. Pratt, listed by M. W. Makemson (1958). *A.J.* **63**, 41.
187. G. v. Schrutka-Rechtenstamm (1939). *Astronomische Nachrichten* **268**, 229.
188. P. J. Morel (1969). *A.J.* **74**, 245.
189. P. Baize (1957). *J. Obs.* **40**, 17.
190. W. J. Luyten and E. G. Ebbighausen (1934). *Publ. Obs. Univ. Minnesota* **2**, 25.
190a. M. M. Dworetsky, D. M. Popper, and D. S. Dearborn (1971). *P.A.S.P.* **83**, 207.
191. W. D. Heintz (1970). *A.J.* **75**, 848.
192. R. G. Hall, Jr. (1952). *A.J.* **57**, 47.
192a. R. G. Hall, Jr. (1949). *A.J.* **54**, 102.
193. A. H. Batten (1967). *Sixth Catalogue of the Orbital Elements of Spectroscopic Binary Systems. Publ. Dominion Astrophys. Obs. Victoria XIII*, 119.
194. R. H. Koch, M. Plavec, and F. B. Wood (1970). *A Catalogue of Graded Photometric Studies of Close Binaries. Publ. Univ. Pennsylvania*, Astr. Series XI.
195. M. S. Snowden and R. H. Koch (1969). *Ap. J.* **156**, 667.
196. R. H. Koch, S. Sobieski, and F. B. Wood (1963). *A Finding List for Observers of Eclipsing Variables*, 4th ed. *Publ. Univ. Pennsylvania*, Astr. Series IX.
197. D. M. Popper (1967). *Ann. Rev.* **5**, 85.

198. K. O. Wright and R. E. Huffman (1968). *Publ. Dominion Astrophys. Obs. Victoria* **13**, 275.

198a. K. T. Johansen (1969). *Astron. Ap.* **3**, 179.

199. R. H. Koch (1967). *A.J.* **72**, 411.

199a. L. Binnendijk (1970). *Vistas in Astronomy* (A. Beer, ed.), Vol. 12, p. 217. Pergamon, Oxford.

199b. E. C. Olson (1968). *Ap. J.* **153**, 187.

199c. B. N. Taylor, W. H. Parker, and D. N. Langenberg (1969). *Reviews of Modern Physics* **41**, 375.

199d. W. G. Melbourne, D. O. Muhleman, and D. A. O'Handley (1968). *Science* **160**, 987.

199e. D. Herbison-Evans, R. Hanbury Brown, J. Davis, and L. R. Allen (1971). *M.N.R.A.S.* **151**, 161.

199f. L. S. T. Symms (1969). *Royal Obs. Bull.* No. 157.

199g. I. W. Roxburgh and P. A. Strittmatter (1966). *M.N.R.A.S.* **133**, 345.

199h. R. P. Kraft and M. H. Wrubel (1965). *Ap. J.* **142**, 703.

199i. C. E. Worley (1969). *Low-Luminosity Stars* (S. S. Kumar, ed.), p. 123. Gordon and Breach, New York.

199j. S. Matsushima and Y. Terashita (1969). *Ap. J.* **156**, 219.

199k. J. Davis and R. J. Webb (1970). *Ap. J.* **159**, 551.

199l. D. M. Peterson and M. Scholz (1971). *Ap. J.* **163**, 51.

199m. D. C. Morton (1969). *Ap. J.* **158**, 629.

199n. G. W. Van Citters and D. C. Morton (1970). *Ap. J.* **161**, 695.

199o. J. L. Greenstein, G. Neugebauer, and E. E. Becklin (1970), *Ap. J.* **161**, 519.

199p. A. Blaauw (1963). *Basic Astronomical Data* (K. Aa. Strand, ed.). Univ. of Chicago Press, Chicago.

199q. P. C. Keenan (1963). *Basic Astronomical Data* (K. Aa. Strand, ed.). Univ. of Chicago Press, Chicago.

199r. R. C. Weast, ed. (1970). *Handbook of Chemistry and Physics*, 51st ed. Chemical Rubber Co., Cleveland.

199s. J. Smak (1967). *Acta Astronomica* **17**, 245.

199t. B. H. Feierman (1971). *A.J.* **76**, 73.

199u. R. Schild, D. M. Peterson, and J. B. Oke (1971). *Ap. J.* **166**, 95.

199v. D. M. Popper (1971). *Ap. J.* **166**, 361.

199w. A. H. Batten, J. M. Fletcher, and F. R. West (1971). *P.A.S.P.* **83**, 149.

199x. D. H. McNamara, H. K. Hansen, and S. K. Wilcken (1971). *P.A.S.P.* **83**, 192.

199y. M. Imbert (1971). *Astron. Ap.* **12**, 155.

199z. W. P. Bidelman (1958). *P.A.S.P.* **70**, 168.

199za. D. M. Popper (1971). *Ap. J.* **169**, 549.

199zb. B. Smith (1948). *Ap. J.* **108**, 504.

199zc. K. T. Johansen (1971). *Astron. Ap.* **12**, 165.

199zd. J. L. Greenstein, J. B. Oke, and H. L. Shipman (1971). *Ap. J.* **169**, 563.

199ze. D. E. Robbins, A. J. Hundhausen, and S. J. Bame (1970). *J. Geophys. Research* **75**, 1178.

199zf. T. Hirayama (1971). *Sol. Phys.* **19**, 384.

199zg. A. Sandage (1970). *Ap. J.* **162**, 841.

199zh. I. R. King (1971). *P.A.S.P.* **83**, 377.

199zi. W. Gliese (1969). *Veröff. Astron. Rechen-Institut, Heidelberg*, No. 22, p. 20.

199zj. R. R. Shobbrook, N. R. Lomb, and D. Herbison-Evans (1972). *M.N.R.A.S.* **156**, 165.

199zk. O. Struve, J. Sahade, S. S. Huang, and V. Zebergs (1958). *Ap. J.* **128**, 310.

199zl. W. D. Heintz (1972). *A. J.* **77**, 160.

PART TWO—STELLAR ATMOSPHERES

200. H. A. Kramers (1923). *Philosophical Magazine* **46**, 836.
201. J. A. Gaunt (1930). *Philosophical Transactions of the Royal Society* A **229**, 163.
202. J. L. Stilley and J. Callaway (1970). *Ap. J.* **160**, 245.
203. E. Vitense (1951). *Z. f. Ap.* **28**, 81.
204. M. S. Vardya (1964). *Ap. J. Suppl.* **8**, 277.
205. A. N. Cox and J. N. Stewart (1970). *Ap. J. Suppl.* **19**, 243.
206. A. N. Cox and J. N. Stewart (1970). *Ap. J. Suppl.* **19**, 261.
207. W. D. Watson (1970). *Ap. J. Suppl.* **19**, 235.
208. R. Wildt (1939). *Ap. J.* **89**, 295.
209. R. Wildt (1939). *Ap. J.* **90**, 611.
210. A. Rosa (1948). *Z. f. Ap.* **25**, 1.
211. N. A. Doughty and P. A. Fraser (1966). *M.N.R.A.S.* **132**, 267.
212. E. Vitense (1953). *Z. f. Ap.* **32**, 135.
213. E. Böhm-Vitense (1958). *Z. f. Ap.* **46**, 108.
214. J. L. Linsky (1970). *Sol. Phys.* **11**, 198.
215. D. Mihalas (1966). *Ap. J. Suppl.* **13**, 1.
216. O. Gingerich and C. de Jager (1968). *Sol. Phys.* **3**, 5.
217. J. R. Auman, Jr. (1969). *Ap. J.* **157**, 799.
218. J.-E. Blamont and R.-M. Bonnet (1966). *Comptes Rendus Acad. Sci. Paris*, Ser. B, **262**, 152.
219. R. Canavaggia, D. Chalonge, M. Egger-Moreau, and H. Oziol-Peltey (1950). *Ann. d'Ap.* **13**, 355.
220. D. Labs and H. Neckel (1962). *Z. f. Ap.* **55**, 269.
221. G. F. W. Mulders (1939). *P.A.S.P.* **51**, 220.
222. G. F. W. Mulders (1935). *Z. f. Ap.* **11**, 132.
223. R. Peytureaux (1955). *Ann. d'Ap.* **18**, 34.
227. J. B. Oke (1964). *Ap. J.* **140**, 689.
228. D. Mihalas (1965). *Ap. J. Suppl.* **9**, 321.
229. S. E. Strom, O. Gingerich, and K. M. Strom (1966). *Ap. J.* **146**, 880.
230. C. H. Payne (1925). *Stellar Atmospheres*, Harvard Observatory Monograph I. The Observatory, Cambridge, Mass.
231. C. H. Payne (1924). *Harvard Circular* 256.
232. H. C. Goldwire, Jr. (1969). *Ap. J. Suppl.* **17**, 445.
233. D. H. Menzel (1969). *Ap. J. Suppl.* **18**, 221.
234. C. E. Moore (1970). *Ionization Potentials and Ionization Limits Derived from the Analyses of Optical Spectra*, Report No. NSRDS-NBS 34. U.S. Department of Commerce, Washington, D.C.
235. G. Elste (1968). *Sol. Phys.* **3**, 106.
236. S. Matsushima (1968). *Ap. J.* **154**, 715.
237. R. G. Athay and R. C. Canfield (1969). *Ap. J.* **156**, 695.
238. O. Gingerich, R. W. Noyes, W. Kalkofen, and Y. Cuny (1971). *Sol. Phys.* **18**, 347.

PART THREE—STELLAR INTERIORS

300. W. A. Fowler, G. R. Caughlan, and B. A. Zimmerman (1967). *Ann. Rev.* **5**, 525.
301. J. N. Bahcall and R. M. May (1968). *Ap. J.* (*Letters*) **152**, L17.
302. J. N. Bahcall and R. M. May (1969). *Ap. J.* **155**, 501.
303. J. N. Bahcall and C. P. Moeller (1969). *Ap. J.* **155**, 511.
304. J. E. Mayer and M. G. Mayer (1940). *Statistical Mechanics*. Wiley, New York.
305. G. Joos, with the collab. of Ira M. Freeman (1958?). *Theoretical Physics*, 3rd ed. Hafner, New York.

306. R. Härm and M. Schwarzschild (1955). *Ap. J. Suppl.* **1**, 319.
307. W. A. Fowler (1958). *Ap. J.* **127**, 551.
308. R. F. Knacke, D. D. Cudaback, and J. E. Gaustad (1969). *Ap. J.* **158**, 151.
309. N. C. Wickramasinghe and K. S. Krishna Swamy (1969). *M.N.R.A.S.* **144**, 41.
310. G. B. Field (1969). *M.N.R.A.S.* **144**, 411.
311. E. E. Becklin and G. Neugebauer (1967). *Ap. J.* **147**, 799.
312. E. E. Kleinmann and F. J. Low (1967). *Ap. J.* (*Letters*) **149**, L1.
313. G. H. Herbig (1966). *Vistas in Astronomy* (A. Beer and K. Aa. Strand, eds.), Vol. 8. Pergamon, Oxford.
314. J. E. Gaustad (1963). *Ap. J.* **138**, 1050.
315. R. J. Gould (1964). *Ap. J.* **140**, 638.
316. S. E. Ananaba and J. E. Gaustad (1968). *Ap. J.* **153**, 95.
317. P. Bodenheimer (1968). *Ap. J.* **153**, 483.
318. L. G. Henyey, R. LeLevier, and R. D. Levée (1955). *P.A.S.P.* **67**, 154.
319. C. Hayashi (1961). *P.A.S.J.* **13**, 450.
320. P. Bodenheimer (1966). *Ap. J.* **144**, 709.
321. I. Iben, Jr. (1965). *Ap. J.* **141**, 993.
322. I. Iben, Jr., and R. J. Talbot (1966). *Ap. J.* **144**, 968.
323. S. S. Kumar (1963). *Ap. J.* **137**, 1121.
324. R. Stothers (1963). *Ap. J.* **138**, 1074.
325. R. Stothers (1966). *Ap. J.* **144**, 959.
326. I. Iben, Jr. (1967). *Ap. J.* **147**, 624.
326a. I. Iben, Jr. (1967). *Ap. J.* **147**, 650.
327. I. Iben, Jr. (1967). *Ann. Rev.* **5**, 571.
328. M. Schönberg and S. Chandrasekhar (1942). *Ap. J.* **96**, 161.
329. S. Torres-Peimbert, E. Simpson, and R. K. Ulrich (1969). *Ap. J.* **155**, 957.
330. W. D. Watson (1969). *Ap. J.* (*Letters*) **158**, L189.
331. I. Iben, Jr. (1966). *Ap. J.* **143**, 483.
331a. I. Iben, Jr. (1966). *Ap. J.* **143**, 516.
332. R. Stothers (1964). *Ap. J.* **140**, 510.
333. R. Stothers (1966). *Ap. J.* **143**, 91.
334. M. Schwarzschild and R. Härm (1958). *Ap. J.* **128**, 348.
335. R. J. Tayler (1969). *M.N.R.A.S.* **144**, 231.
336. J. W-K. Mark (1968). *Ap. J.* **154**, 627.
338. C. Hayashi, R. Hōshi, and D. Sugimoto (1962). *Prog. Theo. Phys.* Suppl. 22.
339. I. Iben, Jr. (1965). *Ap. J.* **142**, 1447.
340. M. Schwarzschild and H. Selberg (1962). *Ap. J.* **136**, 150.
341. M. Schwarzschild and R. Härm (1962). *Ap. J.* **136**, 158.
342. R. Härm and M. Schwarzschild (1964). *Ap. J.* **139**, 594.
343. R. Härm and M. Schwarzschild (1966). *Ap. J.* **145**, 496.
344. P. P. Eggleton (1968). *Ap. J.* **152**, 345.
345. M. Schwarzschild and R. Härm (1967). *Ap. J.* **150**, 961.
346. E. Hofmeister (1967). *Z. f. Ap.* **65**, 164.
347. R. Kippenhahn, H.-C. Thomas, and A. Weigert (1965). *Z. f. Ap.* **61**, 241.
348. R. Kippenhahn, H.-C. Thomas, and A. Weigert (1966). *Z. f. Ap.* **64**, 373.
349. A. Weigert (1966). *Z. f. Ap.* **64**, 395.
350. E. L. Hallgren and J. P. Cox (1970). *Ap. J.* **162**, 933.
351. J. E. Forbes (1968). *Ap. J.* **153**, 495.
352. Y. Tanaka (1966). *P.A.S.J.* **18**, 47.
353. E. E. Salpeter (1955). *Ap. J.* **121**, 161.
354. E. Meyer-Hofmeister (1969). *Astron. Ap.* **2**, 143.
355. E. Hofmeister (1967). *Z. f. Ap.* **65**, 194.

356. G. Rakavy, G. Shaviv, and Z. Zinamon (1967). *Ap. J.* **150**, 131.
357. J. P. Cox and E. E. Salpeter (1961). *Ap. J.* **133**, 764.
358. J. L'Ecuyer (1966). *Ap. J.* **146**, 845.
359. S. C. Vila (1967). *Ap. J.* **149**, 613.
362. V. Castellani, P. Giannone, and A. Renzini (1969). *Ap. Sp. Sci.* **4**, 103.
363. I. Iben, Jr., and J. Faulkner (1968). *Ap. J.* **153**, 101.
364. E. B. Newell (1970). *Ap. J.* **159**, 443.
365. J. P. Ostriker and F. D. A. Hartwick (1968). *Ap. J.* **153**, 797.
366. E. M. Jones (1970). *Ap. J.* **159**, 101.
367. R. L. Sears (1959). *Mém. Soc. Roy. Sci. Liège* **16**, 479.
368. D. Ezer and A. G. W. Cameron (1963). *Icarus* **1**, 422.
369. P. Demarque (1960). *Ap. J.* **132**, 366.
370. P. Demarque (1967). *Ap. J.* **150**, 943.
371a. A. N. Cox, J. N. Stewart, and D. D. Eilers (1965). *Ap. J. Suppl.* **11**, 1.
371b. A. N. Cox and J. N. Stewart (1965). *Ap. J. Suppl.* **11**, 22.
372. A. N. Cox and J. N. Stewart (1962). *A.J.* **67**, 113.
373. G. Keller and R. E. Meyerott (1955). *Ap. J.* **122**, 32.
374. T. R. Carson, D. F. Mayers, and D. W. N. Stibbs (1968). *M.N.R.A.S.* **140**, 483.
375. W. D. Watson (1969). *Ap. J.* **157**, 375.
376. I. Iben, Jr (1963). *Ap. J.* **138**, 452.
377. R. Stothers and C.-W. Chin (1968). *Ap. J.* **152**, 225.
378. M. Simoda and I. Iben, Jr. (1968). *Ap. J.* **152**, 509.
379. P. Demarque and J. E. Geisler (1963). *Ap. J.* **137**, 1102.
380. B. M. Schlesinger (1969). *Ap. J.* **157**, 533.
381. H. Arp and A. D. Thackeray (1967). *Ap. J.* **149**, 73.
382. E. Hofmeister (1967). *Z. f. Ap.* **65**, 194.
383. V. Castellani and A. Renzini (1968). *Ap. Sp. Sci.* **2**, 83.
384. H.-C. Thomas (1967). *Z. f. Ap.* **67**, 420.
385. T. Hamada and E. E. Salpeter (1961). *Ap. J.* **134**, 683.
386. W. B. Hubbard and R. L. Wagner (1970). *Ap. J.* **159**, 93.
387. Y. Terashita and S. Matsushima (1969). *Ap. J.* **156**, 203.
388. J. P. Cox and R. T. Giuli (1961). *Ap. J.* **133**, 755.
389. M. P. Savedoff, H. M. Van Horn, and S. C. Vila (1969). *Ap. J.* **155**, 221.
390. W. D. Watson (1969). *Ap. J.* **158**, 303.
391. G. R. Caughlan (1965). *Ap. J.* **141**, 688.
392. D. L. Moss (1968). *M.N.R.A.S.* **141**, 165.
393. R. Stothers and C.-W. Chin (1968). *Ap. J.* **152**, 225.
394. R. P. Kraft (1961). *Ap. J.* **134**, 616.
395. H. M. Van Horn (1968). *Ap. J.* **151**, 227.
396. T. Kelsall and B. Stromgren (1966). *Vistas in Astronomy* (A. Beer and K. Aa. Strand, eds.), Vol. 8, p. 159. Pergamon, Oxford.
397. H. Copeland, J. O. Jensen, and H. E. Jørgensen (1970). *Astron. Ap.* **5**, 12.
398. M. R. Wehr and J. A. Richards, Jr. (1967). *Physics of the Atom*, 2nd ed. Addison-Wesley, Reading, Mass.
399. M. Schwarzschild (1970). *Quarterly J. Roy. Astron. Soc.* **11**, 12.
400. A. S. Grossman and H. C. Graboske, Jr. (1971). *Ap. J.* **164**, 475.
401. E. Novotny (1972). *Ap. J.* **174**, 425.
402. A. S. Grossman (1970). *Ap. J.* **161**, 619.
403. P. Demarque, J. G. Mengel, and M. L. Aizenman (1971). *Ap. J.* **163**, 37.
404. P. Demarque and J. G. Mengel (1971). *Ap. J.* **164**, 317.
405. P. Demarque and J. G. Mengel (1971). *Ap. J.* **164**, 469.
406. W. D. Arnett (1971). *Ap. J.* **163**, 11.

PART FOUR—THE CALCULATION OF MODEL ATMOSPHERES AND INTERIORS

500. R. S. Kushwaha (1957). *Ap. J.* **125**, 242.
501. D. E. Osterbrock (1953). *Ap. J.* **118**, 529.
502. O. J. Eggen (1969). *Ap. J.* **157**, 287.
503. P. M. Morse (1940). *Ap. J.* **92**, 27.

AUTHOR INDEX

Numbers in parentheses refer to entries in the bibliography. Names containing particles are alphabetized according to the first capital letter.

SUBJECT INDEX

Page numbers referring to tables or figures are italic and preceded by the letter T (table) or F (figure). When pages referring to text include a large proportion of tables or figures, this fact is indicated by the symbol $(T), (F),$ or (T,F) following the page numbers.

Flux *(cont.)*
  examples for Sun, etc., 89–93, 95 *(F)*
  in model atmospheres, 78, 171, 180–83. *F 178–80, 182, 183*
  in model interior, 233
  for Sirius, *F 183*
  solar, 161, 162. *F 15*
  for Vega, 209. *F 183*
Formation of star, 5, 279, 280, 293, 356
Free-free transition, 125–27, 131, 132. *F 99, 101*
  See also Absorption coefficient, free-free
FU Orionis, 279

Galactic clusters, 50, 54, 314, 349, 351, 354–56. *F 294, 350, 352, 353, 355*
  observed, 50, 51, 54, 356. *F 50–53, 294, 349, 354*
Gaunt factor, 128, 131
Giant stars, 18, 19. *T 11, 12. F 19, 20, 50*
  model atmospheres for, 177, 179, 180 *(T,F). T 194*
  model interiors for
    comparison with observations, 349–60 *(F)*
    models and evolution
      general discussion, 319–24 *(T,F)*
      1 $M_\odot$, 324–31 *(T,F). T 378–80*
      5 $M_\odot$, 331–41 *(F). T 390–97*
      30 $M_\odot$, 340–44 *(T,F)*
    sensitivity to assumptions, 344–48 *(F)*
Globular clusters, 49, 50, 54, 319, 349, 351, 354, 355
  observed, 50, 51, 54. *F 53, 348*
Globules, 279
Grains, 278–80
Granulation, 173
Gravitational contraction (expansion)
  at end of main-sequence stage, 302, 305, 306, 323. *F 321*
  energy release by, 235, 245–48, 265
  in giant stars, 322–25, 327, 332–39, 341, 344. *T 342, 343. F 321*
  in helium, carbon, oxygen stars, 363, 366
  in low-mass stars, 297
  in pre–main-sequence stars, 283, 285, 292, 293. *F 290, 292*
  in protostars, 280, 282, 283

Gravity, acceleration due to, 17, 168, 177–79, 196. *T 32–36, 38–41*
Gray atmosphere, 75, 88, 171
Guillotine factor, 160. *T 509*

H (quantity related to flux), 67, 80–82
H⁻ ion. *See* Negative hydrogen ion
Half width, 200, 201, 205
Harmonic law, 22, 30
Harvard-Smithsonian Reference Atmosphere, 188. *T 174, 175*
Hayashi track, 285, 333
Heavier elements
  abundances of, 46, 49. *T 47, 48*
  effect of, on model interiors, 295, 316. *F 295, 345*
  effect of, on spectrum, 6, 7, 9
  and line blanketing, 6, 7, 9, 483. *T 187*
  in photosphere, 179
  in Populations I and II, 49
Helium
  absorption coefficient of, 133, 152, 153
  absorption lines of, 152, 211
  abundance of, 46, 278. *T 49*
  burning of, in stars
    in core, 324, 343, 344, 367. *T 342, 343. F 321, 341*
    in helium stars, 363
    in shell, 324, 331, 337–39, 367
  influence of abundance of, on models, *F 307–9, 346, 347*
  ionization of, 113, 119. *T 114, 118. F 117*
    in stellar interiors, 282, 284, 285, 300, 356
  from nuclear reactions, 249–56. *F 252*
  See also Hydrogen
Helium flash, 324, 326, 327, 330, 331. *T 328, 329. F 330*
Helium stars, 362–64 *(F)*
Helmholtz-Kelvin contraction, 283
  See also Gravitational contraction
Hertzsprung gap, 333
Hertzsprung-Russell diagram
  compared with color-magnitude diagram, 51, 314. *F 311, 312*
  description of, 18, 42. *F 19*
  effect of chemical composition on, 307, 344. *F 307, 308, 345–47*
  effect of mixing length on, *F 310, 348*
  effect of opacity on, 316. *F 310, 313, 318*
  helium stars in, 362–64 *(F)*

DATE DUE